CRISES IN WORLD POLITICS

CRISES IN WORLD POLITICS

Theory and Reality

MICHAEL BRECHER

PERGAMON PRESS

OXFORD · NEW YORK · SEOUL · TOKYO

UK	Pergamon Press Ltd, Headington Hill Hall, Oxford OX3 0BW, England
USA	Pergamon Press Inc., 660 White Plains Road, Tarrytown, New York 10591, USA
KOREA	Pergamon Press Korea, KPO Box 315, Seoul 110–603, Korea
JAPAN	Pergamon Press Japan, Tsunashima Building Annex, 3–20–12 Yushima, Bunkyo-ku, Tokyo 113, Japan

Copyright © 1993 Pergamon Press Ltd

First edition 1993

Library of Congress Cataloging in Publication Data

A catalogue record for this book is available from the Library of Congress

British Library Cataloguing in Publication Data

A catalogue record for this book is available from the British Library

ISBN 0 08 041377 3 Flexicover
ISBN 0 08 041376 5 Hardcover

Printed in Great Britain by BPCC Wheatons Ltd, Exeter

Contents

5. Impact

6. Unified Model of Crisis

7. The Gulf Crisis 1990–91

8. What Have We Learned?

List of Figures and Tables

FIGURES

TABLES

TO EVA

Preface and Acknowledgements

THIS BOOK is the culmination of many years of study and reflection. Although I was unaware at the time of how it would unfold, the long voyage of discovery can be traced to the early 'fifties when I explored the first crisis and war over Kashmir in 1947–48, the enduring issue of the India/Pakistan protracted conflict.[1] Later I turned my attention to Arab/Israel crises and wars—the Suez–Sinai Campaign of 1956–57, the May–June crisis and Six Day War of 1967, and the October–Yom Kippur crisis-war of 1973–74.[2] And since the mid-'seventies I have been immersed in research on interstate crises in the twentieth century, a project that spawned a dozen volumes by scholars from Australia, Canada, Israel, the UK, and the US.[3]

During my frequent visits to South Asia (1951–74) and my lengthy residence in the Middle East (1949–51, since 1969) I became acutely sensitive to the pervasiveness of crisis, conflict and war. Both the India/Pakistan and Arab/Israel protracted conflicts, especially the latter because of active US and Soviet involvement, posed grave dangers to global and regional stability. Early on, I recognized that, in world politics as in domestic political systems and in history, stability often masked domination of the weak by the strong or the poor by the rich, or continued control over colonial lands and peoples (the periphery) by the former imperial powers (the metropole or core). At the same time, I knew that the escalation of crises to wars in the nuclear age and the persistence of conflicts among less powerful states in Third World 'grey zones' of competition between the United States and the Soviet Union made international stability a high value in the last quarter of the twentieth century. Although it seemed unlikely, perhaps impossible, that crises could be prevented or protracted conflicts terminated, their effective management to prevent war was a viable and worthy policy goal.

The first step on the long road to crisis and conflict management was the accumulation of reliable knowledge about the phenomena to be managed in order to prevent runaway turmoil. Viewed from the perspective of the mid-1970s, war had been the object of systematic investigation for half a century, from Wright's ambitious enterprise beginning in the mid-'twenties through Sorokin and Richardson to Singer's Correlates of War project.[4] However, the study of international conflict remained in an embryonic state, despite the pioneering work of the Stanford school.[5] Similarly, work had begun on crisis, both conceptually (McClelland, Robinson, Hermann, Young) and on one celebrated case, the process leading to World War I (O. R. Holsti). The seminal work by Snyder and Diesing came later.[6] Yet much remained to be done. It was an awareness of the danger of crises to global and regional stability and of the gaps in our knowledge about this major source of turmoil that led me to initiate the International Crisis Behavior (ICB) Project in 1975.

How to proceed? There was, and is, no simple and straightforward answer, for contending and contentious schools praise their own and decry other approaches to the generation of knowledge about this or any aspect of world politics: *a priori* versus inductive theorizing; aggregate data analysis versus comparative case study, that is, quantitative versus qualitative method; reliance on a few or on a large number of cases for generalization; and the most fruitful level of analysis, the international system or the state.

I have always been a pluralist in the matter of research strategy. There are, it seems to me, many paths to knowledge, and no single school has a monopoly on truth (Brecher, 1989). Thus I found the debates over methods, from the Bull–Kaplan exchange to the more tolerant discussions by Bueno de Mesquita, Krasner and Jervis, and by Achen and Snidal and George and Smoke to be inconclusive, one of the indicators of immaturity in the discipline.[7]

Theory clearly occupies a central place, whether deductively or inductively derived. Although the former is accorded higher status in the science enterprise, the evidence thus far in the study of world politics is mixed; and, in any event, the choice depends upon a researcher's disposition. Stated differently, the issue of whether formal theory must precede—and take precedence over—empirical investigation remains unresolved. My own disposition has always been in favor of an iterative process—pre-theory, in the form of a framework and taxonomy to guide empirical inquiry, followed by the creation of models and hypotheses, testing, their refinement as the evidence dictates, further testing, and so on.

The stimulus is often a puzzle.[8] In this case, I asked: What is a crisis? How does it differ from conflict, war, dispute, incident? What are the defining conditions of an international (macro-level) crisis and of a foreign policy (micro-level) crisis? What is the logical relationship between them? How does one explain its core dimensions—crisis outbreak, actor behavior, major power activity, the involvement of international organizations, crisis outcome, its intensity and consequences?

This, in turn, led to a related puzzle: What path should be followed and which method(s) should be employed in order to answer these questions and others? My choice, from the outset, was a two-track strategy, flowing from a conviction about the inherent merit of pluralism. One path is in-depth case studies of perceptions and decisions by a single state, using a micro-level model of crisis that I designed to guide research on foreign policy crises in the military-security issue-area and to facilitate rigorous comparative analysis of findings about state behavior under varying stress.[9] The method, "structured empiricism," was developed in earlier research on Israel's foreign policy system and is very similar to George's "structured focused comparison."[10] Both gather and organize data on diverse cases around a set of common questions, permitting systematic comparison. A series of ICB volumes, noted earlier, used this research design and method.

Comparative case study alone, however, and even more so the "crucial case" approach advocated by Eckstein cannot uncover the full range of findings about any phenomenon in world politics.[11] For this purpose, a second path was necessary, namely, studies in breadth of aggregate data on crises over an extended block of time and space. The result was the selection of a large-scale empirical domain, all military-security crises of all states, across all continents, cultures, and political and economic systems, initially from 1929 to 1979, later extended back to the end of 1918 and forward to the end of 1988. In the shaping of this "horizontal" dimension of the project and in the volumes that presented the data and the findings, Jonathan Wilkenfeld and I were academic collaborators in the best sense of the term.

This book employs the above-noted dual strategy of inquiry in a conscious effort at synthesis: of system and actor levels of analysis; of deductive and inductive paths to theory; of qualitative and quantitative methods; and, as a corollary, of in-depth case study and aggregate data, that is, of the evidence from both a small and large number of cases. This is reflected in the structure of the book, whose primary objective is to create a theory of crisis and crisis behavior.

Chapter 1, CONCEPTS and MODELS, defines the key concepts of

the inquiry, crisis, conflict and war, and discusses their interrelationship. It then examines the "state of the art," that is, the literature on this topic. Two general models are presented: Model I (International Crisis); and Model II (Foreign Policy Crisis). And "the tasks ahead" are noted.[12]

Chapters 2–5 have essentially the same structure, focusing on the four phases of an interstate crisis, ONSET, ESCALATION, DEESCALATION, IMPACT. The first half of each of these chapters poses research questions; specifies a phase model; deduces hypotheses; and tests them with aggregate data, namely, the evidence from 390 international crises (system/interactor level) and 826 foreign policy crises (actor level). The second half of each chapter presents an analytical summary of how states coped in ten cases that represent a subset of important and visible military-security crises since the end of World War I: the US in the Berlin Blockade; the USSR in the Prague Spring; the UK in the Munich Crisis; Germany in the Stalingrad Crisis; Israel in October-Yom Kippur; Syria in the first Lebanon Civil War case, 1975–76; India in the border crisis-war with China; Hungary in the Hungarian Uprising; Zambia in Rhodesia UDI; and Argentina in the Falklands/Malvinas case. Thereafter the findings for each phase are compared in terms of: actor attributes—number of decisions, key decision-makers, and their attitudinal prism; situational attributes—crisis trigger, values threatened, duration, system level, number of actors, and violence; and the coping process—information-processing, consultation, decisional forum, and consideration of alternatives. Thus, in accordance with the two-track strategy, both aggregate data (breadth) and case study data (depth) are tapped to test 14 deductively-derived hypotheses about the four crisis phases.

Chapter 6 attempts a 'grand integration' of Models I and II and the four phase models into the UNIFIED MODEL OF CRISIS. This model is applied, in depth, to the GULF CRISIS-WAR of 1990–91, in Chapter 7: each phase is analyzed; hypotheses are tested; and the utility of the model is demonstrated.

Chapter 8, WHAT HAVE WE LEARNED?, recapitulates the main findings about concepts and models, and about each phase and its corresponding period at the actor level, namely, pre-crisis, crisis, end-crisis, and post-crisis. It also attempts to enhance the cumulation of knowledge about crisis by testing 19 hypotheses developed in other works on the subject. And, finally, I speculate on the likely configuration of crises in the next decade, with suggestions for more effective crisis management.

In that context, a series of cataclysmic events occurred since the "cut-off" date for our aggregate data analysis, the end of 1988: the collapse of the communist bloc; the democratization of Eastern Europe; the unification of Germany; and the disintegration of the Soviet Union into 15 independent states. These developments may be said to mark the end of the twentieth century, in terms of world politics. They certainly mark the end of power bipolarity, the dominant trait of the global system since the end of World War II. However, they do not constitute the "end of history."[13] Nor did they usher in an era of interstate tranquillity.

It can be argued that interstate crises and conflicts of the traditional kind will diminish in frequency. However, they continue to flourish in the "new world order," several of them accompanied by intense violence: between Armenia and Azerbaijan over Nagorno-Karabakh; the Gulf crisis-war; and the civil wars transformed into interstate wars in disintegrating Yugoslavia, between Serbia and Croatia, and Serbia and Bosnia-Hercegovina. One of these, the Gulf crisis-war, is dissected in Chapter 7, as noted. The others, and many more that can be anticipated in the next decade, are discussed in the concluding chapter, in "Lessons for the Future." Alas, the conditions most likely to lead to the eruption of interstate crises, often with violence, have not vanished: they have merely become more evident among lesser powers on the peripheries of the global system.

It remains to reaffirm the aims of this book and the project as a whole. The primary intellectual goal, as noted, is to create a valid theory of interstate crisis and crisis behavior. Hence the centrality of the Unified Model, Models I and II, and the four phase models in the pages that follow. The accumulation of empirical data—which took a decade longer than anticipated—generated a rich body of knowledge about every conceivable aspect of the crisis phenomenon. This knowledge is used throughout to test the validity of the models and their derived hypotheses, as well as to measure the intensity and consequences of crises as political earthquakes. As for the case studies, one aim is to illuminate the dynamics of specific crises. More generally, it is to disseminate knowledge about the effects of crisis-induced stress on coping and choice by decision-makers and to discover patterns of crisis management, if they exist.

In terms of policy relevance, the goal is to use knowledge of the past to enhance the quality and effectiveness of crisis management in the future: at the actor level, to enable decision-makers to cope better with crises; and, at the system/interactor level, to reduce the likelihood of crisis escalation to full-scale war or, if war occurs, to expedite termination with minimal adverse fallout for the system and the crisis actors. In the largest sense, the objective is to apply the lessons of history to promote international peace.

Can these policy goals be attained, even in part? Only if the enormous divide between the academy and the national security decision-making community in most states can be replaced by a meaningful dialogue. This is a difficult task and has proved elusive so far, with rare exceptions.

Many have contributed much to this book. Four institutions provided generous funding over the years: the Canada Council, through a Killam senior research fellowship (1976–1979); the Social Sciences and Humanities Research Council (SSHRC) of Canada, through a series of grants (1980–1987, 1990–1992); the Faculty of Graduate Studies and Research, McGill University, through grants, 1987–1990; and the Fonds Pour La Formation De Chercheurs Et L'Aide' A La Recherche (FCAR), a Government of Quebec educational foundation, through a grant (1987–1990).

Colleagues in the International Crisis Behavior Project and graduate students at McGill made my task much easier by their illuminating in-depth case studies. Constraints of space prevent an elaborate testimony to the quality of these works: I have done this in the Foreword to each of the ICB volumes. However, I would like to renew my appreciation of their contribution: to Avi Shlaim (Berlin Blockade); Karen Dawisha (Prague Spring); Peter Wilson (Munich); Geoffrey Jukes (Stalingrad); Adeed Dawisha (Lebanon Civil War I); Steven Hoffmann (India/China Border); Benjamin Geist (Hungarian Uprising); Douglas Anglin (Rhodesia UDI); and Alan Bartley (Falklands/Malvinas).

Earlier versions of the manuscript benefited greatly from a rigorous critique by Ruth Abbey, Hemda Ben Yehuda, Frank Harvey, Patrick James, Janice G. Stein, Yaacov Vertzberger and Jonathan Wilkenfeld. Avi Diskin was helpful on statistical matters. I adopted most of their suggestions—but did not always heed their advice. None of these readers bears responsibility for any errors of fact, faulty analysis or misjudgment.

I am also indebted to David Carment, David Emelifeonwu, Athanasios Hristoulas, and Joel Schleicher for valuable research assistance; to Adam Jones, Sarah Lemann and Maria Marchesi for word processing of the highest quality; and to David Dickinson and Glenda Kershaw of Pergamon Press, for the splendid production of the Work, and for the comprehensive name and subject indices, respectively.

As so often over the decades, I am grateful to my wife, Eva, for encouragement, support, understanding and infinite patience during the years of my preoccupation with a seemingly endless task.

November 1992
Montreal/Jerusalem   MICHAEL BRECHER

CHAPTER 1

Concepts and Models

THE twentieth century is an era of pervasive turmoil. There have been two cataclysmic general wars and many lesser wars in all parts of the world. There has also been a myriad of conflicts, some of them prolonged in time and extending over many issues, such as the East/West, Arab/Israel and India/Pakistan protracted conflicts since the late 1940s. The revolutionary upheavals in Russia and China during and in the aftermath of the two world wars undermined the foundations of global order. So too did economic dislocation, notably the Great Depression of the 1930s, oil-price shocks in the 1970s, and the international debt crisis of the 1980s. The unfolding of *glasnost* and *perestroika* in the USSR under Gorbachev's leadership from 1985 onwards and the eruption of anti-communist "people power" in Central and Eastern Europe, including the Soviet Union, in 1989–91 transformed the Soviet bloc and heralded the end of the Cold War. And the persistent assault on the physical environment, by industrial pollution, the shrinking of rain forests, nuclear power, and ever more awesome weapons of mass destruction, has raised fears about the delicate balance of the ecosystems that sustain the planet. In short, there have been—and continue to be—multiple sources of global disruption, placing the survival of humanity at risk.

One of these is *military-security crises*, the main focus of attention in this book. In order to explain this phenomenon several interrelated tasks must be undertaken. Basic research questions must be posed. Models need to be created to guide the inquiry. Propositions have to be framed and tested with the evidence from crisis, conflict and war since the end of World War I. And the lessons need to be drawn.

The core question can be phrased simply: what does one seek to explain about crises among states? This encompasses a cluster of issues. Under what conditions is a crisis most likely to erupt? Why do some crises escalate to war, such as Entry into World War II (August

–September 1939), while others do not, for example, Cuban Missiles (1962)? What are the conditions in which a crisis is most likely to "wind down"? What are the effects of stress on the ways in which decision-makers cope with crisis? When are states likely to resort to violence in crisis management, for example, the UK in the Falklands/Malvinas crisis-war of 1982? What are the processes leading to choice in situations of high stress? Why do some crises terminate in agreement, as in the Berlin Blockade of 1948–49, while others do not, as in the Berlin Wall Crisis of 1961? Finally, what are the consequences of crises, both for the adversaries and the system in which a crisis occurs, for example, a fundamental change in the Arab/Israel balance of power following the May–June 1967 crisis and the Six Day War?

Stated in terms of purpose, the intellectual aim of this book is to illuminate the meaning of crises in twentieth-century world politics. The policy goal is to enhance the ability of foreign policy decision-makers to cope with turmoil in the future and to learn from the lessons of history in the quest for enduring peace. To these ends I begin with an exposition of concepts and models.

Crisis, Conflict, War

How does one recognize a military-security crisis? The key indicators are threat to basic values, action demonstrating resolve, and overt hostility. Some well-known cases illustrate the stark reality of international crisis. Threatening statements and the mobilization of armed forces by the major powers in the June–August 1914 Crisis dramatized Europe on the brink of war. The Western Powers' threat to integrate their zones of occupation in Germany, followed by the USSR's closure of land access to West Berlin and the US airlift in 1948–49 marked a watershed East/West crisis soon after the collapse of the Grand Alliance in World War II. Soviet missiles in Cuba and the US's "quarantine" of ships en route to the Caribbean indicated another, even more dangerous, superpower confrontation in 1962. Moscow's threat of unilateral military intervention in the October-Yom Kippur crisis-war of 1973 and Washington's nuclear alert generated a brief but intense crisis between the US and the USSR. But these are only among the most dramatic of 390 international crises from the end of 1918 to the end of 1988.[1]

Why should one describe and attempt to explain twentieth-century crises? One reason is that crisis is among the most widely-used verbal symbols of turmoil in the politics among nations. Statesmen often portray their tenure in office as a daily confrontation with crises. Journalists and scholars, too, write about disputes, incidents, riots and rebellions as crises. In sum, crisis is a universal term for disruption and disorder in the global arena.[2]

Another reason is that crisis is closely related to *conflict* and *war*, two other concepts that are essential to understanding world politics. What is an **international crisis**? In essence, it denotes

(1) *a change in type and/or an increase in intensity of disruptive interactions between two or more states*, with *a heightened probability of military hostilities*;[3] that, in turn,

(2) *destabilizes their relationship and challenges the structure of an international system.*[4]

The change or increase in intensity is usually triggered by an act or event: a threatening statement, oral or written; a political act, such as the severance of diplomatic relations; an economic act, like a trade embargo; a non-violent military act, such as the movement of troops; an indirect violent act, that is, against an ally or client state; or a direct military attack. An international crisis can also be initiated by an internal challenge to a regime, verbal or physical, or as an act to strengthen the position of those in power.[5] It may also arise from a technological or geopolitical change in the environment that weakens a state's capacity to protect its vital interests, including its independence.

Whatever the catalyst to a crisis, it generates a perception of threat on the part of the decision-maker(s) of state A. Its response, in turn, leads to more disruptive interactions between A and B, and possibly other states as well, accompanied by a likelihood of violence. In short, an international crisis is characterized by higher-than-normal tension, turmoil and disruption in interstate relations.

An international crisis includes—in fact, it begins with—an external or foreign policy crisis for one or more states. The trigger to a **foreign policy crisis** is perceptual. More precisely, it derives from three inter-related *perceptions* that are generated by a hostile act, disruptive event or environmental change, perceptions of:

(1) *threat to one or more basic values*;

(2) *finite time for response*; and

(3) *heightened probability of involvement in military hostilities* before the challenge is overcome.

In sum, a foreign policy crisis arises from the highest-level political decision-makers' image of pressure(s) to cope with externally-focused stress. It also marks the beginning of an international crisis.

To take a celebrated case: the Cuban Missile Crisis began as a foreign policy crisis for the United States on 16 October 1962, the day President Kennedy learned of the presence of Soviet medium- and intermediate-range ballistic missiles in Cuba; he perceived that development as a grave threat to vital US interests. His response led to a dramatic increase in disruptive interactions between the then-superpowers, thereby setting in motion the international crisis over Cuban Missiles (known by the USSR as the Caribbean Crisis [Sergeev *et al.*, 1990]).

The analytic link between the two levels of crisis can now be formulated succinctly. An international crisis erupts when there is behavioral change by one or more states leading to more hostile interaction. That change in behavior by A triggers a foreign policy crisis for B, through its perception of threat. In short, perception and behavior, state level and system/interactor level, foreign policy crisis and international crisis, are inextricably linked. Thus the phenomenon of crisis can be—and must be—addressed at the two levels of analysis.[6]

Although *conflict* is as old as the human adventure, serious inquiry began only in the mid-nineteenth century, notably by Marx and Engels, social Darwinists such as Spencer and Darwin, and by theorists of power and influence, namely, Mosca, Michels, Pareto and Sorel. In the twentieth century, that continuing inquiry has generated a vast literature on conflict.[7]

Among the most precise definitions of this type of turmoil is that by Gurr (1980: 1–2): "Conflict phenomena are the overt, coercive interactions of contending collectivities." Further, they are characterized by two or more parties engaged in mutually hostile actions and using coercion to injure or control their opponents. This definition is broad enough to encompass political riots, insurrection, revolution and war, but not higher-than-normal interstate tension, with or without violence, that often leads to crises.

International crisis and *international conflict* are not synonymous, though they are closely related. In essence, every crisis reflects a "state of conflict" between two or more adversaries, but not every conflict is reflected in crisis. Moreover, the focus of crisis is (usually) a single issue, whether a border dispute, economic boycott, alleged mistreatment of a minority group, threat to a political regime, etc. Crises occur within, as well as outside, protracted conflicts, for example, the 1964 Ethiopia/Somalia Crisis over the disputed Ogaden territory, and the Iceland/UK Cod "Wars" of 1973 and 1975–76 over fishing rights. Even when a crisis is very long it can be distinguished from a conflict, as with the Jordan Waters Crisis of 1963–64, which was part of the Arab/Israel protracted conflict over many issues, tangible and intangible, since the end of the British Mandate over Palestine in May 1948.

How does one distinguish *protracted conflict* from other types of international turmoil? Protracted conflicts have been defined by Azar *et al.* (1978: 50) as

> hostile interactions which extend over long periods of time with sporadic outbreaks of open warfare fluctuating in frequency and intensity. They are conflict situations in which the stakes are very high. . . . While they may exhibit some breakpoints during which there is a cessation of overt violence, they linger on in time and have no distinguishable point of termination. . . . Protracted conflicts, that is to say, are not specific events or even clusters of events at a point in time; they are processes.[8]

There have been many protracted conflicts in the twentieth century—26 from the end of 1918 to the end of 1988. These include conflicts between Afghanistan and Pakistan, Ethiopia and Somalia, Greece and Turkey, Iran and Iraq, Israel and the Arab states, etc. [see Table 2.2, Chap. 2 below].

Most exhibit all of the traits specified above. In others, notably the East/West Conflict from 1945 to 1990, direct violence between the principal adversaries was conspicuously absent, though proxy wars were widespread, e.g., in Angola, Afghanistan, the Arab/Israel segment of the Middle East; that is, there were no "sporadic outbreaks of open warfare" between the US and the USSR. So too with the Italy/Yugoslavia conflict over Trieste from 1945 to 1953 (Croci, unpub. Ph.D. Diss., 1991). In others, violence was intense and persistent, notably the long-war conflicts between Japan and China from 1937 to 1945, the Axis Powers and the Allies from 1939 to 1945, the Yemen War from 1962 to 1967, the Vietnam War from 1964 to 1975, and the Iran/Iraq War from 1980 to 1988. The non-war conflicts were protracted in all other respects—extended hostile interaction, very high stakes, spillover to many spheres, and conflict processes over time rather than specific events. Thus "sporadic warfare" has been deleted as a defining condition of protracted conflict.

Many crises, too, occur without violence, for example, Remilitarization of the Rhineland in 1936, and Iraq's threat to Kuwait's territorial integrity when the latter attained independence in 1961. Some are characterized by minor or serious clashes, such as a border dispute between Cambodia and Thailand in 1958–59, and the Congo II Crisis in 1964. Others are accompanied by war.

Conceptually, too, crisis is closely linked to *war*. This is so if war is defined as "an exceptional legal condition, a phenomenon of intergroup social psychology, a species of conflict, and a species of violence" (Wright, 1942: II, 685, 700); or, in more concrete terms, as a "conflict involving at least one member of [the] interstate system on each side of the war, resulting in a total of 1000 or more battle deaths" (Singer and Small, 1972: 381). Indeed this is the most important reason for studying the phenomenon of crisis.

Crises are generally identified with acts, events or environmental changes that occur *prior* to the outbreak of military hostilities. Thus Snyder and Diesing (1977: 6–7) defined an international crisis as

> a sequence of interactions between the governments of two or more sovereign states in severe conflict, *short of actual war*, but involving the perception of a dangerously high probability of war. The perceived probability must at least be high enough to evoke feelings of fear and tension to an uncomfortable degree (emphasis added; see also Snyder, 1972: 217).

And Lebow incorporated this sharp distinction into the title of his book, *Between Peace and War: The Nature of International Crisis* (1981).

This view of the two concepts and their relationship to each other has long seemed fundamentally flawed (Brecher, 1977, 1979). The war-crisis link is more complex. International crisis denotes disruptive interaction between states whether or not accompanied by violence. At the actor level, the distinguishing traits of a foreign policy crisis are perceptions of harm—threat to one or more basic values, time pressure, and heightened probability of military hostilities—and the consequent stress which decision-makers experience. Perceptions of harm and stress do not require war. Nor do they vanish with war. Rather, they are exacerbated by war.

Crises occur not only before wars. An invasion, that is, the outbreak of war, can also trigger a crisis, for example, the German attack on 22 June 1941 ("Operation Barbarossa"), triggering a crisis for the Soviet Union. Crises can escalate to war, as with the India/China Border Crisis of 1959–63 and the Football War of 1969 between El Salvador and Honduras. And developments during a war can trigger a crisis for a warring state, as for Germany following the decimation of its Sixth Army in the Battle of Stalingrad (November 1942–February 1943). In short, a crisis can erupt, persist and terminate without violence. The occurrence of war, at any point in the evolution of a crisis, intensifies disruptive interaction and perceived harm and stress. And these have important consequences for decision-making. War, in this perspective, is *one of several crisis management techniques*: verbal, political, economic, non-violent military, and violent; that is, to paraphrase Clausewitz's classic dictum, *war is a continuation of crisis by other means*. War does not eliminate or replace crisis. Rather, crisis is accentuated by war.[9]

This link is highlighted by the concept of *intra-war crisis* or IWC. An intra-war crisis for a state manifests conditions (1) and (2) in the definition of a foreign policy crisis specified earlier, that is, a perceived threat to one or more basic values and an awareness of finite time for response. By its very nature an IWC excludes the third perceptual condition, namely, heightened probability of war. The replacement indicator is perceived deterioration in a state's and/or an ally's military capability *vis-à-vis* an enemy, that is, a perceived *adverse change in the military balance*.

Like crisis itself, IWC applies to both levels of analysis. Thus, just as a foreign policy crisis for a state generates an international crisis, so too a foreign policy crisis for a state during a war generates an international IWC. A measure of its importance is the fact that 30% of all foreign policy crises from the end of 1918 to the end of 1988, 247 of 826, and 19% of international crises, 73 of 390, were IWCs [see Table 2.4, Chap. 2 for the seven types of IWC, with illustrations].

The relationships among *crisis*, *conflict* and *war* are presented in Figure 1.1. As evident, not all crises escalate to war. Some crises occur within, others outside, protracted conflicts. Some crises within and some outside protracted conflicts are accompanied by war. Other logically-possible links are: the overlap of (b) and (e), and (b) and (c) in

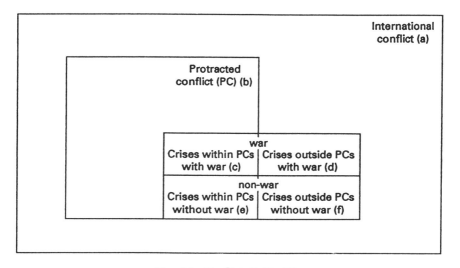

Fig. 1.1 Conflict, Crisis, War

Figure 1.1, that is, the beginning of a protracted conflict in the form of a crisis, accompanied or not accompanied by war; and the emergence of a new international conflict through the eruption of a crisis, with or without war, the overlap between (a) and (d), or (a) and (f). In the most general sense, all types of turmoil are encompassed in international conflict. They comprise, in descending order of conflict space, protracted conflict, crisis, and war, along with other kinds of transnational or interstate disputes over territory, resources, human rights, etc., that do not generate a protracted conflict, crisis or war.[10]

Earlier, it was stated that the major reason for studying crisis is that it is closely linked to conflict and war, all of them crucial concepts and phenomena in world politics. More generally, as G. H. Snyder persuasively argued (1972: 217):

> An international crisis is international politics in microcosm. . . . Such elements as power configurations, interests, values, risks, perceptions, degrees of resolve, bargaining, and decision making lie at the core of international politics; in a crisis they tend to leap out at the observer . . . and to be sharply focused on a single well-defined issue. . . . Thus a crisis is a concentrated distillation of most of the elements which make up the essence of politics in the international system.

State of the Art[11]

Although military-security crises have been pervasive in the twentieth century and were present in all historical eras with autonomous territorial entities (the Middle East, Chinese, Indian and Greek systems of antiquity, the Italian city-state system of the Renaissance, and the Western State system from 1648 to 1939), crisis was only recognized in the 1960s as a distinct phenomenon in world politics.

There are several ways of classifying works on crisis in world politics. One is in terms of substance, with half-a-dozen foci of attention. The first is crisis anticipation, notably McClelland's (1961, 1964, 1968, 1972, 1977) use of events data to map the flow of system-level transitions, which leave measurable traces that are useful as early-warning indicators. He and others influenced by his pioneering work developed sophisticated crisis forecasting techniques in the earliest of the aggregate data projects, the World Events Interaction Survey (WEIS).[12]

Many have tried to explain the failure of crisis (or war) anticipation by states, especially the phenomenon of surprise attack; among others, Wasserman (1960), R. Wohlstetter (1962), Knorr (1964), Holst (1966), Whaley (1973), Ben-Zvi (1975, 1976), Bonham and Shapiro (1976), Shlaim (1976), Handel (1977), Betts (1978, 1982, 1989), Chan (1979), Lanir (1983), Vertzberger (1984), Hybel (1986), Levite (1987, 1989), and Kam (1988). Building upon their contributions, the following chapter will attempt to explain "surprise" with respect to the outbreak (system/interactor level) and initiation (actor level) of crises.

Another substantive focus is the *decision-making process*. A pioneering, complex framework to analyze foreign policy decision-making was constructed by R. C. Snyder, Bruck and Sapin (1962). Paige (1968, 1972) applied this to a major post-World War II crisis, the US decisional response to the eruption of the Korean War in June 1950.[13]

Many other books and articles focused on US decision-making in crises: for example, Allison (1971) and Herek, Janis and Huth (1989) on Cuban Missiles; Halper (1971) on six, and Oneal (1982) on three, post-World War II cases; Shlaim (1983) on the Berlin Blockade, 1948–49; Dowty (1984) on the Lebanon Civil War, 1958, the Jordan/Syria Confrontation, 1970, and the superpower nuclear alert crisis, 1973; Burke and Greenstein (1989) on two US crucial decisions, President Eisenhower's decision not to intervene in the 1954 French/Vietminh battle over Dien Bien Phu, and President Johnson's decision to intervene with fighting forces in the Dominican Republic in 1965; and, more generally, Falkowski (1979).

USSR decision-making, too, has been the object of considerable research, notably: Adomeit's (1982) analysis of Soviet risk-taking and crisis behavior in the Berlin crises of 1948–49 and 1961; Glassman (1975: Chap. 5), G. Golan (1977, 1984: Chap. 8), and Rubinstein (1977: Chap. 8) on Soviet behavior in the 1973 October-Yom Kippur crisis-war; and Valenta (1979, 1984: Chap. 7, 1991), and K. Dawisha (1984) on the 1968 Prague Spring.

Lebow (1981) cast his net much wider, analyzing misperceptions, cognitive closure and coping in 26 crises in which one of the adversaries was a major power, from the Spanish–American War, 1898, to the Middle East Six Day War in 1967.

Others explored the relative influence of specific factors in the decision-making process:

system structure (G. H. Snyder, 1976, Snyder and Diesing, 1977, esp. Chap. VI);

"groupthink" and, more generally, the policy-making group (Janis, 1972, 1989: 231–264, 275–283; Janis and Mann, 1977; Herek, Janis and Huth, 1987);

group setting, both structure and size (Semmel, 1982);

the *military attitude to, and role in*, the *use of force* (Betts, 1977, 1991; George, 1984);

operational codes in crisis behavior (George, 1969a; Hoagland and Walker, 1979);

leadership performance in crisis (e.g., Wallace and Suedfeld, 1988); and the effects of

historical lessons and memories (May, 1973; Falkowski, 1978; Neustadt and May, 1986; Vertzberger, 1986, 1990).

And Morgan (1991) argued, in a general critique of the concept, that "crisis decisions" is, in reality, a subset of "exceedingly difficult" or "complex" decisions that arise in both crisis and non-crisis situations.

The third substantive focus is *crisis management*, both by intermediaries (e.g., Young, 1967; E. Haas, 1983, 1986; Brecher and Wilkenfeld, 1989: Chaps. 5, 6), and how states cope with crises, notably George *et al.* (1971), George and Smoke (1974), Brecher and Wilkenfeld (1989: Chap. 11), Rosenthal, Charles and Hart (1989), and George (1991). Bracken (1983) and Lebow (1987) focused on crisis management in the nuclear sphere. At the conceptual level, Galtung (1965), Bell (1971), Williams (1976), Frei (1982), Lebow and Stein (1987), Winham (1988), and George (1991) contributed to the debate on crisis management.[14]

Closely related to crisis management is the concept and practice of *deterrence*, designed to prevent a military challenge to oneself, to an ally, or to a client state. The pioneering works were by Ellsberg (1959), Kahn (1960, 1962), Schelling (1960), and G. H. Snyder (1961). The most notable works in the second "wave" were George and Smoke (1974), who applied the method of "structured focused comparison" to 11 US cases from 1948 to 1962 and developed a prescriptive theory of deterrence, and Morgan (1977), whose conceptual focus and more rigorous definition of deterrence became the point of departure for much of the subsequent debate. In the third "wave," during the 1980s, the psychological element achieved high visibility through Jervis, Lebow and Stein (1985) and other works. The game theoretical approach was elegantly revived by Brams (1985), Zagare (1987), and Brams and Kilgour (1988).

A special issue of *World Politics* (1989) was devoted to controversies over theories of deterrence, with contributions by Achen and Snidal, George and Smoke, Jervis, Lebow and Stein, and Downs. An acrimonious debate over how to conceptualize, operationalize and test deterrence theory, the usefulness of quantitative methods, and the relevance of context in explaining deterrence outcomes came to a head in an exchange between Lebow and Stein (1990) and Huth and Russett

(1990), building upon several earlier studies (Lebow and Stein, 1987; Russett, 1963; Huth and Russett, 1984, 1988; Huth, 1988a, b). The issue remains unresolved, largely, it has been argued, because too much emphasis has been placed on methodological issues, not enough on the testing of key propositions embedded in conventional and nuclear deterrence theory (James and Harvey, 1992; Harvey and James, 1992).

Another related substantive focus, the *bargaining* dimension of crisis, was the object of several systematic inquiries (Young, 1968; G. H. Snyder, 1972; Snyder and Diesing, 1977: Chaps. II, III, and pp. 480–503; Allan, 1983; and Leng *et al.*, 1979, 1982, 1983, 1987, 1988, 1993 [forthcoming]). Bargaining, as explored in this book, is part of the larger process of crisis management. It will be examined at length in the chapters to follow, both through model-derived propositions and in ten case studies of coping in the onset, escalation and deescalation phases of an international crisis.

By contrast, *initiation* has been underdeveloped in the literature on crisis. It is implied in Schelling's (1966) discussion of the strategies of compellance and deterrence, in Young's (1968) study of bargaining, and in George *et al.*'s (1971) analysis of coercive diplomacy. The major works on initiation are: George and Smoke (1974: Chap. 17); Bueno de Mesquita's (1981, 1985) expected utility theory of initiation of *war*; and Maoz's (1982a, b) studies of the initiation of "serious international disputes" [see Chap. 2, n. 12].

Finally, in contrast to *war termination* [see Chap. 4], little attention has been devoted to *crisis abatement*, the "winding-down" of crises with the least adverse consequences (Hopple and Rossa, 1981: 81–82).

Another mode of grouping the literature is in terms of **models of crisis decision-making** (Hermann and Brady, 1972; O. R. Holsti, 1989). The pioneer in this realm was the "Stanford School," whose *Studies in Conflict and Integration* in the 1960s and 1970s employed a mediated stimulus–response model, with perception as the key variable explaining state behavior (e.g., O. R. Holsti, 1965, 1972; Nomikos and North, 1976). The Stanford Studies emphasized perceptions of threat, time pressure, communication, information overload, and the consideration of alternatives.[15]

Its *hostile interaction* model posits that an expression of hostility by state A towards state B, and reciprocity by B at a higher level of hostility, leads to a spiral of increasingly intense hostility and escalation to violence. A variant is the *conflict-begets-conflict* model, which asserts that state behavior, like human behavior, is a proportional response to an environmental stimulus, more precisely, that ". . . total conflict sent to all conflict partners ought to roughly equal total conflict received" (Wilkenfeld, 1975: 177).[16]

The *individual stress* model identifies stress as the derivative of perceptions—of threat, time pressure, and, in the Hermann (1969b) version, surprise, or, in the author's (1977) definition of a foreign policy crisis specified above, heightened probability of war. There is a wide diversity of views regarding the effects of stress on the quality of decision-making, summarized and assessed by Holsti and George (1975), and Tanter (1975); effects on

> the *search for information and policy options* (Hermann, 1972: 187–211; O. R. Holsti, 1972: 14–17, 119–142; Brecher with Geist, 1980: 235–238, 362–373);
>
> the *ability to assess consequences and choose among options rationally* (Hermann, 1972: 298; Milburn, 1972: 273; Paige, 1972: 52; Robinson, 1972: 23; Morgan, 1977: 178; Brecher with Geist, 1980: 247–249, 358–373); and, at the extreme, on whether or not stress has any *effect on crisis decision-making* (Levi and Tetlock, 1980).

Closely related to the stress model is the *cognitive* model, which argues that decision-making is shaped by psychological biases. The search for alternatives tends to be limited to options consistent with the belief systems of decision-makers. Information processing is complex, and discrepant information is often distorted or rejected outright. The evaluation of alternatives tends to be dominated by a single value. All these and other cognitively-derived biases and shortcomings make optimal choice a chimera (de Rivera, 1968; Axelrod, 1976; Jervis, 1976; Vertzberger, 1986, 1990). And, under the stress of crisis, cognitive limitations on analytic decision-making become more acute (Lazarus, 1966; Holsti and George, 1975; Janis and Mann, 1977; Lazarus and Folkman, 1984, and Janis, 1989).[17]

Another type of psychological approach is psychoanalytic models. One focuses on the role of shame and humiliation in decision-making during crises (Steinberg, 1991a, b). Another explores the effect of crisis-induced stress on decision-making by different types of leader personality (Post, 1991).

The *organizational process* model, or the *cybernetic* model (Steinbruner, 1974; Marra, 1985), argues that the constraints imposed by threat, time and surprise lead decision-makers to rely on SOPS of organizations rather than to engage in a careful search for, and evaluation of, alternatives based upon multiple sources of information. And these decisions tend to be "satisficing," not "optimizing." Allison (1971:

Chaps. 3–4) applied his Model II to the Cuban Missile Crisis. Hazlewood *et al.* (1977) discovered this process in many US responses to crises since 1945. And Levy (1986) found the cybernetic model to be highly salient in the behavior of the major powers during the crisis leading to the outbreak of World War I.

The *cost-calculation* model or Allison's (1971) *rational actor* model—his Model I—or Stein and Tanter's (1980) *analytic* model, or Bueno de Mesquita's (1981) *expected utility* model, postulates that crisis decisions emerge from a careful assessment of risks, costs and benefits of alternative options; that is, decision-makers choose the option that has the greatest expected utility. This they do by multiplying the subjective value of each possible outcome of an action by the probability that it will occur. Moreover, they continuously revise their estimates in the light of new information.[18]

A contrasting approach to probability assessment and risky choice is provided by *prospect theory* (Kahneman and Tversky, 1979). In essence, it argues that "the downside is considerably steeper than the upside; that is, losses loom larger than the corresponding gains. . . . Furthermore, prospect theory implies [in contrast to rational choice theory] that shifts in the reference point induced by the framing of the problem will have predictable effects on people's risk preferences" (Quattrone and Tversky, 1988, 721; also Levy, 1992a; and, for an instructive assessment of early case study attempts to apply prospect theory to international relations, see Levy, 1992b and other contributions to Farnham (1992).

In reflecting on his multiple explanation of US behavior in the Cuban Missile crisis, Allison (1971) suggested that his three models—rational actor, organizational process and bureaucratic—were not mutually exclusive: each captured part of a complex decision-making reality. Stein and Tanter (1980) went further by integrating their three models —analytic, cybernetic and cognitive—and five functions of the decision process—diagnosis, search, estimation and revision, evaluation, and choice—into an overall "multiple paths to choice" model. They postulated that different models may prevail in different stages of decision-making and identified seven possible paths to choice, that is, every conceivable combination of the three models in each of three stages of decision-making, with each path having a distinctive set of traits and consequences. Maoz (1990b: 6.2.1, 7.3, 7.4, 7.5) built on the multiple paths to choice model, which he termed the "MPC framework," and developed an "integrative theory of international processes."[19]

A third approach to classifying works on crises is M. Haas's (1986)

philosophical alternatives. One such cluster is *metaphysical*, which may be idealist (perceptual), materialist (physical, such as information overload or physiological stress), or dualist, combining mental and physical conceptions. Another cluster is *epistemological*, which he terms rationalist versus empirical, along with his notion of crisis as an abstract concept incapable of direct measurement. The last of his philosophical alternatives is *level of analysis* (macro- or system- versus micro- or actor-level). Using a combined typology of metaphysics, epistemology, and level of analysis, Haas grouped 28 studies and definitions of the elusive concept of crisis. He concluded the comparison by noting "a lack of conceptual and empirical consensus" (53).

Another perspective on crisis is O. R. Holsti's (1989: 8–84) dissection of four **levels of analysis**—state, bureaucratic organization, decision-making group, and individual. The rationale was that "each tends to focus on and highlight different aspects of the question [the relationship between crisis and decision-making performance] and to yield a somewhat different modal diagnosis" (13, 11). These levels were compared in terms of: conceptualization of decision-making; sources of theory, insight, and evidence; premises; constraints on rational decision-making; and prognosis—crisis versus non-crisis decisions. Empirical studies of the 1914 Crisis, Cuban Missiles and others were surveyed, as well as theories of crisis management. The upshot was cautious optimism:

> first, "lawlike prescriptions that will enable those who must make decisions in crises to transcend the awful dilemmas they may have to face" are unlikely;
>
> second, "theoretically informed and empirically based diagnoses of the potential frailties and weaknesses in decision-making systems . . . are within reach [and] constitute a not-insignificant contribution toward the prevention of nuclear war";
>
> and finally, there remains the yet-to-be bridged gap between behavioral science and the policy community (65).

Crisis research may also be grouped in terms of the **methodology** employed. It may be *historical* description and analysis, a vast number of works. It may be *crucial case study* (Eckstein, 1975), or *comparative case study*, using a systematic framework of analysis such as "structured focused comparison" (George and Smoke, 1974; George, 1979) or "structured empiricism" (Brecher, 1972, and the ICB studies cited in n.

50 below), or some other variant of comparative analysis (e.g., Lebow, 1981). Or it may be *quantitative, aggregate study* of a large number of cases (McClelland, 1964, 1968, 1972; Gochman and Maoz, 1984; Leng and Singer, 1988; Brecher and Wilkenfeld 1988, 1989; Wilkenfeld and Brecher, 1988).

Since the primary goal of this "state of the art" review is to relate our macro (system/interactor) and micro (actor) definitions to others in the crisis literature, I choose the *level of analysis* mode for special attention, beginning with definitions of crisis from the perspective of a state.

The most widely-accepted view of a foreign policy crisis, in the 1960s and 1970s, was the high threat-short time-surprise formula enunciated by Hermann (1963, 1969a, b, 1972a, b):

> A crisis is a situation that (1) threatens high-priority goals of the decision-making unit, (2) restricts the amount of time available for response before the decision is transformed, and (3) surprises the members of the decision-making unit by its occurrence (1969a: 414).

The Hermann definition owed much to Robinson's initial conception of crisis (1962, 1968, 1972) as a decisional situation with three elements: "(1) identification of the origin of the event—whether external or internal for the decision-makers; (2) the decision time available for response—whether short, intermediate, or long; and (3) the relative importance of the values at stake to the participants—whether high or low" (1968: 511). In essence, Hermann retained two of Robinson's traits, time and threat, but he made significant changes: "restricted" or short time only; and threat to "high-priority goals," not values. And he replaced "origin of the event" with surprise.

Many scholars adopted Hermann's definition. Thus O. R. Holsti, in his innovative study of the 1914 Crisis leading to World War I, defined crisis as "a situation of unanticipated threat to important values and restricted decision time," though he also noted: "there are many usages of the term 'crisis'" (1972: 9, 263, n. 13).[20] So too did: Milburn (1972), in his analysis of crisis management; Nomikos and North (1976), in their rigorous narrative of crisis escalation in 1914; Head, Short and McFarlane (1978), in their study of US decision-making in the 1950 Korean and 1975 Mayaguez crises, though they preferred "important national goals or objectives" to "high-priority goals," and added, as a fourth condition of crisis, a change in the external or internal environment (a precondition in the definition of a foreign policy crisis guiding this inquiry); and Oneal (1982), in his comparative study of US crisis decision-making.

Morse (1972: 127) accepted the short time condition, but not surprise; and he referred to "mutually incompatible but highly valued objectives." A primary emphasis on stress and threat is evident in the Stein-Tanter definition (1980: 58): crisis is "the stress created by the necessity to make important and difficult choices in a threatening environment"; but they too shared Hermann's emphasis on short time for response. Later (1988: 173), Stein adopted the view that focuses on a perceived "threat to basic values" and an anticipation of "limited time to respond." Also in the perceptual mainstream, Lebow's definition (1981: 9–12) focused on three policy-makers' perceptions: of "action or threatened action" that "seriously impairs concrete national interests, . . . bargaining reputation or their ability to remain in power"; "a significant prospect of war" as a result of their response; and "time constraints."

Several actor-level definitions do not emphasize perceptually-derived stress. Hazlewood *et al.* (1977: 79), who examined US Defense Department behavior in external crises from 1946 to 1975, identified crisis "as an extraordinary decision-making activity in which existing decision patterns are disrupted by an emergency . . . that . . . threaten[s] to inflict violence or significant damage to . . . national interests. . . ". They accepted the notion of surprise but emphasized "increased military management activity at the national level."

By contrast, Wiegele (1973, 1985) identified stress as the consequence of information and/or other types of "overload" on the physiological capacity to cope with crisis. Using a Psychological Stress Evaluator, he searched for speech irregularities as indicators of crisis-induced stress among US decision-makers in three cases: the Dominican Republic (1965), the Berlin Wall (1961), and Nixon's Invasion of Cambodia in 1970. In general, "decision makers exhibit negative affect when they must act conflictually in the name of the state [but not so in routine behavior] . . . , as revealed by voice stress analysis" (1985: 168).

Perceived war likelihood is common to the Snyder-Diesing and Brecher definitions, though they specify "dangerously high" (1977: 6–7; Snyder, 1972: 217), compared with "heightened" probability. So too is the exclusion of surprise and *short* time "because they are not logically necessary and some empirical crises do not have these qualities" (1977: 9, n. 7). Yet there are important differences. For Snyder-Diesing, crisis is solely an interaction process; I focus on both interactions, in the macro-level definition and the analysis of international crisis, and the perceptions and actions of one state, that is, an action process, in the micro-level definition and analysis of a foreign policy crisis. Secondly, they ignore the time condition, both its duration and intensity, though I share the view that crises need not be short; in fact, some last many months, even a year or more. And thirdly, "the [Snyder-Diesing] term, probability of war, excludes war itself from the concept, 'crisis' . . . ," whereas I forged a structural link between crisis and war, an intra-war crisis, as indicated in the earlier discussion of these concepts.[21]

Because of the prominence of Hermann's definition of foreign policy crisis, I conclude the actor-level segment of this "state of the art" review by comparing it with my definition presented above. In essence, the latter builds upon, but differs significantly from, that of Hermann on five essential points: (1) the omission of "surprise" as a defining condition; (2) the replacement of short time with finite time for response; (3) the recognition that the change which induces a crisis may originate in the internal, as well as the external, environment of the crisis actor; (4) the concept of "basic values," rather than "high-priority goals," as the object of perceived threat; and (5) the addition of "perceived heightened probability of involvement" in military hostilities, that is, of higher-than-normal war likelihood. These definitional changes merit further discussion.

(1) There are high-threat, heightened probability-of-war, and finite-time situations in the perceptions of decision-makers that do not occasion surprise; that is, they are not unanticipated. For example, the Soviet imposition of the Berlin Blockade in 1948 did not come as a surprise to American decision-makers. But the perceived threat catalyzed a crisis, generated stress, and affected the US's response to the change in the strategic region of Central Europe (Shlaim, 1983).

Hermann and others became increasingly skeptical about the surprise element of crisis. His early simulation analysis (1969b: 69) led to a finding of "no significant relationship between either the time and awareness [surprise] dimensions or the threat and awareness dimensions; however, a significant correlation did occur between decision time and threat." This was reaffirmed by him in a later paper (1972a: 208).

The lower frequency of surprise and doubt about the adequacy of Hermann's overall definition of crisis is evident in Brady's finding (1974: 58): "In sum, . . . the absence of second-order interaction effects leads us to qualify our judgment concerning the [eight-fold] typology's utility. . . . [It] is not as successful as we would have predicted." D. M. McCormick (1975: I, 16) questioned whether surprise could be operationalized at all: "Surprise . . . normally occurs only once when there is an unexpected outbreak of violence. . . . [W]e concluded that surprise is not measurable from content analysis."

Hermann, himself, deleted surprise from his on-going research (Hermann and Mason, 1980: 193), primarily because "previous empirical research failed to establish surprise as generating a measurable result . . .". And surprise was deleted from his revised definition of crisis, which specified as the defining conditions: the perception of "a severe threat to the basic values of their political system"; "relatively short time"; and "an increased expectation that in the near future there will be an outbreak of military hostilities or a sharp escalation of already existing hostilities" (1988: 122).

(2) The lack of validity for short time as a defining condition, too, is demonstrated by the 1948 Berlin Blockade, as well as by the 1967 Middle East Crisis. The former lasted almost a year, the latter three weeks, with Israel's decision-makers willing to delay a military riposte another week or two. It was not the perceived brevity of time that shaped decision-making behavior but, rather, the awareness of the finiteness of time for choice. A response could not be delayed indefinitely; that is, whether a week, a month or longer, there was a realization that decisions for or against war had to be made within some time frame (Brecher with Geist, 1980).

(3) For many states, the change that triggers a foreign policy crisis often occurs within the domestic environment, usually through physical challenges to the political regime by strikes, demonstrations, riots, assassination, sabotage, and/or attempted coups. Most new, Third World states have deeply-penetrated political systems; and domestic changes, some of which derive from foreign sources, may give rise to an image of external as well as internal threat. The assault on Chile's Allende regime in 1973 is a dramatic illustration of this widespread phenomenon in Africa and Latin America (Kaufman, 1988).

(4) High-priority goals as the focus of threat, in Hermann's definition of crisis, has been broadened to basic values. These include core values, which are near-constant and few in number, such as survival of the society and its population, political sovereignty and independence, though even the last two are not universal in time and space. A second value element is context-specific high-priority values. These derive from ideological and/or material interests as defined by decision-makers at the time of a specific crisis. Core values, by contrast, are shared by changing regimes and decision-making groups, as well as by the attentive and mass publics of the state under inquiry. A crisis may be said to exist when the threatened values are not only high-priority for the incumbent élite but also include one or more core values. In short, this view differs from Hermann's in two respects: first, it is values, not goals,

that are under threat in a crisis situation; and second, a crisis implies the involvement of a basic value.

(5) The most important definitional change is the addition of heightened probability of war or, more broadly, higher-than-normal likelihood of involvement in military hostilities, as a defining condition of crisis. In the two cases cited above, decision-makers thought that this would occur before the threat to values was resolved.

Theoretically, perceived probability of war ranges from virtually nil to near-certainty. For a crisis to erupt, however, perception of war likelihood *need not be high*. Rather, it *must be qualitatively higher than the norm* in the specific adversarial relationship. This applies to both states for whom the "normal" expectation of war is "high" and those with a perception of "low" probability of war.

The former comprises states engaged in a protracted conflict, e.g., India and Pakistan since 1947, Israel and the Arab states since 1948. For them, the normal level of perceived probability is "high." However, an unchanging high probability of military hostilities does not generate a crisis. Rather, it is an increase in war likelihood, usually a sharp increase, from "high" to "higher" or "very high," that will trigger a definition of a crisis by the decision-makers of the state(s) concerned. At the other extreme is an adversarial pair with a norm of "very low" expectations of war, e.g., Iceland and the UK prior to 1973. Yet a change in perceived war likelihood in such cases from nil or "very low" to "low," both of which are "low" expectations, will nonetheless trigger a crisis for the state experiencing the rise in perceived likelihood of hostilities.

In sum, it is not "high" probability that is salient to crisis eruption, or "low" probability that is salient to non-eruption. Rather, it is an *upward change* in perceived probability—from a "high" or "low" norm—that helps to trigger a foreign policy crisis. This is one reason why "heightened" or "higher-than-normal" probability is preferred to "high" probability. Another reason is that the term, "heightened," encompasses change from "high" to "higher," and from "very low" to "low," the two types of change in perceived probability discussed above. It also includes a third type, from "low" to "high" likelihood. Thus any manifestation of "high" likelihood is subsumed in the term, "heightened." Finally, *any* of these upward changes creates, for decision-makers, a perception of "high" probability; that is, "higher" and "high" are synonymous for them. For the analyst, however, these are different, conceptually. And what is salient to the explanation of crisis eruption is change. For all of these reasons, the term, "heightened" probability of war is preferred.

Among the three defining perceptual conditions of crisis the most crucial is heightened expectation of war. Threat and time pressure may coexist without a hostile act, event or environmental change being defined, or responded to, as an external crisis. Moreover, a higher-than-normal probability of war necessarily implies a perceived higher-than-normal threat to values, but the reverse does not always obtain. Thus perceived probability of war is the pivotal condition of crisis, with threat and time closely related, as will be elaborated below in the model of foreign policy crisis. Parenthetically, Hermann, who as noted had built in an important way on Robinson's earlier work, later acknowledged the centrality of perceived war likelihood in the concept of a foreign policy crisis: "I accept his [Brecher's] introduction of the expectation of military hostilities as particularly appropriate . . . " (1988: 148, n.3).

In short, all five conceptual departures from the Hermann definition of a foreign policy crisis—*omission of surprise, finite rather than short time, internal as well as external triggers, basic values instead of high-priority goals*, and *heightened probability of war*—are expressed in the definition presented early in this chapter. And it is this fundamentally revised definition (Brecher, 1977) that guided the selection of 826 cases which constitute the ICB's state-level data set from the end of 1918 to the end of 1988. Finally, for the reasons indicated above, the definition used in this book seems to be a more well-rounded, thorough, accurate, precise and realistic indicator of a foreign policy crisis.[22]

I turn now to the "state of the art" on the macro (system/interactor) level of analysis.[23] Existing definitions of international crisis are based upon concepts derived from the systems literature. They can be classified into two types: process, and combined interaction-structure.

Process definitions view international crisis as a turning point at which an unusually intense period of conflictive interactions occurs. According to McClelland (1968: 160–161),

> a crisis is, in some way, a "change of state" in the flow of international political actions. . . . Acute international crises are "short burst" affairs and are marked by an unusual volume and intensity of events. (See also McClelland, 1961.)

Elsewhere (1972: 6, 7) he referred to crisis as

> an unusual manifestation of the interflow of activity between the participants. [Moreover, crisis] interaction is likely to [take the form of effects on the] stability or equilibrium of the system, or disturbance of the normal run of business conducted between actors.

Azar (1972: 184) defined an international crisis in terms of interaction above the threshold of a "normal relations range" (NRR): "Interaction above the present upper critical threshold . . . for more than a very short time implies that a crisis situation has set in."

Two definitions were developed by the *Correlates of War (COW)* Project in the 1980s, namely, a "militarized interstate dispute" (MID), and a "militarized interstate crisis" ((MIC). The former was defined as

> a set of interactions between or among states involving threats to use military force, displays of military force, or actual uses of military force. . . . [T]hese acts must be explicit, overt, nonaccidental, and government sanctioned (Gochman and Maoz, 1984: 587; also Leng, 1987; for the precursor of MID, namely, a serious interstate dispute [SID], see Maoz, 1982a: 7–12).

This "evolves into a *militarized interstate crisis* when a member of the interstate system on each side of the dispute indicates by its actions its willingness to go to war to defend its interests or to obtain its objectives." And these are steps two and three along a ladder of growing belligerence, beginning with an "interstate dispute" and culminating in an "interstate war" (Leng and Singer, 1988: 159).

These definitions tend to emphasize various stages of conflictive behavior among states; to characterize different types of activity; to measure the direction and speed of behavioral change; and to locate shifts that indicate changes in interaction processes. They are all important aspects of crisis analysis. Moreover, clearly defined concepts facilitate these tasks (e.g., Azar, Brody and McClelland, 1972). So do precise scales to rank the behavioral groups (McClelland, 1968; Corson, 1970; Azar *et al.*, 1977).

Yet there are analytical shortcomings. The logic for designating the beginning and end of a crisis was not specified. Changes in process were not related to structure. Causes and effects of systemic crises were not uncovered. The result was a group of essentially empirical studies of international crisis (Azar, 1972; Burgess and Lawton, 1972; Wilkenfeld, 1972; Tanter, 1974; Andriole and Young, 1977; Eckhardt and Azar, 1978).[24]

Combined *structural-interaction* definitions go further, by identifying an international crisis as a situation characterized by basic change in processes that might affect structural variables of a system. Young (1968: 15) stated this view clearly:

> A crisis in international politics is a process of interaction occurring at higher levels of perceived intensity than the ordinary flow of events and characterized by . . . significant implications for the stability of some system or subsystem.

So too did Hermann (1972b: 10):

> In any given international political system, critical variables must be maintained

within certain limits or the instability of the system will be greatly increased —perhaps to the point where a new system will be formed. A crisis is a situation which disrupts the system or some part of the system.

Integrating structure into a process definition serves as a good starting point: by utilizing the dynamic character of interaction with a focus on the effects on structure, these definitions are analytically comprehensive. Yet they suffer from a serious limitation—the crucial concept of structure remains fuzzy; that is, it is difficult to say what structural change would mean in operational terms.[25]

A shortcoming of many international crisis definitions is the mixture of system- and unit-level concepts. This is striking in Wiener and Kahn's (1962) listing of 12 generic attributes of crisis. They included system-level indicators such as a turning point in a sequence of events, a new configuration of international politics as a crisis outcome, and changes in relations among actors. There are also unit-level indicators: a perceived threat to actor goals; a sense of urgency, stress and anxiety among decision-makers; increased time pressure, etc.

Young began with a purely system-level definition, in exploring the role of intermediaries, especially the UN, in crises:

> An international crisis . . . is a set of rapidly unfolding events which raises the impact of destabilizing forces in the general international system or any of its subsystems substantially above "normal" . . . and increases the likelihood of violence occurring in the system (1967: 10).

Soon after (1968: 10, 14), however, when extending his analysis to bargaining among crisis actors, he merged the two levels by defining crises as

> situations perceived by the participants [unit-level] as much more competitive than the ordinary flow of international politics. [Moreover,] crisis concerns the probabilities that violence of major proportions will break out, [a point that] explicitly refers to subjective perceptions about the prospects of violence [unit-level] rather than to a more objective measure of the probability of violence [system-level].

And McCormick (1978: 352) consciously combined Hermann's defining conditions for an actor-level crisis with McClelland's distinguishing trait of a systemic crisis: " . . . a situation between two or more nations characterized by perceptual conditions of high threat, surprise and short decision time, and by behavioral conditions of marked change in their interaction patterns."

In summary, these definitions exhibit three weaknesses. They do not integrate all the key concepts related to international crisis—change in interaction, type of structure, disequilibrium, and instability. They focus excessively on process, with little explanation of its effects on the structure of a system. And they merge systemic concepts with such unit-level concepts as perception, stress and value.

This mixture of levels, conditions and indicators creates conceptual ambiguity. By contrast, several works analyzed crisis at both levels and integrated their findings, while treating foreign policy crisis and international crisis as conceptually distinct. George and Smoke (1974) examined US deterrence policy (actor level) in 11 international crises, from the Berlin Blockade of 1948–49, to Cuban Missiles in 1962. Tanter (1974) attempted to assess the relative potency of event interactions (system/interactor level) and organizational processes (actor level) in explaining the intensity of East/West crises over Berlin. And Snyder and Diesing (1977) integrated bargaining, decision-making and system structure in their analysis of 18 crises, from the Fashoda Incident of 1898 to the 1973 US/USSR nuclear alert crisis. However, in all of these works the primary focus was other than crisis: for George and Smoke, deterrence theory; for Tanter, the East/West conflict; and for Snyder and Diesing, a synthesis of systems, bargaining and decision-making theory.

A qualitatively-different conception of crisis is attributed to the Chinese by Bobrow *et al.* (1977: 204, 205):

first, "While international crises indicate periods of stress and danger, they may also signal opportunities to advance one's interests";

second, "They are recurrent phenomena generated by long-term economic processes and are not unpredictable, sudden flares of belligerency among actors";

third, "They are, at least at their initial stage of development, primarily domestic phenomena and not foreign relations phenomena"; and

fourth, "They are protracted phenomena . . . and their resolution requires persistent struggle, perseverance and patience . . . ".

Thus, "it is fallacious to extrapolate U.S. perceptions of international crisis to the Chinese leadership."[26]

While acknowledging that this is the Chinese view of crisis, the ICB study of twentieth-century crises challenges the conclusion that the phenomenon of crisis is culturally bound. To take the Bobrow *et al.* contentions in sequence:

first, there is no logical incompatibility between stress and opportunity; westerners, too, often perceive opportunities to achieve goals through crises;

second, the Marxist thesis notwithstanding, it is empirically incorrect to assume that all crises, even all Chinese crises, are recurrent phenomena due to long-term economic processes; for example, to explain the China/India crisis of 1959–62 in economic terms may be ideologically sound, but it is empirically fallacious;

third, while some crises originate in domestic pressure, the vast majority do not; and

fourth, not all crises are protracted; this is a confusion between crisis and protracted conflict, a relationship discussed earlier in the context of crisis, conflict and war.

The term, crisis, has an even more profoundly different meaning for the *world system* approach to world politics. According to Wallerstein (1983: 21),

> By crisis in a historical system I shall mean . . . a structural strain so great that the only possible outcome is the disappearance of the system as such, either by a process of gradual disintegration . . . or by a process of relatively controlled transformation. . . . In this sense, a crisis is by definition a "transition" . . . medium-long in length, taking often 100–150 years.

The interstate dimension of crisis is conspicuously absent—consistent with the "world system" denigration of the role of the state in system change and historical evolution. The "world system" definition of crisis specified here is *sui generis*: it uses the same term, crisis, to designate an entirely different phenomenon, namely, irrevocable historical change—"the only possible outcome." So too with its use of the terms, system and transformation. As such, it is not comparable with any of the definitions of international crisis and foreign policy crisis discussed in this chapter.

Other adherents of the "world system" approach acknowledge the existence of "crises within the international state system," but these focus primarily on "the rise and fall of hegemonic states and the competition and conflict accompanying the succession struggle" (Bergesen, 1983: 12). While there is disagreement over the number of hegemony/competition cycles in the world system during the last five centuries —two, according to Bergesen, three (Chase-Dunn, 1979), and four (Modelski, 1978; Hopkins and Wallerstein, 1979)—the set of twentieth-century international crises so defined is very small!

In response to the above-noted conceptual inadequacies, we offered a new definition of international crisis: it incorporates change in *process* and *structure*, and links them to *stability* and *equilibrium*, the four crucial elements of an *international system*. We argued that, in international crises, change varies in quantity and quality. For us, few distortions in process or few challenges to the structure of a system denote low instability, whereas many changes indicate high instability. By contrast, reversible changes in process or challenges to structure indicate equilibrium, while irreversible changes identify disequilibrium.

That, in turn, may or may not lead to system transformation, as illustrated by the Berlin Blockade of 1948–49. The Four Power Agreement on 12 May 1949 left Germany divided, created the foundations of two new international actors, the Federal Republic of Germany (FRG) and the German Democratic Republic (GDR), and changed the balance of power between the superpowers. It also altered the interaction pattern that had existed during the occupation of Germany by the Four Powers. Thus, *inter alia*, our revised definition of international crisis facilitates the study of change in world politics, large and small (Brecher and Ben Yehuda, 1985; Brecher and James, 1986).[27]

From this critique of the "state of the art" on crisis it is clear that, despite abundant theorizing and research, perhaps because of the plethora of definitions, approaches and conceptual frameworks, a widely-accepted *theory of interstate crisis* has not yet been developed.[28]

Crisis Domains/Phases

As noted early in this chapter, the theory of crisis to be presented in this book is based upon the concept of four interrelated *domains/phases* of crisis: onset, escalation, deescalation and impact. These will serve as the primary focus of models and hypotheses, and case studies, in the chapters to follow; that is, their dissection and the presentation of findings about how each unfolds and shapes the succeeding domain and phase will form the major part of the analysis. Here I confront preliminary conceptual questions. What do the domains/phases mean? How do they differ from each other? And what is the nature of their interrelationship?

Onset identifies the initial phase of an international crisis. This coincides with the **pre-crisis** *period* of a foreign policy crisis, in which the non-crisis norm of no (or low) perceived value threat by a state's decision-makers gives way to low (or higher), that is, increasing, threat from an adversary and, with it, low (or higher), that is, increasing stress. Onset/pre-crisis does not refer to any hostile interaction or threat perception, for conflict and stress are pervasive in the twentieth-century global system of fragmented authority and unequal distribution of power and resources. Rather, it is characterized by a change in the intensity of disruption between two or more states and of threat perception by at least one of them, for example, a statement by A threatening to attack B unless it complies with some demand by A.

Operationally, onset is indicated by the *outbreak* of a crisis, that is, the eruption of higher-than-normal disruptive interaction, compared to *non-outbreak*, namely, interaction which may be cooperative or, at most, hostile but minimally disruptive. The onset of an international crisis requires at least two adversaries, one or both of which perceive higher-than-normal value threat and respond in a manner that generates qualitatively higher disruption. And the precipitating change is, generally, region- and issue(s)-specific, except for infrequent system-wide upheavals among states.

Escalation denotes much more intense disruption than onset and a qualitative increase in the likelihood of military hostilities. At the actor level, the counterpart to the escalation phase is the **crisis** *period* of a foreign policy crisis, in which perceptions of time pressure and heightened war likelihood are added to more acute threat perception. The escalation phase and crisis period mark peak distortion and maximal stress, respectively.

Escalation may—but need not—be characterized by a change from *no violence* to *violence* as the primary technique of crisis management; that is, the entire crisis may be non-violent. However, if violence occurs in the onset phase, escalation will be indicated by a shift from *low-level* to *high-level* violence, namely, from minor clashes to serious clashes or war between the adversaries. Whether or not accompanied by violence, the process of escalation usually leads to irreversibility in the sense of consequences for the adversaries, as well as for one or more elements of systemic change—in actors/regimes, power relations, alliance configuration, and rules of the game.[29]

Deescalation is the conceptual counterpart of escalation, that is, the "winding-down" of a crisis, compared to the "spiral" process. At the macro level it is indicated by a reduction in hostile interactions leading to accommodation and crisis termination. At the state level deescalation is operationalized as a decline in perceived threat, time pressure and war likelihood towards the non-crisis norm. As such, it denotes the **end-crisis** *period* and is characterized by decreasing stress for the decision-maker(s).[30] While the danger of crises "getting out of hand," that is, escalating to war, has attracted much more attention from scholars and practitioners, the reduction of hostile, often violent, interactions to a non-crisis norm is a goal of many states, as well as regional and global organizations.

PHASE	ONSET	ESCALATION	DEESCALATION	IMPACT
Interaction	Incipient distortion	Peak distortion	Accommodation	Non-crisis interaction
PERIOD	PRE-CRISIS	CRISIS	END-CRISIS	POST-CRISIS
Perception	Higher-than-normal value threat (Increasing stress)	Acute threat + Finite time pressure + heightened Probability of war (Maximal stress)	Declining threat, Time pressure, Probability of war (Decreasing stress)	Below-crisis level of threat, time, war (Non-crisis stress)

FIG. 1.2   Toward a Unified Model of Crisis: Phases and Periods

Like "onset," "escalation," and "deescalation," the term **impact**, as used throughout this book, refers to both phase and domain. In temporal terms, impact designates the phase following crisis termination, that is, its aftermath, the counterpart of **post-crisis** or **beyond crisis** at the actor level of analysis. Moreover, following normal usage, it identifies the consequences of a crisis, that is, the content of the fourth domain of crisis. Its specific meaning will be apparent from the context in which "impact" is used in the text.

All crises have effects at one or more levels: for the adversaries; for their relationship; and for one or more international systems—the subsystem(s) of which they may be members, other subsystems, the dominant (major power) system and, in the widest sense, the global system. As noted, impact is operationalized by the extent of change in both adversarial relations and the core elements of a system. The task, in this domain, is to describe and explain the "fallout" or legacy of crises.

The domains/phases and periods of crisis, along with the linkages at international and state levels, are presented in Figure 1.2.[31]

As evident, each phase of an international crisis has its counterpart at the state level, a period in a foreign policy crisis. The essential traits of the former are interaction and distortion, of the latter, perception and stress. In terms of sequence, phases and periods are inextricably linked in time; that is, escalation must be preceded by onset, the crisis period follows the pre-crisis period, etc. However, phase and period may diverge, in another sense; that is, the corresponding phase and period do not necessarily begin or end at the identical time.

Phase-change, for example, from onset to escalation, occurs when at least one crisis actor experiences a change from pre-crisis to crisis period; but not all actors need undergo that perceptual change simultaneously. In fact, the evidence indicates that, in a large majority of twentieth-century interstate crises, actors made the "step-level" jump from pre-crisis to crisis period at different points in time, in response to different triggers to escalation. One illustration will suffice.

In the Cuban Missile Crisis, the US crisis period and, with it, the escalation phase, was triggered on 16 October 1962, when the CIA presented to President Kennedy photographic evidence of the presence of Soviet missiles in Cuba. However, the USSR (and Cuba) continued to perceive low threat, no or low time pressure and no or low probability of war until six days later. The catalyst for their step-level change from pre-crisis to crisis period was the official announcement of a US "quarantine" against all ships en route to Cuba. The crisis period for both the US and the USSR, and the escalation phase of Cuban Missiles, came to an end with their agreement on 28 October; and, with it, the crisis entered its deescalation phase. However, Cuba, the third crisis actor, continued at the high stress level of the crisis period until 20 November when it yielded to joint superpower and UN pressure and agreed to the removal of the Soviet IL-28 bombers from the island. With that act, the Cuban Missile Crisis ended for all three actors—and for a fearful world; that is, deescalation gave way to stable equilibrium between the two superpowers. A similar "discrepancy" in *period-change* occurred in the most recent global crisis, the Gulf Crisis of 1990–91.[32]

What one seeks to explain about each of the four domains/phases can be stated in dichotomous terms: for onset, the eruption or non-eruption of a crisis; for escalation, whether or not it leads to military hostilities; for deescalation, whether or not it terminates in some form of agreement, formal, informal or tacit; and for impact, the reduction or increase in tension between the adversaries, and change or no change—in state actors and/or their regimes, the balance of power, the alliance configuration, and the rules of behavior—in the relevant international system following crisis termination. In short, one seeks to uncover the conditions in which an international crisis is most likely to break out, to escalate, to wind down, and to effect change.[33]

This chapter was designed to serve three purposes: to introduce the core concepts—crisis, conflict, and war; to relate the definitions of international and foreign policy crisis to the cumulative body of knowledge on the subject; and to set out the models that guide the inquiry into twentieth-century interstate crises. With the completion of the conceptual overview, I now present two general models to explain international and foreign policy crisis as a whole.[34]

Model I: International Crisis

The factors that explain international crisis can be grouped into four clusters—**system**, **interactor**, **actor** and **situational**. The first two define the contexts (setting) in which a crisis erupts and unfolds through the onset, escalation and deescalation phases, leading to impact. The third comprises actor traits, from age to territorial size. And the fourth refers to attributes of the crisis proper, from trigger to the substance and form of outcome.

The four clusters of independent (explanatory) variables and their relationship to the domains/phases of crisis are presented in Figure 1.3. In essence, the model of international crisis builds upon the linkages specified in Figure 1.2 and depicts a four-phase process that is shaped by varying groups of factors. I turn now to an overview of these explanatory or *enabling* variables, that is, conditions that make most likely the occurrence of onset, escalation, deescalation and impact, through their effect on decision-makers' perceptions and, in turn, on disruptive interaction. Their roles in each phase will be specified and elaborated in subsequent chapters.

One explanatory **system** attribute is the **structure** of the international system under inquiry—the global or dominant system, or a regional subsystem. The pattern of authority may be *hegemonial (unipolar)*, as with the Roman Empire at its height. It may be *polarized (bipolar* or *multipolar)*, for example, US/USSR bipolarity from 1945 to 1962, and the great powers of the inter-World War period, 1919–39, respectively. Or the structure may be *diffuse (polycentric)*, such as the Greek city-state system in the 5th century BC., the contemporary global system since 1963, and most post-World War II regional subsystems. Each of these structural configurations of power and decision affects the situational attributes, from trigger to outcome.[35]

The other system attribute in the model of international crisis is **level**. International crises, with and without violence, occur in the *dominant system* and in various *subsystems*. Yet there are reasons to

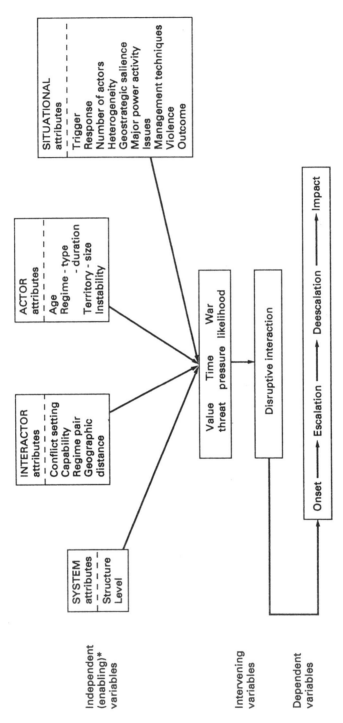

FIG. 1.3   Model of International Crisis

SITUATIONAL
attributes
Trigger
Response
Number of actors
Heterogeneity
Geostrategic salience
Major power activity
Issues
Management techniques
Violence
Outcome

ACTOR
attributes
Age
Regime - type
       - duration
Territory - size
Instability

INTERACTOR
attributes
Conflict setting
Capability
Regime pair
Geographic
distance

SYSTEM
attributes
Structure
Level

Value   Time   War
threat   pressure likelihood

Disruptive interaction

Onset → Escalation → Deescalation → Impact

Independent
(enabling)*
variables

Intervening
variables

Dependent
variables

* Enabling = most likely cluster to cause onset, escalation, etc.

expect that dominant system crises are less likely to generate the intense disruption that characterizes subsystem crises in the twentieth century. Major powers in the dominant system have a primary interest in system stability—except in situations of uncontrollable escalation (June–July 1914, leading to World War I) or when one power perceives an opportunity for hegemony (Entry into World War II, August 1939).[36]

They also tend to use their influence to reduce the incidence of interstate violence. This is partly due to their role as "security managers" and partly because of their greater awareness of the high cost of war, especially in an era of advanced technology, increasingly so after World War I. Minor powers in the dominant system, too, are less likely to initiate crises because of constraints on their freedom of action imposed by the major powers. And both major and minor powers in that system are more cautious about escalating their disputes to violence. Major powers in subsystems, however, have more freedom of action, for interstate politics in subsystems are remote from the primary interests of world powers. Moreover, subsystem actors are not constrained by a "security manager" role, though some regional powers sometimes try to emulate that role (e.g., Iran in the 1970s, Iraq from 1980 to 1991 [Persian Gulf], South Africa in the 1970s and 1980s [Southern Africa]), and possess arsenals of great destructive power. Finally, irreversible escalation in subsystem crises, while rare, can and does occur despite the efforts of the major powers, e.g., the June 1967 Arab/Israel crisis and war.

In sum, system level, like structure, helps to explain the eruption of international crises and the resort to violence in crisis initiation and crisis management.

One **interactor** attribute that is salient to international crises is **conflict setting**. The environment for disruptive interaction among states may be shaped by one or more *protracted conflicts (PCs)*, such as the US/USSR conflict in global politics from 1945 to 1990, or the Greece/Turkey and Ethiopia/Somalia conflicts in the Eastern Mediterranean and East Africa regions since the early 1920s and 1960s, respectively. The context may be free from such a conflict (*non-PC*). Or, at the other extreme, there may be a protracted conflict in which a long war is raging (*long-war PC*), as in Indo-China from 1946 to 1975. As with system structure, each of these types of conflict setting has varying effects on crises. In general, protractedness is expected to generate: more violent breakpoints (triggers); more basic value threats; more violence in crisis management; more activity by the major powers; more involvement and effectiveness of international organizations in crisis abatement; and more ambiguous, less formal, outcomes.

Capability, too, is important in crisis analysis. Capability is a multi-faceted interactor attribute comprising *diplomatic, economic and military resources*. For one thing, behavior during a crisis will vary with the alliance pattern of a crisis actor and its adversary: if the former experiences reliable support from a major power it is likely to act more quickly and with greater resolve than in a situation where it must act alone, especially if the adversary has a major power as a patron. Other elements of behavior will also be affected by the presence or absence of an ally: type of crisis management technique, pacific or violent; disposition to approach an international organization for support; and the size and structure of the decisional unit.

There is also a link between military power and crisis behavior by states with nuclear capability. Where both adversaries possess large stockpiles of nuclear weapons they are likely to be very prudent about using violence to cope with crises, because of the danger of rapid and destructive escalation. States with large or even modest nuclear arsenals may act with greater confidence in their ultimate ability to triumph, when their adversaries have only conventional weapons. Near-nuclear and non-nuclear states will manifest other behavior patterns. In sum, crisis behavior will vary with the extent of the adversaries' nuclear capability at the time an international crisis occurs.

Another interactor variable is **geographic distance** between adversaries. They may be *contiguous*, in the *same sub-region*, on the *same continent*, or *further afield*. State behavior in crises will vary with geographic proximity. Thus crisis actors are more likely to employ violence in crises "close to home," that is, against immediate neighbors, e.g., France/Germany, or within one's own sub-region, e.g., actors in the Near East core of the Middle East, than in more distant regions. It is, all other things being equal, more feasible. There are also likely to be differences in the type of major power activity, for example, the Soviet Union's use or threat of force in the East Berlin Uprising (1953), the Hungarian Uprising (1956), the Prague Spring (1968), and Polish Solidarity (1980–81), all crises within its sub-region, and its behavior in the Arab/Israel crises of 1967 and 1973, verbal threats and military assistance. Of course, geographic distance is only one of a number of independent variables that, together, explain violence in crises.

Turning to the first of the **actor** attributes, **age**, almost all states in Africa, the Middle East and Southern Asia emerged during the global process of decolonization, the "end of empire," in the aftermath of

World War II. *Old* states are expected to behave more prudently than new states in all crisis aspects: whether or not to initiate a crisis; to use violence in crisis management; to press for victory or to accept a compromise outcome. *New* states, because of insecurity, often accentuated by domestic instability, are more likely to view external crises as a compensatory policy device. Of course, more established states are likely to have superior capability which permits and may encourage assertiveness and the exploitation of opportunities for gain. However, this postulate implicitly assumes an interaction effect involving age, capability, and risk propensity in the direction of self-restraint.

The behavior of crisis actors is also likely to vary with political **regime**, both *type* and *duration*. These range from *democracy* to *civil or military authoritarianism*, and from the continuous parliamentary (or presidential) system of the UK (or the US), each for more than two centuries, to many African states, as well as Italy, in which political regimes change rapidly, sometimes more than once during a year.[37] Democracies are expected to respond to crises more cautiously and with less resolve, as did France and the UK in the 1936 Remilitarization of the Rhineland Crisis and Munich in 1938. More generally, variation is likely in many elements of behavior: the type of crisis management technique they will employ, including the extent and intensity of violence; the time span between trigger and major response to the value threat; the level of communication with adversaries; the size and structure of the decision-making unit, etc.

Territory as an actor attribute comprises two dimensions: the *size* of a crisis actor's land base, ranging from the Soviet Union, with more than eight million square miles, to several island states, each with no more than a few hundred square miles; and the *number of borders*, for example, Austria with six contiguous sovereign states, Iceland with none. Some states are contiguous to several major powers, such as Belgium with three in the 1930s. By contrast, all African and South American states, in fact, most states in the global system, have none.

Internal instability is a composite of three actor attributes. *Economic* instability is derived from six elements at the time of a crisis relative to the preceding four years: cost-of-living, unemployment, inflation, food prices, labor disruption, and consumer goods shortages. *Social* instability refers to the extent of societal unrest and mass violence. And *political* instability is indicated by the amount of government instability and regime repression. Some have argued that states beset with internal difficulties tend toward more aggressive external behavior. Others argue for diminished capacity of political leaders to deal effectively with external political situations, like crises, while trying at the same time to maintain their position in the face of internal dislocation. Whichever is correct, domestic instability impinges upon crisis behavior in different phases of an international crisis. Specific effects will be discussed in the presentation of the phase models.[38]

Among the **situational** attributes, the first to occur is **trigger**: as noted, it may be a political, economic, non-violent or violent military act, an event or an environmental change. As such, a trigger generates among decision-makers perceptions of value threat, time constraint on **response**, and heightened probability of involvement in military hostilities before a crisis is resolved. These perceptual changes set in motion a foreign policy crisis for state A. And its *response*, in turn, generates an increase in intensity, and/or a change in type, of disruptive interactions between A and its adversary(ies), that is, an international crisis.

The **number of actors** in a crisis ranges from one state that perceives threat, time pressure, and heightened war likelihood, while its adversary does not, to *n* actors: the largest case in the twentieth century was the 1939 European crisis leading to World War II, with 21 participants. All other things being equal, the larger the number of actors the larger the number of disparate pairs, that is, heterogeneity, and with it, more cleavages and difficulties of accommodation. Moreover, a larger number of actors in an international crisis makes it more salient to the global system, increasing the likelihood of major power involvement, for major powers tend to act as system managers. A larger number of crisis actors also has the potential effect of more coalitions and, with them, a wider scope of disruptive bargaining. Finally, the larger the number of actors in a crisis, the more difficult it is to arrive at a satisfactory solution to competing claims (Olson, 1965). This, in turn, makes it more likely that one or more actors will resort to violence in order to attain their goals.

An international crisis is also influenced by the extent of **heterogeneity** among the adversaries with respect to *military capability, political regime, economic development*, and *culture*. For example, in all the Vietnam War crises involving the US and North Vietnam (1964–75) the adversaries were totally heterogeneous; that is, they differed on all of those dimensions, whereas in US/USSR crises the superpowers differed on political regime and culture. What can be deduced from heterogeneity among crisis adversaries? First, more heterogeneity increases the likelihood that parties to a crisis will try to link new issues to those already in dispute; and this will tend to widen the range of issues in the bargaining process. Moreover, heterogeneity tends to generate misperception, and that increases the likelihood of violence in crisis management. In the largest sense, more differences among crisis adversaries point to more cleavages over which violence is more likely to occur.

Geostrategic salience refers to the location of an international crisis in terms of its natural resources, distance from major power centers, etc. Geostrategic assets vary over time: oil- and uranium-producing regions acquired greater salience since the 1950s; coal-producing regions became less salient. Key waterways and chokepoints like Gibraltar, the Suez Canal, the Straits of Malacca, the Panama Canal, etc., retained their geostrategic relevance over the decades. The extent of geostrategic salience of a crisis explains, in part, its effect on the adversaries and the system in which a crisis occurs. A broader geostrategic salience—to more than one subsystem, to the dominant system and, ultimately, to the global system—indicates more embryonic structural change as a consequence of an international crisis. Thus, a crisis located in a region of geostrategic interest to the dominant system, such as Central Europe throughout the twentieth century, the Arab/Israel conflict zone in the Middle East since 1956, or the Persian Gulf region since 1980, was more significant than one which was salient to a single subsystem, such as South America. More generally, geostrategic salience is likely to affect the number of states that become crisis actors: as the salience of a crisis grows, so too will the likelihood that a state will become a participant. And crises in locations of high geostrategic salience are more likely to induce major power activity, both because they are less sensitive to the costs of involvement in geographically distant crises and because of their role, noted above, of system managers. The Gulf Crisis of 1990–91 is a superb illustration of geographic salience as an explanatory variable in the model of international crisis [see Chap. 7].

Major power activity in international crises incorporates two dimensions—*content* and *effectiveness*. It may take several forms: political, economic or military aid to a crisis actor, and direct military intervention. Effectiveness in crisis abatement extends from the most positive, that is, the single most important contribution, to the most negative, namely, escalating a crisis. Whatever the content, activity by the major powers is important for three crisis domains/phases—escalation, deescalation and impact. There is a a paradox in major power activity during crises. On the one hand, the powers have a strong interest in global system stability and are therefore inclined to act so as to reduce the likelihood of violence in a crisis or to limit its severity and duration, in order to prevent destabilization in major power relations. On the other hand, commitments to clients, in an anarchical system, tend to foster high involvement, that is, military aid or military intervention, which stimulates escalation. Major power activity also contributes to deescalation. The more active the powers in support of clients, the more difficult and complex will be crisis accommodation, for their activity enlarges the legacy of unresolved issues and intra-system tension. Political or economic (low-level) activity, by contrast, generates less intense disruption among clients and thus facilitates a shift to accommodation. But whatever the major powers do, they affect the dynamics of international crisis.

Another explanatory situational attribute is **issues**, which may be *military, political, economic* or *cultural*, or some combination thereof. A crisis issue indicates an object of contention between crisis adversaries. In terms of their relative impact—on adversaries and international systems—military-security issues are more important than any other type of issue, as posited by the Realist school of international relations in its various strands—classical, neo- and structural Realism. Crises involving multiple issues identify more incipient structural change than those dealing with a single issue. As the range of issues increases, so too will the set of actors drawn into a crisis: more topics for bargaining are likely to elicit the entry of additional actors. Moreover, multiple-issue crises have a greater potential to produce change in international relations and, therefore, to induce major power involvement.

Various **crisis management techniques** (CMTs) are used by states to cope with crises. These range from *negotiation, mediation, arbitration* and *adjudication (pacific techniques)*, to *non-military pressure, non-violent military* acts, and, ultimately, to *indirect and direct violence*. Violent behavior generates more acute value threat, fear and mistrust among adversaries than does negotiation, mediation or other pacific CMTs. More intense violence creates more disruption than do minor clashes. And when adversaries resort to war, the ensuing legacy beyond a crisis will be higher tension. Whichever technique of crisis management is used, the content of escalation, deescalation and impact will be affected.

The extent of **violence** in a crisis, a closely-related explanatory variable, ranges from none, through *minor clashes* resulting in few or no casualties, to *serious clashes* short of war, and *full-scale war*. Clearly, hostile physical acts in a crisis are more disruptive than hostile verbal acts; that is, violence is more disruptive than any other type of crisis interaction. And crises that are initiated by, or escalate to, violence are more likely than non-violent crises to gain the attention of major powers, for violent crises have a greater potential to produce fundamental, long-term changes, both for their participants and for one or more international systems.

Finally, among the situational attributes in Model I, **outcome**, both the *substance* and *form* of termination, serves as an independent variable *vis-à-vis* the impact domain of crisis. The bilateral effects of a crisis depend primarily upon who wins, who loses, and whether or not it terminates through an agreement. Thus a disharmonious *definitive* outcome (victory/defeat) is more likely than an *ambiguous* outcome (compromise, stalemate) or a harmonious definitive outcome (perceived victory by all adversaries) to bequeath higher tension beyond a crisis. Moreover, a crisis that terminates in agreement is more likely to lead to mutual satisfaction and, therefore, greater stability than a crisis that ends through a *unilateral act* (invasion, military defeat, occupation, etc.), or *tacit understanding*—or one that *fades*. In short, a definitive outcome, formalized as an agreement, is likely to generate less tension in subsequent relationships among adversaries, despite some notable exceptions, such as the Treaty of Versailles after World War I.

Why do international crises erupt? What explains the change from one domain to another? It may not be possible to establish formal cause-effect links between the explanatory factors specified in Model I and the crisis domains/phases because of the diverse contexts in which crises take place.

In reality, crises are pervasive in *time* and *space*. Indeed, as noted, there was an array of international crises in all regions during the seven decades after the end of World War I. Moreover, they occurred within and outside a *protracted conflict setting*. The ubiquity of interstate crises is also evident for *all system and actor attributes*. They occur in all types of structure—hegemonial, polarized and diffuse; at both system levels—dominant and subsystem; within and outside protracted conflicts; when adversaries are contiguous or remote from each other; when their regimes are identical or discordant, etc. They also occur before and during wars [see Tables 2.1–2.5 in Chap. 2].

Does this mean that international crises are random events? Or are they predictable, at least in probabilistic terms; that is, are there clusters of factors (*enabling* variables) in which crises are *most likely* to occur? Two paths can be followed in search of an answer to this fundamental question. One is to "look at the evidence," to see what pattern, if any, emerges from the data. This may be termed the method of *atomic empiricism*. The other is to deduce the factors that make it most likely for an international crisis to erupt (and for a state to initiate a crisis), etc. I choose the latter, viewing a *deductively-derived, two-level analysis* as a superior path to knowledge about the meaning of crises in the twentieth century. Thus to guide the analysis of crisis I will, in the four chapters to follow, specify and discuss the factors that best explain each crisis domain/phase. These expectations will be tested with two strands of evidence, quantitative and qualitative, that is, from aggregate data and case studies.[39]

It must be emphasized that, notwithstanding the symmetry of arrows in Figure 1.3, not all the explanatory attributes set out in Model I are salient to all domains/phases of an international crisis. Rather, different independent variables help to illuminate one or another aspect of the crisis phenomenon. Thus, all the system, interactor and actor attributes affect the three dependent variables of the crisis proper, namely, onset, escalation and deescalation, but not the outcome domain. Moreover, none of the situational attributes is relevant to onset, for they operate only after a crisis has erupted. Thirdly, different situational attributes help to explain one or more of the other dependent variables. Trigger affects only escalation. The number of actors, heterogeneity, geostrategic salience, major power activity, and issues affect onset, escalation and deescalation. Crisis management techniques and the level of violence affect escalation and deescalation. And outcome impinges only on the impact domain/phase, which begins after a crisis ends.

This discussion raises a crucial theoretical question: are the explanatory variables necessary and/or sufficient for the outbreak of a crisis and its evolution through the four phases?[40] Clearly, they are not necessary conditions, for crises occur, as noted, in every conceivable context of time, space, polarity, conflict setting, etc. Nor are they sufficient to explain any particular domain/phase or crisis as a whole. Rather, they are *enabling* variables: as such, they constitute the *most likely* conditions in which an international crisis will erupt, escalate, deescalate or affect the adversaries and/or the system(s) of which they are members.

This point requires elaboration. A *necessary* condition is one that is always present when a phenomenon occurs. In terms of formal logic, if X is a necessary condition for Y, then X always precedes Y, but Y does not always occur when X alone does, for X on its own may not be sufficient to generate Y. If X is a *sufficient* condition of Y, then Y always occurs when X does; that is, it is enough to have X to have Y. And, for a *necessary and sufficient condition*, Y follows whenever X occurs; and whenever Y occurs it must be preceded by X (Most and Starr, 1982).

Thus, in the case of international crises, if bipolarity were a necessary condition of crisis, it would always be present when a crisis erupts. As noted, it is not. Nor is protracted conflict or any other independent variable in the general model of crisis. Moreover, neither bipolarity nor any of those variables is a sufficient condition of crisis, as delineated in the X–Y relationship specified above.

In Model I, the necessary and sufficient conditions of an international crisis are, *conceptually*: at the system/interactor level, intense disruptive interaction, including a heightened probability of military hostilities, that poses a challenge to some aspect of the international system in which a crisis occurs; and, at the actor level, value threat and its related perceptions—of finite time and heightened war likelihood.

In this context, an important conceptual distinction must be noted. Disruptive interaction and the three perceptions of harm are necessary and sufficient in the sense that they determine the existence of a crisis; that is, they are the defining criteria for identifying an environmental change as triggering a crisis. But they are not causal conditions; they do not explain why that change occurred or when it is most likely to occur. For that dimension of crisis we must turn to clusters of explanatory variables, namely, the system, interactor and actor attributes noted earlier.

In *operational* terms, the presence of the three perceptions of harm is indispensable for, as noted, they catalyze a foreign policy crisis which, in turn, generates an international crisis. As such, the macro-level condition—disruptive interaction—follows inexorably from those at the micro level. Thus to achieve parsimony, the composite perception of harm and disruptive interaction is treated as the *integrated intervening variable* of the Model of International Crisis. And the evidence to test hypotheses derived from this model will focus on the system, interactor, actor and situational attributes, as filtered through the threat-time-war perceptions of decision-makers.

Yet even with this reduced complexity, such logical requirements for a rigorous theory of crisis confront a diverse reality, namely, as noted, the occurrence of twentieth-century interstate crises, often with violence, in a great variety of contexts. Thus our task is to discover the cluster of attributes in which the three-fold perception of harm and disruptive interaction and, therefore, crises is most likely to erupt and evolve. Phase models and hypotheses to be specified in the chapters to follow are designed to explain which combination of enabling attributes is most likely to generate a crisis and to account for its four domains/phases.

An international crisis begins, as noted, with a breakpoint/triggering act, event or environmental change. Once in motion, a crisis continues at a low level of disruption (onset phase) until another set of factors escalates it to more intense disruption. The escalation phase persists until still another group of factors sets in motion a process of accommodation among the adversaries, the deescalation phase, which culminates in termination. Although extinguished, a crisis has spillover effects for the adversaries and, possibly, for one or more systems. As such, it can be likened to an earthquake in a geological system.[41]

To predict the outbreak of a specific crisis between states A and B, possibly, A, B, C, D . . . , at a particular point in time and place, is impossible, just as it is to predict a specific earthquake; for a crisis, that is, a political earthquake, erupts in particular circumstances of the actors, their regimes, capability goals, ideologies, etc., and the cumulative legacy of their past relationship. However, it can be argued that a crisis is most likely to erupt when a particular cluster of system, interactor and actor attributes is present. The first two sets of enabling conditions comprise: a diffuse structure of international system authority (polycentrism); a subsystem setting; a protracted conflict; regime divergence, and geographic contiguity between the adversaries. There are also several actor attributes, which will be examined in the discussion of onset, such as relatively equal capability.

Turning to the second domain/phase, what are the conditions in which an international crisis is most likely to escalate, that is, to become a full-scale crisis, including violence and, possibly, war? The answer lies in a constellation of factors from all four clusters: *system* attributes—polycentric structure and subsystem level; *interactor* attributes—protracted conflict setting, large power discrepancy, geographic contiguity, and regime divergence; *actor* attributes—more acute threat to values, and internal instability in at least one adversary; and *situational* attributes—violent trigger, and several issues in dispute.

The general rationale can be summarized here. War is the most disruptive type of interaction among states. It is most likely to ensue when crucial situational and actor attributes—type of trigger, issues in dispute, threatened values, relative capability, and internal instability —manifest their most negative or conflictive point, namely, the most violent trigger, the largest number of disputed issues, the most basic value threatened, etc. When all of these factors are at the extreme, and when a crisis erupts within an on-going conflict, the likelihood of escalation to war will be highest.

As for the deescalation phase, what leads adversaries during a crisis to bargain, with the goal of a mutually-acceptable outcome?[42] Stated in terms used earlier in this chapter, we seek the enabling conditions in which crises are most likely to wind down to the norm of non-crisis interaction. Deescalation is not exactly analogous to escalation, for almost all crises wind down and terminate, whereas many crises do not escalate to war, for example, the Berlin crises of 1948–49, 1957–59 and 1961, and the Cuban Missile Crisis in 1962. Nevertheless, a group of factors from three clusters would seem to explain the most likely shift from acute disruption to accommodation: an interactor attribute—non-protracted conflict setting; some actor attributes—internal instability and regime type;[43] and several situational attributes—a small number of actors, non-violent techniques of crisis management, and non-military activity by major powers.

This overview of Model I concludes with the impact domain. What constellation explains the extent of fallout from a political earthquake? The crucial variables for effects on the adversaries are the content and form of outcome, that is, as noted, who wins and loses, or whether a crisis ends in a draw, and whether or not it ends in agreement. Another explanatory variable is the intensity (severity) of a crisis.

As will be noted later [Chap. 5], the intensity of a crisis is a composite of six factors specified in Model I [see Figure 1.3]: *number of actors;* type of *major power activity;* scope of *geostrategic salience;* range of *heterogeneity;* number and seriousness of *issues*, and extent of *violence.* The impact of an international crisis is measured by the type and magnitude of *change* in four system attributes; existing *actors* or their *regimes; power configuration; alliance pattern,* and *rules of behavior* (Brecher and James, 1986: Parts 2, 3).

In the largest sense, the more intense a crisis the deeper it will penetrate the structure of an international system; and, over time, the more change it will generate, that is, the greater will be its effects on the system. The scope of systemic impact varies: *no change* (for example, the Aegean Sea Crisis between Greece and Turkey in 1976) *minor change* (in the Middle East alliance configuration, following the overthrow of the Iraq monarchy by a pro-Nasser military regime in the Lebanon/Iraq Upheaval of 1958); *major change* (the creation of a new state and a basic shift in the South Asian balance of power, following the 1971 Bangladesh Crisis); and *system transformation* (of the dominant system of world politics, from multipolarity to bipolarity, the consequence of a large cluster of crises beginning with Entry into World War II in 1939 and ending with the Final Soviet Offensive of 1945).

The model of international crisis presented here specifies the links between explanatory variables, on the one hand, and, on the other, crisis onset, escalation, deescalation and impact.[44] However, system, interactor, actor and situational attributes do not directly cause the eruption, peak distortion, accommodation or legacy of a crisis. Each of these domains/phases is the product of *decisions* and *actions* by states. And they, in turn, are the result of *perceptions* held by foreign policy decision-makers. Thus I turn now to the actor level of analysis.

Model II: Crisis Behavior

The model of international crisis (Model I) is a valuable first approximation to reality. However, it ignores crucial prior and intervening stages, namely, the "black box" of *images* and *behavior* by crisis participants. For example, an international crisis is initiated when State A triggers a crisis for State B, and possibly others. That act, in turn, results from perceptions held by A's decision-makers. They may view the global power structure as an opportunity to achieve goals by triggering a crisis. If engaged in a protracted conflict, they may perceive that a long-term adversary is likely to initiate a crisis—and calculate that preemption is prudent and preferable. In sum, *opportunity* or *threat perception* is likely to induce a decision to trigger a foreign policy crisis for a rival or enemy.

The trigger by state A, whether a verbal statement or a political, economic or military act, creates a perception of threat among the decision-makers of state B and, possibly, others, and in so doing causes the onset of an international crisis. The target state(s) may comply with A's demand or action, leading to abrupt crisis termination, with victory for A and defeat for its adversary(ies). More often, B will respond with one or more hostile acts, leading to more disruptive interaction, with the onset phase evolving through a spiral process to more intense distortion and turmoil.[45] Thus it is imperative to focus on the actor level, as well as on the international level, of crisis analysis. This I now do through a model of state behavior in crisis, presented in Figure 1.4.

The causal links and time sequence will now be summarized.[46] The triggering *act*, *event* or *environmental change* occurs at time t_1. This is the prerequisite for a foreign policy crisis because it stimulates decision-makers' perceptions of value threat and, usually later, of time pressure and heightened war likelihood. These perceptions of crisis—and consequent stress—are generated at time t_2. Decision-makers respond to threatening events by adopting one or more of many coping strategies, such as "satisficing," the avoidance of value tradeoffs, or the reliance on

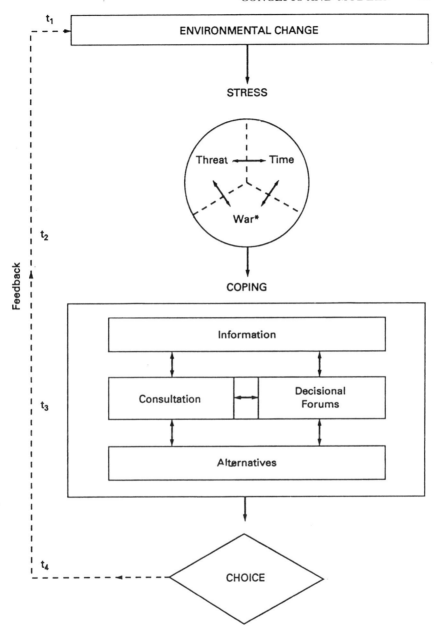

War* = Perceived probability of military hostilities [for non-war crisis]
     = Perceived adverse change in military balance [for intra-war crisis]

FIG. 1.4   Model of State Behavior in Crisis

historical experience, ideology or operational code beliefs as a guide to action.[47] Whichever is selected, coping occurs at time t_3. And choice ensues from coping. More precisely, the perceptions of crisis-induced stress at t_2 are mediated through coping at t_3 and shape decisions at t_4. The direct link to choice is from the decisional forum, which selects one option after evaluating alternatives in accordance with a set of decision rules.

The key concepts of Model II will now be elaborated. *Threat* "concerns harms or losses that have not yet taken place but are anticipated" (Lazarus and Folkman, 1984: 32). Threat perception may be active or passive, strong or weak, and central or peripheral to one's values. *Time pressure* is closely related to uncertainty, notably about the adversary's intentions, the balance of capability, and the quality of information to be processed. In essence, it refers to available time for decision in relation to the deadline for choice; that is, crisis time cannot be equated with clock time (Robinson, 1972: 24–25). And when decision-makers are uncertain, time pressure is likely to be greater.

The *probability of war*, more precisely, of *involvement in military hostilities* or, in an intra-war crisis, *the likelihood of an adverse change in the military balance*, too, is an uncertain element of crisis. Whatever the context, it is uncertainty about value threat, war or adverse change in the military balance, and time pressure that generates a foreign policy crisis.

All three perceptual elements of crisis are interrelated. The more active and stronger a threat and the more central the threatened values, the higher will be the expectation of military hostilities. That, in turn, will intensify the image of crisis. Similarly, the more active, the stronger and the more basic a threatened value, the more limited will be the perceived time to respond. Further, the more intense the time constraint, the higher will be the anticipation of war and the more intense the perception of threat. The reverse links also operate: the higher the perceived war likelihood, the more central, active and strong will be the value threat, and the more limited will be the perceived response time.

Two of these analytic links—between environmental change and threat, and between threat and time—were cogently summarized by Lazarus (1968: 340, 343) as follows:

> The immediate stimulus configuration resulting in threat merely heralds the coming of harm. Threat is thus a purely psychological concept, an interpretation of the situation by the individual. . . . Another, less emphasized factor in the stimulus configuration is the imminence of the confrontation with harm. Threat is more intense when harm is more imminent.

These mutually-reinforcing perceptions, in turn, induce a feeling of psychological *stress*, "a generic term to designate unpleasant emotional states evoked by a threatening stimulus situation . . ." (Janis and Mann, 1977: 50), or a situation "that is appraised by the person as taxing or exceeding his or her resources and endangering his or her well-being" (Lazarus and Folkman, 1984:19). Stress, so defined, applies no less to foreign policy crisis decision-makers than to individuals in their personal lives.

The same is true of *coping*, a process of "constantly changing cognitive and behavioral efforts to manage specific external and/or internal demands that are appraised as taxing or exceeding the resources of the person" (Lazarus and Folkman, 1984: 141).[48] The first reactive, or coping, step by decision-makers is to search for *information* about the threatening act(s), event(s) or change(s). The probe may be conducted through ordinary or special channels. It will be thorough, modest or marginal, depending upon the level of stress. Information may be absorbed with an open mind or may be biased by such factors as ideology or lessons of the past (May, 1973; Vertzberger, 1986, 1990). In short, changes in crisis-induced stress at t_2 cause changes in information processing at t_3.

The inflow of information about a foreign policy crisis leads to *consultation*—with colleagues in the political élite, military and bureaucratic advisors, and possibly others from various interest groups. Consultation may be *ad hoc* or institutional, frequent or infrequent, and may take place within a large or small circle. Coping also requires the creation or activation of a *decisional forum*. As with other aspects of information processing, changes in the intensity of crisis-induced stress will affect the pattern of consultation, the search for and evaluation of *alternatives*, and the type and size of the decisional unit.

Choice follows from the consideration of alternatives. However, several decisions are made during a foreign policy crisis. Moreover, stress changes over time and, with it, the type of behavior. Thus a state-level model must account for changes that occur during a crisis, from its inception, with low stress (pre-crisis period), through rising, higher and peak stress (crisis period), to a declining phase toward normal perceptions of threat, time pressure and war likelihood (end-crisis period).

Viewed in terms of three periods (Figure 1.5), the sequence from trigger to choice is replicated three times: t_1–t_4 (pre-crisis), t_5–t_8 (crisis), t_9–t_{12} (end-crisis). Low threat is perceived in the pre-crisis period, thereby denoting an incipient crisis. The consequent low level of crisis-induced stress leads to n decisions. It is only when feedback from those

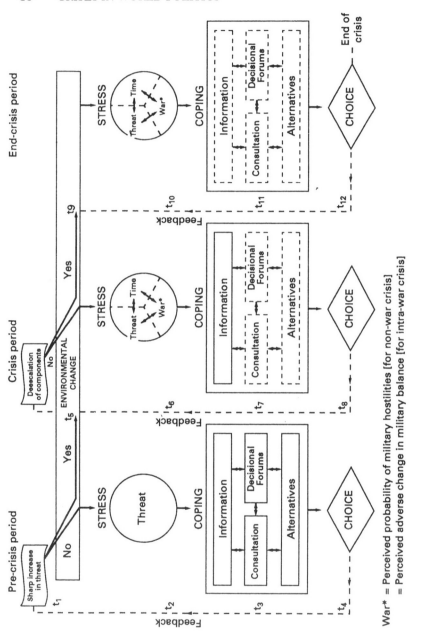

FIG. 1.5   Three-Stage Model of Crisis Behavior

War* = Perceived probability of military hostilities [for non-war crisis]
      = Perceived adverse change in military balance [for intra-war crisis]

decisions to the crisis environment or some other change triggers a sharp rise in threat, along with an awareness of time pressure and heightened war likelihood, that escalation to a fully-crystallized crisis (the crisis period) may be said to begin. Higher stress, in turn, has consequences for coping and choice.

As with the shift from pre-crisis to crisis period, the last threshold, namely, transition to the end-crisis period, occurs when feedback or environmental change triggers a decline in the intensity of crisis perceptions. Stress will lessen, with effects on coping and choice that differ from those in earlier periods. Ultimately, a decision or set of decisions in the end-crisis period will lead to an environmental change that is perceived as no more threatening, no more time constraining, and no more likely to confront a state with war than events or acts in non-crisis periods. At that point a foreign policy crisis comes to an end.[49]

The central question that we seek to answer about crisis behavior is as follows: what are the *effects of changing stress*, derived from changes in perceptions of threat, time pressure and war likelihood, *on coping and choice* by foreign policy decision-makers? One set of questions focuses on the stress-coping link, that is, the effects of escalating and deescalating stress on: the quest for information; the type and size of consultative units; the size and structure of the decisional forum; and on the search for and evaluation of alternatives. Another group of questions aims to illuminate the stress-choice link by uncovering: the *core inputs* into each decision; the perceived cost of the selected option; the gravity of the choice; its complexity, in terms of the issue-area(s) involved; the scope of effects across systems; the type of activity required by a decision; and whether or not a decision is novel.

These questions and the model of crisis behavior guided a series of in-depth case studies of stress, coping and choice in selected twentieth-century crises, from the 1938 Munich Crisis—for France and the UK—to the Gulf Crisis of 1990–91—for the US and Iraq.[50] Together with aggregate studies of 826 state-level cases from 1918 to 1988 they will provide the evidence about foreign policy crises in the chapters that follow.[51] The case studies will take the form of systematic, qualitative illustrations of the coping/choice process in prominent foreign policy crises between 1938 and 1990–91. Comparative findings from these cases will supplement the findings from the aggregate quantitative data.

To illustrate the method, substance and utility of the crisis behavior model (Model II), I present a brief application to Israel's behavior in the 1973–74 October-Yom Kippur crisis-war.[52]

The environmental change that triggered Israel's foreign policy crisis and its pre-crisis period (t_1) was an air battle on 13 September 1973 when 13 Syrian MIGs were shot down against the loss of one Israeli Mirage. Perceiving a threat of possible Syrian retaliation—but not yet time pressure or war likelihood—the Israel Defense Forces (IDF) sent a brigade to the Golan Heights. However, under the influence of "The Conception," namely, the pervasive view among Israel's élites that Egypt (UAR)[53] and Syria were not ready to launch a war, and the evaluation by the IDF Intelligence Branch that the outbreak of war was very unlikely, a (negative) decision was made not to discuss the issue at the full Cabinet meeting on 3 October.

These decisions were taken at t_4, the first choice time-frame specified in the model. But what were Israel's perceptions in its pre-crisis period (t_2)? And how did its decision-makers cope with low stress (t_3)?

At the outset the threatened value was the security of border settlements in the North against Syrian retaliation. By the close of the pre-crisis period, 4 October, the perceived threat changed to a probable joint Egyptian–Syrian attack to regain the Sinai and Golan territories conquered by Israel in the 1967 Six Day War. In short, the value threat was not grave: it did not yet involve Israel's territory *per se*, let alone its existence as a state. As for war likelihood, while war and, certainly, a limited military attack are always viewed as possible in a protracted conflict, there is no evidence of the expectation of war at that stage of Israel's emerging crisis. Time pressure, too, was absent from the initial decision-making process.

Applying the model to coping (t_3), the early news of an Arab military buildup was kept within the IDF élite and the Defense Ministry. Under the shadow of growing but still low threat, the cumulating information was brought to the attention of the "Kitchen Cabinet"—but not to the full Cabinet—a few days before the outbreak of war. The initial effect of increasing threat perception on the consultation process was to seek more advice from IDF officers, the specialists on violence and deterrence. The decisional forum was a large *ad hoc* group, the "Kitchen Cabinet," together with military and bureaucratic advisors. Finally, as for alternatives, the two pre-crisis decisions were reached after limited discussion. There was no search for new options.

The low stress of the pre-crisis period escalated on 4–5 October as a result of three environmental changes (t_5): the hasty evacuation of Soviet dependents from Egypt and Syria; the report by an IDF air reconnaissance mission of reinforced Egyptian deployment in an offensive posture; and an intelligence report from the IDF Southern Command of the extraordinary disposition of Egyptian forces west of the Canal. These events raised the level of Israeli threat perception and introduced two additional elements—an awareness of time pressure to respond and of the higher likelihood of military hostilities (t_6). These perceptual changes marked a shift from the pre-crisis period to the crisis period, with stress later rising to its peak.

On the morning of 5 October the IDF's regular forces were placed on the highest state of alert, and the air force on full alert. Consultation was intense, at an extraordinary informal Cabinet session on the 5th, the "Kitchen Cabinet" at 6.00 a.m. on the 6th, and the full Cabinet starting at 12 noon that day. Fresh information between 3.30 and 4.00 a.m. on the 6th, that an Egyptian–Syrian combined attack would occur before sundown, catalyzed the first two, closely-linked, major Israeli decisions of the crisis period: not to preempt; and to order a large-scale—but not full—mobilization of reserves.

Altogether Israel made 18 decisions during this period. The most important, other than those already noted, were: to launch a general counterattack against Syria (10 October); to cross the Canal (14th); to accept the first cease-fire (21st); to accept the second cease-fire (26th); and to supply Egypt's encircled Third Army, the same day—the last day of the crisis period (t_8).

Turning to perceptions in the crisis period (t_6), the values threatened during the first 30 hours were peace and relative stability. Then, for three days, other values were perceived to be at risk, notably Israel's territory, especially in the North, the lives of Israel's soldiers, and its reputation for military invincibility. As the war continued, the basic value threat took the form of a spiralling cost in human life. The perceived probability of war increased from the early hours of 5 October until 4.00 a.m. on the 6th and then rose traumatically until the Egyptian–Syrian attack. During the next three days there was grave concern about an adverse change in the military balance: Egyptian forces had crossed the Canal and had destroyed the Bar-Lev Line, while Syrian troops had come very close to Israeli settlements on the Golan Heights. And the pressure of time was starkly evident in the unsuccessful pleas to US Secretary of State Kissinger late in the crisis period to delay the coming into effect of the first cease-fire on 22 October. No less compelling was a Soviet signal of intended direct military intervention, creating both an awareness of grave danger and some time constraint if Israel rejected the second cease-fire. In fact, all Israeli decisions of the 1973 crisis period were made under a recognized time constraint.

With respect to coping (t_7), the felt need for information in the crisis period focused on both the battlefront and Washington. As the focus of decision shifted to the bargaining table, the lack of information led to increased stress, notably when Kissinger made no contact with Israel during his Moscow visit on 20–21 October, leading to the first US–USSR-imposed cease-fire. As for consultation, war-induced escalation of stress strengthened the search by senior decision-makers for maximal support, leading to a marked increase in the size of the consultative circle. The "Kitchen Cabinet" was the preeminent decisional forum in the crisis period. The first two decisions were made after a modest cost–benefit evaluation of alternative options. Concern about casualties loomed large in the military moves after 8 October. In contrast to 1967, there was evidence of premature closure in the decision-making process; that is, decisions were made before all available information had been processed and all alternatives carefully assessed.

The second cease-fire, on 26 October, and the withdrawal of the superpowers from the brink—their nuclear alert crisis on 23 and 24 October—set in motion the shift from the crisis period to the end-crisis period (t_9). It was by far the longest period of Israel's Yom Kippur Crisis, lasting from 27 October 1973 to the signing of the Disengagement Agreement with Syria on 31 May 1974.

Israel's psychological environment changed markedly (t_{10}). It perceived less threat from the Arabs by the end of the war; in fact, there was a marked improvement in the military balance, with the IDF bridgehead on the west bank of the Canal secure, Egypt's Third Army encircled, and Damascus within artillery range. At the same time, Israel's military triumph was blurred, its casualties high, including many prisoners, and the political future uncertain. And concern about the reescalation of hostilities to full-scale war vanished only with the Disengagement Agreement of 31 May 1974. Time pressure, too, declined markedly, as evident by the duration of the last period of the crisis.

The task of coping (t_{11}) was made more difficult because of persistent US pressure on specific issues, from the encircled Third Army to the search for an interim agreement with Egypt. This led to an intensely felt need for information about US intentions and likely behavior. All information was processed by the six-member Negotiating Committee, with the Cabinet receiving only a selection of information.

During the protracted negotiations with Egypt and Syria the Cabinet was the principal Israel body for consultation. It was also the sole decisional forum: the Cabinet made or approved all 11 decisions, though the Negotiating Committee played the crucial role. And decisions were generally arrived at only after a careful search for and evaluation of alternatives; for example, the issue of the Geneva Conference—not to attend, to delay, or to attend subject to conditions —was carefully considered before the decision to participate (t_{12}).

As evident from this brief application of the crisis behavior model, the patterns of perception, coping and choice differed in the three periods of Israel's Yom Kippur Crisis. Comparable findings were reported by the other ICB case studies, as will be elaborated in later chapters. Thus the model has demonstrated its efficacy in guiding the analysis of crisis behavior.

Tasks ahead

As with Model I (international crisis), the state-level model (Model II) is necessary but insufficient for a comprehensive analysis of crises in world politics. The reason is that an interstate crisis encompasses much more than the behavior of a single state in a foreign policy crisis. The logical conclusion is to integrate the two models in order to capture the insights provided by each and to portray more accurately the complex reality of crises in the twentieth century.

This holistic approach, the dominant theme of the chapters to follow, is based upon six conceptual guidelines:

(1) the concepts of international and foreign policy crisis denote dynamic processes over time, with separate phases (periods) —onset (pre-crisis), escalation (crisis), deescalation (end-crisis), and impact (post-crisis);

(2) the distinguishing trait of each phase—incipient distortion, peak distortion, accommodation, and non-crisis interaction—and of each period—low, high, declining, and non-crisis stress—can be explained by different sets of enabling variables: system, interactor, actor and situation attributes, acting through perceptions of threat, time pressure and war likelihood;

(3) the two levels of crisis are analytically distinct but interrelated processes, each helping to explain the other, and both integral parts of a larger unified whole;

(4) the models discussed thus far capture parts of a multi-layered reality;

(5) an explanation of cause–effect relationships in an international crisis requires the analysis of images and behavior by the participants, for crisis eruption, distortion and accommodation occur as a result of choices made by their decision-makers; and

(6) a synthesis of the two levels of analysis into a unified model would achieve a comprehensive explanation of the phenomenon of interstate crisis.

The last, crucial task will be undertaken in Chapter 6, after an analysis in breadth and depth of the four domains/phases of crisis.

CHAPTER 2

Onset

IN Chapter 1 it was argued that interstate crises are not random events, despite the diverse settings in which they occur. Further, a preference was indicated for a two-level analysis of the four domains of crisis, emphasizing the dynamic relationship between system/interactor and state levels, from outbreak to legacy. To prepare the ground for the *Unified Model of Crisis* [Chap. 6], several questions will be addressed for each domain/phase of a crisis. The focus on onset is fourfold:

(1) *Under what conditions is an* **international crisis** *most likely to* **break out?**
(2) *When is a state most likely to* **initiate** *a crisis for another member of the global system?*
(3) *What are the conditions in which a state is most likely to be a* **target** *for a* **foreign policy crisis**: *that is, what explains a state's* **vulnerability** *to external crises?*
(4) *How do states* **cope** *with the onset of an external crisis?*

To answer these questions the following research strategy will be employed. A model of crisis onset will specify the factors that explain the *outbreak* of *international crises*, crisis *initiation*, and the *vulnerability* of states to foreign policy crises.[1] Expectations about crisis onset, derived from this model, will then be framed as propositions. Finally, the coping pattern in the pre-crisis period/onset phase will be examined in a representative group of cases.

Model of Crisis Onset

The underlying thesis of the crisis onset model is that an international crisis is most likely to break out, and a foreign policy crisis to be initiated, when a specific group of factors is present. As evident in

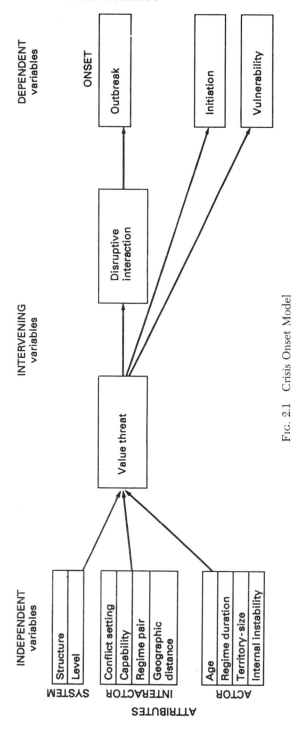

Fig. 2.1   Crisis Onset Model

Figure 2.1, system, interactor and actor attributes serve as independent variables in the onset model. For purposes of this discussion, system comprises static, "hard-shell," contextual attributes, namely, structure and level. Interactor variables are the conflict setting, capability (power discrepancy), regime pair, and geographic distance between the adversaries. The actor attributes are age, regime duration, territorial size, and domestic instability.

All the system and interactor attributes denote reality. Most at the actor level, too, are objective, e.g., regime pair and size. Value threat is perceptual in character. Each of these variables can be grouped into several categories, as follows:

system
>*structure*—multipolarity, bipolarity, polycentrism;
>*level*—dominant system, subsystem;

interactor
>*conflict setting*—non-protracted conflict (non-PC), PC, long-war PC;
>*capability*—positive, negative;
>*regime pair*—democracy, civil authoritarian, military;
>*geographic distance*—contiguous, proximate, remote;

actor
>*age*—new, modern, old;
>*regime duration*—short, medium, long;
>*territory-size*—small, medium, large;
>*internal stability*—low, medium, high;

intervening
>*value threat*—low, medium, high
>*disruptive interaction*—moderate, intense

The dependent variables in the crisis onset model are:

>*outbreak*
>*initiation*
>*vulnerability*

In essence, this model seeks to explain the conditions in which: an interstate crisis is most likely to occur (outbreak); a state is most likely to initiate a foreign policy crisis for another member of the global system (initiation); and a state is most likely to be a target of a foreign policy crisis (vulnerability). The logic underlying the onset model's inferred effects will be specified for each explanatory factor, more elaborately for some, in a more cursory manner for others.[2]

I begin with system **structure**. *Multipolarity* is characterized by a diffusion of power *and* decisional autonomy among several relatively equal units in an international system, at least three, usually more, for example, much of China's classical state system during the Chou dynasty (1122–221 BC), the Italian state system in the fifteenth century, and the Western state system from 1648 to 1939. *Bipolarity* indicates a concentration of power and decision in two relatively equal dominant actors, as with the US and the USSR from 1945 to 1962. And *polycentrism* identifies a hybrid structure with two centers of power and multiple centers of decision, e.g., Napoleonic France and the coalition of England, Austria, Prussia and Russia in the early years of the nineteenth century, and the contemporary global system from the 1962 Cuban Missile Crisis to 1990, when power bipolarity gave way to quasi-unipolarity.

The argument that relates structure to crisis outbreak is three-fold. First, the larger the number of decisional centers in an international system the larger will be the potential number of dyads (pairs). Of the three structures, polycentrism provides the most conducive setting for new system members and, therefore, the likelihood of more competitive and hostile dyads. This is so because polycentrism accords legitimacy to the quest for sovereignty by weak nationalities that are dependencies of major powers. As such, structure enlarges the potential scope of disruptive interaction and, through it, the incidence of crisis outbreak.

A second strand of the structure-outbreak argument is that, in a system of limited resources the pairs are likely to be competitive, that is, adversarial. It is not clear whether states would be more competitive and adversarial in a system with evenly or unevenly distributed resources. Whichever is correct—uneven or even distribution—the postulated link between *limited* resources and *competition/adversary relations* between pairs of states seems valid.[3]

The third element of the postulated link between structure and crisis outbreak relates to constraints. The fewer the system constraints on state behavior, the more likely will there be more-than-normal disruptive interaction and, with it, the eruption of a crisis. And a polycentric structure is characterized by fewer system constraints.[4]

Structure also affects *values* directly. Bipolarity is likely to generate the most basic value threats, that is, perceived threat to the existence of system members, possibly to the bloc leaders as well, and certainly threat to their influence in the system—within their bloc, among non-aligned states, and in the adversary bloc. In polycentrism, by contrast, with looser "rules of the game," states are more likely to perceive threats to territory, political regime, economic welfare, etc. The former are more fundamental values, but the latter will generate more frequent crisis eruptions. In short, all other things being equal, polycentrism is more likely than multipolarity or bipolarity to generate international crises.[5]

The violence aspect of interstate crisis, though relevant to onset/pre-crisis, is central to the escalation phase/crisis period and will be examined at length in that context [Chap. 3]. One point may be noted here. Rivalry and the quest for hegemony within the dominant system in bipolarity will be accompanied by periodic international crises but, infrequently, by outbursts of violence.[6] However, it is the structure with many autonomous actors and fewer system constraints, namely, poly-centrism, that is most likely to generate the disruptive interaction that leads to a violent outbreak.

The system **level** at which interstate crises, like all world politics, take place is *dominant system* or *subsystem*, though more elaborate system rungs or ladders have been constructed (e.g., McClelland: 1955, 1958; Deutsch, 1974: 152–156; Andriole, 1978). The former was defined by Singer and Small (1972:381) as the "Central Sub-System," that is, "the most powerful, industrialized, and diplomatically active members of the interstate system, generally coinciding with the 'European state system'." For the period under inquiry, the dominant system comprised: from the end of 1918 to the end of August 1939, the seven great powers of the inter-World War period—France, Germany, Italy, Japan, the UK, the US, and the USSR, not quite synonymous with Europe; and, for 1945–88, the two superpowers, the United States and the Soviet Union, along with their blocs of allies and clients, organized in NATO and the Warsaw Pact, respectively.

A subsystem, or subordinate system, shares the same attributes as the dominant system; that is, it comprises a set of actors who are situated in a configuration of power (*structure*), are involved in regular patterns of interaction (*process*), are separated from other units by *boundaries* set by a given *issue*, and are constrained in their behavior from within (*context*) and from outside the system (*environment*)" (Brecher and Ben Yehuda, 1985: 17).

More significant are two distinctive traits of a subsystem. First, its members are weaker than their capability counterparts in the dominant system, that is, great powers in both, and minor powers in both. And second, events in the dominant system have a potential for greater impact on the subsystem than the reverse; that is, the former has the power to penetrate the latter more frequently, intensely, and effectively. Whether or not it does so, and its extent, depend on the structure at the two system levels; that is, the likelihood and intensity of penetration will depend on the polarity configuration of both dominant system and subsystems.

The link of system level to crisis outbreak derives from the role conception of major powers in the dominant system. Because of their interest in system stability, with some exceptions noted earlier, they tend to act so as to reduce the incidence of crises, especially in the dominant system. One reason is their shared function as "security managers" of world politics, whether institutionally sanctioned, as in the United Nations Charter in the twentieth century, or self-assumed and informally accepted, as in the Concert of Europe in the nineteenth century. Another reason is that, especially in the nuclear era, the dominant system's major powers are the repositories of "state of the art" technology, and are therefore conscious of the damage that crises can cause for participants and system alike.

At the subsystem level, by contrast, the major powers of the dominant system, irrespective of its structure, prefer to remain aloof, lest crises on the periphery feed back and undermine their relations, ultimately destabilizing the dominant system itself. They tend, therefore, to be permissive about interstate politics in subsystems. Such autonomy reinforces the effect of structure noted earlier, by providing the setting for more, and more disruptive, crises on the peripheries of the global system.

The greater permissiveness of subsystem interstate politics extends to the eruption of crises among adversaries. As such, the level of value threat perceived by the antagonists is likely to be higher: existence will rarely be perceived to be at risk in the dominant system, except in cataclysmic systemic wars; but a threat to existence is not abnormal in subsystem conflicts, wars and crises. This is compounded by the greater tendency of subsystem states to be newer, weaker, smaller and less stable entities (Jackson and Rosberg, 1982). Thus, despite the powers' disposition to aloofness from subsystem interstate conflicts and their greater tolerance of crises between subsystem actors than crises between lesser powers in the dominant system, their power to intervene is omnipresent. Thus the outcome of subsystem crises and, often, the survival of subsystem actors depend ultimately upon the goodwill of the major powers in the dominant system. In sum, subsystem level is a second potent source of value threat and disruptive interaction, leading to crisis outbreak.

The first **interactor** variable in the onset model, **conflict setting**, is grouped into three types. Crises in a *non protracted conflict* are not burdened by long-term hostility between the adversaries, for example, the Soviet Union and communist Hungary in the 1956 Hungarian Uprising. The environment of *protracted conflict* (*PC*), by contrast, is characterized by on-going disputes between the same actors, usually over multiple issues, with interaction fluctuating from acute hostility to relative tranquillity, spillover effects on many aspects of their relationship, and the absence of anticipated termination of the conflict, as illustrated in the Arab/Israel and India/Pakistan conflicts since the late 1940s. *Long-war protracted conflict* exhibits all the traits of a PC, along with continuous warfare, for example, World War II and the second Vietnam War, 1964–75.

Two elements point to a higher likelihood of crisis outbreak among states locked in a protracted conflict. One is the direct effect on perceptions of value threat by the contending parties: in a protracted conflict, rivalry, mistrust, and the persistent expectation of violence from adversaries lead to perceived value threat, especially if a conflict persists for an extended period. The other is the absence of a logical basis for anticipating an interstate crisis in a non-PC setting, whereas crisis is an integral part of the pattern of expectations and behavior in an on-going conflict.

A protracted conflict between two (or more) states not only makes crisis outbreak between them more likely. It also enhances the likelihood of *vulnerability* to crisis. As long as A and B, and possibly others, are caught in the web of protracted conflict, each is "fair game" for the other, that is, a legitimate target. In short, a PC setting, *per se*, makes the participants more vulnerable to external crisis.

Capability, in the crisis onset model, refers to relative strength or power discrepancy; that is, capability is an interactor attribute between (among) adversaries. For the purposes of this book, and the ICB Project as a whole, power was computed for each crisis actor and its adversary in the year a crisis began. The raw power score is the sum of six separate scores measuring: *size of population, GNP, size of territory, alliance capability, military expenditure*, and *nuclear capability*.[7]

Capability has a potent influence on crisis onset through its effect on threatened values. The more favorable a state's power relative to an adversary, the more impervious it will be to hostile acts, events or situational changes. The obverse is equally true: the weaker a state, the graver will be the perceived value threat from an adversary. Moreover, weakness is also likely to lead decision-makers of the target state to adopt change in order to cope with the power discrepancy and the identified value threat.

Where power discrepancy is small or non-existent, the constraint on catalyzing a crisis will be less for either state, because defeat and victory are (almost) equally uncertain. Thus both will be more vulnerable to an external crisis. Moreover, in the absence of power discrepancy there will be a disposition, perhaps need, of the intending initiator to communicate resolve by employing violence; and that renders the target more vulnerable to violent crisis eruption. In sum, all other things being equal, no or low power discrepancy makes crisis occurrence more likely.

Capability also impinges upon crisis initiation. Assuming a rational means-ends calculus by decision-makers, then, all other things being equal, a large power discrepancy between adversaries makes it unnecessary for the stronger state to initiate a foreign policy crisis in order to protect or enhance its national interests. It is likely to do so only if it is dissatisfied with the status quo and initiates an opportunity crisis, e.g., Iraq's invasion of Kuwait in August 1990. Similarly, it is unlikely that a weaker state will draw a stronger adversary into a crisis. By contrast, where power discrepancy is small or nil, the constraint on crisis initiation by either state is less, for defeat and victory are equally uncertain. It can be argued that, if defeat and victory are equally uncertain, maintenance of the status quo will be preferred. However, in accord with power transition theory, it is argued here that, as states approach power parity, the likelihood of either side initiating a foreign policy crisis increases, for reasons cited earlier in the presentation of the onset model. Moreover, the risk and cost of an adversary acting first tend to induce a state to preempt a crisis, especially in a protracted conflict.

There are also reinforcing effects of capability on crisis onset. First, advanced military technology will shrink the distance between a state and its potential crisis/war adversary. A dramatic illustration is the effect of air power and, later, missiles on geostrategic distance during most of the twentieth century. Thus distance/proximity is partly a function of a power gap between the adversaries. Moreover, the larger a state's military capability, the less salient will be its size; that is, power compensates for territory in the quest for security. And power discrepancy in favor of an aggrandizing state will increase the vulnerability of its intended target.

Political **regime**, as noted, is classified as *democracy* and several types of *authoritarianism*. The latter may be *civilian*: communist regimes such as the USSR, Cuba or Vietnam; non-communist republican dictatorships, widespread in the Third World; or monarchical regimes, like Jordan for most of its history and Saudi Arabia. It may be *direct military* rule, e.g., Pakistan 1958–71, 1977–88. It may be *indirect military* rule, in which the armed forces shape policy but act through a subordinate civilian government, such as Panama in the 1980s. And it may take the form of *dual military-political* authority, in which a regime rests on the armed forces and a civilian party or organization, as did Peron's Argentina from 1945 to 1955, and Franco's Spain from 1939 to 1976.

Whether political regimes of adversaries diverge or converge is highly salient to crisis outbreak. Interstate crises, it is argued here, are less likely to occur between democratic states than between states with authoritarian or mixed (democratic/non-democratic) regimes. One reason is that discordant *regime pairs* will accentuate the mutual perception of value threat. Another is that regime differences reinforce distrust. A third is that most democratic states maintain strong economic links with other democracies. And the incentive to maintain harmonious relations is much greater given the impact that mutual non-cooperation might have on domestic economies. In general, regime discordance is an additional interactor source of perceived value threat and disruptive interaction.

A non-democratic regime pair also reinforces the disposition of an authoritarian regime to initiate crises: it accentuates other sources of disruption such as tangible disputes, different economic systems, and competing ideologies. As such, it contributes to more intense hostility, increased fear, and greater willingness to initiate a crisis lest basic values be threatened by an adversary's preemptive act. Moreover, the leaders of authoritarian regimes, both military and civilian, are much freer in choosing paths to goal achievement. And this includes the posing of value threat to adversaries, as well as employing violence, directly or indirectly, as and when deemed necessary. By contrast, decision-makers in pluralist polities and economies are more constrained by diverse interest groups, competing élites, and public opinion from initiating foreign policy crises for other states. In short, democratic adversaries are less likely to initiate foreign policy crises for each other than are authoritarian regimes or mixed adversarial regime pairs. The same reasons explain why democracies are less likely than other regimes to employ violence in coping with external crises (Weede, 1984; Russett, 1990: Chap. 2; Bueno de Mesquita, Jackson and Siverson, 1991; Lake, 1992; Ember, Ember and Russett, 1992; and Chap. 3 below).

Geographic distance, too, affects crisis eruption. For one thing, proximity is more likely to generate a perception of value threat from a hostile neighbor than from a state far from one's borders. Contiguity will sharpen such a perception. Moreover, intense disruption is more likely between contiguous states than between those that are physically apart. Thus, as evident in the array of territorial crises cited later in this chapter, contiguity increases the likelihood of border disputes or wider competitive claims to territory, for example, the 1959–63 India/China Border crisis-war. Ethnic spillovers from one state to another, too, are more likely, for example, in Third World crises such as the Football War of 1969 between El Salvador and Honduras, and the 1985 crisis over Libya's expulsion of Tunisians.[8]

The link between geographic distance and crisis outbreak is accentuated by the *number of borders*. At one extreme, states that are physically remote from all other members of the global system, e.g., Australia, are less likely to be involved in interstate crises. Apart from everything else, they have little opportunity for crisis activity. At the other extreme, states with many borders are likely to be unable to escape involvement in interstate crises—unless they are formally neutralized by the major powers, e.g., Belgium in the nineteenth century, Austria since 1955.

Geographic distance is also conducive to crisis initiation. Neighbors are more likely to trigger crises for each other than for distant states, because their location facilitates the projection of power against an adversary. Proximity tends to overcome the uncertainty about a neighbor's intention and capability. However, caution with respect to crisis initiation will predominate if a state is contiguous to one or more major powers.

Geographic contiguity also accentuates vulnerability to external crisis, that is, state B's proneness to being a target for state A—and *vice versa*. Stated simply, proximity facilitates hostile behavior and disruptive interaction. This is enhanced when the parties are locked in a protracted conflict, for physical proximity is superimposed upon mistrust, fear and longstanding issues in dispute. And when their regimes differ in type, or both are non-democratic, mistrust is reinforced, and communication between adversaries becomes clogged. The result is greater vulnerability to hostile behavior, including the outbreak of an international crisis.

The first explanatory **actor** variable in the crisis onset model is **age**. For one thing, young states have not had the time to develop their economy so as to generate the economic surplus that provides the basis for military power. For another, their political system tends to be non-democratic, primarily because of the often long and violent struggle that culminates in independence, whether from the uniting of disparate groups and territories or from foreign rule or both. Thirdly, they usually suffer from unstable regimes. All of these weaknesses, accentuated by the task of nation-building, make new states more likely to perceive value threats from external as well as internal enemies. That higher propensity for threat perception will predispose them to serve as targets of external crisis; that is, they will be more prone to a paranoia syndrome regarding the intentions of other states. Moreover, because of the decolonization process in the twentieth century, young states emerged in geographic clusters, in the Middle East and Southern Asia and, later, in Africa. Thus adversaries are likely to be territorially contiguous. In terms of the model, all this suggests that age, capability, regime, internal instability, and geographic distance are linked to crisis proneness (to be discussed below).

Age is also salient to initiation. One way of expediting the process of state-building in new states is to externalize obstacles by initiating crises for other states; that is, new states often seek legitimacy and domestic support by redirecting dissatisfaction of their publics to a foreign foe.

Regime duration, too, helps to explain crisis onset. It is, first, salient to crisis initiation. Like new states, regimes of recent origin are beset by perceived insecurity of tenure; and that tends to induce their initiation of foreign policy crises for other states. Moreover, the decision-makers of a new or recently-formed regime will be more prone than those of older regimes to perceive value threats from abroad. Further, like new states, regimes of recent origin are more likely to be confronted with political instability and perceived insecurity of tenure; and that, too, makes them more vulnerable to external crises. Stated differently, this element invites disruptive behavior by adversaries. Established regimes, by contrast, are more secure and more rooted in their societies, and are, therefore, less vulnerable to external intervention.

Territorial size, too, will affect the decision whether or not to initiate an external crisis for another state. Interstate crises are less likely to be catalyzed by small states because the costs of violence, always possible and highly probable once a crisis erupts, would be greater—for their security and, in the case of poor, small states, for their population and resources as well. Conversely, all other things being equal, there are fewer constraints on crisis initiation by a state endowed with large territory because the potential retaliatory damage can be contained more easily.

Size will also affect vulnerability, for a small state is more likely than a large one to perceive a basic value threat, because of its lesser capacity to cope with external sources of threat. Small states in a protracted conflict are even more vulnerable to crisis because of their persistent expectation that a larger adversary may preempt at any time, with graver consequences for the former: its territory is more easily penetrated, and its population centers damaged, by a crisis.

The last explanatory actor variable in the onset model is *internal* **instability**. Instability will affect a decision whether or not to initiate a crisis; that is, it is likely to assist in the quest for protection or enhancement of existing values. The condition of internal turmoil is also more likely to induce decision-makers to externalize their insecure tenure, reinforcing the tendency of young regimes to divert dissent by a foreign adventure, noted earlier.[9]

Domestic instability also helps to explain vulnerability to external crisis. Instability at home will undermine the self-confidence of a state's rulers. Among other consequences is a tendency to exaggerate threatening acts or events that pose a danger to one or more basic values of an unstable regime. More specifically, political instability in State A creates an image of weak resolve to resist demands for concessions by State B. Economic instability undermines a state's ability to cope with threat. And social instability reinforces an image of weakness, which increases the likelihood that B will consider it opportune to trigger a crisis for an unstable, weak and disunited A. In short, A becomes more vulnerable to, that is, a more likely target for, an external crisis by a hostile member of the global system.

The **intervening** variables in the crisis onset model, as noted, are **values** perceived to be at risk and, at the system/interactor level, **disruptive interaction**. The centrality of value threat as the defining condition of crisis onset is evident in the fact that it is directly affected by all ten independent variables; that is, their effects on crisis outbreak, initiation and vulnerability are channelled through the decision-makers' perception of value threat.

Values comprise *economic welfare, territorial integrity, political regime, influence,* the *avoidance of grave damage,* and *existence,* the highest value. It is assumed that crisis actors are more likely to use violence as their primary crisis management technique when their existence is threatened than in situations of any other value threat; further, that there will be variations associated with high, medium and low value threats, as specified above. The differences are likely to be manifested in all facets of behavior: in decision-making—by large or small, *ad hoc* or institutional groups; in response time—slowly or quickly or instantaneously; in crisis management technique—pacific or violent and, if the latter, severe or moderate, central or marginal in coping with crises; in reliance on external support, whether by a major power or an international organization or both, etc. Crisis outcomes, too, are likely to be affected by the gravity of values threatened: the willingness to compromise will be more evident in cases where lesser values are threatened than when a crisis actor perceives its existence to be at stake or perceives grave damage if it yields to adversary demands. In general, it is expected that states will be profoundly affected in their behavior by the gravity of values threatened in a foreign policy crisis.

The economic welfare of Iceland and the UK—more correctly, of their North Atlantic fishermen—was at stake in the Cod War crises of 1973 and 1975–76. China's territorial integrity was threatened by Japan in the 1931–32 Mukden Incident. The political regimes of Nicaragua, Panama, the Dominican Republic and Haiti were threatened by Cuba-assisted invasions of these states by exiles in the 1959 Cuba/Central America Crisis. The regional and global influence of the two superpowers was threatened in the Berlin crises of 1948–49 (the Blockade), 1957–59 (the Deadline), and 1961 (the Wall). And Israel's existence was perceived to be at stake in the 1967 Six Day War Crisis. So too was that of Kuwait and Saudi Arabia in the Gulf Crisis of 1990–91.[10]

Whatever the value threat, it generates higher-than-normal stress for decision-makers. That, in turn, predisposes them to anticipate the outbreak of a foreign policy crisis. Moreover, when a state's decision-makers perceive that a core value is at stake in a conflict or dispute, along with an opportunity to protect or enhance that value, they are likely to initiate a crisis. An international crisis would follow soon thereafter—perhaps instantly, as noted—for a trigger by A and a perception of basic threat by B, and B's response would set in motion more disruptive interaction and, with it, a crisis between them.

The extent of a state's vulnerability to crisis is a function, in part, of the gravity of value threat during disruptive interaction. If the value is perceived as marginal to the target state's interests, a dispute can be more easily resolved without a crisis. However, if a dispute threatens a core value, the target state will perceive a crisis as near-certain and, perhaps, imminent; and it must prepare to cope with the threat and, usually later, time pressure and expected military hostilities as well. In short, the more basic the value threatened, the more likely it is that an interstate crisis will erupt. Parenthetically, proneness to initiation and vulnerability to crisis are intertwined, for the behavior of a crisis initiator is directed to a crisis target. Yet they are not exactly "two sides of the same coin."

In the course of devising the onset model the ten independent variables were also assessed in terms of their effects on each other; that is, a network of effects within the group of independent variables was generated. The results are as follows:

Rank			
1	structure –		8 effects
2	system level –		6
3	age –		5
4	conflict setting –		4
4	capability –		4
4	regime–type (pair) –		4
7	internal instability –		3
8	geographic distance –		2
8	regime—duration –		2
10	territory—size –		1

In purely *statistical* terms, an attempt to infer a causal link between an independent variable and any dependent variable from the number and/or intensity of correlations between the former and other independent variables would be methodologically flawed. At the same time, the overall *theoretical* significance of an independent variable clearly is proportional to the range of its connections with others deemed exogenous. In other words, there is some degree of hierarchy among the independent variables within a theory. Thus, if X_1 is linked to five others, whereas X_2 is connected to only two, one can deduce, *a priori*, that X_1 represents a more central concept within the theory. In this sense, it is permissible—and valuable—to anticipate the relative weight of independent variables before engaging in data analysis.[11]

Data, Propositions and Summary

From the crisis onset model as specified above, it is possible to deduce the conditions in which *outbreak*, *initiation* and *vulnerability* are most likely to occur.

Proposition 1: *An international crisis is most likely to break out when: the dispute between A and B occurs within a polycentric structure; in a subsystem of world politics; in a setting of protracted conflict; when there is no power* *discrepancy between the adversaries; when the regime pair is non-democratic; and when the adversaries are territorially contiguous.*

Proposition 2: *A state is most likely to initiate a foreign policy crisis when the following conditions are present: it is a young or new political entity; it is militarily stronger than its adversary; its regime is non-democratic; it confronts domestic political, social, and/or economic instability; it is geographically contiguous to its adversary; and its territory is large.*[12]

Proposition 3: *A state is most likely to be a target of (vulnerable to) a foreign policy crisis when: it is a young or new political entity; it is engaged in a protracted conflict with one or more states; there is little or no power discrepancy between the adversaries; its political regime differs from that of its adversary; it is confronted with domestic political, economic and/or social instability; it is geographically contiguous to its adversary; its political regime is of recent origin; and its territory is small.*

These propositions are based on the premise that the larger the number of conditions that are present, the more likely it is that decision-makers of the target state(s) will perceive a basic value threat, followed by disruptive interaction; therefore, the more likely it is that an international crisis will break out; and, at the actor level, that a state will initiate an external crisis and a state will be prone to an external crisis [Chaps. 3–5]. (The same assumption applies to hypotheses regarding escalation, deescalation and impact, except that the perception of harm is enlarged to include awareness of time pressure and of heightened probability of involvement in military hostilities.)

As evident, Proposition 1 focuses on the international crisis as a whole and, therefore, on system and interactor variables: actor-level variables are conspicuously absent. By contrast, Propositions 2 and 3 relate to the foreign policy crisis of a state; and its explanatory factors are actor- and interactor-oriented. The difference between Propositions 2 and 3 is even more profound. The former focuses on crisis initiation. The latter, by contrast, is target-oriented. The elements of these two propositions are similar, but the relevant data relate, respectively, to the initiator or triggering entity (state A) and to the target of a crisis (state B).

These are termed *Propositions*, unlike *Hypotheses* for all other phases, because the data for the onset phase are confined to case studies. The ICB Project's aggregate data were coded from the beginning of the crisis period, not pre-crisis. The rationale was that almost all of the independent variables of the onset model—structure, level, conflict setting, geographic distance—are hard-shell factors that change very slowly. Moreover, others, such as capability or regime pair or, at the actor level, size of territory and internal instability, do not change in the pre-crisis period, which is generally weeks or days in duration. Further, as indicated in Chapter 1, perception of value threat is common to both the pre-crisis and crisis periods: it is the sole defining condition of the first, one of three conditions of the second. Thus the findings on Hypotheses 1–3 can be taken to apply as well to the propositions relating to onset/pre-crisis; to the extent that these hypotheses are supported, one can infer support for the propositions regarding onset. To test both would be redundant. This exercise will therefore be conducted for escalation, in the next chapter.[13]

As noted in Chap. 1, none of the explanatory variables in the general macro and micro models of crisis (Models I and II) can be designated as necessary and sufficient conditions. Applying the argument set out there, perceived value threat/disruptive interaction is the defining—necessary and sufficient—condition of the onset phase: a foreign policy crisis and, therefore, an international crisis cannot erupt in the absence of a perceived threat to a basic value; and whenever it is present, a foreign policy crisis ensues—unless it is aborted, a point to be elaborated in the Unified Model of Crisis [Chap. 6].

The first three questions about crisis onset posed at the beginning of this chapter, namely, outbreak, initiation and vulnerability, derived from the theoretical priorities set out in Chapter 1. In order to answer these and other questions to follow, about escalation, deescalation and impact, it was necessary to create a dataset. Using the definitions set out in Chapter 1, we uncovered 390 international crises which incorporated 826 foreign policy crises for individual states, from the end of 1918 to the end of 1988. I pause here to present several 'cuts' of these data, which, *inter alia*, demonstrate the ubiquity of interstate crises in the twentieth century.

The *overall* distribution of international crises by *year* (raw frequency) is presented in Figure 2.2. As evident, there were many peaks and troughs. Ten or more crises erupted in each of 10 years since 1945, with the largest concentration from 1976 to 1981 (68 cases in six years). This was followed by a marked decline in the 1980s, except 1987

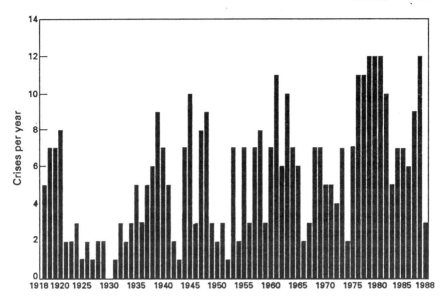

FIG. 2.2   Distribution of International Crises, 1918–88

(37 cases in six years, 1982–86, 1988). At the other extreme, there were 17 years with only one or two crises (none in 1930), notably 1922–31, except for 1924, and again in 1950, 1952 and 1954. Interestingly, the number of crises in any year never exceeded 12, despite the steady sometimes dramatic, increase in the number of sovereign states and, therefore, the number of potential actors in interstate crises after WWII, especially in the 1960s and 1970s. (The raw frequency data do not shed any light on duration, the number of crisis actors, that is, foreign policy crises, ranging from one to 21 [Entry Into WWII, 1939], extent of violence, crisis management techniques, intensity, impact, etc., aspects of crisis to be addressed in later chapters of this book.)

Crises occurred in all *regions* and in all of the seven *decades* since the end of World War I (Table 2.1).

Many of the trends in twentieth-century interstate conflict are confirmed by these data. There was an overall *concentration of crises in the Third World "peripheries" of the global system*. Africa, Asia and the Middle East accounted for two-thirds of the 390 international crises after World War I, compared to only 21% for Europe, the core of the dominant system.[14] There was a *steady decline of interstate turmoil in Europe* after World War II. There were 63 military-security crises in Europe during the first three decades (1919–48), only 20 in the last four (1949–88).[15] The "long peace" in Europe notwithstanding, there was

TABLE 2.1 Distribution of International Crises: Region and Time

	1919–28	1929–38	1939–48	(WWII)°	1949–58	1959–68	1969–78	1979–88	Total
Africa	—	3	2	(2)	6	15	31	46	103 26.4%
Americas	4	6	3	(1)	5	11	7	8	44 11.3%
Asia	4	8	16	(7)	15	16	13	10	82 21.0%
Europe	22	11	30	(17)	7	5	4	4	83 21.3%
Middle East	10	2	10	(4)	10	15	16	15	78 20.0%
Total	40 10.3%	30 7.7%	61 15.6%	(31)	43 11.0%	62 15.9%	71 18.2%	83 21.3%	390 100%

°The figures in this column are part of the 1939–48 cluster of cases. World War II was the largest concentration of intra-war crises (IWCs). See TABLE 2.4.

increasing turmoil in the global system after World War II.[16] By contrast, there was *relative interstate tranquillity in the Western Hemisphere*—no international crises in North America, and only 44 in Latin America, 11% of the total.[17]

Table 2.1 also reveals: a *spiral of crises in Africa* from its first decade of independent states, 1959–68 (15) to two decades later (46); and a very different, *little-changing distribution of crises* over time in the *Americas, Asia and the Middle East.*

Related ICB data indicate that violence was preeminent as the catalyst to international crises in Africa, non-violence in Europe, with the Americas almost evenly divided, and Asia and the Middle East exhibiting considerably more violence than non-violence. The proportions of *violent to non-violent triggers* were: Africa, 72–28%; Americas, 52–48%; Asia, 58–42%; Europe, 34–66% (27–73%, if Europe's World War II cases are excluded); and the Middle East, 57–43%.

Actor-level data on crises are also instructive. Although Africa had the largest number of international crises (103), it had fewer foreign policy crises than Europe or Asia, 175 compared to 224 and 178, and only a few more than the Middle East (170) for the 70-year period. This is one of several indicators of less complex and less intense crises in Africa than elsewhere.[18]

The pervasiveness of interstate crises is also evident in *all system and actor attributes*. As noted, they occurred in all types of structure, at both system levels, within and outside protracted conflicts, when adversaries were contiguous or remote from each other, when their regimes were identical or discordant, etc.

Crises occurred in the inter-World War multipolar structure, e.g., Remilitarization of the Rhineland in 1936, and in bipolarity, e.g., the Berlin crises of 1948–49, 1953, 1957–59, and 1961. And the diffuse pattern of authority, polycentrism, has witnessed over a hundred international crises, from the 1963–65 Malaysia Federation Crisis to the Gulf Crisis of 1990–91.

Viewed in terms of subsystems, US hegemony in Central America has not prevented the Postage Stamp Crisis over territory between Honduras and Nicaragua in 1937, or other crises.[19] Nor was the post-World War II East European subsystem under Soviet hegemony immune to crises, from Communism in Poland in 1946–47 to the Prague Spring in 1968 and Poland Solidarity in 1980–81.

As for *conflict setting*, there were, as noted, 26 protracted conflicts since the end of World War I (Table 2.2). All are (or were) lengthy, most of them several decades or more. Most have fluctuated in inten-

TABLE 2.2   *Conflict Setting of International and Foreign Policy Crises*

	First Crisis/ Conflict Duration	Protracted Conflict	
		International Crisis	Foreign Policy Crisis
AFRICA			
Ethiopia/Italy	(1934–45)	2	3
Ethiopia/Somalia	(1960–	6	8
Rwanda/Burundi	(1963–	1	2
Rhodesia	(1965–80)	11	17
Chad/Libya	(1971–	8	19
Angola	(1975–	9	15
Western Sahara	(1975–	10	14
AMERICAS			
Chaco	(1928–35)	2	4
Essequibo	(1968–	2	2
ASIA			
China/Japan	(1927–45)	7	12
Indonesia	(1945–49)	3	6
India/Pakistan	(1947–	8	16
PRC/Taiwan	(1948–	4	11
Pushtunistan	(1949–	3	7
Korea	(1950–	3	12
Indo-China	(1953–75)	19	39
PRC/USSR	(1969–89)	1	2
EUROPE			
Poland/Lithuania	(1920–38)	3	4
France/Germany	(1920–45)	5	8
World War II	(1939–45)	24°	60
Trieste	(1945–53)	2	5
MIDDLE EAST			
Greece/Turkey	(1920–	9	22
Arab/Israel	(1947–	25	53
Iran/Iraq	(1959–	4	7
Yemen	(1962–90)	6	16
MULTIREGIONAL			
East/West	(1945–89)	19	47
Total		196°°	411°°

°Four of these crises occurred in North and East Africa and the Middle East.
°°The other 194 international crises and 415 foreign policy crises occurred outside of protracted conflicts.

sity, from war to near-accommodation, and back to violence. All have aroused intense animosities among the participants, with spillover to a broad spectrum of issues. Some protracted conflicts comprise recurrent crises over the same issue, for example, the Chad/Libya crises since 1971 over territory, notably the mineral-rich Aouzou Strip. Others exhibit crises over diverse issues, as in the India/Pakistan conflict —Kashmir, the Indus River system, evacuee property, Bengali refugees, East Pakistan/Bangladesh, etc.

No *region* was immune to the disease, with eight PCs in Asia, seven in Africa, four in Europe, four in the Middle East, two in the Americas, and one multi-regional conflict. There was also great variety in the frequency of crises within protracted conflicts: at one end of the spectrum, 25 in the Arab/Israel conflict, along with many more incidents, raids and acts of retaliation, and 19 in the East/West conflict; and at the other, one military-security crisis each in the Rwanda/Burundi and the PRC/USSR conflicts, with two crises in each of three other conflicts —Chaco, Essequibo, and Trieste. There was great variety, too, in the *duration* of protracted conflicts: less than a decade in four of them, Chaco, World War II, Trieste and Indonesia; more than four decades in seven others—Greece/Turkey, East/West, Arab/Israel, India/Pakistan, PRC/Taiwan, Pushtunistan, and Korea; and of these, all but the East/ West conflict continue unabated. In fact, 13 of the 26 protracted conflicts remain unresolved. Yet half of the 390 international crises from the end of 1918 to the end of 1988 occurred outside of an on-going conflict, from Haiti Unrest in 1929–30 to a Honduras/Nicaragua border crisis in 1987.

Diversity is also evident for actor attributes attending crises. They erupt when the value threat is territory, survival of a political regime, influence, or a state's existence. They occur between old and new states, when the power balance is large or small, when a state is/is not beset by domestic instability, etc.

The diversity of actors and location is also evident in a random selection of crises over *territory* during each of the seven decades under inquiry (Table 2.3).

The widespread occurrence of twentieth-century crises extends to *intra-war crises* (*IWCs*). Seven types of environmental change—there may be others—have been uncovered as triggers to crises for states during a war (Table 2.4).

As noted, not all adversaries in an international crisis need be crisis actors: some may not perceive higher-than-normal value threat, time constraint, and/a heightened likelihood of war. Similarly, one or more

TABLE 2.3   *Selected Interstate Crises Over Territory*

Crisis Years	International Crisis	Crisis Adversaries	Disputed Territory
1920	Vilna	Lithuania, Poland	Vilna
1922	Western Anatolia II	Greece, Turkey	Western Anatolia
1923	Corfu	Greece, Italy	Corfu
1932–33	Leticia	Colombia, Peru	Leticia
1937	Amur River Incident	Japan, USSR	Sennufu and Bolshoi islets
1938	Changkufeng Incident	Japan, USSR	Changkufeng hills
1939	Nomonhan	Japan, USSR	Manchukuo/Outer Mongolia frontier
1945–46	Kars-Ardahan	Turkey, USSR	Kars-Ardahan
1947–48	Kashmir I	India, Pakistan	Jammu and Kashmir
1953	Trieste II	Italy, Yugoslavia	Trieste
1955	Pushtunistan II	Afghanistan, Pakistan	Pathanistan
1959–60	Shatt-al-Arab I	Iran, Iraq	Shatt-al-Arab
1961–62	Pushtunistan III	Afghanistan, Pakistan	Pathanistan
1965	Rann of Kutch	India, Pakistan	Rann of Kutch
1968	Essequibo I	Guyana, Venezuela	Essequibo
1969	Shatt-al-Arab II	Iran, Iraq	Shatt-al-Arab
1971	Caprivi Strip	South Africa, Zambia	Caprivi Strip
1977	Belize II	Guatemala, UK	Belize
1977–78	Ogaden II	Ethiopia, Somalia	Ogaden
1981	Peru/Ecuador Border	Ecuador, Peru	Cordillera del Condor
1982	Falklands/Malvinas	Argentina, UK	Falklands/Malvinas Islands
1987	Three Village Border II	Laos, Thailand	Phitsanaloke

actors in an international IWC may not consider their crisis as an IWC: it depends on their relationship to the war then in process. The battle over Dien Bien Phu in 1954 offers a dramatic example.

The siege of the French garrison during the first Vietnam War (1946–54) was an IWC for France, but not for the UK and the US: though they perceived France's predicament as a foreign policy crisis for themselves, they were not at war in Vietnam. And France, as a consequence, behaved very differently from its allies. Ignominious

TABLE 2.4   *Types of Intra-War Crisis*

Trigger to IWC	Number of Cases (International)	Content	State Experiencing Crisis
Entry of major power	4	PRC 'volunteers' into Korean War 1950	US, South Korea
Heightened probability of major power entry	1	Soviet threat during Suez–Sinai War 1956	Israel
Heightened probability of major power exit	1	Fall of Italy 1943	Germany
Technological escalation	5	V-2 bombing, Battle of Britain 1940	UK
Major escalation other than advanced technology	48	Allied landing at Normandy 1944	Germany
Defeat in a significant battle	6	Fall of Dien Bien Phu to Vietminh 1954	France
Internal deterioration	3	Khmer Rouge offensive 1975	Cambodia
Other	5		
Total	73		

defeat led to France's total withdrawal from Vietnam following the Geneva Conference in May 1954. By contrast, the UK and the US, whose perceived value threat was much less grave, successfully resisted strenuous French efforts to draw them into the fighting to defend a strategic base and, by extension, France's colonial war.

The major categories of data for interstate crises from 1918 to 1988 and their distribution may also be noted (Table 2.5).

The final indicator of the ubiquity of interstate crises is the fact that 126 states experienced or initiated one or more foreign policy crises since the end of 1918 [see Chap. 3, Table 3.4 and the accompanying discussion].

Given the ubiquity of interstate crises, one must acknowledge that there are no necessary and sufficient conditions, in the formal sense, to explain the phenomenon of crisis. Therefore what is postulated here regarding onset and in subsequent models is a set of "most likely" or enabling conditions. No more can be achieved at this point in the "state of the art" on crisis, conflict and war.

The crisis onset model addressed the first three questions posed at

TABLE 2.5   *Interstate Crises, 1918–1988: Overall Distributions*

		International Crises	Foreign Policy Crises
Structure	Multipolarity (1918–39)	20%	22%
	World War II (1939–45)	8%	9%
	Bipolarity (1945–62)	24%	25%
	Polycentrism (1963–88)	48%	44%
System Level	Dominant System	18%	27%
	Subsystem	82%	73%
Conflict Setting	Non-Protracted Conflict	50%	50%
	Protracted Conflict	33%	32%
	Long-War Protracted Conflict	17%	18%
Capability I	High	25%	
Power	Medium	30%	
Discrepancy	Low	45%	
	Negative		35%
	No/Low PD		24%
	Positive		41%
Capability II	Small Powers		42%
Power Status	Middle Powers		21%
	Great Powers		25%
	Superpowers		12%
Geographic	Africa	27%	21%
Location	Americas	11%	10%
	Asia	21%	22%
	Europe	21%	27%
	Middle East	20%	20%
	Home Territory		58%
	Sub-region		20%
	Same Continent		10%
	Elsewhere		12%
War Setting	Intra-war Crises	19%	30%
	Non-IWCs	81%	70%
Age of States	Old (pre-1815)		35%
	Recent (1815–1945)		33%
	New (post-1945)		32%
Regime Type	Democratic		38%
	Civil Authoritarian		43%
	Military regime		19%
Regime	Short (0–2 years)		21%
Duration	Medium (3–25 years)		54%
	Long (more than 25 years)		25%
Values	High (existence, avoidance of		
Threatened	grave damage, influence)		46%
	Medium (territory, political system)		42%
	Low (economic, social,		
	limited threat to population, territory)		12%

the beginning of this chapter: what are the most likely conditions for the *outbreak* of an international crisis, the *initiation* of a foreign policy crisis, and for maximal *vulnerability* of a state to an external crisis? Moreover, the pervasiveness of interstate crises in the twentieth century has been demonstrated. Thus I turn now to the fourth question, how do states manage a crisis, for once it erupts, the target state must respond to a perceived value threat; that is, it must cope with a foreign policy crisis.

Coping with Onset

The coping dimension of the pre-crisis period will be described and explained in terms of perceptions, decisions and behavior by ten states confronted with an external crisis (Table 2.6). The ten cases range from pivotal crises in twentieth-century world politics, e.g., Munich (1938), Stalingrad (1942–43), Berlin Blockade (1948) to others that are less well-known. This is deliberate because the purpose of this table and the case studies to follow is to communicate in the most effective way the typologies and their sub-categories. All but two of the typologies correspond to independent variables. Region and Time specify the spatial and temporal settings.

The comparative findings on coping, to be reported after the case studies, can be said to apply to a group of the most prominent interstate crises, without any claim that they are representative in any statistical sense. However, it is reasonable to focus on cases that are easily understood as meriting special attention. In short, the ten crises are representative of a subset of important and visible interstate military-security crises since the end of World War I.

The defining condition of pre-crisis, namely, a perceived threat to one or more basic values, is clearly evident in the ten crises to be explored throughout this book. These may be noted briefly:

for the US in the Berlin Blockade (1948): the preservation of West Berlin as a symbolic Western enclave in communist Europe, and the security of Western Europe;

for the USSR in the Prague Spring (1968): unity of the Soviet bloc, and security of the Soviet Union;

for the UK in the Munich Crisis (1938): avoidance of war and its intolerable casualties, and Britain's influence as a world power;

for Germany in the Battle of Stalingrad (1942): a deep-rooted belief in German military superiority over the Soviet Red Army;

for Israel in the October-Yom Kippur Crisis (1973): security of settle-

TABLE 2.6 Typologies and Case Studies

		Berlin Blockade	Prague Spring	Munich	Stalingrad	October–Yom Kippur	Lebanon Civil War	India/China Border	Hungarian Uprising	Rhodesia UDI	Falklands/Malvinas
STRUCTURE	Interbloc	X									
	Intrabloc		X						X		
	Non-bloc			X	X	X	X	X		X	X
POLARITY	Multipolarity			X							
	World War II				X						
	Bipolarity	X						X	X		
	Polycentrism		X			X	X			X	X
CONFLICT SETTING	Non-PC	X	X	X			X	X	X	X	X
	PC					X					
	Long-War PC				X						
POWER LEVEL	Major Powers	X		X	X						
	Middle Powers					X		X			
	Major/Minor Powers		X	X					X		X
	Middle/Minor Powers						X				
	Minor/Minor Powers									X	
PEACE/WAR SETTING	Non-War	X	X	X			X		X	X	
	Pre-War					X		X			X
	Intra-War				X						
INTENSITY OF VIOLENCE	War				X	X	X	X	X	X	X

	Minor Clashes	No Violence
POLITICAL REGIME		
Democracy/Civil Auth.	X	X
Democracy/Military		X
Civil Auth./Civil Auth.	X	X
ECONOMIC LEVEL		
Advanced Ind./Advanced Ind.	X	X
Advanced Ind./Developing	X	
Developed/Developing		
Developing/Developing	X	X
REGION		
Africa	X	X
Americas		X
Asia	X	
Europe	X	X
Middle East	X	
TIME		
1930s	X	
1940s	X	X
1950s	X	
1960s	X	
1970s	X	X
1980s		X

ments on the Golan Heights and, later in the pre-crisis period, avoidance of high casualties from a joint Egypt-Syria attack;

for Syria in Lebanon Civil War I (1975): the "historic indivisibility" of Syria and Lebanon as part of "Greater Syria," Arab unity, and Palestinian statehood;

for India in India/China Border (1959–62): large tracts of territory regarded as indisputably parts of India, claimed by China, and India's leadership role in the non-aligned Third World;

for Hungary in the Hungarian Uprising (1956): survival of the pro-Soviet Hungarian regime;

for Zambia in Rhodesia UDI (1965): its existence, one year after independence, in the face of anticipated massive economic sanctions by Rhodesia; and

for Argentina in the Falklands/Malvinas Crisis (1982): recovery of sovereignty over long-lost territory, and honor of the armed forces.

In sum, many values were perceived to be at risk: resolve, symbolic presence, military superiority, unity, security, human life, territory, regime survival, honor, status and influence, and existence.[20]

In the larger context within which these ten foreign policy crises unfolded, it is also worth noting the initial trigger-value-response nexus in the onset phase of the relevant international crisis.

Trigger-Value-Response Nexus: Onset Phase

Berlin Blockade (1948)

trigger	decision of intent by the three Western Powers, on 6 March 1948, to integrate their zones of occupation into a West German state and into Western Europe's reconstruction (*political, economic*);
value threat	to USSR's influence in Europe;
response[21]	USSR: walkout of Marshal Sokolovsky from Allied Control Council meeting on 20 March 1948 and imposition of a "baby blockade" on access to West Berlin, on 1 April (*political, economic*).

Prague Spring (1968)

trigger	weakening of pro-Soviet forces in Czechoslovakia culminating in forced resignation

of Novotny as State President on 21 March 1968 (*political*);

value threat
to USSR's influence in Eastern Europe;

response
USSR: the leaders of Eastern Europe summoned to bloc summit meeting at Dresden on 23rd (*political*).

Munich (1938)

trigger
Sudeten German Party's Karlsbad Program on 7 June, demanding greater autonomy for German minority within Czechoslovakia (*internal political*);

value threat
to Czechoslovakia's existence;

response
Czechoslovakia: rejection of SdP demand (*political*).

Stalingrad (1942)

trigger
German offensive on Eastern Front (*violent*);

value threat
to USSR territory;

response
USSR: battles all along Soviet "southern" front (*violent*).

October-Yom Kippur (1973)

trigger
air battle between Syria and Israel on 13 September 1973 (*violent*);

value threat
to Israel's strategic position on Golan Heights;

response
Israel: IDF 7th Brigade dispatched from Negev to North, to confront possible Syrian attack on Israeli settlements (*non-violent military*).

Lebanon Civil War I (1975)

trigger
formation of military cabinet in Beirut on 23 May 1975 (*political*);

value threat
to Syria's hegemony in Lebanon;

response
Syria: "peace mission" dispatched to Beirut on the 25th (*political*).

India/China Border (1959–62)

trigger
China's suppression of Tibet Revolt, March 1959 (*violent*);

value threat   to India's Himalayan borders;
response   India: asylum granted to Dalai Lama, 19
                        March (*political*).

Hungarian Uprising (1956)
trigger   permission granted by communist rulers to
                        rebury Rajk, 5 October 1956 (*political*);
value threat   to survival of Hungary's communist regime;
response   Hungary: armed forces placed on state of
                        alert to confront possible mass upheaval
                        against the regime, 20 October (*non-violent
                        military*).

Rhodesia UDI (1965)
trigger   Rhodesia's threat of economic sanctions
                        against Zambia, 26 April 1965 (*economic*);
value threat   to Zambia's existence;
response   Zambia: to seek international support against
                        Rhodesia threat, 5 May ff. (*political*).

Falklands/Malvinas (1982)
trigger   dispatch of British naval ship to expel Argen-
                        tine "scrap merchants" from South Georgia,
                        on 20 March 1982 (*non-violent military*);
value threat   to Argentina's irredentist claims to Malvinas
                        islands;
response   Argentina: to move to immediate future
                        long-planned invasion of Malvinas islands, 26
                        March (*non-violent military*).

As evident, the triggers to these ten international crises between 1938
and 1982 varied—political, economic, non-violent military, violent,
internal. However, all of these triggers catalyzed perceptions of threat
to important values—existence, influence, territory, political system.
This was one crucial element in the trigger-value-response nexus relating to onset. Moreover, eight of the ten target states responded either
tit-for-tat, e.g., political/political, or with a more intense act, e.g., politi-
cal/non-violent military. The exceptions were Israel in October-Yom
Kippur, a violent trigger and non-violent military response, and India in
India/China Border, a violent trigger and political response.

What follows is an analytical summary of how the crisis actor in each
of these ten international crises, not necessarily the initial target noted
above, coped during its pre-crisis period. Thereafter, the findings will

be compared in terms of *actor* and *situational* attributes, and *coping* processes: specifically, number of *decisions*, key *decision-makers*, and their *attitudinal prism* (actor attributes); crisis *trigger*, *values* threatened, *duration*, *system level*, *number of actors*, *violence* (situational attributes); and *information-processing*, *consultation*, *decisional forum*, and consideration of *alternatives* (coping process).

Once a value threat is perceived, the target state embarks upon a process of coping. As indicated in the Model of Crisis Behavior (Model II), decision-makers seek information about the threat, as well as the intention and capability of the adversary. They consult among themselves and may seek the advice of others within and outside their political and military élites. They also create one or more decision-making forums to seek and evaluate alternative options and to choose among them. The coping process may be rapid or slow. It may occur once or several times during the onset phase, depending upon the reaction of the triggering entity (A) to the target state (B)'s initial response, the number of specific challenges posed by the adversary, and the intensity of hostile interactions. There will be as many responsive decisions as there are challenges, ranging from compliance with an adversary's demands to military action.

The nexus of perceptions, decisions, and coping in the onset phase/pre-crisis period will become evident in the findings from the ten case studies cited above. I begin with two superpower crises, the United States in the Berlin Blockade (1948–49), and the Soviet Union in the Prague Spring (1968), followed by major power crises from multipolarity and World War II, the United Kingdom in the Munich Crisis (1938), and Germany's Stalingrad Crisis (1942–43). Thereafter I shall explore crises for lesser powers from the 1950s to the 1980s.[22]*

BERLIN BLOCKADE (1948–49)[23]

The first of several international crises over Berlin was rooted in the division and occupation of Germany by the victorious Allied powers at the close of World War II: the Potsdam Agreement of July–August 1945 divided Germany into four zones, and Berlin into four sectors, American, British, French and Soviet; but all of Germany was to be treated as a single economic unit under the direction of the Allied Control

---

* Readers who are interested primarily in comparative findings on coping by the ten crisis actors in the pre-crisis period should go directly to Case Study Findings, pp. 117–129.

Council. The Western presence in Berlin was, from the beginning, a geographic and ideological island surrounded by Soviet-occupied communist East Germany.[24]

The onset phase of the Berlin Blockade Crisis, as distinct from the US's pre-crisis period, began on 6 March 1948 when, at their London Conference on Germany, the Western Powers made an unpublicized decision to integrate their zones in Germany into one unit, as part of the economic reconstruction of Western Europe, thereby providing a basis "for the participation of a democratic Germany in the community of free peoples." This followed the Czechoslovak coup, a communist seizure of power in Prague on 25 February. The USSR responded on 20 March, when Marshal Sokolovsky walked out of a meeting of the Allied Control Council, followed by the imposition of a mini-blockade of the Western sectors of Berlin.

The international crisis escalated in June, first with the Western Powers' publication of their London Conference decision, on the 7th, and then on the 24th, when the Soviets imposed a full-scale blockade on all Western land transportation into and out of Berlin. A US airlift followed two days later, with rising tension and the risk of East/West war in the heart of Europe. However, with a US decision on 22 July to refrain from sharp escalatory measures in favor of an expanded airlift and negotiations, the long deescalation phase began.

Talks to break the deadlock began in August 1948. The blockade was virtually dismantled by 21 March 1949. And crisis termination took the form of a Four Power Agreement on 5 May, formalized a week later: Germany was split into two embryonic states, soon to become the democratic Federal Republic of Germany (FRG) and the communist German Democratic Republic (GDR), until the latter was absorbed by the former in 1990.

The pre-crisis period for the US, as well as the UK and France, began on 20 March 1948 with Sokolovsky's walk-out from the Allied Control Council meeting. It lasted until 24 June, when the USSR imposed a full blockade on all land traffic to and from West Berlin. Of the six US decisions during the pre-crisis period two were pivotal: Decision [henceforth D.] 3 on 31 March, when President Truman, in consultation with the State Department, Department of the Army, and the Joint Chiefs of Staff, decided to authorize Military Governor Lucius Clay to send test trains through Soviet checkpoints, with instructions to prevent entry by Soviet personnel but not to shoot except in self-defense; and D. 6 on 23 June, when Clay decided to extend currency reform from the Western zones of Germany to the Western sectors of

Berlin. As with the Soviet walkout on 20 March, these US decisions led to a tit-for-tat reaction: the first triggered a mini-blockade of West Berlin on 1 April; and the second led to the imposition of a full Soviet blockade the day D. 6, marking the beginning of the crisis period for the United States [see Chap. 3].

The three principal US decision-makers were Truman, Clay and Secretary of State George C. Marshall. All shared the Realist view of world politics as essentially a struggle for power to enhance national interests (Carr, 1939; Morgenthau: 1946, 1948). They were also adherents of the "Riga axioms," which viewed the USSR as a revolutionary state with unbounded ideological ambitions to achieve world hegemony, in contrast to the "Yalta axioms," which perceived the Soviet Union as a conventional great power in the international system.[25] The former, crystallized in George Kennan's "Long Telegram" of April 1946 and his anonymous ("X") "Sources of Soviet Conduct" (Kennan, 1947), provided an intellectually persuasive foundation for the concept of "Cold War" and the policy of global containment, pursued by the US for the next four decades.

The "Riga axioms" constituted the US decision-makers' attitudinal prism, that is, the pervasive lens through which specific images of Soviet intentions and actions in a specific confrontation were filtered. Following Shlaim's insightful analysis, this prism comprised four elements: first, as noted, a Realist view of interstate politics as a perpetual conflict of national interests; secondly, the "two-camp" image of irreconcilable, ideologically determined ends and means between the "free world" and communist totalitarianism, which had inherited the image of supreme evil from Nazi Germany; thirdly, a self-image of moral rectitude with a mission to "save the world" from what became known in the 1980s as "the evil empire"; and finally, a set of strategy preferences derived from these images—firmness backed by military superiority, patience and vigilance, resolve and determination, all designed to deter the expansion of Soviet power everywhere in the world. All three US decision-makers, in fact, the Truman Administration as a whole and the professionals of the multi-layered bureaucracy, were committed to these images and self-images, some with a larger emotional component, others due mainly to intellectual conviction. In Shlaim's words (1983, 109): ". . . significant differences existed in style, emphasis and detail. But [there was] a shared hard core of fundamental beliefs and images. . . . This hard-line and hawkish psychological environment constituted the framework for decision, choice and action during the crisis."

The environmental change that triggered the first US post-World War II crisis over Berlin was, as noted, the Soviet walkout from the Allied Control Council on 20 March 1948. Together with other hostile Soviet acts *vis-à-vis* Germany and Berlin, it generated a general US perception of threat from its main adversary in world politics. Yet the collapse of the Council, *per se*, did not pose a direct threat to a basic US value, since Four Power cooperation on Germany had effectively ended earlier. Rather, it implied an embryonic threat to vital Western and American interests—West Berlin as the symbolic enclave of Western values in the heart of Europe and, more generally, the future of West Germany and the security of Western Europe. There were differences among US decision-makers about the probability of war, with Army Secretary Royall the most concerned about an escalation from violent incidents, Clay more sanguine on the whole, and US intelligence estimates optimistic about the avoidance of war at least until the end of 1948. None perceived war as imminent or as likely in the near future. Nor is there evidence of an awareness of time constraints on decision-making regarding Berlin.

How did the US cope with the pre-crisis period (onset phase) of the Berlin Blockade? As expected, there was a more active search for information about Soviet intentions and behavior. Several sources were tapped: the theatre commander, Clay, through teleconferences; CIA estimates; and reports from US envoys in London, Paris, Bonn and Moscow. The result was an increase in the flow of information to Washington. But there is no evidence of concentration at the apex of the US Administration—yet; that is, normal channels of information processing still operated in this phase. Consultation was confined to decision-makers and their official advisors. And the involvement of the President and Secretary of State was limited.

Nor was there a discernible change in the complex pattern of decisional forums on Berlin. Decisions in the pre-crisis period flowed from several centers of authority: some were made by the President, some by the Military Governor, one by the Secretary of State, and one by the Cabinet. And these were generally made without a systematic search for and evaluation of alternatives. While the danger of a complete blockade of Berlin was present in the background, US decision-makers adopted an *ad hoc* approach to choice in this period, partly because of competing foreign policy issues, partly due to the impending presidential election campaign, and partly because of wishful thinking: the Cold War, during which hard choices became the norm, had just begun.[26]

PRAGUE SPRING (1968)

The origins of the Prague Spring Crisis can be traced to domestic unrest and conflict within the Czechoslovak Communist Party during late 1967. This led to the ouster of long-time Soviet loyalist Antonin Novotny as First Secretary on 5 January 1968, and as State President on 21 March. His successor as party leader, Alexander Dubcek, announced a far-reaching "Action Program" which proposed solutions to the country's economic crisis, Slovak pressure for autonomy, the rehabilitation of party leaders purged in the early 1950s, changes in the election system, a new approach to dissent by students and intellectuals, the abolition of censorship, the reduction of economic controls and central planning, reorganization of the security apparatus, etc. More ominously, it pledged "a more active European [independent foreign] policy" for Czechoslovakia, though remaining within the Warsaw Pact and in alliance with Moscow. It was in response to this break with past hard-line policies and, in particular, to heavy pressure from East German and Polish communist leaders that Moscow decided to convene a bloc summit meeting. Thus Novotny's ouster from the presidency and the Dresden summit on 23 March mark the beginning of the Prague Spring onset phase.[27]

The escalation phase began with the publication of the Action Program on 9 April—it had been circulating in Prague in March—and lasted until the invasion of Czechoslovakia by Soviet-led Warsaw Pact forces on 20 August. There were several escalation points, arising from USSR and bloc decisions, as well as from actions by the Czechoslovak reform leaders: growing pressure in Moscow and from bloc leaders for a more visible Soviet military presence on Czechoslovak territory, notably on 14–15 May, 26–27 May, 30 June, 20–21 July, and 7–15 August 1968; and, from Prague, a strong expression of support for the reform program by 60 intellectuals, scientists and writers in an open letter, "Two Thousand Words," which appeared in leading Prague journals on 27 June, as well as passive resistance by Dubcek and his colleagues throughout the spring and summer to pressure from the Warsaw Pact countries, especially the USSR, to pull back from the brink of "counter-revolution."

The deescalation phase was brief, barely a week, from the invasion on 20 August until the Moscow Protocol on the 27th, signed under duress by captive Czechoslovak leaders: it set out the specific measures that they would have to implement on the road to "normalization." With the signing of the Protocol and the return of Dubcek and his colleagues to

Prague, the Soviet leaders resumed their summer holidays! It was the most persuasive evidence that the international crisis over the Prague Spring had come to an end.

The USSR's pre-crisis period began the day after the forced resignation of Novotny as State President, with its decision to convene a bloc summit in Dresden in order to consider the disquieting situation in Czechoslovakia. It ended on 4 May with a meeting between Soviet and Czechoslovak communist leaders, who had been summoned to Moscow for bilateral talks the previous day. Notable among the other eight Soviet decisions in the pre-crisis period were the dispatch of the Warsaw Pact (WTO) commander, Marshal Yakubovsky, to Prague for negotiations on WTO maneuvers in Czechoslovakia, and an informal consensus by a Politburo group to add "mutual brotherly aid" as a principle to govern relations among communist states, including "military assistance" if necessary (18–21 April).

What was the attitudinal prism for Soviet pre-crisis coping with the Prague Spring? The standard themes of Cold War rhetoric are evident in the seven speeches or articles by Soviet leaders during that period: US imperialism as the major source of international tension; its increasingly aggressive posture around the world—militarily in Vietnam, and ideologically in Eastern Europe, supported by *revanchism* in West Germany; and the undermining of Soviet bloc unity by dogmatism (China) and revisionism (Yugoslavia and others).

Only two of these leadership statements were directly relevant to Czechoslovakia, evidence that the Prague Spring was not yet the issue of overriding concern to the USSR: one was by Brezhnev on 29 March to the Moscow City Party Conference, the other by Grishin on 22 April, marking the 98th birthday of Lenin. Although a junior Politburo member, Grishin's hawkish speech in the presence of the Soviet triumvirate—Brezhnev (General Secretary), Kosygin (Prime Minister), and Podgorny (Chairman, Praesidium of the Supreme Soviet)—was the crucial signal of Soviet intentions, to be transformed into reality at the height of the crisis period four months later. Thus, conspicuously absent from his list of principles to govern relations with "fraternal parties" was non-interference; in fact, it was replaced by "brotherly mutual aid," specifically, an assertion of the USSR's intention to "extend to those people whose freedom and independence is threatened by imperialism all-round political, economic, and—if necessary—also military aid." Later, this principle was enshrined as the "Brezhnev Doctrine," the ideological rationale for the invasion of Czechoslovakia by Soviet bloc forces.

The trigger to the USSR's Prague Spring Crisis was, as noted, a cluster of dramatic moves in the ruling Czechoslovak party, notably the replacement of Novotny by Dubcek and the proposal of radical reforms. There were, too, criticisms in the Czechoslovak Party press of past communist rule, and procrastination over planned Warsaw Pact maneuvers in the territory of a strategic Soviet client. The threatened values were the unity of the Soviet bloc and the security of the USSR. Yet time pressure was totally absent from Soviet consideration of the dangers emanating from Prague. And, notwithstanding Grishin's warning, the likelihood of military hostilities between patron and client seemed very remote at the beginning of May 1968. In short, the distinctive traits of the pre-crisis period were present in this case.

How did the Soviets cope with the incipient threat posed by the Prague Spring? A felt need and quest for more information is evident in the communiqué of the Dresden summit meeting in late March. And with the curtailment of traditional sources of information as a result of purges of conservatives from the Czechoslovak party bureaucracy and the security services, Moscow relied more on alternative sources of information, notably the Soviet Embassy in Prague. As for information processing in the narrow sense, it is noteworthy that Brezhnev first referred explicitly to Czechoslovak press reports at the bilateral meetings in Moscow at the very end of the pre-crisis period, a practice to continue on through the crisis period.

Two groups played an important consultative role from the beginning of the onset phase: the Central Committee of the Soviet Communist Party, which convened at the beginning of April 1968 to consider the Prague Spring, at the behest of ideologues within the party *apparat*; and the East German and Polish leaders, Walter Ulbricht and Wladyslaw Gomulka, who urged a harder line towards the Czechoslovak reformists even before the Dresden conclave.

The key decisional forum was the Politburo, but decision-making was not entirely centralized. The Politburo made the two strategic decisions at the beginning and end of the pre-crisis period: to convene a bloc summit meeting in Dresden (D. 1) and to summon the Czechoslovak leaders to Moscow (D. 10). A six-person Negotiating Team for the Dresden summit, to which the Politburo delegated full authority (Brezhnev, Kosygin, Kirilenko, Shelest, Baibakov and Rusakov), made three decisions, one of major substance, namely, not to intervene further in Czechoslovak internal affairs provided the Czech Party carried out its assurances to its bloc colleagues (D. 4). An *ad hoc* group of Politburo members made two decisions, including the floating of the "mutual brotherly aid" principle noted above. The Central Committee made two implementing decisions. And the military were primarily responsible for the dispatch of the Warsaw Pact commander to Prague. In short, several decisional forums operated in the onset phase, under the overall authority of the Politburo. Throughout they seem to have considered many alternative paths to cope with the threat posed by the Prague Spring: persuasion; economic aid; negative sanctions; and, as a possible ultimate technique, force.[28]

MUNICH (1938)

From its seizure of power in Germany in 1933 until the outbreak of World War II the Nazi regime mounted a relentless campaign to restore Germany's "lost territories" and its primacy in Europe. One result was a series of international crises provoked by Germany and directed at major and minor powers alike. These included: Austria *Putsch* (1934); Kaunas Trials (1935), against Lithuania; Remilitarization of the Rhineland (1936), challenging the Versailles Settlement and the interests of seven European states, including France and the UK; *Anschluss* (1938), the merger of Austria into the Third Reich; and the Czech May Crisis (1938), culminating in Munich, the first act in the dismemberment of Czechoslovakia. It was followed in 1939 by Czechoslovakia Annexation, then by Memel, with demands on Lithuania; Danzig, focusing on Poland's port city; and then the climactic crisis of the inter-World War era, Entry into World War II.

During that six-year period of German *revanchism* the Munich Crisis was the decisive turning point on the road to World War II. For most historians (e.g. Watt, 1989), it made war inevitable by an Anglo-French policy of appeasement that was doomed to failure. In the event, it epitomized Europe at the brink of Armageddon for the second time in twenty-five years.[29]

The prelude to Munich as an international crisis was a cluster of threatening words and deeds in the early months of 1938: a speech by Hitler to the *Reichstag* on 20 February, referring to 10 million Germans, six-and-a-half million in Austria, the rest in Sudetenland, whose "right of racial self-determination he would protect" (Taylor, 1979: 378). In March, Austria was annexed. And in May, reports of a concentration of German troops in Saxony, near the Czechoslovak border, triggered the five-day Czech May Crisis. Hitler retreated in the face of British and French threats to intervene if Czechoslovakia were invaded, and the latter's partial mobilization; and the crisis ended on 23 May.

Nevertheless, German pressure on Prague was intensified, through the Sudeten German Party (SdP), whose leader, Henlein, presented demands for much greater autonomy in the Karlsbad Program on 7 June.

That act marked the beginning of the onset phase of Munich as an international crisis. It lasted through the summer, with continuous political and diplomatic efforts to defuse the crisis: a compromise "Third Plan" by Prague on 24 August, in a futile attempt to meet Sudeten German demands; and a pro-German "Fourth Plan" by British mediator Lord Runciman between 3 and 7 September.

The escalation phase began on the 7th with the arrest of SdP members by Czechoslovak police for arms smuggling. On the 12th, at the Nazi Party Congress, Hitler demanded self-determination for the Sudeten Germans. Riots began in Sudetenland the same day. For the next 17 days feverish diplomacy was conducted by the major powers, notably by British Prime Minister Chamberlain interacting with Hitler, who pressed his demands resolutely. Diplomacy took the form of three summit conferences in September: at Berchtesgaden on the 15th, where Chamberlain agreed "in principle" to self-determination for the Sudeten Germans, i.e., merger with Germany; at Godesberg on the 22nd–23rd, where Chamberlain agreed to transmit to Prague Hitler's demand for the territorial transfer of Sudetenland by 1 October; and, after partial British and French mobilization in the expectation of war, at Munich on 28–29 September.

The escalation phase and the Munich Crisis ended with the signing of the Four Power Agreement that sealed the fate of Czechoslovakia; Daladier of France and Italy's Mussolini reinforced the *diktat*. The crisis faded for the USSR sometime in October, once all German-claimed territories had been occupied, and war was averted temporarily.

For the UK, the crisis trigger was a German Government announcement at the end of July designating the Rhineland and areas close to the French, Czechoslovak and Polish borders as "prohibited areas," as well as proclaiming a partial mobilization of German forces, to take effect in September. For Prime Minister Chamberlain and other British leaders, who received the information on 3 August—they were on holiday at the time—this meant a threat to the tranquillity of Europe, along with an emerging time salience.

The initial UK response came on 24 August, in the form of three closely-related decisions: first, to recall Ambassador Neville Henderson from Berlin for a full report on the significance of the German plans;

second, to instruct the Foreign Office to negotiate with Germany secretly so as to establish a personal contact between Chamberlain and Hitler; and third, to instruct Sir John Simon, Chancellor of the Exchequer, to reiterate British policy as laid down on 24 March 1938, in his speech scheduled for 27 August, specifically, to make no direct commitment to the defense of France or Czechoslovakia. Pre-crisis, for the UK, lasted until another, much more threatening speech by Hitler on 7 September.

Although the UK decisions were made formally by the Cabinet, there were four key decision-makers—Prime Minister Neville Chamberlain, the Foreign Secretary, Lord Halifax, the Home Secretary, Sir Samuel Hoare, and Simon. (One day after the crisis period began, the "Big Four" formally became an *ad hoc* "Inner Cabinet" to cope with the crisis.)

The psychological setting for Chamberlain and his colleagues was dominated by fear of war and the need to preserve peace at almost any cost. Several strands coalesced to create this obsession with peace. First, there was an emotionally-rooted belief that a European war on the scale of 1914–18 was irrational, unthinkable, unnecessary and abhorrent. Moreover, a feeling of great anxiety was created by a sense that Britain was militarily unprepared for war with Germany in 1938. And thirdly, in the tradition of "perfidious Albion," it seemed preposterous to the advocates of appeasement for Britain to become embroiled in a distant conflict; a war had to be fought on larger issues.

Among their specific images, perhaps the most noteworthy were that Anglo-German harmony was the key to European peace and that Hitler could be trusted once he realized his "legitimate" aspirations regarding Austria and Sudetenland. British leaders also perceived widespread opposition to war among their people. And there was fear that massive damage could be inflicted by the Germans, especially the *Luftwaffe*. Added to these was Chamberlain's self-image of supreme self-confidence as a political leader who was fated to solve the crisis personally; hence the journeys to Berchtesgaden, Godesberg and Munich to reason with Hitler. Chamberlain's closest aides shared his attitudinal prism and his images and reinforced his conviction, a classic illustration of the negative consequences of "groupthink" in crisis decision-making (Janis, 1972).

The catalyst for the UK's Munich Crisis has already been noted. The perceived value threat was twofold: first, the intolerable casualties to be anticipated in modern war; and secondly, Britain's status and influence as a world power, which would be severely undermined if it failed to prevent Armageddon. Thus Chamberlain was prepared to risk his reputation by personal diplomacy. The cost, in his view, shared by his colleagues, was merely the dismemberment of a distant land and people. Time was salient from the beginning of the onset phase, for the sealing off of borders and partial mobilization could not be ignored. However, while the outbreak of war was clearly possible, it still seemed remote between 3 August and 7 September 1938.

How did the UK cope with the low stress of pre-crisis? There was a modest quest for information, as evident in the increase of diplomatic messages between the Foreign Office and British diplomatic missions, from 4.8 a day during the preceding two months to 6.3 a day in the pre-crisis period (it was to reach 26.2 a day during the high stress, crisis period). This was supplemented by information from Lord Runciman, the informal UK mediator between Germany and Czechoslovakia until 7 September. However, information processing revealed a strong bias in favor of Sudeten "self-determination" through the advocacy of Czechoslovak capitulation, by members of the Cabinet "Big Four," the primary decisional forum, diplomats in Prague and Berlin, and the Foreign Office.

Consultation was restricted in the onset phase to these politicians and civil servants. The Cabinet was rarely called into session during this period. As for alternatives, the only viable option to compliance with Hitler's demands was a public declaration of support for France and Czechoslovakia in a time of crisis and then mobilization of Britain's armed forces. That a declaration was considered and rejected is evident in D. 3, namely, to avoid any public commitment to an ally or the latter's client. The fear of war and indifference to the fate of Czechoslovakia made mobilization unthinkable to UK decision-makers in the pre-crisis period.[30]

STALINGRAD (1942–43)

The Battle of Stalingrad was the only intra-war crisis among the cases examined in this book. At the same time it was one of many significant IWCs during World War II, from the Fall of Western Europe and the Battle of Britain in 1940, through "Barbarossa" in 1941 and Pearl Harbor in 1941–42, El Alamein in 1942–43, the Fall of Italy in 1943, D-Day in 1944, and the Final Soviet Offensive in 1945, to several Pacific theatre IWCs, such as Saipan in 1944, Iwo Jima and Okinawa in 1945, and the End of World War II (Atomic Bomb) Crisis in August 1945.

Half-a-century later, analysts still differ on the relative importance of these battles and campaigns. Yet all agree that in the struggle for the mastery of Europe Stalingrad was decisive in turning the tide of battle between Germany and the USSR. Psychologically, if not materially as well, the former never recovered. For the Soviet Union the triumph at Stalingrad was the psychological catalyst to ultimate victory in the "Great Patriotic War."

Viewed as an international crisis, Stalingrad can be said to have begun on 28 June 1942. That day, the *Wehrmacht* launched a massive summer campaign on the Eastern Front with three aims: to destroy Soviet forces west of the Don River; to capture the oil fields of the Caucasus; and to conquer Stalingrad or destroy it by bombing and heavy artillery. The onset phase, the longest of this IWC, lasted until 19 November. Advance by German forces was slow, with none of the objectives achieved. And on 19–20 November the crisis escalated with the beginning of a massive Soviet counter-offensive northwest and southwest of the besieged city.

The escalation phase continued for 77 days, until the final surrender of the German Sixth Army and ancillary Axis forces on 2 February 1943. The campaign continued, however, with a recovery of German power in the deescalation phase, from 3 February to 24 March, when Field Marshal Manstein's counter-offensive led to heavy Soviet casualties, the surrender of Kharkov, and retreat of the Red Army to the east bank of the Northern Donets River. Thereafter the titanic struggle between the two armies continued at its "normal" level. The intra-war crisis over Stalingrad receded into military history.

Germany's pre-crisis period was triggered by an internal act, namely, its launching of a major offensive on the Eastern Front in June 1942. It lasted 145 days, from 28 June to 19 November, when Germany's perception of threat rose dramatically from an emerging Soviet counter-offensive in and around the besieged city.

There was one strategic decision during the pre-crisis period, formalized as *Führer* Directive 41 on 5 April 1942, to launch a campaign in the East, with the three objectives noted above. There were also 86 Stalingrad-related implementing decisions by Hitler from the end of June to 19 November, but they failed to achieve his goals.[31]

The failure to achieve a decisive military victory, due to the better-than-expected performance of the Red Army, generated a negative, relatively low, value threat for Germany, a threat to the deeply-held belief in Germany military superiority over its Russian (and Marxist) adversaries. However, the loss of territory, grave damage in the form of heavy casualties and defeat in battle, let alone loss of the war, occupation and existence, were beyond the perceptual horizon of the supreme, in fact the sole, German decision-maker in the crisis over Stalingrad, Hitler himself, and even of his principal military advisors during the pre-crisis period. Nor was there any sense of time constraint on decisions, for Germany in the summer of 1942 remained the preeminent power in Europe, holding the initiative in every theatre of military operations. And the third necessary condition of a full-fledged intra-war crisis, a German perception of a likely adverse change in the military balance, was not yet apparent.

How did Hitler perceive the environment for choice and action in the summer of 1942? His belief in German military superiority was part of an attitudinal prism rooted in Nazi ideology. At its core was the philosophy of racism, the doctrine of racial superiority, and the idea of Germany as the master race, with a natural right to rule over inferior races. And such expansion of Germany's right to *lebensraum* could be achieved only by the successful threat or use of force. That ideological component of Hitler's belief system reinforced a widely-shared German belief in cultural ascendancy over Russia, the result of two centuries of interaction, from the reign of Peter the Great onwards. In Jukes' words: "A patronizing Social-Darwinist attitude toward all Slavs, and especially Russians, was long-established in Germany" (173).

From those core attitudes were derived specific images: of the Russians as an "inferior race"; of Marxism–Leninism as an inferior and dangerous ideology; of the Soviet regime as incapable of mobilizing the resources to prevent an overwhelming German victory in the East; of the Red Army as incompetent and unable to withstand an assault by the forces of the Third Reich; of the Russian people as certain, at the first opportunity, to abandon their rulers and to welcome "liberation" by the Germans. That tendency to underestimate his Soviet adversary, its regime, army and people, which was evident in explaining the failure to conquer Moscow in December 1941 as due to the Russian winter, continued to dominate Hitler's perception of the Soviet capacity for war, before, during and after the Battle of Stalingrad.

How did Germany cope with the challenge posed by the pre-crisis period? Like decision-making, information was centralized in Hitler's hands. The primary source was the OKH Intelligence section, whose assessments were presented by the Chief of the Army General Staff at the daily *Führer* Conferences. There was no sense of inadequacy of information, nor a search for additional sources; but the Intelligence reports exhibited little knowledge of the scope, goals or timing of the impending Soviet counteroffensive.

As for consultation, "Hitler did not 'consult' in the normal sense of the word. . . . he rarely left his headquarters, and he discussed events only with a small number of senior officers there [notably Keitel and Jodl until early September 1942]. No Cabinet meetings were held, and even senior Party leaders . . . saw him infrequently" (Jukes, 92).

The basic decisional unit during the Battle of Stalingrad, as during World War II as a whole, was Hitler himself. Formally, he combined the posts of Head of State, Head of Government and Supreme Commander of the Armed Forces. More important, as *Führer*, to whom all officers took an unconditional oath of obedience, and as the charismatic leader who restored Germany to greatness after the ignominy of defeat in World War I, the constraints of the Versailles Treaty, and the catastrophic inflation of the twenties, Hitler stood alone at the apex of power in the Third Reich.

Although the supreme decision-maker, he could not function without advice and information, military and political. The larger decisional forum for all military matters comprised: the *Führer* Headquarters (FHQ), containing the Party Chancellery, headed by Bormann, and the Armed Forces High Command (OKW), headed by Field Marshal Keitel; the latter's most important section was the Armed Forces Command Staff (Wfst), headed by Colonel-General Jodl; and the Army Headquarters (OKH), the key element of which was the Army General Staff, headed by Colonel-General Halder until 24 September 1942, and then by Colonel-General Zeitzler. The main decision-making sessions were the twice-daily *Führer* Conferences at FHQ, attended by representatives of all the military services, the Foreign Ministry, OKW and OKH.

Hitler dominated the decision-making process throughout, making all major decisions, the *Führer* Directives, affecting large operations, on the scale of an Army Group or above, and *Führer* Orders, dealing with a specific operation, such as the capture of a town. There was only one Directive during the Stalingrad Crisis, noted above. There were many Orders, for example, five decrees to the Sixth Army encircled at Stalingrad, in January 1943, to resist to the end. Hitler's decisions were then translated into implementing orders, by Jodl within the OKW sphere, Halder or Zeitzler within the OKH realm.

Hitler's deep-rooted antipathy to the traditional officer class of the *Wehrmacht* led, during the pre-crisis period, to increasingly acrimonious relations with senior military commanders. This culminated in his dismissal of Halder and an Army Group Commander, and threats to dismiss Keitel and Jodl, in September 1942. From October onwards German decision-making relating to the Stalingrad campaign became more and more *ad hoc*, with the *Führer* intervening even more in the execution of operational orders of the most minute kind, no less than 77 interventions in the deployment of divisions or smaller formations during the 145 days of the onset phase.

At the outset, one alternative to an offensive in the South was considered, namely, a renewed assault on Leningrad. The anticipated economic benefits of a sweep to the Volga and Transcaucasia were assessed as more important, though the evaluation was more intuitive than systematic. And there is no evidence of reassessment of the campaign, with a view to revision or replacement, at any time during the onset phase.

In short, the Stalingrad pre-crisis period witnessed an increase in perceived threat, resulting from the failure to achieve set goals. Only with the launching of the Soviet counter-offensive on 19 November 1942 did low-level threat give way to acute stress for Germany, accompanying escalation to the crisis period.

OCTOBER-YOM KIPPUR (1973–74)

From the major powers in the dominant system of world politics I turn to two small states in a conflict-ridden regional subsystem, Israel in the October-Yom Kippur crisis-war of 1973–74, and Syria's initial crisis in the prolonged Lebanon Civil War, which began in 1975.[32]

The setting for the first of these upheavals was a protracted conflict with frequent outbursts of intense violence, with inter-communal and inter-civilizational roots lasting at least a century. Specifically, Israel's victory in the Six Day War of June 1967 led to a vast enlargement of its territory—the West Bank, Gaza, the Sinai Peninsula, part of the Golan Heights, and East Jerusalem. In March 1969 Egypt launched the War of Attrition in an effort to recapture Sinai. A US-brokered cease-fire went into effect in August 1970, but the associated Rogers peace plan remained abortive. Anwar el-Sadat succeeded Gamal Abd-el Nasser in Cairo, and Hafiz al-Asad assumed power in Damascus, both in 1970 and both determined to regain the lost territories. In the spring of 1973 they planned a joint attack on Israel. Israeli forces were mobilized in April 1973 because Egyptian military exercises were misperceived as a prelude to imminent war. It was not to occur until October.

The onset phase of October-Yom Kippur began on 13 September 1973 with an air battle between Israel and Syria. It gave way to escalation on 5 October with evidence of an impending massive disruption in the normally high level of conflictive interaction between Israel and its two most powerful Arab adversaries. The next day it escalated to full-scale war with a surprise attack on Israel by Egypt and Syria. There were several escalation points during the next three weeks.

The deescalation phase began on 26 October, when the second superpower-inspired cease-fire between Egyptian and Israeli forces in the Sinai desert went into effect. The Egypt/Israel segment of October-Yom Kippur terminated on 18 January 1974, when the first Disengagement of Forces Agreement was signed at Kilometre 101 by Generals Elazar and Gamassi. War between Israel and Syria, however, continued for almost another half-year: on 31 May, after a costly mini-war of attrition and a gruelling exercise in shuttle diplomacy by US Secretary of State Kissinger, Israel and Syria signed their (only) Disengagement of Forces Agreement, relating to the Golan Heights. It was still in force—with a UN peace-keeping unit, UNDOF, serving as a cushion—19 years later, in the midst of a long-awaited Arab/Israel peace process.

The preeminent element of the psychological setting among Israel's decision-makers was the "Conception." In essence, it was an extraordinarily simple and erroneous definition of the Middle East situation in 1972 and 1973: Egypt, it was assumed, would not initiate a war against Israel without air power sufficient to dislocate Israel's airfields by deep penetration raids, a capability which it lacked at the time; and Syria would not launch a military strike without the active cooperation of Egypt; *ergo*, as Yigal Allon, Israeli Deputy Prime Minister and a military hero of the 1948 War, declared in June 1973: "They [the Arabs] have no military option at all." The effects of the Conception were to impair Israel's ability to distinguish between signals, that is, authentic clues of an adversary's intent, and *noise*, irrelevant or inconsistent signs pointing in the wrong direction. Specifically, the Conception led to very costly Israeli misperception of the abundant signals in late September and early October 1973 of a concerted Egyptian–Syrian plan to attack Israel.

Among the principal decision-makers, an analysis of Prime Minister Golda Meir's attitude statements indicates three themes: hostility to terrorism; anger at the Arab states' exploitation of the Palestinians, and friendship for the US. Relying mainly on the intelligence estimates of the IDF, she misperceived both Arab intent and capability and the likelihood of war. Allon was skeptical of those estimates in the early days of October; and he was the most dovish of Israel's leaders, calling for peace initiatives and far-reaching territorial concessions for peace, and recognizing that peace required a solution to the Palestinian problem. By contrast, Defense Minister Moshe Dayan advocated a rigid adherence to the *status quo*: continued control over the West Bank and Gaza, and Sharm-e-Sheikh, commanding the sea lines between the Gulf of Aqaba and the Red Sea; and a clear link between withdrawals from Sinai and progress towards peace with Egypt, the concept of "a piece of territory for a piece of peace." Like Allon, he was "gnawed by the mounting suspicion that [the Syrians] could be planning a more basic action," which led to the dispatch of a brigade from Sinai to the Golan Heights. Yet he accepted the crucial decision of 3 October to delay consideration of the Arab threat until the regular Cabinet meeting on the 7th—ironically, a day *after* the Egyptian-Syrian attack on two fronts. And all three Israeli decision-makers rejected the idea of a Palestinian state west of the Kingdom of Jordan, in Israel's historic heartland.

Israel's Yom Kippur Crisis, as noted in Chapter 1, was triggered by an air battle on 13 September 1973 in which 13 Syrian MIGs and one Israeli Mirage were shot down. The initial perceived value threat was to the security of border settlements in the North from possible Syrian retaliation. As the onset phase unfolded, the threat changed to an expected joint attack by Egypt and Syria to regain the Sinai and Golan territories lost to Israel in the 1967 Six Day War. While war or, at least, limited use of force is always perceived as possible in a protracted conflict, Israel's decision-makers viewed the probability of war as very low during the country's pre-crisis period. Nor is there any evidence of an awareness that time constrained Israel's response to the threat throughout the pre-crisis period, that is, from 13 September to 4 October 1973.

Turning to the coping process, the signs of an Arab military buildup were made known initially to the military élite only—the Defense Minister, Chief of Staff, General Staff, and senior officers of the Northern and Southern Commands. As the threat increased, information was brought to the attention of Prime Minister Meir's "Kitchen Cabinet", but not the Cabinet proper a few days before the outbreak of war.

As for consultation, the initial effect of more-than-normal threat and stress on the Prime Minister and Defense Minister was to seek more advice from the specialists on violence, that is, IDF officers. The low level of stress led to a large *ad hoc* decisional forum, namely, the "Kitchen Cabinet" advised by members of the military and bureaucratic élites.

There was no search for new options and limited discussion prior to Israel's two decisions of the onset phase:

D. 1, on 26 September, to warn Syria against military action, backed by the dispatch of the Seventh Brigade from the Negev to the North; and,

D. 2, on 3 October, to delay consideration of the threat until the next regular meeting of the Cabinet on 7 October.

In short, during the low stress pre-crisis period of Israel's October-Yom Kippur Crisis there was a modest probe for information that was processed by a small group; a narrow consultative circle; a decisional forum other than the Cabinet; and limited attention to alternatives prior to choice.[33]

LEBANON CIVIL WAR I (1975–76)

Lebanon was engulfed by a tragic civil war from 1975 to 1991. Its eruption was the culmination of years of gradual social dislocation that led to the polarization of Christian and Muslim communities and pointed to possible disintegration of the "precarious republic" which had emerged as an independent state in 1943 (Hudson, 1968, 1977). From the outset, Syria was enmeshed in the conflict because of its self-image as the patron of Greater Syria, of which Lebanon was, in Syria's view, an integral part. And from the mid-1970s onward the partition of Lebanon was viewed by Damascus as a grave threat, for it would undermine Syria's role as the guardian of Arab unity and, more tangibly, would provide Israel with a pretext to occupy Southern Lebanon up to the Litani River. That, in turn, would significantly enhance Israel's economic and geostrategic capability and alter the balance of power in the long war with the Arab world.

Lebanon's civil war began with reciprocal political terror on 13 April 1975: four members of the Christian *Phalange* (*Kata'ib* Party) were killed by unidentified gunmen; and *it* responded by murdering a busload of Palestinians returning from work. The first international crisis over Lebanon, however, did not break out until the formation of a military cabinet in Beirut on 23 May, posing a threat to Syria's vital interests. (Since Syria was the sole [*state*] crisis actor, the phases of the international crisis were identical to the periods of Syria's foreign policy crisis.)

The onset phase (pre-crisis period) of low threat for Syria's decision-makers lasted eight months, though their perception intensified following the second Egypt/Israel Disengagement Agreement on 1 September 1975. Escalation (crisis) occurred with the Christian expulsion of Muslims from two Beirut slums on 18 January 1976 and the consequent fear by Syria of an impending partition of Lebanon. This phase, too, continued eight months, until an overwhelming defeat of the Muslim-PLO alliance by Syrian forces on 30 September. With that event, all opposition in Lebanon to Syria's hegemony had been overcome, and partition had been averted. The deescalation phase (end-crisis) was dominated by an Arab summit conference in Riyadh/Cairo in October, which legitimized Syria's hegemony in Lebanon by deciding to create an "Arab Deterrent Force," overwhelmingly Syrian in composition. With its arrival in the centre of Beirut on 15 November 1976 to "keep order," the first international crisis arising from Lebanon's civil war came to an end.

The pre-crisis period of Syria's first Lebanon Civil War Crisis lasted from 23 May 1975 to 18 January 1976. All three of its decisions activated direct diplomatic intervention in the form of "peace missions," all of them headed by Foreign Minister Abd-el Halim Khaddam:

D. 1, on 24 May, in response to the formation of a "military Cabinet" in Beirut the previous day;

D. 2, on 28 June, to resolve a political deadlock by brokering the formation of a new cabinet; and

D. 3, on 18 September, to stop the rapidly-escalating fighting between Christians and Muslims.

Throughout its pre-crisis period Syria's Lebanon decisions were taken by a small, *ad hoc* Decision-making Committee dominated by President Asad, and including Khaddam, General Naji Jamil, Chief of the Air Force, and General Hikmat Shihabi, the Chief of Staff. All were committed *Ba'athists* and can be treated as a coherent group with a shared psychological environment.

The pervasive element in their *attitudinal prism* was the "historic indivisibility" of Lebanon and Syria as integral parts of "Greater Syria," whose realization had been frustrated by outside powers, notably France during its tenure as the Mandatory Power in both Lebanon and Syria from 1920 to 1943. Thus the disintegration of Lebanon would be a further blow to an enduring Syrian dream and goal. It would also serve to undermine Arab unity, another high value for Syria's *Ba'ath* leaders.

There were other elements in the worldview of Asad and his colleagues. One was a belief that the partition of Lebanon along communal-religious lines would undermine the Palestinian case for a "secular democratic state" to replace the predominantly Jewish state of Israel: if Arabs of different faiths could not live together in harmony within Lebanon, how could the Palestinians, the Arab states and the world at large expect Jews and Arabs, both Muslim and Christian, to live at peace in a Palestinian state? The Syrian leaders were convinced, too, that the partition of Lebanon would provide Israel with a pretext to occupy all of southern Lebanon up to the Litani River, which would further undermine the "historic indivisibility" of Syria and Lebanon. And that, in turn, would lead to a sharp decline in Syria's influence and status in the Arab world, the Middle East and global politics.[34]

Within that prism were Syrian images of other players in the Arab/Israel conflict, some of those images deeply-rooted. At the global level there was a persistently favorable image of the USSR, based largely upon its supportive roles since the mid-1950s, diplomatically and, most important, through a lavish supply of modern weapons during periods of war and peace. By contrast, Syria's leaders exhibited deep suspicion of US intentions and behavior in the conflict, viewing it as the supreme patron of Syria's mortal enemy. No other global actors were relevant.

Towards the Palestinian national movement, the Resistance, Syria projected a self-image of guardian and disinterested patron, for whom no sacrifice was too much; but the "Greater Syria" concept embraced the West Bank and Gaza and, in fact, the territory of the Kingdom of Jordan and Israel, as well as Lebanon. Of Israel, then and since 1948, the perception was unremitting mistrust and antagonism, with the derivative goal of politicide, that is, to expunge Israel from the international community of states. There was ambivalence towards Egypt, despite their alliance during the October War: for the first five months of the pre-crisis period the image of Egypt was highly positive because of Egypt's favorable view of Syria's behavior in Lebanon; but this image became extremely negative following the signing of the second Egypt/Israel Disengagement Agreement in September 1975. Towards Iraq there was bitter hostility, based upon a conviction that the other *Ba'ath* regime was trying to destabilize Syria's political system. Jordan was perceived positively because of Asad's wish to build a united "Eastern Front" against Israel. So too was the image of Saudi Arabia, despite the ideological gulf between them.

Among the situational attributes, Syria's value threat perception has already been noted—*vis-à-vis* the goals of Greater Syria, Arab unity, and Palestinian statehood. There is some evidence of time being salient, for Syria was quick to respond to the outbreak of civil war with diplomatic pressure on the Lebanese parties to resolve their differences and, at all costs, to avoid partition. It was a role which Syria was to play for the next 15 years, including a massive military presence in Lebanon since 1976, in an unsuccessful effort to impose peace and unity. And while Syrian leaders could not be unaware of the possibility of involvement in military hostilities, the perception of a higher-than-normal probability was not evident until the beginning of the crisis period (escalation phase) in January 1976.

How did Syria cope with the challenge posed by the outbreak of civil war in Lebanon? As always, information was sought about the morass of Lebanon's politics and warring groups; but there is no evidence of an acute felt need for more, and more varied, information on this issue. The President received Foreign Office position papers about the attitudes in other Arab capitals and abroad, reports from the Ministry of Information about developments in Lebanon, assessments from the National Command of the *Ba'ath* Party on Lebanese *Ba'ath* supporters, information about the Palestinian dimension from members of the pro-Syrian *al-Saiqa* Palestinian guerilla group in Lebanon—all filtered by his personal staff, and first-hand reports from Foreign Minister Khaddam and others based upon their three peace missions during the pre-crisis period (there were to be dozens over the next 15 years). Only the last was a new channel of information. And only in the crisis period were the sources of information markedly enlarged.

Asad's decision-making style in all important matters was to consult persons from diverse groups within the Syrian élite: Government, *Ba'ath* Party, Progressive National Movement, armed forces. In the pre-crisis period he consulted only Khaddam, Jamil and Shihabi, for the first two decisions; but they represented key power centers in Syria. And for the third decision the consultation group comprised 11 persons. (In the crisis period it was to be four times as large.)

As for alternatives, while thorough search for and evaluation of options characterized Asad's behavior, the decisions of the pre-crisis period seem to have been taken in accordance with SOPs to protect Syria's vital interests in Lebanon in a phase of relatively low threat, limited time constraints, and less than imminent likelihood of direct involvement in military hostilities.[35]

INDIA/CHINA BORDER (1959–63)

Turning to Asia, I now examine the pre-crisis period of India's prolonged crisis with China over their 2500-mile frontier along the vast range of the Himalayas.[36] But first, a brief overview of the crisis as a whole is in order. The border conflict between Asia's largest and most populous states can be traced to territorial disputes between the British–Indian and Chinese empires. However, the India/China Border Crisis emerged from competing claims between a resurgent communist China and newly-independent democratic India from 1950 onward and the occupation of Tibet by forces of the one-year-old People's Republic of China (PRC) in October 1950. Notwithstanding their *Panch Sheel* (Five Principles of Peaceful Coexistence) Agreement in April 1954 that regulated trade and other relations between the "Tibet region of China" and India, there were spasmodic frontier incidents in the 'fifties. Most disqueting for India was the Chinese construction of a highway across the Aksai Chin, claimed by India as part of the former princely state of Jammu and Kashmir that was integrated into India soon after independence in 1947. India discovered the near-completion of the road by chance in September 1957 and formally protested in October 1958; its Intelligence Bureau had been tracking the road since the early 1950s.

The origins of the prolonged border crisis are linked to the Tibet revolt against China's rule in March 1959, including the flight to India by the Dalai Lama, traditional ruler of Tibet's Buddhists. India's decision, on 15 March, to grant him asylum, if requested, provided the setting for Beijing's charge of Indian intervention in China's domestic affairs and marks the beginning of the onset phase. In reality, the dispute, which had been gestating for at least two years, encompassed large blocks of territory along the 2500 mile arc of the India/China border dominated by the Himalaya and Karakorum mountain ranges. It was awesome in territorial scope.

The onset phase lasted three-and-a-half years. It was marked by: border incidents, such as those at Longju and Kongka Pass in August and October 1959; diplomatic attempts at conflict resolution, notably the Chou En-lai–Nehru summit in Delhi in April 1960 and the Krishna Menon–Chen Yi meeting in July 1962; and strategies and tactics of penetration, encirclement, establishing facts, and buttressing claims by physical presence in "no man's land."

Onset gave way to escalation in September 1962 with the crossing of the Thag La Ridge by Chinese forces on the 8th, the ill-fated Indian

"Operation Leghorn" to "throw the Chinese out" and, dramatically, the Chinese attack in the Eastern and Western Sectors of the disputed border on 20 October. There were two war phases: from 20 to 28 October; and from 16 to 21 November. Indian forces were routed, especially in the North East Frontier Agency (NEFA).

China's announcement of a cease-fire, effective 22 November, and a unilateral withdrawal of PRC forces from 1 December to positions 20 kilometers behind "the line of actual control" on 7 November 1959, marked the beginning of the deescalation phase. Mediation efforts by the Colombo Powers (Burma, Ceylon [Sri Lanka], Cambodia, Indonesia, Egypt, Ghana) dominated the last phase of the crisis. Their proposals were approved by India's Parliament on 25 January 1963 and, in effect, rejected by China, that is, accepted with two "points of interpretation," on 20 April 1963. Thus ended the border crisis; but the border conflict remains unresolved in 1993, long after all the major protagonists—Nehru, Mao, Chou En-lai, Krishna Menon, Chen Yi—had departed from the scene.

India's pre-crisis period lasted three-and-a-half years, until Chinese forces crossed the Thag La Ridge in the Eastern Sector of the disputed border on 8 September 1962. Four sub-phases are evident, each manifesting a broad strategy and several tactical decisions.

Phase 1, 15 March–12 August 1959, the Tibet Revolt and its aftermath: the strategy was to maintain friendly relations with China, yielding neither to PRC nor domestic press and parliamentary pressure; the key decisions were to grant asylum in India to the Dalai Lama (around 15 March) and to inform the latter on 24 April that India would not recognize a "free Government" of Tibet.

Phase 2, 13 August–21 October 1959: a strategy of persuasion and argument with China was adopted on the emerging boundary question; the major decisions, in response to the growing clamor about frontier security, were to release a White Paper of correspondence and notes between India and China during the preceding five years; and to transfer responsibility for the Eastern Sector (North East Frontier Agency or NEFA) from a frontier constabulary, the Assam Rifles, to India's Army; both decisions were announced to Parliament by Prime Minister Jawaharlal Nehru on 28 August 1959.

Phase 3, 21 October 1959–29 July 1961: a strategy of diplomatic pressure on China was added after the humiliating Kongka Pass Incident on 21 October 1959; the major decisions were to reject an implied exchange offer by Prime Minister Chou En-lai at a summit meeting in Delhi, 20–26 April 1960, India to renounce its claims to the Aksai Chin in the Western Sector, China to its claims to NEFA; and to embark upon a systematic study of the conflicting border claims, the Officials' Talks, soon after the summit; India agreed to the latter proposal.

Phase 4, 29 July 1961–7 September 1962: a strategy of non-violent military pressure was adopted; this was expressed in a decision of 2 November 1961 to adopt a "forward policy," that is, in Ladakh, the Western Sector, "to patrol as far forward as possible from our present positions towards the international border and to establish more forward posts there"; and, in the Middle Sector, "as far as practicable, to go forward and be in effective occupation of the whole frontier." Ultimately, NEFA, the Eastern Sector, was included in the "forward policy" as well.

Because of his preeminence in India's political system, formally as Prime Minister and Minister of External Affairs, informally as the dominant figure in the Congress Party who commanded mass adulation, and as the philosopher, architect and engineer of India's foreign policy, Nehru's psychological environment is crucial to the analysis of India's behavior in the crisis with China. His worldview comprised several core elements: a belief in India's potential as a major power; the need for India to remain outside the adversarial camps in the Cold War, in order to achieve the two basic goals of economic development and genuine independence; non-alignment as the policy expression of these goals and as a projection of Indian nationalism into the arena of world affairs, through the concept of an "area of peace" in the Third World; and an ideology of liberalism, humanism and socialism that almost invariably led to a more favorable view of Soviet than of American foreign policy.

Within this attitudinal prism was a romantic image of the Chinese revolution from Sun Yat-sen to Mao Tse-tung, as part of the grand sweep of twentieth-century progress, with Asia and Africa reemerging into the mainstream of modern history. Nehru had a no less romantic view of the India/China cultural relationship since antiquity, free from a legacy of political or military conflict. These elements were partly offset by a Realist strand in Nehru's image—of an aggressive, expansionist China, determined to assert its primacy in Asia, fuelled by a self-image of a superior ideology and civilization. However, war between the Asian giants was utterly remote from his thinking throughout the onset phase. As he remarked on 22 December 1959: "[Local] wars do not take place, are not likely to take place between two great countries without developing into big wars and the big wars without developing possibly—not certainly—into a world war" (as quoted in S. A. Hoffmann, 1990: 123).

The catalyst to the onset of India's China crisis was, as noted, the Tibet Revolt in March 1959 and the flight of the revered Buddhist leader, the Dalai Lama. But in the pre-crisis period other turning points appeared. One was Chou En-lai's letter of 7 September 1959 asserting China's claim to more than 40,000 square miles of what Nehru regarded as indisputable Indian territory: prior to that event he was disposed to an empathetic reading of China's actions. Another was the Kongka Pass Incident on 21 October 1959, noted above. More generally, the implied value threat to India's aspirations at home and abroad became more and more central to Nehru's perception from the autumn of 1959 onward, in light of what he discerned as the PRC's increasingly hostile behavior.

Throughout the three-and-a-half year pre-crisis period Nehru was unaware of any time constraints on decisions relating to the disputed border. Nor did he conceive of war as imminent or likely to occur at all. As major Asian powers, cultures and states, India and China, in Nehru's image, could only do things on a grand scale. In the realm of conflict, this meant full-scale war. Although possible, adverse superpower reaction, among other reasons, made it remote. Little thought was given to a less dramatic Chinese act, such as a limited war, in the form of a punitive raid across parts of the disputed border.

How and how well did India cope with China's challenge in the onset phase? There is no evidence of a felt need for more, or a greater variety of, information about China's intentions or capability. The steady flow of letters between Nehru and Chou and notes between their foreign offices were the primary source, supplemented by (usually critical) articles on Nehru in China's press, notably "The Revolution in Tibet and Nehru's Philosophy" (*People's Daily*, 6 May 1959) and a disquieting note from China's Ambassador to India's Foreign Secretary ten days later, which threatened that China would align itself with Pakistan against India "on two fronts."

Abundant information was provided by India's Intelligence Bureau throughout, but rarely were inferences made by its Director, B. N. Mullik, from unintegrated bits of data. In short, an overall image of China as hostile, pursuing a strategy of incremental expansion to compel India to accept an exchange of territory, could not be dented by signals of impending war. As in many other twentieth-century crises, e.g., the USSR before the German attack in June 1941 ("Barbarossa"), the US before Pearl Harbor in December 1941, and Israel before the October-Yom Kippur War in 1973, India's decision-makers suffered from a conceptual failure in the months before the Chinese attack in October 1962.

Nehru dominated India's decisional forum throughout the onset phase of the India/China crisis. During 1959–60 he consulted the Cabinet Foreign Affairs Committee. But only two colleagues were of consequence—Home Minister Pandit Pant, who urged a more hawkish line until his death in 1961, and Defense Minister V. K. Krishna Menon, a long-time confidante, who pressed a more conciliatory line until the outbreak of war. Several officials in External Affairs were also consulted regularly.

Alternatives were sought and evaluated, but not as parts of a coherent grand design in response to the perceived threat. Rather, they were satisficing options, incrementally formulated as short-term, partial solutions to the developing crisis. The primary goal was an accommodation with China without having to cede territory. Among the options was an idea of leasing the Aksai Chin to China provided India's sovereignty was acknowledged. And for those seeking a political solution, notably Krishna Menon, an exchange of territory was not inconceivable, such as a trade of the Aksai Chin for a strategically valuable slice of territory in the northeast, the Chumbhi Valley. Thus, in coping with the pre-crisis challenge, India's leaders displayed some imagination; but all options were evaluated from the perspective that history and geography made India's case on the border impregnable.[37]

HUNGARIAN UPRISING (1956–57)

Like the Prague Spring of 1968, the Hungarian Uprising was one of many international crises within the Soviet bloc from 1946 to 1980–81.[38] Its roots can be traced to Stalin's death in March 1953 and the effects on the struggle for succession in Moscow, as well as on rivalry among Hungarian communist leaders. Within the USSR Khrushchev emerged triumphant. In February 1956 he sent a shockwave through the bloc with his "secret" de-Stalinization speech to the 20th Party Congress. One result was to question doctrine everywhere in the communist bloc. Another was to generate political crises throughout Eastern Europe, most dramatically in Poland and Hungary. The very foundations of Stalinism and the legitimacy of Soviet rule over its clients were called into question.

In Hungary, the Stalinist leader, Matyas Rakosi, had lost influence to Imre Nagy in July 1953; but he was restored to preeminence in August 1955. However, under the impact of Moscow's rewriting of history and challenges to his leadership by Hungarian intellectuals, Rakosi was ousted on 17 July 1956 and replaced by Ernö Geroe. This was a turning point, a prelude to the Hungarian Uprising as an international crisis. Several other events contributed to rising tension in the summer of 1956, notably a meeting of the intellectuals' *Petoefi* Circle on 27 June, calling for Nagy's return to power.

The onset phase began with a revisionist gesture, the reburial of Laszlo Rajk, the most famous victim of Stalin's purge in the late 'forties, on 5 October. Several hundred thousand attended the symbolic event. Nagy's party membership was restored on the 13th. And Hungary's armed forces were placed on a state of alert on the 20th.

Escalation began with a mass demonstration of Hungarian workers, students and soldiers in Budapest on 23 October. They demanded the withdrawal of Soviet troops, the return of Nagy to power, steps toward democratization in Hungary, and mutual equality as the basis of Hungary–USSR relations. The Hungarian Uprising was now set on an irreversible course. Nagy was catapulted to power and pressed for greater autonomy, including, ultimately, Hungary's withdrawal from the Warsaw Pact. The uprising was crushed by Soviet tanks between 1 and 15 November. Nagy was ousted, and a compliant Kadar was installed as party leader. The crisis lingered on (deescalated) for two months. By January 1957 the tension level prior to the uprising was restored: the last vestiges of independent Hungarian resistance were eliminated; and all evidence of direct Soviet military administration, established at the height of the crisis, had disappeared. In short, the international crisis attending the Hungarian Uprising had terminated.

Three persons dominated Hungary's decision-making in the 1956 crisis: in the pre-crisis period, Geroe, symbol of the remnant of Stalinism, who held power for 100 days as First Secretary of the Party, from 27 July to 25 October 1956; in the crisis period, Nagy, a post-Stalinist popular leader and a precursor of Euro-Communism, who was Prime Minister from 23 October to 4 November; and, in the end-crisis period, Kadar, who succeeded Geroe as First Secretary on 25 October, but was subordinate to Nagy until he was installed by the Soviets in power on 4 November. (He remained there until 1988.)

Three decisions were taken in Hungary's pre-crisis, all of them by Geroe and his principal colleagues, Kadar and Prime Minister Andras Hegedues:

D. 1, on 13 October, to reinstate Nagy into the Party without his having to recant his "errors," but not into a position of influence (a decision designed to appease growing opposition to the "old guard");

D. 2, on 20 October, to place Hungary's armed forces on a state of alert, in order to cope with a possible mass uprising against the regime; and,

D. 3, the same day, to delay action against student dissent until the return of Geroe, Kadar and Hegedues from a visit to Yugoslavia.

D. 2 and 3 were holding actions; all exhibited caution.

The attitudinal prism of those who held power in Budapest during the onset phase was in the classic Stalinist mold, derived from decades of loyal service to the cause of world revolution, in Hungary, Spain and elsewhere. During the summer and early autumn of 1956 Geroe perceived the West in retreat but ever-dangerous to the survival of the socialist camp. In his view, the Party was following a correct path, in the light of "de-Stalinization." And he gravely underestimated the extent and intensity of opposition to the Party's hegemony and its slavish loyalty to Moscow. That gap between perception and reality led to Geroe's ouster two days after the eruption of the crisis period amid a sharp escalation of threat, along with acute time pressure and the expectation of imminent military hostilities.

The catalyst to Hungary's crisis has already been noted, namely, the Rajk reburial. Other developments helped to generate more tension: open ferment among university students in Budapest, beginning on 16 October; and the activation of Soviet forces stationed in Hungary by a state of alert on the 19th. The result was higher-than-normal stress and the perception of a value threat. But for Geroe, unlike Nagy in the crisis period, the value at stake was the survival of the pro-Soviet Hungarian regime and the retention of power by the Hungarian Workers Party. The adversary was internal dissent, not the USSR or the Warsaw Pact states as a group. As evident by the absence of the three most important Hungarian leaders in Yugoslavia from 14 to 23 October and the cautious early decisions, there was no awareness of time pressure for response to the internal challenge. That element and the likelihood of military hostilities were to emerge on 23 October, the day the crisis period began.

How did the Party cope with the emerging crisis? Normally, in communist regimes, all information of political consequence is channelled to the top of the power pyramid. This pattern of information processing was certainly present in the pre-crisis period. Geroe, Kadar and Hegedues were kept fully informed of events at home by their caretaker, Acs. So too was Geroe during his annual vacation in the Soviet Union from 8 September to 3 October (Geroe was, astonishingly, away from Budapest during most of his brief tenure as party leader). Yet there was no sharp increase in the volume of information to Hungary's high-policy decision-makers during the onset phase.

The number of consultations increased slightly, but the consultative circle for all three decisions was limited to the Politburo of the Party. It was to increase drastically from 23 October onwards. Consultation notwithstanding, the felt need for leadership was evident throughout; all acquiesced in Geroe's decisions, as they were to do later when Nagy and then Kadar were in command.

The overriding issue in the pre-crisis period was how to respond to the rapidly growing opposition within Hungary. There were three options, all of which were considered: first, to crush the demands for reform by force and repression, the Stalinist path; secondly, to yield power to the reformers in the Party led by Nagy; and thirdly, to follow a middle path, making concessions but retaining power and communist orthodoxy. The Politburo rejected the first alternative as unfeasible. Geroe rejected the second, on personal and ideological grounds. He tried to implement the third, without success.[39]

RHODESIA UDI (1965–66)

Among the African states none experienced a more threatening foreign policy crisis than newly-independent Zambia in the Rhodesia UDI Crisis of 1965–66. During 1964 and 1965 there was mounting evidence that the minority white regime in Southern Rhodesia (later, Zimbabwe) was planning to issue a unilateral declaration of independence (UDI) from Britain. For Zambia, formerly Northern Rhodesia, the establishment of a hostile white-ruled state posed a grave danger: landlocked Zambia was totally dependent on its larger and wealthier neighbor for rail routes to ports, sources of coal and oil, and power from their jointly-owned hydroelectric stations at the Kariba Dam on the Rhodesia/Zambia border.

From its independence in October 1964 Zambia lived in a state of confrontation with its southern neighbor. However, the Rhodesia UDI Crisis injected a qualitative change in their hostile relationship, for the unilateral declaration of independence (UDI) by the white-ruled, economically and militarily stronger colonial regime in Rhodesia was perceived as a grave threat to Zambia's existence: Lusaka depended upon Salisbury for the three principal sources of its copper-based economy, oil, coal and electricity. The erratic behavior of the colonial power, the UK, further exacerbated that perception.

Since there was only one crisis actor—Rhodesia was the triggering entity and did not perceive a crisis for itself—the phases of the international crisis are synonymous with the periods of Zambia's foreign policy crisis. The onset phase began with an explicit threat by Rhodesia's Premier Smith on 26 April 1965 to expel thousands of workers from neighboring Zambia and Malawi, if the UK acted on Prime Minister Wilson's hint of economic sanctions should Rhodesia resort to UDI. Zambia's response throughout the three-and-a-half month, relatively low-threat, pre-crisis period took the form of contingency planning as it braced itself for the anticipated Rhodesian declaration.

With Salisbury's proclamation of a state of emergency on 5 November, the prelude to UDI on the 11th, the crisis escalated sharply: "Rhodesia's illegal declaration of independence translated a hypothetical situation into a concrete challenge and injected a sense of urgency and realism into the discussions on contingency planning" (Anglin, 1980: 587). Zambia responded with multiple measures, as noted in earlier chapters, including the dispatch of troops to the border, economic sanctions, and the search for foreign support, from the UK, the UN, African states, the US and Canada.

The UK-initiated "quick kill" strategy to compel Rhodesia to rescind UDI failed, largely because of London's refusal to commit the necessary resources. Zambia's economic survival was assured by an Anglo-American-Canadian airlift. At that point the crisis entered a deescalation (end-crisis) "long haul" stage, from 14 January to 27 April 1966. The crisis ended that day when Wilson, in a sharp reversal of policy, announced the initiation of talks with the breakaway Salisbury regime. The tension level returned to the pre-pre-crisis norm. However, the protracted conflict over Rhodesia was to last until 1980 when the white regime gave way to the new state of Zimbabwe after the last of the Rhodesia-related international crises, Rhodesian Settlement.

Zambia's pre-crisis period extended over seven months, from 26 April to 2 December 1965. Two events triggered the perception of higher-than-normal threat in Lusaka: the campaign for the 7 May elections in Rhodesia, designed to secure for Prime Minister Ian Smith a mandate from his white electorate to seize independence, illegally if necessary; and an ominous reply from Salisbury, on 26 April, to London's warning of the serious consequences of illegal action by Rhodesia, namely, Salisbury's threat to "repatriate" (expel) workers from Zambia and Malawi and a warning of the "crippling effects on their own economies" if the UK imposed economic sanctions.

The result was 14 Zambian pre-crisis contingency planning decisions, beginning with verbal defiance of the threatened economic strangulation, by President Kenneth D. Kaunda on 5 May. Other important decisions were:

> to approve an emergency Anglo-American-Canadian airlift of copper from Zambia in the event of Rhodesia's declaration of UDI (25 May);
>
> to renew, at a Commonwealth Conference, an offer of Zambian territory as a British base to cope with UDI (around 18 June);
>
> to appeal to each of Zambia's neighbors for assistance in solving its grave transport problem—first, the Portuguese, for access to their Angolan port of Lubito (around 7 September), then Zaire, via its rail system to the same port (around 16 October), and lastly, Malawi, for access through its rail outlet to the Portuguese Mozambique port of Beira (around 26 October); and
>
> to seek a British Government financial commitment to meet the costs of contingency projects outside Zambia (around 14 September).

In short, Zambia's pre-crisis decisions were designed to elicit international support in its self-perceived struggle for survival.

These decisions, like all others in the UDI Crisis, were taken by an *ad hoc* group of senior Zambian ministers that later became institutionalized as the Cabinet Foreign Affairs Committee: President Kaunda, Foreign Minister Simon M. Kapwepwe, and Finance Minister Arthur N. L. Wina, with Vice-President Kamanga and Home Affairs Minister Chona as frequent participants. All were leading figures in the United National Independence Party (UNIP).

Because of his preeminence, then and later, suffice it to note the psychological environment of Kaunda. His attitudinal prism was shaped by three elements: an intense Christian faith, in which issues and persons were perceived in absolute terms of good or evil; moral outrage against racism; and a commitment to non-violence, a belief strengthened by the message and practice of Gandhi in the struggle for Indian freedom.

As for Kaunda's image of Zambia's adversary, ". . . the Rhodesian rebellion represented an intolerable personal affront to his most cherished beliefs. The Salisbury regime was not merely illegal, colonialist, oppressive and exploitative. More fundamentally, it embodied a satanic racialist ideology. . . . Similarly, Ian Smith as the architect of

UDI was conceived as the anti-Christ" (Anglin, 1993, forthcoming: 42).[40]

Turning to the situational attributes, the catalyst to Zambia's UDI Crisis, as noted, was Rhodesia's 26 April 1965 warning of its intent to pass on to its vulnerable neighbors the economic costs of potential UK sanctions. The value perceived to be at risk was Zambia's very existence, for its independence was barely a year old, its civil service and army were heavily dependent upon British officials and officers, and all of its routes to the outside world ran through Rhodesia. Zambian leaders were not unaware of the time dimension for decisions, but no one could foretell the precise date of UDI. And, despite the gravity of the value threat, they did not perceive war as imminent or likely. In fact, Rhodesia's economic sanctions posed the greatest danger, with military hostilities on the distant horizon.

How did Zambia cope during its pre-crisis period of Rhodesia UDI? Normally dependent on external sources for information, its decision-makers enlarged their search following the initial Rhodesian threat of economic sanctions. This was evident prior to the copper airlift and lesser technical decisions. However, the extent of information search was minimal in the process leading to six decisions, including the military base offer, and moderate prior to four others. More generally, a sense of urgency about information was absent from Zambia's behavior throughout its pre-crisis period.

A similar pattern of consultation is evident: its scope was minimal before making seven decisions, moderate in the course of six others, and extensive in only one case, the decision leading to overtures to Portugal. In short, as long as stress was low, consultation was modest. Formally, a majority of decisions in the onset phase (10 of 14) were taken by Zambia's Cabinet of 12–16 members, with three others by an *ad hoc* group of senior ministers, and only one by the President on his own. Actual decision-making, however, tended to a smaller decisional forum: the Inner Cabinet made seven decisions, and the President alone four others, including all the crucial decisions noted earlier.

As for alternatives, the perceived range of options was limited at eight decision points, and modest at four others. Only with regard to two technical issues did the decision-makers perceive a broad set of options. These were evaluated moderately prior to seven decisions, including the important decisions except one, minimally before three decisions, including the military base offer, and thoroughly before making four decisions, including the copper airlift. On the whole, the low stress of

the pre-crisis period did not generate thoroughness in information processing or in the consideration of alternatives. As with other states'
crises, the pattern of Zambia's decision-making was to change drastically in the crisis period of escalation.[41]

FALKLANDS/MALVINAS (1982)

The last of the ten foreign policy crises to be analyzed in terms of
decisions, decision-makers and their perceptions, and coping, other
than the Gulf Crisis [Chap. 7 below], is Argentina's Malvinas/Falklands
Crisis.[42] While the dispute has deep historical roots—the UK has been
in control of the Falklands since 1833—it lay dormant for decades. For
London, "the issue had an extraordinarily low priority before December
1981. . . . The islands were there, administered by Britain and defended
by 40 Royal Marines. That was all there was to know about them"
(Gamba, 1987: 74). And "Lord Carrington, British Foreign Secretary to
April 1982, is alleged to have admitted that it rated number 242 on the
Foreign Office's list of priorities" (Beck, 1985: 643).

For Buenos Aires, by contrast, the emotional attachment to the
Malvinas as "terra irredenta," a persistent symbol of colonial rule in
Latin America, was an enduring part of the political culture. In times of
national stress the claim to the Malvinas was invoked and reintroduced
to the political agenda of Argentina's rulers. And the claim was pressed
frequently, accompanied by tension between two friendly states with
close economic ties since the late 19th century. So it was once more at
the end of 1981 and the beginning of 1982. As the 150th anniversary of
"foreign" control approached, an insecure military junta initiated an
international crisis, and fought and lost a humiliating war, leading to the
junta's overthrow and the restoration of Argentine democracy.

The crisis began on 9 March, when the Argentine junta decided to
accept in principle a plan to invade the islands.[43] It was transformed into
a threat to the UK with a minor and little-noticed incident on 18 March,
namely, the raising of the Argentine flag in the British dependency of
South Georgia by a group of Argentine "scrap merchants." On the 20th,
London dispatched a vessel from Port Stanley, the principal town in the
Falklands, to expel the intruders. This, in turn, led to Argentina's
second substantive pre-crisis decision, on 26 March—to move ahead to
the immediate future the pre-planned invasion of the Malvinas.

The onset phase included a UK request on 1 April for an emergency
session of the UN Security Council, following the dispatch of Argentine
navy ships to South Georgia on 27 March, and the Council's Resolution

502, on 3 April, calling for an end to hostilities, the withdrawal of all Argentine forces, and a recommendation for a diplomatic solution. Those forces had captured Port Stanley on the 2nd and South Georgia the next day, with minimal losses, triggering the escalation phase. The UK responded on 5 April with a highly-visible embarkation of a large Royal Navy task force to the South Atlantic. Until the end of April the crisis was dominated by an intense US mediation effort conducted by Secretary of State Haig, a replica of Kissinger's shuttle diplomacy in the Middle East in 1973–74, but without success. The war began on 1 May with a British air attack on Port Stanley, Darwin and Goose Green. It ended on 14 June, with severe defeat for 9000 Argentine troops and more than 700 killed, compared to 250 British dead.

As with the other Argentine decisions during the Falklands/Malvinas Crisis, the decision-making group during the pre-crisis period comprised the three-member military junta, General Leopoldo Galtieri, Admiral Jorge Anaya and Brigadier Basilio Lami Dozo, and Foreign Minister Nicanor Costa Mendez. However, the junta needed the consent of the powerful armed forces service councils.

Several elements shaped the decision-makers' psychological environment. One was a deeply-rooted emotional attachment to the Malvinas as "terra irredenta," a feeling widely shared by the nation as a whole. Another was the lure of historical analogy, particularly, the perceived "lessons" of minimal international criticism of India's "liberation" of Goa in 1961 and, even earlier, of US criticism of Britain's behavior in the 1956 Suez Nationalization Crisis: it was believed that these would be replicated in the event of an Argentine invasion of the South Atlantic islands. A third was a complex of military élite attitudes: the armed forces as the creator and central unifying institution of the modern, developed Argentine state; the military as the guardian of national honor, which required the restoration of the Malvinas; and the military's gnawing fear of punishment for its role in the "Dirty War" of the 1970s, when thousands of liberal and leftist civilians disappeared, were tortured or killed; thus the need to retain control of the government, which the recovery of the Malvinas would ensure.

Among the noteworthy specific images were: Galtieri's misreading of British resolve— "I judged it [UK resort to force to retake the islands] scarcely possible and totally improbable. In any case, I never expected such a disproportionate answer. Nobody did" (*The Times* [London], 12 June 1982); and of the likely US posture—"I feel much bitterness towards [President] Reagan, who I thought was my friend" (Hastings, 1983: 142). Anaya's optimism, too, was misplaced: he anticipated that

British resolve would crumble under the weight of losses inflicted by Argentina's navy or South Atlantic weather, or both. And Costa Mendez misread UN receptivity to the UK case for military action, as well as the Soviet Union's likely resort to a veto in the Security Council.[44]

A full-scale Argentine crisis began, as noted, with the departure of the UK task force from the Channel Ports. But the value threat perceived then was apparent from the opening skirmish in South Georgia: it was a threat to a longstanding Argentine commitment to recover sovereignty over the Malvinas. Associated values perceived to be at risk were the collective honor of the armed forces and of the individual services, Galtieri's insecure tenure as President, and more generally, the near-universal self-image of Argentina as a mature, developed independent society. Time, too, was salient in the pre-crisis period, as evident in the decision to push the invasion date forward. However, as Galtieri admitted soon after the defeat, no one perceived war as imminent or its probability heightened. In short, stress in the first month was still relatively low.

How did Argentina cope with the incipient threat? Unlike the crisis period, there was no felt need for more and more varied information. As always, information search and circulation were fragmented among the three branches of the armed forces; and the foreign service had its own separate sources. Consultation, though much more extensive during the war, was not confined to the four decision-makers: each also needed to persuade his active, high-ranking service councils; for example, Anaya needed the approval of eight vice-admirals and 15 rear-admirals. And Costa Mendez regularly consulted the Foreign Office Malvinas Team.

The nine-member Cabinet, of whom six were civilians, was ignored. And the military totally dominated the decisional forum. No alternative to invasion was considered, largely due to the intense commitment to "liberation," but also partly because of the illusions noted earlier—the likely response of the UK, the US, the USSR and the UN. They were abandoned, painfully, only under the impact of events.[45]

Onset/Pre-Crisis: Case Study Findings

The question, to what extent are the ten foreign policy crises "representative," was explored in Table 2.6, in a framework of core typologies for analysis. As a prelude to the main findings on coping in the pre-crisis period, a second cut will now be presented in order to discern the fit of these cases in terms of the propositions on onset/pre-crisis. This is not,

TABLE 2.7 *Propositions and Case Studies on Crisis Onset: Findings*

Propositions on Crisis Onset	Berlin Blockade 1948	Prague Spring 1968	Munich 1938	Stalingrad 1942	October–Yom Kippur 1973	Lebanon Civil War I 1975	India/China Border 1959–62	Hungarian Uprising 1956	Rhodesia UDI 1965	Falklands/Malvinas 1982
1. Outbreak of International Crisis (int)*										
polycentric structure		X			X	X			X	X
subsystem	X				X	X	X		X	X
protracted conflict setting				X	X		X			
no power discrepancy				X	X		X	.		
non-democratic regime pair		X		X				X	X	
territorial contiguity		X		X	X	X	X	X	X	X
2. Initiation of Foreign Policy Crisis (fp)†										
initiator (triggering entity):	USSR	Czecho-slovakia	Germany	Internal Germany[3]	Syria	Internal Lebanon[3]	China	Internal Hungary[3]	Rhodesia	UK
young or new state		X			X				X	
militarily stronger than adversary	X	X	X				X		X	X
non-democratic regime	X	X	X		X	X	X		X	
confronts domestic instability		X					X			
territorially contiguous to adversary		X	X		X		X		X	X
has large territory	X	X	X				X		X	

3. *Vulnerability to Foreign Policy Crisis (fp)*†

target (crisis actor):	US[1]	USSR[2]	UK	Germany	Israel	Syria	India	Hungary	Zambia	Argentina
young or new state					X	X	X	X	X	
in protracted conflict with adversary	X			X	X					
little/no power discrepancy with adversary	X		X	X	X					
different political regime	X		X	X	X	X	X			X
faces domestic instability								X		
territorially contiguous to adversary		X		X	X	X	X	X	X	X
recent regime						X	X		X	
small territory			X		X	X		X	X	X

*int = international crisis (system/interactor level)
†fp = foreign policy crisis (actor level)

1. The target of Soviet behavior in the Berlin Blockade Crisis was the 'Western Powers', i.e., France, the UK and the US. Since the US is the focus of coping in this international crisis throughout the book, Prop. 3 is 'tested' here for the US alone.

2. In the onset phase of the Prague Spring Crisis, the GDR (East Germany) and Poland were the first states in the Soviet bloc to perceive the Czechoslovak reform movement as a threat to their regime. However, the actor that is analyzed for coping in this crisis is the USSR.

3. In the Stalingrad and Hungarian Uprising cases the initiator or triggering entity was the state that became the crisis actor; that is, the trigger was an internal act. In the Lebanon Civil War I case, the initiator was a non-state actor. Thus, for these three crises, Prop. 2 is not relevant.

it must be emphasized, hypothesis-testing in the accepted meaning; but it is instructive nonetheless. What the ten case studies reveal about onset/pre-crisis expectations is set out in Table 2.7.

As evident, half of the relevant elements of Propositions 1–3—90 of 182—apply to these cases. Five occurred in a polycentric structure of global politics; and five focused on the subsystem level. Only three erupted in a protracted conflict setting; and only three were characterized by no power discrepancy, that is, power equality. Four exhibited a non-democratic regime pair. The best fit within Proposition 1, on the *outbreak* of an *international crisis*, is territorial contiguity between the adversaries: it was present in eight of the ten cases.

This pattern is replicated in Proposition 2, on the *initiation* of a *foreign policy crisis*. In only three relevant cases was the triggering entity a new or young state. In four, the initiator perceived military superiority. However, a non-democratic regime and contiguity to one's adversary are evident in six of the seven relevant cases, while four initiators were states with a large territory.

As for *vulnerability* to a *foreign policy crisis* (Proposition 3), the best fit, once more, is territorial contiguity—in eight of the ten cases. Seven target states had a political regime different from the initiator. Six had a small territory. And five were young or new states. Only one crisis actor, Hungary, confronted domestic instability.

Viewed in terms of the ten cases as a group, three fit more than half of the 20 elements of the three propositions on onset/pre-crisis: October-Yom Kippur 14; Rhodesia UDI 13; and India/China Border 12. Two other cases, Stalingrad and Lebanon Civil War I, fit 8 of 14 relevant elements.

The major findings on the case studies focus on actor and situational attributes, and coping during the pre-crisis period of a foreign policy crisis. These are presented in Tables 2.8.A, 2.8.B.1 and 2, and 2.8.C.

As evident in Table 2.8.A, diversity pervades the *actor attributes* in the pre-crisis period of the ten cases. The number of strategic or significant *decisions* ranges from one in three cases—Germany at Stalingrad, Syria in Lebanon's Civil War, and Hungary in the 1956 Uprising—to five for Zambia in Rhodesia UDI, with four each for the USSR and India, three for the UK at Munich, and two each for the US, Israel and Argentina. Diversity is much more striking in the total number of known decisions: the range is from two in Israel's October-Yom Kippur Crisis and Argentina's Falklands/Malvinas Crisis to 87 by Germany during the Battle of Stalingrad. Zambia made 14 decisions, the USSR 10, India seven, the US six, the UK and Syria three each.

TABLE 2.8.A *Onset/Pre-Crisis: Summary of Case Study Findings: Actor Attributes*

International Crisis	Crisis Actor	No. of Decisions°	No. of Decision-Makers°°	Attitudinal Prism
Berlin Blockade	US	2 (6)	3 (8)	Realism, 'Two-Camp' thesis, Moral rectitude, Resolve
Prague Spring	USSR	4 (10)	6 (20)	Stalinism, USSR hegemony in Eastern Europe
Munich	UK	3 (3)	4 (16)	War immoral, Czechoslovakia Remote
Stalingrad	Germany	1 (87)	1 (5)	Nazism, German racial, cultural, military superiority
October – Yom Kippur	Israel	2 (2)	4 (18)	The 'Conception' – no Arab war option
Lebanon Civil War I	Syria	1 (3)	1 (4)	'Historic Indivisibility' of Syria, Lebanon
India/China Border	India	4 (7)	1 (3)	Liberalism-Humanism-Socialism, India/China friendship
Hungarian Uprising	Hungary	1 (3)	1 (16)	Stalinism
Rhodesia UDI	Zambia	5 (14)	1 (16)	Christianity, anti-Racism, Non-Violence
Falklands/Malvinas	Argentina	2 (2)	4 (many)	Irredentism

°The number on the left refers to strategic or tactically significant decisions;
the number in brackets indicates the total number of known strategic, tactical and implementing decisions.

°°The number on the left refers to the principal decision-makers;
the number in brackets indicates the size of the largest decisional forum.

The number of key *decision-makers* in the pre-crisis period was generally very small, despite profound differences in their political systems. There was a preeminent figure in five cases—Germany (Hitler), Syria (Asad), India (Nehru), Hungary (Geroe), and Zambia (Kaunda). There were four persons in the UK (the Inner Cabinet), Israel (the "Kitchen Cabinet"), and Argentina (the military junta and Foreign Minister). The largest group was the six-man Negotiating Committee of the Soviet Politburo in the Prague Spring Crisis. However, in many of these cases there were large institutional groups in which some decisions were made—the Soviet Communist Party Politburo of 20 (including candidate members), the Israel Cabinet of 18, and three states with 16 decision-makers, namely, the UK Cabinet, Zambia's Cabinet, and the Hungarian Workers Party's Politburo. In Argentina, too, decisions required the consent of the large armed services councils.

No indicator exhibits more diversity than the core element of the decision-makers' *attitudinal prism*: Realism (the US); Stalinism (the USSR, Hungary); pacifism (the UK); Nazism (Germany); a "Conception" (Israel); "historic indivisibility" (Syria); Christianity, anti-racism (Zambia); socialism, historical friendship (India), and irredentism (Argentina).

As for the *situational attributes* (Table 2.8.B.1 and 2), there were many types of *trigger* among the ten crises:

> *verbal* act (e.g., the German Government's designation of the Rhineland and other border zones as "protected areas," and an announcement of intended partial mobilization of forces in September, the news of which, on 3 August 1938, triggered a crisis for the UK);
> *political* act (e.g., a Soviet walkout from the Allied Control Council in Berlin on 20 March 1948, for the US);
> *internal* act (the launching of a major offensive on the Eastern Front by the *Wehrmacht* on 28 June 1942, for Germany);
> *non-violent military* act (the dispatch of a British naval vessel from Port Stanley, capital of the Falkland Islands, on 20 March 1982 to expel Argentine "scrap merchants" who had raised the Argentine flag on South Georgia, for Argentina);
> *indirect violent* act (the suppression of the Tibet Revolt in March 1959 by China, for India); and
> *direct violent* act (an air battle between Syrian MIGs and Israeli Mirages on 13 September 1973, for Israel).

Parenthetically, these acts not only catalyzed a foreign policy crisis for

TABLE 2.8.B.1 *Onset/Pre-Crisis: Summary of Case Study Findings: Situational Attributes – Actor Level*

International Crisis	Crisis Actor	Trigger	Values	Time Pressure	War Likelihood	Duration (Days)
Berlin Blockade	US	Political	Resolve, Western presence in Berlin	None	Low	96
Prague Spring	USSR	Political	Bloc unity, Soviet Union security	None	Very low	143
Munich	UK	Verbal	Avoidance of war, Influence abroad	Salient at outset	Very low	35
Stalingrad	Germany	Internal	Image of military superiority	None	No adverse change in military balance	145
October – Yom Kippur	Israel	Violence	Border security, Avoidance of high casualties	None	Very Low	23
Lebanon Civil War I	Syria	Indirect Violence	'Greater Syria,' Arab unity	Salient at outset	Not imminent	241
India/China Border	India	Indirect Violence	Territory, Economic development, Influence abroad	None	Low	1272
Hungarian Uprising	Hungary	Political	Survival of Communist regime	None	Low	18
Rhodesia UDI	Zambia	Verbal	Existence	Vague awareness	Low	211
Falklands/Malvinas	Argentina	Non-Violent Military	Recovery of lost territory, Honor	Salient at outset	Low	27

TABLE 2.8.B.2 *Onset/Pre-Crisis: Summary of Case Study Findings: Situational Attributes – System Level*

International Crisis	System	No. of Actors	Violence
Berlin Blockade	Dominant	4	None
Prague Spring	Subsystem – Central/Eastern Europe	6	None
Munich	Dominant	4	None
Stalingrad	Dominant	2	War
October – Yom Kippur	Subsystem – Middle East	5	Minor
Lebanon Civil War I	Subsystem – Middle East	1	None
India/China Border	Subsystem – South Asia/East Asia	2	Minor
Hungarian Uprising	Subsystem – Central/Eastern Europe	2	None
Rhodesia UDI	Subsystem – Southern Africa	1	None
Falklands/Malvinas	Subsystem – South America	2	Minor

a specific state. They also caused disruptive interaction between the target, the US, the USSR, the UK, etc., and its adversary, the USSR, Czechoslovakia, Germany, etc. As such, these triggers were also visible indicators of the onset of an international crisis or, in cases where the target state was not the first crisis actor, its intensification (e.g. Berlin Blockade).

The pattern of diversity is also evident in the wide range of *values* perceived to be threatened in the ten cases: resolve, symbolic presence, military superiority, unity, security, human life, territory, regime survival, economic development, honor, influence and existence. By contrast, *time* was not salient in the majority of cases during the onset phase; and it was not a source of pressure for decision-makers. Moreover, in nine of the ten cases *war* was perceived as unlikely; the exception was Stalingrad, an intra-war crisis. But the absence of perceived time constraints and heightened war likelihood are "normal" traits of the pre-crisis period.

The *duration* of the pre-crisis period ranged from less than a month for several actors (Argentina, Hungary, Israel) to three-and-a-half years (India), with two cases of more than half a year (Syria, Zambia), two of five months (Germany, USSR), one of three months (US), and one case of barely a month (UK).

Diversity is no less evident in the system/interactor situational attributes. First is the *system level* at which these international crises occurred. Three erupted in the dominant system (Berlin Blockade, Munich and Stalingrad). The other seven took place in various sub-systems: Central/Eastern Europe (Prague Spring, Hungarian Uprising); Middle East (October-Yom Kippur, Lebanon Civil War); South/East Asia (India/China Border); Southern Africa (Rhodesia UDI); and South America (Falklands/Malvinas).

The *number of actors* in the international crises of which these foreign policy crises were a part also varied. There were two single-actor cases—Lebanon Civil War (Syria) and Rhodesia UDI (Zambia), whose adversaries did not perceive a foreign policy crisis for themselves. In four cases the adversarial pairs were crisis actors—Stalingrad (Germany, USSR), India/China Border (India, PRC), Hungarian Uprising (Hungary, USSR), and Falklands/Malvinas (Argentina, UK). There were four actors in the Munich and Berlin Blockade crises (three great powers and Czechoslovakia in the former, only major powers—the US, the USSR, the UK, France—in the latter). There were five actors in the October-Yom Kippur crisis-war (Egypt, Israel, Syria and the two superpowers). And in the Prague Spring there were six crisis actors (USSR, four of its Warsaw Pact allies, and Czechoslovakia).

As for systemic *violence*, war was absent in the pre-crisis period of all cases except Stalingrad, which was an intra-war crisis. Finally, as indicated in the introduction to these case studies, the crises were visibly diverse in terms of ten crucial typologies: they varied in structure, polarity, conflict setting, region, power level, political regime, economic development, peace/war setting, intensity of violence, and decade of occurrence.

In sharp contrast to the diversity in actor and situational attributes, *coping* in the pre-crisis period exhibits marked *homogeneity* (Table 2.8.C).

Information-processing reveals no change in the channels and volume of communication in six of the ten cases; and, where some change occurred, it was confined to a modest increase in the flow of information: an acute felt need for more and more varied information, and resort to unorthodox, novel channels of communication were conspicuously absent in the pre-crisis period.

Consultation tended to be confined to core decision-makers and their technical advisors, civilian and/or military. The only exceptions were the USSR at the outset of the Prague Spring, when other Warsaw Pact leaders enforced consultation on Moscow, and the creation of the "Malvinas Team" in the Argentine Foreign Ministry.

As for *decisional forums*, there were three deviations from the non-crisis norm: the UK *de facto* Inner Cabinet, Israel's "Kitchen Cabinet," and Syria's "decision-making Committee." Yet in the first two of these cases decisions were taken by elected senior ministers, duly authorized by the legislature to play the central role in decision-making in important matters of state. And in the third case Syria's President was the preeminent figure.

Alternatives were considered in several cases, notably by the USSR in the Prague Spring, and by India in the prolonged pre-crisis period of the border crisis with China. However, for the most part, the search for options was minimal. And in many cases the non-crisis pattern obtained, or SOPs were employed.

The conclusion is inescapable: the evidence from the ten case studies reveals a *widely-shared pattern of coping during the pre-crisis period*, despite notable diversity in actor and situational attributes, that is, the crisis configuration.

This central finding may seem counter-intuitive, for it has long been regarded as axiomatic—or an article of faith—that cultural, racial,

TABLE 2.8.C *Onset/Pre-Crisis: Summary of Case Study Findings: Coping Mechanisms*

International Crisis	Crisis Actor	Information	Consultation	Decisional Forum	Alternatives
Berlin Blockade	US	Normal channels and volume	Core decision-makers and advisors	Non-crisis pattern	Non-crisis pattern
Prague Spring	USSR	Modest increase in volume, variety	Central Committee, East German and Polish leaders	Praesidium and its Negotiating Team	Several options considered
Munich	UK	Modest increase in volume	Core decision-makers and advisors	Cabinet 'Big Four'	One option – compliance
Stalingrad	Germany	Normal channels and volume	Core decision-makers and advisors	The *Führer*	One option – Leningrad
October – Yom Kippur	Israel	Normal channels and volume	Core decision-makers and military	"Kitchen Cabinet"	SOPs applied
Lebanon Civil War I	Syria	Normal channels and volume	Core decision-makers	'Decision-making Committee'	SOPs applied
India/China Border	India	Normal channels and volume	PM, few ministers, officials	PM and few ministers	Some options considered
Hungarian Uprising	Hungary	Normal channels, modest increase in volume	Politburo	Politburo	Three options
Rhodesia UDI	Zambia	Modest increase	Core decision-makers and advisors	Mostly Cabinet	Modest evaluation of options
Falklands/Malvinas	Argentina	Normal channels	Armed Services' Councils, Foreign Office 'Malvinas Team'	Military junta and Foreign Minister	No alternative to invasion

historical, political, ideological, and socio-economic differences must result in different behavior. No doubt, this is correct in certain spheres of human action. Yet it is also correct that in other areas those differences do not affect behavior. Perhaps the best example in world politics is the universal quest for power postulated by the Realist School from Thucydides to Morgenthau. And, despite the cogent and, in some respects, persuasive criticism of Realism from many competing interpretations of what moves political entities to act the way they do, it remains beyond question that, throughout history, from the city-states of Greece and their counterparts in the Chinese, Indian and Middle East systems of antiquity, to the principalities of Renaissance Italy and early modern Europe, the polyglot empires of the 17th-20th centuries, and the new nation-states of 19th- and 20th-century world politics, political units sought power, among other aims, notwithstanding their cultural, racial, historical and other differences.

This is not to defend Realism as flawless. Rather, it is to draw attention to the existence of a *universal strand* in interstate politics—and to explain this "counterintuitive" finding as one expression of that strand. Even those who reject Realism's focus on conflict as too narrow a perspective on the complexity of world politics and advocate a corrective emphasis on cooperation operate on the assumption that cooperation has universal application to the diverse units of late-twentieth-century world politics, regardless of diversity in culture, history, political regime, economic system, etc.; and rightly so.

In the context of this inquiry, the discovery of a widely-shared pattern of coping with stress in the pre-crisis period (and, as will become evident, in later periods as well [Chaps. 3 and 4 below]) falls into the same category. Stress is a universal phenomenon, experienced by decision-makers, as indeed by humans in all civilizations, under certain conditions. So, too, the challenge of coping with stress is a universal challenge. Decision-makers of all states need to make choices in situations of complexity and incomplete information. They all attempt to maximize gains and minimize losses, though different cultures may define gains and losses differently. They all seek to enhance the "national interest," though its content may vary.

Theoretically, of course, their coping strategy and behavior could vary greatly. And those who assume or expect such diversity will term the finding of common coping with pre-crisis "counter-intuitive." Others, including the author, who perceive the universal strand in world politics as no less significant, in fact more significant, than the diversity among the members of the global system, are not surprised by the finding of a pattern of common coping on the part of decision-makers of states in crises.

The explanation can be summed up in the concept of *commonality*. Stress is a shared challenge, an indicator of impending danger. States have common traits that outweigh their diversity, especially the need to survive and to minimize harm from external foes. And foreign policy decision-makers, in coping with crisis-generated stress, act as humans do in all comparable situations of impending harm. In essence, the commonality of statehood, stress and human response to expected harm, or gain, overrides all variations among specific states and generates a near-identical pattern of coping in an external crisis. This central finding from the ten case studies, whether regarded as "intuitive" or "counter-intuitive," challenges conventional wisdom and *compels fundamental rethinking about how states cope with interstate crises*, that is, about *crisis management* in world politics.

CHAPTER 3

Escalation

ESCALATION has several meanings in the context of crisis, conflict and war. For some it is a *pre-war* process that leads to war. For others it is an *intra-war* process that enlarges the scope, increases the intensity, or crosses a limit of an on-going war. And for a few the concept has even broader application, extending across the spectrum from *non-violent crisis*, through *conventional war*, to total *nuclear war*.

Stated in terms of this study of twentieth century crises, escalation refers to three distinct processes:

(a) change from *embryonic* to *full-scale* crisis; in terms of *stress*, from low to peak stress;
(b) change from *non-violent* to *violent* crisis; and
(c) change from *no/low* violence to *severe violence*.

These processes unfold at both levels of analysis, as the *escalation phase* of an international crisis, and the *crisis period* of a foreign policy crisis. Each connotes qualitative change in an interstate crisis. Each taps a distinct dimension of escalation; that is, the three processes are parts of a holistic view of escalation. Later [Chap. 6], they will be integrated into a Unified Model of Crisis. As a preparatory step towards that end, this chapter begins with a critique of the literature on the meanings of escalation noted above. The inquiry into escalation that follows thus builds upon—and attempts to contribute to—the cumulation of knowledge about a crucial phenomenon.

Escalation, War, Security Dilemma, Conflict Spiral

The idea of escalation *before* a war is central to the literature on *arms races*. Noteworthy is Richardson's pioneering arms race model (1960a, b). In essence, it argues that any change in an existing military balance enhances the security of one adversary and the *threat* perceived by the other. More important, both are prisoners of assumptions that tend to become self-fulfilling and thereby induce an escalation spiral in the search for superior power; that is, they engage in an arms race. The process is rooted in mutual assumptions and misperceptions. State A may not contemplate a preemptive attack on B, or vice-versa; but each may—in an anarchical state system, is likely to—assume that the other will so contemplate and so act, if it has a sufficient margin of military capability. Thus A will assume that B will attempt to alter the arms balance in its favor. A's assumption will, in turn, predispose it to increase its arms potential. And such behavior will lead B to perceive threat and to respond in kind. In short, the assumptions of A and B become self-fulfilling, driving both to an escalatory arms race. For Richardson, in sum, escalation is built into the *dynamics of the arms race*.[1]

Escalation as a pre-war process was also the focus of the "Stanford Studies" noted earlier. This is evident in O. R. Holsti's (1972) *Crisis, Escalation, War*, which presented the project's major findings on the 1914 crisis leading to World War I and the Cuban Missile Crisis. Although the term was not defined *per se*, escalation, for the Stanford "School," is synonymous with higher crisis-induced stress, a concept that was measured by perceptions of international hostility. Holsti, North and Brody (1968) and Sabrosky (1975), focusing on the crises preceding World War I, found that perceived hostility was the key predictor to interstate violence. More generally, argued the Stanford "School," it affects the decision-making process during a crisis, notably the role of time pressure, patterns of communications, and the search for and consideration of alternatives.

For Rapoport (1960, 1987), escalation is built into the *dynamics of system instability*: the arms system, like any other, becomes unstable when the rates of change in the military balance, not its level, are not constant. In the nuclear era, with the exponential increase in destructive power, escalation is an integral part of the dynamics of non-war superpower confrontation.

The idea of escalatory steps to war, a pre-war process, is also embedded in Lebow's (1987) concept of "miscalculated escalation," one of three sequences from crisis to nuclear war (the others are "preemption" and "loss of control").

> It refers to steps taken up the political-military escalation ladder in a crisis, steps taken to moderate adversarial behavior which instead provoke further escalation. Miscalculated escalation may be the most important sequence to war, because it can be responsible in the first place for a crisis and subsequently for high levels of escalation which threaten war by preemption or loss of control (104).

Leng (1983) and Huth and Russett (1988) found that escalation from crisis to war was driven much more by developments in the international environment and the behavior of one's adversary than by domestic stimuli. And James (1987, 1988) discovered that states were more likely to escalate a military dispute, that is, initiate war when the dispute coincided with an increase in international turmoil and an opportunity to use force successfully.

By contrast, a study of *war initiation* (Romano, 1991) indicated that the decision to initiate war was driven more by perceptions of vulnerability than of opportunity in 11 of 16 cases, ranging from the Suez War, 1956, to the Falklands/Malvinas War, 1982. In only three cases was the decision for war initiation found to be driven more by perceptions of opportunity: Kashmir II, 1965; Somalia/Ethiopia, 1977–78; and Chad/Libya, 1983. In two cases (Iran/Iraq, 1980; Falklands/Malvinas, 1982) it was difficult to determine the relative importance of perceptions of vulnerability and of opportunity. While both perceptions were present in many cases, the effect of the latter tended to focus on the timing of resort to war.[2]

The idea of escalation *during* a war is evident in pre-twentieth century works on military strategy, nowhere more so than in Clausewitz's magisterial *On War* (1976 [1832]; Paret, 1985). For him, the essence of war is to compel one's enemy to do one's will. Thus the aim of the adversaries is total victory; moderation in war is an absurdity. To that end both must act so as to maximize their military power by mobilizing and using all possible resources. And, since victory is the shared yet conflicting goal, the logic of war makes (reciprocal) escalation inevitable: each will raise the stakes and intensity of the contest until one side triumphs. For Clausewitz, in short, escalation is built into the *dynamics of war*.[3]

Among strategic theorists of the contemporary era, escalation is clearly implied in Schelling's seminal work on *The Strategy of Conflict* (1960). But this book focuses primarily on *limited war*, that is, any war less than total war, and on bargaining, via tacit communication, between adversaries in a conflict/war situation. Victory is best achieved through deterrence, or "the skilful *non-use* of military capacity to pursue a nation's objective" (6). However, in the contest over resolve each party will raise the stakes, that is, escalate, to compel the other to yield. For Schelling, then, escalation is built into the *dynamics of bargaining in limited war*.

What is the analytic link between escalation and war? In Smoke's (1977: 17) cogent words:

Escalation is the process by which the previous limits of a war are crossed and new ones established. . . . Conversely, the (expanding) limits of a war are the barriers or thresholds or stages of the escalation process. [That is], limited war and escalation are coextensive. . . . But *limited war* is the static term; *escalation* is the dynamic term.

Smoke also introduced the notion of two images of escalation, the *actor image* and the *phenomenal image*. The former is an *act* by individuals or institutions of a state, the latter "a natural *phenomenon* of war," partly beyond the control of the actors. "To say, 'we shall escalate the war' tends to imply the actor image; to say, 'the war will escalate' tends to imply the phenomenal image." The former focuses on a specific decision at a particular moment, the latter on a process over time. Both images and both levels—micro (state) and macro (system)—complement each other, a view consonant with the central thrust of the integrated approach to crisis in this book.

Escalation, for Smoke, has a built-in upward dynamic, derived from many sources: the wish to take a step toward winning a war, or to act so as to avoid defeat; the willingness to pay a higher price in order to benefit from the "escalation of stakes"; the psychology of decision-makers, namely, the desire to enhance their place in history by winning; and the military requirement of war. Finally, escalation means "crossing the limits of any less-than-all-out war, *limits* being defined in Schelling's way," that is, objective, noticeable (by all parties), discrete saliencies. Thus escalation is *"a step of any size that crosses a saliency"* (21–26, 32).[4]

Adopting a broader view of escalation, Wright (1965) identified it as a process that could occur in any one of four stages of a conflict, from tension through full-scale war. For him, escalation depends upon the growth rate of hostility for each adversary. And that, in turn, derives from the adversaries' perception of six elements: their national interests; the forces immediately available to them; the costs of preparations and hostilities; world pressures for peace; potential military forces; and their vulnerability to destruction.

The first two factors are central in the initial decision to escalate (or terminate) a crisis; the other four become more important in later stages. Using these variables, Wright calculated the probability of escalation for each of 45 selected conflicts since World War I: 9 without violence; 20 that did not escalate, i.e., ended in a cease-fire, with less than 1000 casualties, in less than a year; 14 longer wars, with higher casualties; and two world wars.

An all-encompassing view of escalation was presented by Herman

Kahn, another leading strategist of the post-World War II era. *On Escalation* (1965), which followed his even more controversial *On Thermonuclear War* (1960), was—and remains—innovative in two respects. First, in contrast to the view of escalation as a purely intra-war phenomenon, that is, "the development of small wars into larger ones" (Pruitt and Snyder, 1969: 57), Kahn discerned the roots of escalation and its early stages in a pre-war environment of crisis. Second, he created an elaborate and complex *escalation ladder* of 44 rungs, from non-war to nuclear war.

The first seven comprise non-violent steps, from "political, economic, and diplomatic gestures" and "declarations" in the lowest phase, "sub-crisis maneuvers," through a "show of force," "significant mobilization," etc., in the second phase, "traditional crises," with some steps, such as the "provocative breaking off of diplomatic relations," in stage three, to "intense crises." There are also conventional war steps in the second and third phases, such as "harassing acts of violence" and "large compound escalation." "Barely nuclear war" is step 15; that is, there are no less than 29 additional nuclear war rungs, through four more phases, until the cataclysmic "spasm or insensate war." For Kahn, then, escalation is built into the *dynamics of interstate conflict*.

A severe criticism of Kahn's "escalation ladder" was levelled by Beer (1981: 354, n. 43):

> First, it assumes linearity. Actually escalation may be discontinuous, going back and forth, skipping steps. Second, it assumes uniformity. Higher steps may be steeper . . . and also narrower. . . . Third, it suggests finitude . . . , a fixed number of steps. Actually the number of discrete actions that can be taken can be expanded or contracted by the actors. Finally, it suggests a high degree of rationality. . . . There may be much less rationality at higher levels as the so-called "logic" of the situation becomes overpowering.

"Escalation," wrote Rapoport more sympathetically (1987: 174), "suggests a calibration of conflict intensity, and this is just what *On Escalation* is about." Further, Kahn was making two points: nuclear war is not "the end of everything"; and the advent of nuclear weapons provides opportunities for choice, rather than constituting a paralyzing threat from which there is no escape.

"Few studies of escalation exist," observed a major book in 1977 on this aspect of interstate conflict. "It is mentioned often. But . . . it remains an ancillary aspect of an analysis focused upon deterrence, crisis management, decision-making processes, or something else" (Smoke, 1977: 6). This remains true in 1993. Yet, with the renaissance of strategic thought in the 1960s and beyond, the theme of escalation acquired widespread usage among scholars, policy-makers and the media. The literature on escalation (or what M. Deutsch termed "destructive conflict" [1973, esp. 351–359]) is small. That on escalation and war is large insofar as it spills over to the "causes" of war; but these need not be examined at length here. Suffice it to focus attention on explanations of escalation *to* war, a pattern that includes three traits: rising tension, growing military preparedness, and increasingly hostile actions. These are often accompanied by an arms race, less productive negotiations, more verbal abuse, and more extreme tactics, often leading to war.

Escalation to war is attributed by many to *behavior by a single state* which initiates war to achieve one of several goals: economic gain; political aims, such as the acquisition or restoration of territory (irredentism), the liberation of oppressed groups, or the creation of friendly governments in other states; ideological ends, such as the spread of communism or democracy and market economies; the enhancement of national security or military power in anticipation of future wars; influence; prestige; etc.

Why war: what factors induce states to attempt to achieve these objectives through war? It may be *type of regime*: non-democratic regimes have been found by some to be more likely to externalize their internal sources of disaffection by focusing attention on a foreign "enemy" (Wilkenfeld, 1968, 1969; Rummel, 1983, 1987); but others find no such relationship (e.g., Ross, 1985; Vincent, 1987). More generally, although externalization theory seems logically sound, there is little evidence to support a postulated relationship between internal conflict, real or imagined, and external conflict behavior.[5] Yet there is stronger evidence—and a near-consensus—that democratic regimes do not engage in war *with each other* (Small and Singer, 1976; Chan, 1984; Doyle, 1986; Maoz and Abdolali, 1989; Russett, 1990: Chap. 5; others cited in Chap. 2, p. 61, above, and the evidence presented later in this chapter).

It may be *uncertainty about* security of *tenure* that leads a regime to initiate war, clearly an internal stimulus, or *ideological differences* with the adversary (Rosecrance, 1963). There may be *opportunities for influence and conquest*, created by a power vacuum (Bobrow et al., 1979). Some argue that war results from an exponential *growth in military and economic capability* by a state unaccompanied by higher status in the system, that is, "power inconsistency" (Organski, 1958; Wallace, 1972; Organski and Kugler, 1980; Kugler and Organski, 1989).

This view was also espoused by Howard (1984: 10, 16). For the causes of World War I he quoted, approvingly, Thucydides' (1954) classic explanation of the Peloponnesian War: "What made war inevitable was the growth of Athenian power and the fear this caused in Sparta. . . . You can vary the name of the actors, but the model remains a valid one." Further, Britain feared German hegemony in Europe, and Germany was determined "to achieve a world status comparable with her latent power." Howard agreed with Brodie (1973) that no single-factor explanation of conflict was valid. He also shared Aron's (1966: 7) view: "The stakes of war are the existence, the creation or the elimination of States." And he concluded (18): "The causes of war remain rooted . . . in perceptions by statesmen of the growth of hostile power and the fears for the restriction, if not the extinction, of their own."[6]

The second explanation of escalation to war emphasizes *interactive behavior* that generates a spiral of mutually-reinforcing hostility culminating in war. The process is closely linked to the *security dilemma*, a term coined by Herz who described the dilemma thus (1950: 157, and 1951):

> Wherever . . . anarchic society has existed . . . there has arisen what may be called the "security dilemma" of men, or groups, or their leaders . . . [who] must be, and usually are, concerned about their security from being attacked, subjected, dominated, or annihilated. . . . Striving to attain security from such attack, they are driven to acquire more and more power. . . . This, in turn, renders the others more insecure and compels them to prepare for the worst. Since none can ever feel entirely secure in such a world of competing units, power competition ensues, and the vicious circle of security and power accumulation is on.

Jervis (1976: 67, Chap. 3; 1978) spelled out the link to war:

> . . . the security dilemma can not only create conflicts and tensions but also provide the dynamics triggering war. If technology and strategy are such that each side believes that the state that strikes first will have a decisive advantage, even a state that is fully satisfied with the status quo may start a war out of fear that the alternative to doing so is not peace, but an attack by its adversary. And [in such a situation] . . . even mild crises are likely to end in war.

For others, the quintessential example of the *conflict spiral* is a mutual buildup of arms, as expressed in Richardson's arms race model, summarized above. An arms race may lead to preemption or preventive war. It may enhance the social status of the military which, to preserve its status, initiates war, making its role indispensable (Schumpeter, 1955 [1919]). And, viewed more broadly, *preparation for war* by A may generate goals that B finds threatening, creating the conditions for escalation to war.

Another version of the conflict spiral was set out in North *et al.* (1964: 1):

> If State A . . . perceives itself threatened by State B, there is a high probability that A will respond with threats or hostile action. As State B begins to perceive this hostility directed towards itself, it is probable that B, too, will behave in a hostile (and defensive) fashion. . . . Thereafter, the exchanges between the two parties will become increasingly negative, threatening and injurious. . . . [The result is] rising tensions and conflict escalation [leading] to war.

And for some (Lenin, 1939 [1917]; Choucri and North, 1975), inter-state war may be caused by a conflict over scarce resources.

In the course of an extensive exposition of formal models of crisis bargaining, Snyder and Diesing (1977: 158–159) observed:

> The possibility of escalation is always implicitly present in a crisis. Bargainers are aware of the possibility as a vague risk, but they do not construct a complete escalation ladder in their strategic thinking, planning only a step or two ahead. . . . [T]he typical escalation ladder after 1945 has about four areas: negotiations, or accommodative bargaining (CC), coercive bargaining (DD) including non-violent probes, threats, marshaling of alliance support, troop movements, small faits accompli, etc.; limited violence over a short time period (EE); full war.

There may also be a propensity to war because of: *structural factors*, unanticipated effects of coercive diplomacy (George *et al.*, 1971), and unstable military balances resulting from arms races (Brown, 1987: Part II). Among these factors the most notable centers on the debate over the likely effect of *power distribution* in an international system on peace and war.

Balance of power theorists (e.g., Morgenthau, 1948; Claude, 1962; supported by Ferris, 1973) have argued that relative equality, that is, balanced power, is more likely to produce peace. Preponderant power theorists (Organski, 1958; Organski and Kugler, 1980; Kugler and Organski, 1989, supported by Garnham, 1976, and Weede, 1976) have argued the reverse, on the grounds that a strong power need not employ war to attain its objectives. On the related link of capability and the outcome of war, the evidence supports neither power thesis: initiators are likely to win whether they are stronger or weaker than their target (Maoz, 1983).[7]

There is, too, within the structural approach, an exploration of war as a disease that exhibits a strong "contagion effect" (Alcock, 1972). Many subsequent studies attempted to discover the extent to which the "war virus" spreads among states (Bremer, 1982; Levy, 1982; Starr and Most, 1983, 1985; Siverson and Starr, 1991; and, for Houweling and Siccama, 1985, the "epidemiology of war").[8]

A fourth explanation of escalation to war emphasizes the role of *threat perception*. At one level, war may ensue when decision-makers perceive their goals as incompatible with those of their adversary(ies).

Incompatibility may be viewed as an obstacle to new goal achievement and/or as a threat to the maintenance of an old goal, such as security. Threat perception may lead to preemptive or preventive war. And misperception—of one's self, one's intentions and/or capability, of the adversary's intentions and/or capability—is viewed by some as the primary source of escalation to war (Jervis, 1976; Lebow, 1981: Chap. 6; Stoessinger, 1985: Chap. 8; Vertzberger, 1990: Chap. 1). This "school" emphasizes the cognitive dimension of behavior: distrust generates counter-mistrust and a spiralling process of mutual misperception leading to war.

At the other end of the spectrum is the *rational actor/expected utility* explanation of escalation. Briefly stated, a state that perceives positive expected utility from war will initiate a war, that is, engage in escalation. Viewed as an interactive relationship, escalation will not occur only when state A's positive expected utility from a war with B is less than B's expected loss from a war with A (Bueno de Mesquita, 1981: 86–89, 1985). A variant of this line of argument is that crisis escalation to war is more likely when the initiator estimates for itself positive expected utility relative to its adversary and experiences latent or manifest internal conflict: the former refers to "potentially important sources of domestic strife [that do] *not* have visible referents," such as a "national malaise"; the latter, manifest conflict, "will appear in some open form of (political) expression" (James, 1988: 92–93).[9]

What has been learned about the outbreak of war by quantitative research? Zinnes (1980: 359–360) was modest in her assessment, but optimistic:

> ... a combination of two general types of variables—those that change slowly (governmental structure, level of development, amount of resources) and fast-changing ones (unemployment, civil strife, suicide rates)—does seem to discriminate between nations that become heavily involved in war and those that do not.... Perhaps of greater significance, the nation-state puzzle has shown that we must not become obsessed with attributes of nations to the exclusion of environmental factors....

> Our conclusions are far from earth-shaking.... [T]he mystery is a long way from being solved....

> ... while we surely do not have laws, the empirical findings ... appear to be moving us slowly toward lawlike generalizations.[10]

Midlarsky's (1989a) evaluation of the "state of the discipline" reinforces Zinnes' view that "the mystery is a long way from being solved ...":

> First ... we have not been considering a general theory of war—we have been

considering many different theories that have important areas of convergence but also diverge in essential details. . . .

It is . . . apparent that we are dealing . . . also with conceptualizations of war that cannot be put into a single generic category. . . . [F]uture research may require the systematic delineation among several categories, each of which may require a separate theoretical treatment. Put another way, the search for a theory of war may shortly give way to the search for *theories* of *wars* as the scientific study of war proceeds inexorably forward. . . .

Overall, these studies show that there are many ways to investigate the phenomenon of international warfare, ways that are both analytically rigorous and empirically valid. . . .

This review excludes many explanations of *violence in human relations*, a much broader concept than interstate war: the "part of human nature" school (Lorenz, 1966; Wilson, 1978; Eibl-Eibesfelt, 1979); various psychological drives, notably Freud's (1932) "death instinct"; Fromm's (1941, 1973) "malignant aggression" due to alienation; the "frustration-aggression" nexus (Dollard *et al.*, 1939; Berkowitz, 1962); and "violence as learned behavior." (All of these are discussed briefly in Brown, 1987: Chap. 1.)

The processes noted at the beginning of this chapter—change from embryonic to full-scale crisis, from non-violent to violent crisis, and from low-level to intense violence—give rise to the questions that guide the inquiry into escalation. When does an incipient crisis abort, and when does it develop into a fully-crystallized military-security crisis? Why do some crises run their course with no or low-level violence? What types of interstate crises escalate to war, which do not, and why? What induces a state to escalate a crisis by violence? Why are some states more vulnerable than others to violent escalation?

In operational terms, these questions may be reformulated at both levels of analysis:

1. *When can a low-stress onset phase be expected to escalate to a full-scale international crisis, and when will it abort?*

2. *Under what conditions is international crisis escalation most likely to be violent?*

3. *What conditions are most likely to lead to severe violence during an international crisis?*

4. *What are the conditions that will most likely induce a state to escalate a foreign policy crisis?*

5. *When is a state most likely to employ violence in escalating a foreign policy crisis?*

6. *What are the conditions in which a state is most likely to be vulnerable to violent crisis escalation?*

As in the onset phase, the coping aspect of escalation will also be addressed:

7. *How do states cope with the high stress of the escalation phase/crisis period, whether it is characterized by no, low, or severe violence?*

Several tasks will be undertaken to answer these questions:

First, a model of crisis escalation will be specified that delineates the explanatory, intervening and dependent variables, the postulated relationships among them, and the reasons for these expectations.[11]

Second, hypotheses that logically derive from the model of escalation will be framed.

Third, these propositions will be tested with multiple strands of evidence—quantitative (aggregate data) and qualitative (case study findings)—from crises during the period, end of 1918 – end of 1988. And

Fourth, coping with escalation by the same ten states analyzed in the onset phase will be examined.

Model of Crisis Escalation

A model to explain crisis escalation is inherently complex, for the phenomenon is multi-faceted; that is, the conditions that make change from onset (pre-crisis) to escalation (crisis period) most likely are not necessarily the same as those that best account for change from no violence to violence and change from low violence to war; or, at the state level, the use of violence to initiate escalation, and vulnerability to violent escalation. Thus all variables that help to explain each of these aspects of escalation must be included in the model.

The fundamental postulate of the escalation model is that the dependent variables, escalation, violence, and vulnerability to violence, require the prior presence of three perceptual attributes: more acute value threat, awareness of time pressure and heightened war likelihood; and, at the system level, more intense disruptive interaction between the crisis adversaries than in the onset phase. These are, in short, the defining conditions: as noted in earlier chapters, the dependent variables follow whenever these conditions are present, and whenever the changes to escalation occur they must be preceded by these conditions. Thus the escalation model is parsimonious in its initial formulation: two explanatory variables—perceptually-generated stress and more intense disruption—are causally linked to the changes that constitute escalation.

The model must be enlarged, however. For, while it is logically and empirically correct that the specified conditions lead to escalation, there remains a crucial "black hole" in the explanation of escalation: what generates the necessary and sufficient conditions; or, in operational terms, what makes it most likely that perceived acute threat, time pressure, and heightened war likelihood, and more intense disruption, will emerge and escalate an incipient pre-crisis to a full-scale crisis, often with violence and even war? In formal terms: the composite perceptual attribute and disruptive interaction serve as the model's *intervening* variables, and escalation is the *dependent* variable. But what are the prior *independent* variables?

This question leads to a second postulate of the escalation model, namely, that the process of escalation is most likely to occur when a particular set of **system, interactor, actor** and **situational** attributes is present. The first cluster, as noted in the onset model, comprises relatively static contextual conditions—structure/polarity and system level. Interactor variables are conflict setting, capability, regime pair, and geographic distance. The actor group consists of age and domestic instability. And there are many situational attributes: triggering act/event/change, response, major power activity, number of actors, extent of heterogeneity, and range of issues. These attributes generate the highest likelihood that perceived threat/time/war and, with it, disruption will emerge. And those defining conditions, in turn, serve as the crucial intervening variables that are causally linked to the several meanings of escalation.

The links among the explanatory, intervening and dependent variables in the escalation model are presented in Figure 3.1.

The independent variables in the escalation model are almost synonymous with those specified in the general model of international crisis [Model I] [Chap. 1]. The reason is that escalation is the most complex of the four domains/phases of crisis, in which all four clusters of explanatory variables are highly salient. The operational categories for the situational variables and the defining conditions that were not specified in the onset model [Chap. 2, pp. 53–66] are as follows:

situational
>   *trigger*—non-violent, violent, environmental change;
>   *response*—non-violent, violent;
>   *major power activity*—no/low, high;

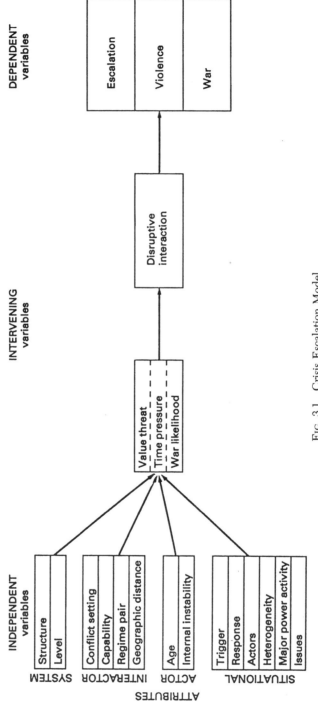

FIG. 3.1   Crisis Escalation Model

number of actors—one, two, three or more;
heterogeneity—none, one, two, three, four;
issues—one, two non-military, military, two including military, three;

intervening
   time pressure—moderate, intense;
   war likelihood—lower, higher;
   disruptive interaction—lower, higher.

I begin with system **structure**. Among the three configurations of world politics from the end of World War I to the end of 1988, polycentrism is the most likely to escalate an incipient crisis and to generate violence, for several reasons. First, as noted, polycentrism imposes fewer constraints on state behavior, including resort to violence. Moreover, all crisis actors in this structure confront more uncertainty about hostile coalitions, given the large number of unaligned states in the global system. And third, the lack of a universally recognized authority in the system means a greater likelihood that, once a crisis is in motion, adversaries will escalate its intensity and use violence to ensure their share of scarce resources.

Since polycentrism is most permissive of violent catalysts to escalation, it is most likely to intensify perceptions of value threat, time pressure, and war likelihood, as well as intensifying disruptive interaction between the adversaries. Bipolarity, in contrast, tends to induce non-violent triggers to the escalation phase, because its major powers are acutely conscious of their role as security managers, especially in dominant system crises. The likelihood of escalation or of violent change is therefore reduced. These arguments merit elaboration.

In a bipolar structure the two major powers possess the interest, as well as the power, to extend their reach to the peripheries of their respective bloc, controlling most of the disruptive interaction between its members and those of the competing bloc. In other system structures, especially multipolarity, the flexible alliance pattern among the major powers reduces the scope and effectiveness of their control over the behavior of lesser powers. For this reason, too, violence is least likely in bipolarity.

System structures also vary in the relative power of potential adversaries. There is more uncertainty and, therefore, a tendency to underestimate one's relative power in multipolarity and polycentrism, because of flexible alignments. The opposite is true of bipolarity, due to a rigid alliance pattern. This means, all other things being equal, a greater likelihood of uncontrollable arms races in polycentrism and multipolarity; for, while arms races also occur in bipolarity—they may even be more intense and prolonged—they will be fewer in number and more easily limited in scope and damage, since fewer actors are effectively involved in the arms control negotiating process. Thus this structural aspect, too, makes polycentrism and multipolarity more prone to crisis escalation and violence.

System **level**, too, contributes to the escalation process. First, the reasoning pertaining to level and an incipient outbreak [Chap. 2] applies to a fully-crystallized international crisis as well. Moreover, as noted in the discussion of the general model of international crisis [Chap. 1] and the model of crisis onset [Chap. 2], dominant system crises are expected to be less intense and less violent than those in subsystems. One reason is the major powers' primary interest in system stability, deriving from their role as security managers of world politics. The other is their more acute awareness of the cost of violence. A violent crisis in the dominant system, from which it is difficult for the powers to remain detached, can undermine their individual status in the power hierarchy, as well as the structure of the system. Thus violence in crises is to be avoided or controlled through major power crisis management. The same attitude—and behavior—by the powers is expected with regard to the target's response. There, too, violence is dangerous and to be thwarted or reduced to prevent costly spillover effects on the dominant system as a whole. Thus the powers tend to limit their resort to violence to crises in which they perceive their most fundamental values to be at stake, that is, when there is "no alternative" for the protection of their existence, influence or core material interests.

In subsystem crises, the use of violence in the escalation phase is more likely for several other reasons. One is that the major dominant system powers are reluctant to assume additional responsibilities as crisis managers and tend to acquiesce in the regional hegemony of major subsystem powers, provided that this contributes to global stability and does not undermine their primacy in world politics. The risk of spillover to the dominant system will vary greatly, from a highly-penetrated Middle East subsystem since 1948, with valuable resources and a geostrategic location perceived to be vital by the major powers, to most subsystems in Africa and Latin America, where neither of these conditions exist. All this strengthens the disposition of major subsystem powers to escalate violence in the crisis period, in order to protect threatened values or to advance interests. They can do so because of their greater freedom of action in their own regional domain.

Disputed issues in subsystem crises and values at stake are no less crucial for adversaries than in dominant system crises. However, in the former, violence, including war, is a more acceptable technique of crisis management and a more widely-used method of behavior to protect basic values. The relative absence of external constraint, legitimacy, pervasiveness in past experience, and the expectation that violence will be used in crises, if necessary, make it much more likely that subsystem crises will exhibit more intense violence as a crisis evolves. The proneness to violence is also true in crises over hegemony in the dominant system (Modelski, 1978; Modelski and Morgan, 1985; Thompson, 1986).

Adversaries in subsystem crises are more likely to be geographically close to each other. This is so because their ability to project power abroad is less than that of their dominant system counterparts. The tendency to military ineffectiveness beyond their neighbors is accentuated by their dependence on the dominant system for inputs of advanced technology. A notable example is the intensely conflictive Middle East, where Egypt, Israel, Jordan and Syria have always depended upon a patron for advanced weapons, especially in the midst of grave violent crises such as the 1967 Six Day War and the October-Yom Kippur War of 1973–74. In short, one effect of physical proximity is to facilitate the resort to violence in crisis management.

Interstate crises that occur during a **protracted conflict** (PC) are more prone than others to escalation, including violence and war. For one thing, an issue in a PC crisis may be limited but it is linked to values in dispute over a prolonged period. Threatened values in non-PC crises, by contrast, are free from the psychological legacy of an on-going conflict. Thus PC crises generate more basic value threats. And these are more likely than low values under threat to induce violence by one or more crisis adversaries.

Such a conflict, over time, also generates more issues in dispute, for it is the essence of a PC that contending issues increase in number and intensity. Mistrust spills over to all domains of interaction, with the result that virtually any issue over which there is less than total understanding and agreement becomes a source of friction, hostility and mutual threat.

Protracted conflict also provides more inducement to violent escalation because of the cumulative effects of such a conflict. Put simply, prolonged, acute and widespread hostility between the same adversaries creates an anticipation of violent behavior in the future. Actors in a PC crisis do not see an end to their conflict and expect a recurrence of violence. Moreover, frequent resort to violence accentuates the image of violence as a protracted conflict norm. And further, the importance of values threatened in a protracted conflict creates a disposition for all contending actors to employ violence, especially because preemptive violence from a long-term adversary is expected. All this puts a premium on violent escalation in a PC crisis, including resort to war. It also generates a disposition to violence in crisis management by the target state.

In crises outside a protracted conflict, adversaries may or may not employ violence: there is no more reason to anticipate a violent escalation than a non-violent one. The type of trigger will depend upon the constellation of a specific crisis, such as the power balance, issues in dispute, geographic distance, regime type, etc. Moreover, even when violence is used there is no *a priori* disposition to resort to full-scale war. In sum, past experience and anticipated future behavior strengthen the likelihood of extreme violence in a crisis during a protracted conflict; they do not in non-PC crises.

A protracted conflict also accentuates the quest for a favorable balance of power, far more so than by adversaries unburdened by a lengthy, complex conflict. Violence must always be anticipated by a rival state, and weaker military capability will stimulate an effort to correct the imbalance. The result is usually an arms race that enhances value threat perception and disruptive interaction. The spiral, in turn, increases the likelihood of crisis escalation, often with violence.

It can be argued that a contrary process is at work in protracted conflicts, namely, that the cumulative experience of PC protagonists in crisis management creates an incentive to minimize violence in recurring crises. However, this tendency is outweighed by the reasons cited above for a propensity to escalate violence. Finally, a PC is more likely between states with perceived power parity. And the consequent uncertainty of crisis outcome further accentuates the tendency to violent escalation.

Capability, defined as power discrepancy, has varying consequences for the use of violence in interstate crises. If power discrepancy is high, a stronger adversary need not trigger a crisis at all, as noted, and certainly not by violence; it can always use violence in a later phase, if necessary. This is so because high power discrepancy gives the stronger state an expectation of victory without violence, while deterring the weaker adversary from employing violence, unless a fundamental value, notably existence or influence, is at stake. Other factors such as surprise and alliance support may change the weaker state's disposition to violent escalation; but the argument here, as throughout the presentation of the escalation model, is based upon the assumption that "all other things are equal."

By contrast, a condition of no or low power discrepancy reduces the credibility of a threat to use force, unless the issue at stake or interest to be protected is central to the regime of one of the parties. Further, in a situation of low credibility a state will be more inclined to employ violence at the beginning of a crisis, in order to demonstrate the credibility of its resolve. It is this disposition, perhaps need, of the intending initiator to communicate resolve by employing violence that renders the target more vulnerable to violent crisis eruption. In sum, no/low power discrepancy increases the likelihood of violent eruption—at the onset phase.

In the escalation phase, when adversaries are equal in power and, more important, the military balance is so perceived, resort to war is unlikely, because of an uncertain outcome and high cost. But when a large power gap is perceived, the stronger actor will be more inclined to use its superior capability, either by escalating from non-violence to violence, or from low violence to war, in the expectation that violence/war will result in goal achievement. Conversely, negative power discrepancy, that is, weakness, will likely lead to non-violent escalation if, in fact, the weaker party escalates at all. The same logic applies to the most likely response to crisis escalation. Positive power discrepancy (relative strength) will induce a violent response, while negative power discrepancy will generate a non-violent response, including, perhaps, compliance with the demand of the stronger actor.

Regimes and regime pairs are expected to vary in their use of violence during interstate crises. The leaders of military regimes are the most likely to rely on violence in the escalation phase, whatever the nature of the initial catalyst. Violence is normal behavior for the military in power. It is the most familiar technique of crisis management, for the military generally achieve and sustain power through violence and tend to use this technique in all situations of stress, internal and external. Violence is also reliable and, in their worldview, legitimate and effective. As threat becomes more acute, in the crisis period, with the addition of perceived time pressure for decision and increasing probability of military hostilities, soldiers in power are likely to employ violence or more severe violence even if alternative techniques of crisis management are available. They extend to interstate relations their normal pattern of behavior (Rummel: 1983, 1985).[12]

Disputes between democratic regimes, as noted, are unlikely to lead to the use or escalation of violence for crisis management. Their ideological dispositions, past experience, and societal constraints make violence, especially war, an option of last resort, even in a phase of rising stress. Along a scale of disposition to violence, a military regime pair will be closely followed by a mixed authoritarian regime pair and civil authoritarian crisis adversaries in the likelihood of resort to violence/war to manage a crisis at its peak (Schweller, 1992).

Geographic distance between adversaries is another autonomous source of crisis escalation. At the extreme, contiguity will increase A's perceptions of more acute threat, time pressure, and the heightened likelihood of military hostilities with B (the defining conditions of the crisis period), given the proximity of B's military forces—and vice versa. Proximity, in turn, makes more likely the use of violence in crisis management by one or more adversaries. First, it is readily available. Secondly, distrust, created or intensified by a crisis, makes both parties more willing to test the other's resolve. Thirdly, the lack of effective system constraints on interstate violence, the essence of an anarchic state system, facilitates the choice of violence, including war, to protect or enhance values that are threatened in a crisis. Finally, mutual fear of possible invasion, alone, puts a premium on resort to violence to escalate a crisis lest the adversary gain an advantage through violent preemption. That tendency, in turn, makes it more likely that targets of crisis initiation will respond with violence.

Age is one of the actor attributes that is salient to the use of violence in crises. Generally, states that attain independence through violence are likely to persist in violent behavior thereafter. The process merits attention because it applies to so many members of the twentieth-century global system. Violent struggle for independence has been a widespread pattern in the Third World since the end of World War II, though some nationalist movements attained sovereignty through negotiations, usually combined with violence (e.g., Rhodesia/Zimbabwe, 1965–80). And some states were recipients of independence through a relatively peaceful transfer of power (e.g., India, Pakistan, Burma and Ceylon in 1947–48, French colonies in North and Equatorial Africa from 1956 onwards, with the notable exception of Algeria). When used for the supreme nationalist goal, violence often acquires an aura of legitimacy. This spills over to a disposition to employ violence after independence, both to sustain domestic power and to confront external adversaries in interstate crises. In short, all other things being equal, older states are less likely to rely on violence. And a successful violent struggle for independence is likely to lead to the later use of violence by states as well.

Escalation to war is more likely when crisis actors are confronted with **internal instability**. The more intense the internal turmoil, the greater the disposition to war. Thus, if violence has not occurred in the onset phase, it will become a virtual imperative when stress rises under the impact of graver threat, time pressure and heightened war likelihood. Reciprocity by the adversary provides another incentive to violence. And when both actors are afflicted with domestic turmoil, war is even more likely. This is reinforced by client–patron relations.

An unstable client is more likely than a stable one to request compensating aid from a patron state, especially military assistance during a crisis, when vital interests are threatened. In such a situation patrons will find it difficult to resist the pressure. And such activity will escalate a crisis sharply if it is directed to strengthen a client's ability to persevere in a crisis and ultimately triumph.

Either may set the escalation process in motion. And the externalization of internal turmoil may not be successful. But it is an attractive way of coping with domestic opposition to leaders, their policy, or both. For the same reason, instability will predispose target states to employ violence in responding to crisis escalation. They will be so inclined for the same reasons that move initiators to act the way they do.

Among the attributes of a crisis that contribute to an understanding of escalation the first in time is **breakpoint/trigger**. A violent trigger is more likely than non-violence to generate perceptions by the target of threatened values, time pressure, and heightened war likelihood. The more intense the violence the more acute will be those perceptions. Moreover, when a catalyst is violent or even a non-violent military act such as mobilization of reserves, the target is likely to respond in kind. When it resorts to violence or a military act to manage a crisis, the initiator is likely to reciprocate, in accordance with the "conflict-begets-conflict" syndrome. The ensuing spiral of disruptive interaction is much more likely than verbal, political or other non-violent non-military triggers to escalate to the most intense form of violence, namely, war. Conversely, if escalation begins with a non-violent act, verbal, political or economic, the target is more likely to eschew violence, in accord with a tit-for-tat strategy.

The **response** of a target state will also impinge upon the escalation process. If its response to a non-violent trigger is moderate violence, the crisis initiator will perceive a higher-than-normal likelihood of war and, therefore, will be likely to counter-respond with equal or more intense violence. If a target's response is war, the initiator will perceive acute hostility and react accordingly. If a target's response is more violent than the trigger, this may create a perception of military weakness on the part of the initial escalating actor. And that perception, in turn, will affect its subsequent behavior. If it perceives the target to be stronger, the actor that set escalation in motion will be less inclined to counter-respond with further violence, lest the upward spiral continue unabated and lead to defeat, with an accompanying high cost in terms of unattained crisis goals. In short, all other things being equal, the type of response by a crisis target will likely shape the course of escalation — non-violence or violence — and, if the latter, its intensity.

Parenthetically, the introduction of violence into a crisis at any time has other consequences. Violence threatens more interests of more states, directly or indirectly, than does non-violence. It raises the tension level, not only for the immediate target, but also for potential future targets. States that are geographically close to the adversaries and/or have alliance commitments are much more likely to enter a crisis when violence is present because of the assumption that this poses a more serious danger, actual or potential, to their interests and cannot be ignored. Violent triggers, in short, have a broader spillover effect, increasing the likelihood that other actors will be drawn into a crisis.

As with violence generally, violent escalation is also expected to draw major powers into a crisis. On the one hand, they are reluctant to become embroiled in disputes that do not directly threaten their interests. On the other, they fear the danger of spillover effects on major power rivalries and, therefore, the implications of violence for global stability. The latter are likely to hold sway, and the major powers are likely to become active in trying to manage risky, violent crises through deterrent and/or reassurance actions, to prevent more intense forms of violence which may engulf them.

The **number of actors** in an interstate crisis, too, affects the escalation process. First, in the absence of more influential countervailing influences, more actors will lead to more, more diverse, and probably more basic values at risk, in the combined perceptions of adversaries. Second, as noted in the discussion of the general model of international crisis (Model I), more actors in an international system generate more dyads (pairs), creating a larger potential of adversarial competition. Similarly, more actors in a crisis lead to more disruptive interaction, with a consequent greater likelihood of violence including escalation to war.

The thrust to violent escalation is reinforced by greater uncertainty about the power balance, with consequences for bargaining strategy and choices at key decision points during a crisis. More precisely, the larger the number of parties in a bargaining sequence, the more difficult it is to attain a solution that will satisfy all concerned. Under such circumstances there is reason to expect that one or more actors will resort to violence in the escalation phase.

This reasoning also applies to the extent of **heterogeneity** among crisis adversaries. The wider their divergence in military capability, economic development, political regime, and culture, the more difficult it is to achieve accommodation, leaving a larger residue of unresolved disputes. That, in turn, creates a larger scope for mistrust and perceived value threat that are more likely to be expressed in violent behavior. Heterogeneous adversaries are also less likely to communicate effectively their intentions and terms of settlement. This too will increase hostility and, with it, a greater disposition to employ violence, in initiating the escalation phase and in responding to threatening behavior. Stated differently, more heterogeneity leads to more misperception and, as a consequence, a more likely resort to violence in the escalation phase.

Major power activity in other states' crises almost always occurs in the escalation phase, that is, after they have become full-scale crises. The more active the major powers in an interstate crisis, the more likely it is that both initiator and target will perceive a more basic value threat—because of the potential damage that can be inflicted by the adversary as a result of aid provided by a patron or otherwise interested major power. Equally, the less active the major powers, the less grave will be the crisis actors' perception of value threat; it will be shaped overwhelmingly by estimates of the intent and relative capability of the main adversary.

A paradox of major power activity in crises is evident with respect to the likelihood of violence. On the one hand, major powers have a strong interest in global system stability, as noted—except when they are in a revolutionary phase of development. They therefore tend to act so as to reduce the likelihood of violence or to limit its intensity, duration and scope, lest ensuing instability cause negative feedback for major power relations and the global system. This takes the form of withholding aid to a client or advice from patrons to both initiator and target of the likely costs of a response that may lead to an escalatory spiral. The overall effect, thus, is likely to be less and less intense violence by the crisis actors. On the other hand, major powers have commitments to allies and clients that call for and expect support in the form of military aid and, if necessary, direct intervention. This second strand of the paradox, more demanding during interstate crises, strengthens the process of escalation to violence or, if it already exists, to war.

A closely-related situational attribute is **issues**. The larger the number of disputed issues in a crisis, the more acute will be the perceived threat to values on the part of all adversaries. Each issue poses a threat to some value and reinforces the negative effect of all other contested issues. That, in turn, contributes to a perception of increasing danger, the need for vigilance and, in general, a conflict spiral between adversaries. The same process, from issues to more mistrust to conflict spiral, generates a greater disposition to violence, both as trigger to the escalation phase and as response by the target. The larger the number of unresolved issues, the more uncertain will be the environment for bargaining and non-violent accommodation by the crisis actors. This will occur unless a difference in preference orderings facilitates a mutually-satisfying trade-off. Given the seriousness of all the issues, log-rolling is anticipated to be rare. In that setting of instability and disruptive interaction, adversaries will be more disposed to resolve the disputes by violent escalation—begetting a violent response.

Finally, multiple-issue crises have more potential than single-issue cases to produce change in the adversaries' relationship and in the international system(s) of which they are members, possibly spilling over to the global system as a whole. Thus they are more likely to attract the attention of major powers because of their far-reaching interests, extending to one or more subsystems. That interest will be reinforced if the adversaries resort to violence, for violent interactions are destabilizing, and major powers, by their involvement, accentuate crisis-generated instability.

Of the three-fold perceptual condition, **value threat**, it was argued in the model of crisis behavior [Model II, in Chap. I], is pivotal. It is the first to emerge in a conflict between two or more states and marks the onset of a foreign policy crisis. Moreover, threat generates an awareness of a higher-than-normal likelihood of military hostilities before the threat is overcome, that is, war likelihood. And both of these create time pressure for response to the value threat and the threat of violence.

The more basic the value(s) at risk, the higher the cost crisis actors are willing to incur to protect them, and the more extreme will be their crisis management (value-protecting) technique, even more in the higher stress crisis period/escalation phase than in the pre-crisis period/onset phase. Violence is the most extreme method to manage a crisis, and war is the most severe form of violence. Thus, if existence or some other core value is perceived to be at stake, the likelihood is very high that violence will be employed, or intensified, to prevent the loss or weakening of that value by a preemptive war on the part of the adversary. In sum, heightened threat is a major source of the peak stress crisis period, along with acute time pressure and heightened war likelihood. And for that reason it increases the likelihood of violence during crisis escalation.

Time pressure, it was noted, refers to available time for decision in relation to the deadline for choice. When decision-makers are uncertain about the adversary's intention and capability, as they usually are in a crisis, time pressure is likely to increase. So too will the perceived **probability of war**.

Most important are the links among the three perceptual conditions. The higher the threat and the more basic the threatened value, the higher will be the perception of war likelihood. Acute threat will also increase the sense of time pressure to respond. And more intense time constraint will increase the perception of war likelihood and the awareness of value threat. Finally, the higher the expectation of war, the more active and basic will be the value threat and the perceived response time. These mutually-reinforcing perceptions induce a feeling of stress. Their interrelationship also provides the logical basis for treating them as a composite intervening variable.

As in the construction of the onset model, the relative weight of the system, interactor, actor and situational attributes was assessed in terms of the "network of effects," that is, effects on each other. The results are as follows:

Rank		
1	structure –	10
2	system level –	7
2	regime (pair) –	7
4	conflict setting –	6
4	capability –	6
4	geographic distance –	6
4	number of actors –	6
8	age –	5
8	major power activity –	5
8	internal instability –	5
11	heterogeneity –	4
11	issues –	4
13	trigger –	3
13	response –	3

In addition, all of these variables affected perceived value threat, time pressure and/or war likelihood. Thus, 90 of the 179 theoretically-possible links (50%) have been operationalized. The six highest rank variables are system and interactor attributes, in that order. The four weakest are situational attributes.

Hypotheses and Findings on Escalation

The first question on crisis escalation posed earlier in this chapter focused on change from an incipient to a fully-crystallized international crisis. In formal terms, as noted, the defining conditions are more acute value threat, time pressure for choice, and heightened war likelihood, perceived by at least one actor, and more disruptive interaction. The presence of these conditions indicates the emergence of the escalation phase/crisis period. The absence of one or more of them indicates an abortive or averted crisis.

Empirically, the defining conditions were present in all ICB cases from the end of 1918 to the end of 1988—826 foreign policy crises and 390 international crises. However, there were many interstate disputes, incidents, etc., that "failed" to qualify as crises, such as a Bulgaria/Greece border dispute in 1931, China's occupation of Tibet in 1950, the Buraimi Oasis dispute in 1955, the Nigerian civil war over Biafra in 1967–70, the 1971 Tupamaro Insurgency in Uruguay, and India/Pakistan border tension over the Sachen Glacier in 1987. Threat was perceived by the decision-maker(s) of at least one state actor in each of these cases and it responded; that is, there was a pre-crisis period and onset phase. However, threat "failed" to become more acute and/or time pressure and/or heightened war likelihood were not perceived.[13]

A more basic question is why this developmental process occurs. Stated in terms of the escalation model, under what conditions is an embryonic crisis (onset) most likely to develop into a full-scale crisis (escalation)? The answer is that the trigger-value-response pattern is most likely to set a spiral in motion when a cluster of other factors is present. Three of them are system or interactor attributes:

- a polycentric structure permits more freedom of action by its autonomous actors; they will feel less constraint in taking steps that are likely to stimulate reciprocal hostility, or escalation;
- a protracted conflict generates long-term mutual mistrust and a mutual expectation of violence, tending to induce more hostile behavior; and

geographic proximity facilitates more hostile behavior between crisis adversaries, whereas distance provides a barrier to escalation.

Their effects are strengthened by the role of several situational attributes:

when more than two actors are engaged in the higher-than-normal hostility of the onset phase, conciliation, compromise and dispute settlement become more difficult, as distrust and uncertainty generate increasing reluctance by all participants to yield to the adversary's demands; that is, the larger the number of actors, the more difficult it is to abort a crisis before it moves beyond the point of no return;

the more heterogeneous the crisis adversaries, with respect to military capability, economic development, political regime and culture, the more likely hostility is to escalate between them; and

if multiple issues are at stake, cutting across simple coalitions of actors, the task of preventing crisis escalation is rendered even more difficult, even if each of the pre-crisis adversaries prefers accommodation: a crisis once set on a spiral path falls victim to its own upward dynamic.

From the escalation model several propositions are derived at the system/interactor level.

Hypothesis 1: *An incipient international crisis is most likely to develop into a fully-crystallized crisis when:*
a crisis occurs within a polycentric structure;
it takes place outside the dominant system;
it is part of a protracted conflict;
the main adversaries are geographically proximate to each other;
there are more than two adversarial actors;
they are heterogeneous in military, economic, political and/or cultural terms; and
there are several cross-cutting issues in dispute.[14]

Two precipitating conditions, type of trigger and response by the adversaries, apply especially to escalation from no violence to violence, and from no/low violence to war, the second and third meanings of this concept. Both violent and non-violent triggers generate perceptions of threat. The former is more likely to set in motion a spiral effect for, as a reciprocal response, violence will virtually ensure that the change from no violence to violence will be sustained. However, a violent trigger to a crisis as a whole (and, therefore, to the onset phase) is not essential to the escalation process. Political or other non-violent triggers will have a similar effect if the value(s) perceived to be at risk are substantive and important for the target state's decision-makers. As such, those triggers, too, will induce reciprocity and a spiral effect. The conflict spiral is reinforced by a tendency to reciprocal response by the target: violent or non-violent triggers tend to beget violent or non-violent responses; and the spiral effect becomes self-sustaining. If the response is "lower" than the trigger in intensity, e.g., a violent trigger and a verbal response, the incipient crisis is more likely to abort. If the response is higher, escalation is virtually certain.

The outbreak of violence as the catalyst to escalation, when there was none in the onset phase, is logically possible and empirically discernible in many combinations of system, interactor, actor and situational attributes. However, violence/war is most likely when a particular set of factors from all four clusters is present at the beginning of the escalation phase. These include all of the factors noted in H. 1.

Two additional interactor attributes help to explain the escalation dynamic to violence/war. One is relative capability; the other is regime pair. When a crisis actor is stronger than its adversary, it is more disposed to introduce violence into a crisis, in the expectation that resort to violence will achieve its objectives. Moreover, if both adversaries are governed by a military regime or they are mixed authoritarian (military/civil), it is much more likely that violence will pervade the change from onset to escalation phase: as noted, decision-makers of such regimes achieved and/or sustained power by violence; it is familiar, legitimate and the preferred technique for coping with crisis as well.

Several situational attributes also serve as explanatory variables. If the type of trigger to escalation is moderately violent or non-violent military, that is, low-intensity violence, and the target's response is tit-for-tat, the spiral to violence or more intense violence is very likely. Moreover, major power activity tends to exacerbate tension between clients engaged in a crisis; military aid facilitates the use of violence by one or both adversaries, and a spiral effect culminating in violence or more intense violence is most likely to ensue.

Two hypotheses on violence are derived from the escalation model:

Hypothesis 2: *An international crisis is most likely to escalate through violence when:*
all of the conditions specified in H. 1 operate;

the adversaries are ruled by military or other types of authoritarian regime;
there is considerable power discrepancy between them; and
major powers are active in supporting clients in the crisis with military aid.

Hypothesis 3: *An international crisis is most likely to escalate to severe violence when:*
all of the conditions specified in H. 1 and 2 operate;
the breakpoint (trigger) to escalation takes the form of a violent act; and
the target responds with equal severity or stronger acts.

The second and third questions about escalation posed earlier in this chapter are closely related. Conceptually, change from no violence to violence in the emergence of a full-scale international crisis, and to severe violence at the peak of a crisis, tap different dimensions of a single, integrated phenomenon. The first refers to the presence or absence of violence, the second, to its extent. Thus they were framed as separate research questions and separate hypotheses: the two questions refer to a scale of violence, ranging from no violence to severe violence. In essence, escalation, at the international/macro level, has three meanings but only two dimensions—change from pre-crisis to crisis, and change from no violence to violence.

The substantive redundancy in H. 2 and 3 derives from the fact that escalation to serious clashes or war is, in essence, an extension of escalation to any form of violence. This is certainly true of the system and interactor attributes—polycentric structure, protracted conflict setting, regime pair, and geographic proximity. As for actor attributes, the more heterogeneous the adversaries, the more they will be prepared to employ severe violence in order to triumph in an external crisis. And the more unstable a crisis actor, the more it will be prepared to risk war abroad, in order to help overcome its domestic problems. Similarly, the more reliable is major power support, the more willing a crisis actor will be to escalate to violence/war in order to achieve its objectives.

What does the evidence from twentieth-century crises reveal about these expectations? The major findings on escalation from an incipient to a fully-crystallized international crisis [H. 1] are set out in Table 3.1.

As evident, four of the expectations set forth in H. 1 are *very strongly* or *strongly* supported, those relating to structure, system level,

TABLE 3.1 *International Crises: Findings on Hypothesis 1*

			Number and Distribution of Cases that Escalated to Full-Scale Crisis			
Independent Variable	Category	No.	%	Category	No.	%
Structure	crises per year, polycentrism	7.27		crises per year, multipolarity[a]	3.72	18
				crises per year, bipolarity	5.31	50
System Level	subsystem		82	dominant system[b]		18
Conflict Setting	PC°		50	non-PC[c]		50
Geographic Distance	'close to home'		76	'more distant'[d]		24
Number of Actors	one crisis actor		41	two or more crisis actors		44
	two involved actors		15	three or more crisis actors		15
				three or more involved actors[e]		85
				(five or more involved actors)		58)
Heterogeneity	low: no differences/one difference		21	high: three or four differences[f]		53
	two differences		26			
Issues	m-s issue alone		50	m-s and another issue		31
	non-m-s issue		12	two non-m-s issues		3
				three issue-areas[g]		4

n = 390 international crises (except for Geographic Distance[d])

°PC, in all tables where it appears = protracted conflict.

a. It can be argued that these findings should be weighted by the number of states in the global system at a specific point in time; that is, the question of proportionality of actors in a system is relevant. Intuition suggests that 2 out of 4 actors or 5 out of 8 is a prominent finding; but that with 2 of 40 or 5 of 80 it is difficult to measure actor influence. This depends on whether the 2 actors out of 40, or 5 out of 80, are major powers or minor powers.

b. Examples of crises at the two levels: dominant system – Remilitarization of the Rhineland (1936); subsystem – Rwanda/Burundi (1964).

c. Illustrations from the three conflict settings: non-protracted conflict – Chinese Eastern Railway (1929), between China and the USSR; protracted conflict – Suez-Sinai Campaign (1956–57), with Egypt, Israel, France, the UK, the US and the USSR as crisis actors; and Rhodesian Settlement (1980), the final crisis in a long-war protracted conflict, with Botswana, Mozambique, Rhodesia and Zambia as direct participants.

d. International crises with more than 2 crisis actors were excluded from this element because of the assumption that multi-actor crises would mask the effect of geographic distance.

e. Illustrations of number of crisis actors: one – Kaunas Trials (1935); two – Football War (1969); three – Ethiopian War (1935–36); four – Basra-Kharg Island (1984); five – Jordan Waters (1963–64); six – Prague Spring (1968); more than six – Entry into World War II (1939 [21 actors]; for illustrations of number of involved actors see note g in Table 3.2.

f. Illustrations of number of attribute differences: none – Cuba/Central America I (1959); one – Kashmir I (1947–49); two – Marshall Plan (1947); three – Trieste II (1953); four – Suez-Sinai Campaign (1956–57).

g. Illustrations of issues: military-security (m-s) issue-area alone – Ogaden I (1964); m-s and other issue – Cyprus II (1967); one non-m-s issue – Haiti Unrest (1929–30); two non-m-s issues – Alexandretta (1936); three issue-areas – Austria *Putsch* (1934).

geographic distance, and heterogeneity. Two—conflict setting and issues—are not. And the finding for number of actors is mixed.[15]

Turning to H. 2, nine types of crisis trigger were operationalized in the ICB Project. These were grouped into three categories: *non-violent*, including external verbal, political, economic, and non-violent military acts, external change, and internal verbal challenge to a regime; *direct violent*, including internal physical violent challenges to a regime; and *indirect violent*, that is, violence directed to an ally or client state.

The aggregate findings on violence *in international crisis escalation* [H. 2 and 3] are presented in terms of the *proportionate frequency of direct violent triggers*, or of *severe violence (war and serious clashes) in the escalation phase*. These are reported in Tables 3.2 and 3.3.

In sum, the data on 70 years of crisis provide *very strong* or *strong* support for five elements of H. 2: structure, system level, geographic distance, conflict setting, and regime type (pair). All five positive findings are statistically significant (code: i or ii).

As for H. 3 (Table 3.3), the evidence on severe violence in international crises is compelling. There is *very strong* or *strong* support for eight of the 12 postulated linkages: conflict setting, geographic distance, number of actors, issues, regime type (pair), major power activity, trigger and response. There is also moderate support for heterogeneity, and modest support for structure, as explanatory variables. Moreover, eight of the 10 supported findings are significant, six of them highly significant (p <0.001). Thus the model has impressive explanatory power for severe violence *during* the escalation phase, much greater than for the likelihood of a violent trigger to escalation.

The findings on trigger and response [Table 3.3] shed light on crucial conditions of severe violence in an international crisis.[16] In this context, the trigger-value-response nexus for the escalation phase of the ten cases provides further, qualitative, evidence.

Berlin Blockade (1948)

trigger	publication by the Western Powers on 7 June 1948 of their London Conference recommendation in March to integrate their zones in Germany (*verbal*);
value threat[17]	Soviet influence in Europe;
response[18]	USSR: Soviet imposition, on 24 June, of a full-scale blockade on all Western land transportation into and out of West Berlin (*economic*).

Prague Spring (1968)

trigger	publication on 9 April of the Czechoslovak Communist Party's "Action Program" setting out the reforms of the Prague Spring (*verbal*);
value threat	survival of the communist regimes in East Germany and Poland;
response	GDR and Poland: pressure on Moscow to take decisive action against Czechoslovak "revisionism" (*political*)

Munich (1938)

trigger	arms smuggling and other offenses by the Sudeten German Party (SdP) (*internal challenge*);
value threat	incipient challenge to Czechoslovakia's sovereignty over Sudetenland, later, to its existence;
response	Czechoslovakia: the arrest of 82 members of the SdP on 7 September (*non-violent military*).

Stalingrad (1942–43)

trigger	a Soviet counter-offensive against German forces at Stalingrad on 19 November 1942 (*violent*);
value threat	the likelihood of massive casualties, and the image of German invincibility;
response	Germany: defense of its encircled Sixth Army (*violent*).

October-Yom Kippur (1973)

trigger	a movement of Egyptian forces towards the Suez Canal and a shift from a defensive to an offensive posture, on 5 October (*non-violent military*);
value threat	peace (war avoidance), danger of high casualties, and Israel's deterrence capability;
response	Israel: large-scale mobilization of reserves (*non-violent military*).

TABLE 3.2 Violence in Escalation of International Crises: Findings on Hypothesis 2

Independent Variable	Category	%	Category	%
			Proportion of Direct Violent Triggers°	
Structure°°	polycentrism	49	multipolarity[b]	32
			bipolarity[a]	21†[i]
System Level	subsystem	40	dominant system[b]	19[i]
Regime Type (Pair)	democratic	27	authoritarian[c]	44[i]
Conflict Setting	PC	47	non-PC[d]	30[ii]
Capability	no/low PD°	48	high PD[e]	25[ii]
Geographic Distance	'close to home'	42	'more distant'[f]	8[i]
Number of Actors	one crisis actor	40	three or more	26[iv]
	two adversaries	48	five or more[g]	38[ii]
Major Power Activity	great powers (1918–39) low	40	great powers (1918–39) high	22[ii]
	superpowers (1945–88) low	39	superpowers (1945–88) high[h]	29[iv]
Heterogeneity	no differences/one difference	47	three or four differences[i]	34[iii]
Issues	m-s issue alone	50	m-s and another issue	29
	three issues	31	non-m-s issue	15
			two non-m-s issues[j]	17[i]

n = 317 cases (390 minus 73 IWCs).

IWCs are excluded from the testing of this hypothesis because they are conceptually related to, but distinct from, the dependent variable, violent escalation. Their inclusion would contaminate the findings in the direction of violent escalation. The reason is that they occur during an on-going war and are therefore more likely to be triggered by violence, irrespective of the effects of specified independent variables. As such, IWC would be performing the confounding function of an independent variable. This note applies to Tables 3.2, 3.3, 3.6, 3.8, 4.1, 4.3, 5.4.

°The proportion of international crises triggered by direct violence was 37%, by indirect violence, 6%, and by non-violent military acts, 16%. For the other 41%, the catalyst was non-violent and non-military.

°°The reported distributions in this table and all others relating to the 14 tested hypotheses are derived from standard contingency table analysis: the categories of the independent variable are interpreted in relation to one value of the dependent variable. Percentages are calculated along the column (dependent variable) scores of a two-by-two contingency table, for both categories of the independent variable. For this and every other independent variable above, the percentage distribution indicated refers solely to the dependent variable category, direct violent trigger.

political, economic, non-violent military, etc. This note applies equally to all subsequent tables (3.3, 3.6, 3.8, 4.1, 4.2, 4.3, 4.4, 5.4, 5.5.1, 5.6) that report the proportional findings of tests on hypotheses.

PD, in all tables where it appears = power discrepancy.

†Code for significance test results:

i $p < 0.001$
ii $p < 0.05$
iii $p < 0.10$ (approaching significance)
iv not significant

Significance tests are performed in this study for supplementary purposes – because the entire population of cases is being analyzed. These tests are used merely to determine whether or not the percentage distributions are statistically meaningful.

a. Examples of violent escalation in different global configurations are: multipolarity – Chaco I (1928–29), between Bolivia and Paraguay; bipolarity – the Catalina Affair (1952), between Sweden and the USSR; and polycentrism – Shaba II (1978), with two African crisis actors, Zaire and Angola, along with Belgium, France and the US.

b. Examples are: Ogaden II (1977–78), between Ethiopia and Somalia (subsystem); and Munich (1938), with Czechoslovakia, France, the UK and the USSR as crisis actors, and Germany as the triggering entity (dominant system).

c. Examples are: non-democratic regimes – Ussuri River (1969), between the PRC and the USSR; mixed pair – Mayaguez (1975), between Cambodia and the US; and democratic – Cod War I (1973), between Iceland and the UK.

d. Examples are: Pushtunistan III, between Afghanistan and Pakistan (1961–62), one of several crises over their long-disputed border (PC); Tet Offensive, between North Vietnam and the US (1968) (long-war protracted conflict); and Libya/Egypt Border (1977) (non-PC).

e. Illustrations are, respectively, Ogaden I (1964), the first of several crises between Ethiopia and Somalia over disputed territory; and Korean War I (1950), between the US, South Korea and Taiwan, on the one side, North Korea and the PRC on the other (high PD).

f. Illustrations are: Suez-Sinai Campaign (1956–57), very 'close to home' for Egypt and Israel; and Dien Bien Phu (1954), which was geographically remote from the crisis actors, France, the US and the UK.

g. Examples for crisis actors are: one – Costa Rica/Nicaragua I (1948–49); three – Lebanon War (1982–83); more than three – Shaba II [five] (1978); for adversaries [involved actors]: two – Amur River (1937); five or more – Entry into World War II [32] (1939).

h. Overall, major power activity in crises exhibited a strong disposition to non-military involvement: for the great powers (1918–39), no involvement in 14 cases (8% of international crises), high involvement in 13 cases (7% of crises); for the two superpowers (1945–88), the comparable figures are 210 cases (37%) and 53 cases (9%). Illustrations for great power activity are: low – Chaco I (1928–29); high – Entry into WWII (1939). For superpower activity: low – Football War (1969); high – Shaba I (1977).

i. Examples for heterogeneity are: no difference – Cuba/Central America I (1959); three or four differences – War of Attrition I (1969).

j. Illustrations for issues are: military-security issue alone – Wal-wal (1934–35); military-security and another issue – Fall of Western Europe (1940); one non-military-security issue – Ifni (1957); two non-military-security issues – Congo I: Katanga (1960–62); three issue-areas – Pushtunistan III (1961–62).

TABLE 3.3 *Severe Violence in International Crises: Findings on Hypothesis 3*

Independent Variable	Proportion of Crises with Severe Violence (Serious Clashes, Full-Scale War)			
	Category	%	Category	%
Structure°	polycentrism†	44	multipolarity[iv] bipolarity[iv]	36 37
System Level	subsystem	40	dominant system[iv]	40
Conflict Setting	PC	52	non-PC[i]	33
Geographic Distance	'close to home'	25	'more distant'[i]	11
Number of Actors				
Crisis Actors	single actor	27	three or more actors[i]	52
Involved Actors	two actors	30	five or more actors[i]	50
Heterogeneity	no difference/one difference	31	two or more differences[iii]	43
Issues	one issue	24	two or more issues, incl. mil.-sec.[ii]	47
Regime Type	democratic	18	authoritarian[i]	33
Capability	no/low PD	48	high PD[iv]	41
Major Power Activity	great powers (1918–39) low	41	great powers (1918–39) high[ii]	67
	superpowers (1945–88) low	23	superpowers (1945–88) high[ii]	45
Trigger	non-violent	30	violent[i]	60
Response	weaker	7	equal/stronger[i]	77

n = 317 cases (390 minus 73 IWCs).

See note on IWCs in Table 3.2.

°See °° n. to Table 3.2.

†Code for significance test results:
i $p < 0.001$
ii $p < 0.05$
iii $p < 0.10$ (approaching significance)
iv not significant

Lebanon Civil War I (1976)

trigger	a Lebanese Christian victory over the leftist Muslim–PLO alliance on 18 January 1976 (*indirect violent*);
value threat	the realization of Greater Syria, along with a danger to national unity;
response	Syria: the dispatch of the Yarmouk Brigade of the Palestine Liberation Army (*non-violent military*).

India/China Border (1962)

trigger	the intrusion of Chinese forces along the Thag La Ridge into India's North East Frontier Province on 8 September 1962 (*violent*);
value threat	to territory claimed by India;
response	India: "Operation Leghorn," to eject Chinese troops (*non-violent military*).

Hungarian Uprising (1956)

trigger	massive demonstrations in Budapest and other Hungarian cities on 23 October calling for the withdrawal of Soviet forces and the return of Imre Nagy to power (*internal challenge*);
value threat	survival of the pro-Moscow communist regime;
response	Hungary: to appoint Nagy as Prime Minister and to invite Soviet troops to restore order in Budapest (*political*).

Rhodesia UDI (1965–66)

trigger	Rhodesia's proclamation of state of emergency on 5 November (*political*);
value threat	increasingly grave risk to Zambia's economic stability and national survival in face of threatened economic blockade by Rhodesia;
response	Zambia: pressure on the UK for an immediate airlift of British army and airforce units to the Kariba power center (*political*).

Falklands/Malvinas (1982)

trigger	the capture of Port Stanley by Argentine forces on 2 April (*violent*);
value threat	to UK-controlled territory;
response	UK: the embarkation of a large Royal Navy task force to the South Atlantic on 5 April, with the aim of restoring UK control over the islands (*non-violent military*).

As evident, the triggers to the escalation of these ten international crises between 1938 and 1982 varied—verbal, political, non-violent military, violent, and internal challenge. All catalyzed perceptions of threat to important values—existence, influence, human life (casualties in war), territory, political system. This was one crucial element in the trigger-value-response nexus relating to escalation. The other, the trigger-response link, is also strongly supported: as postulated in the escalation model, eight of the ten target states responded either tit-for-tat, e.g., political/political, or with a more intense act, e.g., political/non-violent military. The exceptions were India in the border crisis with China, and the UK in Falklands/Malvinas, both with a violent trigger and non-violent military response—initially: later in the escalation phase, the major response of both was full-scale war.

Just as change from an incipient to a full-scale crisis and to violence/war merits analysis at the international level, so too these processes at the state/actor level require attention. The task is to frame and test hypotheses about the conditions in which a state is most likely: to escalate an embryonic crisis, that is, to initiate a full-scale crisis for another state, and to do so by violence; and the conditions that make a state most vulnerable to crisis escalation and to violence.

As a prelude to the discussion of actor-level hypotheses, the "crisis experience" of the members of the global system from 1918 to 1988 is presented in Table 3.4.

The most conspicuous finding is the pervasiveness of the crisis phenomenon in world politics: 99 states triggered one or more crises, and no less than 123 states served as the target of crises. This reinforces the evidence on the ubiquity of crisis reported earlier [Chap. 2, Tables 2.1–2.5].

Twenty states comprise the "high-frequency-of-initiation" group. Four catalyzed more than 30 crises each: the USSR 64; Germany (to May, 1945) 39; the US 35; and Israel 30. Two states initiated 20–29 crises: Turkey 21, and Libya 20. And 14 states triggered 10–19 crises:

TABLE 3.4 *Crisis Experience by States*

State	No. of Crises	No. of Crises Initiated
Afghanistan	5	5
Albania	3	1
Algeria	5	3
Angola°†	12	1
Argentina	3	3
Australia	2	0
Austria	4	1
Bahrain	2	0
Bangladesh	1	0
Belgium	7	2
Bolivia	3	2
Botswana	5	0
Bulgaria	4	3
Burkina Faso	1	1
Burma	1	1
Burundi	1	0
Cambodia (Kampuchea)	6	5
Cameroon	1	1
Canada	2	0
Ceylon (Sri Lanka)	1	1
Chad†	8	5
Chile	2	2
China (pre-1949 and PRC)°†/	21	17
China (Taiwan)	4	3
Colombia	2	1
Congo (Brazzaville)	2	0
Congo (Kinshasa) (Zaire)	4	2
Costa Rica	5	2
Cuba	3	1
Cyprus	3	5
Czechoslovakia /	13	9
Dahomey	1	1
Denmark	2	0
Dominican Republic	5	2
Ecuador	2	2
Egypt (UAR)°†/	22	13
El Salvador	1	1
Estonia	3	1
Ethiopia	5	5
Finland	5	2
France°†/	35	17
France (Vichy)	1	0
Gambia	1	1
Germany (to May 1945)°†/	17	39
Germany (East)	3	3
Germany (West)	2	0
Ghana	1	0
Greece°†/	15	11

TABLE 3.4 *Continued*

State	No. of Crises	No. of Crises Initiated
Grenada	1	1
Guatemala	3	5
Guinea (Indep.)	2	0
Guinea (Portgs.)	0	1
Guyana	2	0
Haiti	3	1
Honduras	6	4
Hungary	10	6
Iceland	2	2
India°/	13	12
Indonesia	8	5
Iran†	12	8
Iraq/	9	11
Israel°†/	24	30
Italy	10	18
Japan°†/	16	19
Jordan°†/	13	2
Kenya	3	1
Korea (North)	2	4
Korea (South)	3	1
Kuwait	3	0
Laos	4	2
Latvia	3	0
Lebanon	8	1
Lesotho	2	0
Libya°/	16	20
Lithuania	8	1
Luxembourg	2	0
Malagasy	2	0
Malawi	1	0
Mali	2	3
Malta	1	0
Mauritania	5	0
Mexico	1	2
Mongolia	0	1
Morocco°†	8	6
Mozambique°	6	1
Muscat and Oman	1	0
Netherlands	11	4
New Zealand	2	0
Nicaragua	12	7
Niger	1	1
Nigeria	3	2
Norway	2	0
Pakistan°†/	14	10
Panama	3	2
Paraguay	2	2
Peru	3	3

State	No. of Crises	No. of Crises Initiated
Poland	10	9
Portugal	2	0
Qatar	0	1
Rhodesia /	5	14
Romania	9	2
Rwanda	1	1
Saudi Arabia†	9	7
Senegal	2	1
Somalia	5	3
South Africa /	4	17
Spain	4	2
Sri Lanka (see Ceylon)		
Sudan	5	0
Sweden	4	0
Switzerland	1	0
Syria°†/	16	10
Tanzania	3	3
Thailand	8	3
Togo	1	1
Tunisia	6	1
Turkey°†/	20	21
Uganda	5	5
UK (Great Britain)°†/	41	16
US (United States)°†/	51	35
USSR (Soviet Union)°†/	38	64
Venezuela	2	4
Vietnam	6	7
Vietnam (North) /	6	12
Vietnam (South)	7	0
Yemen	7	6
Yemen-Aden	2	3
Yugoslavia	12	7
Zambia	9	1
Internally initiated		27
Non-state actor		113
More than one state		54
Other		2
Total:		826

°High vulnerability to foreign policy crises
†High vulnerability to violent crisis escalation
/ High proneness to crisis initiation

Japan 19; Italy 18; (mainland) China, France and South Africa 17 each; the UK 16; Rhodesia 14; Egypt 13; India and North Vietnam 12 each (but North Vietnam and Vietnam together 19); Greece and Iraq 11 each; Pakistan and Syria 10 each.

The ranking changes when the potential for crisis *initiation* is noted. Only ten of these states were independent for the entire 70 years, 1918–88. Israel's "potential" was only 40.5 years, thereby accentuating its role as crisis initiator. So too with Libya (37 years), Rhodesia (14.5), Egypt (52.4), India and Pakistan (41.3), Vietnam (42.8), Iraq (56.2) and Syria (45 years).

The 20 "high frequency of initiation" group accounted for 406 of 826 foreign policy crises, i.e., 49%. Their proportion of all cases triggered by states is much higher, for three categories (internal initiation, non-state actor, and more than one state) catalyzed 194 cases (23.5% of the total). Thus, the high frequency group accounted for 64% of the 632 crises initiated by individual states.

Turning to the dimension of *vulnerability*, some members of the global system have been the target of many foreign policy crises, others of very few, as evident in Table 3.4. Only seven experienced more than 20 crises: the US 51; the UK 41; the USSR 38; France 35; Israel 24; Egypt 22, and (mainland) China 21. Fourteen states each had from 10 to 20 crises: Turkey 20; Germany (excluding the GDR) 19; Japan, Libya and Syria 16 each; Greece 15; Pakistan 14; Czechoslovakia, India and Jordan, 13 each; and Angola, Iran, Nicaragua and Yugoslavia, 12 each. Together, these 21 states account for 435 of the 826 cases during the 70 years, that is, 52.7%. At the other extreme, 20 states, such as Mexico and Switzerland, each had to cope with one crisis, and 24 others with two each, e.g., Australia, Portugal, and Senegal.

These raw figures on number of foreign policy crises must be adjusted because many of the 123 states that were targets of one or more external crises emerged as members of the global system only after World War II: there were only 50 independent states in 1945. Thus among the high-frequency group the US, the UK, the USSR, France and China were independent entities throughout the period for which crisis data have been assembled, end 1918–end 1988, while Israel, as noted, was capable of experiencing foreign policy crises only since its independent statehood in May 1948, and Egypt, since its formal independence was acknowledged in the Anglo-Egyptian Treaty of August 1936.[19]

Using an average number of foreign policy crises per year of independence during the period under inquiry, a different ranking emerges. Angola ranks first, with .92 crises per year, 12 crises since its independence in November 1975. Six of the seven states in the highest absolute frequency cluster remain but in somewhat different order. Angola is followed by the US (.73), Israel (.59), the UK (.59), the USSR (.54), France (.50), and Egypt (.42). Libya, with fewer crises than Egypt, ranks slightly higher in average number per year, .43. Among the other states in the second cluster noted above (12–20 crises), Syria, Pakistan, India, Jordan, Turkey, and Germany, along with (mainland) China, range from .38 to .29 crises per year. Among the others in the absolute high-frequency group, only Japan and Greece remain in the revised ranking with .23 and .21 crises per year, respectively. To this group must be added three other African states: Mozambique (.44), Zambia (.37) and Morocco (.24) crises per year. In sum, 20 states with an average of .20 crises per year of independence or higher constitute the high-frequency group in terms of vulnerability.

The distinction between the "high frequency of initiation" group of 20 states, especially the four most prone to trigger interstate crises, and the other 100+ states is one noteworthy characteristic of the crisis experience. Another is the discrepancy between initiation and vulnerability.

Put simply, not only are some states more "aggressive" in the crisis domain, that is, more prone to initiate crises. Some states are more prone to initiation than to vulnerability—and vice-versa. The most conspicuous, in terms of greater vulnerability, are: Angola (12 crises experienced, 1 initiated), France (35–17), Zambia (9–1), Lebanon (8–1), Lithuania (8–1), Mauritania (5–0), Mozambique (6–1), the Netherlands (11–4), Jordan (13–2), Romania (9–2), the UK (41–16), the US (51–35), and Yugoslavia (12–7). A much greater proneness to initiate crises is evident in the data on four states: pre-May 1945 Germany (17 crises experienced, 39 initiated); Rhodesia (5–14), South Africa (4–17), and the USSR (38–64).

Other findings on crisis experience are worth noting. Some states were prone to violent crisis escalation but were not in either the high vulnerability or high frequency of initiation group—Chad, Iran, and Saudi Arabia. And most states that exhibited a high crisis profile belonged to all three high frequency groups; that is, they were highly vulnerable to crises and to violent crisis escalation, and they were highly prone to initiate crises: China, Egypt, France, Germany (to May 1945), Greece, Israel, Japan, Jordan, Pakistan, Syria, Turkey, the UK, the US, and the USSR.

As for *vulnerability to violence* in the "step-level" jump from pre-crisis to crisis period, research uncovered a "high-vulnerability-to-violent escalation" group of 20 states. Together they experienced 207 foreign policy crises in which the crisis period was triggered by violence: these constitute 49% of all violent escalation cases (422), 51% of all of those states' crises (403), and 25% of all crises (826) from the end of 1918 to the end of 1988.

Major powers of the post-World War I era are the most conspicuous members of that group: the US, 25 (of 51) cases with violent escalation; the USSR, 17 (of 38); the UK, 15 (of 41); and France, 14 (of 35) cases. These are followed by a cluster of 16 states: Egypt and Japan, each with 11 cases whose crisis period was triggered by violence; Angola, China, Germany (including East Germany, 1955–88), Greece and Israel, 9 each; Chad, Iran, Jordan, Syria, Turkey and Zambia, 8 each; and Morocco, Pakistan and Saudi Arabia, 7 each. At the other extreme, 19 states were free from violent crisis escalation, e.g., Guyana and Norway. And 31 states each confronted one such crisis, e.g., Argentina, Denmark and Romania.

As with vulnerability to crisis outbreak, the ranking of the "high-vulnerability-to-violent" escalation group must be adjusted by the number of years of independence, that is, the factor of potential vulnerability: 9 of the 20 states emerged after World War II, compared to China, France, Germany, Greece, Iran, Japan, Saudi Arabia, Turkey, the UK, the US, and the USSR that were independent throughout the period, 1918–88. Viewed in terms of the average number of crises escalated by violence per year of independence during the period under inquiry, the ranking of vulnerability to violent escalation changes considerably. Angola has the highest per annum frequency (.69), followed by the US (.36) and Zambia (.33). These are followed by Chad (.28), the USSR (.24), Israel and Morocco (.22), Egypt and the UK (.21), and France (.20). The net cluster comprises Jordan (.19), Syria (.18), Pakistan (.17), Japan (.16), China, Germany and Greece (.13). The lowest frequency of violent crisis escalation is shared by Iran, Saudi Arabia and Turkey (.11).

Another distinction is important in this context, namely, the incidence of *direct* and *indirect violent* triggers: the latter refers to violent acts aimed at an ally or client state of the target, or an internal revolt in another state (e.g., Israel's attack on Syria's Golan Heights in June 1967, triggering a foreign policy crisis for the USSR). In this perspective, the four major powers comprise a distinct cluster, each with fewer crises escalated by direct than by indirect violence (the US 11–14; the UK 6–9; the USSR 7–10; and France 4–10). This indicates that major powers often experience crisis escalation by violence as a consequence of their patron role *vis-à-vis* client states. None of the other members of the 20 vulnerable-to-violence group had more than three indirect-violence cases: Turkey had 3, Germany, Israel, Japan, Jordan, Libya and Syria had 2 each; five other states—China, Egypt, Greece, Pakistan and Zambia—each had one indirect violence case. And four states (Angola, Chad, Iran and Morocco) experienced only direct violent triggers.

Based upon the reasoning set out in the escalation model, three propositions at the actor level are presented here:

Hypothesis 4: *A state is most likely to escalate another state's incipient (pre-) crisis to a full-scale crisis (crisis period) when*
it is ruled by a non-democratic regime;
it is engaged in a protracted conflict with its adversary(ies);
it has a favorable power relationship with its adversary(ies);
its adversary is geographically contiguous;
it is a young or new political entity; and
it is experiencing acute internal instability.

The findings on escalation of foreign policy crises are reported in Table 3.5.

TABLE 3.5   *Escalation of Foreign Policy Crises: Findings on Hypothesis 4*

Independent Variable	Proportion of Full-Scale Foreign Policy Crises			
Initiator's:	Category	%	Category	%
Regime Type	democratic	33	authoritarian	67
Conflict Setting	PC	50	non-PC	50
Capability	high negative PD	15	high positive PD°	59
Geographic Distance	'close to home'	82	'more distant'	18
Age	old states	34	new states	66
Internal Instability	increasing	24	decreasing†	2

n = 826 cases

°The other cases escalated by states exhibited low negative PD (9%), low positive PD (12%), and no PD (5%).

†The other 74% of the cases showed no change in internal instability for the initiator.

As evident, the data provide *very strong* support for five of the six elements in this hypothesis—regime type, capability, geographic distance, age and internal instability.

As for the dimension of violence:

Hypothesis 5: *A state is most likely to escalate a crisis from no violence to violence when all of the conditions specified in H. 4 operate; and when*

it is receiving major power military support.

The findings on the role of violence in escalation are set out in Table 3.6.

TABLE 3.6 *Violent Escalation of Foreign Policy Crises: Findings on Hypothesis 5*

Independent Variable	Proportion of Foreign Policy Crises Escalating Through Violence			
	Category	%	Category	%
Regime Type°	democratic	18	authoritarian†[i]	36
Conflict Setting	PC	33	non-PC[iii]	26
Capability	negative PD	31	positive PD[ii]	21
Geographic Distance	'close to home'	36	'more distant'[i]	4
Age	old states	22	young states[i]	44
Internal Instability	increasing	64	decreasing[ii]	26
Major Power Activity	low	35	high[iv]	26

n = 579 cases (826 minus 247 IWCs).

See note on IWCs in Table 3.2.

°See °° n. to Table 3.2.

†Code for significance test results:
  i $p < 0.001$
  ii $p < 0.05$
  iii $p < 0.10$ (approaching significance)
  iv   not significant

In short, four of the seven elements of this hypothesis exhibit *very strong* support from the aggregate data—regime type, geographic distance, age, and internal instability. There is also *moderate* support for conflict setting. The first and second of these findings are highly significant ($p < 0.001$).

Two hypotheses on vulnerability are deduced from the escalation model.

Hypothesis 6: *A state will be most vulnerable to crisis escalation when*
it is not an actor in the dominant system;
it is ruled by a non-democratic regime;
it is engaged in a protracted conflict with one or more states;
it has an unfavorable power relationship with its adversary;
it is geographically contiguous to its adversary;
it is a young or new state; and
it is experiencing acute internal instability.

As for the dimension of violence,

Hypothesis 7: *A state is most likely to be vulnerable to violent crisis*
escalation when
all of the conditions specified in H. 6 operate in its foreign policy
crisis;
its regime is of short duration; and
its territory is small.

The aggregate findings on vulnerability to escalation are set out in Table 3.7.

In sum, the data on 70 years of interstate crises in the twentieth century exhibit *very strong* or *strong* support for four of the seven elements in H. 6, system level, regime type, geographic distance, and internal instability. Proneness to foreign policy crises does not, however, seem to be related to conflict setting, power discrepancy or age. The finding for capability is, in fact, counterintuitive—stronger states seem to be more vulnerable than weaker states to a foreign policy crisis. This finding, parenthetically, is consistent with power transition theory.

The major findings on vulnerability to direct violent crisis escalation [H. 7] are derived from the data on the total number of 826 foreign policy crises minus IWCs and missing data, that is, 540 cases (Table 3.8).

Overall, the evidence on foreign policy crises during most of the twentieth century supports 8 of the 9 postulated linkages in H.7: four *very strongly*—system level, geographic distance, age, and regime type; two *strongly*—capability and regime duration; and two *moderately*—conflict setting and size of territory. However, only two of the supported findings—regime type and regime duration—are statistically significant. Four others approach significance.

The qualitative findings on the three perceptual conditions of vulnerability to (violent) escalation [H. 6 and 7] are also instructive.

TABLE 3.7 *Vulnerability to Full-Scale Crisis: Findings on Hypothesis 6*

Independent Variable	Distribution of Foreign Policy Crises by Vulnerability			
	Category	%	Category	%
System Level	subsystem	73	dominant system[a]	27
Regime Type	democratic	38	authoritarian[b]	62
Conflict Setting	PC	50	non-PC[c]	50
Capability	negative PD	36	positive PD[d]	56
Geographic Distance	'close to home'	78	'more distant'[e]	22
Age	old states (pre-1815)	37	modern states (1815–1945)	31
			new states (post-WWII)[f]	32
Internal Instability	Increasing	26	Decreasing[g]	2

n = 826 cases

a. As indicated in the notes to Table 3.1, the comparable figures for international crises are: subsystem – 82%, dominant system – 18%. Illustrations of foreign policy crises: Bolivia and Paraguay in the 1928–29 Chaco I Crisis (subsystem level), and crises for the GDR, the USSR, France, the FRG, the UK, and the USA in the 1961 Berlin Wall Crisis (dominant system level).

b. Illustrations of regime types: democratic – the UK in the Chanak Crisis of 1922; civil authoritarian – Iran in Shatt-al-Arab II, 1969; military – Chile in Beagle Channel II, 1978–79.

c. Examples of foreign policy crises in different conflict settings, with non-violent triggers: non-protracted conflict – information concerning a US decision to support an anti-Guatemala regime 'liberation movement', on 12 December 1953, triggered a crisis for Guatemala; (East/West) protracted conflict – the German Democratic Republic (GDR)'s erection of a wall separating East and West Berlin on 13 August 1961 triggered Berlin Wall crises for the US, the UK, France and West Germany; and long-war protracted conflict – a threat by US Secretary of State Dulles to use nuclear weapons against the People's Republic of China (PRC), communicated via India's Prime Minister Nehru on 22 May 1953, triggered a crisis for the PRC during Korean War III.

d. Power equality accounts for 8% of the cases. Further examples of foreign policy crises with different levels of power discrepancy: the US in the Cienfuegos Base Crisis (1970), no power discrepancy *vis-à-vis* its adversary, the USSR; Jordan in the 1963-64 Jordan Waters Crisis, with positive power discrepancy, because of an Arab coalition in that case (Egypt, Syria, Lebanon, Jordan) against Israel; and the USSR in the Azerbaijan Crisis (1945–46), with negative power discrepancy *vis-à-vis* its adversarial coalition, comprising the US, the UK and Iran.

e. For illustrations of actor-level crises in terms of geographic distance, see note f. to Table 3.2.

f. The equal distribution is misleading, however. The last group had a much shorter time-span as potential crisis actors than 'old' states (China, France, Iran, Japan, Russia, Turkey, the UK) and 'modern' states (the US, Central and East European, as well as South American states), all of which were independent for the entire 70-year period under inquiry. 'New' states encompass most Middle East and South Asian states since the 1940s; African states since the 1960s or 1970s. All this indicates a much greater concentration of crises in 'new' states.

g. The other 72% of the cases showed 'normal' instability; for illustrations of actor-level crises in terms of internal instability, see note g. to Table 3.8.

TABLE 3.8 *Vulnerability to Violent Crisis Escalation: Findings on Hypothesis 7*

Independent Variable	Category	%	Proportion of Direct Violent Triggers	
			Category	%
System Level°	subsystem	35	dominant system[a]	8†[iv]
Conflict Setting	PC	34	non-PC[b]	26[iii]
Geographic Distance	'close to home'	45	'more distant'[c]	4[iii]
Age	old states	17	new states[d]	37[iii]
Regime Type	democratic	17	authoritarian[e]	36[ii]
Capability	negative/no PD	34	positive PD[f]	18[iv]
Internal Instability	increasing	26	decreasing[g]	63[iv]
Regime Duration	short	46	long[h]	26[ii]
Territory-Size	small	30	large[i]	21[iii]

n = 540 cases (826 minus 247 IWCs and 39 missing data).

See note on IWCs in Table 3.2.

°See °° n. to Table 3.2.

†Code for significance test results:
  i $p < 0.001$
  ii $p < 0.05$
  iii $p < 0.10$ (approaching significance)
  iv not significant

a. Illustrations of foreign policy crises escalated through direct violence are: subsystem – Iraqi Nuclear Reactor (Iraq) (1981); dominant system – Ussuri River (USSR) (1969).

b. Examples of direct violent triggers to a fully-crystallized crisis are: protracted conflict setting – Pakistan's first (1949–50) crisis with Afghanistan in the protracted conflict over Pushtunistan; the US's Pueblo crisis (1968) (non-PC); and the breakthrough by the British Eighth Army at El Alamein on 23 October 1942, an intra-war crisis for Italy and Germany (long-war PC).

c. Illustrations of geographic distance categories regarding direct violent escalation are: home territory – Qibya (Jordan) (1953); sub-region – Yemen War II (Saudi Arabia) (1964); same continent – Stalingrad (Germany) (1942–43); elsewhere – Pueblo (US) (1968).

d. Direct violent triggers in the three age categories are: old states – Leticia (Colombia) (1932–33); modern states – Suez-Sinai Campaign (Egypt) (1956–57); new states – Congo I: Katanga (Congo) (1960).

e. Examples of the three regime type pairs are as follows: the firing by Icelandic gunboats on British fishing trawlers on 14 May 1973, triggering Cod War I between Iceland and the UK (democratic/democratic); the shooting down of a Swedish flying boat by two Soviet fighters on 16 June 1952, the trigger to Sweden's Catalina Affair (democratic/civil authoritarian); and a *coup d'état* that overthrew the ruler of Yemen on 26 September 1962, escalating foreign policy crises for Saudi Arabia and Jordan, setting in motion the protracted Yemen War (1962–67) (civil authoritarian/civil authoritarian).

f. Illustrations are as follows: Israel in the 1982 Lebanon War, power equality (no power discrepancy) *vis-à-vis* Syria; Pakistan in the Kashmir I Crisis (1947–48), low negative power discrepancy *vis-à-vis* India; the USSR in Congo II (1964), high negative power discrepancy *vis-à-vis* the coalition of Belgium, the US and the Congo.

g. Illustrations of direct violent escalation are: increasing instability – Six Day War (Israel) (1967); normal (in)stability – Bay of Pigs (Cuba) (1961); decreasing instability – Uganda/Tanzania I (Tanzania) (1971).

h. Illustrations are: Nagomia Raid (1976), a Rhodesia 'hot pursuit' operation into Mozambique, barely a year after the latter attained its independence; and, for a relatively longstanding regime, Syria's al-Biqa Missiles Crisis (1981), initiated by an Israeli air attack on Syrian missile sites in Lebanon.

i. Examples are: Israel's Tel Mutillah Crisis (1951), escalated by Syria (small state); and, for a large state, India's first Kashmir Crisis (1947–48), escalated by Pakistan's support for an incursion by pro-Pakistani 'Azad Kashmir' tribesmen.

Values. A more acute threat perception than in the pre-crisis period [Table 2.8.B.1, Chap. 2] is clearly evident in the crisis period of the ten cases examined throughout this volume [Table 3.10.B.1 below]:

the US (Berlin Blockade, 1948)—reputation for resolve, along with the continuation of its pre-crisis values at risk, namely, preservation of West Berlin as a western enclave in communist Europe, and West European security;

the USSR (Prague Spring, 1968)—reinforcement of the pre-crisis values, bloc unity and Soviet national security;

the UK (Munich, 1938)—peace in Europe, as in the pre-crisis period, but much more acutely perceived;

Germany (Stalingrad, 1942–43)—its military hegemony, specifically, the likelihood of massive casualties, possible destruction of the Sixth Army, possible loss of Army Group A, trapped in the Caucasus, and the image of German invincibility;

Israel (October-Yom Kippur, 1973)—initially, peace (war avoidance), thereafter, the danger of high casualties, and its deterrence credibility;

Syria (Lebanon Civil War I, 1976)—the same pre-crisis core value, namely, the realization of Greater Syria, along with national unity, that is, the danger of disunity in Syria proper;

India (India/China Border, 1962)—territorial integrity (more acute danger to NEFA in the Eastern Sector and Ladakh in the Western Sector), along with national security, and the policy of non-alignment;

Hungary (Hungarian Uprising, 1956)—at first, survival of the communist system and the old regime, as in the pre-crisis period; then, under Nagy, survival of the reform regime and protection of Hungary's newly-asserted independence from Moscow;

Zambia (Rhodesia UDI, 1965–66)—increasingly grave risk to economic stability and national survival because of Zambia's vulnerability to a paralyzing economic blockade by Rhodesia; and

Argentina (Falklands/Malvinas, 1982)—more acute threat to recovery of lost territory and to honor as the tide of battle pointed to Argentina's humiliating defeat.

Time Pressure. As noted [Table 2.8.B.1, Chap. 2], there was no time pressure in the pre-crisis period of six cases, low salience in the other four; by contrast, it was high in five cases from the beginning of the crisis period and increasingly salient in the other five [Table 3.10.B.1 below]:

the US (Berlin Blockade, 1948)—time was finite but not short; high salience resulted from the imposition of a full-scale Soviet blockade on 24 June 1948, as evident in the US response the next day, the decision to launch an airlift; time pressure declined thereafter;

the USSR (Prague Spring, 1968)—there was growing awareness among Soviet decision-makers of a deadline for decisive military action to contain the Prague Spring virus, as evident in the moving of troops across the Czechoslovak border on 26–27 May and other decisions;

the UK (Munich, 1938)—time became highly salient on 7 September and remained high until the signing of the Munich Agreement at the end of the crisis period;

Germany (Stalingrad, 1942–43)—time pressure was high from the beginning of the crisis period, triggered by the Red Army's counter-offensive at Stalingrad on 19–20 November 1942; it remained acute until the surrender of the Sixth Army on 3 February 1943;

Israel (October-Yom Kippur, 1973)—time was highly salient from the first day of the crisis period (5–6 October), as evident in the large-scale mobilization of Israel's reserves and the (unused) plan for preemption; it remained high until the second ceasefire (26 October) that ended the crisis period;

Syria (Lebanon Civil War I, 1976)—time was salient on the first day of the crisis period, 18 January, with the Maronite Christian victory over Syria's clients at the time; time pressure was accentuated by the growing danger of Lebanon's partition along sectarian lines;

India (India/China Border, 1962)—time was highly salient with the approach of winter, and time pressure became very high with the Chinese attack on 20 October, until the end of the crisis period;

Hungary (Hungarian Uprising, 1956)—time for decisions was short, and pressure became increasingly intense, because of growing demands by Soviet envoys in Budapest;

Zambia (Rhodesia UDI, 1965–66)—time salience increased steadily and was expressed in the making of 13 of the 16 decisions in the crisis period; and

Argentina (Falklands/Malvinas, 1982)—time became highly salient with the dispatch of a British naval task force on 5 April; its intensity increased with the outbreak of war and the near-certainty of military defeat.

War Likelihood. As noted [Table 2.8.B.1, Chap. 2], this was low or very low in eight of the ten cases during the pre-crisis period, and not imminent in Syria's crisis over Lebanon; by contrast, the perceived likelihood of involvement in military hostilities (or war likelihood) in the crisis period was high in four cases, steadily increasing in five others, with one intra-war crisis, Stalingrad [Table 3.10.B.1 below].

the US (Berlin Blockade, 1948)—the perceived likelihood of (inadvertent) war increased sharply with the full Soviet blockade on 24 June and remained high until the crisis period ended on 22 July;

the USSR (Prague Spring, 1968)—the perceived need for Warsaw Pact military intervention increased steadily from the Soviet/ Czechoslovak summit on 5–6 May until the decision on 20 August to crush the Prague Spring by force;

the UK (Munich, 1938)—the expectation of war became acute with the news of 7 September that Hitler planned to invade Czechoslovakia on 19–20 September;

Germany (Stalingrad, 1942–43)—the perception of a grave adverse change in the military balance on the Eastern Front increased steadily as the Red Army's pincers closed around the Sixth Army;

Israel (October-Yom Kippur, 1973)—a very sharp rise in the perception of war likelihood occurred after 4.00 a.m. on 6 October, compared to a Military Intelligence probability estimate of "lower than low" nine hours earlier; and a perceived grave challenge to the military balance existed during the first three days of the war;

Syria (Lebanon Civil War I, 1976)—the defeat of its clients in Beirut and the increased danger of Lebanon's partition sharply increased Syria's perceived likelihood of the need to intervene militarily;

India (India/China Border, 1962)—until 20 October, when war broke out, India's decision-makers perceived a low likelihood of full-scale war; they expected continued Chinese small-scale incursions in NEFA and Ladakh;

Hungary (Hungarian Uprising, 1956)—a Soviet invasion was perceived as possible from the beginning of the crisis, but the likelihood of invasion escalated dramatically on 30 October;

Zambia (Rhodesia UDI, 1965–66)—sub-war hostilities, including commando-style incursions and sporadic air raids from Rhodesia, were perceived as highly likely, but not full-scale war; and

Argentina (Falklands/Malvinas, 1982)—war was perceived as very likely when the Royal Navy task force embarked on 5 April, and inevitable as it approached the disputed islands.

With the completion of the testing of hypotheses on escalation and the presentation of aggregate findings, I turn to the final question on this aspect of twentieth-century crises: how do states *cope* with the peak stress period of a foreign policy crisis?

Coping with Escalation

Once a crisis escalates, the target state must cope with the stress posed by more acute value threat, heightened probability of war, and time constraints on choice. The fundamental question is whether or not diverse states exhibit a shared or dissimilar pattern of coping with escalating stress in an external crisis. As with the pre-crisis period, I will examine the decisions, perceptions and behavior of the ten states that represent the typologies specified earlier: structure, polarity, conflict setting, power level, political regime, economic development, peace/war setting, intensity of violence, region, and time. The same sequence of cases will be followed, beginning with crises for the superpowers, the US (Berlin Blockade) and the USSR (Prague Spring), and ending with Argentina's crisis-war over the Falklands/Malvinas.°

BERLIN BLOCKADE (1948)

The US's crisis period over the Berlin Blockade lasted 28 days. It began on 24 June 1948, when the Soviet Military Command in Germany severed all land communication between West Berlin and the three Western zones. It ended with a crucial decision by President Truman on 22 July, to reject a proposed armed convoy to break the blockade, in favor of an expanded American airlift to the encircled city.

As in the pre-crisis period, there were three key *decision-makers*: President Truman, Secretary of State Marshall and General Clay, the US Military Governor in West Germany. Most of the second echelon from the pre-crisis period continued to serve in the US decisional unit—Defense Secretary Forrestal, Army Secretary Royall, Under-Secretary of State Lovett, and Clay's deputy from the State Department, Murphy, along with Army Under-Secretary Draper.

Of the ten US decisions in the crisis period, four others are worth noting:

Clay's initiative in launching an airlift, on 25 June 1948;

° Readers who are primarily interested in comparative findings on coping with crisis escalation by the ten actors should go directly to "Case Study Findings," pp. 215–226.

Truman's decision the next day to place the airlift on a full-scale, organized footing;

a decision on 15 July to dispatch B-29 bombers to US bases in the UK; and

the decision by the President on 19 July, after extensive consultation, to do whatever was necessary to exercise US rights in Berlin.

The *attitudinal prism* of US decision-makers during the pre-crisis period, shaped by the "Riga axioms," continued into the crisis period: prisms do not change quickly. Thus the Soviet Union was regarded as totalitarian, aggressive, expansionist, an "evil empire" that threatened the most vital interests of the United States and its Western allies. Yet there were changes in perceptions of the values at stake and of Soviet bargaining tactics. In essence, decision-makers in Washington viewed Moscow's behavior as ominous, a high-risk strategy that could lead to war. By contrast, those "in the field," Clay and Murphy, perceived the USSR as risk-averse and almost certain to withdraw from the brink of war if the US maintained and demonstrated its resolve.

Truman's decision to stand firm on Western rights in Berlin at all costs was predicated on the deep-rooted perception of the Soviet Union as a threat to US interests and world peace, to be countered only by unmistakable evidence of US resolve and bargaining from a position of strength. Beyond the Soviet threat to Berlin was the image of a threat to all of Germany and to the democracies of Western Europe. The US President was sensitive to the risk of war and was convinced that the Soviets might well resort to military incidents to test US resolve; but he was also convinced of the high cost of retreat. And it was he who made the decision to stay in Berlin, often in the face of dissenting advice.

Marshall tended to share Truman's image of Soviet intentions, strategy and tactics. For him, too, the blockade was designed to undermine the unification of the three Western zones in Germany. He was concerned about the risks of escalation that, in his view, could not readily be controlled. His approach was pragmatic; but awareness of Soviet conventional military superiority led him to oppose any form of military confrontation to cope with the Berlin Blockade. By contrast, Clay exhibited the hardest line, viewing the Blockade as the most serious threat to Western security interests since Hitler in the late 'thirties; a failure by the US to sustain its resolve in Berlin would be, for him, fraught with the gravest consequences.

The values perceived to be at risk were fundamental: "America's policy in Germany, its entire policy in Europe, and, more broadly, its global position *vis-à-vis* the principal Cold War adversary, particularly its reputation for firmness and resolve" (Shlaim, 1983: 270).[20]

Whereas the US perception of war likelihood during the crisis period was relatively low, the imposition of a full-scale blockade by the Soviets led to a sharp increase in the expectation of war. The dominant view among US decision-makers—Truman, Marshall and their Washington aides—was that war was more likely to occur inadvertently than as a result of deliberate Soviet choice. Clay and Murphy viewed the possibility of war as remote. The Washington image prevailed and, with it, the choice of an airlift over a much more risky armed convoy.

The Soviet blockade also created an awareness of time pressure at the beginning of the US's crisis period. Clay was the most sensitive to the time dimension, as evident in his immediate response, his decision on 25 June to launch the airlift. So too with his rejected proposal of an armed convoy: its prospects for success, in his view, would diminish over time. For the Washington decision-makers, time was finite but not brief. It was highly salient until the airlift was formalized as US government policy. Thereafter the awareness of time constraints on decisions declined.

Among the coping mechanisms of US leaders, a felt need for *information* became apparent with the escalation of the crisis. The primary source of information for Washington was Clay, the US Military Governor in Germany. Information exchange and processing was also institutionalized in a US–UK–France committee. Moreover, normal cable traffic between Washington and London increased and was supplemented by correspondence between Marshall and Foreign Secretary Bevin. Information processing for the senior decision-makers was eased by the creation of the Berlin Group in Washington, headed by Bohlen, an expert on the USSR. In short, increasing stress had profound effects on the volume, type and processing of US information relating to the Berlin Blockade.

The consultative circle became broader and the *consultative* process more intense. In a potential war situation the President relied more on advice from the military, especially the Joint Chiefs of Staff, who strongly advised against an armed convoy. Yet Clay was consulted personally by the President, as were two prominent Republicans, Senator Vandenberg and John Foster Dulles, undoubtedly to broaden the scope of support for risky decisions on Berlin in the crisis period. In general, high stress led to a search for consensus across the spectrum of US politics.

US *decisional forums* varied from the President alone to the National

Security Council, with 20 participants. Most decisions were taken by small, *ad hoc* groups, in contrast to the broadening of the consultative circle under increasing stress. The most significant change during the crisis period was the preeminence of President Truman as the "decision-maker of last resort." Clay and Marshall offered advice and took some initiatives. But the President made the crucial decision to stay in Berlin. In short, decision-making under high stress became centralized under the President, using *ad hoc* forums instead of institutionalized procedures.

Many *alternatives* to an airlift were considered in the crisis period, ranging from planned withdrawal to the use of nuclear weapons. However, the evaluation of options tended to be intuitive rather than analytic, that is, without a careful calculus of costs and benefits, and a ranking, of the various alternatives. Decision-makers were more concerned with short-term goals, particularly the flow of essential supplies to beleaguered West Berlin. Even on the core decision, to stay in Berlin, there is no evidence of a comprehensive assessment of all known options. Rather, the response to the most profound crisis confronting the US since the end of World War II was primarily affective. In sum, as in many other crises, escalation and increasing stress led to improvised procedures in the consideration of alternatives.

PRAGUE SPRING (1968)

The crisis period of the USSR's Prague Spring was triggered by the failure of a Soviet–Czech bilateral summit on 4–5 May 1968 to solve the dispute. It ended on 20 August with the invasion of Czechoslovakia by Warsaw Pact forces and the ouster of the Dubcek reformist regime.

Escalation was evident at once, in the first of 37 Soviet decisions during the crisis period, namely, Decision [henceforth D.] 11, by the Politburo on 5 May, to renew press attacks on the reform movement, to initiate military maneuvers near the Czechoslovak border, to mobilize support from the Soviet bloc and, most ominously, to approve contingency plans for a possible invasion (the first 10 USSR decisions of the Prague Spring Crisis, it will be recalled, were made during the pre-crisis period).

Not all the Soviet decisions were important. Some were declaratory, others implementing, and still others preparation for action to cope with the increasingly acute threat posed by the Czechoslovak aim of "socialism with a human face." The key decisions, other than Decision 11, may be noted briefly:

D. 12, on 7 May, to convene a summit in Moscow the next day, with Poland, the GDR, Hungary and Bulgaria;

D. 13, on the 8th, to accept a greater role for East bloc leaders in managing the crisis over the Prague Spring;

D. 14, on 14–15 May, to press for maneuvers and the stationing of Soviet troops in Czechoslovakia;

D. 15, on 26–27 May, to authorize the dispatch of military units into Czechoslovakia, as a warning signal to an impending meeting of the Czech Communist Party Central Committee;

D. 16, on 6 June, to support the Dubcek leadership within the Czech Communist Party;

D. 21, on 27 June, to protest the publication of a non-Party radical Czech "2000 Words" manifesto;

D. 24, on 10 July, to transfer operational control over any future military action from the Warsaw Pact to the Soviet High Command;

D. 34, on 20–21 July, to demand the immediate stationing of Soviet forces in Czechoslovakia;

D. 35, the same day, to launch a full-scale invasion of Czechoslovakia before 26 August unless Dubcek agreed to end the reform movement and to permit the permanent presence of Soviet forces;

D. 37, on 31 July, to give Dubcek one more chance, and to hold a multilateral Soviet bloc meeting in Bratislava;

D. 39, on 13 August, to demand immediate Czechoslovak fulfillment of commitments undertaken at the Bratislava conclave; and

D. 44, on 17 August, to launch the invasion on the 20th.

The key Soviet *decision-makers* were: Brezhnev, General Secretary of the Communist Party of the Soviet Union; Prime Minister Kosygin; Podgorny, Chairman of the Praesidium of the Supreme Soviet; Suslov, Secretary of the Central Committee; and Shelest, First Secretary of the Ukrainian Central Committee.

Their *images* were similar, but not identical, though most perceived the Prague Spring as a grave threat to the cohesion and stability of the Soviet bloc under Moscow's hegemony. For Brezhnev, the core value at risk was the ideological consensus underlying the Soviet system and its path to socialism. Kosygin perceived a greater threat from a Soviet bloc invasion to crush the Czechoslovak reform movement, especially its adverse effect on East/West detente, a precondition to reform of the Soviet economy, than from the Prague Spring itself. Podgorny shared Brezhnev's concern and was a strong advocate of military intervention.

Suslov was primarily concerned with the threat from Maoist "perversion" of Marxism–Leninism and seemed willing to accept moderate reform in Prague in order to maintain bloc unity against China. And Shelest viewed the Prague Spring as a dangerous precedent for opposition to Moscow domination over his own fiefdom, the Ukraine.

Evidence of escalation from the pre-crisis to the crisis period is abundant. A more acute Soviet perception of *threat to values* at the beginning of May 1968 resulted from several mutually-reinforcing events: calls for a special Czechoslovak Party Congress, designed to provide formal authority for the reform program; growing press attacks on the Soviet Union and the policies of the discredited Novotny leadership; Prague's refusal to hold joint spring maneuvers in Czechoslovakia; and demonstrations on May Day in support of Dubcek.

Time pressure, too, is evident during the crisis period. As noted, the USSR decided on 26–27 May to begin moving troops across the border on the eve of a Czechoslovak Central Committee session, in an effort to prevent the complete ouster of pro-Soviet conservative elements in the party hierarchy. During the summer there was growing awareness in Moscow of a deadline for decisive military intervention, namely, a scheduled meeting of the Slovak Party Congress on 26 August, with the Fourteenth Party Congress, due to convene on 9 September, lurking in the background. Time became increasingly salient, culminating in the decision to invade on 20 August.

In the pre-crisis period there had been no serious consideration of a military option. That began, as noted, only after the failure of the 5–6 May summit; that is, an awareness of likely *involvement in military hostilities* emerged. It gathered momentum during the next three months, intensifying with each failure to overcome the dispute by persuasion. (Apropos, there were 50 speeches, statements and interviews by Soviet Party and military leaders relating to the Prague Spring during the crisis period.) Until the end of July the preferred military option was to prop up party conservatives in Prague with Soviet troops already in Czechoslovakia. Thereafter, decision-makers opted for military invasion. In sum, the three necessary conditions of a crisis period were present from 5 May to 20 August, as the USSR's foreign policy crisis escalated to the point of decisive action.

Coping mechanisms and processes, too, underwent conspicuous change during the Soviet Union's crisis period. A more intense perceived need, and search, for information is apparent in the steady flow of (33) delegations to and from Moscow, especially in the 25 negotiating sessions until 28 July. In all, there was active participation by members of the Politburo, the Central Committee and the military High Command. Additional translators were mobilized by the Soviet Embassy in Prague, with information proceeding swiftly and directly to the highest level decision-makers in Moscow.

The Soviet *consultative circle* included senior military officers and East European leaders from the outset of the Prague Spring Crisis. However, their role and direct participation intensified during the crisis period, the former because of the increasing likelihood of war, the latter at their insistence. The military, in particular, became an active pressure group, with specific aims: to hold maneuvers in Czechoslovakia and to station troops permanently near the latter's frontier with West Germany. And the Warsaw Pact Party/State leaders successfully asserted their claim to consultation because of the implications of the Prague Spring for their own retention of power (e.g., Brezhnev's acceptance on 15 August of the appeal by Hungary's leader, Kadar, to be allowed to mediate between Moscow and Prague). The Soviet leadership also consulted their own Central Committee, formally until late July, informally thereafter.

The Politburo remained the USSR's *decisional forum*, as evident in the decisions cited above. But within that body primary responsibility for crisis management, as noted, rested with Brezhnev, Kosygin, Podgorny, Suslov and Shelest. They participated in many of the negotiating sessions with Czechoslovak and other Warsaw Pact leaders. And they contributed half of the statements and speeches relating to the crisis. The military, too, were active in the public debate but took their lead from the Politburo.

Perhaps the most striking characteristic of Soviet decision-making in the crisis period was the wide range of *alternatives* explored:

> political exhortations and pressure, positive and negative economic incentives, the permanent stationing of troops as a limited and sufficient objective; the use of these troops to support a comeback by Czechoslovak conservative elements; and the disposition of Pact troops in and around Czechoslovakia as a form of minatory diplomacy . . . [along with] the use of third-party intermediaries ranging from [East German leader] Ulbricht to Kadar to [French communist leader] Rochet to Tito . . . (K. Dawisha, 1984: 315).

Although contingency plans for a military invasion seem to have been considered on the first day of the crisis period (D. 11), it was the option of last resort, to be implemented only after all else failed to achieve Soviet objectives.[21]

MUNICH (1938)

Britain's full-scale Munich Crisis was catalyzed by three seemingly unrelated events on 7 September 1938: an editorial in *The Times* advising Prague to yield to Hitler's demand by transferring Sudetenland to Germany; a call for rebellion by the Germans in Czechoslovakia, issued by the Nazi leader in Sudetenland after a conference with Hitler; and a report by the German *chargé d'affaires* in London to Foreign Secretary Halifax that Hitler had decided to invade Czechoslovakia on 19 or 20 September. Together, those events generated three high-stress British perceptions: of a grave *value threat*, the breakdown of peace in Europe; of *time pressure* for decisions, given Hitler's timetable for invasion; and of a *heightened probability* that the UK would become involved in *military hostilities*, almost certainly full-scale war, over "a far away country between people of whom we know nothing" (Chamberlain's derisive comment in a broadcast to the nation on 27 September [1939: 274–276]).

The UK's crisis period was relatively short, from 7 to 30 September, and very intense. There were several indicators of behavioral change from the pre-crisis period, notably: many more decisions (16–3) in a slightly longer time span, 23 days to 14 days; extraordinary channels of information flow; a broadening of the consultative circle, and a somewhat larger role for the full Cabinet in decision-making. I turn now to these dimensions of the UK's decision process relating to the peak of the Munich Crisis.

Many of its decisions are worth noting:

D. 5, on 13 September, by the Inner Cabinet, to send a message to Hitler requesting a personal meeting with Prime Minister Chamberlain;

D. 6, on 15 September, by Chamberlain at Berchtesgaden, the first of three summit meetings, to accept in principle Germany's claim to Sudetenland, a decision endorsed by the Cabinet two days later;

D. 8, on 18 September, by the Inner Cabinet, to dispatch to Czechoslovak President Beneš a set of Anglo-French proposals for Czech capitulation on Sudetenland, that is, a direct transfer of the territory without a plebiscite, along with a qualified guarantee of Czechoslovakia's new boundaries, proposals that were ratified by the Cabinet the next day;

D. 10, on 20 September, by the Inner Cabinet, to warn Prague that its rejection of the Anglo-French proposals would lead to its isolation, to face Germany alone;

D. 12, on 23 September, by the Cabinet, to withdraw its opposition to Czechoslovakia's mobilization of its armed forces;

D. 13, on 25 September, by Chamberlain, to write Hitler urging a Joint Commission on Sudetenland, with an implied threat that Britain would go to war if Czechoslovakia were attacked;

D. 15, on 27 September, by Chamberlain, to set in motion mobilization of the British fleet;

D. 18, on 29 September, by Chamberlain, to sign the Munich Agreement, calling for the complete Czech evacuation of Sudetenland by 10 October; and

D. 19, on 30 September, by Chamberlain, to initiate an Anglo-German Declaration (signed the same day).

The key *decision-makers* remained the Big Four of the UK Cabinet, Chamberlain, Halifax, Hoare and Simon. Their *psychological environment*, too, remained essentially unchanged during the crisis period: their belief that European peace was the highest value to be protected and that this was attainable with "minor" sacrifices by a small people in Central Europe; an intuitive sense that Hitler could be trusted to honor his commitments; a pervasive fear of war and, especially, of the destructive power of the *Luftwaffe*; and the conviction that Britain was unprepared for war.

These images led to steadily-increasing British pressure on Prague to yield Sudetenland, along with a willingness by London to accept almost all of Hitler's demands. Among the Big Four, only Halifax dissented occasionally from the consensus beliefs, notably at a Cabinet meeting on 25 September, when Chamberlain urged that Prague be pressed to accept the more far-reaching concessions worked out with Hitler at Godesberg. It was not without influence, for that day the Prime Minister, in a message to Hitler, implied that the UK would fight if Czechoslovakia were attacked. (There were other more vocal dissenters in the Cabinet, notably Duff-Cooper and Stanley.)

The three necessary and sufficient conditions of the crisis period —more acute value threat, time constraints and heightened war likelihood—and accompanying high stress were increasingly evident in the statements and actions of UK decision-makers after 7 September 1938, especially during the 72 hours before the signing of the Munich Agreement by Chamberlain, Daladier, Mussolini and Hitler. How then did the UK cope with crisis escalation?

As stress rose there was a felt need for more *information*; and new sources were tapped. For one thing, regular diplomatic transmission increased sharply, from 6.3 messages a day to and from the Foreign Office in London during the pre-crisis period to 26.2 messages a day in the high stress crisis period. There was, too, increased communication with Heads of Government of other major powers: French Premier Daladier visited London on 18–19 and 26 September; there were several exchanges of telegrams between Chamberlain and President Roosevelt; and information was sought from Mussolini as well. Moreover, extraordinary channels were created by Chamberlain's summit strategy—three meetings with Hitler in two weeks, with information about the latter's real intentions in the crisis a fundamental goal. And a special emissary, Horace Wilson, was used to transmit and to uncover information at the height of the crisis, on 26 and 27 September. In short, the volume, range and intensity of information increased markedly during the UK's Munich crisis period.

The *consultative circle*, too, underwent marked change. The almost exclusive reliance on the *ad hoc* Inner Cabinet of the Big Four in the pre-crisis period gave way to the larger, institutional group, the full Cabinet, in the crisis period: there were 8 and 6 meetings, respectively, a ratio of 1.33:1, in the low stress phase, compared to 2 and 8 meetings, a ratio of 1:4, in the high stress phase. Moreover, the range of consultation was broadened, with Anglo-French meetings of political or military leaders on 19, 20, 26 September. There was also extensive communication with members of the Commonwealth, notably Canada and Australia. British diplomatic specialists were consulted in both periods, notably Vansittart, Cadogan and Wilson of the Foreign Office, Henderson in Berlin, Newton in Prague, and Perth in Rome.

As evident in the summary of coping during the crisis period [Table 3.10.C below], Chamberlain remained the preeminent decision-maker, with the Inner Cabinet the most important *decisional forum*. However, the full Cabinet became increasingly influential, its role changing from a decision-ratifying body to a decision-influencing and, in some instances, a decision-making body: Chamberlain's dominance and the centrality of the Inner Cabinet declined conspicuously during the peak stress phase, from 24–30 September.

With rising stress, from 7 to 21 September, the search for and evaluation of *alternatives* increased as well. Noteworthy were the Anglo-German cooperation option, adopted by Chamberlain as a summit strategy and operationalized at Berchtesgaden and, later, at Godesberg and Munich; and the Anglo-French cooperation option, expressed in their Joint Proposals of 18 September. During the peak stress stage, in the last week of September, other options were considered and adopted: to signal Britain's intention to stand by France and to support Czechoslovakia if it were invaded by Germany, following a meeting with the French on 25 September; a "timetable" alternative to Hitler's demands at Godesberg; mobilization of the navy; and the use of Mussolini as a mediator to avert a war, all on the 27th.

In sum, the UK's Munich crisis period reveals sharp changes in British behavior under the impact of higher stress: it affected information search, flow and processing, the consultation process, the decisional forums, and the consideration of alternatives.[22]

STALINGRAD (1942–43)

The escalation of Germany's Stalingrad Crisis was triggered by a massive Soviet counter-offensive north and south of the besieged city on 19–20 November 1942. Although the attack *per se* was not a surprise, its scope and intensity were not anticipated by the *Führer* Headquarters or the German High Command.

Hitler remained the sole *decision-maker* throughout the crisis period, and his Daily Conferences continued to be the forum in which decisions crystallized. But all required his approval. And many, including minute operational orders, were initiated by him.

As in the pre-crisis period there was only one German strategic decision: on 22 November, Hitler ordered the Sixth Army to withdraw eastward into Stalingrad, not westward out of the Soviet encirclement. The decision was made, as so often, against the clear advice of his generals, in this case, Zeitzler, Jodl, Field Marshal Manstein, Paulus, who commanded the Sixth Army, and Air Force Chief of Staff Jeschonnek, who challenged Goering's assurance that all the requirements of the beleaguered German troops could be met by an airlift. There were also many tactical and implementing decisions relating to the Battle of Stalingrad and, especially, the fate of the Sixth Army: 16 in the last 10 days of November 1942; 32 in December; 17 in January 1943; and 1 in the first two days of February, a total of 66 such decisions.[23]

The most important of these was a decision on 9 December to attempt to relieve the Sixth Army, beginning on the 11th or 12th, for the besiegers had become the besieged. Hitler's behavior during that 12-day episode clearly reveals the adverse effects of escalating stress on crisis decision-making. On the 13th he avoided a decision on the withdrawal of Army Group A from its precarious position deep in the

Caucasus. Requests for an attempted breakout of the Sixth Army from its encirclement were rejected on the 17th, 19th and 22nd. An utterly contradictory decision was made on the 21st, authorizing the Sixth Army to break out, provided it could still hold Stalingrad! And on the 23rd the relief effort was abandoned.

In January 1943 the drama of Germany's most disastrous single defeat in World War II moved towards its *dénouement*. Yet Hitler could not conceive of the "loss" of Stalingrad. And his obsession extended to a persistent refusal, to the bitter end, to permit the Sixth Army to surrender. That month, he rejected Soviet surrender terms on the 9th, Paulus's requests on the 22nd and 23rd to negotiate surrender, and a plea to make a final attempt to break out or fly out senior officers, on the 24th. In an empty gesture, Hitler decided to promote 118 senior German officers at Stalingrad, on 31 January, three days before the final surrender.

The escalation of Germany's Stalingrad Crisis, following the Soviet counter-offensive, was reflected in far more acute *value threats* than in the pre-crisis period. One was high and steadily increasing casualties, with the annihilation of 20 German divisions a distinct possibility. (It was to be made certain by Hitler's stubborn and foolhardy and, some might argue, irrational decisions.) Another was the danger that Army Group A would be trapped and destroyed in the Caucasus. And, thirdly, the most important for Hitler, was the threat to his image of German military invincibility, especially against a foe regarded as inferior.

Time became increasingly salient from 20 November 1942 onwards, both to extricate the Sixth Army from the tightening vise of the Red Army and to achieve the orderly withdrawal of Army Group A from the Caucasus. The military were acutely aware of time constraints; Hitler was not—never in the case of Stalingrad, and belatedly regarding the fate of Army Group A.

As for the perception of a likely *adverse shift in the military balance*, there is one compelling indicator of awareness by Hitler's military advisors: they made 11 requests for authority to attempt a breakout from the counter-siege at Stalingrad, between 22 November 1942, barely two days after the Soviet assault, and 30 January 1943, three days before the end. On three occasions they sought permission to negotiate a surrender. All fell on deaf ears. The generals, at least, were aware that the impending destruction of one German army, part of another, and four armies of Germany's allies would have far-reaching implications for morale in the *Wehrmacht* and for its capability to resist multiple invasions by the Anglo-American-Soviet Grand Alliance, some already initiated, others planned. Their correct perception was soon to become a reality. Hitler's misperception would lead to the collapse of Germany, its occupation, and its partition for 45 years.

As for coping mechanisms and processes, the flow of *information* to and from the Sixth Army was maintained by radio, after the severance of land links on 22 November 1942. There is no evidence of a felt need for more information by Hitler or the German High Command as the tide of battle worsened and the losses spiralled. The problem was not volume or quality of information, but, rather, Hitler's closed mind to any information or assessment that clashed with his definition of the situation (e.g., expert evaluations that an airlift to the Sixth Army was doomed; information from the Romanian forces in November about a major buildup of Soviet forces, presaging a counter-offensive; and Rommel's assessment on 28 November that North Africa could not be held against the Anglo-American invasion force). All were rejected or ignored by Hitler.

The *consultative circle* broadened somewhat during Germany's Stalingrad crisis period. Manstein imposed his presence and, ultimately, his view on the need to try to save the Sixth Army; but it was too late. Goering was consulted briefly on the airlift. Rommel's advice to withdraw from North Africa was heard but rejected. Admiral Dönitz, the successor to Raeder as naval commander, was also consulted. But the core consultative group remained the daily meeting at *Führer* Headquarters with a few military advisors. As noted, this also served as the *decisional forum* where Hitler made his Stalingrad and other decisions, sometimes with, often without, their support.

Hitler gave no attention to a possible Soviet counter-attack at Stalingrad, perhaps because he was then preoccupied with North Africa and France: on 5 November 1942 he decided, belatedly, to reinforce Rommel's *Afrika* Corps, a decision that was aborted by the Anglo-American landing in Tunisia two days later; and on 8 November he decided to invade unoccupied France. Nor was an immediate response made to the Soviet offensive between 19 and 22 November, when the advance units of the Red Army pincer movement from north and south first met. Thereafter, several *alternatives* were proposed, all but one were considered, and most were rejected by Hitler:

withdrawal to the west, that is, abandoning the Volga line, proposed by Jodl on the 21st and by Paulus on the 23rd—before the vise encircling the Sixth Army was closed;

withdrawal to the east, that is, holding the Volga line at Stalingrad
—Hitler's ultimate choice on 9 December;

withdrawal to the southwest and linking up with existing German
forces, suggested by Manstein on the 25th; and

a land attack to relieve the Sixth Army, approved by Hitler on 2
December, but unsuccessful.

A related alternative was withdrawal from North Africa, recommended by Rommel; it was rejected by Hitler. And a more far-reaching option, not considered, was to end the war with the Soviet Union; it was proposed by Mussolini on 1 December and by his Foreign Minister on the 18th. Hitler could rarely be moved from his obsession about holding Stalingrad at all costs. On the issue of Army Group A he was slightly more flexible; and it successfully withdrew from its exposed position deep in the Caucasus by late January 1943.

Hitler had failed to cope with escalating stress during the Stalingrad Crisis. By the end of the crisis period Germany had suffered an ignominious defeat, with calamitous losses. The military balance changed irrevocably. And Germany never recovered from the Battle of Stalingrad. It was a, perhaps the, turning point in the European theatre of World War II.

OCTOBER-YOM KIPPUR (1973)

Israel's crisis period encompassed the 30 hours of perceived basic value threat, finite—very short—time, and heightened probability of war, from the morning of 5 October to the outbreak of war at 14.00 (Israel time) the next day, and the entire Yom Kippur War, until the second cease-fire on 26 October. In coping with very high stress, 18 decisions were made. Ten were important:

D. 3 and 4 on the morning of 5 October, to place IDF forces on the highest state of alert and to empower the Prime Minister and the Defense Minister to mobilize all reserves if necessary (the first two Israeli decisions were made in the pre-crisis period);

D. 5 and 6, taken within minutes on the morning of the 6th, not to launch a preemptive military strike against Egypt and Syria, and to order large-scale but less than full mobilization;

D. 11, in the evening of 10 October, to launch a general attack on Syria's Golan Heights;

D. 13, in the afternoon of the 12th, to accept a US-suggested (abortive) cease-fire in place;

D. 14, in the evening of 14 October, to launch a counter-attack across the Suez Canal;

D. 16, at midnight on 21/22 October, to accept a US-USSR call, via the UN Security Council, for a cease-fire;

D. 19, in the afternoon of 26 October, to accept a second cease-fire (that terminated the fighting with Egypt); and

D. 20, the same evening, to yield to US pressure on the issue of supplies to Egypt's encircled Third Army.

The *attitudinal prism* among Israel's decision-makers at the beginning of the crisis period, in fact, until the Egyptian-Syrian attack, was the "Conception," namely, the view that the likelihood of an Arab military strike was "lower than low." The Prime Minister's *images* focused on half a dozen issues: the likelihood of war; the unwisdom of Israeli preemption; the infamy of the attacking Arab states; Israel's aims; the cease-fire; Soviet culpability, and US aid.

Mrs. Meir remained uncertain about the outbreak of war until the early morning of the 6th. She perceived the grave risk of forgoing US aid if Israel preempted. She reaffirmed her image of total Arab responsibility for the absence of peace, which was restated as Israel's primary objective. She perceived and accused the Soviets of major responsibility for the war. And throughout the crisis period she was preoccupied with the need not to alienate the US or, in more positive terms, to ensure a steady and massive flow of arms support.[24]

During the first 30 hours of Israel's Yom Kippur Crisis the *value* perceived to be at risk was peace. In the ensuing days of dramatic escalation, the basic values were human life, due to the sharp increase in casualties, and the IDF's deterrence credibility. Reports at the time notwithstanding, survival was never at stake in the 1973–74 crisis —though the gravity of Israel's military setback during the first 72 hours of the war reportedly led to the near-use of nuclear weapons (Hersh, 1991).

The perceived *probability of war* remained "lower than low" (the phrase used by the IDF's Director of Military Intelligence on the evening of 5 October). It rose traumatically from 4.00 a.m. (Israel time) on the 6th until the Egyptian–Syrian attack that afternoon. And for three days there was grave concern over the adverse military balance, for Egypt had crossed the Suez Canal and had destroyed the Bar-Lev Line, and Syrian forces had come perilously close to Israeli settlements on the Golan Heights, as well as to the hub of Israel's vital National Water Carrier in the North.

Time pressure, totally absent in the pre-crisis period, was evident throughout Israel's crisis period. On the first day it imposed a demand for immediate consideration of both mobilization and preemption. It seriously influenced the Israeli decisions to press forward on the west side of the Canal and to recapture positions on the Golan Heights. And towards the close of the crisis period time salience was reflected in the unsuccessful Israeli pleas to Secretary of State Kissinger to delay the coming into effect of the first cease-fire, on 22 October, and even more, in Israeli awareness of the grave danger of direct Soviet military intervention, on the 24th, if it rejected the second cease-fire.

The coping process, too, differed markedly from the pre-crisis period. The felt need for *information*, from the battlefronts and Washington, became intense with the outbreak of war. Special measures were taken to ensure a flow of reliable information to Mrs. Meir and the Cabinet as quickly as possible, from Defense Minister Dayan, Chief of Staff Elazar and special military advisor Bar-Lev, and from Foreign Minister Eban and Ambassador Dinitz in the US. High stress was also manifested in the exchange of notes between Meir and Nixon three times during the war, her abortive attempt on 9 October to visit the US President, and daily communication with Kissinger, including his visit on the 22nd after arranging a joint superpower call for a cease-fire during an urgent visit to Moscow. In short, not only was the volume of information very high. The flow was also between the highest level decision-makers.

Israel's *consultative circle* increased from the "Kitchen Cabinet" of four to seven available ministers on 5 October, to the full Cabinet of 18 thereafter. Moreover, the escalation of stress led its decision-makers to seek advice from both civil servants and military officers, with special reliance on the latter. Other politicians were ignored.

Among the noteworthy features of Israeli decision-making in the high-stress crisis period was the great variety of *decisional forums*. Six of the 18 decisions were made by the full Cabinet; seven by the Prime Minister in consultation with other ministers and, sometimes, the Chief of Staff, that is, by Mrs. Meir's "Kitchen Cabinet"; two by the General Staff with the Defense Minister; and one each by the Prime Minister and Defense Minister, the two of them with IDF officers, and by the Prime Minister together with a few ministers. The prominent role of the "Kitchen Cabinet" was unique among Israel's crises. And, while the General Staff was consulted frequently, it was not a decision-making unit.

The first two decisions of the crisis period, the alert and authorization to mobilize reserves, were made after a modest cost-benefit analysis. So too were several wartime decisions, for example, to cross the Canal only after weakening Egypt's armored strength. The two strategic decisions on 6 October, hours before the war, one against preemption, the other in favor of large-scale mobilization, were made on the basis of historical legacy, notably the 1967 crisis and war, and intense time pressure. From 8 October onward, the main calculus for decisions on military moves was to save lives and equipment because of heavy losses in the early days. There was continuing reliance on a large group, the Cabinet, to evaluate *alternatives* and make choices. Little attention was given to short-run goals. And there was evidence of premature closure, under the impact of escalating stress.

LEBANON CIVIL WAR I (1975–76)

The pre-crisis period of Syria's initial crisis in the prolonged Lebanon Civil War escalated in January 1976: in the course of renewed heavy fighting between Maronite forces and the leftist Muslim–PLO alliance, the Christians occupied, and expelled the inhabitants of, two Muslim ghettos in Beirut, *al-Karantina* and *al-Maslakh*. Syria, perceiving the imminent collapse of the Muslim-Palestinian alliance and the danger of a *de facto* partition of Lebanon, made its first (strategic) decision of the crisis period, namely,

> D. 4, on 18 January, to deploy in Lebanon the Yarmouk Brigade of the Syrian-controlled Palestine Liberation Army (PLA); (the first three decisions, it will be recalled, were made in the pre-crisis period).

The other six decisions of Syria's crisis period, two of them strategic, four tactical, may be noted briefly:

> D. 5, on 19 January, to dispatch Syria's Foreign Minister, its Chief of Staff and its Chief of the Air Force and National Security to Lebanon to try to arrange a cease-fire;
>
> D. 6, on 15 March, to defend the Lebanese President's palace against an advancing Lebanese Arab Army force by intervening indirectly through Syria-directed PLA and *al-Saiqa* units;
>
> D. 7, on 28 March, to impose an embargo on all supplies to leftist Muslim forces;
>
> D. 8, on 8 April, to warn the leftist Muslims that Syria would invade Lebanon if they did not moderate their intransigence;

D. 9, on 31 May, a strategic decision, to dispatch Syrian army units into Lebanon in an effort to "save Lebanon" by ending the civil war; and

D. 10, on 22 September, another strategic decision, to threaten a direct attack by Syrian army units unless PLO forces withdrew from Mount Lebanon within five days.

These decisions were taken by the nine-member *ad hoc* decision-making Cabinet, which replaced the four-member *ad hoc* decision-making committee in the pre-crisis period. But not all nine persons were participants in all decisions. In addition to President Asad, Foreign Minister Khaddam, Deputy Defense Minister Jamil, and Chief of Staff Shihabi, the *decision-making forum* included Prime Minister Ayyoubi, the Assistant Secretary-General of the ruling *Ba'ath* Party, al-Ahmar, the Assistant Secretary-General of the party's Regional Command, Bajbouj, Air Force Security Head, al-Kholi, and the head of *al-Saiqa*, Mohsen. Thus, as stress escalated, the Party High Commands were more directly involved in decision-making, as was the Air Force and the pro-Syrian component of the PLO.

The *psychological environment* of Syria's decision-makers remained essentially unchanged in the crisis period. Central to their *attitudinal prism* was a conspiracy theory, namely, that the civil war in Lebanon was part of a grand design by "imperialist" and "Zionist" forces to undermine the Arab world's capability to defeat the challenge of Zionism, in particular, to reverse the Arab gains from the 1973 war.

Among the Syrian *images* was a threat to the indivisibility of Syria and Lebanon, with its inevitable spillover effects on the stability and unity of Syria. Specifically, the "confessional" or communal character of Lebanon's civil war—Christian, Muslim, Sunni, Shia, Druze, etc.—posed the danger of polarizing sectarian loyalties in Syria, where the minority Alawi held sway.

Until the end of May 1976 Syria's image of the USSR was positive. Thereafter Soviet condemnation of Syria's direct intervention in Lebanon led to a reciprocal negative perception of the USSR. By contrast, Syria's perception of US hostility, a near-constant in Syria's foreign policy, decreased because of Washington's mediatory role between Syria and its arch-enemy, Israel. Syria's image of the Palestinians was favorable in the crisis period. And of Israel, as almost always, Syria's image was one of extreme hostility.

How did Syria cope with its perception of more acute value threat, pressure of time, and higher likelihood of military hostilities, that is, with the escalation of its Lebanon crisis? The volume of *information* increased, in response to greater felt need. Sources became more diverse—*Ba'ath* members, friendly Palestinians and Syrian soldiers operating in Lebanon, direct telephone communication between Asad and Lebanese politicians, and frequent delegations of Lebanese leaders visiting Damascus. And, with the escalating stress, information was directed to the top of the authority pyramid.

The *consultative circle* varied from the core group of four—Asad, Khaddam, Jamil and Shihabi—to large groups from several élites: the National and Regional Commands of the *Ba'ath* Party; non-*Ba'ath* members of the Progressive National Front; the Minister of Information, and several military and civilian advisors to the President. Thus consultation was confined to the four key *decision-makers* on the road to D. 5–8. At the other extreme, 43 persons were drawn into the consultation process before D. 4, and 41 before D. 9, both strategic decisions. Similarly, the *decisional forum* varied from the original *ad hoc* committee of four, in making D. 5–8, to the *ad hoc* decision-making Cabinet of nine, in making D. 4, 9, 10.

The consideration of *alternatives*, too, varied with the perceived significance of the issue for choice. It was most thorough in arriving at the three strategic decisions of the crisis period. Thus, prior to D. 4, according to Asad himself, the clear options were: not to intervene, at the cost of a near-certain collapse of "the Resistance" (Muslim–Palestinian alliance); and to intervene, at the possible cost of war with Israel. In the case of the even riskier decision to intervene directly with Syrian troops, the decision-makers sought and assessed likely responses from several potential actors, notably Israel and Iraq. The intention to intervene was communicated to the US, indirectly to Israel, via Washington, to several Arab states, Lebanese leaders and the PLO. Only when reassuring responses were forthcoming, especially the signal from Israel—Prime Minister Rabin declared, "Israel is in no hurry to intervene in Lebanon"—was D. 9 formalized on 31 May 1976. A careful evaluation of alternatives was evident, as well, before D. 10 on 28 September 1976 to attack the leftist forces in the mountains around Beirut. By contrast, assessment was perfunctory before the less significant, that is, less costly, Syrian decisions of the crisis period. In short, there was a clear correlation between the likelihood of involvement in military hostilities and the extent of search for, and evaluation of, alternatives.[25]

INDIA/CHINA BORDER (1962)

There were two stages in India's crisis period: pre-war, from 8 September 1962, when Chinese "border guards" crossed the (India-defined) international border at the Thag La Ridge into the North East Frontier Agency (NEFA), until 19 October; and the war, from 20 October to 21 November. Both, especially the latter, exhibited a marked escalation from the leisurely, three-and-a-half year pre-crisis period and onset phase.

During the six-week pre-war sub-phase India made one strategic decision, on 10 or 11 September—to expel the Chinese from the Thag La Ridge area, by force if necessary. Several operational decisions, mostly concerned with the movement of troops to the mountainous terrain, were made between the 11th and the 17th to implement "Operation Leghorn." There was also a responsive political decision on the 18th, agreeing to a Chinese proposal for talks in Beijing, to begin on 15 October. And thereafter, five more tactical decisions were made, with the cumulative effect being to transform India's policy, in Delhi and in NEFA, to a defensive posture. Three of them are worth noting:

on 7–8 October, to avoid the preemptive use of force and to attempt positional maneuver in the disputed area;

on 11 October, to postpone Operation Leghorn indefinitely; and

on 17 October, to hold the Indian positions in and around the Dhola post, in the Thag La Ridge area, through the winter.

India's behavior in the pre-war sub-phase was shaped by an essentially unchanged *attitudinal prism* discussed earlier: first, a belief that the border dispute was primarily a manifestation of China's hostility toward India; second, a conviction that Chinese forces would continue to infiltrate and occupy Indian territory all along their frontier unless met by firm countermeasures; and third, major war was highly unlikely, and India's resolve would lead to talks on the border dispute.

Until war erupted on 20 October 1962 Nehru retained his underlying *image* of war between India and China as virtually impossible. For one thing, he could not perceive a Chinese military strike that was less than a full-scale invasion of India; that is, war between India and China would have to be a "big" war, with the possibility of escalating to a world war, something the superpowers would not permit. For another, if China invaded India, both the US and the USSR would prevent grave damage to India, with the Soviets compelling China to withdraw. As with the flawed Israeli "Conception" of likely Arab behavior in 1973, it was a misperception of historic proportions.[26]

As for the specific *value threat* posed by the Thag La Ridge incident of 8 September, Nehru perceived this as a tactical ploy to compel India to negotiate the NEFA border, as well as the Western Sector in Ladakh, recalling Chou En-lai's implied offer of a barter deal in April 1960. To forestall such a disadvantageous basis of negotiation required India's resolve in NEFA. China would withdraw from the brink.

Defense Minister Krishna Menon, too, perceived full-scale war as unthinkable, an image reinforced by discussions with China's Foreign Minister, Chen Yi, in July 1962. Rather, as always, Pakistan was the primary enemy. Yet Menon did not dissent from Nehru's and the prevailing view that Chinese troops must be compelled to withdraw behind the Thag La Ridge by limited force, if necessary.

The Thag La Ridge incident, *per se*, did not pose a major threat to India: many such incidents had occurred since 1959. However, it was perceived as China's reactivation of the Eastern Sector of the border dispute after three years of quiet. Further, it required an Indian tit-for-tat reaction, lest China interpret India's acquiescence as weakness and accelerate its limited incursions across the vast arc of the Sino/Indian frontier. In that sense, India's perception of threat became more acute after 8 September.

Time, too, became salient: the approach of winter imposed a deadline, late October, for the implementation of Operation Leghorn. And, while a heightened probability of war was nowhere in evidence, India's decision-makers did anticipate a very high likelihood of *involvement in military hostilities* before the border crisis was resolved.

The war sub-phase of India's 1962 crisis period began on 20 October with a simultaneous Chinese attack in NEFA and Ladakh, the Eastern and Western Sectors of their disputed border. The immediate reaction by Nehru and virtually the entire political and military élites of India was shock and surprise, for full-scale war, as noted, was not anticipated. This was followed by a sense of betrayal and, then, painful recognition that the assumptions underlying India's policy towards China and the border conflict were fundamentally flawed.

The best expression of this image shift was Nehru's lament on 25 October, during the lull between the two Chinese offensives: "we were getting out of touch with reality . . . and we were living in an artificial atmosphere of our own creation." There was also dismay at Moscow's pro-China posture during the war sub-phase, which coincided with the Cuban Missile Crisis, and the non-aligned attitude of the non-aligned world, except Egypt and Yugoslavia, to "unprovoked Chinese aggression."

While India's territorial integrity was at risk from the beginning of the crisis period, the perceived threat to territory now became acute. Dramatic defeat on the battlefield added two other important values to those at stake, namely, India's security and its carefully nurtured role as the preeminent non-aligned state.

Among the nine Indian decisions during the war sub-phase, four are noteworthy:

> on 26 October, to transfer troops from the Punjab to NEFA and the Sikkim border, despite Pakistan's openly pro-China stance during the war;
>
> on 28–29 October, to seek emergency military equipment from the US;
>
> on 31 October, to remove Krishna Menon as Defense Minister; and
>
> on 19 November, to request immediate American air cover for Indian cities against possible Chinese bombing.[27]

Nehru was the preeminent decision-maker throughout the crisis period. However, during his lengthy absence abroad (8 September–1 October), tactical decisions were made by an *ad hoc* group of civil servants and military officers under the firm direction of Krishna Menon, even after his departure for the UN General Assembly in New York on 18 September.

During the pre-war sub-phase the felt need for *information* increased, with the Krishna Menon-led committee seeking more information from the Director of the Intelligence Bureau, Mullik, from Army Headquarters, and from the Head of the Eastern Command, General Sen. However, until the war began, new information was filtered through a rigid lens. Information processing was compounded by the problems of overload and the presence of considerable "noise" among the signals of China's intentions and plans *vis-à-vis* the border crisis. During the war there was much greater receptivity to incoming information, including the flow from foreign powers, notably the US.

The daily meetings at the Defense Ministry remained the principal *decisional forum* for day-to-day crisis management throughout the pre-war sub-phase. Only after the outbreak of war, around 24 October, did Nehru begin to chair its sessions. And by that time more basic policy decisions were taken by the Emergency Committee of the Cabinet (formerly its Foreign Affairs Subcommittee), consisting of Nehru, Krishna Menon, Home Minister Shastri, Finance Minister Morarji

Desai (both to become Prime Minister in the post-Nehru era), Planning Minister Nanda, and Krishnamachari, Minister of Economic and Defense Coordination.

The *consultative circle* was broadened under the impact of war: among the politicians, Krishnamachari and, with Menon's decline, Morarji Desai and the new Defense Minister, Chavan; among the civil servants, Foreign Secretary M. J. Desai, and Mullik; and, among the generals, Kaul, Thapar, and his replacement toward the end of the war, Chaudhuri.

Because of their hardshell *attitudinal prism*, Indian decision-makers did not engage in a careful search for, or evaluation of, strategic *alternatives* during the pre-war sub-phase. Even tactical options, notably over Operation Leghorn, were not subject to systematic cost-benefit analysis. This negative approach changed under the initial impact of war. But with the second Chinese offensive in November, a preoccupation with the immediate future shaped India's decisions, as in Nehru's unprecedented appeal for US air cover and implied willingness to enter a military alliance with Washington.

HUNGARIAN UPRISING (1956)

The crisis period for Hungary began as an internal upheaval on 23 October 1956: students in Budapest, defying a ban on demonstrations, led a mass rally of 200,000 to 300,000, formally in support of Polish reformers but in reality the vanguard of a demand for radical political change in Hungary. There were two sub-periods. In the first, from 23 to 29 October, the decision-makers' primary attention and all 13 decisions focused on the internal challenge to the communist regime and to their own power.

Seven were concessions to the revolutionaries, such as rescinding the ban on demonstrations, ousting Geroe as First Secretary and replacing Hegedues as Premier by the reformer, Imre Nagy, admitting opposition parties to the government, and disbanding the AVH (secret police). Five were designed to restore communist control, such as a defiant speech by Geroe, the invitation to Soviet troops to restore order, and the introduction of summary trials and executions.

At the same time, the external dimension of Hungary's national, traumatic crisis was an integral part of the decision-makers' *attitudinal prism*. As old-line communists ruling a small state occupied by Soviet forces, Geroe, Hegedues, Nagy and Kadar could not but be acutely aware that the USSR would actively oppose any potential threat to the communist bloc's cohesion under its hegemony. Ambassador Andropov was Moscow's pro-consul in Budapest; and Khrushchev's dispatch of two senior Praesidium (Politburo) members, Mikoyan and Suslov, to Budapest on 24 October to restore order and communist control, by political means if possible, was the first of many signals that the threat of Soviet military intervention was present from the beginning of the crisis period.

During the second sub-period, from 30 October to 4 November, the source of Hungary's threat perception shifted from a now-supportive mass public to the Soviet Union: Moscow's conciliatory gesture on the 28th, agreeing to withdraw its troops from Budapest, gave way two days later to massive reinforcement of the Soviet occupation force, to implement a Soviet Communist Party Politburo decision on the 30th (unknown to Hungary's reform rulers for several days) to crush the Hungarian Uprising by force. Thus the last nine decisions of Hungary's crisis period focused on the high risk of Soviet military intervention, including a warning to the Soviet High Command to withdraw its forces from Hungary and a threat to proclaim Hungary's neutrality if Soviet troop movements in Hungary continued.

Four of Hungary's 22 crisis period decisions were important:

D. 7, on 23 October, to invite Soviet troops to restore order in Budapest; (D. 1–3 were made in the pre-crisis period);

D. 9, the same day, to appoint communist reform leader Imre Nagy as Prime Minister;

D. 11, on 25 October, to replace Geroe as First Secretary of the Hungarian Workers Party by Kadar (who held that post until 1988); and

D. 21, on 1 November, to proclaim Hungary's neutrality and its exit from the Warsaw Pact.

These decisions, according to Hegedues, emerged "from chaos and confusion." They were "hastily taken, contradictory, ill-considered and impractical," some "on direct orders from Moscow, others under the intense pressure of fighting." The key *decision-makers* were then-First Secretary Geroe, supported by Hegedues, from 23 to 25 October, and Premier Imre Nagy from 26 October to 4 November. (The decisional forums, as will be noted below, were much larger.)

Perceived *value threat* was very high throughout the crisis period: at first, survival of the communist system and the old regime; later, survival of the reform regime and newly-asserted independence from Moscow. *Time pressure*, too, was felt from the outset and with increasing intensity. It was expressed in round-the-clock meetings of the party/state leadership to cope with rapidly-changing dramatic events, in the lack of sleep, and in continuing demands from high-level Soviet envoys—Mikoyan, Suslov and Andropov—and from the mass movement in the streets for immediate decisions to satisfy their conflicting aims. Time was finite—and short. As for the *likelihood of military hostilities* with outside actors, while always possible because of the large Soviet garrisons near the capital and vital Soviet interests, its perception by Hungary's leaders escalated sharply from 30 October onwards.

How did they cope with the multiple challenges posed by escalating stress? There was a steady and increasing flow of *information* to the party and state leaders via several radio stations, telephone, a stream of delegations from an aroused public, and the Soviet Embassy and Politburo envoys. Together they generated a marked increase in the daily rate of communications between Hungary's decision-makers and their diverse constituencies. Moreover, Nagy felt a need for more information and acted accordingly, by appointing a close associate to monitor and classify the inflow of information from diverse sources, and by assuming the foreign affairs portfolio in order to maintain direct contact with Western diplomats. Information was funnelled immediately to the top of the power pyramid, to Nagy during most of the crisis period (as to Geroe in the pre-crisis period and the first two days thereafter, and to Kadar in the end-crisis period). And it was the principal decision-maker, Nagy (or Geroe or Kadar), who shaped the evaluation of the information day by day. In short, the normal channels of information were short-circuited under the impact of rising stress.

The *consultative circle* expanded markedly at the beginning of the crisis period, far beyond the Politburo's 16 members under Geroe. It comprised the Central Committee of the Hungarian Workers Party (79 members), the Party Secretariat (6), the Council of Ministers (28), leaders of the opposition parties (10), Nagy followers (10), and Soviet envoys representing the Kremlin, at varying times, from 40 to 100 persons. As stress increased so too did the frequency of consultation, at party headquarters and, after 26 October, at the parliament building, the new seat of power exercised by the Council of Ministers. So too did the felt need for face-to-face proximity among the decision-makers.

The principal *decisional forum* in the early days of Hungary's crisis period was First Secretary Geroe, invariably supported without dissent by other members of the Politburo gathered at party headquarters. According to Hegedues, it was "an amorphous body, Central Committee, Politburo, Presidential Council and Council of Ministers at one and the same time."[28] And throughout, the role of the individual leader, first Geroe and then Nagy, was decisive. There was a felt need for effective leadership and a willingness to acquiesce in the leader's decisions. Dissent was rarely expressed in the high-level meetings, e.g., over the disbanding of the secret police, and the inclusion of opposition parties in a new Cabinet. After the 26th the Council of Ministers made the key decisions, with Premier Nagy the central figure in the decision-making process. The key institutional body, from 30 October onwards, was an Inner Cabinet acting in the name of the Council of Ministers.

While the sessions at party and, later, government headquarters were frequent, lengthy and continuous, there was no systematic search for or evaluation of *alternatives*. Daily, often more frequently, decisions were dictated by the demands of the moment, as the party and governmental élites struggled to survive in the face of massive pressure from within and outside Hungary, from supporters and critics, friends and enemies simultaneously. At the outset, the options took the form of a simple dichotomy: to use force against, or to make concessions to, rebellion in the streets. For Geroe, the options of a multi-party system or withdrawal from the Warsaw Pact or Hungary's neutrality were beyond his rigid belief system. And, while Nagy was more open-minded, he did not seriously consider inviting Western military intervention or even military resistance to the Soviet invasion. Geroe followed the well-established Stalinist path of repression, without assessing the available information, possible consequences or the feasibility of alternatives. Nagy pursued a path of verbal innovation combined with caution in internationalizing the escalating conflict with Hungary's communist patron. Choices tended to be arrived at instinctively.

RHODESIA UDI (1965–66)

The trigger to Zambia's crisis period was a verbal act by the white regime in Salisbury, led by Rhodesia's Prime Minister, Ian Smith, namely, the proclamation of a state of emergency on 5 November 1965. Although justified as a response to a "threat to security," it was perceived by President Kaunda and his colleagues as a prelude to UDI, the long-feared Unilateral Declaration of Independence by Rhodesia from British colonial rule. This event sharply increased Zambia's threat perception—of a hostile and much more powerful neighbor capable of strangling its economy and, therefore, putting its existence as an independent state at risk.

The crisis period lasted from 5 November 1965 to 13 January 1966, with two sub-periods. The first four weeks, until 2 December, were dominated by Zambia's pressure on the UK to adopt a military response to Rhodesia's rebellion. Thereafter, the emphasis was on economic survival, in the form of decisions to cope with Rhodesia's retaliation against UK-imposed sanctions, supported by Zambia, among many other states.

There were 16 Zambian decisions in the crisis period (compared to 14 in the pre-crisis period), seven in the military sub-period, nine concerned with economic measures. The most important are as follows:

D. 15, on 6 November, to warn Smith of the grave consequences of his actions (implemented by Kaunda in a radio speech the next day);

D. 16, on 12 November, to deploy a company of troops at each of the three border crossing points, a symbol of defiance in response to Rhodesia's UDI the previous day;

D. 17, the same day, to introduce limited sanctions by making Rhodesian currency and money orders no longer negotiable for Zambian economic transactions;

D. 18, on 17 November, to press for an immediate airlift of British army and air force units in order to ensure Zambia's continued access to the vital Kariba power installations;

D. 19, on 21 November, to reject an offer of OAU military intervention;[29]

D. 22, between 6 and 12 December, not to comply with an OAU Council of Ministers resolution on the 3rd calling for the severance of diplomatic relations with London if the Rhodesian rebellion were not crushed by 15 December;

D. 24, on 17 December, to approve a UK-initiated, and US-supported, airlift of oil to Zambia and voluntary oil sanctions against Rhodesia; and

D. 30, on 13 January 1966, to cooperate fully with Prime Minister Wilson's "Quick Kill" strategy, specifically, to implement full Zambian sanctions on imports from Rhodesia, except for coal and power.

That Kaunda and his colleagues experienced high stress in the aftermath of UDI is beyond doubt. This was evident in no less than 477 statements expressing perceptions of *value threat* (82% of the total), *likelihood of military hostilities*, and *time constraints* (9% each) in the crisis period. (Parenthetically, as anticipated by the crisis behavior model set out in Chapter 1 [Model II], the concentration on value threats was even higher in the pre- and end-crisis periods, 95% and 91%, respectively.)[30]

Four sets of values were given virtually equal attention in the Zambian statements during the crisis period: economic interests; belief system/ideology; national security, and external support. As for the image of time constraints on Zambian decision-making, an awareness of short time was expressed in—and influenced—13 of the 16 decisions (81%) in the crisis period (compared to 29% and 25% of the pre- and end-crisis decisions). Typical of this perception was Foreign Minister Kapwepwe's warning to the OAU on 3 December 1965: "Time is against us in Zambia." From the outset of its UDI Crisis Zambia was aware of Rhodesia's marked military superiority; but there was no anticipation of military hostilities until the rebellion was proclaimed. And thereafter, Kaunda expected commando-style incursions and possibly sporadic air attacks, rather than full-scale war.

How did Zambia cope with the higher stress of the crisis period? While a quest for *information* is evident in the pre-crisis period, escalation was marked by persistent complaints of its inadequacy. "Our queries are met with a conspiracy of silence," was a frequent lament by Kaunda. And that, in turn, increased the stress level. Illustrative of the search for information was the process preceding D. 22, to dissent from the OAU conditional call for the severance of diplomatic relations with the UK. Zambia's decision-makers sought information about: its moral and legal obligations to the OAU; the risk of Zambia's political isolation in Africa; the danger that OAU-inspired sanctions might dissuade Britain from assisting Zambia's quest for alternative outlets to the sea; and the possibility of a dramatic, negative preemptive act by London. Similarly, D. 23, to dispatch goodwill ministerial missions to Moscow and Washington, was partly in search for information about the superpowers' likely future roles in the UDI Crisis. In aggregate data terms, the evidence shows a thorough probe for information prior to 7 of the 16 crisis period decisions, compared to 4 of 14 pre-crisis decisions, that is, 44% and 29%, respectively. And decision-makers were more receptive to new information in the pre-crisis than in the crisis period.

In general, the frequency and scope of *consultation* by Zambia's decision-makers broadened as stress became more intense. Apart from the search for advice, consultation was designed to enlist support for a preferred option—or opposition to an undesired option. Sometimes it took the form of active lobbying, as with the oil airlift decision. At other times Zambia's leaders played an educational role, for example, making

OAU members aware of the risk of an African military solution to the crisis or the danger of diplomatic sanctions against Britain. And on still other occasions it was in search of legitimacy for the option about to be chosen.

Broad consultation is evident in, among other things, the decisional process leading to dissent from the OAU call for diplomatic sanctions against Britain. Kaunda sought support within his parliamentary caucus, the National Council of the governing party, and the Cabinet. He recalled half a dozen ambassadors to African states. And he wrote to the other African Heads of State to justify his preferred option. The consultative circle was multi-layered.

Among the four types of consultative group, the political élite was the most salient throughout, being consulted on virtually all decisions; and it was the principal consultative group in the process leading to 50% of the crisis period decisions (compared to 43% of pre-crisis and none of the end-crisis decisions). Interestingly, as stress increased, the extent of participation by bureaucrats rose from 57% to 75%, and of external interests, from 50% to 87% of the decision processes. Only the corporate élite was virtually ignored—throughout the crisis. Even more striking, the Cabinet was consulted before only 9% of the decisions in the crisis and pre-crisis periods, 14% of the end-crisis decisions.

There were three *decisional forums* during Zambia's UDI crisis period: the President alone; an *ad hoc* group of 3–6 senior ministers, and the Cabinet (12–16 persons). As stress increased so too did Cabinet participation, from 21% of decisional units in the pre-crisis period to 31% in the crisis period. The main reasons for larger, and institutional, forums were Kaunda's commitment to consensus, increasingly evident as stress increased, and his strategy of drawing others into shared responsibility for difficult choices. Cabinet sessions were sometimes *pro forma*; but with rising stress they became longer, acrimonious and more substantive. Yet dissent never threatened ultimate agreement, largely because of Kaunda's preeminent role as the decision-maker of last resort.

The findings on *alternatives* in Zambia's UDI crisis period are mixed. On the one hand, as stress rose the extent of search for options declined—an extensive search, from 36% to 19%, with a moderate search rising from 21% to 31%. One reason was escalating stress. Another was redundancy; that is, the same issues kept recurring—OAU military intervention, requiring D. 12, 19 and 33, appeals for British aid, the focus of D. 8, 25 and 30, alternative outlets to the sea, the issue of D. 2, 6, 7, 9, 11, 14, 24, 27 and 28, and demands for British retaliation, the substance of D. 3, 18 and 20. Thus, as the crisis continued, the need for a search for new alternatives declined; most of them had already been uncovered. Nevertheless, the evaluation of alternatives improved under rising stress: thorough evaluation rose from 29% of the pre-crisis decisions to 44% in the crisis period; and combined moderate and thorough assessment rose from 79% to 94% of the decisional tasks. Only in the case of Kaunda's acceptance of Wilson's "Quick Kill" strategy (D. 30) is there evidence of premature closure, a trait generally associated with decision-making in the crisis period.

In sum, rising stress led to a more thorough search for and evaluation of information and alternatives. Perceived policy options narrowed. The "lessons of history" were salient throughout, namely, mistrust of the intentions of the white regime in Rhodesia, and faith in British integrity. Cognitive rigidity increased somewhat; and short-run concerns shaped images and choices. Yet, on the whole, Zambian decision-makers grasped the reality of the challenge posed by UDI with greater insight than their UK patron.

FALKLANDS/MALVINAS (1982)

Argentina's crisis period was triggered by the news that a large Royal Navy task force had set sail from Southampton on 5 April 1982 en route to the South Atlantic. The rapidity and magnitude of the UK response to Buenos Aires' attempt to seize control of the long-disputed Falklands/ Malvinas islands came as a shock to the military junta. It was one of many misperceptions and miscalculations by the Argentine leaders.

As in the pre-crisis period the key *decision-makers* were General Leopoldo Galtieri, Admiral Jorge Anaya and Brigadier Basilio Lami Dozo, the ruling military junta. They made two crucial decisions during the crisis period, which lasted until defeat and surrender on 14 June:

first, to reject a potentially viable peace proposal by Peru's President Belaúnde, on 2 May; and

second, to dispatch military negotiators to the UN on 1 June, with the authority to accept any "honorable settlement."

There was also a tactical decision with far-reaching implications for the future conduct of the war: on 2 May Admiral Anaya recalled the Argentine fleet to port, following the sinking of the *General Belgrano*; that effectively removed the navy from the war with the UK.

Much of Argentina's crisis period was devoted to a search for crisis termination without full-scale war: its decision-makers were unprepared, and they sought to avoid war because they were aware of British naval superiority, even in the South Atlantic zone close to the Argentine heartland. That search took the form of intense mediation efforts: first, by the United States, through Secretary of State Haig's shuttle diplomacy (Washington–Buenos Aires–London) from 8 to 28 April, with several American proposals, all ultimately rejected by Buenos Aires; second, the Peruvian President's promising mediation plan, that appeared to be on the verge of Argentine acceptance when the *General Belgrano* was torpedoed by a British nuclear submarine on 1 May, with 300 Argentine casualties, and British paratroops landed at Port Stanley, Darwin and Goose Green the same day; and third, mediation by the UN Secretary-General from 10 to 21 May. All were of no avail.

To a large extent this was due to the persistence of the core elements of the junta's *attitudinal prism* during Argentina's crisis period. One was the deep-rooted national commitment to the "liberation" of the Malvinas Islands from British colonial rule. Another was the pervasive conception of the military's rightful primacy in Argentine society. And a third was a proud self-image of Argentina as a mature, developed Euro-American state.

As the crisis escalated, however, there were some changes in specific *images*. The most visible was disenchantment with the US, on whose benevolent neutrality or support the junta had counted: "I feel much bitterness towards Reagan, who I thought was my friend," said Galtieri after Washington issued a statement on 30 April supporting the UK. It was another serious misperception. Moreover, his optimism of the pre-crisis period gave way before the end of May to the awareness of certain defeat. By contrast, Admiral Anaya remained optimistic that the British would be defeated by the Argentine Navy, especially its air arm, or by South Atlantic weather.

How did Argentina's decision-makers cope with the rising stress of the crisis period? They tried to offset their military inferiority by enlisting support from other states and organizations: first and foremost from the US, as noted; then from the UN; throughout the crisis period, from Latin American states, via the OAS, which responded with a resolution on 29 May condemning UK behavior and calling upon the US to withdraw its support of the British; and, finally, symbolically, from the Non-Aligned Movement, which Galtieri addressed on 2 June at its Havana meeting under Castro's chairmanship. None of these efforts was successful, except for verbal support from the Americas.

Information processing remained fragmented during the crisis period, an expression of the deep divisions among the Argentine military. Each service sought more information under stress; but pride and jealousy could not overcome the "fief-like structure" of the junta, even with respect to sharing information and intelligence about the enemy's plans. (More serious was the lack of coordination in operational planning and military operations.)

The pattern of *consultation*, too, remained essentially unchanged: at first it was confined to the four principal decision-makers; it was then extended to their respective service councils, each large and disunited. Some civilian leaders were consulted by Galtieri, to the chagrin of the military. But the Cabinet, with a civilian majority, continued to be ignored.

The military also continued to dominate the *decisional forums* during the crisis period. The three-member junta stood at the apex of the decisional pyramid. Galtieri's presidential staff was headed by senior army and navy officers. No decisions could be made without the approval of all the service councils. Even the Foreign Ministry Malvinas Team was dominated by its military members. As one commentator observed perceptively: "The Argentine military establishment is a porous system of baronial powers and privileges and competing, and overlapping, intelligence systems. Its 'three republics' . . . percolate their views from the ranks of colonels and generals and the junta then smooths the positions into policy . . ."[31]

The commitment to "liberating" the Malvinas created a rigid posture toward search for *alternatives* to military action. Yet alternatives were considered as the stress level rose and the outcome, humiliating defeat, became more certain. A compromise proposal, involving mutual withdrawal and the right of self-determination by the islanders, without a precondition of Argentine sovereignty, was considered, seemingly accepted, and then reneged upon, by the junta on 11–12 April. Other proposals were made to Haig on 21 April, based upon lengthy consideration, calling for mutual withdrawal of forces and a UN-supervised transition to Argentine sovereignty by the end of 1982, which London rejected. Most important, serious consideration was given to the Peruvian President's proposal for a cease-fire, mutual withdrawal of forces, and subsequent talks on the future of the islands: but for the sinking of the *General Belgrano* at the same time, it would probably have been accepted by Argentina. After talks at the UN proved fruitless, the crisis escalated to full-scale war, ending with the surrender of Argentine forces on 14 June, the end of Argentina's crisis period. Four days later Galtieri was removed from office.

Escalation/Crisis: Case Study Findings

As with onset/pre-crisis, the findings on the ten case studies in the escalation phase/crisis period take two forms: first, the extent to which they fit the relevant cluster of hypotheses; and second, a comparative analysis of coping during the crisis period, in light of the actor and situational attributes of each case.

The fit of the ten cases is presented in Table 3.9.

Viewed in terms of specific hypotheses and their component parts, the crises from Munich (1938) to Falklands/Malvinas (1982) are as "representative" as in the onset phase/pre-crisis period. The range of "fitness" is very broad: from territorial contiguity, all ten cases [H. 6], and reciprocal or stronger response, all seven cases [H. 3], excluding the three obverse cases—see n.1 to Table 3.9, to internal instability, one case [H. 6], and high major power activity, two cases [H. 2].

Viewed in terms of each case study as a whole, October-Yom Kippur is the best fit, with 20 of the 28 elements. The least representative is Hungarian Uprising, 10. As noted, H. 4 and 5 are not relevant to Lebanon Civil War I because the crisis initiator was a non-state actor; and Berlin Blockade, Munich and Rhodesia UDI were coded for the obverse of H.2, 3 and 5, as specified above. Overall, of the 280 individual elements in the seven hypotheses, the ten cases fit 131 of the 255 reported, relevant elements (51%).[32]

The major findings from the ten case studies of the crisis period are summarized in Tables 3.10.A, 3.10.B.1 and 2, and 3.10.C.

As evident in Table 3.10.A, there is great diversity in the *actor attributes* of the ten states during their crisis period. The *number* of strategic or otherwise significant *decisions* ranges from one in Germany's crisis to 13 for the USSR in the Prague Spring, the second largest gap being two in Argentina's crisis and 10 in Israel's October-Yom Kippur Crisis. The range is even broader for the total number of known strategic, tactical and implementing decisions, 67 for Germany, two for Argentina and seven for Syria, the second largest gap being the USSR (37) and the US in the Berlin Blockade (10).

There is less variation in the number of key *decision-makers*, from one in the crises for Germany, Syria, Hungary and Zambia (Hitler, Asad, Geroe/Nagy and Kaunda) to five in the Soviet Prague Spring Crisis. However, at the other extreme, the largest number of decision-makers on any decision ranged from four in the Stalingrad case (Hitler, Keitel, Jodl and Halder/Zeitzler) to 100 in Hungary's chaotic Uprising

TABLE 3.9 Hypotheses and Case Studies on Crisis Escalation: Findings

Hypotheses on Crisis Escalation	Berlin Blockade 1948	Prague Spring 1968	Munich 1938	Stalingrad 1942	October–Yom Kippur 1973	Lebanon Civil War I 1975	India/China Border 1959–62	Hungarian Uprising 1956	Rhodesia UDI 1965	Falklands/Malvinas 1982
1. Escalation to Full-Scale Crisis (int)°										
polycentric structure	X	X			X	X			X	X
subsystem level					X	X	X		X	X
protracted conflict setting	X	X		X	X		X			X
territorial contiguity	X	X	X	X	X	X	X	X	X	X
more than two crisis actors	X		X		X					
high heterogeneity	X	X	X		X	X			X	X
several issues	X	X	X	X	X			X	X	
2. Escalation through Violence (int)°										
(the conditions in H. 1); and	1		1						1	
authoritarian regime pair		X		X				X		
high power discrepancy		X				X		X		
high major power activity				X	X					X
3. Escalation from No/Low to Severe Violence (int)°										
(the conditions in H. 1 & 2); and	1		1						1	
violent trigger				X			X			X
reciprocal or stronger response		X		X	X	X	X	X		X
4. Escalation to Full-Scale Crisis (fp)†										
initiator	US[2]	Czechoslovakia	Czechoslovakia	USSR	Egypt	non-state actor[3]	PRC	Hungary	Rhodesia	Argentina
authoritarian regime	X	X	X	X	X		X	X	X	X
protracted conflict setting	X		X	X	X		X		X	
favorable power relationship	X			X	X		X	X	X	X
geographic contiguity	X	X	X	X	X	X	X	X	X	X

	USSR	GDR, Poland[4]	Germany	Germany	Israel	Syria	India	USSR	Zambia	UK
increasing internal instability			X	X						X
5. Escalation through Violence (fp)† (conditions in H. 4); and	1			1					1	
initiator receiving military support from major power				X	X		X			
6. Vulnerability to Crisis Escalation (fp)† target:										
not a dominant system actor		X			X	X	X		X	
authoritarian regime	X	X	X	X		X		X	X	
protracted conflict setting	X		X	X	X					X
weaker than initiator	X								X	
territorial contiguity	X	X	X	X	X	X	X	X	X	X
young/new state		X			X	X	X		X	
increasing internal instability		X								
7. Vulnerability to Violent Crisis Escalation (fp)† (conditions in H. 6); and										
target:										
regime – short duration						X			X	X
small territory					X	X			X	

°int = international crisis (system/interactor level)

† fp = foreign policy crisis (actor level)

1. In the Berlin Blockade, Munich and Rhodesia UDI crises there was no violence. Thus H.2, 3 and 5 were coded for the obverse of the dependent variable, i.e., non-violent trigger to escalation, no violence in the escalation phase, and non-violent initiation, along with the obverse for the independent variables: for H.2, democratic regime pair, low major power activity, low power discrepancy, and the obverse of the seven conditions specified in H.1; for H.3, non-violent trigger, weaker response, and the obverse of the 10 conditions specified in H.1 and 2; and for H.5, initiator not receiving military support from a major power, and the obverse of the six conditions specified in H.4. The results are not reported in this table.

2. The initiator of escalation in the Berlin Blockade Crisis was the 'Western Powers'. For this element, the US is designated the initiator.

3. Since the initiator to escalation of Syria's Lebanon Civil War I case was a non-state actor, H.4 and 5 relating to the initiator are not relevant to this coding.

4. In the Prague Spring Crisis, the GDR and Poland were the first states to perceive more acute value threat, time pressure, and heightened probability of war. As such, they are designated the target.

TABLE 3.10.A *Escalation/Crisis: Summary of Case Study Findings: Actor Attributes*

International Crisis	Crisis Actor	No. of Decisions[°]	No. of Decision-Makers[°°]	Attitudinal Prism
Berlin Blockade	US	4 (10)	3 (8)	unchanged – 'Riga Axioms'
Prague Spring	USSR	13 (37)	5 (20)	'Brezhnev Doctrine'
Munich	UK	9 (16)	4 (16)	unchanged – peace highest value, Hitler trustworthy, Czechoslovakia distant
Stalingrad	Germany	1 (67)	1 (4)	unchanged – USSR militarily inferior, Russians inferior 'race', Stalingrad surrender inconceivable
October – Yom Kippur	Israel	10 (18)	4 (18)	unchanged – the 'Conception', initially; then, Arab infamy, Soviet culpability, US friendship
Lebanon Civil War I	Syria	3 (7)	1 (9)	unchanged – 'Imperialist-Zionist conspiracy' against Syria, danger of spillover of Lebanese partition and turmoil to Syria's unity and vital interests
India/China Border	India	5 (19)	2 (6)	unchanged – China hostile, 'forward policy' necessary to prevent infiltration, war unlikely
Hungarian Uprising	Hungary	4 (22)	1 (100)	inadmissibility of internal upheaval, initially; then, certainty of Soviet opposition to reform movement
Rhodesia UDI	Zambia	8 (16)	1 (16)	unchanged – UK trustworthy; Rhodesia's white regime perfidious
Falklands/Malvinas	Argentina	2 (2)	4 (many)	unchanged – Irredentism

[°]The number on the left refers to strategic or tactically significant decisions; the number in brackets indicates the total number of known strategic, tactical and implementing decisions.

[°°]The number on the left refers to the principal decision-makers; the number in brackets indicates the size of the largest decisional forum.

(members of the Politburo, Council of Ministers, etc.), and from the six members of the Emergency Committee of India's Cabinet in the 1962 India/China border war to the full membership of the Soviet Communist Party Politburo (20, including candidate members) in the Prague Spring Crisis, and "many" in the Argentine case (the three military service councils).

The actors' *attitudinal prism*, by contrast, reveals great diversity: the US's "Riga Axioms" in the Berlin Blockade; Israel's "Conception" in October-Yom Kippur; UK appeasement in the Munich Crisis; Germany's denigration of Soviet arms and the Russian people at the Battle of Stalingrad; Syria's conspiracy thesis at the height of the Lebanon Civil War; Zambia's basic trust in British intentions *vis-à-vis* Rhodesia UDI, and Argentina's irredentism over the Malvinas Islands. The "Brezhnev Doctrine" in the Prague Spring Crisis was an innovation, although its essential content characterized Soviet behavior towards clients from 1917 onwards; so too with the initial rejection of internal turmoil by old-guard Hungarian communists in 1956 and their intuitive awareness of active Soviet opposition to any attempt to overthrow Moscow's control.

Among the *situational attributes* (Tables 3.10.B.1 and 2), there is marked variation in all except two of the necessary and sufficient conditions of the crisis period, that is, high or increasing *time salience* in the making of decisions, and the higher-than-normal *likelihood of war*/involvement in military hostilities. Thus many different *triggers* are evident: violent acts, as in the Germany, Syria and India crises; non-violent military acts, as in the US, Israel and Argentina crises; political acts (the USSR, Hungary); and verbal acts (the UK and Zambia).

Values perceived to be at risk, too, were varied: reputation for resolve (the US in the Berlin Blockade) and for military invincibility (Germany and Israel in Stalingrad and October-Yom Kippur, respectively); peace (the UK in Munich and, initially, Israel); regional hegemony (the USSR in the Prague Spring, and Syria in Lebanon's Civil War); territory and non-alignment (India in the India/China Border Crisis); territory and honor (Argentina in the Falklands/Malvinas case); survival of a political regime (Hungary); and economic stability, affecting survival as an independent state (Zambia in Rhodesia UDI).

The *duration* of the crisis period also exhibits diversity. At the extremes were Hungary (less than two weeks) and Syria (eight months). There were three cases whose crisis period lasted from three weeks to a month (the US, Israel and the UK). Four other cases lasted from two to three months (Germany, India, Argentina and Zambia). And the

TABLE 3.10.B.1 *Escalation/Crisis: Summary of Case Study Findings: Situational Attributes – Actor Level*

International Crisis	Crisis Actor	Trigger	Values	Time Pressure	War Likelihood	Duration (days)
Berlin Blockade	US	Full-Scale Soviet Blockade 24 June 1948	Reputation for Resolve	High – until airlift decision	High	28
Prague Spring	USSR	Failure of bilateral Summit 4-5 May 1968	Bloc unity, Soviet hegemony	High	Steadily increasing	107
Munich	UK	Call for rebellion in Sudetenland + report of Hitler invasion plan 7 September 1938	Peace	High	Steadily increasing	23
Stalingrad	Germany	Soviet counter-offensive 19–20 Nov. 1942	Massive casualties, loss of Army Group A, image of *Wehrmacht* invincibility	High	Intra-war	77
October – Yom Kippur	Israel	Shift of Egyptian forces from defensive to offensive posture 4 October 1973	Peace, initially; then, human life and reputation for invincibility	High	Low initially; then very high	22

Lebanon Civil War I	Syria	Christian Lebanese military victory, expelling Muslims from two Beirut areas 18 January 1976	'Greater Syria,' Internal Syrian unity	Increasing salience	Steadily increasing	256
India/China Border	India	Chinese incursion at Thag La Ridge 8 September 1962	Territory, Resolve, National Security, Non-Alignment	Increasing salience	Steadily increasing	75
Hungarian Uprising	Hungary	Student-led demonstration for reform 23 October 1956	Survival of communist system; then, survival of reform regime + independence from Moscow	Increasing salience	Low, first phase; then very high	13
Rhodesia UDI	Zambia	Rhodesia's proclamation of emergency 5 November 1965	Economic Stability; National Security	Increasing salience	Sub-war hostilities anticipated	70
Falklands/Malvinas	Argentina	Dispatch of British Navy task force to South Atlantic, 5 April 1982	Recovery of lost territory, Honor	Increasing salience	Steadily increasing	71

TABLE 3.10.B.2   *Escalation/Crisis: Summary of Case Study Findings:*
Situational Attributes – System Level

International Crisis	System	No. of Actors	Violence
Berlin Blockade	Dominant	4	None
Prague Spring	Subsystem – Central/Eastern Europe	6	Minor
Munich	Dominant	4	None
Stalingrad	Dominant	2	War
October – Yom Kippur	Subsystem – Middle East	5	War
Lebanon Civil War I	Subsystem – Middle East	1	Serious Clashes
India/China Border	Subsystem – South Asia/East Asia	2	War
Hungarian Uprising	Subsystem – Central/Eastern Europe	2	Serious Clashes
Rhodesia UDI	Subsystem – Southern Africa	1	None
Falklands/Malvinas	Subsystem – South America	2	War

USSR's Prague Spring crisis period continued for three and a half months.

The *number of actors* in the international crisis of which the specific foreign policy crisis was a part also varied. As noted, there were two cases with only one crisis actor—Lebanon Civil War I (Syria) and Rhodesia UDI (Zambia), though each perceived an adversarial source of threat, Israel and Rhodesia, respectively; and there were other *involved actors* in these cases. In Stalingrad, the Hungarian Uprising, Falklands/Malvinas and India/China Border the adversaries, the USSR, the USSR, the UK and China, were crisis actors. And there were several multiple-actor cases: Berlin Blockade and Munich four each; October-Yom Kippur five; and Prague Spring, with six actors.

Finally, among the situational attributes, the intensity of *violence* varied. There was no violence in the escalation phase of three cases —the US (Berlin Blockade), the UK (Munich), and Zambia (Rhodesia UDI). There were minor clashes in the USSR's Prague Spring, and serious clashes in two cases, Syria in Lebanon's Civil War, and Hungary in the 1956 Uprising. And full-scale war raged in four crisis periods —Stalingrad, October-Yom Kippur, India/China Border, and Falklands/Malvinas.

Notwithstanding the conspicuous variation in actor and situational attributes, the evidence on coping (Table 3.10.C) reveals a *common response to the challenges posed by crisis escalation*. First, all of the crises except Stalingrad, the only IWC, exhibit a felt need and quest for more *information* by decision-makers experiencing rising stress. For the US in the Berlin Blockade there was an increase in cable traffic, a joint information processing committee with its British and French allies, and the Berlin Group in Washington. In the Prague Spring, a steady flow of delegations to and from Moscow generated a large body of fresh, reliable information to the USSR on the basis of which options were framed and evaluated, and choices made. In the Munich Crisis, extraordinary channels played a notable role in providing British Prime Minister Chamberlain and his colleagues with the necessary information for assessment as a prelude to choice. In Syria's crisis, too, information increased in volume and intensity, with old and new channels in Lebanon contributing to the flow. With slight variations, this was the common information pattern for nine of the ten states during their period of highest stress.

Consultation was broader and, generally, more intense as stress increased. This was true of the role of East European communist leaders and the Soviet military in the decision-making process of the USSR culminating in the crushing of the Prague Spring. The British Inner Cabinet of four consulted the full Cabinet, French leaders, and members of the Commonwealth before making the fateful UK decisions concerning Czechoslovakia in 1938. Prime Minister Meir's "Kitchen Cabinet" of four consulted the full Cabinet of 18 and many others in Israel's October-Yom Kippur crisis period. President Asad broadened the Syrian consultative circle to 43 for some crucial decisions relating to its first crisis in the Lebanon Civil War. And in Hungary's 1956 crisis, from 40 to 100 persons were consulted at the height of the crisis. The only exception was Argentina in the Falklands/Malvinas Crisis.

A similar pattern of enlargement is evident in *decisional forums* during the crisis period. While the President remained the decision-maker of last resort, *ad hoc* groups and the National Security Council were used to make US decisions to cope with the Berlin Blockade. In the UK's Munich Crisis the full Cabinet became an important decisional unit, supplementing the four-member Inner Cabinet. In Israel the Cabinet of 18 tended to replace the "Kitchen Cabinet" as stress increased. In India the Emergency Committee of the Cabinet emerged as the principal decisional forum at the height of the Sino/Indian border war. And in Zambia an *ad hoc* committee of 3–6 senior ministers

TABLE 3.10.C *Escalation/Crisis: Summary of Case Study Findings: Coping Mechanisms*

International Crisis	Crisis Actor	Information	Consultation	Decisional Forum	Alternatives
Berlin Blockade	US	Felt need + quest for more	Broader, more intense	President, NSC, *ad hoc* groups	Planned withdrawal; armed convoy; airlift; nuclear weapons, etc.
Prague Spring	USSR	Felt need + quest for more – via many delegations	Military and East European leaders	Politburo	Political pressure; economic incentives; stationing troops in Czech. to support conservatives; third party intermediaries; military invasion
Munich	UK	Felt need + quest for more; extraordinary channels	Broader – full Cabinet, France, Commonwealth, etc.	Inner Cabinet, Cabinet	Anglo-German cooperation; support Czechoslovakia in war
Stalingrad	Germany	no felt need or quest for more	Broader	*Führer* daily meeting	Withdrawal of 6th Army to west; withdrawal to east; withdrawal to southwest; relief operation, etc.

October – Yom Kippur	Israel	Felt need + quest for more	Broader, more intense	Cabinet, "Kitchen Cabinet", PM + Ministers, Defense Minister + General Staff	Full, large-scale, no mobilization; preemption; many tactical alternatives during war
Lebanon Civil War I	Syria	Felt need + quest for more	Broader (4–43 persons)	ad hoc decision-making Cabinet	To intervene/not to intervene; directly/indirectly
India/China Border	India	Felt need + quest for more	Broader	ad hoc Defense Minister-led committee, then Emergency Committee of Cabinet	None pre-war; then de facto military alliance with US
Hungarian Uprising	Hungary	Felt need + quest for more	Broader (40–100 persons)	First Secretary + Politburo members; then PM + Cabinet members	To use/not to use force against internal upheaval; political versus armed resistance to Soviet troops
Rhodesia UDI	Zambia	Felt need + quest for more	Broader	President; ad hoc/group of 3–6 ministers; Cabinet (12–16)	Search declined; evaluation increased
Falklands/Malvinas	Argentina	Felt need + quest for more	No change	No change	Search unchanged; evaluation increased

became the core decisional group for President Kaunda's response to UDI. Here too Argentina was the exception.

As for *alternatives*, the pervasive trait of the crisis period is extensive search for and careful evaluation of options. The US considered a planned withdrawal, an armed convoy, and the use of nuclear weapons, apart from the airlift, at the height of the Berlin Blockade. The Soviets exhausted an array of options before resorting to military intervention to crush the Prague Spring: political pressure; economic incentives; third party intermediaries, and stationing troops near the capital. Other actors, too, sought and/or considered several options before making difficult choices at the peak of their crises.

In sum, *the crisis period, too, witnessed a common pattern of coping by diverse states* before their crisis entered the deescalation or winding-down stage. Stated differently, the commonality of the phenomenon of crisis overcame the marked differences among these states and in the configuration of their external crises to generate a shared response to escalating and peak stress. As in the pre-crisis period, this ought not to be regarded as a counter-intuitive finding, except for those to whom all crises are, *a priori*, unique events. And the explanation for this shared pattern of crisis management, set forth at the end of Chapter 2, applies to its persistence in the crisis period as well.

CHAPTER 4

Deescalation

UNLIKE the escalation process, the "winding-down" of interstate crisis, that is, deescalation, has been neglected in works on world politics. This is evident in several overviews on crisis. Tanter (1979) focused on crisis anticipation, crisis decision-making, and crisis management (a synonym for coping as used in this book). O. R. Holsti (1979, 1989) concentrated on models of crisis, but not on deescalation *per se*. Hopple and Rossa (1981) reported on descriptive studies, explanatory works, determinants of crisis, and crisis decision-making/management. And M. Haas (1986) presented philosophical alternatives, metaphysical approaches, paradigms of crisis, epistemological aspects, facet theory, and correlates of crisis. On deescalation, Hopple and Rossa noted the shortcoming on deescalation thus:

> Research on the abatement and resolution of international crises is sketchy and decidedly descriptive in nature. The quantitative work ... does not attempt systematically to answer the question of why crises abate.... Research and analysis of crisis warning, forecasting, and management have been dominant; consequently, the empirical base and conceptual foundations for exploring, describing, and explaining crisis resolution are weak (81–82).

Indifference to the winding-down of violent conflict was lamented in a review of the first 11 years of *The Journal of Conflict Resolution* (Converse, 1968: 476–477): "I get the feeling that, for most JCR contributors, once a war happens, it ceases to be interesting." Yet this attitude is not surprising, for scholars, like most policy-makers since the dawn of the nuclear age, have been primarily interested in averting an outbreak of war, with its high costs for people and societies everywhere on a shrinking planet. Once war erupts their interest shifts: for policy-makers, to victory; for scholars, to least disruptive accommodation.

A rare but sparse treatment of crisis termination is to be found in Snyder and Diesing's innovative work on crisis, conflict and system (1977: 18–19). They noted several means of peaceful crisis termination:

yielding by the loser, i.e., the weaker party; explicit negotiation, the most likely path when the adversaries possess approximately equal bargaining power and reliable information; tacit bargaining, used when the parties seek to end a crisis without formally resolving the basic issue in conflict; and fading away. Two alternative conditions of non-violent crisis termination were cited: recognition by the weaker actor of its weakness; or recognition by both parties of the danger of continued confrontation. And, as noted earlier, crises often escalate and "terminate" in war.

A rare analysis of *nuclear* crisis deescalation also merits attention. Davis and Wolf (1992) focused on "behavioral factors," that is, "the mindsets, fears, and perceptions of decision-makers, along with their styles, under stress, for both decision-making and action" (77) in situations without a large-scale nuclear exchange. They developed a cognitive process model of decision-making, with hierarchies of variables and clear decision rules. Their conclusions were that:

> Cognitive processes contribute to . . . "the fog of termination." . . . Negative feelings about opponents . . . can result in dangerous misperceptions of opponent actions. . . . Other common cognitive processes . . . can also seriously impede efforts to terminate. . . . [and] [some] "non-rational" cognitive processes . . . could cancel each other out and others might favor successful termination (100).

Concentrating on non-superpower nuclear crisis deescalation, Martel (1992) cited three deescalatory measures: avoiding an alert of nuclear forces when tension increases and reducing their readiness during a crisis; forgoing actions indicating an increased perception of war; and terminating hostilities that generate pressure to employ nuclear weapons. Deescalatory measures are termed voluntary. They depend on rational actors. And, in essence, they "are an intrinsic part of the thinking that spawned the theories of deterrence and crisis management in the 1950s and 1960s" (217). Deescalatory measures, in short, "are a supremely rational choice, because they provide *a form for thinking about how to terminate a crisis prior to the use of nuclear weapons*" (217, 219–220). Finally, deescalation measures can be useful if four conditions exist: cooperation between the adversaries; agreement on the benefit of termination; a consensus on the avoidance or limited use of nuclear weapons; and agreement by the adversaries that deescalatory measures can help terminate nuclear crises. In sum, the deescalation aspect of interstate crisis has been neglected, a major shortcoming which this chapter is designed to help overcome.

This task is facilitated by the intricate conceptual link between crisis and war, delineated early in this inquiry into twentieth-century crises

[Chap. 1, pp. 6–8 and Fig. 1.1]. In essence, it will be recalled, war is a subset of crisis; that is, all wars are, *ipso facto*, crises, but not all crises escalate to war. Moreover, as noted, war does not eliminate or replace a crisis; rather, crisis is accentuated by war. And further, war can be viewed, *inter alia*, as one of several crisis management techniques—verbal, political, economic, non-violent military, and violent. Given the crisis-war link, war termination may be treated as a surrogate for crisis termination, the end point of crisis deescalation. And fortunately, there has been considerable discussion of war termination. Thus a critique of the "state of the art" on war termination can serve as a prelude to the analysis of crisis deescalation.

War Termination

The task of presenting such a review is complicated by disagreement on the scope of the literature on war termination. Brams and Kilgour (1987: 567) incorrectly termed it "sparse." Fox (1970: 2), Ikle (1971: 151), and Stein (1975: 1) observed, correctly, that it is much smaller than work on the initiation of war and the dynamics of escalation.[1] And, at the other extreme, Handel (1978: 9) exaggerated its volume as "prodigious, if not overwhelming." Yet it is not insubstantial if one includes the first four of his five categories:

(1) normative studies, notably the utopian work of Kant, Abbé St. Pierre, Rousseau and Bentham;

(2) economic explanations of the optimal conditions of war termination (e.g., Keynes, 1920; Boulding, 1946; Mantoux, 1952);

(3) international law treatises, focusing on the formal requirements for cease-fire, armistice, and truce agreements, the legal position of belligerents, the role of third parties, including international organizations in pacific settlement (e.g., Oppenheim-Lauterpacht, 1952; Schwarzenberger, 1968; Stone, 1954);

(4) diplomatic history, that is, abundant in-depth case studies of how wars ended; and

(5) theory of international relations, at three levels, following Waltz (1959): individual (e.g., Nicolson, 1933; George and George, 1964); state (Butow, 1954, 1961; Craig, 1955; Huntington, 1957; Finer, 1962; etc.); and international system (Kecskemeti, 1958; Rapoport, 1960; Fox, 1970; Ikle, 1971).

Almost a decade before Handel's "Critical Survey," Carroll (1969: 295–296) identified five clusters of questions about "How Wars End":

"(1) Questions of definition and classification (of war endings);
(2) Questions of a descriptive or quantitative nature about . . . historical experience;
(3) Questions of an analytical nature about the processes by which wars are brought to an end;
(4) Evaluative questions concerning war outcomes . . . and their consequences; [and]
(5) Questions of policy . . ."

It was Phillipson (1916) who first noted three modes of war termination—cease-fire, conquest, and peace treaty; he added a fourth, unilateral declaration. Stone (1954) added a fifth mode, namely, armistice.[2] On the resolution of international conflicts, as distinct from but encompassing wars, K. J. Holsti (1966: 274–282) specified six modes of outcome that built upon Boulding's (1962) categories:

"(1) avoidance or voluntary withdrawal" (e.g., the USSR's withdrawal of its 1960 demand for a 'troika'-type UN Secretary-Generalship);
"(2) violent conquest";
"(3) forced submission or withdrawal," resulting from a threat to use force;
"(4) compromise";
"(5) award," that is, submission of the conflict to arbitration or adjudication; and
"(6) passive settlement," that is, acquiescence in a new *status quo*, without a formal agreement (e.g., the partition of Korea after World War II).

The dominant view has been that war termination is definitive in substance; that is, wars end in victory/defeat (Calahan, 1944: 18; Kecskemeti, 1958: 9; Coser, 1961: 349). Yet Coser also wrote: "Indeed, most conflicts end in compromises . . ." (352). Seabury and Codevilla (1989) also focused on these two types of war termination, along with "How Wars Start" and "How Wars are Fought." In their colorful language, wars end as a negotiated "happy ending" (compromise), or as one of several variations of defeat/victory—"capitulation," "the peace of the dead" (conquest), "the peace of the prison" (occupation), and "the peace of cultural conquest."

The victory/defeat dichotomy conceals much about outcome: Carroll (1969: 305) discerned no less than 15 meanings accorded to the term "victory." These fall into four categories: victory as interpreted in a military sense; as a relationship between the warring parties; as a relationship between war aims and war outcome; and victory in terms of gains and losses. Whatever the substantive outcome—victory/defeat, stalemate, or compromise, the alternative outcomes used in the ICB Project—war endings, according to Carroll (1969: 298–299), arose from one of the following: piecemeal conquest of territory; withdrawal of forces by one or more parties; dissolution of a belligerent government; oral agreement; political agreement; and extermination or expulsion of the forces of one side or more; that is, war termination occurs with or without formal or informal agreement.

The question, when do wars end, has been subject to diverse interpretations. For Wright (1942: 226), the average duration of 278 wars from 1450 to 1930 was 4.4 years, with variations according to type and period.[3] Coser (1961: 347–348), by contrast, emphasized certain termination "markers," such as the capture of a capital city, that are recognized as salient by both adversaries. Klingberg (1966: 167) came to the conclusion that one could not "predict accurately during a war how long the war will last." And Barringer (1972) viewed war termination as one of six phases in a larger conflict: it occurred when the weaker party perceived the negative balance of forces as likely to continue and when great power intervention in support of the adversary was perceived by at least one of the parties as likely if the war escalated.

The historical evidence on war termination is instructive. According to Wright (1970: 52–53), less than half (137) of the 311 cases of "war in the material sense" from 1480 to 1970 ended formally with a peace treaty. Viewed over the centuries: one third of the wars in the 16th and 17th centuries terminated through a peace treaty, half in the 18th century, two-thirds in the 19th, six-sevenths in the first two decades of the 20th century, declining to half in the inter-World War period, and none thereafter. In sum, a curvilinear pattern is evident for peace treaty outcomes. Focusing on the 20th century, Carroll (1969: 297) reported that, while all but one of the 21 large-scale international wars ended in peace treaties, armistice, truce or cease-fire agreements, only two of 36 civil, revolutionary, and anti-colonial wars ended in an armistice or a cease-fire.

Carroll (1969: 313–315) summed up the diverse views on how and when wars end, with a set of nine variables that shape the decision to continue or terminate a war: war aims; the military situation at the time of choice; morale, or war moods; costs; vulnerability to destruction; potential resources for continued fighting; domestic conditions; external conditions, and available terms of peace. However, she acknowledged that her formulae, based upon these factors, "are purely speculative, vastly oversimplified, and in practice, useless for predictive purposes" (see also Carroll, 1970).

There are several competing hypotheses on why wars end. Richardson (1948; Rapoport, 1957: 282–298) attributed termination to changing war moods that spread like an epidemic, i.e., irrational mass behavior. Wars, in this view, end when a sufficient proportion, half, of the population becomes infected with war weariness.

Kecskemeti (1958, 1970) invoked two "rational" criteria to explain the termination of armed conflict: the principle of "irreversibility" regarding the military outcome—a victory/defeat situation; and the principle of "correspondence between effort and stake," that is, a calculus of the relative importance of costs and benefits. The two "principles" reinforce each other (1970: 105). Wright (1965), too, viewed war termination as a function of calculation, of "costs of . . . hostilities," "world pressures for peace," and "vulnerability (of forces) to destruction." So too did Ikle (1971), arguing that decision-makers engage in a cost-benefit analysis—military gains versus intolerable destructive activity by the enemy.

In that context, a few attempts have been made to apply game theoretic models to explain war termination. Wittman (1979) termed the necessary condition a belief by the adversaries that "agreement [to terminate] makes both sides better off; for each country the expected utility of continuing the war must be less than the expected utility of the settlement" (744). Further, war termination is not an imposed act; it requires the assent of both sides. And, counter-intuitively, his rational actor model indicated that a reduction of hostilities and/or an increase in the likelihood of winning a war may reduce the probability of termination.[4]

Brams and Kilgour (1987) applied two variable-sum games, a Deterrence Game based upon Chicken and a New Deterrence Game—Winding-Down. Their main finding was that, "in principle, winding down in either game is possible. Yet in order not to destabilize the cooperative outcomes . . . , the players must upgrade the level of their retaliatory threats against departures by their opponents from these outcomes." Thus "deescalation cannot be safely pursued without strengthening threats of reprisal if cheating is detected" (568, 570).

Rapoport (1960) distinguished between "gamelike" and "fightlike" wars, whose outcome will depend upon rational and irrational considerations, respectively. And Fox (1970: 1) cited as factors favoring war termination:

> world political pressures for peace, constraints [on the full use of] the coercive forces available, competing high-priority domestic policy objectives, the translation of battlefield results into . . . moderated war objectives [and] the continuous calculus of sacrifices still to be made and gains still to be realized.

Stein (1975) noted that war termination, unlike war initiation, is a reciprocal action, except in cases of unilateral withdrawal (e.g., of PRC forces from NEFA and Ladakh in the 1962 India/China border war [see below]). More important, war termination was linked to the concept of conflict reduction, which was defined as

> that process which facilitates movement toward a relationship of conflict management within cooperation rather than cooperation within conflict. It initiates and reinforces changes in the rules of the game between the participants, as it deescalates the intensity of means used in the dispute and reduces the costs. . . . The object is not the legal but the political termination of hostilities . . . (16–17).

War termination may be followed by renewed escalation, rather than conflict reduction. But it is most likely to be enduring when it is linked to a process of conflict reduction through negotiation of the core issues in dispute.

In a rare foray into termination of nuclear war, Cimbala (1987) related the concepts of conventional war termination, crisis management and coercive diplomacy, and crisis escalation to the problem and possibility of war termination. However, a theory of how nuclear wars end is conspicuously absent.

By contrast, the most imaginative analysis of war termination, as of crisis escalation, is that by Kahn (1970). Consistent with his earlier work: "The possibility of thermonuclear war is here faced and its termination probed, in view of the fact that the missiles for such a war are already in existence and its actuality is therefore not truly 'unthinkable'" (133). In essence, he delineated Six Basic (and Omnipresent) Thermonuclear Threats and 11 Types of War Outcome.

The first threat is Large Escalation or "Eruption," defined as "a sudden move up the 'escalation ladder' to very large attacks," which could result in total destruction of the target (139). The second is a Nuclear Talionic Reprisal, that is, a nuclear tit-for-tat. The third is Exemplary (and/or Reprisal) Attacks, "an equitable response to previous injury or wrong"; this includes all nuclear talionic reprisals, though not all reprisal attacks are talionic (142). The fourth threat is "Noblesse Oblige" (or Potlatch) Response, designed to display how much one cares for a client. The fifth is Competition in Bearing Costs (or "Pain") by the nuclear adversaries. And the sixth is Competition in Risk-Taking, that is, "manipulating the risk of war in order to obtain foreign-policy advantages" (145).

For Kahn, there are both "rational" and "irrational" outcomes to thermonuclear war, which can vary in type, scope and intensity. The 11 Types of War Outcome are the counterpart to the 44 steps on his Escalation Ladder (1965), discussed in Chapter 3. They range from: (1) Unconditional and total victory, and (2) Substantially complete victory, each of which may not be Pyrrhic, to (10) Major and/or substantially complete defeat, and (11) Unconditional and total surrender, each of which may not be Pyrrhic for the opponent. In between are clear but limited success and failure, ambiguous but clear success and failure, and a neutral outcome. Among the forms of outcome, he emphasized a cease-fire, *ad hoc* or conditional, with several possibilities, such as nuclear and conventional cease-fire, and nuclear cease-fire with continued conventional war.

In assessing each of these outcomes, three variables were emphasized by Kahn: political, physical and social-psychological, measured by élan, morale and social disruption. A state may succeed on one of these criteria and fail on one or both of the others. Success or failure is measured by: the level of damage to noncombatants; relative costs to the adversaries; comparison with what would have happened in the absence of a war; and the difference between actual and expected outcome, for example, in World War I, the expectation of a short war followed by unambiguous victory/defeat, compared with the reality of a long, destructive war in which even the victors suffered enormous losses. Despite his emphasis on the distinct possibility of, and the capacity for, coping with limited thermonuclear war, which does not put human survival at risk, Kahn had no illusions about the possibility of the ultimate horror, "spasm war": "Accidents can happen, staffs can disobey orders, misunderstand, or miscalculate; decision-makers can act wildly, irrationally" (147–148). Chilling as this may be, Kahn's focus on thermonuclear war is unique in the war termination literature. Moreover, he situated this extreme type of war in the broad context of crisis, conflict and war, as the highest point in his escalation ladder. He also compelled us to think about how to terminate such a destructive war. And by treating war termination as the end point of deescalation, his work is especially relevant to an analysis of crisis deescalation.

Model of Crisis Deescalation

As noted in the "state of the art" review above, much less attention has been devoted to deescalation than to escalation in the crisis–conflict –war literature. Further, this disparity reflects a preoccupation with the danger of crises getting out of hand. It is also true that deescalation is not the exact opposite of escalation, for almost all crises wind down and terminate, apart from a few that fade, whereas many do not escalate to war (e.g., Berlin Blockade, 1948–49, Cuban Missiles, 1962). At the same time, deescalation, too, has both theoretical and practical relevance.

It is, first, the conceptual counterpart to escalation, the winding-down of crises compared to the spiral process. Moreover, it is an integral part of the crisis phenomenon. Thus a unified model of crisis [Chap. 6 below] would be incomplete without an explanation of accommodation between adversaries leading to termination of an international crisis and, at the actor level, of why and how a state's foreign policy crisis ends.

In policy terms, the decline of disruptive, often violent, interaction among states to a non-crisis norm is a goal of many members of the global system, including major powers and international organizations, as well as crisis actors themselves. All other things being equal, the graver the challenge to an international system, global, dominant or subsystem, the greater the concern of decision-makers.

There are several ways in which this domain of crisis can be analyzed. The most creative thus far has been in terms of bargaining among adversaries leading to deescalation. According to Snyder and Diesing (1977: 195–198), there are three types ("dimensions") of bargaining process: accommodative, coercive, and persuasive:

> The accommodative dimension is the convergence of the "bargaining positions" of the parties toward a settlement, through a sequence of "bids" or proposals for settlement—i.e., demands, offers, concessions. . . .

> Coercive bargaining is the bilateral process of asserting firmness, making threats and warnings, and exerting pressure in various ways to influence the other party to accept one's will or one's latest bid. It includes the threat of harm; in crises, the threat of war. . . .

> Persuasion is akin to coercion in that its aim is to influence the adversary to concede, to accept one's own demands. Unlike coercion, however, it does not involve threatening harm to the other party if he does not concede. . . .

> Both coercive and accommodative moves (threats and concessions) present the adversary with a *choice* between a pair of outcomes, one of which is certain, the other uncertain. . . . Persuasion helps him make these choices to one's own advantage . . .

Thus accommodative bargaining is the deescalation counterpart to coercive bargaining in the escalation phase.

A formal method of analyzing the bargaining process is through game theory. Various typologies of games have been developed to capture the full range and nuances of bargaining by crisis adversaries. Among their nine games, Snyder and Diesing (1977: 41–48, 482) specify four that fit the notion of deescalation, for they encompass the possibility of negotiated compromise that the adversaries prefer to no agreement. Two are mixed motive symmetric games: Chicken (e.g., Berlin Blockade, 1948–49 [Britain, France, the US vs. the USSR]), and Prisoner's Dilemma (Berlin Deadline, 1957–59 [the US vs. the USSR]); both are adversary games in which the parties' interests are sharply opposed, but a negotiated compromise is sought and achieved. Two are asymmetric games: Called Bluff, a misperception game that is Prisoner's Dilemma for one player, Chicken for the adversary (the US [Prisoner's Dilemma] vs. the USSR [Chicken] in Cuban Missiles, 1962); and Bully, in which player A is unwilling to compromise but prefers B's capitulation to its demands rather than war or no agreement (the UK vs. France in the 1898 Fashoda Crisis).[5]

Another valuable typology of bargaining games was specified by Leng (1987: 182–195, building upon Leng and Gochman, 1982, and 1993: Chap. 4), to correspond with six types of "militarized dispute." Three of them fall within the domain of deescalation:

Standoff—both parties are firm; both use threats, which lead to a spiral; but it tapers off because neither wants uncontrolled escalation; they prefer war to surrender but compromise to war (Berlin Wall, 1961);

Dialogue—"Both sides pursue accommodative bargaining strategies either through conciliatory influence attempts by each, or by one party employing an appeasing strategy and the other succumbing to its appeal. The level of escalation is low, while the level of reciprocity is high" (first Moroccan Crisis, 1905–06); and

Prudence—one party is assertive, leading to rapid submission by the other; that is, A escalates conflictive action, B responds with accommodative behavior (Austria *Anschluss*, 1938).[6]

Bargaining is, as noted, one path to the analysis of deescalation. Another is to discover the conditions in which crises are most likely to wind down to a non-crisis norm of interaction. This path examines several themes. Most important, what explains the *process* of deescalation? Further, how long do international crises last and why, that is, what explains their duration? And third, how do crises end, or what explains the form of termination? To these questions I now turn.

As with onset and escalation, the necessary and sufficient conditions of deescalation derive from the general crisis models specified in Chapter 1. The decline of one or more actor perceptions—of value threat, time pressure for choice, and war likelihood—marks the beginning of the end-crisis period. The three perceptual conditions, as noted, are closely intertwined. Escalation to a full-blown crisis requires the presence of all three. However, in the deescalation phase they do not necessarily decline simultaneously or at the same pace. If war becomes less likely, time will be less salient, but value threat may persist.

These actor-level conditions are also inextricably linked to a decrease in their counterpart at the international crisis level—the intensity of disruptive interaction and the consequent challenge posed to the existing structure of the relevant international system(s). Only when perceived value threat, time pressure and war likelihood, disruption, and challenge to stability return to their non-crisis norm is the deescalation process complete; it culminates in crisis termination.

As with onset and escalation, one seeks to explain the factors that are most likely to generate change in the contours of interstate crisis; specifically, from intense disruption to accommodation, along with declining value threat, time pressure and war likelihood, leading to crisis termination. Elements from three variable clusters enter the optimal configuration, as evident in Figure 4.1.[7]

There are interactor attributes, namely, non-protracted conflict setting, power equality, that is, capability, and regime convergence. Also salient to explaining deescalation of an international crisis leading to agreement is one actor attribute—internal instability. And there are four situational attributes: a small number of crisis actors; political and/or economic (low) activity by the major powers; high involvement by the relevant international organization(s), global and/or regional; and reliance by the adversaries on non-violent techniques to manage their crisis.

The rationale for three of these explanatory variables—conflict setting, capability and regime pair—is the obverse of their expected effects in the onset and escalation phases. Suffice it to summarize the argument. A crisis outside of an on-going conflict is not burdened by cumulative hostility and mistrust, thereby reducing a major psychological obstacle to the acceptance of compromise and accommodation by the crisis actors (e.g., the winding-down of an Arab/Israel crisis, compared to the Cod War crises of the 1970s between Iceland and the UK).

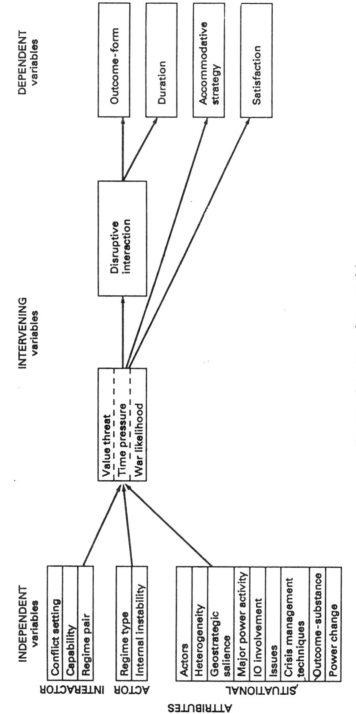

FIG. 4.1 Crisis Deescalation Model

Democratic regimes reduce the likelihood of miscommunication and misunderstanding in the bargaining process because mutual familiarity with, and acceptance of, the formal and tacit rules, principles, norms and institutions of the interstate system facilitate mutual understanding of signals and verbal exchanges between adversaries. And a perception of relatively equal power between adversaries, whether individual states or coalitions, makes compromise more acceptable once escalation has reached its peak, often in war, with its attendant high cost and a likely stalemate, because no or low power discrepancy means that neither is likely to triumph.

As for the number of actors, fewer participants in a crisis means fewer adversarial pairs, a less complex set of issues and less disruptive interaction, even during the escalation phase. These make accommodation less difficult and less time-consuming.

The paradox of major power activity in interstate crisis was also noted in the analysis of escalation [Chap. 3]. On the one hand, interest in system stability encourages behavior to reduce crisis intensity and duration. On the other, commitments to clients tend to foster high activity, that is, military or semi-military intervention, which stimulates escalation. Low (verbal, political, economic) activity, by contrast, generates less intense disruption among adversarial clients and facilitates accommodation.

By contrast, the prospects for deescalation are enhanced by high international organization involvement in managing an interstate crisis. Crisis adversaries are often incapable of winding down their crisis by direct negotiations. Thus the role of a third party is crucial in "saving face," in creating a forum for negotiating a truce, cease-fire, or armistice, in a violent crisis, or an agreement, formal, informal or tacit, to terminate a non-violent crisis: neither adversary needs to initiate accommodation and bear the perceived cost of displaying weakness. Moreover, the IO can provide good offices, conciliation or active mediation to assist accommodation.[8] And it lends the legitimacy of the international system to any agreement reached. In sum, the thrust of IO activity in crises is to incorporate the terms of a solution into a formal document, such as a League of Nations or UN resolution or a report of the results of its good offices or mediation. More generally, IO intervention tends to promote compromise, that is, encourage agreement.

Non-violent crisis management, too, eases the deescalation process. It is less disruptive than violence. It is less likely to induce reciprocal violence by an adversary. And it reduces the time required to achieve accommodation and crisis termination.

A closely-related aspect of deescalation is the duration of crises. During the twentieth century some were very short, one less than a day, the shooting down of a Libyan plane by Israel on 21 February 1973. Others were very long, a year or more (e.g., Berlin Deadline, from 15 December 1957 to 15 September 1959). Clearly, duration is not the product of chance. Thus this discussion will focus on identifying the important factors that determine the length of crises; that is, why some last a long time, while others are very short. The most plausible *a priori* candidate is the idea that duration is a function of intensity; that is, the less intense a crisis, the shorter it is likely to be.

This expectation derives from the effects of a group of factors which, together, measure the intensity of a crisis.[9] The postulated link of each variable to duration will be stated here briefly; the argument assumes that "all other things are equal."

(1) number of actors: few participants generate a less complex set of disruptive interactions; this requires less time for effective bargaining and accommodation between the adversaries;

(2) heterogeneity: fewer differences among crisis adversaries, regarding military capability, economic development, political regime, and culture indicate fewer cleavages and, therefore, the need for less time to achieve mutual accommodation;

(3) geostrategic salience: the more distant an interstate crisis from major power centres and/or the less valuable the natural resources of the crisis region, the easier it will be, and the less time will be required, for the parties to bargain effectively and achieve satisfactory crisis termination;

(4) major power activity: political or economic support for clients engaged in interstate crises, as noted, causes less intense disruption than military activity; this, in turn, facilitates the winding-down process, thereby shortening a crisis;

(5) issues: fewer issues in contention require less complicated value tradeoffs in the course of negotiation; they are also likely to draw fewer actors into an international crisis, with reduced heterogeneity, further easing the process of deescalation; and

(6) violence, which is more disruptive than any other technique of crisis management and is likely to induce reciprocal violence—"violence begets violence"; thus non-violent techniques will reduce the time needed for accommodation.

Each of these situational attributes helps to explain the duration of crises; their combined and, often, reinforcing effects, indicating the intensity of a crisis, is postulated as the optimal predictor of duration. Outcome is a multi-faceted dimension of interstate crisis. One aspect merits attention here. When, that is, under what conditions is an international crisis most likely to terminate in some kind of agreement? The explanatory variables relating to form of outcome were explicated earlier in the analysis of deescalation. One is conflict setting (PC/non-PC). Another is major power activity (high/low). A third is involvement by international organizations (IOs) (high/low). And a fourth is the type of crisis management technique employed by crisis actors (violent/pacific). The reasoning that guided the selection of all of these factors was specified in the discussion of the deescalation process. In essence, it is the exact opposite of the rationale relating to escalation.

Thus far the deescalation model has been presented and tested in terms of interaction, a winding-down of tension between crisis adversaries; and explanations have been offered for its three dimensions —process, duration, and form of outcome. However, like onset and escalation, deescalation must be probed at the actor level as well. Here the focus is on state behavior in the end-crisis period of a foreign policy crisis. Two questions are pertinent. The first links bargaining to prior choice of crisis management technique: why do a state's decision-makers choose to wind down a crisis by adopting an accommodative strategy, with the goal of mutually-acceptable termination? Stated in terms of games discussed earlier, why do they choose some version of Snyder and Diesing's Hero, Leader or Protector, or Leng's Dialogue? The second question focuses on the attitudes to crisis outcome, that is, the conditions in which a state is most likely to be satisfied.

One factor that is likely to induce an accommodative strategy is the type of conflict setting. More precisely, the prospects for this choice will be enhanced if a crisis occurs in a non-PC environment, for the issue(s) in dispute will not be exaggerated by a cumulation of hostility, distrust and fear of the adversary's intention and capability.

A second explanatory variable is power discrepancy. If a state perceives itself or its supportive alliance as militarily superior to its adversary or the adversarial coalition, it is unlikely to adopt an accommodative strategy. If it perceives power equality or inferiority *vis-à-vis* its adversary, such a strategy will be more attractive in pursuit of crisis goals.

Regime type, too, will impinge upon behavior in the end-crisis period. All other things being equal, a democracy will be more positively disposed to winding down a crisis by reliance on pacific techniques of crisis management, with the aim of achieving a mutually-acceptable agreement: both the political system and political culture of a democratic state predispose its decision-makers to follow a non-violent path towards crisis termination.

The presence or absence of domestic stability will also be relevant to the choice of bargaining strategy. The more stable a state, the more willing it will be to accept a compromise agreement in order to end a crisis. And because it is stable it can more readily absorb the cost of concessions in the interest of deescalation and termination.

Still another factor that affects behavior in the end-crisis period is the extent of major power activity in a crisis. If a patron is reluctant to provide military assistance to an ally or client state, the latter will be more inclined to adopt an accommodative strategy; that is, weakness induces compromise and concessions.

Similarly, the degree of IO involvement in the quest for crisis abatement, especially, the extent of IO willingness to support a state's objectives, will influence its choice of crisis management technique: it is more likely to deescalate tension if it perceives IO backing for its claims and aspirations.

As for attitudes to crisis outcomes—when is a crisis actor most likely to be satisfied—the key explanatory variables are: a non-protracted conflict setting; high activity (military support) by a major power; low involvement by the relevant international organization(s); and perception of victory or stalemate (rather than defeat or compromise or stalemate). The logic underlying these expectations may be noted briefly. If a crisis erupts within a protracted conflict, adversaries will (correctly) perceive it as merely an episode in an on-going struggle; whatever the outcome, the larger conflict will continue. Thus, no matter what the specific outcome, it is less likely that an actor would be satisfied.

Moreover, if a major power is militarily active in support of an ally or client, the outcome is likely to be satisfactory to the recipient, for such aid will enhance its capability. As for the role of international organizations, the most likely effect of high involvement would be to promote accommodation among the conflicting parties; therefore, a less satisfying outcome would ensue for any of the protagonists than would be the case if they were left to their own devices. Finally, if an actor perceives full achievement of its goals in a crisis, satisfaction would be more likely than if it perceives defeat, stalemate or compromise. In sum, a combination of these conditions is most likely to generate satisfaction with a crisis outcome.

Hypotheses and Findings on Deescalation

Several expectations about deescalation—process, duration, and outcome—are implied in the model on this domain of crisis. The task now is to frame these as hypotheses and to test them against the evidence of 390 international crises, encompassing 826 foreign policy crises, from the end of 1918 to the end of 1988. Thereafter, the case studies analyzed in earlier chapters will be examined in terms of how decision-makers coped with the challenge of the declining stress, end-crisis period, culminating in diverse outcomes. I begin at the system/interactor level, the deescalation process, *per se*.

Hypothesis 8: *An international crisis is most likely to terminate through a formal or semi-formal agreement when:*
a crisis unfolds in a non-protracted conflict setting;
the adversaries are relatively equal in military power;
there are few adversarial actors;
the major powers are not highly active in the crisis;
the international organization is highly involved in pursuit of pacific
*   settlement; and*
the adversaries rely on non-violent crisis management techniques.

As for the dimension of crisis duration,

Hypothesis 9: *The less intense an international crisis, the shorter it is likely to be; specifically, when there are/is:*
few adversarial actors;
low-level, i.e. non-military, activity by the major powers;
low geostrategic salience;
little heterogeneity among the adversaries;
few issues in contention; and
non-violent crisis management techniques.

What does the evidence from twentieth-century crises indicate about the deescalation process and the duration of this phase?

The findings on deescalation [H. 8] are presented in terms of the proportion of crises that terminate through an agreement (Table 4.1).

In sum, there is *strong* support for one expectation regarding the form of winding down a crisis [H. 8], great power activity, *moderate* support for the number of adversaries, and *modest* support for conflict setting. Only the first of these findings is statistically significant.

TABLE 4.1   *Deescalation of International Crises: Findings on Hypothesis 8*

	Proportion of Crises Terminating in Agreement			
Independent Variable	Category	%	Category	%
Conflict Setting°	PC°°	50	non-PC†[iv]	59
Capability	no/low PD°°°	55	high PD[iv]	63
Number of Actors	one crisis actor	47	four crisis actors[i]	53
	few adversaries	67	five or more adversaries[iv]	52
Major Power Activity	great powers (1918–39) low	73	great powers (1918–39) high[ii]	41
	superpowers (1945–88) low	55	superpowers (1945–88) high[iv]	55
IO Involvement	low	57	high[iv]	53
Crisis Management Techniques	non-violence	55	violence[iv]	56

n = 315 cases (390 minus 73 IWCs and 2 missing data).

See note on IWCs in Table 3.2. The inclusion of cases that occur during a war would contaminate the findings on deescalation, as well as on violent escalation.

°See °° n. to Table 3.2.

°°PC, in all tables where it appears = protracted conflict.

°°°PD, in all tables where it appears = power discrepancy.

†Code for significance test results:
  i $p < 0.001$
  ii $p < 0.05$
  iii $p < 0.10$ (approaching significance)
  iv   not significant

The findings on crisis intensity and duration [H. 9] are presented in terms of the likelihood of shorter crises (Table 4.2).

In sum, all six elements of H. 9 are supported by the evidence from 70 years of crises: three *very strongly*—number of actors, geostrategic salience, and issues; two *strongly*—major power activity (very strong support for the inter-World War great powers), and crisis management techniques; and one *moderately*—heterogeneity. All of these findings, except the last, are statistically significant, two of them—issues and crisis management techniques, and part of a third—superpower activity, highly so (p <0.001).

Two hypotheses at the actor level are also derived from the deescalation model.

TABLE 4.2 *Intensity and Duration of International Crises: Findings on Hypothesis 9*

Independent Variable	Proportion of Short-Duration Crises			
	Category	%	Category	%
Number of Actors°	two	43	four or more[ii]	14
Major Power Activity	great powers (1918–39) low	34	great powers (1918–39) high[ii]	4
	superpowers (1945–88) low	36	superpowers (1945–88) high[i]	24
Geostrategic Salience	minimum	34	maximum[ii]	9
Heterogeneity	none	40	maximum[iv]	28
Issues	one	44	three[i]	12
Crisis Management Techniques	non-violence	39	violence[i]	21

n = 388 cases

°See °° n. to Table 3.2.

†Code for significance test results:
  i   p < 0.001
  ii   p < 0.05
  iii p < 0.10 (approaching significance)
  iv   not significant

Hypothesis 10: *A state is most likely to adopt an accommodative strategy in crisis management when:*
its crisis occurs in a non-protracted conflict setting;
its power is equal or inferior to its adversary;
it is governed by a democratic regime;
it is characterized by domestic stability;
it receives non-military support from a major power; and
its claims are supported by the involved international organization.

The final expectation about the deescalation domain of crisis relates to a participant's attitude to the substantive outcome.

Hypothesis 11: *A crisis actor is most likely to be satisfied with the outcome when:*
its crisis occurs outside an on-going conflict;
it receives military support from a major power;
the relevant international organization is perceived as supportive; and
the actor perceives victory.

What does the evidence of 70 years of foreign policy crises reveal about these hypotheses?

The findings on accommodative strategy [H. 10] are presented in terms of type of primary crisis management technique (Table 4.3).

TABLE 4.3   *Deescalation of Foreign Policy Crises: Findings on Hypothesis 10*

Independent Variable	Proportion of Foreign Policy Crises with Accommodative Strategy (Pacific Crisis Management)			
	Category	%	Category	%
Conflict Setting°	PC	33	non-PC†[i]	38
Capability	low PD	44	high PD[ii]	35
Regime Type	democracy	43	authoritarian[i]	33
Internal Stability	increasing	37	normal[iv]	37
Major Power Activity	great powers (1918–39) low	51	great powers (1918–39) high[i]	40
	superpowers (1945–88) low	34	superpowers (1945–88) high[i]	20
IO Involvement	non-support	31	support for crisis actor[iv]	43

n = 540 cases (826 minus 247 IWCs and 39 missing data).

See notes on IWCs in Tables 3.2 and 4.1.

°See °° n. to Table 3.2.

†Code for significance test results:
  i   p < 0.001
  ii   p < 0.05
  iii   p < 0.10 (approaching significance)
  iv   not significant

In short, five of the expectations about the conditions most likely to lead to a state's adoption of an accommodative strategy are supported by the evidence, one *strong*-to-*moderate*, three *moderately*, one *modestly*. Only the link to internal instability is not supported. All of the supported conditions, except IO involvement, are significant ($p = < 0.001$ or 0.01).

The findings on satisfaction with the outcome [H. 11] are presented in terms of the proportion of crises characterized by crisis actor satisfaction (Table 4.4).

As evident, all four actor-level elements of the hypothesis that specifies the most likely conditions of satisfaction with a foreign policy crisis outcome are supported: one of them *very strongly*—the content of

TABLE 4.4   *Attitude to Crisis Outcome: Findings on Hypothesis 11*

	Proportion of Foreign Policy Crises Satisfaction with Outcome			
Independent Variable	Category	%	Category	%
Conflict Setting°	PC	42	non-PC†[i]	59
Major Power Activity	great powers (1918–39) low	31	great powers (1918–39) high[ii]	46
	superpowers (1945–88) low	50	superpowers (1945–88) high[ii]	69
IO Involvement	non-support	32	support for crisis actor[i]	58
Outcome-Substance	victory	96	defeat, compromise, stalemate[i]	17

n = 589 cases (826 minus 237 missing data)

°See °° n. to Table 3.2.

†Code for significance test results:
  i   p < 0.001
  ii   p < 0.05
  iii p < 0.10 (approaching significance)
  iv   not significant

outcome; one *strongly* — IO involvement; and two *moderately* — major power activity and conflict setting. All four of these positive findings are statistically significant, three of them highly significant (p < 0.001).

As with the pre-crisis and crisis periods, the qualitative evidence from the ten case studies on the end-crisis period is instructive.

The US (Berlin Blockade) — with the US Government's National Security Council (NSC) decision on 22 July 1948 in favor of an expanded airlift and negotiations, US perceptions of harm declined, especially the likelihood of war with the USSR and reduced time pressure on US decisions, with consequent lower stress for decision-makers.

The USSR (Prague Spring) — the successful invasion of Czechoslovakia on 20–21 August 1968 led to an immediate sharp reduction of Soviet perceptions of value threat and the elimination of the time element, and with that less stress.

The UK (Munich) — no end-crisis period, for crisis termination and the abrupt elimination of stress for British decision-makers occurred with the signing of the Four Power Agreement at Munich on 30 September 1938 [see below].

Germany (Stalingrad)—Manstein's counter-offensive in February–March 1943, the recapture of Kharkov, and the forced withdrawal of some Soviet forces to the east of the Donets River overcame the perceived adverse change in the military balance and acute stress resulting from the defeat at Stalingrad.

Israel (October-Yom Kippur)—the end of the fighting with Egypt on 26 October 1973 set in motion a visible decline in all three Israeli perceptions of harm—less threat, less time pressure on decisions, and reduced likelihood of further military hostilities with accompanying casualties.

Syria (Lebanon Civil War I)—its defeat of PLO-Muslim forces near Beirut on 28–30 September 1976 catalyzed reduced threat perception and time constraint and, thereby, the beginning of Syria's end-crisis period, though it did not change its image of a 'Zionist-Imperialist' conspiracy against Syria's vital interests.

India (India/China Border)—China's announcement of a cease-fire and unilateral withdrawal, on 21 November 1962, was perceived by India as the end of military hostilities in the near future, reduced value threat and no more time pressure, heralding the beginning of deescalation.

Hungary (Hungarian Uprising)—with the suppression of the popular uprising by 3 November, the newly-installed Kadar regime correctly perceived less value threat for Hungary, that is, its regime, and the beginning of deescalation of its crisis.

Zambia (Rhodesia UDI)—with a UK verbal commitment, on 13 January 1966, to crush the Rhodesian rebellion, Zambia's decision-makers perceived a sharp reduction in value threat, catalyzing the beginning of deescalation.

Argentina (Falklands/Malvinas)—Argentina's end-crisis period began early in June with a perception that military defeat was imminent and time was irrelevant; value threat remained high, but accommodation to the harsh reality was perceived as inevitable.

Coping with Deescalation

Coping with a foreign policy crisis is not confined to its onset or escalation phases. Even after a crisis peaks, and stress begins to decline, decision-makers are confronted with challenges. If a crisis has been triggered by, or has escalated to, war, how to wind down the violence without sacrificing basic values? If a crisis has been free from violence even in its escalation phase, how to restore non-crisis normalcy with one's crisis adversary(ies)? Thus the task of coping with end-crisis (deescalation) differs from that of the earlier periods. In essence, it is to manage the deescalation process so as to achieve crisis termination and conflict reduction at minimal cost.

In accordance with the underlying thesis of this book, one expects that the behavior of dissimilar states under conditions of varying stress levels will be essentially the same regarding the coping process. This was discovered for the pre-crisis and crisis periods of the ten cases. The same pattern of commonality or shared coping process is also expected in the end-crisis period, for the reasons noted earlier. Thus the question guiding the case studies to follow is: did states as different as the US and the USSR, Zambia and Argentina, etc., exhibit a fundamentally similar coping process; or were coping processes distinctly at variance from one another?

The vast majority of foreign policy crises undergo an end-crisis period and deescalation (Brecher with Geist, 1980: Part III; Brecher and Wilkenfeld, 1989: 23–24, 210–211, 216–218). Among the ten cases examined throughout this volume, only one, the UK's Munich Crisis, terminated with the end of the crisis period, on 30 September 1938, as noted; that is, the three defining perceptual conditions of a foreign policy crisis returned to their non-crisis norm for the UK that day. This is evident from three events.

The initialling of the Munich Agreement by the Four Powers in the early hours of the 30th heralded the transfer of Sudetenland from Czechoslovakia to Germany without resort to force. Thus the primary UK goal during this crisis, the avoidance of war, was assured, at least in the short run. Moreover, the signing of the Anglo-German Declaration by Chamberlain and Hitler the same day pointed to an improvement in relations, another British goal during the Munich Crisis. And most important, the British Prime Minister, the most influential UK decision-maker, perceived the end of the crisis on 30 September. Just after his return from Munich that day he gave the Cabinet the "assurance that 'as things had turned out, he felt that they could safely regard the crisis as ended'" (whereas perceptions of value threat, time pressure and war likelihood were clearly visible at the Munich Conference) (T. Taylor, 1979: 900, as quoted in P. Wilson, 1984: Chap. 3, 24 and n. 25).

In the other nine cases, by contrast, crisis termination was less abrupt. The duration of the deescalation phase varied. So too did its intensity and the crisis outcome. There were also variations in the number of decisions, information processing, consultation, the consideration of alternatives, and the type and size of decisional forums. But all of these cases experienced an end-crisis period that can be differentiated from the escalating crisis period. To these cases of deescalation I now turn. The sequence followed in the analysis of pre-crisis and crisis will be replicated, beginning with the two superpower cases, the US in the Berlin Blockade and the Prague Spring Crisis for the USSR.[*]

BERLIN BLOCKADE (1948–49)

The winding-down of the first US crisis over Berlin did not begin with a change in the external environment or a Soviet conciliatory gesture. Rather, it was an internal American act: on 22 July 1948 President Truman's National Security Council (NSC) rejected the use of force in favor of an expanded airlift and negotiations. The choice of a non-coercive path to crisis resolution set deescalation in motion, for it reduced *time pressure* on US decisions while permitting a search for a solution without a dangerous risk of war or the loss of basic values.

Unlike the time dimension, US *values* were perceived to be at risk throughout the end-crisis period. These were: the symbolic importance of its continued physical presence in the city; its prestige; its reputation for resolve; Western plans to form a West German state; and the unhindered economic recovery of non-communist Western Europe. Only when the USSR offered to lift the blockade without requiring the sacrifice of any of these core US values did threat perception return to the pre-crisis level.

Still another pattern is evident with regard to the US perception of *war likelihood* in the end-crisis period. Generally, it was much lower than in the crisis period. But, when the Soviet Military Governor, Marshal Sokolovsky, announced in early September 1948 that air maneuvers would be held in the Berlin area, the NSC viewed the risk of war as serious. Truman himself thought the world close to war and assured Defense Secretary Forrestal in mid-September that, if necessary, he would order the use of nuclear weapons. This, in fact, was the basis of one of the most crucial US decisions in the end-crisis period: on 16 September the National Security Council instructed the military to plan for the use of nuclear weapons in case of war, with the ultimate decision left to the President (Decision [henceforth D.] 20).

The other 12 US decisions to manage deescalation can be grouped

---

[*] Readers who are interested primarily in comparative findings on how the nine states coped with deescalation should go directly to "Case Study Findings," pp. 272–286.

into several clusters. Two involved the expansion of the airlift (D. 19 and 25, on 7 September and 22 October 1948). Four dealt with a Western approach to the UN to help resolve the crisis (D. 21, 22, 26 and 27, on 21 September, 26 September, 26 October, and 24 December). The currency question was a central topic throughout. Moscow's insistence that the ruble be the sole currency for Berlin was conditionally accepted by Secretary of State Marshall on 3 August 1948, provided that the currency would be subject to quadripartite control (D. 17, the first of the end-crisis period). This was followed by Marshall's rejection of a Soviet draft agreement on currency and the larger Berlin issue, a week later (D. 18).

All the other US decisions focused on direct negotiations between Washington (or the three Western Powers) and Moscow:

D. 23 — on 4 October, Marshall and British Foreign Secretary Bevin agreed to oppose a proposed meeting of the Council of Foreign Ministers as long as the blockade was still in force;

D. 24 — on 5 October, Truman, yielding to Marshall's protest, abandoned his plan to send Chief Justice Vinson on a peace mission to Moscow;

D. 28 — on 1 February 1949, Truman and newly-appointed Secretary of State Acheson agreed to probe, through a secret channel, Stalin's signal on 31 January that the blockade could end without the Western Powers having to terminate the monetary union of their zones in Germany; and

D. 29 — on 29 March, Truman approved the procedure for the Jessup–Malik secret talks.

Those talks led to crisis termination, in the form of the Four Power accord on 5 May 1949, to the effect that all restrictions imposed since 1 March 1948 would be removed on 12 May. The Western *quid pro quo* was acceptance of a Council of Foreign Ministers meeting on 23 May "to consider" the future of Germany and problems relating to Berlin, including the currency question. Thus ended the US end-crisis period, its foreign policy crisis, and the Berlin Blockade international crisis as a whole.

There was no change in the *attitudinal prism* of US decision-makers during the end-crisis period, the essentials of which were discussed in the preceding chapter. For Truman the two key perceptual elements were fear of appeasement (*à la* Munich, 1938) and the projection of an appearance of resolve, strength and firmness. Marshall perceived the Soviets as realistic, rational and pragmatic; he therefore did not perceive war as likely. And Acheson, his successor, placed the highest value on the demonstration of US resolve and the denial of Soviet control over the western zones of Germany at all costs, for the future of Germany was perceived as the key to the outcome of the Cold War.

The principal US *decision-makers* in the end-crisis period were the same as in the crisis period, namely, Truman, Marshall, and Clay, the Military Governor of West Germany, with Acheson succeeding Marshall as Secretary of State in January 1949. Truman's role was less crucial, partly because deescalation had set in, but more important because he was preoccupied with the presidential campaign in the autumn of 1948. Clay's role, too, declined once war receded into the realm of the unlikely. Marshall played the central role from 22 July to the end of 1948, and Acheson thereafter, as diplomacy became the central thrust of US crisis management in the Berlin Blockade Crisis. Others with lesser roles in the decision-making group were Defense Secretary Forrestal, until his retirement in March 1949; Army Secretary Royall; Under-Secretary of State Lovett, until his resignation in January 1949; Bohlen, head of the Berlin Task Force throughout; and Professor Jessup of the Columbia University Law School, who negotiated the final terms of the agreement with Soviet UN Ambassador Malik.

The volume of incoming *information* remained high in the end-crisis period, but its processing was increasingly left to subordinate officials. Marshall and Lovett kept the President informed of major developments; but the President did not "read the cables." And the Secretary of State relied heavily on Bohlen for information processing. The task was complicated by the need to coordinate negotiating steps with London and Paris, with the UK capital as the clearing house for multiple strands of information.

Consultation, too, became very complex. It was coordinated by the US Ambassadors in London and Moscow, the Military Governor in Germany and the UN Representative, as well as between the US Joint Chiefs of Staff and the UK Combined Chiefs of Staff. There were also frequent consultations among the foreign ministers, especially in Paris during the autumn of 1948, among Marshall, Bevin and Schuman. Acheson, too, consulted his British and French counterparts in April 1949. And within the US political system, Republican leaders were consulted, notably Senator Vandenberg and Dulles, the foreign affairs advisor to the Republican presidential candidate, Governor Dewey of New York. As deescalation unfolded, the consultative circle became smaller. And as the danger of war receded, the military became less active in the consultation process. The experts of the State Department bureaucracy became more important. In sum, the reduction of stress led to less involvement of the President and the military, with a return to institutionalized procedures for consultation.

A return to normalcy is also evident in the US *decisional forum*. There, too, the role of the President declined sharply; he was rarely involved, except in the September "war scare." The Secretary of State was the central figure. And the National Security Council was important in enhancing the airlift and in planning for possible war. The Cabinet, as always, was ignored.

As for *alternatives*, a paradox is evident: the search for options declined, and their evaluation became more rigid. The reason is that successful crisis management—the airlift and, to a lesser extent, negotiation from strength, diminished the inducement to search for other alternatives. Moreover, Acheson was less sympathetic than Marshall to the ideas emanating from the State Department's Policy Planning unit and its head, Kennan. The consideration of alternatives—withdrawal or mobilization for war—was undertaken by the Defense Department and the Joint Chiefs of Staff. In short, declining stress in the end-crisis period led to less open-minded and less analytical evaluation of options by decision-makers, but more intense search for options by both diplomatic and military specialists of the US government.[10]

PRAGUE SPRING (1968)

The Prague Spring end-crisis period for the USSR was among the shortest of the ten crises: it began with the invasion by Soviet-led Warsaw Pact forces on the night of 20–21 August and ended on the 27th with the signing of the Moscow Protocol by Czechoslovak leaders. During that week the Politburo of the Soviet Communist Party made four interrelated decisions:

D. 48—on 22 August, it reversed course and decided to negotiate directly with the Czechoslovak leaders in Moscow;

D. 49—on 23 August, it agreed to include Dubcek and Cernik in the negotiations;

D. 50—on 23–24 August, it decided to treat the imprisoned Czechoslovak leaders as the formal representatives of the Czechoslovak party and state; and

D. 51—on 24–25 August, it decided in favor of a formal protocol that would specify the necessary measures to be taken by Prague on the "road to normalization."

There was no change in the *psychological environment* of the Soviet decision-makers, either in their *attitudinal prism* or in their specific *images*: the time span was too brief for a shift from deep-rooted attitudes. Thus, even though there was a sharp change in tactics 48 hours after the invasion, from "military imposition" to "negotiated imposition" (K. Dawisha, 1984: 334), this did not reflect a change in conception or perceptions of the challenge posed by the Prague Spring. This may seem curious, but a stable psychological environment does not preclude a change in tactics: in this case, to negotiate with the Czechoslovak leaders was regarded as the most effective path to "normalization."

Two of the three indicators of end-crisis were evident within hours of the military intervention: Soviet perceptions of both *threat* and *war likelihood* declined as a result of the successful invasion and acquiescence by the Western Powers. Moreover, popular resistance, though widespread, was passive. Yet threat, to Soviet ideological hegemony in eastern Europe, remained, for the Czechoslovak communists had succeeded in convening the Extraordinary Fourteenth Party Congress and had elected a reform-minded Central Committee. Moreover, *time salience* increased. In fact, it was the failure of the pro-Moscow faction in the Czechoslovak Party to assert control in Prague that induced the Soviets to opt for direct negotiations with the Dubcek-led reformists. At the end of the day, with the signing of the Moscow Protocol, the three perceptual conditions had returned to their pre-Prague Spring levels, marking the termination of the Soviet end-crisis period and the international crisis as a whole. While tension persisted for months over conflicting Soviet/Czechoslovak interpretations of the Protocol, it was not of crisis proportions.

Contrary to the expectations of Model II [Chap. 1], the Soviet leaders exhibited a greater felt need for *information* in the end-crisis period. This focused on two related issues: popular reaction to the invasion, and the direction of the Czechoslovak Party in light of the Extraordinary Congress. Enhanced search, in this case, was accompanied by improved quality of information, as a result of the presence in Czechoslovakia of Soviet troops and security forces in large numbers, with most of the Czechoslovak communist leaders in detention. Moreover, information processing during the week of the end-crisis period remained essentially unchanged; that is, the most salient information went directly to the Negotiating Committee of the Politburo.

Nor was there any change in the pattern of *consultation*. The two crucial groups during the crisis period, other than the Soviet party leadership *per se*, namely, the East European leaders and the Soviet military, remained active during the week of invasion and negotiation. The former, in fact, were present in Moscow for the signing of the Protocol, although they did not participate in direct negotiations with the discredited Czechoslovak leadership.

The Politburo of the Soviet Party remained the basic *decisional forum* in the end-crisis period, as evident in the summary of decisions above. However, a core group of five—Brezhnev, Kosygin, Suslov, Podgorny and Ponomarev—played the key role in the negotiations leading to the Moscow Protocol. (It was, in informal terms, the Politburo Negotiating Committee minus Shelest.)

In contrast to the crisis period of the Prague Spring, there was neither a comprehensive search for nor careful consideration of *alternatives*, partly, no doubt, because of the brief time span, one week. Rather, after two days the Soviet decision-makers made a *volte face* from military to diplomatic coercion, in an attempt to meet the challenge posed by the Fourteenth Party Congress. No other options were considered. They did not seem to have a well-thought-out alternative strategy if coercive diplomacy failed to oust the reformists.

In sum, Soviet coping during the end-crisis period, with respect to information, consultation and decisional unit, was a continuation of the much longer and more threatening crisis period. Only the alternatives aspect of the coping process differed in the two periods of the Prague Spring Crisis.[11]

STALINGRAD (1943)

The end-crisis period for Germany in the IWC over Stalingrad can be dated to the surrender of the Sixth Army and the fall of the city on 2 February 1943. The *dénouement* was anticipated for weeks. Moreover, while anguish over the loss continued for months, the acute stress of the final weeks ended abruptly. Further, while Germany had suffered a major defeat, Army Group A had been successfully extricated from the Caucasus, thereby preventing a total collapse on the Southern Front. And the Soviet offensive, which continued until 19 February, achieved no further spectacular encirclement of Axis forces. In fact, Field Marshal Manstein's counter-offensive, from 20 February to 24 March, recaptured Kharkov and forced Soviet forces back across the Donets River.

All this led to a reduced German perception of *value threat*, despite the initial shock to its assumed military superiority over an "inferior" people. Other threats arose during the end-crisis period, notably, possible Allied landings at various peripheries of "Fortress Europe"—Norway, Portugal, Greece; but these did not seem grave in the winter of 1943.

Time pressure, too, declined, as evident in the sharp reduction in the number of German decisions relating to the Stalingrad area of the Eastern Front. There were 13 in the 50 days of the end-crisis period (compared to 67 in the 75 days of the crisis period), that is, one in four days compared to almost one a day. Even more pointed, Hitler's interventions in lesser operational matters declined sharply: from 1.23 per day in the pre-crisis period, rising to 1.66 per day in the crisis period, and dropping to .55 per day in the end-crisis period—none of the last being related to Stalingrad.

As for the perceived military impact, the defeat at Stalingrad dramatized an adverse change at the beginning of the end-crisis period. By the end of the crisis, however, after Manstein's victorious counter-offensive, the balance seemed more favorable once more.

The pattern of Germany's coping during its Stalingrad deescalation phase did not exhibit basic change. The processing of *information* at the *Führer* HQ Daily Conferences continued in force. The flow of information, too, remained unaffected. By mid-February 1943, however, with German forces on the offensive once more, Hitler's interest in information from the Eastern Front declined.

Nor did his preference for minimal *consultation* change except in one noteworthy case: he was more open to Manstein's advice about the scope, goals and direction of his February–March offensive, summoning the Field Marshal to his HQ and visiting him in the field, in February. For the rest, Hitler continued the practice of considering reports and issuing directives, rather than consulting subordinates, military or civilian.

There was one *de facto* change in the *decisional forum*: from 19 February to the end of Manstein's counter-offensive on 25 March, his field HQ became the decisional unit for the southern sector of the Eastern Front. The evidence is stark: from 1 to 24 March 1943 Hitler made only four decisions relating to that Front, only one of these to the southern sector. There was also an attempt to reduce Hitler's dominant influence over operational decisions by persuading him to appoint a Commander-in-Chief East—there was one for the Western Front and another for the Southern Front—but Hitler did not yield; and the senior field commanders did not press the issue. He remained the preeminent, virtually the sole, decision-maker throughout the Stalingrad end-crisis period.

As for *alternatives*, there were only two operational questions, both noted above, on which options were considered before decisions were made. One was whether to stand fast, as at Stalingrad, or to yield territory, with Hitler finally accepting Manstein's case in favor of flexibility. On the other, whether or not to appoint a Commander-in-Chief of the Eastern Front, he refused. In short, the end-crisis period of the Stalingrad Crisis exhibits German perceptions of declining threat, time pressure and adverse change in the military balance, and lower stress, but few changes in the pattern of coping.[12]

OCTOBER-YOM KIPPUR (1973–74)

Large-scale fighting in the Sinai Desert ended on 26 October 1973, with the coming into effect of the second cease-fire. That event, following the avoidance of nuclear confrontation between the two superpowers on the 24th and 25th, set in motion a decline in Israel's level of *threat* perception and in its decision-makers' image of *time pressure* for decisions; that is, it marked the beginning of Israel's end-crisis period and, with it, the deescalation phase of the Egypt/Israel segment of the October-Yom Kippur Crisis in which Egypt, Israel, Syria, the US, and the USSR were crisis actors.

The cease-fire on 26 October seemed precarious, particularly in light of the fate of its predecessor four days earlier. Egypt was determined to save its encircled Third Army from destruction. Israel insisted upon an immediate exchange of prisoners. And the OPEC oil embargo was creating growing fear in Western Europe and Japan. In that setting, Israel's Cabinet, on 30 October, authorized Prime Minister Meir's visit to Washington the next day in order to shore up US support for its objectives arising from the war (D. 21).

It was during the Meir visit (31 October–4 November) that the draft of the Six-Point Agreement with Egypt was hammered out in tense meetings with President Nixon and Secretary of State Kissinger. The latter secured Sadat's acceptance at meetings in Cairo on 6–7 November. And the next day, after further discussions with Under-Secretary of State Sisco, Israel's Cabinet approved the agreement (D. 22). This process became a precedent for the pattern of Israel–Arab–US negotiations throughout the end-crisis period: shuttle diplomacy by Kissinger; the painstaking search for common ground, sometimes to a microscopic degree; Israel's insistence on a political *quid pro quo* for territorial concessions, as expressed in the dictum, "a piece of peace for a piece of territory"; and increasing US involvement, including assurances and economic and military aid to both adversaries.

The method was successful. In the South, it led to the Egypt/Israel Disengagement Agreement on 18 January 1974, terminating Israel's (and Egypt's) end-crisis period and their segment of the October-Yom Kippur Crisis. In perspective, it also served as the first step on the road to Camp David and the Peace Treaty of 1979.[13] In the North, after renewed fighting and a month of arduous, US-mediated negotiations, it culminated in the Israel/Syria Disengagement Agreement of 31 May 1974. Despite frequent incidents, including open warfare in Lebanon in 1982, that agreement remained in force as the foundation of stability on the Golan Heights into the early 1990s.

The other nine Israeli decisions in the Yom Kippur end-crisis period focused on two issues, the Geneva Peace Conference and the Disengagement Agreement. Three merit attention:

D. 24—the Cabinet, on 25 November, approved Kissinger's compromise proposal to convene the Geneva Peace Conference under US-USSR auspices and UN chairmanship;

D. 27—after more heated discussions with Kissinger, the Cabinet decided, on 17 December, to participate in the Conference but not to negotiate with Syria unless it released the list of Israeli POWs. (The Conference convened on the 21st, adjourned and vanished into history; Syria did not attend); and

D. 31—the Cabinet, on 17 January 1974, accepted the Disengagement Agreement with Egypt.

The winding-down of Israel's crisis with Syria was both easier and more difficult than accommodation with Egypt. It was easier because the military outcome of the October-Yom Kippur War for Syria was unqualified defeat: Israel had crossed the 1967 cease-fire line and was entrenched close to Damascus. At the same time, Israel's withdrawal, even a few kilometers on the Golan Heights, would have placed its settlements on the Heights, as well as towns and villages in northern Israel, within Syrian artillery range. The negotiation process was further complicated by a crisis of confidence in the Government of Israel caused by the war. (In the event, Labor emerged from the 31 December 1973 general election with a reduced plurality—from 58 to 51 seats, out of 120 in the *Knesset*. Meir finally formed a new government, which lasted a month, and resigned immediately after the Disengagement Agreement with Syria was signed on 31 May 1974.)

Kissinger succeeded in extracting a list of Israeli prisoners in Syria, Israel's *sine qua non* for negotiations, during a brief shuttle in February 1974. And during a persistent 27-day shuttle in May between Damascus and Jerusalem, with side trips to Riyadh, Amman and Cairo, he succeeded in finding a basis for accommodation. The key issues were the same as in the negotiations with Egypt: an exchange of prisoners; the extent of Israel's withdrawal from occupied territory; the size of forces to remain in the areas of thinned-out forward lines; and the size and composition of the UN force in the buffer zone between the forward lines.

All of these contentious issues were resolved. The prisoner exchange was implemented with the signing of the Disengagement Agreement. In the Sinai, the IDF pulled back 20 kilometers from the Suez Canal and further in the South; on the Golan Heights, Israel withdrew from part of the principal city, Quneitra, as well as from one of the surrounding strategic hills. The contending forces were drastically reduced in the forward area. And a UN force, UNDOF, was created, serving as an effective buffer into the early 1990s. However, Egypt successfully resisted Israel's pressure to move from "maintenance of the cease-fire" to termination of the "state of belligerency." And Syria refused to include a cessation of terrorist activities in the cease-fire. The US compensated Israel with several "Memoranda of Understanding," notably, assuring Israel the right of passage for Israel-bound goods through the Canal, and according legitimacy, *a priori*, if Israel exercised self-defense in case of raids from Syrian-controlled territory across the demarcation line.

The decline in value threat, as noted, is one indicator of change from crisis to end-crisis period. After 26 October 1973 Israel perceived less threat: from the Arabs, with Egypt's Third Army encircled on the east bank of the Canal and Damascus within artillery range; and from the superpowers, because Washington and Moscow had averted a nuclear collision. There were other sources of concern, notably, pressure from the US for territorial concessions and uncertainty about military aid from Israel's patron; but these were of a lesser order of significance.

As for the military indicator of deescalation, by the end of the October-Yom Kippur War, that is, by the end of the crisis period, Israel's leaders perceived a positive shift in the military balance. The IDF was firmly entrenched on the west bank of the Canal, with a vise-like grip on Egypt's Third Army. And in the North Israeli forces were perilously close to Syria's capital. Israel had once again proved its military superiority, though not as decisively as in 1967 or 1956. Finally, compared with the crisis period, 5–26 October, Israel's decision-makers did not feel any time pressure for decisions, military or political.

In sum, deescalation, that is, the winding-down of stress, was already visible when the second cease-fire took effect, on 26 October 1973; and by 18 January 1974, with respect to Egypt, by 31 May, vis-à-vis Syria, the three perceptual sources of high stress had returned to the levels that obtained prior to the onset of the October-Yom Kippur Crisis.

Contrary to the expectation of Model II on end-crisis behavior [Chap. 1], Israel's coping did not differ from that of the crisis period. Persistent US pressure on specific issues (e.g., the freeing of Egypt's Third Army from IDF encirclement) led to an intensely felt need for *information* about US intentions and likely behavior. The enhanced search was expressed in frequent visits of senior decision-makers to Washington: Meir, 1–4 November; Foreign Minister Eban, 20–24 November; and Defense Minister Dayan, 5–7 December and 4–5 January 1974. Moreover, the processing of new information underwent a change in the less stressful end-crisis period: all information went first to a four-person Negotiating Committee comprising Meir, Dayan, Eban and Deputy Prime Minister Allon; for the negotiations with Syria it was enlarged to include Peres and Rabin. The Negotiating Committee then reported, as it saw fit, to the full Cabinet.

During the prolonged negotiations of the 1973–74 end-crisis period the Cabinet remained the principal forum for consultation. One opposition leader, Begin, several civil servants, and three generals, too, were consulted, making a *consultative group* of 24. In contrast to the crisis period in 1973, the Israeli Cabinet was the sole *decisional forum*: it made or approved all 11 decisions of the end-crisis period.

There were no threat or time constraints on Israel's consideration of *alternatives* in the 1973–74 end-crisis period. In fact, Israel's decision-makers examined options very carefully at every decision point. Thus the alternatives of not attending the Geneva Peace Conference, delaying, and attending subject to conditions, such as not sitting together with Syria's delegates, were considered and chosen before the final decision to participate. The same was true with respect to the terms of a Disengagement Agreement with Egypt and, later, with Syria. Each of these agreements was a turning point in the winding-down of Israel's crisis with its two Arab adversaries. The latter also denoted the termination of Israel's nine-month foreign policy crisis and of the October-Yom Kippur Crisis as a whole.[14]

LEBANON CIVIL WAR I (1976)

With the decisive defeat of PLO and leftist Lebanese Muslim forces in the hills above Beirut, as a result of Syria's offensive on 28–30 September 1976, the latter's perception of threat declined, and time ceased to be a constraint on decisions; that is, the crisis period gave way to end-crisis in Syria's initial foreign policy crisis of Lebanon's prolonged civil war (1975–1991). This period lasted almost seven weeks: Arab League resolutions in Riyadh and Cairo during October created an Arab Deterrent Force of 30,000, almost entirely Syrian; and on 15 November Syrian forces, implementing those resolutions, reached the centre of Beirut.

There were three Syrian decisions during its end-crisis period:

D. 11—President Asad, on 30 September, halted the Syrian offensive and offered peace talks to the Palestinians, in an effort to neutralize them by diplomatic means and to isolate the Druze forces from the leftist coalition;

D. 12—the *ad hoc* decision-making committee of four decided, on 11 October, to launch a second offensive against the Palestinian-Lebanese Muslim alliance in order to improve Syria's bargaining position at the forthcoming Arab summit conference; and

D. 13—the enlarged Cabinet decision-making group of nine decided, on 15 October, to participate in a mini-Riyadh summit, aimed at a resolution of the Lebanon conflict.

There were no basic changes in Syria's *attitudinal prism* during the end-crisis period. They continued to evaluate developments in Lebanon as part of a plot by "imperialist and Zionist" forces to undermine Syria. Further, they viewed the Palestinians as lending themselves to this international conspiracy. Soviet behavior was perceived as negative, at first; but antagonism declined later in the end-crisis period. Perceptions of the US were ambivalent. The Druze "national movement" under Kamal Jumblatt was viewed in negative terms. Egypt was perceived in positive terms, after the reconciliation between Sadat and Asad. So too was Jordan. Towards *Ba'athist* Iraq, by contrast, there was continued hostility. And antipathy to Israel was even more marked.

Nor was there change in the pattern of *information processing* during Syria's end-crisis period. Information continued to be sought and acquired from Lebanon, through *Ba'athist* members, Palestinian sympathizers and Syrian soldiers acting in Lebanon as "truce supervisors." President Asad was in regular telephone communication with Lebanese leaders. And Lebanese delegations flocked to Damascus to see Asad and offer their evaluations of the rapidly-changing constellation of forces and events in and around Beirut.

Consultative groups varied in Syria's end-crisis period. Asad apparently acted alone in making D. 11—to offer the Palestinians peace talks. The core committee of four, Asad, Khaddam, Jamil and Shahabi, was the consultative unit for D. 12, to launch another major offensive against the Palestinian-left Muslim alliance. But D. 13, which indicated a major shift in policy, involved the consultation of 41 persons.

The same diversity is evident in *decisional forums*. Asad was the sole decision-maker in D. 11. The four-person *ad hoc* committee made D. 12. And the nine-member decision-making Cabinet made D. 13.

A thorough search-cum-evaluation process characterized strategic D. 13, as with all strategic decisions in Syria's Lebanon Civil War I Crisis of 1975–76. Asad's disposition was conveyed by three senior advisors: political advisor on foreign affairs al-Dawoodi; Minister of Information Iskander; and Khidhr, Director-General of Arab Affairs in the Foreign Ministry:

> Very rarely, indeed extremely rarely, would the President take an important decision without prior evaluation and consultations within the Government and sometimes from outside it, such as university professors. Consultations usually centre on important members of the Party and sometimes the Progressive National Front. . . . He [Asad] rarely makes an instinctive decision. [In the Lebanese Crisis], as the crisis worsened and the possibility of war increased, the evaluation process was widened and was made more rigorous (A. I. Dawisha, 1980: 179–180).

In sum, Syria's decision-makers were aware of the complexity of their environment for decision, in all three periods of the crisis. Further, their strategic decisions, including D. 13 in the end-crisis period, were the product of rational choice, the outcome of lengthy meetings in which all high-level interest groups participated. Third, they were primarily concerned with long-term interests. Fourth, options were carefully evaluated before choices were made. And finally, ideological considerations were important in Syria's decision-making throughout.[15]

INDIA/CHINA BORDER (1962–63)

India's end-crisis period was triggered by a verbal act: on 21 November 1962 the PRC announced a cease-fire beginning at midnight and a unilateral withdrawal of Chinese forces starting 1 December "to positions 20 kilometers behind the line of actual control . . .". In the Western and Middle Sectors of the disputed border, the "control line" was that "which existed between China and India on November 7,

1959"; the "control line" in the Eastern Sector—NEFA—would be "the illegal McMahon Line."[16]

India responded with the first of its three important end-crisis decisions, on 22–24 November 1962: to accept the Chinese cease-fire and withdrawal, *de facto*, but not to yield to the demand that India, too, withdraw 20 kilometers behind the PRC-designated "line of actual control" on 7 November 1959 (first proposed in a note from Chou Enlai to Nehru that day). To accept this demand would have been tantamount to formal abandonment of the Aksai Chin part of Ladakh in exchange for Chinese withdrawal from NEFA, a barter deal that India had rejected at the Nehru-Chou summit in April 1960, and ever since. Yet, in Hoffmann's words (226), "India's refusal to grant legitimacy to China's 'line of control' would not change the fact that India was now forced to tolerate it. . . . [and] that *de facto* toleration has continued (for the most part) since 1962."

The second Indian decision, on 12–13 January 1963, was to accept the Colombo Proposals, a set of suggestions that were framed at a conference in Ceylon's (Sri Lanka's) capital on 10–12 December 1962 by six Non-Aligned Asian and African states: Burma, Cambodia, Ceylon, Egypt, Ghana and Indonesia. Overall, these Proposals "tilted" in favor of India. China was asked to withdraw 20 kilometers from the cease-fire line, only in the Western Sector, while India would not have to withdraw anywhere. Further, a demilitarized zone would be established in the Ladakh area of Chinese withdrawal, with both sides permitted to establish civilian posts "to be agreed upon" and, with calculated vagueness, "without prejudice to the rights of the previous presence of both India and China in that area." In short, India's posts in the disputed territory would be there by right, not by Chinese permission. Not surprisingly, India's Parliament gave its formal approval, on 25 January 1963. The PRC did not, and has not, to the present day. (It did not formally reject the Colombo Proposals but, rather, added two "points of interpretation"; and these constituted *de facto* disavowal of the Colombo mediation effort.)

India's third decision was not directly related to the border dispute but clearly derived from the military defeat in October–November 1962: the Emergency Committee of the Cabinet, with subsequent Cabinet approval, decided, in mid-February 1963, to double the amount spent for defense the previous year. The massive increase was designed to implement a new three-year defense plan—to recruit new mountain divisions and to improve border communications, with more transport, supplies, and weaponry. (The three-year plan, followed by a five-year plan, was to make India the preeminent military power in South Asia.)

There were changes among India's key decision-makers during the end-crisis period. Nehru remained the dominant figure, though the shock of the border war and signs of illness in early 1962 were beginning to take their toll. Two newcomers were Y. B. Chavan, the new Defense Minister and a senior Congress leader who had been Chief Minister of Maharashtra, and General J. N. Chaudhri, the newly-appointed Chief of Army Staff. Mullik, Director of the Intelligence Bureau, and Foreign Secretary M. J. Desai continued to be Nehru's principal bureaucratic aides. And expert advice, as in the past, flowed from the China specialists in the Ministry of External Affairs.

Nor was there a basic change in the *psychological environment* of India's decision-makers. Rather, the war reinforced the *attitudinal prism* and *images* formed during the three-and-a-half years of the crisis with China. Central to the beliefs of Nehru and others was that China's hostile behavior towards India was motivated primarily by the goal of primacy in Asia: for this purpose, India had to be seen by Asia's states and peoples to be irresolute, ineffective and militarily weak. Further, in the PRC's on-going rivalry with the Soviet Union for communist leadership, India's Non-Alignment had to be shown as a cover for allegiance to the West. Other Chinese objectives, in this view, were to undermine India's economy, Nehru's leadership, and the viability of democratic socialism. Given these beliefs and perceptions, along with a feeling of China's betrayal of India's oft-displayed friendship, it seemed natural to Nehru to seek military assistance wherever possible; and that meant, first and foremost, the US and the UK. This he continued to do even after the war ended, with discreet inquiries about a tacit air defense pact, under the terms of which they would defend India's cities while the latter engaged the Chinese, if fighting resumed.

As in the end-crisis period of other foreign policy crises, India's perception of *threat* declined sharply between 22 November 1962 and 28 February 1963. Yet, as long as the border dispute remains unresolved and the PRC is aligned with India's other hostile neighbor, Pakistan, the level of threat perception remains higher than in the non-crisis years preceding the outbreak of the India/China Border Crisis in March 1959.

Time pressure for decisions was no longer observable after the Chinese withdrawal in December 1962, though concern about the long term was evident in India's decision to set in motion a military buildup, along with the three-year defense plan. Similarly, the resumption of large-scale fighting seemed less and less likely months after the cease-fire and the withdrawal of PRC forces as pledged on 21 November 1962. The likelihood of *military hostilities* remained higher than in the non-crisis years before 1959, but much lower than the crisis period of October and November. In short, all three perceptual indicators of crisis declined, though a residue of uncertainty about China's intentions and India's capability continued beyond India's end-crisis period and, more generally, the traumatic 1962 crisis and war.

How did India cope with the challenge of the end-crisis period? The search for, and flow of, *information* declined once the fighting ended. However, Nehru remained closed to the increasing evidence of the debacle and its causes. He did not acknowledge the failure of India's generals to stave off defeat, especially in NEFA, placing the blame instead on brigade commanders and more junior officers. Nor did he recognize his own errors: in misperceiving China's intentions, despite the abundance of information that signalled a Chinese attack; in military appointments, notably General Kaul to command Operation Leghorn, designed "to throw the Chinese out"; and in management of the war. Only with respect to improving relations with the West and long-term military planning was information processed effectively.

Consultation underwent significant change in India's end-crisis period. Nehru consulted more widely. In particular, the six-member Emergency Committee of the Cabinet, an *ad hoc* body during the war, became the principal and regular forum for consultation on foreign and defense issues, including anything to do with China, notably the Colombo Proposals and the military buildup. Its membership remained unchanged: Nehru, Chavan, Morarji Desai, Shastri, Krishnamachari and Nanda.

The key decision-makers were noted earlier. Suffice it to add that in the end-crisis period the Emergency Committee served as both a consultative unit and *decisional forum*. It was there that the major issues were discussed and choices made. As for *alternatives*, search declined in a phase of declining stress. At the same time, options were considered very thoroughly. Thus ways were devised to accept the substance of the PRC cease-fire-withdrawal announcement without according it legitimacy. And India's interpretation of the Colombo Proposals was adopted by the mediators. In this aspect of coping with crisis, India was very successful during its end-crisis period.

HUNGARIAN UPRISING (1956–57)

The end-crisis period of the Hungarian Uprising is unique among the case studies in this volume. By the time it began, on 4 November 1956, Hungary was occupied by Soviet troops. There was no autonomous government. The Kadar regime, formed that day, was almost totally dependent on General Grebbenik, commander of Soviet troops in Hungary. As *de facto* ruler, he told the Greater Budapest Workers' Council, bluntly, on 17 November: "You have to understand that it is not the Kadar Government which is in control here but the Soviet Military Command; and it has the power to force the Hungarian workers to return to work."[17] Finally, Hungary's adversary was not the USSR, the patron of the new regime; rather, it was domestic opposition to the ouster of the Nagy government and the occupation of Budapest and most of Hungary by a foreign power.

Nonetheless, the external crisis arising from the Hungarian Uprising did not end on 3 November. There was an end-crisis period (and deescalation phase) of declining *threat* perception, increasing irrelevance of *time pressure* on Hungary's decisions, and the absence of *war likelihood*—between Hungary and the Soviet Union. In Geist's words (180), it lasted until January 1957, "when the last vestiges of independent resistance to state terror were eliminated, crushed, silenced, and the vestiges of direct Soviet military administration disappeared. . . . There was still tension, but it was the kind of tension that had existed for years . . .".

Three decisions were taken, two of them primarily domestic in focus:

D. 1—on 4 November, the Soviet rulers decided to form a new government in Budapest, led by Kadar;

D. 2—on 21 November, the Kadar-led Government of Hungary agreed to allow Nagy and his entourage, seeking asylum in the Yugoslav embassy, to go home unharmed; and

D. 3—at the end of November, Hungary's government decided to deny entry to a UN Special Commission of Inquiry.

The dominant, perhaps sole, motive of the new Kadar regime was survival. That meant either negotiating a compromise with the two principal sources of dissent, the Workers' Councils and the Writers' Union, or their suppression. It tried to do the former, without success, until a secret visit of Soviet Politburo member, Malenkov, in early December 1956. He accomplished the latter by January 1957. (And the remaining Workers' Councils were dissolved in November 1957.)

Kadar's survival also depended on a solution to the Nagy problem. In fact, this was the key issue of the end-crisis period. Despite their guarantee (D. 2 noted above), the Soviets arrested Nagy and his entourage outside the Yugoslav embassy on 22 November and deported them to Romania on the 27th, after all efforts to persuade him to recant failed. This was the crucial decision and action of the end-crisis period, for which Kadar took formal responsibility. (In 1957, they were secretly returned to Hungary; and in June 1958, Nagy and three of his associates were hanged. They were rehabilitated 31 years later with the overthrow of communist rule.)

Turning to coping mechanisms, there is no evidence about the flow of *information* to the core leadership group in the Hungarian government/ party. However, as in the pre-crisis and crisis periods, it can be inferred that all information was channelled directly to the senior decision-makers. And they, in turn, were in constant touch with Soviet leaders in Moscow and Budapest.

Like Hungary's end-crisis period as a whole, the *decisional forum* was abnormal. The ultimate source of decisional power, as noted, was the Soviet Military Command in Hungary and, beyond it, the Soviet Communist Party Politburo. To the extent that authority existed in Hungary, it was concentrated in the hands of Kadar, who held the two key posts of First Party Secretary and Prime Minister. The key decisional unit was a directorate of four Politburo members—Kadar, Muennich, the Minister of Armed Forces and Public Security, Minister of Industry Apro, and Kossa, the Minister of Finance. The Politburo of 11 was the highest executive body of the Hungarian Socialist Workers Party (the reconstituted Communist Party), formally responsible to a 23-member Central Committee. But, as Kadar admitted 25 years later: "Who elected that body [which first met on 2 December 1956]? Obviously, it elected itself. There was no other solution under the circumstances" (quoted in Geist, forthcoming: 181).

The *consultative circle* in Hungary's end-crisis period was restricted: the eight members of Kadar's government; the Politburo of 11; and, at the outer limit, the 23-member Central Committee. As for *alternatives*, they were considered carefully: to release, deport or arrest Nagy and his aides; to negotiate with, or suppress, the Workers' Councils and the Writers' Union; to cooperate with, or obstruct, the UN inquiry. Kadar denied it entry.[18] Soon thereafter the crisis over the Hungarian Uprising ended, with a pro-Soviet regime ensconced in power. It remained there until the democratic upheaval of 1989.

RHODESIA UDI (1966)

Zambia's end-crisis period was triggered by Prime Minister Wilson's seemingly new commitment to crush the Rhodesian rebellion, conveyed persuasively during his visit to Lusaka on 13 January 1966. It was in that atmosphere of euphoria that Zambia made its "Quick Kill" decision the same day, calling for sweeping sanctions against the Smith regime in white-ruled Rhodesia, along with an agreement to receive a British military mission and, in general, acceptance of British policy on Rhodesia. The deescalation phase was aptly characterized as "trust in Britain," more specifically, "misplaced trust [by President Kaunda] in Prime Minister Wilson's good faith," from 14 January to 27 April 1966.[19]

The first two of Zambia's four end-crisis decisions were designed to survive the shock of anticipated Rhodesian retaliation and the high cost of sanctions:

D. 31—around 24 January, to take a series of measures to "gird for the crunch," including steps to sustain partial production of the copper mines and minimum exports, to continue and possibly expand the Anglo-American-Canadian airlift, to mobilize financial support around the world, and to minimize the disruptive domestic effects of sanctions and shortages; and

D. 32—on 5 February, to stockpile a three-month supply of essential commodities.

The other two decisions came after the *de facto* 15 February deadline for Zambia's implementation of its "Quick Kill" sanctions strategy:

D. 33—on 26 February, to oppose an ultimatum on force or other extreme measures against Rhodesia at that time, during a meeting of the OAU Council of Ministers, while at the same time pressing for mandatory sanctions and OAU collective assistance to Zambia; and

D. 34—on 8 March, to suspend the "Quick Kill" strategy indefinitely, possibly permanently, in favor of the "Long Haul" strategy aimed at bringing down the white Rhodesian regime.

The long wait for firm British action against the rebel regime in Salisbury proved to be in vain. On 27 April, soon after his election victory (31 March), Prime Minister Wilson informed Parliament of his intention to seek "talks about talks" with Premier Smith of Rhodesia. Kaunda heard the news from the BBC! He felt bitter and betrayed by a trusted friend. But with that event Zambia's crisis over UDI came to an end. It was the prelude to a protracted conflict over Rhodesia which ended in 1980 when Rhodesia gave way to the new state of Zimbabwe.

There is abundant evidence of reduced stress in the end-crisis period, despite the worry about Rhodesia's likely countermeasures against an economically vulnerable Zambia. The number of articulated perceptions of threat, time, and war likelihood by Zambia's decision-makers declined drastically, from 477 in the 70-day crisis period to 109 in the 103-day end-crisis period: value threat perceptions declined from 391 to 99, and time pressure statements from 16 to 4.

All of Zambia's end-crisis decisions were made by the Cabinet of 16. However, as earlier, the pivotal *decision-maker* was President Kaunda, with four other ministers playing an important role: Vice-President Kamanga; Foreign Minister Kapwepwe; Home Minister Chona, and Finance Minister Wina.

How did they cope with what seemed to be a continuing survival crisis? The *information* probe was slightly more extensive than in either the crisis or pre-crisis periods: it was thorough in the process of making 2 of the 4 decisions, compared to 7 of 16, and 4 of 14 decisions in the earlier periods. A similar pattern is evident with regard to receptivity to information: it was open-minded in 3 of 4 decisions, compared to 11 of 16, and 7 of 14 decisions, respectively. To take one illustration: before deciding on the "Long Haul" (D. 34), Zambia's decision-makers "were amply served by a steady flow of published reports and private briefings. . . . [T]he avalanche of information received from reliable sources [about major oil leaks] . . . compelled them to reconsider and eventually reverse their policy" (Anglin, forthcoming 1993, 276–277).

The primary motives of *consultation* in Zambia's crisis seem to have been the need to solicit support and to ensure legitimacy for a preferred policy option—from élite groups within the state and from important external actors. Both the frequency and variety of consultation increased markedly with the intensification of stress, throughout Zambia's crisis. Thus, in the end-crisis period, "intense" as opposed to "moderate" or "limited" consultation did not precede any decision, compared to one-fourth of the decisions in the crisis period. As in the earlier periods, political leaders were the group most often consulted, with the corporate community at the other extreme. The bureaucratic élite became more active over time, as did external actors, mainly the UK and Tanzania; and there was no decline in their activity during the low stress end-crisis period, for example, consultations with the Commonwealth and the OAU before arriving at D. 34—the "Long Haul."

The most notable change in Zambia's *decisional forum* from crisis to end-crisis period was the growth of ministerial and Cabinet units at the expense of the President. Kaunda made none of the four decisions alone, compared to 30% of the crisis period decisions, though he was a member of the decisional unit for all decisions. The explanation for this broadening of the decisional base was Kaunda's firm commitment to consensus-style politics. Although he was the repository of executive authority, the President usually opted for shared responsibility in difficult and potentially divisive decisions. And though the Cabinet almost invariably ratified decisions, they were often made by the President or by Kaunda and his senior ministers.

As for *alternatives*, search was never extensive in the end-crisis period, compared to 36% and 19% of the decisions in the pre-crisis and crisis periods. Moreover, thorough evaluation of alternatives declined from 44% in the crisis period to 25%. Specifically, in "girding for the crunch" (D. 31), the decision-makers gave little attention to alternative approaches to the challenge that lay ahead. There was more consideration of options in deciding how to cope with OAU militancy (D. 33), and to acknowledge the failure of the "Quick Kill" sanctions policy (D. 34). In sum, there were some continuities in Zambia's behavior during its Rhodesia UDI Crisis. There were also important changes in coping with deescalation.

FALKLANDS/MALVINAS (1982)

Argentina's end-crisis period was brief. It began on 2 June, when President Galtieri offered to accept "any helping hand" in his hour of need, when junta member Brigadier Lami Dozo denied that Argentina had received military aid from the USSR, and when Foreign Minister Costa Mendez sought support from the Non-Aligned Conference in Havana. By then the outcome of the war was certain, as Galtieri acknowledged in a plaintive speech on Army Day, 29 May: "I have no more weapons, nor cannons nor tanks. . . . We have no more ships or planes to be manned" (quoted in Bartley, 1984: 16).

There was an inconclusive meeting between the President and the army High Command on 4 June. He consulted trade union and party leaders the next day. There was acrimonious debate within the service councils as humiliating defeat drew near. A visit by Pope John Paul II on 11–12 June was of no consequence. On the 14th Argentine forces at Port Stanley surrendered without a fight, a decision made by General Menendez, the local commander, to the chagrin of the junta. A *de facto* cease-fire took effect on the 16th. And on the 18th President Galtieri was removed from office by his fellow generals. Argentina's end-crisis period was over; and, with it, the international crisis over the Falklands/Malvinas.

Coping during the end-crisis period was a continuation of earlier attempts to manage Argentina's gravest foreign policy crisis in the twentieth century. *Information* was sought and processed by each branch of the military, among whom traditional jealousy remained a serious barrier to coordinated policy: "Mirroring the fief-like structure of the junta, the services lacked cohesion and promoted over-reliance upon military espionage . . ." (cited in Bartley, p. 42).

Consultation, too, continued to exhibit this "fief-like structure." Members of the junta and the Foreign Minister consulted among themselves. Each then consulted his military or diplomatic service, especially its service council. The President and the Interior Minister also consulted civilian politicians. Coordination was absent.

During the end-crisis period the junta remained the preeminent *decisional forum*. Even the Foreign Ministry's Malvinas Team was dominated by its military members. But other than the painful acquiescence in defeat, the cease-fire decision, the junta did not act as a decision-making body during the last two weeks of the crisis. More often than not, the choice was not to act. As for the consideration of *alternatives*, there was none. The Argentine decision-makers observed the approaching *dénouement* almost as spectators: the outcome was determined by the fighting and surrender on the ground.

Throughout their "opportunity" crisis, which became a nightmare, Argentine decision-makers suffered the ills of very high stress. The norm of a few hours' sleep each day from the end of March to mid-June led to physical exhaustion. The evidence indicates that they became increasingly incapable of processing information and arriving at decisions (Charlton, 1989). This was compounded by the dispersion of decision-making centers—Buenos Aires (the junta), Commodore Rivadavia (the military command), and Port Stanley (field operations). The division of responsibilities between political and military committees was blurred. And clarity of leadership was absent. But the most fatal flaw in Argentine decision-making was misperception of the likely UK response, the inability to consider that London would take resolute military action. The result was a foreign policy catastrophe.

In sum, Argentina's coping in the Falklands/Malvinas Crisis was inept and ineffective. It misperceived the UK's likely response to the surreptitious landing of troops. It misjudged the balance of forces. It miscalculated the likely US role and world opinion generally. The price was high, for Galtieri, the junta, the military, and Argentina.

Deescalation/End-Crisis: Case Study Findings

The findings on deescalation/end-crisis are presented in two formats, as in the earlier phases and periods: the extent of fit of the ten cases with Hypotheses 8–11; and the evidence of coping in the end-crisis period, in light of the specific actor and situational attributes.

As evident in Table 4.5, there is a close fit between the conditions in H. 8 and three of the 10 cases explored in depth: Prague Spring, five of the six elements; Munich and Hungarian Uprising, four elements each. H. 10, too, exhibits a close fit. Munich (UK) and Rhodesia UDI (Zambia) met five of the six conditions. And three other cases—Prague Spring (USSR), Stalingrad (Germany), and Lebanon Civil War I (Syria)—fit four conditions.

H. 11 reveals the closest fit among the hypotheses on deescalation. One crisis—Lebanon Civil War I (Syria)—matches all four conditions. And in four other cases—India/China Border (PRC), Hungarian Uprising (USSR), Rhodesia UDI (Rhodesia), and Falklands/Malvinas (UK)—three of the four postulated conditions were present.[20]

Viewed in terms of each international crisis as a whole, three of the 10 cases exhibit two-thirds or more of the combined elements of H. 8–11: Munich, Hungarian Uprising, Lebanon Civil War I. And two other cases—Prague Spring and Rhodesia UDI—fit 60% of the postulated conditions. Taken together, the 10 cases fit 91 of the 172 reported relevant elements in H. 8–11 (53%).

Many individual elements of the hypotheses on winding-down of crisis exhibit a strong fit. In H. 8, nine of the 10 cases match the condition on IO involvement. Eight cases fit the condition of H. 10 regarding capability. And in H. 11, nine cases fit the condition relating to crisis outcome, while eight cases fit the conflict setting condition.

The major findings from the case studies of coping in the end-crisis period are summarized in Tables 4.6.A, 4.6.B.1 and 2, and 4.6.C.

Among the *actor attributes* (Table 4.6.A), variation is evident in the number of *decisions*. Thus, important (or strategic) decisions range from one (Argentina) to five (Israel), with the USSR, Germany and Zambia each exhibiting two such decisions, and the US, Syria, India and Hungary, three each. The range is considerably wider for the total number of decisions, from two (Argentina) to 13 (the US and Germany), and 11 for Israel.

TABLE 4.5 *Hypotheses and Case Studies on Crisis Deescalation: Findings*

Hypotheses on Crisis Deescalation	Berlin Blockade 1948–49	Prague Spring 1968	Munich 1938	Stalingrad 1942–43	October–Yom Kippur 1973–74	Lebanon Civil War I 1975–76	India/China Border 1962–63	Hungarian Uprising 1956–57	Rhodesia UDI 1965–66	Falklands/Malvinas 1982
8. Termination in Agreement (int)°[1]										
non-protracted conflict setting										
equal capability among adversaries		X	X			X		X	X	X
few actors		X	X							
low major power activity		X	X	X				X		
high IO involvement		X	X	X	X	X	X	X	X	X
non-violent crisis management	X	X	X	X		X		X		X
9. Low Intensity Leads to Short Duration (int)°[2]										
few actors	2	2	2	2	2	2	2	X	2	X
low major power activity								X		X
low geostrategic salience								X		X
low heterogeneity between adversaries								X		
few issues										X
non-violent crisis management										
10. Accommodative Strategy (fp)†[3]	US[4]	USSR	UK[5]	Germany	Israel	Syria	India	Hungary	Zambia	UK
non-protracted conflict setting			X	X				X	X	
power equality or inferior power	X	X	X	X	X	X	X	X	X	X

Table 4.5 Continued

Hypotheses on Crisis Deescalation	Berlin Blockade 1948–49	Prague Spring 1968	Munich 1938	Stalingrad 1942–43	October–Yom Kippur 1973–74	Lebanon Civil War I 1975–76	India/China Border 1962–63	Hungarian Uprising 1956–57	Rhodesia UDI 1965–66	Falklands/Malvinas 1982
democratic regime	X	X	X	X	X	X				
domestic stability	X		X	X		X	X		X	
non-military support from major power	X	X	X			X			X	X
support from relevant IO		X		[6]			X	X	X	X
11. *Satisfaction with Outcome*[7] (*fp*)†	US	Poland	France	Germany[8]	Israel	Syria	PRC	USSR	Rhodesia	UK
non-protracted conflict setting		X	X	X	X	X	X	X	X	X
military support from major power	X	X	X			X	X	X	X	X
support from relevant IO				[6]		X	X	X	X	X
perception of victory	X	X	X	X	X	X	X	X	X	X

*int = international crisis (system/interactor level)

†fp = foreign policy crisis (actor level)

1. H.8, in its present form, cannot be coded for eight of the ten international crises: Prague Spring, Munich, Stalingrad, Lebanon Civil War I, India/China Border, Hungarian Uprising, Rhodesia UDI, and Falklands/Malvinas ended through a unilateral act, respectively by: the USSR-led Soviet bloc invasion; the imposition of surrender by the four Munich powers on Czechoslovakia; the destruction of Germany's Sixth Army by Soviet forces in 1942; the entry of Syrian forces into Beirut; the PRC's unilateral ceasefire and withdrawal; the Soviet military intervention in Hungary; the UK's initiation of talks with Rhodesia; and the victorious British expeditionary force in the Falklands. In some of these cases, a facade of agreement, i.e., a formal document, was signed, e.g., the Four Power Agreement (*diktat*) at Munich, and the Moscow Protocol, by the captive Czechoslovak communist leaders. All of these cases were therefore coded as the obverse of the dependent variable; that is, termination in non-agreement (imposed outcome) is most likely when a crisis occurs in a protracted conflict setting; with unequal capability among the adversaries; many actors; high major power activity; low IO involvement, and violent crisis management. The obverse coding for these eight cases relating to H.8 is reported here.

2. H.9 can be coded in the form specified above in two cases only – Hungarian Uprising and Falklands/Malvinas. Five of the other cases were of high intensity and long duration, that is, the obverse conditions: Berlin Blockade, Prague Spring, Munich, Stalingrad, October Yom-Kippur. Since the qualitative findings presented in this table are illustrative, the coding for these obverse cases is not reported here. And the other three were 'mixed', that is, low intensity and long duration: Lebanon Civil War I, India/China Border, Rhodesia UDI. As such, they cannot be coded.

3. Hypothesis 10, as framed, cannot be coded for five of the ten cases because the crisis actors in these international crises did not adopt an accommodative strategy. Thus these cases (the USSR in the Prague Spring, Germany in Stalingrad, Syria in Lebanon, Civil War I, India in India/China Border, and the UK in Falklands/Malvinas) are coded for the obverse, that is, the non-adoption of an accommodative strategy, in accordance with the decision rule set out in n.1.

4. In the Berlin Blockade Crisis, the three Western Powers adopted an accommodative strategy directed to peaceful termination, from 22 July 1948 onwards. The US, as the focus of coping in this case, throughout the book, is used here to test the fit for H.10.

5. Several actors in the Munich Crisis adopted an accommodative strategy directed to peaceful termination. The UK, as the focus of coping in this case, throughout the book, is used to test H.10.

6. There was no functioning IO during WWII.

7. The coding for (dis)satisfaction with a crisis outcome exhibits great variety: three of the four crisis actors in the Berlin Blockade case (the US, the UK, France) were satisfied, the USSR was not. Five of the crisis actors in the Prague Spring Crisis (the USSR, Poland, the GDR, Hungary and Bulgaria) were satisfied with the outcome in 1968, Czechoslovakia was not. Similarly, France and the UK were satisfied with the Munich outcome in 1938, Czechoslovakia and the USSR were dissatisfied. In the 1962–63 India/China Border Crisis, the former was dissatisfied, the latter was satisfied. In light of this diversity and the purpose of this table, one satisfied state will be used to test the fit for each hypothesis.

8. Germany, the only crisis actor in the Stalingrad case, was dissatisfied with the outcome and is therefore coded for the obverse, that is, a PC setting, no military support from a major power, etc.

TABLE 4.6.A *Deescalation/End-Crisis: Summary of Case Study Findings: Actor Attributes*

International Crisis	Crisis Actor	No. of Decisions*	No. of Decision-Makers**	Attitudinal Prism
Berlin Blockade	US	3 (13)	3 (8)	unchanged – Realism, Resolve, Fear of appeasement
Prague Spring	USSR	2 (4)	5 (20)	unchanged – Brezhnev Doctrine
Munich	UK	—	—	—
Stalingrad	Germany	2 (13)	2 (3)	unchanged – Germany's racial and military superiority
October – Yom Kippur	Israel	5 (11)†	4 (21)	unchanged – mistrust of Arabs, especially Syria, trust in US
Lebanon Civil War I	Syria	3 (3)	1 (9)	unchanged – 'Imperialist–Zionist' conspiracy, indivisibility of Syria and Lebanon
India/China Border	India	3 (3)	1 (5)	unchanged – China hostility deep-rooted
Hungarian Uprising	Hungary	3 (3)	1 (11)	Soviet occupation necessary to survival of Communist regime in Hungary
Rhodesia UDI	Zambia	2 (4)	1 (16)	unchanged initially; then, UK betrayal of trust
Falklands/Malvinas	Argentina	1 (2)	4 (many)	unchanged – Irredentism

*The number on the left refers to strategic or tactically significant decisions; the number in brackets indicates the total number of known strategic, tactical and implementing decisions.

**The number on the left refers to the principal decision-makers; the number in brackets indicates the size of the largest decisional forum.

†Refers to Israel/Egypt segment of this crisis.

Variation is more conspicuous in the total number of *decision-makers* during the end-crisis period. At one extreme, there were 21 in Israel's October-Yom Kippur Crisis (members of the National Unity Government), 20 in the USSR's Prague Spring (the Politburo), and even more in Argentina's Falklands/Malvinas Crisis (the combined membership of the [military] service councils). At the lower end, there were three in Germany's Stalingrad Crisis and five in India's border crisis-war with China.

At first glance, the number of key decision-makers in the end-crisis period shows less variation, with a preeminent leader in four crisis actors—Asad (Syria), Nehru (India), Kadar (Hungary), and Kaunda (Zambia), and, except for a specific military campaign, Hitler in Germany. At the other extreme were the five members of the Soviet Negotiating Committee, four in Israel's Negotiating Team, and four in Argentina's case (the military junta and the Foreign Minister). There were three key US decision-makers (Truman, Marshall/Acheson and Clay), and Hitler, with Manstein, in Germany's end-crisis Stalingrad case. In fact, the variation is greater, for, between the preeminent decision-maker and the total number there was an intermediate cluster in some cases: a four-member *ad hoc* committee in Syria's Lebanon end-crisis; a four-member directorate within the Hungarian Communist Party Politburo; and a group of four senior ministers with whom Kaunda often shared decision-making responsibility. In short, pre-crisis and crisis variation, in the number of decisions and the number of decision-makers, persisted in the end-crisis period.

The *attitudinal prism*, by contrast, reveals no change in the end-crisis period in seven of the nine cases. However, this is not surprising, for specific attitudes and, even more so, a core world view change slowly. They are unlikely to change during the course of a single crisis, even a very long one such as the India/China Border Crisis.

The two deviant cases can be readily explained. In the Hungarian Uprising, the Kadar Government, appointed by the Soviet Military Command on the first day of the end-crisis period, did not perceive the USSR as its foreign policy adversary. Rather, as noted, the regime and its leaders were totally dependent upon Soviet occupying forces for their survival and for the survival of communism in Hungary. In sum, their image of the Soviet Union from 4 November 1956 onwards was fundamentally different from that of Nagy and his colleagues during the crisis period. In Zambia's crisis, perceived by Kaunda and others as threatening its survival, British Prime Minister Wilson's decision in April 1966 to open talks with the rebel regime in Rhodesia came as a

TABLE 4.6.B.1 *Deescalation/End-Crisis: Summary of Case Study Findings: Situational Attributes – Actor Level*

International Crisis	Crisis Actor	Trigger	Values	Time Pressure	War Likelihood	Duration (days)
Berlin Blockade	US	Internal – US decision to enlarge airlift, 22 July 1948	Reputation for Resolve, Western presence in Berlin	Reduced	Lower, except for few days	295
Prague Spring	USSR	Violence – invasion of Czechoslovakia, 20–21 August 1968	Reduced threat	Increased	Lower	7
Munich	UK	–	–	–	–	–
Stalingrad	Germany	Non-violent military – Surrender of Sixth Army, 2 February 1943	Reduced threat	Reduced	Positive change in military balance	51
October – Yom Kippur	Israel	Non-violent military – cease-fire, 26 October 1973	Reduced threat	Reduced	Much lower re Egypt, still high re Syria	217

Lebanon Civil War I	Syria	Violence – defeat of PLO-Muslim forces, 30 September 1976	Reduced threat	Reduced	Still high	47
India/China Border	India	Verbal – PRC announcement of unilateral cease-fire, 21 November 1962	Reduced threat	Reduced	Lower but still high	98
Hungarian Uprising	Hungary	Non-violent military – Soviet occupation of Budapest, 3 November 1956	Reduced threat	Reduced	Nil	60
Rhodesia UDI	Zambia	Verbal – PM Wilson's oral commitment to crush Rhodesia rebellion, 13 January 1966	Reduced threat	Reduced	Lower	104
Falklands/Malvinas	Argentina	Internal – perception of imminent military defeat, 2 June 1982	Military defeat, failure to regain	Reduced	Adverse change in military balance	16

shattering betrayal of unqualified trust; the trauma also changed their attitudinal prism.

Among the *situational attributes* (or crisis components) (Tables 4.6.B.1 and 2), there is a noticeable decline in perceived value threat, time pressure for decisions, and war likelihood (or negative change in the military balance), as postulated in Model II (state behavior) [Chap. 1]. Only two of the nine cases reveal a persistence of *value threat*: the US in the Berlin Blockade, because the outcome of the enlarged airlift, the self-generated trigger to the end-crisis period, remained uncertain and, with it, the US reputation for resolve, as well as the viability of a continued Western presence in Berlin; and Argentina's increasing awareness that "liberation" of the Malvinas, the core value prompting its initial invasion, was beyond its grasp. A reduced value threat was perceived in all other cases.

Similarly, the sole exception to a perceived reduction of *time pressure* was the USSR in the Prague Spring: while its invasion of 20–21 August 1968 was successful, Moscow was acutely aware of strong opposition at the Extraordinary Fourteenth Congress of the Czechoslovak Communist Party and, therefore, the need to arrive at an agreement quickly with the perpetrators of the Prague Spring. Thus time remained salient during the entire week of the end-crisis period, until the Moscow Protocol was concluded with Dubcek and his colleagues.

Perceived *war likelihood/military hostilities*, too, exhibited a marked decline, as postulated. The only exception was Syria in the Lebanon Civil War. Despite its victory over the PLO–Muslim coalition, further Syrian military involvement was likely, given the complexity of the struggle for power among Christians, Muslims, Druze and Palestinians — and Syria. A further (partial) exception was Israel's perception of high war likelihood with Syria after its Disengagement Agreement with Egypt on 18 January 1974. And in India's end-crisis period it was uneasily aware of a possible resumption of war with China, though the likelihood declined in the aftermath of the unilateral PRC withdrawal starting 1 December 1962.

Triggers to the end-crisis period exhibit greater variation. Three were violent: the successful Warsaw Pact invasion, for the USSR in the Prague Spring; Syria's military triumph over PLO–Muslim forces, in its Lebanon Civil War I Crisis; and the advance of British forces at Port Stanley, for the UK in the Falklands/Malvinas Crisis. Three were non-violent military in form: Germany's surrender at Stalingrad; the cease-fire, for Israel in the October-Yom Kippur crisis-war; and the Soviet occupation of Budapest, for Hungary in the Hungarian Uprising. Two were verbal acts: China's announcement of a unilateral withdrawal, for India in the border crisis-war; and the British Prime Minister's pledge to compel Rhodesia to rescind UDI, for Zambia. Finally, there was one internal trigger, namely, the US's expanded airlift decision, during its Berlin Blockade Crisis.

There is even greater variation in the *duration* of the end-crisis period. For the USSR (Prague Spring) it was one week, and for Argentina (Falklands/Malvinas), 16 days. At the other extreme, the US's winding-down process during the Berlin Blockade Crisis lasted almost 10 months, and Israel's October-Yom Kippur end-crisis period, seven months. In between were Zambia and India, each slightly more than three months; Hungary, two months; and Germany and Syria, each one-and-a-half months.

TABLE 4.6.B.2   *Deescalation/End-Crisis: Summary of Case Study Findings:
Situational Attributes – System Level*

International Crisis	System	No. of Actors	Violence
Berlin Blockade	Dominant	4	None
Prague Spring	Subsystem – Central/Eastern Europe	6	Minor
Munich	Dominant	—	—
Stalingrad	Dominant	2	War
October – Yom Kippur	Subsystem – Middle East	5	War
Lebanon Civil War I	Subsystem – Middle East	1	Serious Clashes
India/China Border	Subsystem – South Asia/East Asia	2	None
Hungarian Uprising	Subsystem – Central/Eastern Europe	2	None
Rhodesia UDI	Subsystem – Southern Africa	1	None
Falklands/Malvinas	Subsystem – South America	2	War

The *number of crisis actors* in the deescalation phase of the international crisis as a whole, as distinct from adversaries, varied as well: one in the Lebanon Civil War I and Rhodesia UDI crises; two in the Stalingrad, India/China Border, Hungarian Uprising, and Falklands/Malvinas cases; four in the Berlin Blockade, five in October—Yom Kippur, and six in the Prague Spring.

Finally, among the situational attributes, the range of *violence* varied: no violence in the deescalation phase of four international crises—Berlin Blockade, India/China Border, Hungarian Uprising, Rhodesia UDI; minor clashes in the Prague Spring; serious clashes in the Lebanon Civil War; and full-scale war in the winding-down phase of three cases—Stalingrad, October-Yom Kippur, and Falklands/Malvinas. In sum, variation in both actor and situational attributes is no less striking in the end-crisis than in the pre-crisis and crisis periods.

The pattern of very similar *coping* uncovered in the two earlier periods is substantially replicated in the end-crisis period of the nine crises (see Table 4.6.C). It is evident, for the most part, in the *information* domain. Either the felt need and quest for information, that is, its volume or processing, or both, were unchanged in seven of the nine cases: the USSR, Germany, Israel, Syria and Argentina, regarding both aspects; the US with respect to volume; and Hungary as far as processing was concerned. There were some changes, however. In the US case, processing reverted to bureaucratic subordinates—as expected during a phase of declining stress. In the India case, the flow of information declined, as expected, but processing became more rigid, primarily because of the profound distrust of any PRC actions following the perceived Chinese betrayal of India's friendship. Finally, in the Zambia case, the volume of information increased slightly but, as expected, receptivity was greater than in the crisis period. In sum, the information pattern in the end-crisis period was very similar for a group of diverse states; but it did not accord with the expectation of more change from the crisis period, in both volume and processing.

As for *consultation*, the findings are more mixed. The process was essentially unchanged in four cases: the USSR, Germany (except for the addition of Manstein), Syria and Argentina. It was broader in three cases. The US consulted intensely with the UK and France, on both the military and diplomatic steps to deescalation of the Berlin Blockade. Israel enlarged the élite groups that were consulted in coping with the mini-war of attrition and tough bargaining with Syria. And in India the Emergency Committee of the Cabinet emerged as Nehru's main consultative body during the diplomatic battle over the Colombo Proposals. In two cases the consultative group was narrower: in Hungary, a reduction from approximately 100 to the new 23-member Central Committee of the ruling party; and in Zambia, much less consultation outside the political leadership and senior bureaucrats.

The *decisional forums* exhibit continuity from the crisis period in six crises: the USSR—the Politburo and its (now informal) Negotiating

Committee; Germany, except for the autonomy of decision granted to Manstein by Hitler; Israel—the Cabinet; Syria—the President, the *ad hoc* decision-making committee, and the *ad hoc* decision-making Cabinet; Zambia—the President, senior ministers and the Cabinet; and Argentina—the military junta and the Foreign Minister. Changes occurred in the other three cases: in the US, a much less active President, at first because of Truman's preoccupation with the election campaign in the autumn of 1948, and later because of the steady decline in war likelihood; India, where the Emergency Committee of the Cabinet became the central decisional, as well as consultative body; and Hungary, a unique case in which the Soviet Military Command in Hungary was the dominant decisional unit, with the Hungarian Politburo and its four-member directorate acting in a subordinate capacity. Overall, then, continuity outweighed change in the end-crisis decisional forums.

In the search for and consideration of *alternatives* there was more variation. Search remained careful in the Israel and Syria cases. It declined in the US, the USSR, Germany, India, and Zambia crises, as expected in the lower-stress end-crisis period. And neither Hungary nor Argentina engaged in a search for options. As for evaluation, it remained careful in five cases—Germany, Israel, Syria, India and Hungary. It was less careful than in the crisis period in the USSR and Zambia cases. It was more rigid in the US crisis—because the airlift strategy was working. And there was no evaluation, and no options, in the Argentina crisis.

Two themes emerge from these findings on deescalation/end-crisis. First, the case studies exhibit more commonality than diversity during the winding-down phase of an interstate crisis; at the same time, there was more variation in coping with deescalation than with onset or escalation. Second, the sharp differences between coping with low and high stress, in the pre-crisis and crisis periods, do not extend to the shift from crisis to end-crisis; rather, continuities are conspicuous. Why is this so?

Earlier, deescalation/end-crisis was termed the obverse of the escalation phase/crisis period—winding down versus the spiral process. Conceptually, this remains valid. However, implicit in this idea was the view that the step-level change from crisis period to end-crisis period is the mirror image of the change from pre-crisis period to crisis period. In reality, these step-level changes, especially as they relate to coping, are not identical. By the time a crisis actor enters the winding-down, end-crisis period, it has been through the peak period of stress; and that has

TABLE 4.6.C *Deescalation/End-Crisis: Summary of Case Study Findings: Coping Mechanisms*

International Crisis	Crisis Actor	Information	Consultation	Decisional Forum	Alternatives
Berlin Blockade	US	Unchanged in high volume, but processing by subordinates	Diplomatic and military – UK, France, Republican Party leaders	Secretary of State and NSC; declining role of President	Search declined, evaluation more rigid
Prague Spring	USSR	Unchanged in volume and processing	Unchanged – East European leaders and Soviet military	Unchanged – Politburo and its Negotiating Committee	Neither comprehensive search nor careful evaluation
Munich	UK	–	–	–	–
Stalingrad	Germany	Unchanged in volume and processing	Unchanged, except Manstein	Enlarged – addition of Manstein	Search declined, evaluation on two issues
October – Yom Kippur	Israel	Unchanged processing	Broader – Cabinet, Opposition leader, bureaucrats, generals	Cabinet	Careful evaluation

Lebanon Civil War I	Syria	Unchanged in volume and processing	Unchanged – 4–43 persons	Unchanged – President, decision-making Committee, decision-making Cabinet	Careful search and evaluation
India/China Border	India	Decline in flow, rigid processing	Broader, especially 6-member Emergency Committee of Cabinet	Enlarged – Emergency Committee of Cabinet	Search declined, careful evaluation
Hungarian Uprising	Hungary	Processing unchanged	Narrower – 8–23 persons	Abnormal – Soviet Military Command, four-person Hungarian Politburo directorate, 11-person Politburo	Careful evaluation
Rhodesia UDI	Zambia	Volume slightly more, processing more open	Narrower	Unchanged, but ministers and Cabinet more important	Search declined, evaluation less thorough
Falklands/Malvinas	Argentina	Unchanged in volume and processing	Unchanged	Unchanged	No search or evaluation

left its imprint on perceptions even while acute tension is declining. Thus a kind of inertia and time lag tend to operate in the coping process: many characteristics of coping in the crisis period, e.g., the active search for information and special decisional forums, are likely to continue into the winding-down end-crisis period. In this sense, the crisis period spills over into end-crisis, muting the differences between crisis management at the peak and during the downswing of an inter-state crisis.

The pattern of very similar coping in the ten foreign policy crises acquires added significance in light of the conspicuous diversity in the extent of: involvement by the major powers; geostrategic salience; heterogeneity, and issues. These situational attributes, along with the number of actors and the extent of violence, the diversity of which was discussed above, combine to generate the overall intensity of a crisis [see Table 5.3 and the accompanying discussion for diversity in intensity scores].

Crisis termination, the "normal" end of the deescalation process, is also the logical point to assess another crucial crisis dimension, namely, the *intensity* or severity of an international crisis. This will be done in the first part of the following chapter, as a prelude to the analysis of crisis impact.

CHAPTER 5

Impact

INTERSTATE crises vary along many dimensions: the context in which they erupt, notably their polarity, conflict setting and region; the relative power of adversaries; their territorial and population size; level of economic development; type of political regime; the extent of violence; outcome, etc. This diversity is evident from little-known cases since the end of World War I, as well as from celebrated cases of the contemporary era as presented in Table 5.1.

These crises also vary in *intensity* and *impact*, two other crucial dimensions of the crisis phenomenon. What is meant by intensity? Can it be measured and crises ranked along this dimension? If so, what elements enter into such an assessment? What is their relative weight in the calculus of intensity? And how, if at all, can one achieve clarity and precision about the intensity of a specific crisis? Similarly, what is meant by impact? Can it be measured, and crises ranked, in terms of their consequences? What criteria should be used, and what weights should be accorded to the relevant factors? These questions serve as the focus of this chapter.

As an analytic point of departure, the two dimensions refer to different types of change in different time frames. Intensity is a composite of situational attributes during an international crisis. The term refers to the volume of *disruptive change* among crisis actors from onset to termination and denotes the extent of *instability*. Impact is a composite of effects on a system, as well as on the adversaries, after the end of a crisis. The term refers, in system terms, to the extent of *structural change* or irreversibility and thus denotes the presence or absence of *(dis)equilibrium*.[1] In short, whereas intensity refers to disruptive interaction while a crisis is in motion, impact refers to structural change after a crisis.

TABLE 5.1 *Selected Crises: Various Dimensions*

International Crisis (Little-Known)	Polarity	Conflict Setting	Region	Capability (Power Discrepancy)	Territory – Size	Political Regime	Violence	Outcome – Content
Bessarabia (1919–20)	Multipolar	non-PC°	Eastern Europe	High	Large/Medium	Civil Authoritarian/ Civil Authoritarian	Serious Clashes	Definitive†
Leticia (1932–33)	Multipolar	non-PC	South America	Low	Medium/Medium	Military/Democratic	Serious Clashes	Definitive
Junagadh (1947–48)	Bipolar	PC	South Asia	Low	Large/Small	Democratic/ Democratic	Minor Clashes	Definitive
Qalqilya (1956)	Bipolar	PC	Middle East	Low	Small/Small	Democratic/Civil Authoritarian	Serious Clashes	Ambiguous°°
Malaysia Federation (1963–65)	Polycentric	non-PC	Southeast Asia	Low	Medium/Large	Democratic/Civil Authoritarian	Minor Clashes	Definitive
Belize I (1975)	Polycentric	non-PC	Central America	Low	Medium/Medium	Democratic/Military	Serious Clashes	Definitive
Three Village Border (1987–88)	Polycentric	non-PC	Southeast Asia	Low	Medium/Medium	Civil Authoritarian/ Civil Authoritarian	Serious Clashes	Ambiguous

(Well-Known)

Case								Outcome
Invasion of Ruhr (1923)	Multipolar	PC	Western Europe	High	Medium/Small	Democratic/ Democratic	Minor Clashes	Ambiguous
Entry into WWII (1939)	Multipolar	non-PC	Eastern Europe	High	Medium/Medium	Democratic/Civil Authoritarian	Full-Scale War	Ambiguous
Azerbaijan (1945–46)	Bipolar	PC	Middle East	High	Large/Large	Democratic/Civil Authoritarian	No Violence	Definitive
Suez–Sinai War (1956–57)	Bipolar	PC	Middle East	Low	Small/Medium	Democratic/Military	Full-Scale War	Ambiguous
Berlin Wall (1961)	Bipolar	PC	Central Europe	High	Large/Large	Democratic/Civil Authoritarian	No Violence	Ambiguous
Cuban Missiles (1962)	Bipolar	PC	Central America	Low	Large/Large	Democratic/Civil Authoritarian	Minor Clashes	Definitive
War in Angola (1975–76)	Polycentric	PC	Southern Africa	Low	Medium/Large	Civil Authoritarian/ Civil Authoritarian	Full-Scale War	Ambiguous
Falklands/Malvinas (1982)	Polycentric	non-PC	South America	Low	Medium/Large	Democratic/Military	Full-Scale War	Definitive

Code:
°PC = protracted conflict
†Definitive Outcome = victory or defeat for all crisis actors
°°Ambiguous Outcome = stalemate or compromise for at least one crisis actor

Indicators and Index of Intensity

One indicator is the *number of crisis actors*; that is, the state or states whose decision-makers perceived an act, event or change, abroad or at home, as a catalyst to basic value threat, finite time for response, and more likely involvement in military hostilities before the threat dissipates. Underlying this indicator is the premise that, all other things being equal, the presence of more state actors in a crisis indicates the likelihood of more hostile interaction. The extent of *involvement by major powers* is another indicator of intensity. Was there any activity? If so, was it primarily verbal, political, economic or military support for one of the adversaries? Or did one or more major powers engage in military intervention?

A third factor that contributes to intensity is *geostrategic salience*. Were the location of a crisis and the actors' resources salient to one, a few, many or all members of the global system? Still another element is the extent of *heterogeneity* among the adversaries. Did they vary in military capability or were they all major (or minor) powers? Were they states with post-industrial or pre-modern economies, or did they exhibit diverse levels of development? Were their political regimes divergent or similar? And did they reflect one or more cultures and belief systems? Moreover, what was at stake; that is, were the *issues* political, economic, cultural or military, or a combination of these? Finally, was there interstate *violence* in the crisis; if so, to what extent? These six elements, together, indicate the intensity of an international crisis.

They also point to links between the two levels of analysis, a central theme of this inquiry. The number of crisis actors is inescapably linked to the micro or state level. The extent of major power involvement spills over the two levels. Geostrategic salience and the range of issues represent the macro or system/interactor level, *par excellence*. Interstate violence corresponds to process or patterns of interaction. And heterogeneity synthesizes the two levels. These indicators, with illustrations, will now be examined.

International crises from the end of 1918 to the end of 1988 reveal great variation in the *number of actors*. There were four cases with more than six direct participants: Entry into World War II (1939) 21; Pearl Harbor (1941–42) 10; Remilitarization of the Rhineland (1936) 7; and Angolan War (1975–76) 7. (The Gulf Crisis, 1990–91, too, falls into this category, with 14 crisis actors [Chap. 7 below]).[2] At the other extreme were crises with only one state that perceived a crisis for itself, from Russia in the Russian Civil War (1918–20) to Nigeria in the

Nigeria/Cameroun Border Incident (1987). To tap that variation, a six-point scale was generated, the highest point assigned to cases with six or more actors, the lowest point indicating one crisis actor.[3]

Involvement, as noted earlier, refers to the extent of major power adversarial activity in an international crisis. Three assumptions guided the construction of a scale for this indicator of intensity. First, direct confrontation between major powers generates the most intense disruption, as in Entry into World War II (1939). Further, their high involvement, that is, military intervention or aid, or covert activity (e.g., the US and the USSR in October-Yom Kippur, 1973–74), signifies more potential system change than low involvement, namely, political or economic support for a client state, or no involvement (e.g., the second Punjab War Scare between India and Pakistan, in 1987). And third, high involvement by several major powers is more disruptive than other combinations of activity such as one with high, others with low, involvement, or even one as a crisis actor, others marginally involved; in the latter case (e.g., the 1968 Prague Spring), the major powers' adversarial roles are muted and systemic effects are lessened.

These assumptions generated two six-point scales of involvement by the major powers, one for the great powers of the inter-World War period, the end of 1918 to August 1939, another for the two superpowers, the US and the USSR, from September 1945 to the end of 1988. The latter will be discussed here. Maximal involvement, that is, both superpowers as crisis actors (point 6), was evident in Cuban Missiles, among others.[4] Slightly less intense involvement (point 5) combines one superpower as a crisis actor, the other highly (militarily) involved, as in the 1984 crisis over Nicaragua MIG-21s. Both powers were involved militarily but not as crisis actors (point 4) in Kars-Ardahan (1945–46), an early Cold War crisis arising from a Soviet claim to Turkish territory. Much less adversarial involvement combines one superpower as a crisis actor, the other not involved or only marginally so (point 3), e.g., Communism in Poland (1946–47), with muted US political activity, and the US's Invasion of Grenada (1983), in which the USSR stood aside. There were also cases with one superpower highly involved, the other little or not at all (point 2), e.g., Invasion of Laos I (1953–) and the 1984 Sudan/Ethiopia Border Crisis, with the US sending military aid to France in the former, the Soviets to Ethiopia in the latter, and the other superpower remaining aloof. Finally, at the lowest point in the scale (1), both superpowers were uninvolved in many crises. These range from the first India/Pakistan crisis over Kashmir in 1947–48 to the last intra-war crisis of the prolonged Iran/Iraq War in 1988.

Geostrategic salience, as noted, refers to the importance of an international crisis in terms of its proximity to/distance from major power centers and its natural resources. Such assets vary over time. Thus uranium- and oil-producing regions acquired greater salience from the 1950s onwards, while coal-producing regions became more peripheral to interstate politics and conflict. Even key waterways for a century or more—Gibraltar, the Suez Canal, the Strait of Malacca, and the Panama Canal, entry-exit points, respectively, between the Atlantic Ocean and the Mediterranean, the latter and the Indian Ocean, the latter and the South China Sea, and the Pacific and Atlantic Oceans—declined in importance with the vast changes in military technology since the end of World War II.

Illustrative of the change is the Strait of Hormuz, which links the industrialized world (Western Europe, North America and Japan) and a region with vast oil reserves that produced 40% of the annual world oil supply in the 1970s and 1980s, the Persian Gulf. Yet the frequent partial blockages of oil transport through that waterway during the Iran/Iraq War (1980–88) did not cause major economic disruptions in the world economy or draw the major powers into Gulf War I. Alternative routes for the export of Middle East oil, along with other sources of petroleum, reduced the geostrategic salience of the Strait of Hormuz.[5] Nonetheless, these choke points and waterways remain not insignificant in the last decade of the twentieth century.[6] The result of these assumptions and arguments is a five-point scale of geostrategic salience: to the global system (point 5); to the dominant system and more than one subsystem (4); to the dominant system and one subsystem (3); to more than one subsystem (2); and to one subsystem (1).[7]

The extent of *heterogeneity*, as noted, is measured by the number of differences between any pair of crisis adversaries on four attributes—military capability, economic development, political regime and culture. For this purpose every crisis actor was classified in terms of these attributes at the time of its crisis. Four categories were used for *military capability*: superpower; great power; middle power; and small power—most states in the global system in most international crises from 1918 to 1988.[8] Heterogeneity is said to exist, with respect to military capability, when any pair of crisis adversaries belongs to more than one of the four levels of power.[9]

Actors were also categorized in terms of *economic development*, as post-industrial (e.g., the US, Germany, Japan in the 1970s and 1980s), developed (Australia, Canada), and developing (Third World states). For this indicator, heterogeneity exists when any adversarial pair is identified with more than one level of economic development.[10] *Political regime*, too, is an indicator of heterogeneity. States are grouped as: democratic (West European states, the US and Canada, among others); civil authoritarian (communist states, most Middle states, and many Latin American states for most of the 70 years); military (Egypt from 1952 to 1970, most African states most of the time from 1958–1988, etc.); and dual authority (e.g., Argentina from 1945 to 1955, Spain from 1939 to 1976, Turkey from 1980 to 1983).[11] The fourth element of heterogeneity is *culture*, referring to belief system, ideology, language, etc.[12] The values for this indicator of intensity are scored in ascending order, from no heterogeneity (point 1) to total heterogeneity (point 5).[13]

Issues, too, enter the calculus of crisis intensity. The myriad of specific disputes between states were grouped into four *issue-areas*, that is, clusters of issues with a shared focus: *military-security*, which incorporates disputes over territory and borders, military incidents, and war; *political-diplomatic*, comprising all issues that impinge upon sovereignty; *economic-developmental*, including issues arising from nationalization of property, disputes over raw materials, economic boycott, foreign debt; and *cultural-status*, comprising issues of ideology, symbols, disputes over language, etc.

Two assumptions guided the construction of an issue scale: first, that an international crisis over a military-security issue is more intense than a crisis concerned with any other issue-area; and second, that crises over multiple issues will generate more change than a single issue crisis, in the relations between adversaries, in the international system in which the crisis occurs, or in both. These assumptions led to a five-point scale: crises involving three or more issue-areas (point 5); two issue-areas, including military-security (4); a military-security issue alone (3); two issue-areas other than military-security (2); and one non-military issue-area (1).[14]

The extent of *violence* in an international crisis is the last of the six intensity indicators. A four-point scale descends from full-scale war (point 4), through serious clashes short of war (3), to minor clashes resulting in few or no casualties (2), and no violence (1).[15]

In order to measure the intensity of an international crisis an index was created from the six indicators examined above: number of actors, (major power) involvement, geostrategic salience, heterogeneity, issues and violence. The **Index of Intensity** (or **Index of Severity**, the term used in earlier ICB publications) is based upon a weighted summation of the indicators. The weight of each indicator, in turn, was derived from its causal links to the other indicators; that is, it was created deductively. Since there are six indicators of intensity, and each, formally, can be causally linked to any of the others, there exists a theoretical maximum of 30 potential direct linkages.

In fact, geostrategic salience is immune to effects of all other indicators of intensity. The reason is that salience is a function of resources and distance associated with location, relatively static elements. As such, they are impervious to the number of actors or major power involvement, etc., in a specific crisis or even a cluster of crises within a defined region or limited time frame. Thus the maximum number of effects of any single indicator, except geostrategic salience, is four: salience can theoretically affect all five other indicators. This reduces the maximum number of potential direct linkages to 25. None of the indirect linkages was incorporated into the index. The logic underlying the derived linkages and assigned weights are presented in Figure 5.1.

All four direct linkages are postulated for *actors*. First, the number of actors in an international crisis will affect the extent of major power involvement, all other things remaining unchanged. The rationale is that more direct participants in a crisis extend its scope of system relevance. This, in turn, makes higher involvement by the powers more likely because, as system managers, regardless of the polarity configuration, they will be more concerned with a crisis that may set in motion far-reaching changes in the system(s) in which a crisis occurs.

The number of actors also affects heterogeneity, for, *a priori*, more direct participants increases the set of paired comparisons between them. And, as noted in the discussion of deescalation, more dyads increase the likelihood of disparate or conflicting pairs. Thus a larger number of actors is expected to generate more heterogeneity in a crisis.

Also linked to the number of actors is the range of issues. Once again, more participants enlarge the number of potential coalition structures. And these, in turn, will induce the linking of issues operating in a crisis to other latent potential sources of discord. Stated differently, more actors will increase the scope of bargaining in a crisis. And that will complicate the task of achieving accommodation among the adversaries.

The fourth causal link between actors and other indicators of intensity is the disposition to violence in a crisis. More participants in a crisis bargaining process make a collectively satisfying outcome more unlikely. In that setting, one or more crisis actors will be more disposed to use violence to attempt to attain their goals.

Major power *involvement*, too, is causally linked to all other indicators of intensity except geostrategic salience. To begin with the number of actors: when superpowers or great powers are active in a crisis

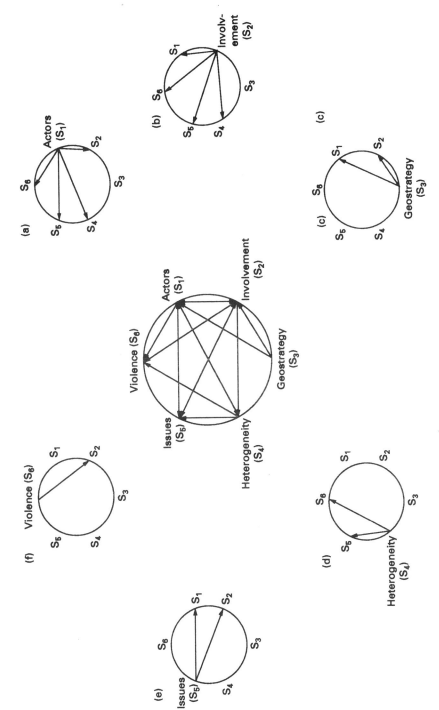

Fig. 5.1 Indicators of Intensity: Network of Effects

their involvement is likely to draw in other states. Stated differently, the actions of major powers will have more spillover effects on the global system and subsystems and on their members; that is, the behavior of major powers will have more far-reaching implications than the behavior of minor powers for developments beyond their immediate domain. This is evident in both threats or cooperative acts.

The involvement of major powers also ensures greater heterogeneity, except in crises when lesser powers are aloof. Put simply, their presence enhances the likelihood of at least one disparate dyad, in power terms; there may be other sources of heterogeneity as well. Thus major power participation in a crisis raises the probability of diversity among actors in a crisis setting.

A link to issues can also be inferred. For one thing, when major powers become involved in a crisis, the range of issues is likely to expand, simply because it is of the essence of major power status to be sensitive to, and to seek satisfaction on, multiple issues. Major powers can also, more readily than lesser powers, introduce new issues to a bargaining process through which participants seek crisis accommodation and termination.

Finally, major power involvement in an international crisis is expected to cause a lower level of violence. This applies especially to superpowers in the nuclear age because of their capability of mass destruction and their awareness of that awesome reality. The "rules of the game," framed by them, impose cautious self-restraint on their use of violence in general and carefully calibrated violence in crises so as to avoid miscalculation and untoward escalation to a level of mutually intolerable cost. Even for great powers in a non-nuclear era, crisis involvement is likely to diminish the resort to violence in the interest of crisis stability, except for powers seeking hegemony or a revision of the *status quo*.

Geostrategic salience is expected to affect two other intensity indicators directly, number of actors and major power involvement. The logic of the first linkage can be stated thus: the more significant a region in which a crisis erupts, in terms of its resources and proximity to the dominant system, the more likely it is that a state within or closely related to that system will be drawn into the hostile interaction between the main adversaries; the stakes of such a crisis and the potential effect of its outcome, beyond the direct relationship of the adversaries, compels greater concern and a willingness to assume costs by states whose interests are not initially involved in the dispute.

As for the second link, physical distance will be much less of a barrier to major power involvement than for lesser powers because of their technological capability. More important, their self-assumed and, often, legitimized role as system managers is likely to induce their involvement in crises whose geostrategic salience extends beyond the main adversaries and their subsystem to the stability of the dominant system and, even more, of the global system as a whole. None of the other three intensity indicators is directly influenced by the geostrategic salience of a crisis.

Heterogeneity, too, is expected to affect two other indicators of crisis intensity. One is the range of issues. Why is this so? First, the disparity between crisis adversaries increases the probability that they will operate with different perceptions of their bargaining environment. Further, this is likely to lead some actors to introduce new issues and to link them to those already under consideration. All other things being equal, this will tend to increase the number and range of issues raised by crisis participants.

A link between heterogeneity and violence can also be inferred. The more diverse the crisis adversaries, especially if they are grouped in coalitions, the more difficult it is for them to communicate effectively their objectives and terms for accommodation. That complication in crisis bargaining will, in turn, increase the likelihood of resort to violence by one or more adversaries, as a consequence of miscommunication and faulty signalling. In short, misperception by heterogeneous adversaries is more likely to result in violent crisis management techniques, with spiralling effects on their mutual behavior. None of the other three indicators of intensity is directly influenced by heterogeneity.

Issues, too, are expected to affect two other indicators of intensity. One is the number of actors, for more issues in contention are likely to draw more states into a crisis; that is, additional foci of bargaining are likely to attract the interest and/or concern of actors who were indifferent to earlier sources of dispute among crisis adversaries.

The extent of major power involvement will also be influenced by the range of issues. Multiple-issue crises have a greater potential than single-issue cases to effect change in adversarial relations and the international system in which a crisis occurs. Once again their role as system managers is more likely to induce major power involvement in crises that have broader implications such as system stability than in crises that are remote from major power concerns, that is, on the periphery of the dominant system. In sum, as with geostrategic salience and heterogeneity, a weight of 2 is assigned to issues.

Violence, the last of the six indicators of intensity, is expected to affect only one other indicator, namely, major power involvement. The basis of this inferred link is the primacy of military-security issues over all others, an assumption discussed above. In substantive terms, inter-state violence is likely to generate concern on the part of major powers because of their system-wide interests. More specifically, violent crises signify disruptive interactions that have the potential to create fundamental changes in the system in which disruption occurs: major powers cannot be impervious to the destabilizing effects of military hostilities. However, conventional wisdom notwithstanding, violence is not causally linked to any other intensity indicators.[16]

The outcome of the deductive derivation of linkages among the intensity indicators is the following assignment of numbers to the weights: w_1 (actors) = 4, derived from four effects; w_2 (involvement) = 4 (four effects); w_3 (geostrategic salience) = 2 (two effects); w_4 (heterogeneity) = 2 (two effects); w_5 (issues) = 2 (two effects); and w_6 (violence) = 1 (one effect).[17]

Case Studies of Intensity

BERLIN BLOCKADE

There were four direct participants in this crisis, all of them major powers. The first to perceive a threat to basic values was the USSR, as a consequence of the Western intention, announced on 6 March 1948, to create an integrated West German economy and state, as part of the anti-communist, US-led Western bloc. The trigger for the US, France and the UK was the Soviet walkout from the Allied Control Council on 20 March. For all three Western Powers that act created a perception of high threat to a core value, namely, the legitimacy of Western interests in Berlin and, by implication, in Germany as a whole. Thus the *number of actors* indicator of intensity was 4 on the six-point scale.

Involvement by the major powers was at the maximum, 6 on the six-point scale. All four powers perceived a threat to basic values—the future of Germany and their relative influence in Europe, as well as time constraints on choice, and the increased likelihood of war. They were actively involved throughout the crisis, with grave risks for the security of all (e.g., the US President's decision on 31 March 1948 authorizing General Clay to send test military trains through the Soviet zone and checkpoints). The possibility of violence was ever-present, with potential far-reaching consequences for the global system.

The *geostrategic salience* of the first Berlin crisis, too, was very high, 5 on the five-point scale. This derived from the centrality of Germany in the struggle for global hegemony between two irreconcilable political, economic and belief systems and, in terms of traditional state rivalry, between the US and the USSR which, more than ever in the post-World War II period, stood apart from all other states in the power hierarchy. The profound cleavages in their worldview and emerging bloc interests ensured that the Berlin Blockade and successor crises, the Deadline (1957–59) and the Wall (1961), would score among the highest on this indicator, that is, they were salient to the global system, and on overall intensity. All three are included in the cluster of most intense crises since the end of World War I.

Heterogeneity in the first Berlin crisis was not quite at the maximum. It was visible in the sphere of political regime, three democracies versus communism in the Soviet Union. It was also present regarding military capability for, while the US and the USSR were at the same level as superpowers, the France/USSR and UK/USSR pairs each exhibited a qualitative difference in power, with the two West European states as "great powers" in 1948. There was, too, an enormous gap in the cultural domain, with respect to ideology/belief system, language and religion. Only in the economic arena can the difference between any adversarial pair be regarded as quantitative rather than qualitative. All four actors had industrialized economies; a "post-industrial" advanced economy was not yet a reality, even for the US. Thus Berlin Blockade scored 4 on the five-point scale for this indicator of intensity.

Several *issues* were at stake in this international crisis. Preeminent was the military-security issue-area, for Berlin Blockade and its outcome impinged directly on the military balance between East and West, including a heightened probability of full-scale war at escalation peaks of the crisis period. Political-diplomatic issues, too, were in dispute, including the likely transfer of sovereignty to a newly-created West Germany by the Western Powers and, in the larger sense, the balance of influence between the two coalitions in Berlin, Germany, Europe and the world. And, finally, cultural-status issues were at stake through the clash over ideology and symbols, and the status of the occupying powers in Berlin and Germany as a whole. Thus, the issues indicator was accorded 5 on the five-point scale.

The only indicator of intensity on which Berlin Blockade ranks very low is *violence*. There were "near-miss" incidents. And, as indicated in the discussion of the US Berlin crisis, senior decision-makers, including President Truman and Secretary of State Marshall, were much less sanguine than Military Governor Clay that the Soviets were bluffing. The danger of armed conflict seemed real. It was that sense of the risk of war that led to caution amidst resolve, firmness rather than bluff or intimidation in US behavior. The same can be inferred from Soviet behavior, such as non-interference with the airlift or military trains proceeding to Berlin from the Western sectors. In short, while violence did not occur, the heightened probability was present throughout the first Berlin crisis, especially during the escalation phase. Yet the absence of violence reduced its overall intensity, through a score of 1 on the four-point scale.

The combined scores for Berlin Blockade lead to an *overall intensity* of 8.25 on the ten-point scale, making it among the most intense crises during the 70-year period of inquiry. This score is derived from the equation for overall intensity specified earlier. The relevant data and calculus are presented in Table 5.2.[18]

TABLE 5.2   *Overall Intensity: Berlin Blockade*

Indicator	Weight	Assigned Score
Actors	4	4
Involvement	4	6
Geostrategy	2	5
Heterogeneity	2	4
Issues	2	5
Violence	1	1

$$\text{Intensity Index}^{\circ} = S' = 0.134 \left(\sum_{k=1}^{6} w_k \, s_k \right) - 1$$

Where S = Severity Index; s_k = kth indicator ($k = 1, \ldots, 6$); and w_k = weight assigned to kth indicator.

$$0.134 \, (4(4) + 4(6) + 2(5) + 2(4) + 2(5) + 1(1)) - 1 = 8.25$$

°The coefficient used in the conversion to a 10-point scale is derived as follows: the lower and upper boundaries (minimal and maximal weighted scores) for intensity are 15 and 82: in order to convert these scores to a 10-point scale, it is necessary to multiply by 0.134 and subtract 1 from each value.

PRAGUE SPRING

As in Berlin Blockade and most international crises, the actors did not enter Prague Spring simultaneously. The crisis period for East Germany and Poland was triggered by the official publication of the Czechoslovak Central Committee-approved "Action Program" on 9 April 1968: party leaders Ulbricht and Gomulka were acutely sensitive to the virus of liberalism in Prague and the clear danger of spillover to their own hard-line regimes. For the USSR, as noted, the failure of the one-day bilateral summit with the Czechoslovak communist leaders on 4 May escalated its foreign policy crisis. Bulgaria and Hungary became seriously alarmed over the situation in Czechoslovakia after a summit meeting with three other Warsaw Pact members in Moscow on 8 May. Military intervention to terminate the Prague Spring now seemed a real possibility. Hungary was reluctant to become involved, and the stability of Bulgaria's regime seemed to be at stake. And for Czechoslovakia, while the threat of military intervention was perceived from early May onward, time constraints were not, until the invasion on 20 August. Only then were all three conditions of its crisis period perceived by Dubcek and his colleagues. Thus Prague Spring was at the maximum for the *number of actors* indicator, 6 on the six-point scale.

Superpower *involvement* in the Prague Spring fits the pattern of US/USSR behavior in crises within the other's acknowledged regions of primacy: when either was a direct participant in an international crisis within a subsystem in which it was the preeminent power, the other was either not involved or only marginally so.[19] This was replicated in the Prague Spring Crisis. The USSR was deeply involved from the outset, perceiving a grave threat to bloc unity and its own national security. It used various means of pressure, direct and indirect, to cajole the Prague reformers into submission. It considered the option of military intervention from early May 1968 onwards. But only as a last resort did it conceive and direct the Warsaw Pact invasion in August. The only US involvement was a condemnation by President Johnson immediately after the invasion and a brief suspension of negotiations with the USSR regarding SALT I. Thus Prague Spring, like all other international crises cited above, was coded "one superpower a crisis actor, the other low or no involvement," leading to a score of 3 on the six-point scale for involvement.

Prague Spring was highly salient to Eastern Europe, for it openly challenged bloc unity under USSR hegemony. And it was so perceived by decision-makers in Moscow and the other Warsaw Pact members.

This was its primary *geostrategic salience*. At the same time its implications for the dominant system of the superpowers extended the salience of this crisis beyond one subsystem. Had the experiment in reform succeeded, the Prague Spring would probably have set in motion a wave of political change in Eastern Europe heralding the end of the Warsaw Pact and the dismantling of the communist bloc. This would have meant the serious weakening of the USSR in the global balance of power, as occurred in the East European upheaval of 1989. In the event, the Prague Spring was crushed, delaying that transformation for two decades. During those years the bloc was frozen and Soviet hegemony was enshrined in the Brezhnev Doctrine, proclaimed at the peak of the crisis: as noted, it enunciated the limited sovereignty of members of the "socialist commonwealth," and the Soviet Union's right, and duty, to intervene anywhere in the bloc where socialism was threatened. In sum, Prague Spring was salient to the dominant system of world politics and one subsystem, scoring 3 on the five-point scale.

In terms of *heterogeneity*, there were few attribute differences among the adversarial pairs in the Prague Spring Crisis. Even if one takes the most extreme dyad, the USSR and Czechoslovakia, one finds far more qualitative symmetry than difference. The political regime of both was communism, even though the Czechoslovak leaders were engaged in a heroic effort to reform the system in the direction of "socialism with a human face." The Soviet economy was much larger, given its population and resources, but the level of economic development was the same, namely, a developed, though not a post-industrial economy. Thirdly, there were strong cultural affinities between the two principal adversaries in this crisis. The one notable difference was military capability, the USSR a superpower, even more so in Eastern Europe than in the global system, and Czechoslovakia a small power. The upshot is a very low score for Prague Spring, 2 on the 5-point scale for heterogeneity.

Issues, by contrast, were at the maximum in the Prague Spring. The military-security issue-area was pivotal from the beginning of the crisis. The conflict was not over territory or borders but rather over the unity of the Soviet bloc and the East/West military balance. The sovereignty of Czechoslovakia and, by implication, of all Warsaw Pact members, was at stake, in light of the claims asserted by Moscow via the Brezhnev Doctrine, that is, a political-diplomatic issue. And a basic ideological conflict over the paths to socialism (cultural-status) lay at the heart of the Prague Spring. Thus this crisis was assigned 5 on the five-point scale for issues.

The last of the intensity indicators, *violence*, was minimal in the Prague Spring. The unwillingness of Dubcek and his colleagues to resist militarily became apparent in July over the "Prchlik affair."[20] In the event, the invasion was brief and decisive. Within 36 hours the Czechoslovak road and communications network was under the control of the Warsaw Pact invaders. The Czechoslovak army had been neutralized. All military objectives had been attained. There were minor clashes only, leading to a score of 2 on the four-point scale for violence.

Taken together, the individual scores lead to an overall intensity of 6.77 on the ten-point scale, sufficient to include Prague Spring in the cluster of most intense crises since the end of World War I.

MUNICH

The four crisis actors entered the Munich drama at different times. Czechoslovakia's crisis period was triggered by two events on 7 September: the detention of SdP members, which seemed to put an end to hopes for a compromise solution through the Runciman Mission; and Hitler's order to Henlein to break off all negotiations with Prague. For Britain and France, a full-fledged crisis was catalyzed by Hitler's violent speech on 12 September, portending a descent into irreconcilable conflict. And one week later, President Beneš' request that Moscow reaffirm its commitment to come to the assistance of Czechoslovakia as provided in the Soviet-Czech Defense Pact generated a crisis for the USSR. In terms of the *number of actors* indicator, then, Munich scored 4 on the six-point scale.[21]

There was very high involvement by the major powers in the Munich Crisis. Three of the seven great powers in the inter-World War dominant system, France, the UK and the USSR, were crisis actors. A fourth, Germany, was the catalyst to the crisis through its incessant demands for the annexation of Sudetenland. In fact, but for Germany, this crisis could not have occurred. Moreover, all of these states engaged in intense political and military activity throughout the crisis, including mobilization of reserves and threats and counter-threats of war. And two other major powers were involved actors: Italy, which offered diplomatic support to its German ally and was a signatory of the Munich Agreement; and, marginally, the US, through personal appeals by President Roosevelt to all actors on 26 and 27 September to refrain from the use of force. Only Japan among the major powers was aloof. Thus the *involvement* indicator scored 6 on the six-point scale.

Munich also scored the maximum on *geostrategic salience*. First, the balance of power in the dominant system of world politics during the 1930s was at stake. This centrality of Munich derived from the vast resources and military capability of the direct participants, including the then-formidable armed forces of Czechoslovakia. Munich was also salient to several subsystems, Western Europe, Central Europe and Eastern Europe, though these overlapped, geographically, with the dominant system of the great powers. Finally, war among the major European powers was a highly probable outcome, with near-certain spillover consequences for global politics as a whole, as the outbreak of war in Europe demonstrated a year later. Thus this indicator of intensity scored 5 on the five-point scale.

There was much less *heterogeneity* among the adversarial pairs in the Munich Crisis. The most extreme and appropriate dyad for analysis is Germany/Czechoslovakia. In any event, none of the other crisis actors was a pure adversary or pure ally of either of the main protagonists. They differed fundamentally in political regime, extreme civil authoritarianism versus democracy. They also differed in the cultural domain, with respect to language, ideology, and belief system. However, both were advanced industrial economies. And, while Germany was stronger militarily, the gap in capability in the subsystem in which the crisis occurred, that is, Central Europe, was narrow in 1938. This was especially so in light of the theoretically important Czechoslovak access to military aid, through its defense pacts with both France and the USSR: Germany could not know—and did not until late in the crisis—that these were unreliable assets for a small state in acute distress. In sum, there were two attribute differences, thus 3 on the five-point scale for heterogeneity.

Munich encompassed important issues. First and foremost was the military-security issue-area. The most visible dispute was over Czechoslovak territory. Threats of war were incessant. Forces were mobilized by all the crisis actors, as well as Germany. The peace of Europe seemed to be at risk. It was a military-security issue *par excellence*. In addition, the political-diplomatic issue-area was involved. Czechoslovak sovereignty was being compromised. Germany aspired to hegemony in Europe. The relative influence of France, Germany, the UK and the USSR would certainly be influenced by the outcome of Munich. And finally, cultural-status issues were part of this complex crisis. Hitler trumpeted the doctrine of "racial self-determination." The clash between Nazism and democracy was clearly evident. Ethnic conflict between German and Czech-speaking communities in

Czechoslovakia was both symbol and substance. Thus the *issues* indicator scored 5 on the five-point scale.

Only on the violence indicator does Munich exhibit low intensity. Although violent SdP demonstrations occurred daily in Sudetenland, and armies were mobilized in expectation of war, there was no interstate violence in the Munich Crisis, as in the Cold War inter-bloc crisis over the Berlin Blockade a decade later, and the other Berlin crises to follow. Thus Munich scored 1 on the four-point scale for *violence*.

Taken together these scores generate an *overall intensity* of 7.98 on the ten-point scale, placing Munich in the group of most intense international crises since the end of World War I.

STALINGRAD

Despite its prominence in World War II military history, there were only two crisis actors in the Stalingrad IWC. For the Soviet Union, the German campaign of 28 June 1942, directed ultimately to Stalingrad's capture or destruction, posed another serious challenge, of the same order as the siege of Leningrad; that is, it was an intra-war crisis, a grave threat to Soviet forces defending Stalingrad in the face of a massive onslaught. For Germany, by contrast, the Red Army's counter-offensive on 19–20 November signalled possible disaster: on that day Germany's crisis period became a reality. While Hungarian forces, too, were decimated at Stalingrad, and Italian and Hungarian armies had to be withdrawn from the Eastern Front, it was a full-fledged intra-war crisis for the USSR and Germany. Thus, for the *number of actors* indicator of intensity, Stalingrad scored 2 on the six-point scale.

Major power involvement in the Stalingrad Crisis was high. Two of the powers, the USSR and Germany, were crisis actors, with the USSR, as the triggering entity for Germany's crisis period and its exclusive adversary as the momentous battle raged for months. At the same time, none of the other major powers of the pre-1945 era was a crisis actor. And only Italy was directly involved, through the presence of its 8th Army on the satellite front near Stalingrad. Thus this crisis scored high, but not at the maximum, on the *involvement* indicator, 4 on the six-point scale.

The location and context of the Stalingrad Crisis ensured the maximum score for *geostrategic salience*, 5 on the five-point scale. Europe in 1942–43 was still the core of the global system, even though two of the seven major powers, the US and Japan, were "off-shore islands," geographically distant from the core. Any crisis in Europe was salient to the dominant system. This salience was accentuated by the setting for Stalingrad, that is, a world war in which the fate of peoples, states, nations, ideologies, political and economic systems, and influence were at stake. Moreover, the outcome at Stalingrad portended consequences far beyond the battlefield or the specific casualties, gargantuan though they turned out to be. It had implications for the ultimate triumph or defeat of the Allied or Axis Powers and, therefore, for the question, "who would inherit the Earth" when peace eventually came. Thus Stalingrad received the highest possible score for this indicator of intensity.

Although the adversaries at Stalingrad differed in some respects, heterogeneity ranked lower than involvement or geostrategic salience. The political regimes of Germany and the USSR were fundamentally opposed, though both were civil authoritarian in form: while both were dictatorships, one was based upon, and rationalized by, fascism and racism, the other by communism. Moreover, they were vastly different in the cultural domain—in language, belief system, historical tradition, literature, music, etc. At the same time there was no qualitative difference in military capability or economic development. Both were great powers in the hierarchy of the state system from 1918 to 1945. And while Germany may have been more advanced economically, they both fell into the category of developed economy. In short, they differed on two of the four attributes, leading to a mid-point score on this indicator, 3 on the five-point scale of *heterogeneity*.

Stalingrad focused primarily on military-security issues. First and foremost the crisis concerned territory, including the Caucasus and the Ukraine, two areas with crucial resources of oil and grain for both protagonists. The cultural-status domain was also relevant, for ideology, symbols and non-material values were integral parts of the struggle between the armies of Germany and the USSR throughout their epic four-year war. Thus the *issues* indicator scored 4 on the five-point scale.

As for the intensity of violence, Stalingrad was one of the four full-scale war cases in this analysis, along with India/China Border, October-Yom Kippur, and Falklands/Malvinas. Measured by the size of armies in combat, the scope of weaponry and firepower, the number of casualties, and the decisiveness of outcome, Stalingrad stands apart, except for the last criterion, which it shares with China's triumph against India. Like those crises, it scored 4 on the four-point scale for *violence*.

The upshot of this analysis is an *overall intensity* score for Stalingrad of 5.97 on the ten-point scale, considerably lower than the three major power crises discussed earlier or the Arab/Israel crisis to follow [Table 5.3 below].

OCTOBER-YOM KIPPUR

There were five crisis actors during this Middle East crisis-war. The deployment of Egyptian forces toward the Suez Canal on 5 October 1973 and a change from defensive to offensive posture triggered the crisis period for Israel. On 10 October, after several days of setbacks and heavy losses—the war began on the 6th—Israeli forces reversed the tide of battle in the North, advancing, slowly, toward Damascus, triggering a crisis for Syria. The rejection of a US-initiated cease-fire in place, by Egypt and Syria on 12 October, triggered a crisis for the US, which feared a possible direct military confrontation with the USSR, the patron of the two Arab states. A crisis for Egypt was triggered on 18 October, when President Sadat belatedly became aware of the worsening military situation following Israel's successful crossing of the Suez Canal on the 16th and the consequent threat to the Egyptian Third Army. And Israel's continued advances after the first of two superpower-imposed, UN-formalized cease-fire agreements on 22 October triggered a crisis for the USSR. Thus, in terms of the *number of actors* indicator, October-Yom Kippur was among the most intense, 5 on the six-point scale.

The Middle East crisis-war of 1973–74 was even more intense in terms of superpower involvement. The US and the USSR were adversarial crisis actors, as evident in the Soviet threat of direct military intervention in Sinai on 24 October, and the US counter-threat, signalled by a strategic nuclear alert the same day. Only the Cuban Missile Crisis was more acute in the nuclear sphere of superpower behavior.

More tangibly, both superpowers provided massive arms and equipment to their client states during and after the October-Yom Kippur crisis-war: the Soviets began their airlift-sealift on 8 October, the US on the 14th. And at the end of the war the US extended an additional $2.2 billion in emergency military assistance to Israel, while the Soviets rapidly replenished the depleted arsenals of Egypt and Syria. Moreover, both cease-fire agreements were worked out by the patron powers. The UN Security Council adopted a joint US-USSR resolution to that effect on 22 October and authorized the creation of a UN force to police the Golan Heights. This was replicated in a second UN cease-fire resolution on the 25th, after the Soviet threat, the US counter-threat, and US pressure on Israel to abandon its encirclement of Egypt's Third Army.

Then, as an active mediator for two months, Secretary of State Kissinger brokered the (first) Egypt/Israel Disengagement Agreement of 18 January 1974, involving Israel's partial withdrawal, the exchange of prisoners, the reduction of forces in Sinai, and the establishment of a UN buffer zone between the combatants.

A crucial role was also played by the US in securing the Israel/Syria Disengagement Agreement. On 2 May Kissinger began a month of shuttle diplomacy between Damascus and Jerusalem. The US-induced agreement, on 31 May 1974, followed the pattern of Egypt/Israel disengagement—limited Israeli withdrawal, exchange of prisoners, the thinning of forces on the Golan Heights, and a UN buffer zone. It also terminated the Middle East crisis-war for Israel, Syria, the US and the USSR. Thus October-Yom Kippur scored 6 on the six-point scale for major power *involvement*.

The *geostrategic salience* of this crisis, too, was the maximum, 5 on the five-point scale. Two elements made October-Yom Kippur salient to the global system as a whole: the Suez Canal's role as a crucial link in the transportation nexus between Europe, on the one hand, and East Africa and Southern Asia, on the other; and the vast oil resources of the Middle East. The region's strategic significance was accentuated by two other factors: it was a "grey zone" of superpower competition in which the US and the USSR perceived the necessity of high involvement lest their adversary enhance its influence; and its proximity to the Muslim regions of Soviet Central Asia enhanced its high salience, especially to the USSR because of possible adverse spillover from turbulence in the Muslim Middle East. As always since the Suez–Sinai crisis-war of 1956–57, an Arab/Israel international crisis has higher geostrategic salience than crises in any other Third World regional subsystem.

October-Yom Kippur was also characterized by maximal *heterogeneity*, that is, differences among adversarial pairs on all four attributes. There was a marked power discrepancy, for each of the regional protagonists was confronted with a hostile superpower. Moreover, underdeveloped Arab economies faced the then-most advanced post-industrial state in the global system, the US. Types of political regime, too, were heterogeneous—democracy in the Israel-US coalition, a mixture of authoritarianism in the Egypt–Syria–USSR coalition. And Islam confronted Judaism in the cultural domain. This diversity was accentuated by Arab non-recognition of Israel's legitimacy as a sovereign state in the "Arab world." Thus October-Yom Kippur scored 5 on the five-point scale for this indicator of intensity.

Both military and political issues were at stake in October-Yom Kippur. Egypt and Syria, as noted, were motivated primarily by the reconquest of territory lost in the June 1967 Six Day War. More generally, borders remained in dispute. For the Middle East crisis actors the regional military balance, too, was at stake. And for the superpowers the issue was influence in a resource-rich, strategic region of mainly non-aligned states. Thus the *issue* indicator for this crisis scored 4 on the five-point scale.

Finally, October-Yom Kippur was among the most intense of all post-World War II international crises in terms of violence: full-scale war for 20 days; very high casualties; staggering losses of equipment; a battle involving more than 2000 tanks; and a threat of one superpower's intervention, countered by the other's implied threat to use nuclear weapons. Thus the *violence* indicator registered 4 on the four-point scale.

Together, the indicators generated an *overall intensity* of 9.18 on the ten-point scale, making October-Yom Kippur one of the most intense crises from the end of 1918 to the end of 1988.

LEBANON CIVIL WAR I

The *number of actors* indicator for this crisis was minimal, as noted, 1 on the six-point scale. The extent of *involvement* by the major powers, too, was very low. US activity was political, serving as a conduit between Syria and Israel, relaying intentions and information to the two principal state antagonists in Lebanon during the past four decades. (Israel remained aloof from the internal war because Syria did not cross the "red line" of the Litani River.) The USSR supported Syria until its 1 June 1976 invasion of Lebanon, which Moscow strongly opposed; arms deliveries were halted briefly. Thus, on this indicator, too, Lebanon Civil War I scored 1 on the six-point scale.

Other Middle East international crises (Suez-Sinai Campaign [1956], Six Day War [1967], October-Yom Kippur [1973–74]), scored very high on *geostrategic salience*, namely, 5 on the five-point scale: they were salient to the global system because of their strategic location and/or oil resources. Unlike those Arab/Israel crisis-wars, Lebanon was on the geographic periphery of a conflict zone that was of great concern to major powers in the dominant system. Further, it lacked oil. It was the weakest state in the subsystem. And its political fate—restored unity and sovereignty, partition, merger with Syria, etc.—was of interest only to Syria and Israel and, in rhetorical terms, to other Arab states. In short, Lebanon Civil War I had minimal salience. Thus, it scored 1 on the five-point scale for this indicator of intensity.

The task of measuring heterogeneity in this international crisis is complicated by two factors: first, the absence of a second crisis actor serving as Syria's adversary; and second, the fact that the state of Lebanon since 1975 has been more a fiction than a reality. Nonetheless, for this purpose the dyad is Syria/Lebanon. Syria's military capability was much larger, a great power in subsystem terms compared to a small power. They also differed in political regime, Syria's civil authoritarianism under the *Ba'ath* Party versus Lebanon's confessional democracy. In the economic sphere, Lebanon was much more highly developed than Syria, especially in the realm of banking, finance and commerce. Only in culture was there more kinship—in language, tradition, a veneer of French culture as a result of their colonial experience and, for a slight majority of Lebanese by 1975, Muslim faith as well. Thus this crisis scored high for *heterogeneity*, 4 on the five-point scale.

The issues indicator was minimal in Lebanon Civil War I. There was no military-security issue at stake for Syria or Lebanon—or Israel. Nor were the political-diplomatic or economic-developmental issue-areas involved. Rather, one issue was at risk, namely, Syria's influence and its status in the Arab world, especially among the Palestinians, whose cause Syria has long claimed as its own. Thus this crisis scored 1 on the five-point scale for *issues*.

By contrast, there was widespread violence in Lebanon Civil War I. It was not a full-scale war; but it was intense, with heavy casualties and prolonged fighting among Syrian forces and those of Christian, Muslim, Druze and Palestinian militias. Thus it scored 3 on the four-point scale for *violence*. The upshot of these individual scores was a low *overall intensity*, 2.08 on the ten-point scale.

INDIA/CHINA BORDER

The two protagonists entered this international crisis at approximately the same time, both catalyzed by the Tibet revolt. For the PRC the trigger was India's decision to give asylum to the Dalai Lama. For India it was the Chinese accusation of fomenting rebellion in Tibet and undermining China's unity, including control over Tibet. There were no other direct participants. Thus the *number of actors* indicator of intensity scored 2 on the six-point scale.

The extent of superpower *involvement*, too, was low. The US, along with Australia, Canada and the UK, sent substantial aircraft and other military equipment to India. The USSR was involved politically, through several statements via *Pravda*, calling on India to accept China's cease-fire proposals but, in general, attempting to steer a neutral path between a communist ally and a non-aligned friend. China was alienated. And India was disappointed by Moscow's "even-handed" posture between what it regarded as the aggressor and the victim of aggression. Thus India/China Border registered 2 on the six-point scale.

Nor was *geostrategic salience* high for this international crisis. It posed great danger and had serious implications for stability and the balance of power in South Asia as a subsystem, particularly because of the embryonic China-Pakistan alignment against India. It also symbolized the PRC's hegemony in East Asia; no other state in that regional subsystem could compete with China's military capability, though Japan was already much stronger economically. More to the point, despite the fact that Asia's giants were its protagonists, this crisis was irrelevant to the dominant system of East/West conflict at the time, vastly overshadowed by the danger of nuclear war posed by Cuban Missiles. For these reasons India/China Border scored 2 on the five-point scale for this indicator of intensity.

Among the four attributes that comprise the basis for assessing extent of heterogeneity, India and China differed on two. The political regime of China was communist, while India adhered to parliamentary democracy, with a formal constitution and federalist features. There were also enormous differences in the cultural domain: language (Hindi and many other distinct languages versus Chinese dialects); belief system (Hinduism and Islam versus Maoism, superimposed on Confucianism); music, art, literature, etc. However, they were both economically underdeveloped, at approximately the same level of modernity. And their military capability was comparable—two great powers in subsystemic terms, South Asia and East Asia. Thus this international crisis scored 3 on the five-point scale for *heterogeneity*.

There was one overriding issue in India/China Border, namely, territory. Yet the PRC had other objectives: to weaken India's image in the Third World; to undermine the stability of the Nehru government; to portray democracy as an inefficient alternative to communism, etc. But these were not objects of contention, i.e., issues, in the crisis. Rather, this is a classic example of the primacy, in fact, exclusivity, of the military-security issue-area in a crisis. For this reason India/China Border scored 3 on the five-point scale for *issues*.

Of all the intensity indicators only violence was at the maximum in this international crisis. Although of brief duration, a full-scale war raged between India and China for a week in October and another week in November. Large forces were involved, the number of prisoners was high, and Indian troops were expelled from substantial blocks of territory in the North East Frontier Agency (Eastern Sector) and Ladakh (Western Sector). Thus *violence* registered 4 on the four-point scale.

Combining the individual scores, India/China Border registered 3.82 on the ten-point scale for *overall intensity*, far below the minimum for the cluster of most intense crises in 70 years.

HUNGARIAN UPRISING

For both Hungary and the Soviet Union the trigger to the crisis period was the mass demonstration of 23 October 1956. The communist leaders in Budapest viewed it as a serious threat to the communist regime and to their own power. Moscow saw it as a threat to Soviet hegemony, not only in Hungary but in Eastern Europe as a whole. Yet, despite the spillover effects, they were the only *crisis actors*. Thus this intensity indicator scored 2 on the six-point scale.

The extent of *involvement* exhibited a decade-old pattern in intra-Soviet bloc crises. The USSR was a very active crisis actor, engaged in the highest possible involvement, direct military intervention. The US protested against Soviet behavior and supported the UN's muted criticism of its repressive policies. However, in essence, the US acquiesced in the reassertion of Moscow's hegemony in Hungary. The result was 3 on the six-point scale for involvement.

The *geostrategic salience* of the Hungarian Uprising was higher. Hungary is located in the heart of Europe, on the western edge of the Warsaw Pact. Its borders with neutralized, pro-West Austria and non-aligned communist Yugoslavia enhanced the importance of its location. And 1956 was the height of the East/West Cold War. Hungary's revolt against Soviet domination and its possible exit from the USSR's security zone made the Uprising highly salient to the dominant system of world politics, polarized between US- and USSR-led military alliances, profoundly distrustful of each other. And it was also salient to the stability of the East European subsystem. Thus Hungarian Uprising scored 3 on the five-point scale for this indicator of intensity.

There was moderate *heterogeneity* in this international crisis. First and foremost was the vast difference in military capability: the USSR was a global superpower, Hungary a minor power, even in terms of the East European subsystem. Moreover, they differed basically in the cultural domain—ethnic background, language, religion, etc. However, they shared a communist political regime, although the Hungarian leaders sought autonomy from Moscow's domination. And while the Soviet economy was much larger and, in military technology, much more advanced, the economies of the two adversaries were developed. In short, the Hungary/USSR dyad was heterogeneous on two of the four attributes, leading to a score of 3 on the five-point scale for this indicator.

The primary issue in contention was military and political control of a client by a patron state. Hungary pressed for the withdrawal of Soviet forces so that it could be free to choose its foreign policy, including non-alignment in the Cold War. For the Soviet Union this posed a grave challenge to its military hegemony throughout the bloc, which it regarded as a natural "security zone" for the USSR as a state, as well as for the "communist camp." This, in turn, had implications for the East/West military balance. In short, the military-security issue-area was at the core of this crisis. At the same time political-diplomatic issues were also in dispute, including sovereignty over Hungary and Soviet influence in Eastern Europe. Thus Hungarian Uprising scored 4 on the five-point scale for *issues*.

As for *violence*, the Soviet invasion led to armed resistance by sub-stantial segments of the Hungarian people. Even though Nagy and his colleagues decided against the military option, that is, to avoid direct confrontation by the armed forces, there were serious clashes in Budapest and elsewhere, especially until 14 November and, more spasmodically, until January 1957. Violence was more intense than in the Prague Spring: it scored 3 on the four-point scale for this indicator. The individual scores for intensity in Hungarian Uprising led to an *overall intensity* of 4.76 on the ten-point scale.

RHODESIA UDI

Since Zambia alone experienced a foreign policy crisis, Rhodesia UDI scored 1 on the six-point scale for *number of actors*. There was exten-sive *involvement* by the UK, military, political, diplomatic and econ-omic. However, this indicator of intensity for post-World War II cases is measured by the extent of superpower involvement. And US activity was confined to economic aid, while the USSR remained aloof. Thus this indicator, too, was at the minimum, 1 on the six-point scale. So too with *geostrategic salience*: Rhodesia UDI was relevant only to the Southern African subsystem; even the challenge to the UK posed by

Rhodesia's action did not make this crisis salient to Western Europe or any other international subsystem. Thus it scored 1 on the five-point scale for salience.

As for heterogeneity, the adversaries differed on all but one of the four attributes. Rhodesia was much stronger, militarily, a middle power in subsystem terms, while Zambia was a very weak minor power: it was incapable of defending itself, as evident in its persistent request for a British military presence to guard key installations. While both antagonists were underdeveloped economies, Rhodesia was much stronger in this realm, too, because of its stranglehold over key raw materials that, as noted, were vital for Zambia's survival. And in the cultural domain, a black African state confronted a white-settler, European regime, with antagonistic values and ideologies; it was the remnant of the old imperial order versus the new post-colonial era. Only in terms of political regime were they similar. Both were civil authoritarian, in the guise of democratic forms. Rhodesia had a severely restricted franchise—democracy for a minuscule minority; and Zambia's regime was dominated by a charismatic president, who remained in power until 1991, when he was ousted in a democratic election. In sum, Rhodesia UDI scored 4 on the five-point scale for *heterogeneity*.

This crisis was also intense with respect to issues. First and foremost, Zambia's economic survival was perceived to be at stake. Sanctions were imposed in the struggle against UDI. Rhodesia threatened to use its economic power to counter opposition from Zambia and the international community. Access to oil, coal and electricity was at the heart of the crisis. At the same time, there was a considerable military-security dimension. Forces were mobilized by the principal antagonists and moved to their border. British troops and planes were stationed in Zambia to protect it from invasion or harassment. There were frequent threats of military action by Rhodesia. The OAU discussed the possible dispatch of an African armed force to assist Zambia. Thus this crisis registered 4 on the five-point scale for *issues*.

There was no *violence* in Rhodesia UDI, despite high tension and frequent threats to use force; hence, a score of 1 on the four-point scale. Taken together these indicators sum to a very low *overall intensity*, 2.62 on the ten-point scale.

FALKLANDS/MALVINAS

The UK was the first crisis actor in an intercontinental crisis at the southern tip of the Americas: its trigger was the 18 March flag incident.

Argentina perceived a full-scale crisis on 5 April with the news that a large British task force was en route, determined to evict Argentine forces from the islands. Thus Falklands/Malvinas registered 2 on the six-point scale for the *number of actors* indicator.

Even more than in Rhodesia UDI the UK was highly involved in this international crisis: it was a crisis actor engaged in full-scale war. However, the *involvement* of both superpowers was limited to the political-diplomatic arena. The US, as noted, was a high-profile mediator, including direct communications between President Reagan and British and Argentine leaders. The USSR was marginally involved, making an unsuccessful offer of arms to Argentina in return for diplomatic support for Soviet policies. Such superpower involvement is classified as "low," leading to a score of 1 on the six-point scale for this indicator of intensity.

In an earlier era, before the construction of the Panama Canal, the location of the Falklands/Malvinas islands was of geostrategic consequence, as the passageway between Atlantic and Pacific Oceans. Long before 1982, however, the islands had become peripheral to the main lines of sea communication between the Americas and Europe, on the one hand, the Far East and Southern Asia, on the other. Nor do they have confirmed natural resources, though rumors of substantial oil deposits surfaced during the crisis. Yet any territorial residue, such as the Falklands/Malvinas islands, was salient to Latin America, especially to the Southern Cone, centered on Argentina. Moreover, given the crucial role of the UK, and the likely effects on relations between Argentina and the European Community, this crisis was also *geostrategically salient* to Western Europe. Despite a highly visible US presence, it was not relevant to the dominant system of world politics. Thus it scored 2 on the five-point scale.

In sharp contrast with the three indicators discussed above, heterogeneity was at the maximum in the Falklands/Malvinas Crisis. The UK's military capability was markedly superior to that of Argentina, even in the South Atlantic, a regional great power compared to a middle power. So too with economic development. Despite its decline after World War II, the UK remained an advanced industrial state. Argentina was still in the throes of underdevelopment. In terms of political regime, the role model for democracy in much of the world confronted a military dictatorship. And finally the UK and Argentina were far apart in the cultural sphere—language, religion, worldview, music, art, etc. Thus Falklands/Malvinas scored 5 on the five-point scale for *heterogeneity*.

There were two closely-related *issues* in this international crisis. One was a conflict over territory, with Argentina and the UK expending large resources to restore, and to retain, control over the islands. The full-scale war that ensued from this crisis reflects the importance of the military-security issue-area. The ultimate object of contention was sovereignty, both antagonists persisting with longstanding claims; that is, Falklands/Malvinas also focused on the political-diplomatic issue-area. Thus it scored 4 on the five-point scale for this indicator.

Violence was at the maximum, namely, full-scale war: it was one of the relatively few major wars in the 1980s. Thus it scored 4 on the four-point scale. Summing the intensity scores for Falklands/Malvinas leads to an *overall intensity* of 4.09 on the ten-point scale.

It remains to compare the scores for intensity assigned to each of the ten crises. These are presented in Table 5.3.

As evident, several of these international crises rank high in terms of *overall intensity*, sufficient for their inclusion in the category, "most intense" international crises during the 70-year period under inquiry.[22] These are Berlin Blockade, Prague Spring, Munich and October-Yom Kippur. What are the similarities and differences among them?

All were multiple actor-cases, two of them with 4 actors, one with 5, and one with 6. Major power involvement was at the peak in three of these crises; only in Prague Spring was a superpower, the US, virtually uninvolved. All of these crises were geostrategically salient to the dominant system of world politics; and three of them—all but Prague Spring—had global salience.

There was much greater variety with respect to heterogeneity—from one attribute difference (Prague Spring) to differences on all four attributes (October-Yom Kippur). Issues exhibit the least variation: three cases encompassing three or more issue-areas, one case affecting two issue-areas, including military-security. And violence resembles heterogeneity in its variation. It is noteworthy that only one of these cases was characterized by full-scale war (October-Yom Kippur); one had minor clashes; and two were without violence.[23]

One final theme from the case study findings on intensity merits attention. As evident in Table 5.3, there was great variety among the ten cases for all six indicators. They ranged from:

1 to 6 crisis actors;
no involvement by major powers to their participation as crisis actors (points 1 and 6);
minimal geostrategic salience, that is, to one subsystem, to global system salience (points 1 and 5);

TABLE 5.3 *Selected International Crises: Components of Overall Intensity*

International Crisis	Crisis Actors	Major Power Involvement	Geostrategic Salience	Heterogeneity	Issues	Violence	Overall Intensity
Berlin Blockade	4	6	5	4	5	1	8.25
Prague Spring	6	3	3	2	5	2	6.77
Munich	4	6	5	3	5	1	7.98
Stalingrad	2	4	5	3	4	4	5.97
October – Yom Kippur	5	6	5	5	4	4	9.18
Lebanon Civil War I	1	1	1	4	1	3	2.08
India/China Border	2	2	2	3	3	4	3.82
Hungarian Uprising	2	3	3	3	4	3	4.76
Rhodesia UDI	1	1	1	4	4	1	2.62
Falklands/Malvinas	2	1	2	5	4	4	4.09

minimal to maximal heterogeneity, that is, adversarial differences on 1 to 4 attributes (points 2 and 5); a non-military single-issue case to crises with spillover to three or more issue-areas (points 1 and 5); and from no violence to full-scale war (points 1 and 4).

This diversity is also clearly evident in the scores for overall intensity: there were two cases with low intensity (Rhodesia UDI, Lebanon Civil War I); two with modest intensity (Falklands/Malvinas, India/China Border); two with moderate intensity (Stalingrad, Hungarian Uprising); two with high intensity (Munich, Prague Spring); and two with very high intensity (October-Yom Kippur, Berlin Blockade).

Impact: Indicators and Index

In the analysis of concepts [Chap. 1] it was noted that the consequences of interstate crises unfold at two levels: first, for the relationship between adversaries beyond a crisis, especially their relative power; and second, for one or more international systems. To capture the multiple effects, *impact* is measured by four indicators of system change: change in power distribution, in actors, in rules of the game, and in alliance configuration.

Power change encompasses the number of power centers and the hierarchy of power in an international system. To tap both types of change a four-point scale was generated for this indicator of impact: change in the composition of states at the top of a power pyramid (point 4); change in the ranking of the five most powerful states in the dominant system or the relevant subsystem (3); change in the relative power of crisis adversaries (2); and no change in their relative power (1).

Change in the membership of the power élite in an international system (point 4) is infrequent. Notable examples of exit from the dominant system's major powers are associated with World War II intra-war crises: France in June 1940, after the Fall of Western Europe; Italy in November 1943, after the Fall of Italy; Germany in May 1945, after the Final Soviet Offensive; and Japan in September 1945, after the End of World War II (Atomic Bomb) IWC. All of these changes were the direct result of that war and are incorporated in the maximal overall impact, 10 on the ten-point scale, accorded to the last two of these crises.

Changes in entry or reentry into the club of major global powers are also rare: France, after the Final Soviet Offensive that led to the end of World War II in Europe; the People's Republic of China, after its victory in the China Civil War of 1948–49; and West Germany, after the triumph of the Western Powers in the Berlin Blockade Crisis and the creation of the Federal Republic of Germany, in 1949. At the regional subsystem level, Israel entered the Middle East power élite after defeating several Arab armies in the Israel Independence crisis-war of 1948–49. And North Vietnam became a major power in Southeast Asia following its military triumph over France at Dien Bien Phu in 1954.

Crisis-induced changes in ranking among the most powerful members of an international system (point 3) are also discernible: the emergence of Japan to preeminence in East Asia after the Mukden Incident of 1931–32; Germany's primacy in Europe following the Fall of Western Europe in the spring of 1940—the forced withdrawal of British forces at Dunkirk and the German occupation of Belgium, the Netherlands and part of France; Israel's rise in the hierarchy of the Middle East subsystem as a result of its military triumph over Egypt in the 1956 Suez-Sinai Campaign, and even more dramatically after the devastating defeat of Egypt, Syria and Jordan in the Six Day War of 1967. And India became the superpower of South Asia as a result of the 1971 Bangladesh crisis-war, which significantly diminished the power of Pakistan through the creation of a new state out of former East Pakistan.

The largest group of international crises in terms of this indicator of impact (156 of 390 cases from end-1918 to end-1988, or 40%) exhibited a change in the relative power of adversarial crisis actors, large or small (point 2). This was identified with any of the following combinations of perceived outcome: victory/defeat; victory/stalemate; victory/compromise; compromise/stalemate, and compromise/defeat.[24] In these mixed outcomes, victory denoted an accretion of power, defeat a diminution of power, and compromise/stalemate an increase in power for the former, a decrease for the latter. In most cases scored as point 2 the power change was minute. In none of these outcomes was there a change in the composition of the power élite or in the ranking of states in the relevant subsystem.

The second most frequent cluster of cases in terms of power change—99 (25.4%)—was no change in relative power (point 1). These were identified with any perceived identical outcome by the principal crisis adversaries, that is, victory/victory, defeat/defeat, compromise/compromise, stalemate/stalemate.[25]

Change in *actors* is of two kinds: regime change, whether in orientation or type; and the creation, preservation or destruction of an independent state (or states). It is assumed, first, that the latter is more significant, for a state is a more durable structure than a regime; and second, that change in regime type is more consequential than change in policy direction. These assumptions generated a four-point scale to tap this indicator of impact: formation, maintenance or elimination of one or more states (point 4); change in regime type (point 3); change in regime orientation (point 2); and no change in actors or regimes (point 1).

The most extreme type of actor change was not infrequent in the 1918–88 period, 23 cases (5.9%). Notable examples are the following: in Europe, elimination of Austria for 17 years following the *Anschluss* (1938); in the Middle East, preservation of Israel's statehood as a result of victory in the Israel Independence crisis-war (1948–49); in South Asia, creation of a new state from the former territory of East Pakistan, as a consequence of the Bangladesh Crisis (1971); in Southeast Asia, preservation of Indonesia's independence, proclaimed in 1945, as a result of Indonesia Independence III (1948–49); and in Africa, the maintenance of Gambia's statehood, despite the Gambia Coup Attempt (1982).

Changes in regime type were almost as frequent—20 (5.2%). Non-communist regimes gave way to communist governments in several European states as a result of international crises and USSR intervention soon after World War II.[26] In the Middle East, the Suez Canal Crisis (1951–52) and the Lebanon/Iraq Upheaval (1958) led to dramatic change in Cairo and Baghdad, from a civil authoritarian monarchy to a military regime. In Southeast Asia, the regime of Prince Sihanouk gave way to a military group headed by Lon Nol after the Cambodia Crisis (1970). In Africa, Nouakchott II (1977) led to a change in regime. And in the Americas, the aftermath of the Grenada Crisis was the replacement of a Marxist regime by democracy.

Rules of the game are norms derived from law, custom, morality or self-interest that serve as guidelines for behavior by system actors. According to Young (1989: 16), "rules are well-defined guides to action or standards setting forth actions that members are expected to perform under appropriate circumstances." A rule indicates the relevant subject group, the behavioral prescription, and a specification of the circumstances under which the rule is operative. Young discussed the three types of rules that are associated with international regimes. One is *use* rules, e.g., rules that pertain to the use of international air space, which frequently takes the form of limitations on the exercise of rights. Another is *liability* rules: these spell out the locus and extent of responsibility in cases of injury arising from the action of individual parties under the terms of a regime. The third type is *procedural* rules: these deal with the handling of disputes or the operations of explicit organizations associated with regimes.

Kratochwil (1990) defined a rule as a type of directive that simplifies choice by drawing attention to factors which an actor has to take into account. Four types of rule were delineated: *Instruction* rules; *tacit* rules; *explicit* rules; and *practice* rules. In the area of international relations, tacit rules function as "devices for keeping the international game within certain bounds of mutual expectations and thus half-way predictable" (82). Explicit rules become necessary when the interacting parties do not share a common history or culture, and because of the imprecision of tacit rules, especially when a large number of participants play the game. Practice rules are characterized by specificity and the constitutive nature of a given "performance" (92): a classic example is the Latin dictum, *clausula rebus sic stantibus*; that is, an agreement is binding on the parties only as long as the conditions attending its creation remain unchanged.

Rules may be formal or informally codified. They may be violated frequently. However, they remain valid as long as state actors acknowledge their legitimacy and behave accordingly. Even when states initiate violence they usually invoke the right of self-defense. Given this pattern of behavior, rules of the game tend to change very slowly. Such changes comprise: change in the content of existing rules; the creation or elimination of rules; and modification of actor consensus about a system's rules of behavior.

Two assumptions underlie the assessment of crisis-generated rule change in an international system. First, to institutionalize rules requires more time than to forge a consensus about informal norms of behavior. Thus changes in codified rules are more significant for the affected system. Moreover, it is assumed that a change in content follows a shift in the extent of consensus rather than the reverse, and that dissensus, in turn, leads to change in permissible rules of behavior. A conspicuous example relates to the rules on prisoners of war: terrorists were traditionally excluded from this status; but the consensus on their exclusion has declined during the 1980s and early 1990s.

These considerations led to the construction of a four-point scale to measure crisis-induced rule change: creation/elimination of codified or tacit rules of the game (point 4); increase/decrease in actor consensus on codified rules (point 3); increase/decrease in consensus on tacit rules (point 2); no change in tacit or codified/institutionalized rules (point 1).

There have been few cases of maximal impact on rule change in an international system. A notable example in Europe is the "Brezhnev Doctrine" enunciated during the Prague Spring Crisis (1968). Then and for the next two decades East European interstate relations were guided by the primacy of USSR (bloc leader) interests rather than the conventional principles of state sovereignty and non-intervention. In the Middle East, a tacit rule, that is, an unwritten and unstated agreement or understanding, governed Syrian and Israeli behavior in Lebanon from 1976 to 1981. It was broken by Israel during the Biqa Valley Missiles Crisis (1981), with grave consequences including the Lebanon War a year later. In aggregate terms, there were only 18 cases of 390 (4.6%) during the 70 years in which rules of the game were created or eliminated. In the Middle East, there were only two cases (0.5%), and in Africa, three (0.8%).

There were also relatively few cases of change in consensus on codified rules (point 3). A notable illustration is the cumulative decline in consensus among the four victorious allied powers, the US, the USSR, the UK and France, on the 1945 Potsdam rules governing Berlin, as a result of the three major crises, the Blockade (1948–49), the Deadline (1957–59), and the Wall (1961). Overall, there were nine such cases of rule change in the Middle East (2.3%), and three in Africa (0.8%).

A decline in consensus on tacit rules was a more frequent consequence of international crisis outcomes, especially in the Middle East—11 cases (24%). It was evident in Black September (1970), as well as in the Iraqi Nuclear Reactor Crisis (1981), when Israel preemptively destroyed what was perceived as a gravely-threatening military-industrial nuclear complex in Iraq. Most crises, however (183, or 46.9%), had no effect on rules of the game (point 1), whether informal or institutionalized: in Africa, with fewer and less developed rules, 47 (12.1%) of the cases had some effect.

Change in *alliances*, the fourth indicator of crisis impact, refers to shifts in the structure or functioning of alliances within an international system. These comprise the formation or elimination of an interstate alliance, and changes within an existing alliance, both in number of members and extent of cohesiveness. A scale to measure these changes was based upon two assumptions: first, that change in the number of alliances will have greater consequence than change within an existing alliance; and second, that change in the number of alliance members will have the greatest effect of all alliance attributes. The result was a four-point scale to tap this indicator of impact: formation or elimination of an alliance (point 4); entry or exit of an actor into or from a formal or informal alliance (point 3); increase or decrease of cohesiveness within an existing alliance (point 2); and no change in alliance configuration (point 1).

There have been many international crises that induced the maximal impact of alliance change (20 of 388, 5.1%). A notable example in Europe was the sundering of the 1935 Franco-Soviet alliance as a consequence of the Nazi-Soviet Pact in late August 1939, which triggered the momentous Entry into World War II Crisis. In the largest sense, that crisis, by the time it had fully run its course in six years of global war, shattered the entire alliance structure of the inter-World War period, 1918–1939. In East Asia, the Sino-Soviet alliance of 1950 followed the China Civil War of 1948–49 and lasted for a decade. In the Middle East, the October-Yom Kippur crisis-war (1973–74) led to the replacement of an Egypt-USSR alliance dating, informally, to the mid-1950s, by a new Egypt-US alignment which continues into the early 'nineties.

Changes in the membership of an existing alliance, too, have occurred in various subsystems.[27] There were even more cases of increase/decrease of cohesiveness within an existing alliance (41, or 10.5%) (e.g., increasing cohesion within the Warsaw Pact under Soviet domination as a result of the Prague Spring). Yet the vast majority of international crises during the 70-year period had no effect on alliances (e.g., Middle East [72%], Africa [70%]). This completes the descriptive analysis of the indicators of impact.

As with crisis intensity, an *Index of Impact*, designated an *Index of Importance* in earlier ICB publications, was created from the individual indicators. The weights were arrived at deductively through an assessment of the potential links among them. Since there are four indicators, there is a maximum of twelve possible direct linkages. The actual weight assigned to any indicator is based upon the number of causal links posited with others. These are presented in Figure 5.2.

Change in power will affect each of the other indicators of impact. When the power configuration of an international system changes, for example from bipolarity to multipolarity, or the reverse, so too does the extent of actor autonomy. Thus, if power becomes more dispersed, states will have greater flexibility in shaping their foreign policy behavior towards other states. But if a system becomes more polarized, freedom of choice will be curtailed. In short, shifts in power distribution are postulated as likely to affect the foreign policy orientation of states, that is, cause actor change.

Power change will also affect an alliance configuration. For one thing, coalition dynamics reflect changes in the dispersion of capability among

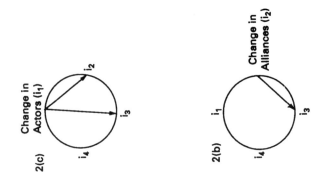

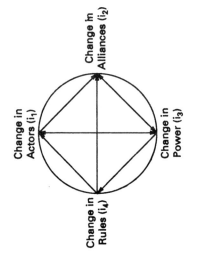

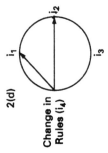

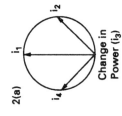

FIG. 5.2 Indicators of Impact: Network of Effects

system members. Moreover, alliances, which provide security for those who might otherwise perceive themselves as vulnerable, undergo changes as the power constellation and consequent perceived threat changes.

Rules of the game are also sensitive to shifts in power. In an anarchic society such as twentieth-century world politics, law generally reflects the preferences of actors capable of reacting decisively to perceived violations. Although even the most powerful actors face constraints, knowledge of the power hierarchy in the global system or a subsystem will generally provide insight into how rules are likely to be interpreted in a given crisis. In sum, the indicator, power change, scores the maximum in the scope of impact.

Change in the number or type of *actors* is expected to influence two of the other three indicators of impact. First, it is likely to affect an existing alliance pattern: if an actor exits from, or enters into, a given subsystem, it will affect the calculations of other actors. Thus actor changes may stabilize or solidify coalitional arrangements, since alliances are often designed and used by states to cope with the enduring security dilemma.

Changes in actors will also influence power distribution. Clearly, the addition of an actor to, or deletion from, an international system will affect the distribution of power in that context. Moreover, a new regime in a state, with objectives and values different from its predecessor, is likely to alter the power hierarchy in the system.[28]

Change in *rules of the game*, too, is expected to affect two indicators of impact. One is actors: prevailing norms will influence the conduct of actors in interstate relations. As norms change, so too will the beliefs of decision-makers as to what constitutes permissible foreign policy behavior and thereby behavior itself.

Rules change will also influence alliances. For one thing, it may make an alliance more—or less—attractive to one or more members. For another, evolving rules can also stimulate the formation of new alliances in response to newly-perceived problems. Third, rule changes affect the perceptions of potential and actual alliance partners. Thus rules of the game are likely to affect alliance dynamics.[29]

Change in alliances will affect only one other indicator of impact, namely, power distribution. If an existing alliance collapses or a new one is formed, or even if an alliance becomes more or less cohesive, such change will affect the ability of states in these coalitions to coordinate their behavior, enhancing or diminishing their capability. This, in turn, will affect the hierarchy of power within and between alliances and, more generally, in the system(s) of which those states are members.[30]

In sum, the weights for the impact indicators are as follows: x_1 (power change) = 3, derived from three effects; x_2 (actor change) = 2 (two effects); x_3 (rules change) = 2 (two effects); x_4 (alliance change) = 1 (one effect).

The time frame for assessing the impact of an international crisis is approximately three years, whereas intensity is confined to the duration of the crisis. Given the character of systemic changes, a shorter time period would be insufficient for them to unfold. A longer period would make it difficult to disentangle the effects of a specific crisis from the competing effects of other crises and conflicts occurring during the same extended time frame.[31]

Crisis Impact Model

The task of a model of crisis impact is to explain the two levels noted earlier, bilateral effects and system consequences. The independent and dependent variables of the model and the direction of crisis impact are presented in Figure 5.3.

The *bilateral effects* of an international crisis depend primarily upon the *content* and *form* of *outcome*: that is, who wins, who loses, or whether the crisis ends in a draw (content); and whether or not it terminates through some kind of agreement (form). It is expected that a disharmonious definitive outcome (victory/defeat) is more likely than an ambiguous outcome (compromise, stalemate) or a harmonious definitive outcome (victory/victory) to bequeath higher tension and instability beyond a crisis. Moreover, if a crisis terminates in a formal or semi-formal voluntary agreement the bilateral effect is more likely to be mutual satisfaction and, therefore, more stability than if a crisis ends by a unilateral act or tacit understanding, or if it fades. In sum, a definitive outcome, formalized as an agreement, is most likely to generate less tension in subsequent interaction between adversaries.

Bilateral effects are also influenced by the *overall intensity* of a crisis, the composite independent variable which, according to this model, explains systemic impact. The six indicators of intensity (actors, involvement, geostrategic salience, heterogeneity, issues and violence) and the four indicators of impact (change in power, actors, rules and alliances) were operationalized and illustrated earlier. Thus it suffices to state the reasons for the choice of intensity and its components as explanatory variables for crisis impact.

The general thesis of the crisis impact model is as follows: *destabiliz-*

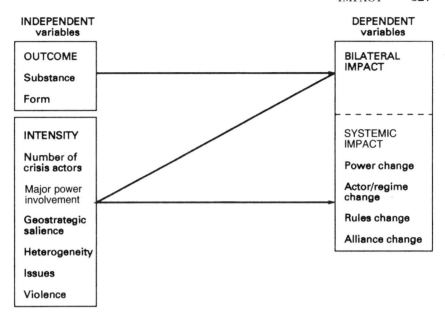

Fig. 5.3 Crisis Impact Model

ing effects during a crisis (intensity) will penetrate the structure of one or more international systems and, over time, will generate change (impact), large or small. The causal links between each component of intensity and impact will now be specified.

Actors. The larger the number of direct participants, the more disruptive a crisis is likely to be, and the more widespread will be embryonic change during a crisis; that is, more actors are likely to generate more hostile interactions, requiring more time for accommodation; more intensity, in turn, will lead to more negative "fallout" for future interaction between the adversaries and for the international system in which a crisis takes place—and, possibly, others as well (greater impact).

(Major Power) Involvement. Their role as crisis adversaries indicates more intense disruption and incipient structural change than any other type of activity; thus more active support by major powers for a client or ally engaged in a crisis, i.e., military intervention compared to political involvement, or stronger opposition to its adversary, makes crisis accommodation more complex and termination more difficult; more intensity has the effect of enlarging the crisis legacy of unresolved issues and intra-system tension (greater impact).

Geostrategic Salience. The broader the salience of a crisis, the more change is portended in the relations among adversaries and/or the system(s) of which they are members; thus a crisis that erupts in a region of geostrategic interest to the major powers (e.g., Central Europe in the twentieth century) will be more intense than a crisis in a peripheral subsystem (e.g., Africa); neither the adversaries, in subsequent interaction, nor the relevant international system(s) can be immune to the consequences—more far-reaching impact;

Heterogeneity. The wider the divergence between adversaries, regarding military capability, economic development, political regime and culture, the more difficult it is to achieve accommodation (more intensity); this is likely to leave a larger residue of unresolved issues, thus extending the negative impact of a crisis outcome.

Issues. More issues in dispute complicate the process of crisis accommodation and make it less likely that all will be resolved (more intensity); this, in turn, will have more destabilizing consequences for the system in which a crisis occurs, as well as for the adversaries (greater impact).

Violence. More intense violence leads to more mistrust, more dissatisfaction, and higher post-crisis tension (impact) within the system.

The impact model probes the phenomenon of international crisis as a *political earthquake*. And the indexes of intensity and impact were designed to measure its strength, both at the time it occurs, the counterpart of a physical upheaval on the earth's landscape, and the scope and depth of its consequences for political actors and systems. With these indexes and data about international crises for actors in global politics during a 70-year period, 1918–1988, one is able to test several hypotheses that derive from the crisis impact (or "crisis-as-earthquake") model. The findings will also test the validity of the model.

Hypotheses and Findings on Impact

At the *bilateral* level, a general hypothesis merits attention:

Hypothesis 12: *The impact of an international crisis on relations between adversaries is most likely to be higher tension when:*
   the outcome is definitive and disharmonious (victory/defeat);
   a crisis ends without agreement;
   there are several crisis actors;
   the major powers are highly involved;
   the crisis has high geostrategic salience;

the adversaries are heterogeneous on many dimensions;
there are several issues in dispute; and
there is a high level of violence during the crisis.

None of these conditions is necessary. Rather, as with the independent variables specified in all other hypotheses, each is sufficient in the sense that any one is expected to generate interactor tension after a crisis. The more that are present, the greater will be the impact.

The findings on the bilateral impact of an international crisis are presented in Table 5.4.

In sum, six postulated linkages in H.12 and part of a seventh are supported by the aggregate evidence: two and part of a third, *very strongly*—heterogeneity, issues, and great power activity; two, *moderately*—form of outcome and number of actors; and two, *modestly*—geostrategic salience and violence. Three of the supported findings are highly significant (p < 0.001), and another is significant. The discrepancy in the effects of great power and superpower activity is noteworthy.

At the *system* level, two related general propositions are worth probing:

Hypothesis 13: *The higher the intensity of an international crisis, the greater will be its systemic impact, high intensity being expressed by:*
several crisis actors;
high major power activity;
high geostrategic salience;
high heterogeneity;
several issues; and
severe violence.

It will be evident that many narrow-gauge, system-focused hypotheses are nested within this overarching proposition. There are 24 logically-possible bivariate hypotheses—individual linkages between any of the six components of intensity and the four components of impact. A few may be cited:

(13a)   the broader the geostrategic salience of an international crisis, the greater the likelihood of a change in alliance configuration;

(13b)   the more active the major powers in an international crisis, the more far-reaching will be the shift in power distribution;

TABLE 5.4 *Bilateral Effect of International Crises: Findings on Hypothesis 12*

	Proportion of International Crises Leading to Higher Tension			
Independent Variable	Category	%	Category	%
Outcome-Substance°	victory/defeat	39	compromise†[iii]	36
Outcome-Form	unilateral act	49	agreement[iv]	39
Number of Actors	one crisis actor	39	five or more crisis actors[ii]	59
	two adversaries	46	five or more adversaries[iv]	46
Major Power Activity	great powers (1918–39) low	28	great powers (1918–39) high[i]	68
	superpowers (1945–88) low	54	superpowers (1945–88) high[iv]	42
Geostrategic Salience	low	42	high[iv]	50
Heterogeneity	very low	23	high[i]	50
Issues	one non-m-s°°	24	two or three, incl. m-s[i]	48
Violence	none	40	severe[iv]	49

n = 294 cases (390 minus 73 IWCs and 23 missing data).
IWCs are excluded from the testing of this hypothesis because they are conceptually related to, but distinct from, the dependent variable. Their inclusion would contaminate the findings in the direction of higher tension. The reason is that they occur during an on-going war and are therefore more likely to generate tension, irrespective of the effects of specified independent variables. As such, IWC would be performing the confounding function of an independent variable.

°See °° n. to Table 3.2.

°°m-s = military-security

†Code for significance test results:
i $p < 0.001$
ii $p < 0.05$
iii $p < 0.10$ (approaching significance)
iv   not significant

(13c) the wider the range of disputed issues, the more extensive will be the cross-cutting effects and consequent changes in alliances;

(13d) more violence will lead to more change in rules of the game; and

(13e) more issues in dispute will cause more changes in regime orientation.

The evidence on the link between intensity and impact is presented in Tables 5.5.1 and 2.

TABLE 5.5.1   *Intensity and Impact of International Crises: Findings on Hypothesis 13*

Independent Variable	Proportion of Intensity Indicators Leading to High Impact			
	Category	%	Category	%
Number of Crisis Actors°	three or fewer	18	four or more[†i]	63
Major Power Activity	low	19	high[i]	40
Geostrategic Salience	low	20	high[i]	50
Heterogeneity	no/low	15	high[i]	24
Issues	one	17	several[i]	31
Violence	low	16	high[i]	30

n = 273 cases with impact scores

°See °° n. to Table 3.2.

†Code for significance test results:
  i   p < 0.001
  ii   p < 0.05
  iii p < 0.10 (approaching significance)
  iv   not significant

TABLE 5.5.2   *Overall Intensity and Overall Impact: Findings on Hypothesis 13*

		Impact	
		Low	High
Intensity	Low	82%	18%
	High	33%	67%

n = 273 cases with impact scores

In sum, all six elements of Hypothesis 13 which, together, constitute the Index of Intensity, are supported: number of crisis actors, major power activity, and geostrategic salience, *very strongly*; heterogeneity, issues, and violence, *strongly*. And all of these are highly significant ($p < 0.001$). The link between overall intensity and overall impact also shows *very strong* support for the expected association; more than four-fifths of all cases at the low-intensity/low-impact end of the scales, and two-thirds of all cases at the high end of the scales.

The most crucial question about the domain of crisis impact relates to different types of impact. These comprise:

> *system transformation*, in Gilpin's terms, "*systems change*," that is, "a major change in the character of the international system itself" (1981: 41) (e.g. End of World War II [Atomic Bomb] Crisis, 1945);
> *substantial change*, for Gilpin, "*systemic change*," that is, "change within the system . . . , in the international distribution of power, the hierarchy of prestige, and the rules and rights embodied in the system" (42) (Six Day War, 1967, for the Middle East subsystem);
> "*interaction change*," that is, "modifications in the political, economic, and other interactions or processes among the actors in an international system," including "alliance formation, regime change, and transnational relations" (43–44) (Berlin Blockade, 1948–49, for the dominant system); and
> *minor/no change* (Falklands/Malvinas Crisis, 1982).

What combination of situational attributes is most likely to lead to a wide-ranging (system-transforming) impact? An answer is suggested by

Hypothesis 14: *The systemic legacy of an international crisis is more likely to be transforming when all the conditions specified in H. 13 are present, and:*
the more extreme the catalyst (trigger) to escalation;
the more severe the violence employed in crisis management;
the longer the crisis; and
the less formal the outcome.

While the rationale for these expectations has been delineated in earlier discussions, it is well to recapitulate the reasoning.

Trigger. A hostile physical act is more threatening than a verbal act; and a scale of intensity is evident among the former, from non-military pressure through non-violent military, indirect violent, to direct violent catalysts to crisis; the more extreme a trigger, the more mistrustful will the target be of the crisis initiator, even after the termination of a crisis.

Crisis Management Technique: Violent behavior generates more fear and mistrust than does negotiation, mediation or other pacific techniques; more intense violence—full-scale war or serious clashes-—creates more hostility for a longer period than do minor clashes; and when adversaries resort to war, the legacy will be higher tension, system instability and, often, disequilibrium.

Duration. The longer a crisis lasts the deeper will be hostility between the adversaries and mistrust of each other's intentions, which often spills over to allies and clients, enveloping much, if not all, of the system; if a lengthy crisis is characterized by extreme violence, in the trigger, in coping, or both the adverse effects will be even more profound.

Form of Outcome. If a crisis ends through a formal agreement, its legacy will be greater trust than crisis termination through a unilateral act, usually hostile, such as invasion, military defeat, occupation, etc.; similarly, a tacit understanding will generate less trust than a semi-formal agreement, and the latter less good faith than a formal agreement.

The findings on "systemic effect" are presented in Table 5.6.

TABLE 5.6   *Systemic Effect of International Crises: Findings on Hypothesis 14*

| Independent Variable | Proportion of International Crises Leading to High Impact | | | |
	Category	%	Category	%
Trigger°	violent	31	non-violent†[iii]	22
Crisis Management Techniques	intense violence	27	negotiation[i]	15
Duration	long[iii]	26	short	21
Outcome-Form	formal agreement	20	less formal[ii]	37

n = 273 cases with impact scores

°See °° n. to Table 3.2.

†Code for significance test results:
  i $p < 0.001$
  ii $p < 0.05$
  iii $p < 0.10$ (approaching significance)
  iv   not significant

In sum, four new elements in H. 14 are supported by the evidence, two of them—crisis management technique, and form of outcome—*strongly*, the other two, *moderately*. Moreover, as noted, all six elements of intensity are strongly linked to impact.

Case Studies of Impact

The ten interstate crises will now be examined in terms of the concept and index of impact. The same sequence as that in earlier chapters will be followed, beginning with the two superpower-dominated cases. Unlike the earlier periods, the emphasis here will be on the international crisis as a whole (e.g., Berlin Blockade, Prague Spring), for impact is clearly a system/interactor level concept.°

BERLIN BLOCKADE

To assess the impact of the first Berlin crisis requires a discussion of its content, both long- and short-term. The East/West protracted conflict, of which this crisis was a dramatic episode, had its roots in a world transformed by World War I and the Bolshevik Revolution of 1917, leading to an irreversible cleavage between Western democracy and Soviet communism. The Cold War was an outgrowth of the territorial and ideological division of Europe at the end of World War II, when the two main victors, the US and the USSR, confronted each other across the "no man's land" of Central Europe, from the Baltic to the Mediterranean.

The early skirmishes in their competition for hegemony took several forms. One was a cluster of military-security crises between 1946 and the spring of 1948: Communism in Poland; Turkish Straits; Greek Civil War; Communism in Hungary; Truman Doctrine, and the Marshall Plan, culminating in the communist seizure of power in Prague, Communism in Czechoslovakia. But it was the Berlin crisis in 1948–49 that created the first watershed in East/West relations after World War II. Put simply, the Cold War crystallized in the long, drawn-out test of resolve between US decision-makers headed by Truman and their Soviet counterparts under the direction of Stalin; the UK and France played a secondary role.[32]

These observations reinforce the reasoning for the high overall intensity accorded to Berlin Blockade. That crisis posed grave challenges to

---

° Those who are interested primarily in comparative findings on the impact of the ten cases should go directly to pp. 351–356.

the dominant system of world politics while the crisis unfolded, with grave implications for the global system, only three years after the triumph of the major power alliance in World War II. First, it created a mutual perception of a high risk of war between the US and the USSR. Second, it tested the resolve of both emerging superpowers to prevent the other's successful penetration of their respective spheres of influence in Europe. Rules of the game, laid down at the Potsdam Conference in 1945, were undermined. And existing alliances were found wanting. All this became clear during one of the longest superpower crises on record (March 1948–May 1949).

What, then, were the actual consequences of the Berlin Blockade Crisis for its adversaries and for the international systems of which they were members? At the bilateral level, the outcome was victory for the Western Powers, defeat for the USSR, in the form of an agreement that recognized Western rights in Berlin. As such, it denoted a change in their relative power, as did Cuban Missiles 14 years later, though in both cases a face-saving formula for the Soviet Union was devised: respectively, a Council of Foreign Ministers' meeting "to consider" the future of Germany, the tradeoff for Soviet termination of the Berlin blockade; and a US commitment not to invade Cuba, the tradeoff for withdrawal of all Soviet nuclear missiles from the island. But there was no change in the composition of the global system's power élite (point 4) or in the ranking of élite members (point 3). Thus *power change* for this crisis was 2 on the four-point scale.

The effect of the Berlin Blockade Crisis on actors was profound. Two states were created in 1949 from the ashes of Germany as a direct consequence of this first East/West crisis over Berlin, the Federal Republic of Germany (FRG) and the German Democratic Republic (GDR). Both were to serve as key members of the two competing coalitions led by the US and the USSR. Thus *actor change* generated by Berlin Blockade was the maximum, 4 on the four-point scale.

The impact of this crisis on rules of the game, too, was far-reaching, though less than the maximum. The Potsdam rules (1945), calling for mutual non-intervention in each others' sectors in Berlin, were shattered by the Blockade, not to be restored until the Four Power agreement in 1971, and then to be dramatically replaced by the unification of Germany in 1989–90. With the breakdown of that consensus in 1948–49 the way was open for other assaults on East/West rules of the game, notably in Korea a year later. North Korea challenged the 1945 rules governing a partitioned peninsula into pro-Soviet and pro-US zones and regimes by invading the South in June 1950. In one crisis during that war the US threatened to use nuclear weapons on the battlefield. Thus, on this indicator of impact Berlin Blockade scored 3 on the four-point scale for *change in rules*.

The most far-reaching effects of this crisis relate to alliance configuration, nothing less than the creation of a new alliance. While embryonic structures of a Western alliance emerged prior to Berlin Blockade, notably the five-member Western European Union (WEU) in 1947, the thrust to a tight alliance, led by the US, was a direct result of the trauma of Berlin Blockade: NATO, the most potent military alliance of the post-World War II era, was formalized in 1949, within months of the end of the crisis over Berlin; and in 1955 it incorporated West Germany into its ranks. The USSR responded more slowly, but with less pressure, for its troops were in effective occupation of all its client states by 1949. Its institutional response to NATO, the Warsaw Pact, was formalized in 1955, reflecting the tight polarization between the two camps that was ushered in by the Berlin Blockade Crisis. Thus this case scored 4 on the four-point scale for *alliance change*.

The relevant data and method for calculating overall impact are presented in Table 5.7. Applying the equation, the Impact Index generates an *overall impact* score for Berlin Blockade of 7.00 on the ten-point scale, placing it in the high impact group of crises since 1918.[33]

TABLE 5.7   *Overall Impact: Berlin Blockade*

Indicator	Weight	Assigned Score
Power Change	3	2
Actor Change	2	4
Rules Change	2	3
Alliance Change	1	4

$$\text{Impact Index}^\circ = \text{I}' = 0.375 \left(\sum_{j=1}^{4} u_j\, i_j \right) - 2$$

Where I = Impact Index; i_j = jth indicator (j = 1, . . ., 4); and u_j = weight assigned to jth indicator.

$$0.375\,([3 \times 2] + [2 \times 4] + [2 \times 3] + [1 \times 4]) - 2 = 7.00$$

°The coefficient used in the conversion to a 10-point scale is derived as follows: the lower and upper boundaries (minimal and maximal weighted scores) for impact are 8 and 32: in order to convert these scores to a 10-point scale, it is necessary to multiply by 0.375 and subtract 2 from each value.

PRAGUE SPRING

As with the Berlin Blockade twenty years earlier, the Prague Spring Crisis posed several challenges to the dominant system, as well as to Eastern Europe as a subsysem. First, by questioning Moscow's hegemony within its own bloc, the Czechoslovak reform leaders undermined the image of the USSR as a superpower: if it could not prevent disarray among its clients or sustain its control over a client's political regime, the Soviet Union would forfeit its claim to equal superpower status with the US in world politics generally. Second, if Prague were successful in introducing "socialism with a human face," the near-certain spillover of revisionism to most other Soviet clients would undermine the continued viability of Moscow's highly-valued East European "security zone." Finally, spillover from the Prague Spring to latent dissent in the bastion of communism itself could not be ruled out, as was to be demonstrated in 1990–91, in the aftermath of the over-throw of communist regimes throughout Eastern Europe. Not without reason, then, Soviet decision-makers perceived the Prague Spring as a grave danger to their power at home and in Eastern Europe and their status as a superpower abroad.

What were the actual consequences of the Prague Spring Crisis? The coalition of military forces was overwhelmingly in favor of the Warsaw Pact invaders. Minor clashes occurred, as noted, but the outcome was never in doubt: victory for Moscow and its clients, defeat for Prague. The result was a relative shift in power to the former. However, both the composition of the power élite and the ranking of members within the East European subsystem (points 4 and 3) remained the same. It was, in short, a minor *power change*: Prague Spring scored 2 on the four-point scale for this indicator of impact.

Actor change, too, was modest. There was no fundamental change in state membership of the system: none was eliminated; nor was a new state created (point 4). Moreover, there was no change in regime type (point 3): Czechoslovakia remained communist in form and content. Rather, change occurred in regime orientation, with the restoration of a hard-line communist government under Husak, totally subordinate to the Kremlin and its pro-consuls in Prague. Thus this crisis scored 2 on the four-point scale for *actor change*.

Nor was there a basic structural change in alliance configuration. The Soviet bloc remained intact. No member withdrew from the Warsaw Pact, though Romania remained aloof from the invasion, and Hungary was less than enthusiastic. Yet change did occur, in the form of greater (imposed) cohesiveness within the alliance. Dissent, the experiment in domestic reform, and attempted loosening of the alliance by a client were crushed by the bloc leader. Soviet control over Eastern Europe was strengthened. The alliance became tighter because of the fright caused by the near-success of Dubcek and his colleagues. In formal terms, Prague Spring scored 2 on the four-point scale for *alliance change*.

The strengthening of Soviet control over its East European clients was justified by a major change in the rules of the game. Until the Prague Spring the USSR adhered to the principles of state sovereignty and non-intervention in the internal affairs of other countries in the Soviet bloc, notwithstanding its military suppression of the Hungarian Uprising in 1956. But, as noted in the discussion of the escalation phase of Prague Spring [Chap. 3], the Soviet perception of grave value threat led to the enunciation of the "Brezhnev Doctrine" at the height of that crisis. In essence, it proclaimed a higher principle to govern relations in the "socialist commonwealth," namely, the right and obligation of "fraternal members" to intervene in the domestic affairs of a member-state if the unity of the bloc were threatened. That doctrine became the basis of enforced unity through compliance with Moscow's will, hence greater cohesion, for the rest of Brezhnev's tenure in office, during the brief periods of his successors, Andropov and Chernenko, and formally, Gorbachev, until the 1989 apologies by Warsaw Pact members, including the USSR, for the 1968 invasion of Czechoslovakia. Thus, for *rules change*, Prague Spring scored 4 on the four-point scale.

The combination of these individual scores was an *overall impact* score of 5.50 on the ten-point scale, the minimum for inclusion in the group of high impact international crises since the end of World War I.

MUNICH

To assess the impact of Munich (and two other cases, Stalingrad and Lebanon Civil War I) is made more difficult by the fact that their effects are blurred by other international crises on the same issue(s), either soon after or in a continuing sequence over time. For Munich both types of "contamination" were at work: Czechoslovakia Invasion, in March 1939, the consummation of the dismemberment process initiated by the Munich Crisis; and Entry into World War II (August–September 1939), followed by 28 intra-war crises culminating in the End of World War II (1945).[34]

If one subsumes the impact of Munich into the cluster of 1939–45 crises associated with global war, its overall impact score would be 10.00 on the ten-point scale. However, this would be a distorted assessment because the maximum score for change in the distribution of power, actors, rules of the game and alliances was a consequence of the total cluster of crises during that six-year period. At the same time, to identify the impact of Munich with its predecessor, Czech. May Crisis, and its sequel, Czechoslovakia Annexation, would be to narrow the scope of the effects of Munich to that state's fate; and this would be unduly restrictive. Thus for purposes of this analysis the impact of Munich will be assessed outside of these two clusters, for one is too broad in time and space, the other too narrow.

The Munich Agreement of 30 September 1938 was an emphatic victory for Germany and, to a lesser extent, Italy. It was a devastating defeat for Czechoslovakia and, although not so perceived by British and French decision-makers at the time, a defeat for the UK and France as well. In terms of *power change* it marked a significant shift in the ranking of the power élite within the dominant system of world politics. While Germany's reascent to high power status and military capability was a process dating to 1933, Hitler's diplomatic triumph in the Munich Crisis was a watershed: it catapulted Germany to the front rank of the major powers in Europe, coequal with Britain, France and the USSR. This was dramatically demonstrated in less than a year, by the triumphant German Blitzkrieg in Poland and, eight months later, by the destruction of the armies of France, Belgium and the Netherlands, and the enforced withdrawal of all British troops from the continent. Thus Munich was assigned 3 on the four-point scale for this indicator of impact.

The effect of Munich on actors was even more profound. Less than six months after the Four Power Agreement on Sudetenland, the process of obliterating Czechoslovakia as an independent state was completed. A two-day crisis, Czechoslovakia Annexation (14–15 March 1939), led to the merger of Bohemia, Moravia and Slovakia into, or under the control of, the Third Reich, exactly a year after the annexation of Austria. In short, the direct impact of Munich was the elimination of a state, point 4 on the four-point scale for *actor change*.

The legacy of the Munich Crisis to rules of the game was also far-reaching. Until September 1938 Hitler's Germany acquiesced in the principles of state sovereignty and territorial integrity, the traditional pillars of global order. Even the *Anschluss* with Austria had adhered to legal formalities: the newly-appointed Nazi Chancellor, Seyss-Inquart, secured the passage of a law by the Austrian Government on 13 March

1938 annexing Austria to Germany. But, while the seizure of Sudetenland was legitimized by the Munich Agreement, it represented the breakdown of consensus on the above-noted principles. And the events of the next year, from the dismemberment of Czechoslovakia to the assault on Poland, reflected the impact of the Munich Crisis. Thus it was scored 3 on the four-point scale for *rules change*.

The consequences of Munich for the major power alliance configuration were to unfold rapidly. The failure of France and the USSR to protect Czechoslovakia against the German political onslaught, which both were obligated to do under the terms of bilateral agreements with Prague, shattered the 1935 Franco-Soviet Pact, regarded by the signatories and others as the basis for the containment of aggressive renascent German power. More generally, it undermined the reliability of all alliance commitments by major powers to minor ones. And as the events from September 1938 to the outbreak of World War II revealed, French and Soviet behavior, despite their alliance commitments, encouraged Hitler in the belief that the Western Powers would stand aside as he proceeded to establish German hegemony throughout Central and Eastern Europe. As such, post-Munich alliance changes facilitated the road to war. Thus, the Munich Crisis scored the maximum on *alliance change*, 4 on the four-point scale.

Taken together, the individual scores lead to an *overall impact* of 8.13 on the ten-point scale, making Munich one of the most consequential of all international crises since 1918.

STALINGRAD

The Stalingrad Crisis, as noted, was unique among the ten cases examined in this book: it was the only intra-war crisis. At the same time it was one of many significant IWCs during World War II, from Fall of Western Europe and Battle of Britain in 1940, through "Barbarossa" and Pearl Harbor in 1941–42, El Alamein in 1942–43, Fall of Italy in 1943, D-Day in 1944, and Final Soviet Offensive in 1945, to several Pacific theatre IWCs, such as Saipan in 1944, Iwo Jima and Okinawa in 1945, and the End of World War II (Atomic Bomb) Crisis in August 1945.

Half a century later, analysts still differ on the relative importance of these battles and campaigns. Yet all agree that in the struggle for the mastery of Europe, Stalingrad was decisive in the tide of battle between Germany and the USSR. Psychologically, if not materially as well, the former never recovered. For the Soviet Union the triumph at Stalingrad was the psychological catalyst to ultimate victory in the "Great Patriotic War."

Stalingrad, an intra-war crisis *par excellence*, falls within the largest single cluster of crises associated with any war since 1918. Like Munich, if its impact is subsumed within Entry into World War II and the array of IWCs that followed from 1939 to 1945, its overall impact score would be 10.00 on the ten-point scale. However, as with the Munich Crisis, not all the consequences of six years of global war can be attributed to a single battle, not even a turning point like the 1942–43 Battle of Stalingrad. Thus, for purposes of this inquiry, its impact will be assessed independently.

As noted in earlier discussions [Chaps. 3 and 4, on Escalation and Deescalation], the Battle of Stalingrad was a major defeat for Germany and a decisive victory for the USSR. The result was far-reaching *change in the distribution of power*. The decimation of Germany's Sixth Army and the loss of at least 400,000 front-line troops, as well as enormous stocks of weapons, constituted a shift in relative power between the two adversaries on the Eastern Front. (Italian and Romanian losses at Stalingrad were marginal to this balance.) But the outcome at Stalingrad had a much greater impact, measured by power change.

After Stalingrad, Germany was no longer the preeminent military power in Europe. That process, a shift in rank within the power élite of the dominant system during World War II, was slow to unfold. Neither Hitler and his generals, nor their opponents, recognized the power change that had occurred until much later. Yet in substantive terms Stalingrad weakened the ability of the *Wehrmacht* to withstand further assaults in the future from East and West, including the greatest combined air-land-sea operation in military history, D-Day, in June 1944, and the relentless advance of the Allied armies all along the Eastern and Western Fronts, culminating in total victory in early May 1945. Although it is difficult to disentangle one battle from a complex war, Stalingrad marked the "beginning of the end." And, viewed in the minimal time frame for assessing impact, namely, three years, the composition of the power élite in the global system was transformed before February 1946: Germany, Italy and Japan were reduced to lesser powers; and the USSR occupied coequal status with the US at the apex of the world power pyramid. The contribution of Stalingrad to that momentous power change was immense though not exclusive, leading to a score of 3 on the four-point scale for this indicator of impact.

The Battle of Stalingrad also had a profound effect on actors/regimes in the dominant system. As the first decisive defeat of German forces in the East, it contributed enormously to the collapse of Nazi Germany and the emergence of two independent successor states in 1949, the FRG and the GDR. It would be incorrect to attribute that climactic development solely, or even primarily, to Stalingrad and, therefore, wrong to score actor change for that international crisis at the maximum. However, insofar as the Battle of Stalingrad pointed the way to Germany's surrender two years later, it seems reasonable to "credit" this IWC with a change in regime type: the 1945 partition of Germany was accompanied by a drastic shift in regime for both successor states, namely, communism in East Germany-GDR, and democracy in West Germany-FRG. Thus Stalingrad was accorded 3 on the four-point scale for *actor change*.

In sharp contrast to the far-reaching effects of the Stalingrad Crisis on the power configuration and on actors, there was no discernible legacy to rules of the game. Although it was a battle of great intensity and enormous casualties, the then-existing rules of war were not violated. Nor was there a change in consensus about such codified or tacit rules in subsequent warfare on the Eastern Front—as a direct effect of Stalingrad. Thus it scored 1 on the four-point scale for *rules change*.

As with actor change, Stalingrad did not have direct effects on alliances. There were far-reaching changes from 1945 onward, notably the collapse of the wartime Grand Alliance. But this and other alliance changes resulted from the end of World War II and ideological conflict, not from victory/defeat at Stalingrad *per se*. However, as with the reasoning about actor change, the contribution of that IWC to the military outcome in Europe was such as to justify assigning a high, though not the highest, score to *alliance change*—3 on the four-point scale.

Taken together the individual scores for Stalingrad lead to an *overall impact* score of 5.50 on the ten-point scale.

OCTOBER-YOM KIPPUR

The very high intensity score for October-Yom Kippur reflects the multiple challenges this crisis posed to the structure of several international systems. At the global level, the Arab oil embargo of 1973 undermined the economic stability of Western Europe and Japan. Moreover, less developed states and regions came under grave pressure as a result of the unleashing of a powerful economic weapon. Alliances were tested. The pre-1973 hierarchy of power in the Middle East was assaulted. And rule dissensus widened. What then was the impact of October-Yom Kippur in the years that followed?

The Arab/Israel subsystem experienced major changes in the distribution of power. Israel, since its triumph in 1967, had been the preeminent regional actor in terms of military capability. After the 1973–74 war, however, its brief tenure as regional superpower gave way to relative power equality among Egypt, Israel and Syria. It was, in effect a return to the power hierarchy after the 1956–57 Suez-Sinai War, though Syria emerged relatively stronger after October-Yom Kippur.[35] In sum, the shift in power rank within the Arab/Israel subsystem generated a score of 3 on the four-point scale for *power change*.

No actor was eliminated as a result of this international crisis. Nor were new states created. However, change in regime orientation is discernible. At the outset of October-Yom Kippur, Egypt was a Soviet client, though less overtly than in the Nasser era, especially 1956–70. That dependence persisted during most of the 1973 war, as evident in the crucial role of the Soviet airlift-sealift from 8 October onward. Syria's dependence was even greater, throughout the crisis-war. However, a shift in orientation towards the superpowers began, largely because of the rescue of Egypt's Third Army through US political pressure on Israel, and Israel's partial withdrawal from the Suez Canal, in accordance with the US-brokered Disengagement Agreement of January 1974. This change in Egypt's foreign policy orientation, in turn, strengthened the Syria–USSR relationship. And the US airlift to Israel, starting on 14 October, reinforced the latter's dependence on its American patron for arms, economic aid, and political and diplomatic support. In short, October-Yom Kippur registered 2 on the four-point scale for *actor change*.

Informal rules were maintained during the 1973–74 war, except for a brief resort to surface-to-surface missiles by Syria, causing heavy damage and casualties to an Israeli *kibbutz*, and a retaliatory bombing of urban centers by Israel. Much more consequential was the setting in motion of a change in the basic rules of the Arab/Israel game, dramatized by President Sadat's journey to Jerusalem and his speech before the *Knesset* in November 1977, with an offer of formal peace in exchange for land. The deeply-rooted Arab consensus goal, namely, Israel's destruction, was shattered by the ensuing Camp David Accords (1978) and the Egypt–Israel Peace Treaty (1979). That breakdown in consensus led to a score of 3 on the four-point scale for *rules change*.

Several alliance changes resulted from the October-Yom Kippur upheaval. Most European members of NATO denied landing rights to

US aircraft in its airlift to Israel, causing deep cleavages in the Western alliance. More significant, the alliance between Egypt and Syria crumbled under the weight of divergence of policy toward the superpowers, especially during the negotiations leading to the disengagement of forces. Later, the Sadat peace initiative of 1977, gestating during the aftermath of the October-Yom Kippur crisis-war, was to sunder the pattern of alliances among Arab states based upon a consensus view of Israel's illegitimacy as a state. Egypt was to be ostracized for a decade. And it took 13 years for normal relations to be reestablished between Cairo and Damascus. Thus this Arab/Israel crisis scored 4 on the four-point scale for *alliance change*.

The legacy of October-Yom Kippur was a transformation of the Middle East subsystem, especially regarding rules and alliances, and basic change in the balance of influence between the superpowers in that region. Taken together, these effects led to an *overall impact* of 6.63 on the ten-point scale.

LEBANON CIVIL WAR I

The Lebanon crisis of 1975–76 was similar to a long-war crisis in that the Lebanon civil war, which it catalyzed, continued unabated for 16 years. As such, its impact was part of a larger and lengthy process. Nonetheless, the effects of this particular episode can be assessed.

The outcome was victory for Syria, leading to an enhancement of its influence in Lebanon—the beginning of a permanent Syrian military presence—and of its status in the Arab world. Its adversaries, the Muslim–PLO coalition, suffered a defeat, as did the weak Lebanon government, whose writ became even more limited with the arrival of the Syria-dominated Arab Deterrent Force in Beirut. This constituted a shift in power within Lebanon in Syria's favor. However, there was no fundamental change in the Middle East or intra-Arab power élite (point 4), nor a change in relative rank within that hierarchy. Thus Lebanon Civil War I scored 2 on the four-point scale for *power change*.

The effect on actors was less visible. Lebanon and its complex confessional political system survived the crisis and continued to exist throughout the civil war. Stated in terms of impact, no actor was eliminated or created (point 4). Nor was there any change in regime type (point 3) or even in the orientation of the increasingly irrelevant Government of Lebanon (point 2). There was, in short, no impact in this domain, that is, 1 on the four-point scale for *actor change*.

By contrast, the crisis of 1975–76 did affect the rules of the game relating to Syria's relations with Lebanon. Although a long-aspiring power in that subregion and accepted as the most influential "outside" power, Syria acquiesced in the principle of Lebanon's sovereignty. With its military intervention in 1975–76, however, the consensus over that crucial principle broke down. From that time onward Syria's intervention in all aspects of Lebanon's affairs became the norm; and, as a direct outgrowth of Lebanon Civil War I, Lebanon increasingly became occupied territory. That situation was legitimized in the 1989 Taif Agreement on the basic revision of Lebanon's 1943 constitution and, even more so, Lebanon's formal acceptance of Syria's hegemony in the two states' 1991 bilateral cooperation agreement. In sum, there was a breakdown in consensus on *rules of the game*, thus a score of 3 on the four-point scale for this indicator of impact.

As with actors, the first international crisis of Lebanon's civil war had no long-term effects on the alliance configuration, neither within the system of Arab states nor in Lebanon itself. Syria's defense of Lebanese Christians against their Muslim-PLO adversaries was short-lived. In fact, shifting alignment wih the contenders for power in Lebanon became the pattern of Syria's behavior, designed to prevent any Lebanese group, militia, party or coalition from attaining power in all of Lebanon and threatening Syria's hegemony. Thus the alliance shifts were transient, with cohesiveness varying throughout the civil war. The result is a score of 1 on the four-point scale for *alliances*.

The summation of these individual scores for Lebanon Civil War I generates an *overall impact* of 3.63 on the ten-point scale.

INDIA/CHINA BORDER

The border crisis and war between India and China reached its peak (October–November 1962) when the gravest superpower confrontation after World War II, Cuban Missiles, brought the US and the USSR close to nuclear war. Whether this was coincidence or by (China's) design remains unclear. Moreover, conflict and war between the two most populous states in the world, exemplars of democracy and communism—and undisguised competitors for leadership—in the Third World of Asia and Africa, posed serious challenges to the global system. First, victory for India or China might have spillover effects on future attitudes and behavior of Third World states towards competing ideologies, political regimes and economic systems. Moreover, their foreign policy orientation, including non-alignment with the superpowers in an intense Cold War era, might be affected by the outcome of a contest between India and China. Third, India's commitment to non-alignment was under stress, as the dictates of war led to visible dependence on the US and the UK for military aid. And finally, the future balance of power in Asia was at stake in the *dénouement* to the process of change from near-allies to open enemies in the relationship between Asia's largest powers. What then was the impact of the 1962–63 border crisis and war?

The outcome to the war in NEFA and Ladakh was unqualified victory for China and humiliating defeat for India. Clearly it constituted a shift in the relative power between the adversaries. Initially it portended fundamental change in the composition of the power élite in Asia as well. That did not materialize, for India remained a major power. In fact, its military power increased substantially, and even more so after its triumph in the war with Pakistan over Bangladesh (1971). Yet in the aftermath of the 1962 war the image and reality of a shift in rank among the leading Asian powers penetrated the perceptions of decision-makers in Asia and in the dominant system. Thus India/China Border registered 3 on the four-point scale for *power change*.

Notwithstanding the definitive outcome, victory/defeat, the effect of India/China Border on actors/regimes was limited. No state was eliminated or created (point 4). Nor was India's democratic regime swept aside by the dramatic setback (point 3) or even undermined, though individuals, notably Krishna Menon, were swept from power, and even Prime Minister Nehru's primacy was challenged briefly. This does not mean, however, that the effect of this international crisis was nil. What seems to have occurred, haltingly, was a change from pro-Soviet non-alignment to a posture of "equidistance" in India's policy towards the superpowers. It was not a fundamental change in regime orientation but it did constitute a considerable shift. And since India was the leading non-aligned state for most of the history of the Non-Aligned Movement, the change was consequential. Thus India/China Border scored 2 on the four-point scale for *actor change*.

This crisis also had a modest effect on *rules of the game*. Prior to the 1962 border war China adhered to a policy of non-interference in the affairs of South Asia, particularly in the longstanding India/Pakistan conflict over Kashmir. An emerging alignment with Pakistan from 1959 onward led the PRC to make increasingly pro-Pakistan statements on the dispute. But the tacit rules dictated no overt interference from China. This changed in the aftermath of the border war. Thus in September 1965, during the second India/Pakistan war over Kashmir, China mobilized forces and threatened to cross the still-disputed northeast India/China border to reduce the pressure on Pakistan in the west. That crisis fizzled out but it reflected a declining consensus in rules of the game regarding China and South Asia. Thus India/China Border scored 2 on the four-point scale for this indicator of impact.

Finally, there was a modest effect of this international crisis on alliance configuration. China had already begun the process of withdrawal from the USSR-dominated "communist camp." Soviet neutrality during most of the India/China border crisis-war hastened the Sino/Soviet split, but it did not catalyze a basic change in the communist world's alliance pattern. India, as noted, sought military aid from all countries but, especially, from the US, the UK and the Commonwealth. While it did not abandon non-alignment, the pillar of its foreign policy since 1949, it became more receptive to Western aid and more neutralist on the multiple issues that divided the superpowers in the Cold War; that is, as noted, its policy became one of "equidistance" from Moscow and Washington. As such, this expressed less attachment to the then-pro-Soviet posture of the Non-Aligned Movement. Thus India/China Border registered 2 on the four-point scale for *alliance change*.

The combination of individual scores for India/China Border generated an *overall impact* of 5.13 on the ten-point scale, below the minimum for inclusion in the high impact group of crises since 1918.

HUNGARIAN UPRISING

The Hungarian Uprising was not the first upheaval in the post-World War II Soviet bloc: it was preceded by the East Berlin Uprising in June–July 1953. Yet the events in Budapest in October–November 1956 posed a challenge to the East European subsystem and, indirectly, to the dominant system of world politics. Had Premier Nagy achieved his government's proclaimed intention of withdrawing from the Warsaw Pact, it would have seriously undermined the unity of the bloc, Soviet primacy in Eastern Europe and, therefore, Soviet capability *vis-à-vis* the US and the West generally, in their struggle for global hegemony. Moreover, if Hungary's revolt had succeeded and a softer version of communism had been introduced in Budapest, this would almost certainly have spilled over to other members of the bloc. That process was aborted 12 years later in Czechoslovakia (Prague Spring); but it came to fruition in 1989 all over Eastern Europe. What, then, was the actual impact of the Hungarian Uprising?

Its suppression by Soviet troops and tanks and the decapitation of the reform leadership was a victory for the USSR and a defeat for Hungary:

for years thereafter the Kadar regime was even more dependent than its predecessors upon Moscow and its representatives in Budapest. That definitive outcome signalled a shift in relative power in favor of the USSR. However, there was no change in the composition of the power élite within the East European subsystem (point 4 of power change), nor a change in ranking within the existing power hierarchy (point 3). Thus Hungarian Uprising scored 2 on the four-point scale for *power change*.

The effect on actors/regimes, too, was modest. There was no change in the membership of the Soviet bloc in Eastern Europe (point 4). Nor did Hungary's regime change fundamentally (point 3). Rather, the effect of this international crisis and its outcome was a reversion to the compliant client of the pre-October 1956 era; that is, the ouster of Nagy and his "liberal" colleagues led to a shift in regime orientation, point 2 on the four-point scale for *actor change*.

Rules of the game within the communist bloc were also affected by the outcome of Hungarian Uprising. One of the fundamental tacit rules since the days of the Cominform (1947) was acceptance by formally sovereign East European states of Soviet hegemony in the "communist camp" and submission to the dictates of the ideological and political leadership in Moscow, the "bastion of socialism," in its global struggle with the capitalist powers of the West. The Hungarian reform movement of 1956, like its successor in Prague in 1968, symbolized a decline in consensus on that tacit rule. However, Hungarian Uprising did not catalyze a new rule of intra-bloc relations (point 4), as did Prague Spring, namely, the Brezhnev Doctrine. Nor did the events of the late 1950s indicate a breakdown in the East European consensus on rules of behavior (point 3). Thus the 1956 crisis scored 2 on the four-point scale for *rules change*.

The failure of the Hungarian Uprising did not cause major change in the *alliance pattern* within Eastern Europe. The Warsaw Pact remained intact. Hungary did not withdraw. Soviet troops continued to be stationed on Hungarian territory—until shortly after the collapse of the bloc, the Pact, and the "communist camp" in 1989. Yet the 1956 upheaval did affect the cohesiveness of the communist alliance. The patron state reasserted its control even more emphatically in the years that followed the Uprising. And the clients read the lesson of its suppression as a clear warning of the fate that would befall attempts to assert their independence from Moscow or change the nature of their regime. The next attempt occurred 12 years later and failed. Twelve years after the Prague Spring still another revolt occurred, in Poland;

but Solidarity failed as well—until the collapse of Soviet power in Eastern Europe. In sum, change was confined to increased cohesiveness in the alliance within the Soviet bloc, thus 2 on the four-point scale for this indicator of impact.

The individual scores for Hungarian Uprising generate a score for *overall impact* of 4.0 on the ten-point scale.

RHODESIA UDI

Despite the grave threat perceived by Zambia, namely, its existence as an independent state, the impact of Rhodesia UDI was minimal, even less than its intensity. The outcome for Rhodesia was victory, expressed in the UK decision on 24 April 1966 to hold talks with the breakaway regime. For Zambia it was compromise: its existence was no longer at immediate risk; but all other objectives remained elusive, notably the end of the white regime in Salisbury and reliable, alternative sources for crucial commodities. This combination, victory/compromise, reflected a modest *power change*, that is, a slight shift in favor of Rhodesia. Thus on this indicator of impact Rhodesia UDI scored 2 on the four-point scale.

There was no discernible change in the sphere of actors: not the elimination or the creation of a new state (point 4) (this was to occur 14 years later and cannot be "credited" to the first crisis in the Rhodesia cluster); not a change in regime type (point 3) (civil authoritarianism remained in place even after the replacement of Rhodesia by Zimbabwe); and not even a change in regime orientation (point 2) by either Zambia or Rhodesia. The absence of *actor change* leads to a score of 1 on the four-point scale.

The same is evident for *rules of the game*: Zambia and Rhodesia, and the principal non-African actor, the UK, played by the same rules after Rhodesia UDI as before. Thus this indicator, too, registered 1 on the four-point scale. And no change occurred in the alliance pattern. Zambia remained a non-aligned state. And Rhodesia continued its path of assertive isolation from all other African entanglements and any further afield. This reality was accorded 1 on the four-point *alliance scale*. The result was a very low score for *overall impact*, 2.13 on the ten-point scale.

FALKLANDS/MALVINAS

The 1982 crisis-war in the South Atlantic marked the dramatic reentry of the UK into the domain of crisis, conflict and war after two decades of virtual inactivity. Only six of its 41 foreign policy crises from 1918 to 1988 occurred after 1961: one dealing with East Africa Rebellions (1964); two over a fishing dispute with Iceland, Cod War I and II (1973 and 1975–76); two in defense of a remnant of empire, in Central America, Belize I and II (1975 and 1977); and Falklands/Malvinas. In fact, this was the sole UK international crisis from 1977 to 1990.

For Argentina the role of crisis actor in international military-security crises was even rarer. It was so involved only in two cases of a longstanding dispute with Chile over the Beagle Channel (1977–78, 1978–79). The second crisis ended through papal mediation. And the dispute was solved by a Vatican-mediated treaty in 1984. But Argentina's attempt to regain control over the Malvinas Islands was of a different order, a supreme example of the influence of irredentism in foreign policy decisions.

Despite its high visibility—the war was a global media event—Falklands/Malvinas did not pose a serious challenge to any international system while it unfolded, not the South American subsystem nor Western Europe, the location of its two principal actors, let alone the dominant system. The main reason was its remoteness from any power centre, in sharp contrast to Central Europe and the Middle East. What impact did it have in the years that followed?

The outcome, it will be recalled, was decisive victory for the UK and traumatic defeat for Argentina. This represented a clear shift in relative power between two historic friends: Argentina was the UK's strongest link with any state in Latin America, especially in economic relations. But the outcome to Falklands/Malvinas did not alter the composition of the power élite in the South American subsystem (point 4) or even the ranking among its strongest powers, Argentina and Brazil (point 3). Thus it registered 2 on the four-point scale for *power change*.

The most significant consequence of the Falklands/Malvinas crisis-war was in the realm of actors/regimes. More precisely, the military junta that had ruled Argentina since 1977 had tried to reinvigorate the "national honor" and restore the declining basis of its political power by seizing the disputed islands in an act of bravado. They failed and paid a high price—ouster from power, ignominy and imprisonment. With them the military regime itself crumbled and was replaced by a civilian and democratic government. It was, in short, a basic change in regime type, leading to a score of 3 on the four-point scale for *actor change*.[36]

In contrast to this fundamental change—Argentina experienced two democratic elections since 1983, and democracy continues to flourish—there was no effect on rules of the game: no new rules of behavior; no breakdown in the consensus on codified rules; and no change in consensus on tacit rules (points 4, 3, and 2, respectively). Diplomatic relations between Argentina and the UK were severed early in the crisis. But with the help of UN good offices they negotiated a return to normalcy: diplomatic relations were restored in 1990. Thus, with respect to *rules change*, Falklands/Malvinas scored 1 on the four-point scale.

There was a modest effect on alliances. While the US played an active, pro-UK mediatory role and later openly espoused the British case, several European states were either neutral or pro-Argentine. This was evident in NATO's response to British attempts to secure open support from the Western alliance, as the OAS had supported the claims of Argentina. NATO demurred, to the dissatisfaction of the UK and, to a lesser extent, the US. In sum, there was a decrease in cohesiveness within NATO and, to a lesser extent, in the OAS as a result of Falklands/Malvinas. The former was reminiscent of, but much less divisive than, that which occurred during and as a result of two other crises: the NATO split during the Suez/Sinai War (1956), with the UK and France strongly opposed by the US, to the extent of the latter cooperating with their common enemy, the USSR; and October-Yom Kippur (1973–74), with almost all NATO members refusing to facilitate the US airlift to Israel. In sum, Falklands/Malvinas scored 2 on the four-point scale for *alliance change*.

The individual scores for this international crisis generated an *overall impact* of 4.0 on the ten-point scale, well below the high impact group.

Impact/Post-Crisis: Case Study Findings

The findings on impact/post-crisis, as on all other phases and periods, will be presented in two formats: first, an indication of the extent to which the ten interstate crises fit H. 12–14; and then, an analysis of the impact of these cases.

Compared with the early phases and periods of the Unified Model, the impact data (Table 5.8) reveal a fit of 58% — 104 of the 180 elements of the three hypotheses combined. The range is less wide, from victory/defeat outcome, in eight of the ten cases, to many crisis actors, high major power activity, and high geostrategic salience, in four cases [all, H. 12].

Among the 10 international crises, the best fit is October-Yom Kippur, 15 of the 18 elements, followed by Stalingrad (13) and Berlin Blockade (12). At the other extreme, Prague Spring fits only eight elements.

TABLE 5.8 *Hypotheses and Case Studies on Crisis Impact: Findings*

Hypotheses on Crisis Impact	Berlin Blockade 1948–49	Prague Spring 1968	Munich 1938	Stalingrad 1942–43	October – Yom Kippur 1973–74	Lebanon Civil War I 1975–76	India/China Border 1959–63	Hungarian Uprising 1956–57	Rhodesia UDI 1965–66	Falklands/ Malvinas 1982
12. *Bilateral Effect – Higher Tension (fp)*†										
victory/defeat outcome	X	X	X	X		X	X	X		X
termination through unilateral act		X		X		X	X	X	X	X
many crisis actors	X	X	X		X					
high major power activity	X		X	X	X					
high geostrategic salience	X		X	X	X					
high heterogeneity between adversaries	X				X	X			X	X
several issues	X	X	X	X	X			X	X	
severe violence	X	X		X	X	X	X	X		X
13. *High Intensity Leads to High Impact (int)*°[1]										
several crisis actors	X	X	X		X	X	X	X	X	X
high major power activity	X		X	X	X	X	X	X	X	X
high geostrategic salience	X		X	X	X	X	X	X	X	X
high heterogeneity	X				X		X	X		X

several issues	X	X	X		X	X		X
severe violence			X			X	X	
14. Far-reaching Systemic Impact (int)°²								
(the conditions in H.13); and violent trigger	X	X	X		X	X	X	X
severe violence in crisis management			X		X	X	X	
long duration	X	X	X		X		X	
form of outcome other than mutual agreement		X	X	X				

°int = international crisis (system/interactor level)

†fp = foreign policy crisis (actor level)

1. Five of the 10 cases (Lebanon Civil War I, India/China Border, Hungarian Uprising, Rhodesia UDI, and Falklands/Malvinas) exhibited relatively low intensity, though India/China Border approaches the threshold for high impact (see Table 5.9). Thus they were coded for the obverse conditions in H.13, that is, few crisis actors, low major power activity, etc.

2. The same five cases did not have a 'far-reaching... impact' and were thus coded for the obverse of the conditions specified in H.14.

Of the ten cases, five scored very high or high on overall impact [Table 5.9 below]: Berlin Blockade, Prague Spring, October-Yom Kippur, and Munich and Stalingrad as part of the World War II cluster. (Even if assessed on their own, Munich was, as noted, a political-diplomatic turning point on the road to World War II; and Stalingrad was a military turning point in shaping the outcome of that war.)

As evident in Table 5.8, the high intensity scores (20 of 30 [H. 13]) relate to these five cases. October–Yom Kippur is a perfect fit—six of six elements. Berlin Blockade fits five elements, Munich, four; but Prague Spring, an intra-Soviet bloc crisis, fits only two elements. The other five cases which, as noted, were characterized by low intensity and relatively low impact, are coded for the obverse of the specified conditions. As such, India/China Border fits five of these elements, and all the other cases, four each. As for the other postulated conditions of far-reaching impact [H. 14], Stalingrad fits all four, October–Yom Kippur, three, among the high overall impact crises.

Four crises noted earlier as among the most intense group over the 70-year period [Table 5.3] were also among those with the highest impact, along with Stalingrad (Table 5.9). However, the ranking differs. On the ten point scale for overall intensity the rank order was: October-Yom Kippur, Berlin Blockade, Munich and Prague Spring. For overall impact the order is Munich, Berlin Blockade, October-Yom Kippur, and (equal) Prague Spring and Stalingrad.

Basic power change resulted from the outcome of three of these five

TABLE 5.9   *Selected International Crises: Components of Overall Impact*

International Crisis	Power Change	Actor Change	Rules Change	Alliance Change	Overall Impact
Berlin Blockade	2	4	3	4	7.00
Prague Spring	2	2	4	2	5.50
Munich	3	4	3	4	8.13
Stalingrad	3	3	1	3	5.50
October – Yom Kippur	3	2	3	4	6.63
Lebanon Civil War I	2	1	3	1	3.63
India/China Border	3	2	2	2	5.13
Hungarian Uprising	2	2	2	2	4.00
Rhodesia UDI	2	1	1	1	2.13
Falklands/Malvinas	2	3	1	2	4.00

cases; that is, Munich, Stalingrad and October-Yom Kippur all generated or contributed to a basic shift in ranking among the most powerful states in the relevant international system, the dominant system for the first two, the Middle East subsystem for the third. (The effect of the first two, however, as noted, was contaminated by Entry into World War II [1939] and the many IWCs that followed.) The other two high impact cases, Berlin Blockade and Prague Spring, led only to a change in relative power between the adversaries.

These international crises had an even greater effect on actors. Two of them, Munich and Berlin Blockade, scored the maximum on this component; that is, they led to the elimination of an actor (Czechoslovakia in 1939) and the creation of new actors (Federal Republic of Germany and German Democratic Republic, both in 1949). And one, Stalingrad, contributed to a change in regime type—in the Western and Soviet zones of Germany from 1945 onwards. Prague Spring and October-Yom Kippur led only to a change in regime orientation.

In the domain of rules change, too, four of the high impact cases had far-reaching consequences. Prague Spring generated a new rule to govern relations within the communist bloc after 1968. And Munich, Berlin Blockade and October-Yom Kippur all led to a breakdown of an existing consensus about system rules.

Finally, there were significant alliance changes in the aftermath of all but one of these crises. Munich led to the sundering of the Franco-Soviet alliance. Berlin Blockade led to the formation of NATO. October-Yom Kippur catalyzed the collapse of the Egypt-Syria alliance which triggered the 1973–74 Middle East crisis and war. And within months of Stalingrad the German-Italian alliance had collapsed. Only Prague Spring was followed by modest change in the Warsaw Pact.

One final theme from the case study findings on impact merits attention, even emphasis. As evident in Table 5.9, there was great variety among the ten cases for all but one of the four indicators—power change:

  from change in relative power among adversaries to a shift in ranking among the most powerful states in a system (points 2 and 3);
  from no change whatsoever in actors/regimes to maximal actor change, that is the creation and elimination of one or more actors (points 1 and 4);
  from no change in rules of the game to the creation of a new rule of behavior (points 1 and 4); and

from no change in alliances to the formation or elimination of a new alliance (points 1 and 4).

This diversity is also clearly evident in the scores for overall impact. There was one case with very low impact (Rhodesia UDI); three with modest impact (Hungarian Uprising, Falklands/Malvinas, Lebanon Civil War I); one with moderate impact (India/China Border); two with moderately high impact (Stalingrad, Prague Spring); and three cases with very high impact (Munich, Berlin Blockade, October-Yom Kippur).

A comparative analysis of state behavior in ten foreign policy crises revealed that, despite great diversity in system, actor, and situational attributes, there was a remarkable similarity in the pattern of coping with external military-security crises, especially in the pre-crisis and crisis periods. The comparative analysis of impact among the international crises of which these foreign policy crises are a part reinforces this theme.

These findings are directly pertinent to the unresolved and often acrimonious debate about *universality* and *particularism* in concepts, models, theories, and substance, in the study of crisis, conflict and war, and in the larger domain of world politics. The uniqueness school of thought will have to contend with these findings about universality in crisis, conflict and war, among many other clusters of evidence about commonality in human behavior.

CHAPTER 6

Unified Model of Crisis

THE most challenging task of this book is to synthesize the two levels of analysis and the four crisis domains into a unified model. As indicated at the close of Chapter 1, this was to be attempted after onset, escalation, deescalation and impact were explored at the system/interactor and state levels in breadth and depth. With the completion of that theoretical and empirical inquiry [Chaps. 2–5], the task of synthesis now compels attention.

What is the meaning of "unified model"? In essence, it is a heuristic device to explain interstate crisis as a whole. To achieve that goal it builds upon the logic of Model I (international crisis) and Model II (foreign policy crisis) and integrates them into Model III (interstate crisis). Moreover, it attempts to incorporate the phase models—for onset, escalation, deescalation and impact—into a holistic model. Thirdly, its empirical data are drawn from the findings on the hypotheses that were derived from the phase models, findings that were based upon two strands of evidence: aggregate, quantitative data on 70 years of crises (1918–1988), and qualitative data from ten case studies. Finally, in the next chapter the Unified Model of Crisis (henceforth also cited as UMC) will be applied to the Gulf crisis-war of 1990–91.

The synthesis to follow is based upon the conceptual guidelines set forth in Chapter 1, "Tasks Ahead." Four chapters later, these merit recapitulation. The concepts of international and foreign policy crisis denote dynamic processes over time. The key traits of each phase and period, distortion and stress, are explained by clusters of enabling variables, system, interactor, actor and situational, operating through decision-makers' perceptions of value threat, time pressure and probability of war (military hostilities). The two levels of analysis are distinct but interrelated. Models I and II capture segments of complex reality. And cause-effect relationships at the international level require the analysis of images and behavior by the crisis actors (state level). The task of integrating the two levels of analysis is demanding. Without a synthesis, however, a theory of interstate crisis cannot be achieved.

Onset/Pre-Crisis

How does an interstate crisis begin? As will be recalled, it erupts as a foreign policy crisis for a state, through one of three kinds of trigger: a hostile act, a disruptive event, or an environmental change. The catalyst may be internal or external.

There are several types of external triggering act, all initiated by an adversary state, more than one state, an alliance, or a non-state actor. It may be verbal, an accusation, protest, demand or threat by one or more states against another: state A may issue a threat to expel B's citizens if B persists with propaganda against A's leaders. State A may commit a hostile political act, such as severing diplomatic relations with B, forming an alliance with a rival of B, or renouncing a treaty between them. It may impose an economic embargo on B's exports or nationalize the property of B's citizens and corporations on its territory. It may take non-violent military action, such as a mobilization of reserves, maneuvers, a show of force, or a change from a defensive to an offensive posture. It may also resort to indirect or direct violence, attacking B's client or launching an assault on B's territory.

An interstate crisis may also be set in motion by one of several types of external change: the development of a new weapon or weapon system or, more generally, an innovation in military technology that affects the balance of power between adversaries; a sudden challenge to a state's legitimacy by an international organization or a group of states; change in the configuration of the global system or the salient regional subsystem, etc. Alternatively, an internal verbal or physical challenge to B's regime may occur with the support of A's leaders. It may take the form of a *coup d'état*, assassination, act of terror or sabotage, demonstration, strike, mutiny or revolt. It may be a fall of government or proclamation of a new regime.

The variety of triggers is evident in some of the case studies examined throughout this book.

The UK's Munich Crisis was catalyzed on 3 August 1938 by news of Germany's dual announcement—partial mobilization of its armed forces, to take effect in September, and designation of the Rhineland and other border zones as "prohibited areas" (*verbal act*).
Moscow's walkout from a meeting of the Allied Control Council on

20 March 1948 triggered the US's pre-crisis period in its Berlin Blockade Crisis (*political act*).

Exactly 34 years later, on 20 March 1982, the dispatch of a British armed vessel from Port Stanley, to expel a group of "scrap merchants" who had symbolically raised the Argentine flag on South Georgia, induced Argentina's Falklands/Malvinas Crisis (*non-violent military act*).

China's suppression of the Tibet Revolt in March 1959 catalyzed India's lengthy pre-crisis period in the India/China Border Crisis (*indirect violent act*).

An air battle between Syrian MIGs and Israeli Mirages on 13 September 1973 triggered Israel's October-Yom Kippur Crisis (*direct violent act*).

Germany's Stalingrad Crisis was initiated by its decision to launch a major offensive on the Eastern Front in June 1942 (*internal act*).[1]

There is, in short, an array of triggers to interstate crises. However, in order for B to experience a crisis, the catalyst, whether it is an act, event or environmental change, must be perceived by B's decision-makers as a source of higher-than-normal value threat. That perception, in turn, generates modest stress, indicating the beginning of B's pre-crisis period. However, the change is not yet, and may not develop into, an international crisis.

Stated in terms of the Unified Model, the outbreak of a foreign policy crisis is a defining condition of an international crisis. It is necessary but not sufficient; that is, the pre-crisis period for a state is a prerequisite to, but not synonymous with, the onset phase. This distinction is evident in the schematic representation of the UMC (Figure 6.1).

Whether or not B's pre-crisis will set an international crisis in motion depends upon its perception and response. If it ignores A's trigger as posing a marginal or transitory threat—and does nothing—B's incipient foreign policy crisis will be aborted and an international crisis will not ensue. There are many such "failed" interstate crises in twentieth-century world politics [Chap. 3, n. 13].

More often than not, B will perceive a trigger as seriously threatening and will respond, in accordance with the dictates of a universally-shared security dilemma (Herz, *op. cit.*, and Chap. 3, p. 136 above), that arises from the underlying anarchy of the interstate system, as conceptualized by several strands of Realism (Carr, 1939, Morgenthau, 1948, Waltz, 1979, Gilpin, 1981). B's preliminary response may be a verbal, political, economic, non-violent military, or violent act (the same categories as

360

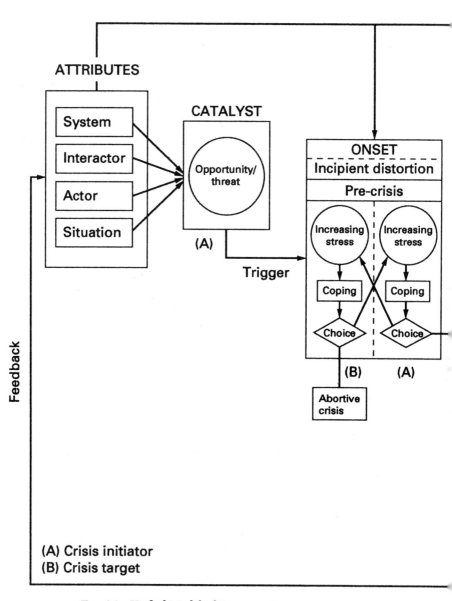

FIG. 6.1   Unified Model of Interstate Crisis

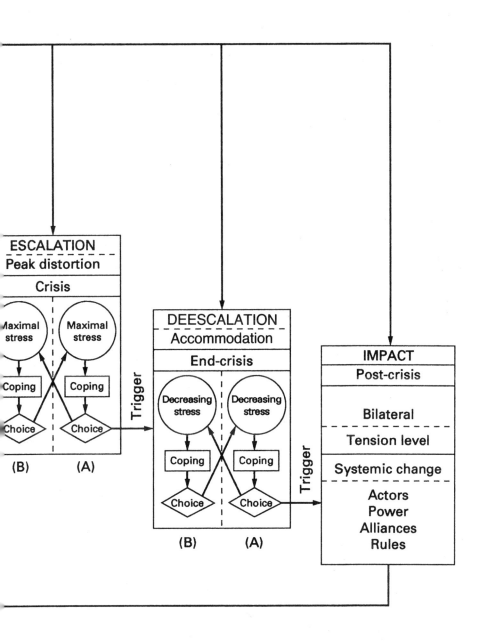

triggering acts); or it may take the form of a multiple response, including or excluding violence. Whatever B's response, other than "do nothing" or compliance, it will generate a reciprocal perception of threat by A's decision-makers and, with it, A's pre-crisis period. If A responds, more-than-normal hostile interaction between A and B would follow. That, in turn, would transform a pre-crisis period into the onset phase of an international crisis, characterized by incipient distortion. Considerable time—days or weeks—may elapse between pre-crisis and hostile interaction. However, once "the battle is joined" between A and B, that is, once an international crisis erupts, its outbreak is antedated to the time of B's initial perception of value threat; for that, as noted, is the *sine qua non* of an international crisis. (The analysis of the Gulf Crisis [Chap. 7] will clarify the linkage.)

If this process describes the link between the two levels of analysis at the beginning of an interstate crisis, what explains the change from non-crisis to pre-crisis and then to onset? An unambiguous, theoretically valid causal formula is not possible because, as indicated early in this book, interstate crises are pervasive in time and space, affecting virtually all members of the global system. What is possible is to specify the cluster of enabling variables, that is, the system, interactor and actor attributes, whose presence makes the outbreak of an interstate crisis most likely. The more of these conditions that are present, the more likely is the jump from non-crisis to incipient foreign policy crisis and the onset of an international crisis.

These conditions were derived from the *crisis onset model*, the first phase model, and were specified in **Proposition 1** [Chap. 2].
A foreign policy crisis and an international crisis are most likely to be catalyzed when:
> *the dispute between A and B underlying the perceived value threat occurs within a polycentric structure;*
> *it erupts within a subsystem of world politics, and*
> *in a setting of protracted conflict;*
> *there is no power discrepancy between the adversaries;*
> *their political regimes are non-democratic or mixed; and*
> *the adversaries are geographically contiguous.*

Three other puzzles about "crisis takeoff" were addressed in the discussion of onset/pre-crisis [Chap. 2] and merit renewed attention in the context of the Unified Model. First, what enabling variables explain the most likely set of conditions for crisis initiation by a state? Further, what makes a state most likely to be a target of threat; that is, what conditions explain a state's vulnerability or proneness to foreign policy crises? Finally, if A's action triggers B's pre-crisis period and generates low stress, what does the UMC indicate as the most likely pattern of coping in that initial period of an interstate crisis?

The task of explaining foreign policy crisis initiation confronts the same reality as the outbreak of international crises, namely, pervasiveness. Thus it is necessary to specify *the most likely conditions in which a state will trigger a military-security crisis for another member of the global system*. These, too, were indicated in the discussion of onset/pre-crisis, in **Proposition 2**, namely,

when the state
is a young or new independent entity;
is militarily stronger than its adversary;
has a non-democratic regime;
confronts internal political, social and/or economic instability;
is geographically contiguous to its adversary; and
has a large territory.

As for vulnerability to crisis, great variation was noted in the number of foreign policy crises experienced by states in the twentieth century —from 51 (the US) to 1 (20 states). Yet no fewer than 123 states were targets of external crises. Thus a universal *a priori* formula to explain vulnerability or proneness is not possible. However, a set of enabling variables was specified in Chapter 2 as the most likely conditions in which a state would be a target for such a crisis.

The postulated *conditions of maximal vulnerability* for a state, as specified in **Proposition 3**, *are when:*

it is a young or new state;
it is a participant in a protracted conflict;
it is relatively equal in military power to its adversary(ies);
it suffers from domestic turmoil;
it is geographically contiguous to its adversary(ies);
its political regime differs from that of its adversary(ies);
its political regime is of recent origin; and
it is a small state.[2]

Given the prevalence of low stress among the adversaries, their behavior (*coping*) during the pre-crisis period is likely to take the form of a preliminary probe of each other's intention, capability and resolve, to test what Ellsberg termed their "critical risk." According to this model,

> there is some threshold of risk that is the maximum risk a party can stand without capitulating or conceding. If the credibility (probability) of the adversary's [com-

mitment] to stand firm is perceived [by actor A] as higher than this threshold, [then actor A] must give in; if it is lower, the party will continue to stand firm. In other words, the party estimates whether the likelihood of the adversary's being really committed to firmness is too high to take a chance or low enough to be worth risking. (Snyder and Diesing, 1977: 50; also 198–207.)

The parties may negotiate, formally or informally, bilaterally or indirectly through a third party. They may accept mediation by an international organization or a mutually-trusted state. They will try to enlist support from one or more major powers in the form of economic aid, diplomatic pressure on the adversary and/or pledges of military assistance, if necessary. Where alliance commitments exist these will be invoked. In their absence a crisis actor may attempt to forge a coalition. It may seek legitimacy for its intended course of action by attempting to enlist the involvement of the global and/or regional organizations, usually in the form of statements or resolutions supporting its cause.

All of these external acts are designed to bolster a crisis actor's bargaining power in the pre-crisis period. Bargaining is not likely to be of the coercive diplomacy type, for the heightened probability of military hostilities and time pressure are not yet, or are only dimly, perceived by the adversaries, and the value threat is still modest in the onset phase. In short, the adversaries are likely to select one or more pacific techniques of crisis management, notably negotiation or mediation.

For the same reasons—low value threat, unawareness of time constraint, and the perception of war as unlikely—decision-making in the pre-crisis period will differ little from its non-crisis norm. Decision-makers will not exhibit a more intense search for *information* about the disputed issue(s) or the adversary's intention and behavior. Normal channels will persist, with little change in the volume or variety of incoming information. The processing of information will remain essentially the function of bureaucrats. And their "gatekeeper" role on the type and amount of information to flow upwards to senior decision-makers will, as in non-crisis situations, have a profound effect on the latter's (mis)perceptions and behavior in the pre-crisis period. The one exception to this non-crisis norm of information processing is interstate crises in which pre-crisis is characterized by very high value threat, despite the absence of perceived heightened probability of war and little, if any, time pressure: in this situation, information-processing will resemble that of the crisis period, with direct involvement by senior decision-makers, e.g., the UK in Munich 1938.

Consultation, too, is likely to follow the non-crisis norm. The cost of miscalculation and erroneous decisions is still small in the onset phase/pre-crisis period, for involvement in military hostilities is viewed as remote, and grave values are not, usually, yet at risk. Senior decision-makers will become more active, simply because a new or enhanced threat is perceived, requiring attention and response by those authorized to decide and act for a state. They will meet more frequently and seek more advice from military and civilian advisors, but without a display of pressure for rapid choice.

They may be open-minded about *alternative* ways of responding to the perceived threat, though not averse to reliance on standard operating procedures to cope with the challenge. And the *decisional forum* is likely to remain the non-crisis unit, whether Cabinet, National Security Council, Politburo, Revolutionary Command Council, Standing Committee, or other institutional variants. In general, the decision process will be unhurried and largely free from dysfunctional stress.

The case studies in this book provide strong, but not unqualified, support for the expected coping pattern in the pre-crisis period. There was no change in information processing in six of the ten cases; and change in the other four was confined to a modest increase in information flow. Decision-makers did not exhibit an acute felt need for more, and more varied, information, and did not resort to extraordinary channels of communication. As for consultation, the only exceptions to the UMC's anticipated behavior were the USSR's consultation with leaders of other Warsaw Pact states in the Prague Spring Crisis, and the formation of an *ad hoc* group, the "Malvinas Team," by Argentina's Foreign Ministry, in the Falklands/Malvinas Crisis.

Similarly, seven of the ten cases adhered to a non-crisis norm for decisional forums in the pre-crisis period. The exceptions were the UK's "Inner Cabinet" (Munich, 1938), Israel's "Kitchen Cabinet" (October-Yom Kippur, 1973), and Syria's "decision-making Committee" (Lebanon Civil War I, 1975). Finally, some alternatives were considered in four of the ten cases during the pre-crisis period: Hungary in the Hungarian Uprising (1956); India in the India/China Border Crisis (1959–62); Rhodesia in the UDI Crisis (1965); and the USSR in the Prague Spring (1968). But the search for options in all of these was minimal. In short, coping with pre-crisis did not differ markedly from the non-crisis norm. The fundamental reason was a modest value threat and the perceived remoteness of military hostilities or time pressure for choice.

Many of these cases also illustrate the search for external support from major powers, allies and/or an international organization. In the

Munich Crisis the UK (and France) sought US support for their plans to yield to Germany on Czechoslovakia's Sudetenland. During the Battle of Stalingrad Germany employed the armies of lesser allies, Italy, Hungary and Romania, in an effort to protect its flanks. In the Berlin Blockade the three Western Powers relied on each other in the struggle with the Soviet Union over Berlin and Germany. In the Hungarian Uprising the USSR mobilized the (passive) support of its Warsaw Pact allies; and in the Prague Spring Crisis the Soviet Union demanded, and received, political and, later, military support from its Warsaw Pact allies against Czechoslovak revisionism. In Rhodesia UDI, Zambia sought military, economic and diplomatic backing from its patron, the UK. And in the Falklands/Malvinas Crisis, Argentina sought support from the OAS and, marginally, from the Non-Aligned Movement and the USSR, while the UK invoked its "special relationship" with the US, sought NATO backing, and requested UN intervention.

In the Unified Model, the duration of the onset phase is postulated as flexible. As will be clarified below, this phase will continue as long as the initial value threat for all crisis actors remains fundamentally unchanged, and decision-makers' perceptions are free from heightened expectations of war or acute time pressure; and, at the international level, as long as disruptive interaction is modest. Thus the duration of onset may be very brief, less than a day, or very long, many months, even longer. Indeed a crisis may erupt without a distinct onset phase, especially when it is triggered by A's unanticipated military attack on B, or vice-versa. In such cases the onset and escalation phases of hostile interaction are fused, as are the pre-crisis and crisis periods for one or more of the actors.

The number of decisions, too, is expected to vary greatly, from one to many. This will depend upon several situational attributes: the duration of the onset phase; the number of actors at that stage; the geographic distance between the adversaries; the gravity of values at risk; and the extent of salience to major powers. Whatever the individual linkage (e.g., more and/or more basic threatened values pose more of a challenge and generate more decisions), there is likely to be fewer decisions during onset/pre-crisis than in the escalation phase/crisis period.[3] Adversaries may make and implement several decisions without altering the initially-low level of distortion and crisis-induced stress. This static process is presented, schematically, in the Onset/Pre-Crisis box of Figure 6.1. So too is the dynamic process in a prototype crisis.

As evident, the key concepts are trigger, stress, coping and choice. In response to a perceived opportunity or a perceived threat from an external or internal source, A triggers a perception of low value threat by B, generating low stress. B's decision-makers, engaging in preliminary crisis management, cope with modest threat and stress through several mechanisms [see Figure 1.4]. They process information essentially as in a non-crisis period. Their consultation pattern, too, adheres to a non-crisis norm. They may, but often will not, seek fresh options on how to respond to the challenge. Alternatives are assessed by the established non-crisis decisional forum. Choice takes the form of one or more decisions designed to meet the perceived threat. Time is irrelevant. And military hostilities are viewed as remote.

As indicated by the upward arrows within the Onset/Pre-Crisis box, B's choice (decision) and its implementation will, in turn, catalyze low value threat and low stress for A. Like B, A's coping will correspond to a non-crisis norm, that is, to established routines of information processing, consultation with bureaucratic subordinates, limited if any search for alternatives, assessment of options in the institutionalized decisional forum and, more often than not, a decision that follows standard operating procedures.

This mutual process of perception, coping and choice at the state level will generate modest distortion at the interactor level. There may be only one action-reaction exchange. There may be many. This will depend upon whether the decision-action behavior of A and/or B sustains or alters the existing level of perceived threat and stress. If the former, the adversaries are signalling a preference to continue in the onset/pre-crisis mode of modest disruptive interaction. That mode of interacting decisions and actions may be repeated several, even many, times. However, as evident in the Berlin Blockade, Prague Spring, Munich, and other interstate crises [Chap. 2], mistrust is more likely to cumulate during this static, intra-phase/intra-period process and, with it, self- and mutually-induced stimuli to escalate disruptive interaction. How long it will take for cumulative mistrust or misperception, or both, to break the circular process charted in the Onset/Pre-crisis box cannot be determined *a priori*.

How and when does the initial phase change occur, that is, from onset to escalation? Is it a particular type of decision by one of the adversaries? Is it a cumulation of actions and interactions by the crisis actors? Is the "step-level" jump a function of a shift in perceptions? More generally, is there a focal point, an act, event, environmental or perceptual change, or some combination thereof, that designates the change in phase?

The UMC identifies the indicator of phase change. The key is a new constellation of system and/or interactor and/or actor attributes, strengthened by some traits of the crisis itself, that generates for at least one of the adversaries an image of more acute value threat, along with an awareness of time pressure and an increasing expectation of involvement in military hostilities before the disruptive challenge is overcome. With that fundamental perceptual change, that is, a deepening of the anticipation of harm, the onset phase will move to more intense action and reaction that heralds the escalation phase. The actors will experience a corresponding change from pre-crisis to crisis period. The termination dates for phase and period are often, but need not be, identical. And when phase/period change in an interstate crisis occurs the coping pattern undergoes basic change as well.

Escalation/Crisis

The term "escalation" has several meanings in relation to interstate crisis. Three have been addressed in this book and must be integrated into the Unified Model. One refers to change from incipient to full-scale crisis or, in formal language, from onset phase to escalation phase and, at the state level, from pre-crisis period to crisis period. Another indicates change from non-violent to violent crisis and, closely related, change from no/low level to severe violence, also at both levels of analysis. The third focuses on behavior or crisis management, that is, how decision-makers cope under increased stress. Each of these is an analytically distinct aspect of escalation. I begin with a fourth meaning, phase/period-change.

Escalation in this sense refers to a dynamic process in the evolution of a crisis: it denotes a shift from one "state of a system" or equilibrium to another. At the system/interactor level, the indicators of escalation are an increase in the intensity and/or a change in the type of disruptive interaction between adversaries, including a heightened probability of military hostilities. At the state level the indicators are a perception of more acute value threat, awareness (or, if it existed in the pre-crisis period, greater awareness) of time constraint on choice and, unlike pre-crisis, an image of substantial increase in the probability of war.

How does escalation begin? As specified in Figure 6.1, the process from pre-crisis period to onset phase is replicated. State A may commit a hostile act against B or vice-versa. It may be verbal, political, economic, non-violent military or violent. Or the catalyst may be a disruptive event or environmental change. The target may comply, that is, yield to the adversary's demand, in which case the crisis will terminate abruptly in victory/defeat, the counterpart to "abortion" in the onset phase. This is a rare response because of *raison d'état*. More likely, the target will perceive the trigger as communicating a step-level change in hostility and respond accordingly. The combination of A's trigger and B's response, or vice-versa, completes the initial jump from onset/pre-crisis to escalation/crisis.

Some crises gestate slowly; that is, they undergo a lengthy onset phase in which the adversaries do not threaten or employ violence, or engage in coercive diplomacy. This pattern operates when lesser values are at stake, not existence or influence or territorial integrity; and especially when time, though salient, is not crucial to the outcome.

Other crises crystallize quickly, with a short onset phase and the early threat or use of violence. This pattern tends to correlate with high values at risk. The determining factor for the time frame of a crisis is the type and level of threatened value(s). The reasoning derives from Model II. Where minor values are at stake, time pressure will be absent or minimal, and war will be perceived as unlikely, thus making escalation remote and, therefore, imposing no/few demands on the adversaries to abandon pre-crisis behavior. Where basic values are perceived to be under threat, a premium is placed on violence, and the time for choice and action will be restricted. In short, the duration of the onset phase will, as noted, be a function of the gravity of values threatened and, to a lesser extent, the awareness of time constraints on choice.

Sooner or later behavior will generate for at least one of the actors perceptions of more acute value threat, a heightened probability of war and time pressure, inducing more disruptive interaction and, thereby, a jump to the escalation phase. As with the onset phase, its beginning is dated back to the three-fold perception, for the same reason: its presence, indicating a shift from pre-crisis to crisis period for the relevant state(s), is also the necessary condition of phase-change.

The shift from onset to escalation is an integral part of the crisis process, except in those cases that abort or "fail" to materialize. The key question in this context is: *under what conditions is escalation most likely to occur?* The answer emerges from the *crisis escalation model* [phase model II] presented in Chapter 3: there, a cluster of enabling variables that make the "great leap" most likely were specified [**Hypothesis 1**] and tested. These conditions are:

crisis occurrence within a polycentric structure,
outside the dominant system, and
in a protracted conflict setting;

geographic proximity between the adversaries;
more than two adversaries in the onset phase;
heterogeneity between them; and
several cross-cutting issues in dispute.

Escalation also evokes an image of violence, in two respects: the role of violence in the shift from one phase to another and from pre-crisis to crisis period; and the change from no/low-level to severe violence, that is, to serious clashes or war during an interstate crisis.

Although not theoretically necessary, the step-level jump from onset to escalation phase and from pre-crisis to crisis period is most likely to be catalyzed by a threat of violence or its actual use. Stated in terms of the UMC's trigger categories, phase and period change toward more acute tension and conflict will probably result from: non-violent military, indirect violent or violent acts; an event portending resort to violence; or a situational change that facilitates violence, such as an innovation in weapons technology or a shift in the balance of power. Even if the trigger is a verbal, political or economic act, it will contain an implied threat of violence. By contrast, the catalyst to crisis onset will most likely involve non-violent acts, non-violent events, or non-military environmental changes.

Two questions about violence in crisis escalation were addressed in this book. *Under what conditions is the trigger to the escalation phase/crisis period most likely to be some form of violence?* And *why should this be so?* The first question was explored in Chapter 3 and led to two propositions [**Hypotheses 2 and 3**], which were tested with the evidence of international and foreign policy crises from the end of 1918 to the end of 1988. The enabling variables for violent escalation of an international crisis [**Hypothesis 2**] were postulated as:

all of the conditions for a jump from onset to escalation specified in H. 1, along with
    military or other types of authoritarian regime;
    power discrepancy between the adversaries; and
    military aid by patrons to clients engaged in the crisis.

As for escalation of an international crisis from no/low to severe violence [**Hypothesis 3**], all of the conditions in H. 1 and 2 are relevant. The two additional enabling conditions are:

the trigger to escalation takes the form of a violent act; and
the target responds with equal severity or stronger acts.

At the state level, the cluster of conditions most likely to induce an actor to escalate another state's pre-crisis to a fully-crystallized foreign policy crisis [**Hypothesis 4**] was postulated as follows:

it is ruled by a non-democratic regime;
it is engaged in a protracted conflict with its adversary(ies);
it has a favorable power relationship with its adversary(ies);
its adversary is geographically contiguous;
it is a young or new state; and
it is experiencing internal instability.

As for violence, **Hypothesis 5** postulated the most likely conditions to induce a state to employ violence in escalating a crisis as:

those specified in H. 4, along with
military support from a major power; and
heterogeneity vis-à-vis its adversary regarding political, military, economic and/or cultural aspects of development.

Why should violence be expected in the trigger to crisis escalation? The point of departure is that disruptive interaction has already been generated in the onset phase: without it the non-crisis norm in interstate relations would persist; that is, a crisis would not have begun. However, the level of disruption remains low. Stated formally, escalation signifies a step-level jump in the pattern of hostility, a qualitative increase in the intensity or a change in type of disruptive interaction. For that to occur the trigger must be a much more powerful inducement to change—in disruptive interaction between adversaries, in decision-makers' perceptions of threat, time pressure and war likelihood, and in crisis management. The most powerful catalyst is violence, actual, threatened or implied.

The process of step-level change from pre-crisis to crisis, and onset to escalation, was analyzed in ten case studies [Chap. 3]. To illustrate the hypotheses regarding escalation with in-depth evidence, the triggers to escalation and the pre-crisis period for a specific state are summarized here.

For the US in the Berlin Blockade, the catalyst to escalation was the severance by the Soviet Military Command of all land communications between West Berlin and the three Western occupation zones in Germany on 24 June 1948 (*non-violent military* act); as a result, the existing low-intensity pattern of East/West hostile interaction was transformed, with a high risk of resort to force.

The USSR's Prague Spring Crisis was triggered by the failure of a Moscow bilateral summit on 4–5 May 1968 to solve the Soviet/ Czechoslovak Communist Party dispute (a *political* act, presaging a willingness to resort to patron violence against a client, if necessary).

A fundamental change in the UK's Munich Crisis occurred on 7 September 1938 when the semi-official British newspaper, *The Times*, advised Prague to yield to German demands, the Nazi leader in Sudetenland openly called for rebellion, and the British Foreign Secretary learned of a German plan to invade Czechoslovakia on 19 or 20 September: this cluster of *verbal* acts and events, with war visible on the horizon, altered the UK's crisis abruptly.

The massive Red Army counter-offensive on 19–20 November 1942 transformed the Battle of Stalingrad from an anticipated decisive victory for Germany to potential disaster, a quantum leap in its Stalingrad Crisis (*direct violent* act).

The shift of Egypt's forces along the Suez Canal from a defensive to an offensive posture, discerned on 5 October 1973, indicated a sharp increase in the likelihood of attack, the trigger to escalation for Israel in the October-Yom Kippur Crisis (*non-violent military* act).

Syria's crisis period in Lebanon Civil War I was set in motion by a Christian Lebanese military victory over the Left-Muslim alliance in Beirut on 18 January 1976; the internal Lebanese balance was undermined and, with it, Syria's hegemonial role in Lebanon (*indirect violent* act).

China's military incursion at Thag La Ridge in India's North East Frontier Agency (NEFA) on 8 September 1962 transformed a three-year onset phase of minor disruption and low stress, catalyz-ing the escalation to war for India in the India/China Border Crisis (*direct violent* act).

The Hungarian Uprising underwent a qualitative change for Hungary with a huge student-led demonstration for reform on 23 October 1956 (internal event).

Rhodesia's proclamation of a state of emergency on 5 November 1965 was perceived by Zambia as marking a fundamental change in its UDI Crisis (a *political* act, presaging economic strangulation and, possibly, resort to force by Rhodesia).

The dispatch of a British naval task force to the South Atlantic on 5 April 1982 indicated to Argentina's decision-makers a heightened probability of war in the near future, a visible escalation of its Falklands/Malvinas Crisis (*non-violent military* act).

As evident, all but one of these triggers to escalation were violent or military acts, or indicated the threat of violence. A crucial effect was the qualitative increase of stress among decision-makers. That, in turn, had consequences for coping in the crisis period [see below].

The first of two aspects of vulnerability to be addressed was the *most likely conditions in which a state would be a target of a foreign policy crisis*. These were specified in **Hypothesis 6**, as the state being:

an actor outside the dominant system;
ruled by a non-democratic regime;
engaged in a protracted conflict;
militarily weaker than its adversary;
geographically contiguous to its adversary;
a young or new state; and
afflicted with acute internal instability.

Vulnerability to violent crisis escalation [**Hypothesis 7**] is most likely when:

all of the conditions specified in H. 6 are present, and when
    a state's regime is of short duration; and
    its territory is small.[4]

There are many differences between onset and escalation, and between pre-crisis and crisis. Two arise from the definition of these phases and periods. One is the extent of disruptive interaction: it is more intense in the escalation phase. The other is the depth and scope of perceived hostility held by decision-makers: low value threat in the pre-crisis period; acute value threat, reinforced by time pressure and heightened probability of war, in the crisis period. This perception, in essence a more basic anticipation of harm, points up a third difference: it generates higher stress than in the pre-crisis period. And that, in turn, has a profound effect on the behavior of decision-makers in the two periods. Still another difference relates to the number of decisions. But first, the variation in the number of decisions within each period merits attention.

In terms of the Unified Model, this depends upon several situational attributes. One is duration: all other things being equal, a *caveat* that applies to all of the postulated linkages here, a longer period will generate more decisions than a shorter one. A second is the number of actors: the larger the number of players, the greater the likelihood that each will make more decisions to cope with a more complex environment, complexity being defined in terms of uncertainty about the intent, capability and resolve of adversaries and potential patrons, allies or clients. Another is the geographic distance between adversaries: the more proximate their borders, the more likely it is that there will be more intense disruption caused by, and generating, more decisions to protect or enhance the threatened value(s). A fourth element affecting variation in decisions within a period is the number of values at risk: more values require more decisions to cope with anticipated harm, even assuming that the value threat is low. And a fifth relevant crisis trait is the extent of salience for major powers: the more a crisis impinges upon the interests of major powers, the more involved they will be, the greater the ensuing challenge for the adversaries and, therefore, the more decisions they will have to make.

Returning to the comparison by period, the UMC postulates that the number of important decisions is likely to be higher in the crisis period. *Strategic* decisions have been defined as "broad policy acts, measured by significance for a state's foreign policy system as a whole, duration of impact, and the presence of a subsidiary cluster of decisions. Those subsidiary clusters, to operationalize that policy act, constitute *tactical* decisions" (Brecher, 1972: 374).

The reason is a combination of higher stakes, emergent time salience, and greater expectation of war in the crisis period. Pre-crisis, as noted, is generally confined to low value threat and low stress. The demands on decision-makers are proportionate to the threat-stress level. They perceive little need to make hard choices, that is, core decisions about an incipient crisis, such as whether to engage in war or diplomacy, whether or not to shift resources to the military sphere, to embark upon a search for external support, etc. These and other problems of decision are not urgent. The threat posed in the pre-crisis period is not such as to induce an abnormal pattern of choice. Time does not impose constraints. And the perceived remoteness of military hostilities leads to an avoidance of decisions whose consequences cannot be anticipated. The tendency, therefore, is to make few, if any, strategic or even tactical decisions, lest options to cope with escalation of a crisis be foreclosed.

Once more the ten case studies are instructive. In eight cases there were *more strategic and tactical decisions in the crisis period*, even though the *pre-crisis period was longer* in almost all cases, as evident in Table 6.1.

Along with these differences, there is a conspicuous conceptual

TABLE 6.1   *Strategic/Tactical Decisions: Pre-Crisis and Crisis Periods*

International Crisis	Crisis Actor	Duration (days)		Number of Decisions	
		Pre-Crisis	Crisis	Pre-Crisis	Crisis
Berlin Blockade	US	96	28	2	4
Prague Spring	USSR	143	107	4	13
Munich	UK	35	23	3	9
Stalingrad	Germany	145	77	1	1
October – Yom Kippur	Israel	23	22	2	10
Lebanon Civil War I	Syria	241	256	1	3
India/China Border	India	1272	75	4	5
Hungarian Uprising	Hungary	18	13	1	6
Rhodesia UDI	Zambia	211	70	5	8
Falklands/Malvinas	Argentina	16	71	2	2

similarity between the two phases/periods. As with onset/pre-crisis, escalation/crisis may be analyzed as a static, intra-phase/intra-period process and as a dynamic inter-phase/inter-period process. Both of these interrelated concepts in the Unified Model are presented in the Escalation/Crisis box of Figure 6.1.

Once an act, event or environmental change triggers the threefold perception of harm that marks the beginning of a crisis period, and the target state responds, escalation is set in motion. This phase, too, may be brief or lengthy. It, too, may be characterized by one, albeit more intense, action-reaction exchange, or many interactions. It may be non-violent or violent, more likely the latter for reasons noted earlier. Major powers may or may not become involved in support of a client or ally; they are more likely to do so than in the onset phase. This also applies to international organizations.

The core concepts of onset/pre-crisis are also central to an understanding of intra-phase, intra-period escalation: trigger, stress, coping, choice. In essence, as evident in Figure 6.1, onset/pre-crisis is replicated, but at a higher level of disruptive interaction and stress. The step-level jump occurs as the result of a catalyst that generates B's image of much greater and imminent harm, including the heightened probability of military hostilities. That perception generates higher stress and compels B to cope with a more dangerous challenge.

According to the Unified Model, its decision-makers will adopt more elaborate crisis management techniques. They will engage in a more intense search for information and process it, quickly, at the highest level. They will broaden the scope of consultation, to draw upon the expertise of specialists in violence, and, possibly, include competing élites in order to enhance national unity. They may create an *ad hoc* decisional forum in order to expedite and enhance the efficiency of the decision-making process. And they will embark upon a more careful search for, and consideration of, alternatives to manage the crisis. Time becomes highly salient. Military hostilities will be viewed as increasingly probable. Stress will be high. Choice is more likely to be novel, to deal with a more serious threat.

As in onset, too, hostile interaction is not constant; that is, there may be escalation points within the escalation phase. If non-violence prevails, a military buildup may increase by spurts or sharp increases. If military hostilities have begun, the buildup will become more intense, involving more forces, qualitatively different weapons, the search for allies, and/or an extension of the war in terms of territory. In short, the level of stress and disruptive interaction, while higher than in pre-crisis/onset, may fluctuate as well during crisis/escalation. There may also be rising, higher and highest sub-phases of escalation.

In this context, the difference between escalation point and escalation phase merits further discussion. Acts or events such as mobilization of reserves, movement of forces to the adversary's border, or more extreme language of threat are escalation points, that is, specific markers of more disruptive interaction. But they operate below the new and higher threshold of distortion created by the phase-change from onset to escalation. (There may also be deescalation points during the deescalation phase [see below].)

Stated in terms of the UMC, escalation points are not synonymous with phase-change from onset to escalation (or from escalation to deescalation). That occurs only when an act, event or environmental change causes a fundamental change (expansion or contraction) in perceptions of impending harm and disruptive interaction. Moreover, once the jump to the escalation phase occurs there is no turning back, that is, no reversion to the lower level of disruptive interaction that characterizes the onset phase. In sum, an escalation point designates a specific increase in disruptive interaction within a phase. The escalation phase refers to a general pattern of higher distortion. The former constitutes change within existing bounds. The latter creates new boundaries and new upper and lower thresholds of interaction.

The third meaning of escalation relates to coping with the challenge of a full-scale crisis. In some respects adversaries will follow the pre-crisis pattern. They will seek to uncover each other's intention, capability and resolve, that is, to assess their "critical risk." But the emphasis of the search will shift: to the adversary's disposition to use violence or diplomacy (or both) to achieve its objectives; to relative military capability; and to the likelihood that the adversary will stand fast on its demands, rather than compromise or yield. More important, this search and all other aspects of crisis management during the crisis period will be much more intense because of the higher stress generated by the threefold perception of harm—of more acute value threat, time pressure and heightened war likelihood. Crisis actors will also negotiate, directly or indirectly, and will seek support from one or more major powers, other states and international organizations. Moreover, because the stakes are higher and the risks greater than in the pre-crisis period, actors are more likely to adopt a strategy of coercive diplomacy as the basis for crisis bargaining.

Bargaining will take the form of verbal and physical acts. If violence has not yet occurred, actors will employ various means short of war to compel their adversary to yield or at least compromise. They may mobilize reserves and/or place armed forces on alert. They may hold visible maneuvers. They may threaten to use violence, if necessary. They may activate commitments, that is, draw upon "promissory notes" of allies and friends to provide assistance in situations of crisis or war. And they may seek legitimacy from international organizations and law for demands that are based upon *raison d'état* and superior power.

If violence erupts in the crisis period, either as the trigger or in the course of bargaining, coercive diplomacy will give way to the strategy of force, designed to achieve victory at minimal cost—in casualties, weapons, morale, national unity, status in the international system, and the image held by friends, enemies and neutrals. The extent of force will vary, depending upon the gravity of values at risk, the importance of the issues, the relative power of the adversaries, and the pressures imposed by time, other actors and international institutions for crisis termination.

The use of violence as a crisis management technique is much more likely in the crisis period/escalation phase than in pre-crisis/onset, for reasons cited earlier. Whatever its scope and severity, violence will intensify disruptive interaction and generate higher stress, for the target and, assuming reciprocal violence, for the initiator as well. In general, coping with escalation in a context of violence is more stressful than coping with pre-crisis or with a non-violent crisis period.

Given the presence of perceived basic threat, time constraints and heightened probability of war, the Unified Model postulates that *decision-making* in the crisis period will differ markedly from non-crisis and pre-crisis norms. Higher stress will create a stronger felt need for *information* about: the adversary's intention, capability and resolve; the attitudes of a patron, major powers, and other states; and the likely reaction of all these parties to the use of violence, its legitimate scope, severity and purposes. That need, in turn, will stimulate a more thorough search for information from multiple sources and a more careful assessment of its contents. In short, there will be a more active focus on the acquisition and evaluation of information in the crisis period.

Higher stress, the UMC contends, will also affect information processing. Bureaucrats will play a lesser role, and senior decision-makers will become more directly involved. Many of the laborious and time-consuming intermediary layers will be eliminated, with more information being elevated rapidly to the top of the organizational pyramid. The result is that senior decision-makers' perceptions under high stress will be formed largely from their direct access to information relevant to a crisis. Sources of information will be broadened. And higher stress will create a tendency to rely on extraordinary and improvised channels. This, in turn, will reinforce the central role of these channels in the information sphere of crisis management.

Consultation, too, will undergo substantial change in the crisis period. In contrast to pre-crisis/onset, the cost of miscalculation and decisional errors will be high. Military hostilities are more likely. And if they have occurred, more intense violence is expected. That, too, accentuates stress. Under these conditions, decision-makers are likely to broaden the consultative network and seek the views of persons outside the core decisional group, especially when existence or some other core value is at stake, so as to maximize national unity at the peak of a crisis. For these reasons, too, decision-makers will consult more frequently among themselves, deriving reassurance and confidence from more face-to-face contact. They will also rely on *ad hoc* forms of consultation.

The search for, and consideration of, *alternatives*, too, will not be impervious to the higher stress of the crisis period. Because basic values are under threat, decision-makers will enlarge the scope of their search for viable options. And that search will occupy a considerable part of the time allocated to crisis decision-making. Moreover, given the greater reliance on group problem-solving, noted above, alternatives will be assessed with greater care. However, because of perceived time constraints on choice, decision-makers will be more concerned with the immediate than the long-term future. And, notwithstanding the conventional wisdom about a curvilinear (inverted U) relationship between stress and decision-making performance, the group context for evaluating alternatives under higher stress and the presence of grave value threats are likely to enhance, not diminish, the care with which alternatives are considered.

According to the UMC, change will also occur in the *decisional forum* during the high-stress crisis period. The institutional unit for choice in non-crisis and pre-crisis periods will tend to give way to an *ad hoc* or combined *ad hoc*-institutional body, usually small and homogeneous in composition and devoted to the political leader to whom this group provides advice about the most cost-effective path to crisis management. At the same time, the members of the decisional unit will exhibit a greater felt need for decisive leadership. There seems to be a meaningful correlation between available time for choice and dissensus/consensus: the longer the decision time, the greater will be the conflict within a decisional forum. But once a decision is reached, the greater will be the likelihood of a consensus.

For the crisis period, too, the ten cases examined in this book provide substantial evidence in support of the Unified Model's postulates. There was a felt need for more information in all cases except the sole intra-war crisis, Stalingrad. The crisis actors also intensified and diversified their search: more cable traffic and a tripartite information processing committee among the Western Powers (the US, Berlin Blockade); many delegations to and from Moscow and Prague, bringing first-hand information (the USSR, Prague Spring); envoys to and from Damascus (Syria, Lebanon Civil War I); and extraordinary channels of communication (the UK, Munich).

The pattern of consultation was broader in all cases except Argentina (Falklands/Malvinas). It included East European leaders and the Soviet military establishment in the USSR's Prague Spring Crisis. Chamberlain's "Inner Cabinet" consulted the full British Cabinet, French and Commonwealth leaders in the highest stress phase of the UK's Munich Crisis. A similar enlargement of the consultative circle is evident in Israel's Yom Kippur Crisis, far beyond the "Kitchen Cabinet," in Syria's Lebanon Civil War I Crisis, from nine to 43 persons, and in Hungary's 1956 crisis, almost 100 persons.

Ad hoc decisional forums flourished in the crisis period of six of the ten cases: several such US groups in the Berlin Blockade; the UK's "Inner Cabinet" (Munich); Israel's "Kitchen Cabinet" (October-Yom

Kippur); Syria's "decision committee" (Lebanon Civil War I); a Defense Minister-led committee during the pre-war part of India's escalation phase (India/China Border); and an informal group of 3–6 ministers under Kaunda's leadership in Zambia's UDI Crisis. It should be noted, however, that many of these *ad hoc* groups operated within a larger decision-making framework in which the institutionalized unit played a key role—the President and National Security Council (US), the Cabinet (UK, Israel), the President and Cabinet (Zambia).

The evidence on alternatives provides even stronger support for expected behavior in the crisis period. Options were sought and thoroughly assessed in eight of the ten cases. Two illustrations will suffice. Germany weighed, and ultimately rejected, several options at the peak stress crisis period of the Battle of Stalingrad: withdrawal of its 6th Army to the west, east or south-west, and an attempted relief operation to break its encirclement by the Red Army. And Hungary's rulers pondered whether or not to use force against mass protests in Budapest and elsewhere, and whether to oppose Soviet forces politically or with armed resistance, in the Hungarian Uprising.

There is also evidence of attempts at coalition-building and legitimation of policy preferences, that is, efforts to elicit support from allies, clients, major powers and/or international organizations during a state's crisis period. This was a continuation of pre-crisis behavior but at a higher level of intensity. The US counted on British and French support throughout the Berlin Blockade in 1948–49. The USSR expected and received loyalty from its Warsaw Pact clients during the escalation phase of the Prague Spring, when they contributed forces to the invasion. Zambia persistently but unsuccessfully sought UK assistance in trying to cope with its UDI Crisis. And during its Falklands/Malvinas crisis period, Argentina pleaded with the OAS to rally behind a fellow Latin American state against the "imperialist" UK.

What produces the next phase-change in an interstate crisis? According to the Unified Model, as long as action-reaction behavior by the adversaries sustains the existing high level of mistrust, hostility, disruptive interaction, and stress, or as long as cost-benefit assessments by the main protagonists remain unchanged, the escalation phase will persist. However, sooner or later, an act or event will indicate a willingness to accommodate, by reducing maximal demands or offering concessions. Mutual mistrust will diminish. Signals of openness to compromise may appear. One or more of these developments portends another phase-change, from escalation to deescalation. This is preceded, at the actor level, by a shift from crisis to end-crisis period, with a winding-down of overt hostility.

Deescalation/End-Crisis

Most analysts of interstate crisis focus on the peak stage of disruptive interaction and stress, that is, on what the UMC terms the escalation phase and the crisis period. Onset and deescalation, and their state-level counterparts, pre-crisis and end-crisis, are neglected as marginal to the crisis phenomenon. The reasons, simply stated, are: greater interest in the drama of violence and high tension associated with escalation; and the greater significance of that phase for subsequent relations between the adversaries, as well as for the regional and, sometimes, global balance of power. Yet this view is fundamentally flawed, conceptually and empirically.[5]

As with any societal phenomenon, crisis is most creatively analyzed as a dynamic process, not a static object. Viewed holistically, it exhibits an evolution through phases and periods. It emerges, sometimes erupts, from a non-crisis norm of no or low stress and no or low disruptive interaction (pre-crisis period/onset phase). Unless aborted, it moves through a stage of rising tension and hostility, usually accompanied by violence, toward a peak of perceived harm and disruption (crisis period/ escalation phase). And at some point the adversaries engage in a process of accommodation that leads to crisis termination (end-crisis period/ deescalation phase). Crisis, so viewed, is an integrated whole, whose "peripheral" phases/periods are inextricably linked to escalation. Onset creates the conditions from which the upward spiral of conflict develops. And deescalation captures the winding-down of hostility, disruption and perception of harm. It is, conceptually, a natural evolution. Empirically, as noted, onset and escalation sometimes occur simultaneously, that is, as a violent eruption of a full-scale crisis. So, too, escalation and deescalation may be fused, through an abrupt termination of a crisis. However, these are infrequent occurrences. Moreover, simultaneity and fusion are illusory; they only mask processes at work, however short and difficult to discern they may be.[6]

The concept of deescalation, like escalation, has several meanings. First, it refers to the winding-down of a crisis, a process of accommodation by the adversaries. As such, it is characterized by a decline in the perceptions of threat, time and war likelihood towards their non-crisis norms and in the intensity of disruptive interaction. In this sense deescalation denotes phase-change and period-change—no different, conceptually, than the change from onset to escalation, and from pre-crisis to crisis.

At the actor level, deescalation has two additional meanings. One is a strategy of crisis behavior designed to achieve the goal of accommodation between the conflicting parties. This strategy is precisely the obverse of a strategy of force that aims at an imposed victory/defeat outcome, compared to a voluntarily arrived-at mutual compromise. An accommodative strategy, then, is associated with a decrease in tension and perceived harm which, in turn, leads to less disruptive interaction and distortion in the relationship between adversaries.

Deescalation also captures the dimension of satisfaction with a crisis outcome. Several pairs of perceived outcome can be identified: all crisis actors are satisfied; all crisis actors are dissatisfied; and a mixed pair—A satisfied with the outcome, B not, or vice-versa. The success or failure of deescalation, in this sense, is measured by the extent to which the adversaries are dissatisfied with the outcome: deescalation is often the result of at least one party's dissatisfaction with the costs entailed by the crisis.

How does deescalation begin? Several scenarios are theoretically possible and are evident in twentieth-century crises. This phase may begin *force majeure*, that is, when one actor achieves a decisive military victory and imposes the conditions of crisis termination. In such a case deescalation may take a few days to run its course. However, it may last weeks or months until a cease-fire, armistice or peace agreement is framed and implemented. But whatever the duration, the link between escalation and deescalation is laid bare—winding-down grows out of the peak disruption created by war and its outcome.

At the other extreme of scenarios for the transition to deescalation is a mutual signalling of a wish to terminate a crisis. This may occur in the context of a costly war of attrition in which victory is unattainable by either adversary. It may also emanate from a rational calculus by the decision-makers of both adversaries that, in game-theoretic terms, a strategy of cooperation will generate a more positive payoff than a strategy of defection. Such a calculus may occur before military hostilities have erupted or during a war, with a coincidence of perceptions that continuing the war will increase one's losses, whereas accommodation (cooperation) will increase one's gains.

If the adversaries arrive at this assessment more or less simultaneously, phase-change from escalation to deescalation would occur abruptly and is likely to be of brief duration. If there is a time lag in the adversaries' shift from a strategy of defection to one of cooperation, deescalation may still begin—as long as the mutual perception of the relative military balance has convinced both that military victory is either impossible or too costly relative to the anticipated gains. That awareness need not be, and rarely is, simultaneous. One of the conflicting parties may make a bid for termination. The adversary may find the terms unacceptable or sub-optimal, in which case a bargaining process will ensue. Its intensity and duration will depend upon the parties' assumptions of the military balance, before or during a war.

There are other scenarios for deescalation. However, all of them exhibit the crucial indicator of phase-change from escalation to de-escalation: at least one crisis actor must perceive a decline in value threat and/or time pressure and/or war likelihood (an adverse change in the military balance, if war has broken out). That perceptual shift marks the beginning of a "crisis downswing" towards the pre-crisis level of perceived harm and, eventually, to the non-crisis norm.

Stated in terms of the UMC, phase-change is a function of period-change. And period-change, from crisis to end-crisis, begins with a decline in one or more of the perceptions of threat, time and war likelihood and their derivative, high stress—the defining conditions of a full-scale foreign policy crisis. When an actor-level crisis begins to diminish, stress declines, with consequences for coping. And this, in turn, leads to less disruptive interaction, marking the beginning of the phase-change from escalation to deescalation.

What does the evidence of the ten case studies examined throughout this book indicate about the beginning of the end-crisis period?

> The Berlin Blockade began to wind down for the US on 22 July 1948 when President Truman's National Security Council opted for an expanded airlift and negotiations, instead of force, as the path to crisis termination ([internal] *political* act).
>
> The USSR's Prague Spring Crisis began to deescalate with its invasion of Czechoslovakia on 20–21 August 1968 (*violent* act).
>
> Germany's end-crisis period in the Battle of Stalingrad began with the surrender of its 6th Army and the capture of the city by Soviet forces on 2 February 1943 (*non-violent military* act).
>
> The cessation of hostilities on its southern front and the second cease-fire with Egypt, on 26 October 1973, marked the start of deescalation/end-crisis in Israel's October-Yom Kippur crisis-war (*non-violent military* act).
>
> Syria's end-crisis period in the 1975–76 Lebanon Civil War I case began with its defeat of Palestinian and Left Muslim forces near Beirut on 30 September 1976 (*violent* act).

The winding-down of India's prolonged border crisis with China began on 21 November 1962, when the latter announced an immediate cease-fire and a unilateral withdrawal of forces starting 1 December to a point 20 kilometers behind "the line of actual control" (*verbal* act).

Hungary's end-crisis period in the Hungarian Uprising can be dated to 4 November 1956, when a new communist government headed by Kadar took office, backed by Soviet military power (*political* act).

Deescalation of Zambia's Rhodesia UDI Crisis began on 13 January 1966 when Prime Minister Wilson, on a visit to Lusaka, indicated a new UK commitment to crush Rhodesia's rebellion (*verbal* act).

Argentina's end-crisis period in the Falklands/Malvinas Crisis began on 2 June with several statements by its leaders seeking aid from any source, in the final stage of its war with the UK (*verbal* act).

In sum, as postulated in the UMC, there was great variety in the triggers to deescalation and the beginning of the end-crisis period: three verbal, two political, two non-violent military, and two violent acts.

How long will the deescalation phase last? Several variables will determine its duration. One is the number of crisis actors. All other things being equal, the fewer the adversaries, the less complex will be the accommodation process. Value tradeoffs, involving mutual concessions, will be easier for the conflicting parties to identify and to measure and, therefore, to accept as a fair compromise. Any increment beyond a two-actor crisis game adds to the complexity of the accommodation process: the dynamics of negotiation; the ability of each party to assess multiple combinations of gains and losses; the communication of bids and counter-bids; the greater likelihood of misperception; mistrust of one or more adversaries' intention regarding crisis accommodation; and the framing of a package to satisfy minimal demands and achieve mutual satisfaction.

This analysis of the link between number of actors and duration of deescalation applies to a crisis in which the adversaries' relative equality of power dictates a compromise outcome. However, if crisis escalation includes war and a decisive victory/defeat outcome, the duration of deescalation is likely to be short, as noted, only long enough for the victor to frame surrender terms for the vanquished.

The duration of deescalation will also be influenced by the extent of major power activity. The less involved the powers are in a crisis, the longer will be the process of accommodation by the adversaries. If major powers are active militarily in support of a client, they can exert pressure in favor of a compromise outcome to a crisis; and this they will prefer so as to minimize the risk of major power confrontation and the consequent threat to stability and equilibrium in the global system. Low-level activity, verbal, political or economic, will reduce the major powers' leverage with clients or non-client adversaries in the accommodation process.

Several other factors will affect the duration of the deescalation phase. One is the geostrategic salience of a crisis. The more remote it is from the vital interests of the major powers, the less likely it is that they will intervene and, therefore, the less influence they will exert on crisis termination. This absence, in turn, will tend to make deescalation longer. In such a case its evolution will depend largely on internal dynamics between the lesser powers that are the crisis adversaries. Moreover, the more heterogeneous the crisis actors, the longer will be the accommodation process. Differences in political regime, and/or culture, level of economic development, and military capability will compound misunderstanding, misperception and mistrust and make the search for a compromise solution more difficult to attain. Thirdly, the type of crisis management techniques will affect the duration of deescalation. If a crisis escalates to war, accommodation will be more difficult, unless one party achieves decisive military victory and can impose the terms of war termination. Where the outcome of military hostilities is inconclusive, the accommodation process will be more complex and longer.

Two other closely-related explanatory variables are the number and importance of issues in dispute between the crisis adversaries. The fewer the issues, the shorter will be the deescalation phase, because the quest for mutual compromise will be easier to achieve. Similarly, the less basic the perceived values at stake, the less difficult will be the framing of terms that will be mutually acceptable to the conflicting parties.

The ten case studies are also instructive on the duration of the end-crisis period, as well as on the form of termination.

> The US's crisis over the Berlin Blockade ended with the Four Power Accord of 5 May 1949 that removed all restrictions imposed by the USSR since 1 March 1948, in exchange for a meeting of the Council of Foreign Ministers to "consider" the future of Germany ($9\frac{1}{2}$ months, *formal agreement*).

The Prague Spring Crisis for the USSR terminated on 27 August

1968 with the signing of the Moscow Protocol by Czechoslovak communist leaders, who acquiesced in the "Brezhnev Doctrine," acknowledging Soviet hegemony in Eastern Europe (one week, *imposed formal agreement*).

Germany's intra-war crisis over Stalingrad ended on 24 March 1943 with the successful conclusion of Manstein's counter-offensive, including the recapture of Kharkov (seven weeks, *unilateral act*).

The Egypt/Israel and Israel/Syria Disengagement Agreements on 18 January and 31 May 1974 marked the end of Israel's end-crisis period in the two segments of its October-Yom Kippur crisis-war (12 weeks *vis-à-vis* Egypt, 31 weeks *vis-à-vis* Syria, *formal agreement*).

The winding-down of Syria's Lebanon Civil War I Crisis ended on 15 November 1976 when its forces, implementing the Riyadh and Cairo resolutions of October legitimizing Syria's hegemony in Lebanon, reached the centre of Beirut (47 days, *unilateral act*).

The deescalation of the India/China Border Crisis, for India, but not the still-unresolved conflict over borders, came to an end during the last fortnight of February 1963, when India's Cabinet approved the recommendation of its Emergency Committee to double the defense expenditures of the preceding year in order to implement a three-year plan to expand India's military capability (almost 14 weeks, *faded*).

Unlike eight of the other cases, the termination of Hungary's end-crisis period in the Hungarian Uprising cannot be precisely identified. By early January 1957 Soviet direct military rule ended, as did the remnants of domestic resistance (approximately two months, *faded*).

The end-crisis period of Zambia's Rhodesia UDI Crisis came to an end on 27 April, when newly-elected Prime Minister Wilson told Parliament that he would seek "talks about talks" with Rhodesia's Premier Smith (99 days, *unilateral act*).

Argentina's end-crisis period ended with a *de facto* cease-fire and military defeat in the Falklands/Malvinas crisis-war (14 days, *imposed formal agreement*).

As with the triggers to the end-crisis period, there was great variety in both the duration and form of termination of this period. The former comprised: one week; two weeks (two cases); seven weeks (two cases); two months; three months; almost eight months; and 9½ months. The latter included: four formal agreements; three unilateral acts; and two faded outcomes.

The three meanings of deescalation, namely, the winding-down process, the strategy of accommodation, and satisfaction with a crisis outcome, were explored at length in Chapter 4 [phase model III]. For each, a most likely occurrence proposition was framed and tested against the evidence of 70 years of interstate crises. These will now be summarized as integral parts of the Unified Model.

Under what conditions is an international crisis most likely to wind down and terminate in an agreement? As specified in **Hypothesis 8**,

successful crisis accommodation is most likely to occur when:
a crisis unfolds in a non-protracted conflict setting;
the adversaries are relatively equal in military power;
there are few adversarial actors;
the major powers are less active in the crisis;
the international organization is highly involved in quest of a peaceful settlement; and
the adversaries rely on non-violent crisis management techniques.

As for crisis duration, *the less intense an international crisis, the shorter it is likely to be* [**Hypothesis 9**], that is, *when there are/is:*
few adversarial actors;
low-level, non-military, activity by the major powers;
less heterogeneity among the adversaries;
low geostrategic salience;
few issues in contention; and
non-violent crisis management techniques.

As indicated in earlier discussions of the UMC, crisis actors may adopt one of several strategies of crisis management, notably, deterrence, compellance or accommodation. According to **Hypothesis 10**, *a state is most likely to adopt an accommodative strategy when the following conditions are present:*
its crisis occurs in a non-protracted conflict setting;
its power is equal or inferior to that of its adversary;
it is governed by a democratic regime;
its internal conditions are stable;
it receives non-military support from a major power; and
it receives support for its claims from the relevant international organization.

When is a crisis actor most likely to be satisfied with a crisis outcome? According to **Hypothesis 11**, this will occur under the following conditions:

a state's foreign policy crisis takes place outside an on-going conflict;
its patron major power does not provide military assistance;
it receives support from the involved international organization;
it perceives the outcome as a victory or compromise, not a defeat or stalemate; and
it does not suffer an adverse change in the power balance vis-à-vis its adversary after the crisis.[7]

Earlier in this chapter, several differences between onset/pre-crisis and escalation/crisis were noted. A similar comparison can be made between escalation/crisis and deescalation/end-crisis. The volume of disruptive interaction is expected to decline in the latter, as will the intensity of perceived harm on the part of crisis actors. These differences flow from the definition of the two phases and periods. However, they are also empirically supported. As a result, the decision-makers' stress level will decline. And behavior will be correspondingly affected. Finally, the number of decisions in the end-crisis period, too, is expected to decline, relative to the peak crisis period.

The ten cases exhibited these changes as a crisis deescalated. Disruptive interaction continued, but at a distinctly lower level of intensity. This occurred because the crisis actors perceived a lower value threat and, with it, less stress from time pressure and/or expectation of war or an adverse change in the military balance. In some cases this was due to a cease-fire or armistice agreement during a war (e.g., India in the border crisis-war with China, Israel in the October-Yom Kippur crisis-war). In other cases it was due to a compromise (the US in the Berlin Blockade). In still others it occurred because of a military victory (the USSR in the Prague Spring) or the assertion of superior military power (Syria in Lebanon Civil War I). These two characteristics of deescalation/end-crisis also sometimes accompanied military defeat (Germany at Stalingrad, Argentina in the Falklands/Malvinas crisis-war).

In all of these cases, whatever the trigger and duration, there was a decline in both perceived harm and disruptive interaction. That, in turn, led to less stress for decision-makers. Whether as a result of a cease-fire or more formal termination of hostilities, or a military victory or even defeat, or a faded outcome, the world looked less menacing to decision-makers than in the crisis period. Stated in terms of the UMC and the definition of crisis, high stress, derived from a composite perception of harm, diminished in the end-crisis period.

The number of decisions in this period, too, is expected to decline for all of these reasons. In particular, there will be fewer occasions when difficult choices have to be made. Put simply, "the worst is over" and "the end is in sight." The substance of crisis termination will not always be attractive to decision-makers—imposed agreement or compromise or stalemate, and often defeat, with its attendant high costs. But these outcomes are usually beyond their control, the result of inferior military power or bargaining skills, or external pressure by major powers, or the failure of allies to provide necessary aid, or several of these together. As such, they can "breathe more easily" and adapt to the new circumstances created by the end of a foreign policy crisis. Because it is often beyond their control, stress diminishes and options for end-crisis choice are restricted. Thus fewer decisions will be made in the end-crisis period.

The evidence on strategic and tactical decisions made in that period is instructive, especially relative to its duration (Table 6.2).

TABLE 6.2   *Strategic/Tactical Decisions: End-Crisis Period*

International Crisis	Crisis Actor	Duration (days)	Number of Decisions
Berlin Blockade	US	287	3
Prague Spring	USSR	7	2
Stalingrad	Germany	50	2
October – Yom Kippur	Israel	84	5
Lebanon Civil War I	Syria	47	3
India/China Border	India	99	3
Hungarian Uprising	Hungary	approx. 65	3
Rhodesia UDI	Zambia	105	2
Falklands/Malvinas	Argentina	14	2

(The Munich Crisis did not have an end-crisis period)

As evident, the number of decisions was not responsive to the length of deescalation. The explanation lies in the essence of strategic decisions: as turning points in a crisis, they occur rarely. It is inefficient to change grand—or even lesser—strategy frequently, whereas it is efficient to be flexible about implementation.

All of the themes relating to the preceding phases and periods apply to deescalation/end-crisis as well, with appropriate changes because of declining perceptions of harm, stress, etc. (Its static and dynamic processes are formalized in the Deescalation/End Crisis box of Figure 6.1.) As with the preceding periods, too, the core concepts apply to end-crisis, namely, trigger, stress, coping and choice. What sets end-crisis in motion is the obverse of the upward spiral of escalation; that is, when a decline in one or more of the perceptions of harm—threat, time and war likelihood—is triggered by a less menacing act, event or environmental change, end-crisis and deescalation begin. Generally, interaction will be less intense and hostile, although violence may persist, along with major power and international organization involvement. The shift to end-crisis/deescalation is no less a step-level change. The change takes the form of a perception of less threat, less time pressure and decreasing probability of war (or an improvement in the military balance), leading to a lower level of stress and disruptive interaction.

The distinction between phase change and point change applies to deescalation as well. The latter designates a specific decrease in disruptive interaction—a conciliatory statement by an adversary, its partial withdrawal of forces or their shift to a defensive posture, a mediatory role by a major power or an international organization, or another state, that assists the process of accommodation, etc. The deescalation phase, by contrast, denotes a general pattern of lower distortion. Deescalation points represent changes within the bounds of a downward spiral of hostility as the parties move towards crisis termination. When that point is reached, the deescalation phase and the international crisis as a whole come to an end. Perceptions of harm revert to the non-crisis norm. So too does the intensity of disruptive interaction. The storm of escalation gives way to relative calm, though the basic issues in dispute between crisis adversaries often persist, as does their underlying conflict.

Because of the downward spiral, coping (crisis management) will differ in the end-crisis period. The search for knowledge about the adversary's intent, resolve and capability, that is, its "critical risk," which is crucial to coping in the crisis period, is now expendable. The focus will be, rather, on accommodation and crisis termination. Thus the adversaries will seek to involve the global and/or regional organization in facilitating an agreement, with minimal disruptive interaction. If they are small powers they will attempt to persuade their patron to assist the winding-down of disruption so that the parties can more readily reach a mutually-satisfying outcome.

Adversaries will also continue to engage in bargaining, with verbal, political and, if deemed necessary, physical acts as well. If violence erupted in the onset or escalation phase, the weaker actor will attempt to achieve better terms of war termination by preemptive bidding. If violence did not occur in a crisis, the strategy of coercive diplomacy will give way to flexible negotiation, with each actor attempting to reduce losses and maximize gains in the negotiations that are central to the accommodation process. Bargaining will encompass threats, promises, and the inducement of future benefits to accrue from a less harsh outcome. It may also involve one or more major powers attempting to protect a client from the high cost of defeat.

The coping mechanisms employed by crisis actors on the path to termination will also undergo change. The quest for *information* about the adversary's capability and intention, the attitudes of major powers and IOs, etc., will be less intense than in the crisis period. And information processing is expected to revert to the pre-crisis norm, with bureaucrats playing the crucial role of determining the flow of information to the top of the decisional pyramid. *Consultation* with persons or groups, which tends to expand in the escalation phase, is expected to contract, as less stress is experienced by decision-makers. The *decisional forum* is also likely to revert to its institutional, pre-crisis norm, for the need to elicit support from a broad cross-section of the political public, to share the burden of difficult decisions, diminishes in the new environment of less risk to core values and less stress. The search for, as well as consideration of, *alternatives* will involve much less decision time because the stakes will be perceived as less important by the decision-makers. Time becomes less salient. Military hostilities will be less probable (or the military balance less adverse). Stress, too, will decline. And choice is likely to be of the standard operating procedure, routinized type.

Unlike the pre-crisis and crisis periods, the UMC's postulates about end-crisis coping are not strongly supported by the evidence from the nine case studies (Munich, as noted, did not have a deescalation phase). Thus the volume or processing of information, or both, remained essentially the same as in the crisis period for seven of the nine crises: the USSR, Germany, Israel, Syria and Argentina (both volume and processing), the US (volume), and Hungary (processing). Among the changes: information processing in the US returned to the bureaucrats; India's volume of information declined; and receptivity to information in Zambia was greater than in the crisis period.

As for consultation, the process remained the same in four cases—the

USSR, Germany, Syria and Argentina. It was broader in three cases: US consultation with the UK and France regarding the winding-down of the Berlin Blockade; Israel's enlarged network of consultation about the negotiations and bargaining with Syria; and Nehru's consultation with the Cabinet's Emergency Committee during India's negotiations with China over the non-aligned states' Colombo Proposals. In Hungary and Zambia the consultative circle became much narrower and smaller. The three cases of broader consultation were participatory democracies. All the rest were authoritarian regimes, civilian or military.

In six of the nine cases the decisional forum of the crisis period continued through end-crisis: the USSR's Politburo and its Negotiating Committee; Hitler for Germany; Israel's Cabinet; Syria's President and the *ad hoc* decision-making Committee and Cabinet; the President, senior ministers and Cabinet in Zambia; and Argentina's military junta and Foreign Minister. By contrast, the US President was much less active in end-crisis decision-making on the Berlin Blockade; the Emergency Committee of India's Cabinet became its decisional, as well as consultative, unit in the initial accommodation process with China; and in Hungary, a foreign body, the Soviet Military Command, dominated decision-making as the Hungarian Uprising gave way to relative tranquillity.

The one aspect of coping in which the postulates of the Unified Model are strongly supported is that of alternatives. The search for options in the end-crisis period declined in five cases—the US, the USSR, Germany, India, and Zambia; and it was non-existent in Hungary and Argentina. However, evaluation remained careful in five cases—Germany, Israel, Syria, India and Hungary. It was less so in the USSR and Zambia, and more rigid in US behavior over the airlift strategy to break the blockade in Berlin. In sum, coping with accommodation in these crises exhibits more continuity than change from coping in the crisis period.

Impact/Post-Crisis

Thus far the Unified Model has focused on interstate crisis *per se*, that is, on an autonomous phenomenon with clear boundaries. Stated formally, the UMC has offered an explanation for eruption (onset/pre-crisis), crystallization (escalation/crisis), and the winding-down process (deescalation/end-crisis), leading to termination. However, the end of a crisis does not mark the end of its role in the on-going flow of world politics. Crises have multiple effects, on the actors, on their relations, and on one or more international systems. The UMC tries to capture this post-crisis dimension by the concept of impact.

Although it is treated, schematically, as another domain/phase of crisis [Figure 6.1], impact differs from the other three phases in several respects. Its time frame is arbitrary, 3–5 years after crisis termination, for reasons set out earlier. It has no coping dimension. It is less precise than onset, escalation and deescalation, and their actor-level periods, pre-crisis, crisis and end-crisis; that is, empirical traces of impact/post-crisis are more difficult to discover than the evidence of a crisis proper. There is also less consensus on its scope and direction. Nonetheless, while recognizing these constraints, the UMC contends that the boundaries and content of the impact domain/phase can be designated and its effects measured, though with less confidence than the measurement of its conceptual counterpart for the crisis proper, namely, intensity.

The concept of impact is a heuristic device to capture the consequences of an interstate crisis. At the bilateral level, the task is to discover how a crisis affects subsequent relations between the adversaries. Operationally, its legacy is defined in terms of greater or less distrust, hostility and tension. And the tangible indicator is the occurrence or non-occurrence of one or more military-security crises between the adversaries in the five years following crisis termination.

What determines this aspect of impact? According to the Unified Model, the crucial explanatory variables are outcome, both content and form, and the intensity of a crisis. The UMC postulates that, all other things being equal, a clear, zero-sum, victory/defeat outcome is much more likely to have a negative impact than a blurred, ambiguous outcome, in which none of the adversaries achieved all of its goals during a crisis or when the *status quo ante* remained unchanged. Either of these outcomes, compromise or stalemate, will reduce the likelihood of more hostile relations after a crisis has ended.

The UMC also contends that the form of outcome has spillover effects on post-crisis relations between the adversaries. Thus a crisis which ends through agreement—a cease-fire, truce or armistice, in case of violence, or a formal document setting down the procedure for dispute settlement, or even an exchange of letters of peaceful intent—is much more likely to leave a positive residue on relations between the adversaries than termination through a unilateral act, such as decisive military invasion or even humiliating unilateral withdrawal, or by covertly-inspired regime change in the adversary.

The intensity of a crisis, it will be recalled [Chap. 5], is a composite of six situational attributes that are measured from onset to termination: number of actors; extent of major power involvement; scope of geostrategic salience; range of heterogeneity between the adversaries; number of conflictive issues; and degree of violence. Combined as an index of intensity, these indicators generate the overall intensity of an interstate crisis. Most important, according to the Unified Model, intensity and impact are causally linked: simply put, the more intense a crisis, the greater the impact is likely to be for the relations between the adversaries and, more broadly, for the relevant international system(s), global, dominant and/or subordinate.

As with intensity, it was argued that impact can be measured, but as a post-crisis dimension [Chap. 5]. More generally, crisis impact is the indicator of an international political "earthquake." Indeed, a Richter-type ten-point scale was devised to measure the "fallout" of an interstate crisis on the landscape of world politics. Moreover, like overall intensity, the overall impact of a crisis is the product of a set of situational attributes. Its indicators are types of change generated by a crisis during a three-year period after termination.

One is the extent of change in the distribution of *power*. This ranges, in ascending order, along a four-point scale, from no change, if the outcome is compromise or stalemate, to change in relative power between the adversaries, to a shift in ranking within the power hierarchy, to the inclusion of a new state in, or the exclusion of a pre-existing member from, the apex of the power pyramid.

Another indicator of impact is *actor* change. As with power, there may be no change. However, a crisis may affect the political regime of one or more adversaries, either their foreign policy orientation or, more basically, the regime type, for example, a crisis-induced shift from authoritarianism to democracy or the reverse. In rare cases, a crisis may lead to the creation, elimination or restoration of a state, as with Bangladesh as a result of the 1971 India/Pakistan crisis-war.

Alliances, too, may or may not undergo change as a consequence of an interstate crisis. To capture this aspect of impact, another four-point scale was constructed, ascending from no change, through an increase or decrease in cohesiveness within a pre-existing alliance, to the entry or exit of an actor into or from an alliance, to the formation or elimination of an alliance, as with the transformation of the alliance configuration as a result of the Entry into World War II Crisis of 1939 and the six-year upheaval that followed. Finally, and most difficult to measure, interstate crises may generate changes in rules of the game, formally or informally.

How to measure the impact of an interstate crisis was a crucial methodological task, a prerequisite to systematic empirical research on the consequences of crises. Even more important was a theoretical task, namely, to generate, deductively, the conditions of most likely impact on interactor relations and the system(s) of which they are members. To this end the UMC postulated expectations about change at both levels of analysis, indicated the underlying logic, and framed these assumptions in a form that could be tested. The result was three multivariate hypotheses about crisis as a political earthquake. They are cumulative, in the sense that many independent variables, the components of intensity, recur, with additional variables in the first and third of these hypotheses.

One focuses on the bilateral legacy. **Hypothesis 12** postulates that

the impact of an international crisis on subsequent relations between the adversaries is most likely to be high tension when:
   the outcome is definitive and disharmonious (victory/defeat);
   a crisis ends without agreement;
   there are many crisis actors;
   the major powers are highly involved;
   the crisis has high geostrategic salience;
   the adversaries are heterogeneous on many aspects;
   there are at least several issues in dispute; and
   there is intense violence during the crisis.

The second and third expectations relate to systematic consequences. **Hypothesis 13** specifies the direct intensity-impact link. Thus, *the higher the intensity of an international crisis, the higher will be its impact, high intensity being expressed by:*
   many crisis actors;
   high major power activity;
   high geostrategic salience;
   high heterogeneity;
   at least several issues in dispute; and
   intense violence.

Hypothesis 14 is a logical extension of H. 13, for it addresses the broadest possible scope of impact, namely, system transformation. Thus it postulates that *the systemic legacy of an international crisis is most likely to be transforming when:*
all of the conditions specified in H. 13 operate, and when

the catalyst to crisis escalation is extreme;
violence is the primary crisis management technique;
the crisis is of lengthy duration; and
the outcome is other than formal agreement.

The logic underlying these expectations and the findings from the testing of these hypotheses were set out earlier [Chap. 5] and need not be repeated. Suffice it to recall a high degree of support for many of the individual linkages incorporated in the three hypotheses relating to impact.[8]

In that context, the UMC postulates a close link between intensity and impact. The case study findings on these two aspects of interstate crisis were reported earlier [Tables 5.3 and 5.9]. Their association is noteworthy. In general, using 5.00 as the high-low divide, all of the high overall intensity cases scored high on overall impact as well: October-Yom Kippur: 9.18–6.63; Berlin Blockade: 8.25–7.00; Munich: 7.98–8.13; Prague Spring: 6.77–5.50; and Stalingrad: 5.97–5.50. Similarly, four of the low overall intensity cases also scored low on overall impact: Lebanon Civil War I: 2.08–3.63; Rhodesia UDI: 2.62–2.13; Falklands/Malvinas: 4.09–4.00; and Hungarian Uprising: 4.76–4.00. The only serious anomaly was India/China Border: 3.82–5.13.

To recapitulate: impact merits attention on several grounds. Conceptually, it is an integral part of the phenomenon of crisis viewed holistically: without this post-crisis dimension, the analysis would be incomplete. Moreover, as evident in Figure 6.1, the impact domain/phase provides an indispensable dynamic link between a specific, time- and space-bound disruption, an interstate crisis, and global politics writ large. Without impact, the dynamism of the UMC is confined to the perception-decision-behavior-interaction flow from phase to phase and period to period, within an interstate crisis *per se*. Impact traces the feedback from a crisis to the system, interactor and actor attributes of the larger environment from which the crisis originated. As such, it links crisis to the array of events, acts and changes that, together, constitute the flow of world politics.

In that larger vista, world politics encompasses crisis, conflict and war, and other forms of disruption, along with a myriad of cooperative transactions and interactions among the many layers of actors in the global system. Thus interstate crisis is but one of many sources of global instability and disequilibrium. Nevertheless, its capacity for disruption is enormous, as evident in some of the transforming crises of the twentieth century: the 1914 Crisis, which revolutionized the structure of world politics, destroying and creating states as a result of the military upheaval that followed; the Entry into World War II Crisis, which exceeded its predecessor in the scope of change—bipolarity, global decolonization amidst the decimation of empires, etc.; and Cuban Missiles which, in the post-Cold War perspective of the 1990s, stabilized superpower relations in an era of rapid, potentially destructive technological change. For all of these reasons, impact is no less crucial than the other three domains/phases of interstate crisis. And finally, in policy terms, the ability to trace post-crisis impact can enhance the way in which decision-makers, sensitized to potential multiple consequences, will respond to future incipient crises among the ever-growing number of autonomous members of the global system. (This point will be elaborated in Chap. 8.) Such is the *raison d'être* for the inclusion of the impact phase/post-crisis period in the Unified Model of Crisis.

This model, it should be clear by now, does not purport to represent reality. Rather, like all models, it is an analytical device designed to explain reality, in this case the phenomenon of interstate crisis. To explain the meaning of crises in the twentieth century, several paths have been pursued in this book. The first was to elucidate the logic of two general models—international crisis [Model I] and foreign policy crisis [Model II], and four phase models—onset, escalation, deescalation and impact. The explanatory factors in each model were specified, along with their anticipated effects. These independent variables were then combined into clusters (propositions and hypotheses) which were postulated as explaining one or more dimensions (or aspects) of interstate crisis (outbreak, initiation, vulnerability, escalation, the role of violence, outcome, etc.). Thereafter, these clusters and their constituent parts were tested against the real world, namely, the evidence of 390 international crises and 826 foreign policy crises from the end of 1918 to the end of 1988, supplemented by evidence from ten case studies and an in-depth study of the Gulf Crisis [Chap. 7].

In none of these analyses were assumptions made about the scope or potency of the independent variables, other than the *a priori* derivation of their effects on other such variables [Appendix A]. Thus in order to complete this presentation of the Unified Model it is necessary to compare their explanatory power as postulated by the model, that is, the dimensions (aspects) of crisis they try to explain.

The key to this comparison is a summary of variables, phases, clusters of hypotheses, and crisis dimensions they attempt to explain (Table 6.3).

Of the 24 independent variables that were specified in the phase models, eight attempt to explain crisis aspects in three of the four

TABLE 6.3 *Unified Model: Scope of Explanation*

Variables: Multiple-Phase	Phase	Propositions & Hypotheses	Dependent Variables: Aspects of Crisis			
			Onset	Escalation	Deescalation	Impact
Conflict Setting	Onset Escalation Deescalation	P. 1,3; H. 1–7,8,10–11	Outbreak Vulnerability	Outbreak Initiation Vulnerability Role of Violence (in all three above)	Termination – Agreement Accommodative Strategy Satisfaction	
Capability	Onset Escalation Deescalation	P. 1–3; H. 2–5,8,10	Outbreak Initiation Vulnerability	Initiation Role of Violence (in Outbreak)	Termination – Agreement Accommodative Strategy	
Regime Type	Onset Escalation Deescalation	P. 1,2 H. 2–7,10	Outbreak Initiation	Initiation Vulnerability Role of Violence (in Outbreak)	Accommodative Strategy	
Internal Instability	Onset Escalation Deescalation	P. 2,3 H. 4–7,10	Initiation Vulnerability	Initiation Vulnerability Role of Violence (in two above)	Accommodative Strategy	
Number of Actors	Escalation Deescalation Impact	H. 1–3,9,12,13		Outbreak Role of Violence	Termination – Agreement Duration	Higher Tension (Bilateral) Greater Legacy (System)
Heterogeneity	Escalation Deescalation Impact	H. 1,2,5,9,12,13		Outbreak Role of Violence	Duration	Higher Tension Greater Legacy

TABLE 6.3 Continued

Variables: Multiple-Phase	Phase	Propositions & Hypotheses	Dependent Variables: Aspects of Crisis			
			Onset	Escalation	Deescalation	Impact
Issues	Escalation Deescalation Impact	H. 1–3,9,12,13		Outbreak Role of Violence	Duration	Higher Tension Greater Legacy
Major Power Activity	Escalation Deescalation Impact	H. 2,4,8–13		Role of Violence Initiation	Termination – Agreement Duration Accommodative Strategy Satisfaction	Higher Tension Greater Legacy

Variables: Dual-Phase	Phase	Propositions & Hypotheses	Dependent Variables: Aspects of Crisis			
			Onset	Escalation	Deescalation	Impact
Structure	Onset Escalation	P. 1 H. 1,2		Outbreak	Outbreak Role of Violence	
System Level	Onset Escalation	P. 1 H. 1,2		Outbreak	Outbreak Role of Violence	
Geographic Distance	Onset Escalation	P. 1–3 H. 1–7		Outbreak Initiation Vulnerability	Outbreak Vulnerability Role of Violence	
Age	Onset Escalation	P. 2,3 H. 4–7		Initiation Vulnerability	Outbreak Vulnerability Role of Violence	
Regime Duration	Onset Escalation	P. 3 H. 7		Vulnerability	Vulnerability Role of Violence	

Variables: Single-Phase	Phase	Propositions & Hypotheses	Dependent Variables: Aspects of Crisis			
			Onset	Escalation	Deescalation	Impact
Trigger	Escalation Impact	H. 2,14		Role of Violence		Greater Legacy
Geostrategic Salience	Deescalation Impact	H. 9,12,13			Duration	Higher Tension Greater Legacy
Outcome – Substance	Deescalation Impact	H. 11,12			Satisfaction	Higher Tension
Size	Escalation	H. 2,3		Role of Violence		
Response	Escalation	H. 3		Role of Violence		
Crisis Management Technique	Deescalation	H. 8,9			Termination – Agreement Duration	
IO Involvement	Deescalation	H. 8,10,11			Termination – Agreement Accommodative Strategy	Satisfaction
Power Balance Change	Deescalation	H. 11			Satisfaction	
Outcome: Form	Impact	H. 12,14				Higher Tension Greater Legacy
Violence	Impact	H. 12,14				Higher Tension Greater Legacy
Duration	Impact	H. 14				Greater Legacy

phases. Eight relate to two phases. And eight are phase-specific. No independent variable cuts across all phases. I turn now to the most salient themes of the three clusters.

The *multiple-phase* variables encompass three of the four types of independent variable discussed in the phase models: *interactor* (conflict setting, capability, and regime type); *actor* (internal instability); and *situational* (number of actors, heterogeneity, issues, and major power activity). System variables are conspicuously absent from the cluster with broadest scope. All eight purport to explain, in part, the processes of escalation and deescalation. Four also focus on the unfolding of an interstate crisis, its onset, while the other four relate to consequences or impact.

These variables exhibit considerable diversity in scope, both in the range of propositions and hypotheses of which they are a part, and the aspects of crisis which they attempt to explain. At one extreme of the scope spectrum are *heterogeneity* and *number of issues*, which are elements in only six of the 17 propositions and hypotheses; at the other is *conflict setting*, which is included in 12 of them; in between, in descending order, are *capability* and *regime type*, *major power activity*, and *number of actors* and *internal instability*.

A wide range is also evident in the aspects of crisis which these variables attempt to explain. Once more, conflict setting claims the broadest scope of explanatory power: in the onset phase, the outbreak of international crises and the vulnerability of states to foreign policy crises; all aspects of the escalation phase, that is, the crystallization of an incipient crisis, initiation and vulnerability, and the role of violence in all these aspects of crisis; and, for deescalation, the winding-down process, along with the likelihood of a state adopting an accommodative strategy and the extent of satisfaction with the crisis outcome.

The minimal scope of explanation among the multiple-phase variables is shared by heterogeneity and issues, which differ on one aspect: violent escalation of a foreign policy crisis is within the ambit of the former, escalation from no/low to intense violence, of the latter. The main difference between the two groups of these wide-ranging variables is that conflict setting, capability regime type, and internal instability seem to be irrelevant to the impact of a crisis, while number of actors, heterogeneity, issues, and major power activity do not shed any light on crisis onset.

The eight *dual-phase* variables are even more diverse. Two are systemic, namely, structure and level; one, geographic distance, is interactor; two are actor variables, age and regime duration; and three are situational factors—trigger, geostrategic salience, and outcome. Generally, as expected, these variables enter into fewer hypotheses than the multiple-phase cluster, only two or three. But there are two notable exceptions. Geographic distance recurs in 10 propositions and hypotheses, second in frequency to conflict setting among all the explanatory factors. And age is included in six hypotheses, the same as heterogeneity and issues at the lower threshold of the multiple-phase cluster.

That anomaly, narrow scope in terms of phases addressed but inclusion in many propositions and hypotheses, is also evident in the range of crisis aspects that geographic distance and age purport to explain: the former, all dimensions of onset and escalation; and the latter, most of them. Contrary to expectations, too, is the very narrow scope of structure and system level, three propositions and hypotheses each. However, they relate to the most crucial aspects of the crisis phenomenon, the outbreak of an international crisis, its crystallization, and the role of violence in the step-level jump from onset to escalation.

The *single-phase* independent variables claim the least explanatory power. One, territorial size, focuses on onset. Another, response, is confined to escalation. Three of these factors attempt to explain deescalation, namely, crisis management technique, international organization (IO) involvement, and change in the power balance. And the final three are confined to impact.

Two of these phase-specific variables, IO involvement and violence, are parts of three hypotheses, exhibiting the same scope as three of the dual-phase variables and more than three others in that cluster. IO involvement offers an explanation of several aspects of the winding-down process, and, at the state level, of the adoption of an accommodation strategy by a crisis actor. And violence purports to explain two aspects of the impact phase—higher tension and system transformation.

In light of the data in Table 6.3, it seems appropriate to prune the large number of independent variables in the UMC. Using the theoretical criterion of scope of crisis dimensions addressed, nine of the 24 independent variables in the UMC are eliminated, namely, those that enter into only one or two propositions and hypotheses, with a correspondingly narrow explanatory reach: trigger; response; regime duration; primary crisis management technique; territorial size; outcome—form; outcome—substance; duration of crisis, and power balance change.[9] Bearing in mind that the remaining 15 explanatory factors (of the original 24) illuminate the four distinct phases of a complex phenomenon, this is not unreasonable.

A no less severe test will be the evidence from the real world, in addressing the question: are the postulated linkages between these variables and crisis aspects supported and, if so, robustly or modestly? If the evidence from twentieth-century crises, to be reported in Chapter 8 [Table 8.2 and the accompanyng discussion] disconfirms the expected effects, the necessary conclusions will have to be drawn.

What functions, then, have been performed by the Unified Model of Crisis? In the largest sense the UMC guided and shaped an inquiry into the meaning of crises in the twentieth century. It provided the intellectual rationale for the phase models. It generated the logic for the inferences derived from these models. And it specified these in the form of propositions and hypotheses. As such, it made possible the testing of theoretical expectations with the abundant evidence of interstate crises, facilitating the crucial confrontation between theory and reality. In so doing, the Unified Model has laid claim to being the core of a *scientific research program* (Lakatos, 1970) on crisis, conflict and war, for it aims to discover which logically-derived assumptions about crises and state behavior are falsified and which are confirmed.

CHAPTER 7

The Gulf Crisis 1990–91

THE Unified Model was designed to analyze any interstate crisis. To test its explanatory power this chapter will apply the model to one of the most dramatic and intense military-security crises in the twentieth century.

The roots of the Gulf Crisis of 1990–91 are embedded in the collapse of the Ottoman Empire after World War I, the creation of Iraq in 1920, the longstanding UK protectorate over Kuwait, and its transfer of independence to the al-Sabah emirate in 1961. However, it was President Saddam Hussein's perception of an opportunity for Iraq's aggrandizement in 1990 against a small, immensely wealthy and militarily weak neighbor that generated, first, a *threat crisis* for Kuwait and a *bilateral international crisis* (Iraq/Kuwait), and soon thereafter, a *global crisis*. The dynamics of that process and how the actors coped with, that is, managed or mismanaged, their crisis are the central concerns of this analysis.

As indicated in the model, an interstate crisis begins when the first actor perceives value threat, but not yet a heightened probability of war, or time pressure for response to the threat, the two other defining conditions of a full-scale foreign policy crisis for a state. Kuwait was the first actor in the Gulf Crisis. And it perceived a higher-than-normal threat to values on 17 July 1990. On that day Iraq's President denounced Kuwait (and the United Arab Emirates [UAE]), not for the first time, for exceeding their OPEC production quotas, thereby reducing oil prices and oil revenues for Iraq, allegedly to the amount of $14 billion. More disquieting was a threat to use force if they did not curb their excess output: "If words fail to afford us protection, then we will have no choice but to resort to effective action to put things right and ensure the restitution of our rights" (*FBIS–NESA*, 17/7/90).[1] It was that threat and the renewed accusation that triggered a perception of value

404

threat for Kuwait's decision-makers, that is, its *pre-crisis period* and, with it, the *onset phase* of the Gulf Crisis as a whole.

Onset

In the Unified Model, *periods* and *phases* are treated as analytic categories. As such, they are demarcated precisely—their trigger, termination and dates. In reality, however, periods and phases are parts of a dynamic, integrated whole, namely, an interstate crisis. Each is influenced by, and derives from, acts, events and/or environmental changes in the preceding period of phase—or developments prior to the eruption of a specific crisis. So it was with Kuwait's pre-crisis period and the onset phase of the Gulf Crisis.

Several system and interactor attributes generated an *opportunity crisis* for Iraq in the last half of July 1990. The long war with Iran (1980–88) was over, with Iraq the perceived victor, though the outcome seemed more like a stalemate. While Iraq had not attained hegemony in the Gulf region, it was clearly one of the two major regional powers, with a formidable military arsenal, including a million-man army, advanced Soviet tanks and planes, a stockpile of chemical and biological weapons, etc. At the same time, it had incurred large debts to Arab Gulf states in order to finance the war. Its economy was in need of a massive infusion of funds for reconstruction. And it had an insatiable desire for more advanced weapons, including a nuclear capability. Nearby was affluent but vulnerable Kuwait, whose legitimacy as a state Iraq had challenged from its independence in 1961, the occasion for an earlier Iraq-created interstate crisis.[2] Moreover, they had longstanding territorial disputes, notably over the strategic islands of Bubiyan and Warba at the northern end of the Gulf and the invaluable Rumaila oil field.

The major power constellation, too, seemed favorable to Iraq. Although the Soviet Union, Iraq's principal patron and arms supplier for two decades, was now suffering the effects of upheaval in Eastern Europe and at home, the US had supported Iraq throughout Gulf War I (the Iran/Iraq War, 1980–88) and beyond.[3] And President Bush was perceived by Baghdad as unlikely to intervene in a conflict in a "faraway country between people of whom we know nothing"[4] especially while he was savoring victory in the Cold War. Everything seemed ripe for extracting economic and territorial concessions from Kuwait and, if necessary, using force to annex Kuwait as Iraq's long-coveted 19th province.

Evidence of an opportunity/threat crisis, initiated by Iraq and directed against Kuwait, is abundant. The prelude began almost five months before the crisis erupted: on 24 February 1990, at the first anniversary meeting of the Arab Cooperation Council (ACC) (Egypt, Iraq, Jordan and Yemen), held in Amman, Iraq's President warned that, in the aftermath of the collapse of the Soviet empire in Eastern Europe, the Arabs had to be careful to resist US attempts to establish hegemony in the Middle East. He also expressed anger at the behavior of lesser Gulf region oil-producing states. This accusation became specific on 30 May at a closed session of the truncated extraordinary Baghdad Arab summit, when Saddam Hussein charged Kuwait and the UAE with violating OPEC production quotas: "This is in fact a kind of war against Iraq . . . we have reached a point where we can no longer withstand pressure" (*FBIS–NESA*, 19/7/90).

The pre-crisis period for Kuwait was characterized by mixed signals —hostile Iraqi acts, disruptive events, and reassurance by outside actors—from 17 July, the trigger date, until 1 August. The most important of these will now be summarized.

16–19 July: Iraq deployed 35,000 troops, tanks and rockets from three élite divisions within 10–30 miles of the Kuwaiti border, raising Kuwait's level of perceived threat (*non-violent military* act);

18 July: Iraq's Foreign Minister Tariq Aziz charged that Kuwait had stolen $2.4 billion worth of Iraqi oil from the disputed Rumaila oil field (*FBIS–NESA*, 18/7/90) (*verbal* act);[5]

24 July: the United States announced a joint military exercise with the UAE and the dispatch of two KC-135 aerial refuelling tankers, as well as two additional warships, in a show of force designed to "lay down a marker for Saddam Hussein" (*verbal* act by patron state);[6]

25 July: Iraq demanded $2.4 billion compensation from Kuwait (*verbal* act);

27 July: under Iraq's pressure, the "minimum reference" oil price was raised by OPEC from $18 to $21 a barrel (Iraq had demanded $25 a barrel) (*external change*);

1 August: the Jidda talks between senior Iraqi and Kuwaiti officials, which began the previous day, collapsed (*political* act).[7]

There is no evidence of Kuwait's perception of higher-than-normal value threat arising from Saddam Hussein's charges before 17 July. Moreover, Kuwait's ruler seems to have perceived low (or no) probability of war until the last moment. As late as 27 July Kuwait had not moved any of its forces to the border. They were put on full alert and deployed north of Kuwait City—by the two senior army commanders. "But the emir. . . overruled them and ordered the troops back to their garrisons. Based on experience [he] assumed Saddam could be placated with money" (Schwarzkopf, 1992: 293). On 1 August Kuwait's Ambassador to the US reportedly said: "We came to the conclusion that Saddam Hussein was not going to invade." And the then-Defense Minister, Nawaf al-Ahmad al-Sabah, allegedly ordered Kuwaiti tanks near the Iraq border not to fire on the invaders (Gargan, *NYT*, 24/5/91, A5).[8]

Saudi Arabia, too, was apparently taken by surprise: an astonished King Fahd, on being told of Iraq's invasion of Kuwait, reportedly asked: "Are you sure?" (Lamb, *Los Angeles Times*, reprinted in *The Gazette* [Montreal], 1/12/90). And, until a few hours before the attack, US leaders and almost all officials perceived the probability of war as very low. This view was reinforced by Saudi Ambassador Prince Bandar who reported that his uncle, King Fahd, had been assured by Egyptian President Mubarak, King Hussain of Jordan and others that Saddam Hussein had given them personal assurances he would not invade Kuwait. The three pro-US Arab leaders reportedly conveyed these assurances directly to President Bush and asked him not to do anything to upset the Arab handling of an intra-Arab dispute (Oberdorfer, *Washington Post Magazine*, 17/3/91, 40). "In effect," as Draper (1992b: 38) remarked, "US policy before the Iraqi invasion of Kuwait was not made in the United States. It was little more than a mirror-image of what friendly Arab rulers were telling the United States to think."[9]

There are several reasons for Kuwait's low-profile attitude to earlier Iraqi threats in 1990 (February, May) and to threats in the last fortnight of July. First, the norm in Iraq/Kuwait relations was a persistent challenge to Kuwait's legitimacy as an independent state: the basis of Iraq's contention was the fact that from 1875 until the end of the Ottoman Empire, Kuwait had been part of the province (*vilayet*) of Basra, which was included in an independent Iraq in 1920. Iraq's claim was pressed by all rulers after the end of the British Mandate in 1932, by Hashemite kings until the overthrow of the monarchy in 1958, by General Qassem, who attempted to annex Kuwait in 1961 [see n. 2, Chap. 7], and, from 1968, by the *Ba'ath* regime. Even after Iraq recognized Kuwait's independence, there were prolonged border disputes on the mainland and over the islands of Bubiyan and Warba, long coveted by Iraq. There were clashes in 1973 and 1976. A standstill agreement was signed in

1977 and, reportedly a fuller border accord in 1984. Moreover, twice in the 1980s Saddam Hussein pressed for naval facilities and a long-term lease to the islands, which blocked Iraq's exit to the Gulf. And in August 1988, only weeks after the end of the Iran/Iraq War, discussions over the unresolved Iraq/Kuwait border resumed, again in December 1988 and February 1989. But there were no Iraqi threats of invasion.[10]

A second reason was Kuwait's open support for Iraq in its war against Iran (1980–88), including $10–15 billion of interest-free loans and grants and unrestricted access to Kuwait's Gulf ports. The ruling al-Sabah family of the emirate found it difficult to imagine that Iraq would reward its support in Gulf War I with a military assault. And third, accusatory rhetoric is a core element of the political culture of inter-Arab politics.[11]

It remains to summarize the onset phase of the Gulf Crisis in terms of the Unified Model. The duration of this phase was 16 days, from 17 July to 1 August 1990, though there was a "pre-onset" background dating back to Saddam Hussein's harsh criticism of Kuwait (and the UAE) on 24 February. When, on 17 July, he repeated these charges and added a threat to take action in order to protect Iraq's interests, that verbal act served as the trigger to Kuwait's perception of higher threat than normal, that is, its pre-crisis period. That development, in turn, marked the beginning of the onset phase.

Kuwait was the only crisis actor in the onset phase, with Iraq playing the role of initiator or "triggering entity." Egypt and Saudi Arabia provided good offices in a failed attempt at third party intervention to assist peaceful conflict resolution—the Jidda meeting on 31 July–1 August. All of the major powers, except the US, were totally uninvolved. Washington sent mixed signals in the last week of July, including a minimal show of force in the Gulf, that implied indifference to intra-Arab disputes [see pp. 413–415 below].

Disruptive interaction increased modestly, in the form of escalatory rhetoric by Iraq and the movement of troops close to Kuwait's border during the last fortnight of July. There was no violence during the onset phase. Nor did the verbal or even the non-violent military hostility presage resort to force, let alone the total conquest of Kuwait. Egypt's Mubarak and Saudi Arabia's Fahd, based upon their interpretation of an assurance from Saddam Hussein that he would not use force, persuaded Bush that the "mini-crisis" would pass quickly, without adverse consequences. The onset phase terminated with the deadlock at Jidda on 1 August; but it was not an abortive or "failed" crisis. The next day, onset gave way to escalation as a result of Iraq's invasion and occupation of Kuwait.

In terms of the Unified Model's actor level of analysis: Iraq's renewed demands for economic compensation and territorial revision, in the last two weeks of July, were perceived by Kuwait as a low value threat—until Iraq's invasion. Kuwait tried to cope through direct negotiation. Its army was put on alert; but so remote was war in its perception of a likely scenario that the alert was terminated on 1 August. Time was moderately salient for Kuwait from the 24th, when talks with Iraq were arranged by Egypt and Saudi Arabia. And while war may have been perceived in the last half of July as possible, Kuwait's decision-makers did not anticipate war as probable—until it erupted. Thus Kuwait's pre-crisis period and the onset phase of the Gulf Crisis are dated 17 July–1 August 1990.

Escalation

In the Unified Model, it will be recalled, *phase change* and *period change* are "step-level" in character. Thus the jump from onset to escalation occurs with qualitatively more intense disruptive interaction. Similarly, the shift from pre-crisis to crisis is evident in perceptual change for at least one crisis actor, namely, more acute value threat, along with heightened probability of war and finite time constraints on behavior. Moreover, phase change derives from period change; that is, the three-fold perception of harm and consequent response mark the jump from onset to escalation. Finally, not all crisis actors experience period change simultaneously. In fact, one or more may move from pre-crisis to crisis long after the escalation phase begins.

In the Gulf Crisis, Kuwait was the first actor to experience period change. The trigger to its crisis period was Iraq's invasion at 2.00 a.m. (Gulf time) on the 2nd of August: Iraqi tanks reached the capital swiftly and conquered the emirate within six hours. That act triggered a sharp escalation of Kuwaiti threat perception, in fact, a threat to its existence as a state, along with an acute awareness of war and time pressure. The invasion also transformed Kuwait's foreign policy crisis into a bilateral (Iraq/Kuwait) international crisis. Stated in terms of the Unified Model, Iraq's opportunity crisis and the pre-crisis period of Kuwait's threat crisis, comprising the onset phase, underwent step-level change to become Kuwait's crisis period, thereby setting in motion the escalation phase [See Figure 7.1 below].

If Iraq's conquest of Kuwait had been ignored by all major global and regional powers, the Iraq/Kuwait crisis would have remained bilateral and brief. However, Saudi Arabia and, more important, the United States, Iraq's principal adversary throughout the Gulf Crisis, also perceived the occupation of Kuwait and its huge oil resources as a basic value threat [see below]. The US's immediate response led to a further qualitative change.

The invasion occurred at 6.00 p.m. on 1 August 1990 (EST). At 11.20 p.m. a White House statement condemned Iraq's invasion and called for "the immediate and unconditional withdrawal of all Iraqi forces" from Kuwait and the restoration of its legitimate government, demands that were sustained for seven months through diplomacy and war. Moreover, executive orders froze Iraqi and Kuwaiti assets in the US, the latter valued at $30 billion. That initial US response, including the President's ambiguous remark at a press conference on 2 August, "We're not ruling any options in, but we're not ruling any options out," transformed the bilateral Iraq/Kuwait Invasion crisis into the global Gulf Crisis of 1990–91.

The process leading to the bilateral crisis illuminates the inextricable link between opportunity and threat crises. As evident, what A (Iraq) regarded as an opportunity crisis, leading it to initiate a foreign policy crisis for B (Kuwait), became a threat crisis for the latter; that is, A's decision and action generated stress for B. And it was Kuwait's perceived threat, time pressure and war certainty, followed by its response, the immediate request for aid from the major powers and the UN, that led to more disruptive interaction and, with it, an international crisis.[12]

There were many actors in the Gulf Crisis. However, Iraq and the United States stand apart and will be the main focus of this analysis. The rationale is two-fold. One reason is the essential reality of this crisis. While most of the 28 states in the US-led Coalition contributed to the military buildup in the Gulf region and supported the UN resolutions to wrest Kuwait from Iraq's control, by force if necessary, only six were actively involved in the war against Iraq: the US, Saudi Arabia, the UK, France, Egypt and Syria. And ultimately the outcome depended upon a test of arms between Iraq and the US, from 17 January to 28 February 1991. On the other side, Jordan, Yemen and the PLO, among others, supported Iraq diplomatically, politically and economically. And the "Arab street" in many states rallied to its cause. But Iraq was alone when crisis escalated to war. In short, this was fundamentally a two-actor game between the US and Iraq. Moreover, this is a parsimonious model to operationalize; and given the Unified Model's complexity, that is a virtue—for both reader and author!

In the onset phase of the Gulf Crisis (17 July–1 August 1990), neither Iraq nor the US perceived value threat, let alone heightened war probability and time pressure. For both, value threat burst upon the scene on 2 August: the trigger for the US (as well as for the UK and other members of what was to become the Coalition) was the invasion of Kuwait; for Iraq, it was condemnation of its invasion by the US and the UN. These acts marked the beginning of the pre-crisis period for both states. Their crisis period was to come much later in the escalation phase and at different times.

Many *values* were perceived to be at risk from the outset. For the *US*, the invasion and occupation of Kuwait was viewed as a threat: to its *influence* in the Gulf region, jeopardized by the conquest of one client, Kuwait, and an imminent threat to another, more valuable client, Saudi Arabia; to *stability* in the Middle East, a prerequisite to the untrammelled flow of oil to the US and its allies around the world; to *economic well-being* for the US and the world economy, especially the cost and availability of Middle East oil; and to the fragile, emergent post-Cold War *new world order*.

For *Iraq*, the immediate, hostile US response to its conquest of Kuwait threatened several crucial values: significant *economic gains*—Kuwait's assets world-wide and its valuable oil reserves—designed to overcome serious economic difficulties created by the prolonged Iraq/Iran War (Gulf War I); its improved *access to the Gulf*, afforded by Kuwait's 310-mile coastline; Iraq's ambition to be the *hegemonial power in the Gulf region*; and its goal of *preeminence in the Arab world*. Thus, for Iraq, too, the first condition of a foreign policy crisis, a perceived threat to basic values, was present from 2 August onwards.

US condemnation of Iraq's invasion of Kuwait almost certainly came as a surprise to Saddam Hussein. From as early as the spring of 1982, Washington had tilted in favor of Baghdad during Gulf War I, viewing Iran's Islamic fundamentalist leadership as a much greater threat to US interests than Ba'athist ideology or Iraq's aspirations in the Gulf region. During Gulf War I US covert aid to Iraq included the transmission of valuable classified intelligence about Iranian troop movements acquired by satellite reconnaissance, and the indirect sale of very large quantities of US arms, via Iraq's Arab allies, as well as US high technology usable for military purposes. That military support for Iraq continued even after the end of the Iran/Iraq war in 1988 (Waas, *Village Voice* [New

York], 18/12/90, 27–37; Hersh, *NYT*, 26/1/92, A1, 12). In fact, from 1985 to 1990 the US Government approved export licenses for Iraq valued at $1.5 billion, of which $500 million was shipped (Farnsworth, *NYT*, 25/6/91, A11).[13]

In another signal of patronage, President Reagan and the State Department blamed *Iran* for the sinking of the USS *Stark* in the Persian Gulf by *Iraq* in May 1987, killing 37 US seamen. Most conspicuous was the US's deafening silence on Iraq's use of chemical weapons against both Iranian forces and its own Kurdish citizens in 1988. On the contrary, the President blocked Congress-approved sanctions against Iraq for its mass murder of Kurds.

President Bush continued Reagan's pro-Iraq policy. This US posture was formalized in a secret White House document, National Security Decision Directive (NSDD) 26, in October 1989, that termed "normal relations" with Iraq in US "longer term interests" and urged "economic and political incentives for Iraq to moderate its behavior and to increase our influence with Iraq." (Sciolino, *NYT* 29/5/92, A3). That directive guided US policy towards Iraq until its invasion of Kuwait.

US policy was linked to—and was dramatically uncovered by—the Banca Nazionale del Lavoro (BNL) scandal in Atlanta, involving the illegal transfer of an estimated $5 billion in loans to Iraq and other countries. Specifically in 1989 and 1990 the Bush Administration reportedly "frustrated its own criminal investigators and regulators examining Iraq's role in a multibillion dollar bank fraud scheme in Atlanta," which helped to finance Iraq's massive purchases of arms and advanced military technology (Baquet, *NYT*, 20/3/92, A1, 9).

The essence of "Iraqgate" or "the BNL affair" was admirably summarized as evolving through three stages: first, charges by Democratic Congressmen of a wrong policy—currying favor with Saddam Hussein before his invasion of Kuwait; then, charges that "the policy was not only flawed but criminal. . . ."; and, thirdly, "accusations that the [Bush] Administration was less than thorough in its investigation of a huge fraud scheme at the Atlanta bank." The upshot was charges of one or more coverups and the appointment of a special investigator. (Sciolino, *NYT* 18/10/92, E4).

Specifically, three questions "lie at the heart of the affair":

". . . in its zeal to influence Mr. Hussein, did the Bush Administration ignore evidence that some of this aid was diverted to Iraq's buildup of weapons? Did it try to delay indictments of high-level Iraqi officials accused in a United States bank fraud? And did the President's aides lie to Congress in an attempt to conceal the full scope of their failed courtship of Iraq?" (Sciolino, *NYT*, 9/8/92, E18).[14]

This policy of active support was reinforced by several negative or confusing signals in 1990 that generated Hussein's perception of the likely US response—acquiescence in, if not a "green light" for, his behavior towards Kuwait.[15]

One was the relatively moderate criticism of his threat on 2 April 1990 to "make fire eat up half of Israel if it tried to do anything against Iraq," with a proud boast, "we have the binary chemical" weapon (*FBIS–NESA*, 3/4/90). The White House termed Hussein's remarks "particularly deplorable and irresponsible"; and President Bush "found those statements to be bad," urging that they "be withdrawn."[16] The threat to Israel was renewed at the Arab League summit in Baghdad on 30 May.

Another signal of a friendly US disposition was sent ten days after Saddam Hussein's threat to destroy half of Israel: during a visit of five US Senators to Baghdad, Republican Minority Leader, Robert Dole, conveyed to Saddam Hussein the President's wish for "better relations with Iraq." A week after Hussein's undisguised threat to Kuwait and the UAE on 17 July, noted earlier, the State Department's spokesperson, Margaret Tutwiler, noted: "We do not have any defense treaties with Kuwait, and there are no special defense or security comitments to Kuwait." However, in seeming contradiction, she also declared that the US was "strongly committed to supporting the individual and collective self-defense of our friends in the Gulf with whom we have deep and longstanding ties." (This was the exact wording of an instruction to Ambassador April Glaspie on 19 July; see n. 17 to Chap. 7 for this and other cables during the last half of July 1990.)

The most important signal of likely US behavior was the reported statement by the US Ambassador to Iraq, at a meeting with Iraq's President the next day, on 25 July:

> . . . we have *no opinion on the Arab-Arab conflicts, like your border disagreement with Kuwait*. . . . The instruction we had [at the US Embassy in Baghdad during the late 1960s] was that we should express no opinion on this issue and that the issue is not associated with America. [Secretary of State] James Baker has directed our official spokesmen to emphasize this instruction . . . (emphasis added).

In short, the US would remain aloof from an Iraq/Kuwait conflict.[17]

The policy of conciliation received its most authoritative expression in a follow-up message from Bush to Saddam Hussein on 28 July, amidst reports of the massing of Iraqi forces near the border with Kuwait. It's tone was a model of reassurance, without the slightest hint of deterrence:

". . . we believe that differences are best resolved by peaceful means. . .

"Let me reassure you, as my Ambassador, Senator Dole and others have done, that my Administration continues to desire better relations with Iraq. We will also continue to support our other friends in the region with whom we have had long standing ties. We see no necessary inconsistency between these two objectives. . .

I completely agree that both our Governments must maintain open channels of communication to avoid misunderstanding and in order to build a more durable foundation for improving our relations" (Text in Gordon, 25/10/92, A14).

Finally, on 31 July, less than two days before the invasion, the Assistant Secretary of State for the Near East and South Asia reinforced the Tutwiler and Glaspie signals by informing the House of Representatives Sub-Committee on Europe and the Middle East:

> We have no defense-treaty relationships with any of the [Gulf] countries. We have historically avoided taking a position on border disputes or on internal OPEC deliberations. . . .

Asked what the US would do if Iraq invaded Kuwait, Kelly replied:

> That, Mr. Chairman, is a hypothetical or a contingency question, the kind of which I cannot get into (Subcommittee on Europe and the Middle East, 1990, 14).

The fact that Kuwait did not want a formal US defense commitment did not alter the signal to Iraq, namely, that the US would not become embroiled in its dispute with Kuwait. As for the President's and Secretary of State's responsibility, one commentator with long experience in the State Department remarked: ". . . maybe Mr. Bush and his top aides were blinded by their 'friendly' mindset toward Saddam and by their inattention to a situation they did not comprehend—until there was no choice but war" (Gelb, *NYT*, 17/7/91, A21). Later, this mild rebuke gave way to severe criticism of an act of omission in the Bush-Baker 'soft'-line message, which senior Pentagon officials had opposed at the time, in vain.

"Never once in the week prior to the attack—as Iraqi troops on the disputed border massed to over 100,000—did Mr. Bush ever say, or even hint that the U.S. would respond to Iraqi aggression with force.

Mr. Bush said nothing about force for one very good reason: He had no idea he would use force. . .

. . . The question is whether Saddam had good reason to read Mr. Bush's diplomatic passivity, particularly in the week before Aug. 2, as a tacit go-ahead.

The answer is very probably yes.

In calculating whether he could get away with gobbling up Kuwait, Saddam's only worry was Washington ... Perhaps he would have attacked no matter what. He heard nothing from President Bush. He attacked" (Gelb, *NYT*, 22/10/92, A27).

One thing seems certain: whatever the intentions of Baker and Bush, Iraq's President did not interpret the US Ambassador's words or, even more, the US President's message as signalling US resolve to act militarily to defend Kuwait against an Iraqi invasion. Not surprisingly, Saddam Hussein expected that the US and the non-Arab world generally would acquiesce in the invasion of Kuwait. Hence, too, his surprise at the US/UN condemnation.[18]

These signals may explain the negative input to Hussein's crucial decision to invade Kuwait, namely, his perception that there were no serious obstacles from the Western world. But what was the positive input, that is, what were his motives and goals? These were, in part, the obverse of the threatened values noted earlier. One was the enormous economic gain that would accrue to Iraq from Kuwait's Midas-like wealth and oil resources. Another was territorial aggrandizement. A third was geopolitical advantage, that is, ready access to the Gulf. A fourth was the opportunity to overcome domestic pressures, arising from the burdens of prolonged war against Iran (*FBIS–NESA*, 7/8/90 and 13/8/90).

Closely related was the nature of Saddam Hussein's political regime in Iraq. Ultimately he ruled through pervasive fear; and a system of fear within necessitates action abroad to reinforce the ruler's credibility for sustaining fear at home. Finally, there were personal motives: his aspiration to dominate the Gulf region and, ultimately, establish his preeminence in the Arab world; and recognition as a heroic figure, in the tradition of Nebuchadnezzar and Saladin, and in the twentieth century, Nasser. These were heady dreams. Put simply, Saddam Hussein thought he could get away with it, at little or no cost. So it seemed in late July 1990.

Conspiracy was a crucial element of Hussein's view of the world. He seemed to perceive a "multilateral conspiracy" after Iraq's "military success over Iran in 1988." It was, in his view, spearheaded by the US and Israel which, allegedly, could not tolerate an Iraq with "beefed-up military muscles." Saudi Arabia and several Gulf emirates were also involved in the "conspiracy." And their excess output of oil "spelled economic ruin for Iraq." "Something in all this may have corresponded to the truth," observed Gorbachev's Middle East envoy, to whom these charges were conveyed by Hussein on 5 October 1990; "something was a figment of his imagination, the result of overwrought suspicions. But *that is what he really believed."*

The core of Saddam Hussein's perception and likely behavior was suggested by his response to Yevgeni Primakov's question: "Doesn't it seem to you that just like the Israelis, you have a Masada complex? He nodded his head." Most important, in this context, "If I have to fall to my knees and surrender or fight, Saddam said, I will choose the latter." Yet there was another, contradictory strand in Saddam Hussein's complex psychological makeup: "As a realist I understand the true state of affairs. Yet I cannot resolve the question of Kuwait if it is not tied up with the solution to other problems of the region" (Primakov, *Time*, 4/3/91 [emphasis added]).[19]

That the perceived *possibility* of war between Iraq and the US was higher on 2 August than a day, a week or a month earlier is beyond question. Bush seemed surprised, dismayed and angry in his public responses to the invasion on 2 and 5 August (*NYT*, 6/8/90, A7). And an atmosphere of "shock and frustration" reportedly prevailed when he and his advisors met on 2 and 3 August to confront Iraq's invasion (Friedman and Tyler, *NYT*, 3/3/91, A1, 18, 19).

The possibility of war increased incrementally during the next three months, as evident in the military buildup by both the US and Iraq from early August 1990 onward [see Pre-War I: Crisis Management, below]. But Bush and Baker were at pains to diminish the likelihood of war and to qualify references to war with "if force becomes necessary." In fact, the concentration of US forces in the Gulf region was central to a strategy of *compellance* (Schelling, 1960), using gradually-escalating pressure to coerce Iraq's withdrawal from Kuwait without resort to force—if possible. The two key elements of this strategy were: the deployment of US forces to deter an Iraqi attack on Saudi Arabia, and UN economic sanctions to compel Iraq to withdraw from Kuwait.

The task of establishing "turning point" dates in the evolution of perceived *war likelihood* by US (or Iraqi—or any other) decision-makers is made more difficult by the fact that Bush, like Saddam Hussein, did not think linearly about the prospects of war. He was subject to mood swings, sometimes believing that war could be averted, sometimes thinking that war was inevitable. Nonetheless, the fragmentary evidence indicates the following perceptual "turning points" for the US:

2–6 August 1990—*higher-than-normal possibility* of war against Iraq;
7 August–29 October—*increasing possibility* of war;

30 October–28 November—*heightened probability* of war;
29 November 1990–16 January 1991—war *very highly probable*, but
not certain.

US leaders did not perceive war as significantly more likely until the
President's secret approval of a military plan, on 30 October, to launch
an air and naval strike against Iraq in mid-January 1991 and a ground
campaign in February, and its partial implementation in the form of an
announcement by Bush on 8 November to deploy at least 150,000 more
troops to the Gulf region. That decision/announcement was a major
self-induced escalation point with respect to perceived war probability:
its stated purpose was "to ensure that the coalition has an *adequate
offensive military option should that be necessary* to achieve our common goals" (emphasis added). [See below for the making of the
"prepare for war" decision.] A month later, another escalation point
occurred, namely, the passing of Security Council Resolution 678, on 29
November 1990: that external disruptive event authorized the "use [of]
all necessary means," clearly implying force, to achieve Iraq's withdrawal from Kuwait. [See below for the making of Resolution 678.]
Thus the second defining condition of the crisis period—a perception of
higher-than-normal probability of war—is evident from 2 August 1990,
certainly from 7 August, when the decision to deploy US troops to Saudi
Arabia was announced; but high probability, as distinct from
heightened probability, came much later—with the 30 October
decision.

So, too, did the third necessary and sufficient condition of a fully-
crystallized foreign policy crisis, the time dimension. US awareness of
time pressure was not apparent during the first three months of the
Gulf Crisis, despite occasional speculation in the US media that climate
and religion imposed time constraints—the desert heat for much of the
year and the Muslim month of fasting, *Ramadan*, in March–April.
There was not a single reference to a deadline for Iraq's withdrawal
from Kuwait in the first 11, mostly-US-sponsored, resolutions on Iraq's
invasion passed by the UN Security Council. Indeed, it was not until 30
October 1990 that time acquired salience in US perceptions and
decisions.

This is evident in comments by Administration officials while reflecting on the 30 October decision/8 November announcement.

"We're not prepared to give this guy unlimited time, whoever's side
time is on." Specifically, "only the threat of early war" could persuade
Saddam to withdraw.

There was also concern that US forces in the Gulf region might "lose their edge" if the crisis went on too long.

Further, their presence was a "point of vulnerability" for the Saudi regime, which would be aggravated if they remained "for a prolonged period."

Finally, domestic support and/or coalition cohesion might erode if military action were long delayed (Rosenthal, *NYT*, 10/11/90, A1; Gordon, *NYT*, 13/11/90, A1, 14; and Friedman and Tyler, *NYT*, 3/3/1991, A18).

And, in the gestation of the "prepare for war" decision, the generals designated 1 January–15 February 1991 as the "window of opportunity" for a large-scale military assault on Iraq's forces.

As with the perception of war likelihood, the Security Council resolution of 29 November 1990 was a major escalation point in terms of time salience: it specified, unambiguously, the deadline of 15 January 1991 for Iraq's withdrawal from Kuwait. Thus each day after Resolution 678 was approved, time constraints increased, for a failure to act after the deadline would have destroyed US credibility among friend and foe alike. In short, it was the emergence of self-induced time pressure, with the 30 October decision to launch an attack against Iraq in January –February 1991, that explains the dating of the US pre-crisis period as 2 August–29 October 1990.

Iraq's role in the onset phase, as noted, was that of triggering entity: it catalyzed a threat crisis for Kuwait and, later, for the US and many other states, thereby setting in motion the Gulf Crisis. As such, Iraq did not perceive any of the three defining conditions of a foreign policy crisis; that is, it was not yet a crisis actor. *Value threat*, marking the beginning of its pre-crisis period, emerged on 2 August, with the strong US critical response hours after the invasion of Kuwait. However, the other two necessary conditions of a crystallized foreign policy crisis—perceived heightened probability of war and time pressure—were not in evidence in Iraq's statements or behavior for many months.

Like its main adversary, Iraq's military buildup during the summer and autumn of 1990 [see below, pp. 423–424] aimed at war avoidance. Its counterpart to the US strategy of compellance was *deterrence*, designed to persuade Washington that the cost of war in US casualties would far exceed any benefits. To that end Iraq dispatched more and more troops to Kuwait, exceeding the US-led Coalition forces in the Gulf region until very late in the escalation phase.

That Saddam Hussein perceived the possibility of war with the US as higher after 2 August than before seems certain. First, the "hands-off" signals from US officials were dramatically erased by the instant condemnation of the invasion from the White House. More important, on 15 August Iraq's President offered to accept all of Iran's conditions for a formal end to the Iran/Iraq War—an exchange of prisoners-of-war, withdrawal from occupied Iranian territory, and restoration of their 1975 treaty regarding the Shatt-al-Arab waterway—in order to free more than one hundred thousand Iraqi troops for the Kuwait front.

As with the US perception of *war likelihood*, Iraq's evolving expectation of war can be summarized as follows:

2 August—war with the US *more possible* than previously;
3 August–28 November—*increasing possibility* of war;
29 November 1990–16 January 1991—war *much more likely*.

Iraq's perception of the possibility of war grew incrementally from early August to late November. Yet Iraq remained impervious to the qualitative change in US behavior and resolve, though it responded, tit-for-tat, to the escalating US military buildup. While its perception of threat, notably to the annexation of Kuwait, intensified over the months, *time* seemed irrelevant. And its expectation of war remained relatively low—until the UN authorized the use of force by the US-led Coalition.

Although Saddam Hussein viewed US intentions through a conspiratorial lens, more important in the shaping of his behavior was a misperception of US resolve: in essence, the US would shrink from the formidable cost of all-out war. Throughout the Gulf Crisis, Hussein remained skeptical of Bush's resolve to employ massive violence—until massive violence was initiated by the US and its allies on 17 January 1991. He dismissed Bush's persistent warnings that the US would resort to force, if necessary. He rejected all attempts at mediation then and later, in fact until a month after the outbreak of war. Yet he could not be unaware of the qualitative change in the probability of war and the UN-sanctioned deadline for Iraq's withdrawal from Kuwait. Thus Iraq's pre-crisis period is dated 2 August–28 November 1990.

The basic difference in the perceptions of war likelihood and of time pressure by the two protagonists lay in the date of acute awareness. For the US, the decision of 30 October 1990 to launch a war against Iraq in mid-January, partly manifested in its 8 November military buildup, made war much more likely. For Iraq, it did not; Iraq was not even aware of the decision. Similarly, the combination of a deadline for withdrawal and the Security Council's authorization of resort to force by the Coalition, on 29 November 1990, made war seem very highly probable for the US, with time acutely relevant. For Iraq, it made war more likely and generated initial awareness of time pressure.[20] Thus, the time frame of periods for the principal adversaries and of the escalation phase was as follows:

the US: pre-crisis—2 August–29 October 1990;

crisis   —30 October 1990–28 February 1991;

Iraq: pre-crisis—2 August–28 November 1990;

crisis   —29 November 1990–28 February 1991.[21]

The escalation phase of the Gulf Crisis, in accordance with the "decision rules" of the Unified Model, lasted from 2 August 1990 to 28 February 1991.

Some may question the choice of late October and late November as the beginning of the crisis period for the main protagonists, arguing that a full-scale foreign policy crisis began for both the US and Iraq with the invasion of Kuwait. But what is meant by "full-scale"? That event catalyzed the pre-crisis period for the US, as President Bush remarked many times during the next seven months: "This conflict *started* August 2 when the dictator of Iraq invaded a small and helpless neighbor" (*NYT*, 17/1/91, A14 [emphasis added]). Within hours, as noted, the stern US response triggered Iraq's pre-crisis period.

The Unified Model's rules on change in phases and periods are precise. Onset, as noted, begins with the entry of the first actor (or actors) into an interstate crisis, that is, the day it perceives higher-than-normal threat to one or more basic values. The onset phase ends with the exit of the first actor(s) from its pre-crisis period, that is, the day its perception deepens and broadens to comprise more acute value threat, along with time pressure and a heightned probability of war. The emergence of these three conditions of a full-fledged foreign policy crisis marks the beginning of that actor's crisis period. That process, in turn, leads to more disruptive interaction and, with it, the beginning of the escalation phase. So it was in the Gulf Crisis.

To clarify this demarcation of the escalation phase for the Gulf Crisis and the pre-crisis period for the US and Iraq, it is crucial to apply the concepts of international and foreign policy crisis. A sharp increase in disruptive interactions between Iraq and the US—and between many other dyads such as Iraq/Kuwait and Iraq/Saudi Arabia—erupted with the invasion of Kuwait and continued until the end of the Gulf crisis-war. Moreover, that situational change generated, objectively, a greater possibility of military hostilities between Iraq and its adversaries, notably the US, in the light of the immediate US reaction cited above. And war had already erupted between Iraq and Kuwait.

As for the second condition of an international crisis: Iraq's invasion posed a challenge to the Gulf regional balance, the inter-Arab balance and, potentially, the Arab/Israel balance, that is, to the structure of the Middle East subsystem. It also represented a potential challenge to: US influence in the Middle East; to the structure of the world economy, especially the price and supply of oil; and to the viability of US/USSR cooperation to assure peace and stability in the post-Cold War global order, based upon the principles of territorial integrity and independence.

Thus, both defining conditions of a full-scale *international* crisis were present from 2 August 1990: Iraq's invasion of Kuwait on that day marks the beginning of the escalation phase. This is not, however, synonymous with the beginning of the crisis period for either or both of the principal adversaries: for the US, only two of the defining conditions, and for Iraq, only one of the three conditions of a fully-crystallized *foreign policy crisis* were present in early August [see Figure 7.1].

Before exploring how the two main adversaries coped in the escalation phase, one persistent hypothetical question merits attention: could Iraq have been deterred from invading Kuwait? In an attempt to answer this question and, more generally, to derive lessons from Gulf War II, Davis and Arquilla (1991) applied an experimental interdisciplinary methodology: alternative models of Saddam Hussein's reasoning from February 1990 to February 1991 were devised, and his behavior was explained retrospectively. Their conclusions were that: US efforts to deter Saddam Hussein's invasion of Kuwait by actions in late July 1990 would not have succeeded; nor could his withdrawal have been achieved soon after the invasion, even with a compromise over the disputed islands and the Rumaila oil field; and third, that only the US-led ground campaign persuaded Iraq's leader to accept a cease-fire. In short, deterrence could not have succeeded.

The same answer to this intriguing question was given by Stein (1992), though for different reasons. Three "distinct but not mutually exclusive explanations [were offered]. . .

a poorly designed [US] strategy that would have confused a fully rational adversary bent on expansion; an adversary who was motivated by a mixture of opportunity and need, and made serious tactical miscalculations about the scope of military action; and an adversary who framed the problem in such a way that the choice was between open confrontation and long-term sabotage. Any one of these conditions could have defeated deterrence and reassurance. Together, they made deterrence of the attack against Kuwait hopeless." (170)

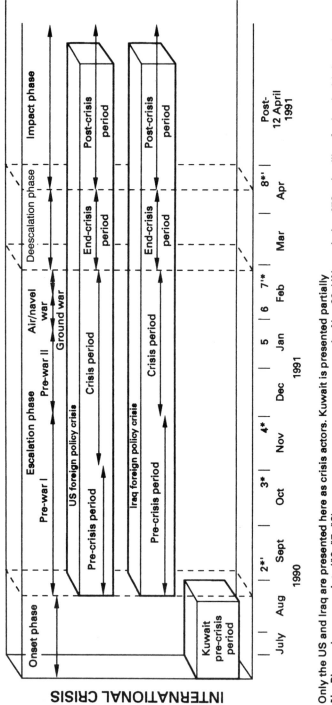

FIG. 7.1 Gulf Crisis – Phases & Periods

Only the US and Iraq are presented here as crisis actors. Kuwait is presented partially

*' – Phase change – points (*2, *7, *8)
* – Period change – points (*3, *4, *7, *8)

1 – July 17: Saddam Hussein denounced Kuwait for exceeding OPEC quota and threatened to use force.

2 – Aug 2: Iraq's invasion of Kuwait – the Emirate conquered within 6 hours.

3 – Oct 30: US decision to launch a war against Iraq in Jan-Feb 1991.

4 – Nov 29: UN resolution 678 – deadline for Iraqi withdrawal imposed and authorization of resort to force to coalition.

5 – Jan 17: Massive air-naval war by US and Allies against Iraq.

6 – Feb 24: Ground war against Iraq by US and Allies.

7 – Feb 28: Iraq's acceptance of Bush's 27 Feb. Unilateral ceasefire and all UN Security Council resolutions.

8 – Apr 12: UNSC resolution 678 (3 April) – after permanent ceasefire went into effect.

These speculations are highly plausible 'what if' conjecture. What is clear from the available evidence is that the U.S. did not attempt to deter Iraq in July 1990. Rather, as indicated earlier (n. 9), the American national security community was, as so often, taken by surprise.

Pre-War I (2 August–28 November 1990)

CRISIS MANAGEMENT

How did Iraq and the US cope during the lengthy pre-war phase? Both actors pursued a leisurely tit-for-tat strategy in direct hostile interaction. There were frequent escalation points, especially in the *military buildup*. The most important of these will now be noted briefly.

3 August: Iraqi forces (60,000) were concentrated on the Saudi Arabian border.

5 August: Saddam Hussein ordered the formation of 11 additional army divisions.

7 August: US forces (6000–15,000 and four tactical fighter squadrons) were deployed in Saudi Arabia.

8 August: the US announced that up to 50,000 troops might be dispatched to Saudi Arabia to press for Iraq's compliance with UN resolutions; Bush declared that "a line has been drawn in the sand" (*NYT*, 9/8/90, A1); Iraq's Revolutionary Command Council (RCC) responded by annexing Kuwait, "in a comprehensive, eternal, and inseparable merger" (*FBIS–NESA*, 9/8/90).

11 August: the upper limit of US forces was raised to 200,000.

16 August: Iraq took thousands of foreigners—American, British, French, Japanese, etc.—as hostages, some of whom were sent to Iraqi military and industrial targets as "human shields" against air attacks by the US-led Coalition.[22]

18 August: US ships in the Gulf fired warning shots over the bows of two Iraqi tankers; Iraq termed the US and UK blockade "an act of war."

22 August: Bush mobilized 40,000 reservists to active duty, the first such call-up since the 1968 Tet Offensive in the Vietnam War.

21 September: the RCC called on Iraq's citizens to prepare for "the mother of all battles"; by then Iraq had 430,000 troops in the South and in Kuwait, in defensive positions.

23 September: Hussein threatened to attack Saudi Arabian oil fields, unfriendly Arab states and Israel if UN economic sanctions began to "strangle" Iraq.

 8 *November:* Bush ordered *at least* 150,000 more American troops to the Gulf region, to achieve "an adequate offensive option" (*NYT*, 9/11/90, A12).

19 *November:* Hussein responded to Bush's 8 November escalation by announcing the deployment of 250,000 more troops to Kuwait and southern Iraq, making a total of 680,000 (*FBIS–NESA*, 19/11/90).

Tit-for-tat extended to mutual *denunciation* by the Iraqi and American leaders: Bush condemned Saddam Hussein as "worse than Hitler" and compared Iraq's invasion of Kuwait to Nazi Germany's invasion of Czechoslovakia in 1939; and, on 15 October 1990, he invoked the image of a war crimes trial: "Hitler revisited. But remember, when Hitler's war ended, there were the Nuremberg Trials" (*NYT*, 16/10/90, A19). Hussein accused Bush of lying. Yet the adversaries were not averse to *bargaining.* Notable was Saddam Hussein's "peace initiative," an offer on 12 August to discuss Iraq's withdrawal from Kuwait in return for: an end to UN economic sanctions, imposed by the Security Council on the 6th; immediate withdrawal of foreign forces from Saudi Arabia, to be replaced by Arab forces, other than those of Egypt; the end of Israel's occupation of the West Bank and Gaza, the Golan Heights, and southern Lebanon; and Syria's withdrawal from Lebanon (*FBIS–NESA*, 13/8/90).[23] On the 19th Hussein offered to release the foreign hostages, in return for a Security Council-guaranteed, US-approved withdrawal of US forces from the region or a "clear, unequivocal commitment, in writing" by Bush to withdraw all US and allied forces from the region, along with a lifting of the UN blockade of Iraq" (*FBIS–NESA*, 20/8/90). The next day the US rejected this proposal until Iraq met the three conditions of the Security Council resolutions of 2 and 19 August—complete, unconditional Iraqi withdrawal from Kuwait, the restoration of the Emir's regime, and the release of all hostages.

Yet, on 1 October Bush implied sequential "linkage" between the Kuwait and Palestine issues, in a speech to the UN General Assembly: "in the aftermath of Iraq's unconditional departure from Kuwait, I truly believe there may be opportunities . . . for all the states and the peoples of the region to settle the conflicts that divide the Arabs from Israel" (*NYT*, 2/10/90, A12). On 23 October 330 French hostages were released by Iraq, followed by a trickle of British, German, Austrian, Japanese and other First World hostages. And on 18 November Hussein and the RCC, in an attempt to delay a Coalition attack, announced the conditional release of all Western hostages, in stages, beginning Christmas Day and ending on 25 March—"unless something happens to disturb the atmosphere of peace" (*FBIS–NESA*, 19/11/90).

In sum, bargaining between the principal adversaries in the first pre-war sub-phase of escalation (2 August–28 November 1990) included verbal and political acts, non-violent military shows of force, rare resort to violence, displays of resolve, and conciliatory gestures.[24]

For the US and Iraq, *coping* in Pre-War I comprised several strands. The military buildup was central for both actors, as noted. In addition, the US expended vast resources to forge a world-wide coalition, in order to compel Iraq's withdrawal from Kuwait, and to mobilize global system legitimacy for the Coalition's actions, through UN Security Council resolutions. Iraq, apart from deploying more than half a million troops to defend its newly-acquired "19th province," sought external support from other Arab states and non-state organizations, from traditionalist and fundamentalist Islam, and from the "Arab street," in order to expel the "infidels" entrenched in the land of Islam's holiest Holy Places.

Coalition-building is fraught with difficulty. The task is made more complicated by the stress of a military-security crisis. When the initiator is a superpower, when it aspires to a world-wide alliance, including such disparate elements as all major powers and Arab, European and Asian states, and when prospects of war and domestic turmoil cannot be dismissed, the task is awesome. To that challenge President Bush and Secretary of State Baker devoted immense energy during the escalation phase of the Gulf Crisis, until war erupted in mid-January 1991.

Creating a viable anti-Iraq coalition was inextricably linked to the other strand of US crisis management, because the attainment of legitimacy meant, largely, the undoing of Iraq's aggression against Kuwait under UN auspices. Achieving authorization for military sanctions, if they proved necessary, was a formidable undertaking because it required the consent or at least acquiescence of the other four permanent members of the Security Council, the only UN body that could legitimize these strong measures of collective security. If the major powers were prepared to participate in a US-led global coalition, their support in the UN and, therefore, global legitimacy would follow. However, other powers, especially France and the USSR, had their own vital interests to protect and enhance.

The UK posed no problem for the US's coalition-building effort throughout the Gulf Crisis. Prime Minister Thatcher (and, from early

December 1990, Prime Minister Major), as well as Parliament, opposition parties and British public opinion, shared the Bush–Baker conviction that Hussein's behavior was intolerable and that Iraq's military power posed a grave danger to American, British and, more generally, to Western and global interests in the Gulf region, namely, assured oil to the industrialized economies and Middle East stability.[25] More tangibly, the UK was the only Western member of the Coalition other than France to deploy more than symbolic forces to the Gulf region. Thus, from the beginning of the Gulf Crisis, the US could, and did, rely on UK support within the UN Security Council and in the creation of a military alliance to compel Iraq's ouster from Kuwait by force, if necessary. The "special relationship" between London and Washington was reinvigorated under the stress of crisis.

China's behavior was not likely to pose a serious problem for the US-led Coalition. Its strategic and economic interests in the Gulf region were modest. More important, its primary foreign policy interest after the suppression of the pro-democracy movement in June 1989 was restored respectability, especially in the US, the principal source of advanced technology and, potentially, large-scale investment to help China achieve its ambitious goal of modernization by the year 2000. Its options were clear: to join the global diplomatic coalition in defense of collective security and thereby regain respectability; or act as a "spoiler" by using its veto in the Security Council to deny UN legitimacy for US aims. China chose the former path, by voting in favor of all UN resolutions during Pre-War I. Yet it was a maverick member of the Coalition, trying to enhance its image in Washington and, at the same time, to maintain its credibility in the Third World.

France's role in the Coalition was uncertain because of national interests and status. First, France had cultivated a close relationship with Iraq for almost two decades and was, after the USSR, the most important contributor to its military-industrial complex. Moreover, French interests in the *Maghreb* — Algeria, Morocco and Tunisia — dictated caution in any French policy directed against an Arab state. Third, a large immigrant community of Arabs from North Africa reinforced that constraint. Fourth, France vied with the US and the USSR for influence in the Arab world and the Middle East. And finally there was France's deep-rooted need "to go it alone," as evident in its continued aloofness from the West's military alliance since de Gaulle's withdrawal of French forces from the unified NATO command in 1966. Notwithstanding these concerns, France was loyal to the US-led Coalition: it voted in favor of all 11 Security Council resolutions from 2 August to 28

November 1990; and it dispatched modest land, air and naval forces to the area of conflict. The reason would seem to lie in France's overriding interest during the Gulf crisis-war—to avoid alienating Western Europe's ultimate military protector on an issue that the US President had categorically defined as a "vital interest" and to which he had irrevocably committed his prestige.

Among the major powers in the Coalition, the most problematic was the USSR. Three strands, not easily reconciled and the cause of uncertainty for US decision-makers, were evident in Soviet behavior. One was strong, persistent verbal support for the UN resolutions and the US determination to expel Iraq from Kuwait. Another was a refusal to participate in the military buildup in the Gulf region or military hostilities against Iraq. And the third was a high-profile attempt to mediate between the conflicting goals of the two main adversaries. These roles were pursued simultaneously during the entire crisis.

There were several reasons for Soviet ambivalence. First, the USSR had been a patron of Iraq for two decades, through a formal treaty of friendship dating to 1972 and as the largest supplier of advanced weapons for Iraq's army; it was reluctant to sever these longstanding ties. Moreover, despite the end of the Cold War the two superpowers continued to compete for influence in the oil-rich and strategically-valuable Middle East. Third, Iraq and the Gulf zone were perilously close to the USSR, and events there could spill over to its Muslim-majority Central Asian republics. And fourth, during the early months the Soviets worried about the fate of the 10,000 Soviet citizens in Iraq and Kuwait, including 7830 military and industrial advisors. The result was a complex Soviet posture on the Gulf Crisis from its inception, as evident in a brief summary of Soviet behavior during Pre-War I.

3 *August:* a Joint Statement by Baker and Foreign Minister Shevardnadze condemned "the brutal and illegal invasion of Kuwait" and called for "an international cutoff of all arms supplies to Iraq" (Keller, *NYT*, 4/8/90, A6).

11–13 *August:* contrary to the US contention that it had ample authorization for the use of force to ensure Iraqi compliance with the UN embargo, the Soviet UN delegate insisted that this first be approved by the moribund Military Staff Committee of the Security Council, which had not met since 1946, and that a fresh resolution under Article 42 of the Charter was necessary.[26]

25 *August:* largely as a result of Soviet opposition to an unrestricted use of force, Security Council Resolution 665, approved that day,

permitted minimal force necessary to secure Iraq's compliance with economic sanctions.

4 September: Shevardnadze proposed an international conference on the Israel/Palestine issue and other Middle East problems, to be linked with the Kuwait crisis (Clines and Text, *NYT*, 5/9/90, A17).

9 September: at their Helsinki talks, Bush and Gorbachev reaffirmed the Baker-Shevardnadze Joint Statement of 3 August and their support for the five Security Council resolutions passed until then; moreover, they pledged "to act individually and in concert to reverse Iraq's conquest of Kuwait." At the same time, they did not conceal their differences over: the timing of—and authorization for—the use of force to ensure Iraq's compliance with UN demands; Soviet participation in policing the embargo; "linkage" between the invasion of Kuwait and other Middle East issues; the Arab states as possible mediators; and the continued presence of Soviet military experts in Iraq.[27]

4–5 and late October: Moscow pursued the path of direct mediation, through Gorbachev's emissary to Baghdad, Yevgeni Primakov.[28]

29 October: Based upon Primakov's assessment of Saddam Hussein's views, Gorbachev once more urged a diplomatic solution. (This policy continued for almost a month, when the USSR finally approved the US draft of what became Resolution 678.)

The task of winning the support of lesser powers for a US-led coalition was easier. The Arab front-line states in the Gulf region, notably Saudi Arabia, identified quickly with the objective of undoing Iraq's aggression against a fellow-member of the Gulf Cooperation Council (GCC). Indeed, without Saudi Arabia's formal invitation to the US to come to its defense, with ready access to Saudi bases, the anti-Iraq coalition would have been still-born.

The greatest disappointment for the US was the reaction of the other two economic superpowers, Germany and Japan. Both invoked constitutional constraints to justify their abstention from the military coalition in the Gulf region. Germany tried to compensate by financial contributions to cover part of the cost of the Gulf crisis-war, $1.2 billion before the outbreak of war, an additional $5.5 billion later. Japan, too, tried to compensate by pledging large sums of money—initially $2.2 billion and, later, $11 billion more—for the Coalition and to ease the financial burden of the Gulf Crisis for exposed states, notably Egypt, Jordan and Turkey.

A notable success in the US coalition-building effort was the active role of two important Arab states other than Saudi Arabia, namely, Egypt and Syria. On 6 August President Mubarak agreed to allow the *USS Eisenhower*, a nuclear-powered aircraft carrier, to pass through the Suez Canal en route to the Gulf. More important, he was instrumental in achieving a majority at the emergency summit meeting of the Arab League in Cairo on the 10th, 12 of 21, in favor of (a) condemning Iraq for invading and occupying a fellow Arab state, and (b) sending Arab troops to defend Saudi Arabia and the Gulf emirates. Moreover, by the beginning of November Egypt had reportedly deployed almost 20,000 troops to Saudi Arabia for the defense of the kingdom and the liberation of Kuwait. The Syrian contingent was smaller and slower to arrive, 7500 by late November.

The second strand of US crisis management, its *quest for legitimacy*, was a major success. Through a relentless series of Security Council resolutions, the US harnessed the authority of the world body in support of its consistent minimal demands: Iraq's unconditional and complete withdrawal from Kuwait; the restoration of the legitimate government of the emirate, and the release of all foreign hostages by Iraq. These resolutions are summarized in Table 7.1.

In sum, the main themes of the Security Council's resolutions on the Gulf Crisis during Pre-War I were: unconditional and total withdrawal of Iraqi forces from Kuwait (Res. 660); mandatory economic sanctions until Iraq complied with the Council's resolutions (Res. 661); nullification of Iraq's annexation and restoration of the Emir's government (Res. 662); and Iraq's responsibility for war damages and economic losses—implied reparations (Res. 674). Taken together, the 11 Security Council resolutions from the eruption of the Gulf Crisis until 28 November (Pre-War I) indicated a steady escalation of UN pressure on Iraq to comply with the demands of the world community. However, that process was, to a large extent, reactive, a function of events as they unfolded, not of a preordained plan (Sciolino and Pace, *NYT*, 30/8/90, A1, 15).

Iraq's pre-war coping, too, was devoted partly to trying to forge a wide-ranging coalition. There were several constituencies: the mass public of Arab lands from Mauritania to the Gulf; friendly Arab states; traditionalist and fundamentalist Islam; the Third World generally; and, despite their savage eight-year war (1980–88), Iran.

To this end Saddam Hussein, Iraqi ministers and Iraq's media employed many techniques: rallying the impoverished many in the overcrowded streets of Arab cities against the extraordinary affluence of the few, in a call for the redistribution of Arab wealth; mobilizing

TABLE 7.1   *UN Involvement in Gulf Crisis: Pre-War 1*

Resolution	Date	Vote	Content
660	02/08/90	14–0°	Iraq's invasion condemned; demanded that "Iraq withdraw immediately and unconditionally all its forces" to 1 August positions; Iraq and Kuwait called upon "to begin immediately intensive negotiations" on their disputes.
661	06/08/90	13–0†	Mandatory global economic sanctions imposed.
662	09/08/90	15–0	Iraq's annexation of Kuwait on 8th declared "null and void".
664	18/08/90	14–0°°	Demanded release of all foreign hostages by Iraq.
665	25/08/90	13–0†	Minimum force authorized to impose UN economic sanctions.
666	13/09/90	13–2°°	Humanitarian food supplies to Iraq and Kuwait to be determined by Security Council.
667	16/09/90	15–0	Iraq condemned for "aggressive acts" against foreign embassies and personnel in Kuwait.
669	24/09/90	14–1°	Committee on Sanctions created under Res. 661 entrusted to examine requests for assistance.
670	25/09/90	14–1°	All air links with Iraq to be severed.
674	29/10/90	13–0†	UN members invited to make claims for financial compensation.
677	28/11/90	(15–0)	Iraq condemned for attempting to change demographic composition of Kuwait's population.
(678 (686 (687 (688			to be discussed later in the text)

° Yemen not participating in the vote   † Cuba and Yemen abstaining
°°Yemen abstaining   ††Cuba and Yemen opposed
° Cuba opposed

Sources: The content summary and quoted passages are based upon the following UN Security Council documents: S/RES/660 (1990), 2 August 1990; S/RES/661 (1990), 6 August 1990; S/RES/662 (1990), 9 August 1990; S/RES/664 (1990), 18 August 1990; S/RES/665 (1990), 25 August 1990; S/RES/666 (1990), 13 September 1990; S/RES/667 (1990), 16 September 1990; S/RES/669 (1990), 24 September 1990; S/RES/670 (1990), 25 September 1990; S/RES/674 (1990), 29 October 1990; S/RES/677 (1990), 28 November 1990.

the poor Arab states against the oil-rich kingdoms, emirates and sheikhdoms of the Gulf region; invoking the symbols of Islam and the historic struggle against the infidels from the West; appealing to former colonies in the Third World against the "new colonialism" of the US and its allies; and most visibly, posing as the champion of the Palestinians in their struggle for independence against the most unifying symbol in the Arab world, the "Zionist entity," that is, the State of Israel. Many of these symbols were used to reinforce one another, for these diverse groups—Arab, Muslim, the poor, non-white, and ex-colonial—had shared memories and anger *vis-à-vis* the major Western powers.[29]

Saddam Hussein also invoked religion to buttress his cause. Using extreme Muslim symbols, he appealed to the "Arab street" and public opinion in the Islamic world generally, over the heads of their governments. In fact, he openly called for the overthrow of the ruling families in Saudi Arabia, the Gulf emirates and sheikhdoms, and President Mubarak of Egypt (e.g., *FBIS–NESA*, 13/8/90, 46). This seemed an aberration for a secular Arab nationalist nurtured in pan-Arab *Ba'ath* ideology. It was extreme, shrill, persistent—almost daily—and not without effect during the escalation phase and beyond. These religious symbols, often accompanied by appeals to the poor and to anti-colonialist sentiments, led to mass demonstrations in support of Iraq—in Jordan and Yemen, among Palestinians in the West Bank and Gaza, in the *Maghreb* states and in the Sudan, with the Muslim Brotherhood and its affiliates taking the lead.

For most Arab states, Iraq's behavior created consternation and a dilemma: how to respond to the destruction of one Arab League member by another? To condemn Iraq would create an image of aligning oneself with the West, the former dominant powers in the Middle East. To support Iraq meant undermining the core principle of territorial integrity and sovereign independence of all members of the Arab family. The result was either neutrality or, for most, only rhetorical support for one of the protagonists, Iraq or the UN Coalition.

These mixed reactions were evident at the Arab League summit in Cairo on 10 August. A majority of 12 voted in favor of a seven-point resolution: Saudi Arabia, Kuwait, the United Arab Emirates, Qatar, Oman and Bahrain, all oil-rich states from the Gulf region; and Egypt, Syria, Lebanon, Morocco, Somalia and Djibouti. Libya and the PLO joined Iraq in outright rejection of the resolution. Jordan, Mauritania and Sudan masked their opposition by approving "with reservations." Algeria and Yemen abstained. And Tunisia was absent.

The main provisions of the seven-point resolution were: condemnation of Iraq's invasion of Kuwait, its "threats to Gulf states," and "massing troops" on Saudi Arabia's borders; a demand for the withdrawal of Iraq's forces from Kuwait; a call for the restoration of the Emir's Government; and, operationally, support for UN economic sanctions, and the dispatch of Arab troops to Saudi Arabia and the lesser Gulf states to defend against a possible Iraqi invasion (Kifner, *NYT*, 11/8/90, A1, 6). In fact, as noted, only Egypt and Syria—and, symbolically, Morocco—actually sent military contingents.

What were the key *decisions* of the main protagonists in the first prewar sub-phase of escalation and the date of their implementation?

Iraq

To invade Kuwait—2 August 1990;
To annex Kuwait—8 August, and its proclamation as Iraq's 19th Province, on 28 August;
To offer a conditional withdrawal from Kuwait—12 August;
To accept Iran's terms for the termination of Gulf War I—15 August;
To take foreign hostages en bloc—16 August.

the US

To condemn Iraq's invasion of Kuwait and demand complete, unconditional withdrawal—1–2 August 1990;
To freeze Iraqi and Kuwaiti assets in the US—2 August;
To seek UN approval for global mandatory economic sanctions—6 August;
To begin a military buildup of US forces in the Gulf region—7 August;
To prepare for war against Iraqi forces in Kuwait—8 November.

The intricacies of Iraq's decision-making are almost impossible to fathom—for a Westerner. Suffice it to note that Saddam Hussein was the ultimate if not sole decision-maker, certainly on crucial issues such as the Gulf Crisis. It has been suggested (Dunnigan and Bay, 1991: 375) that orders to invade Kuwait were issued less than half a day before the attack; if so, it was an impulsive decision. US decision-making is less of an enigma. In its pre-crisis period (2 August–29 October) the crucial decisions were: to deploy troops to Saudi Arabia and the Gulf region, for this marked direct US military intervention in the Gulf Crisis; and to prepare for war in mid-January 1991. Despite the fragmentary evidence, it is possible to present a preliminary analysis of these decisions.

The *decision to intervene* was taken from 2 to 4 August, the result of (at least) three meetings of the National Security Council.[30] The first, starting at 8.00 a.m. (EST) on 2 August, was long and inconclusive. CIA Director Webster expressed grave concern about a likely invasion of Saudi Arabia, with 100,000 Iraqi troops concentrated in Kuwait, many of them only 10 miles from the Saudi border. Treasury Secretary Brady drew attention to Iraq's control of 20% of known world oil reserves, which would increase to 40% if Saudi Arabia were seized by Saddam Hussein, and the consequence of higher oil prices. Bush responded with an expression of resolve: "Let's be clear about one thing. We are not here to talk about adapting [to higher oil prices]. We are not going to plan how to live with this" (Friedman and Tyler, *NYT*, 3/3/91, A18).

Defense Secretary Cheney reported that Air Force KC-10s, large aerial refuelling planes, had been moved to Saudi Arabia. General Powell informed the group that a squadron of F-15 fighter planes was on alert, ready to move to Saudi territory, if the Saudis agreed. General Schwarzkopf (1992:298) "laid out the options [of what could be done immediately] as [Powell] had instructed. . . [noting that] we could make certain moves with our air and sea power to demonstrate US determination and, if necessary, punish Iraq." Energy Secretary Watkins proposed bombing Iraq's oil pipelines to Turkey and Saudi Arabia. White House Chief of Staff Sununu urged an economic embargo; but Budget Director Darman observed that, historically, this technique was ineffective. Both Powell and Cheney advocated a defensive goal—to protect Saudi Arabia, not the liberation of Kuwait. However, they differed sharply on the scope of a US military response: at a joint meeting the previous night the Chairman of the JCS favored a limited punitive strike, such as the bombing of the Iraq–Saudi Arabia pipeline; the Defense Secretary wanted "a full range of options, including the maximum use of force" to be presented to the President (Tyler, *NYT*, 15/3/91, A14).

Bush seemed frustrated by the lack of a clear course of action: "But we just can't accept what's happened in Kuwait just because it's too hard to do anything about it" (Woodward, 1991: 229). At that stage he favored more economic sanctions, along with a diplomatic effort to compel Iraq to withdraw from Kuwait. No decision was reached.

Schwarzkopf's recollection of that first NSC meeting is instructive. Brent Scowcroft, the National Security Advisor, UN Ambassador Thomas Pickering, and Cheney "made interesting contributions, but other Cabinet officers [CIA Director Webster was singled out] who should have helped assess the new developments seemed quite unprepared." Further, Bush displayed an open mind and did "not make snap judgments or decisions before he had the complete picture." Most important, barely 14 hours into the US crisis, "[h]e considered an attack on the Saudis to be cause for war"—in reply to Powell's query about "laying down a red line with regard to Saudi Arabia" (1992: 297–298).

A second meeting of the NSC was held on the 3rd of August. Scowcroft advocated a hard line, arguing that Iraq's invasion could not be tolerated because it posed a fundamental threat to the balance of power in the Middle East. Bush concurred. Economic sanctions were discussed. So too was a CIA estimate that Iraqi forces could capture the Saudi capital, Riyadh, in three days. Scowcroft urged two parallel paths: the use of force, if necessary, to prevent an attack on Saudi Arabia; and the overthrow of Saddam Hussein by covert means. Bush ordered the CIA to start planning a covert operation for that purpose. (It was formally authorized on the 17th, to be achieved through Iraqi dissidents, not assassination [Woodward, 1991: 237, 282].) But there was still no decision about military intervention.

Bush had phoned King Fahd on the afternoon of 2 August. They agreed that the invasion and conquest of Kuwait were unacceptable, but no decision was reached. Scowcroft told Saudi Ambassador Bandar on the 3rd: "The Bush position was that the United States was *inclined* to help in any way possible" (Woodward, 1991: 240). The President reportedly gave Bandar a personal pledge to stand by Saudi Arabia: "I give my word of honor, I will see this through with you" (*ibid*, 241). And Powell told Schwarzkopf: "The President was ready to consider sending troops" (1992: 298). But none of these constituted an irrevocable US decision to intervene.

That decision emerged, indirectly, from the third meeting of the NSC, at Camp David, on 4 August, after an extensive briefing by Schwarzkopf on the Central Command's Operations Plan 90–1002 dating to the early 1980s. Two scenarios were sketched: in Woodward's words, a "deterrence piece," to defend Saudi Arabia (Tier I), that would require a US military buildup of 200,000–250,000 in the Gulf region and would take 17 weeks to implement; and a "warfighting piece" (Tier 2), designed to expel Iraq's forces from Kuwait, which would need 8–12 months and a much larger buildup. Schwarzkopf, in his memoirs (1992: 300–302), did not specify the number of troops required. The "contingency plan for the *defense* of Saudi Arabia," he told the President, would require bases in Saudi Arabia and take three months. The expulsion of Iraq from Kuwait would need "a whole lot more troops and a whole lot more time," at least six additional divisions with a "time frame: 8–10 months. I heard a few people around the table gasp."

The decision to commit US forces was taken by "the Principals" between the 4 August meeting and the morning of the 5th (Schwarz-kopf, 1992: 302): Bush, Vice-President Dan Quayle, James A. Baker III, Cheney, Scowcroft, John H. Sununu, Powell, and Webster. It did not relate directly to the Tier Two option; rather, it was to have Bush phone Fahd, to try to persuade him to invite US forces and to offer large-scale military aid. Bush confirmed the time of this decision and his perceived value threat, in an address to Congress on 11 September: "Within three days [of the invasion], 120,000 Iraqi troops with 850 tanks had poured into Kuwait, and *moved south to threaten Saudi Arabia*. It was then that I decided to check that aggression" (*NYT*, 12/9/90, A20, emphasis added). Powell had correctly anticipated this development by telling Schwarzkopf on 2 August: "I think we'd go to war over Saudi Arabia, but I doubt we'd go to war over Kuwait" (Schwarzkopf, 1992: 297).

It took two days to implement that decision. The major obstacle was Saudi hesitation, even though Saudi Arabia's leaders perceived a much graver value threat than did Bush and his advisors. The President reassured Fahd by phone on the 4th that the US would stand by Saudi Arabia and proposed sending a high-level delegation headed by the Defense Seretary to discuss the dispatch of US forces. Fahd delayed 14 hours before accepting a mission headed by Cheney, undoubtedly because of the perceived high political cost:[31]

There are three versions of the meeting with the King of Saudi Arabia on 6 August 1990. According to Woodward (1991: 270), the essence of Cheney's *démarche* to Fahd was as follows:

> The President asked me to emphasize four things. The United States is prepared to commit a force to defend Saudi Arabia that can do the job.... [T]o be successful, we have to have forces in place.... Time is of the essence.... Third point: After the danger is over, our forces will go home.... Fourth, it will be far more dangerous if we wait.... I'd like to receive your approval to proceed with introduc-ing U.S. forces.

Fahd reportedly relented. Yet, even when he decided to invite US troops, he specified two conditions, in writing: they would leave Saudi Arabia when the Iraqi threat was overcome; and offensive military action would require prior Saudi approval (Friedman and Tyler, *NYT*, 3/3/91, A18). According to Schwarzkopf (1992: 305–306), "Fahd responded sharply to one of [the royal princes present, who had been urging caution]: 'The Kuwaitis did not rush into a decision, and today they are all guests in our hotels'." He then "turned to Cheney and said in English simply, 'Okay'." The first stage of Plan

90–1002—to dispatch 6000–15,000 troops—was announced by Bush on 7 August.

The gestation of the *"prepare for war"* decision lasted almost a month.[32] In early October the President pressed the Pentagon for a briefing on an offensive military operation. Schwarzkopf's initial plan, presented by his chief of staff to "the Principals" at a meeting in Washington on 11 October, called for three stages of air attacks: on Iraq's command, control and communications centers; on its infrastructure of bases, roads and transportation; and on Iraqi ground forces, including the Republican Guard divisions. This was to be followed by a direct ground assault on Iraqi forces in Kuwait. Bush and Cheney rejected the last phase as certain to be too costly in terms of casualties. Schwarzkopf himself derided the proposed "straight-up-the middle charge right into the teeth of the Iraqi defenses," which he attributed to his "planning wizards" (1992: 356).

During a visit by Powell to Saudi Arabia on 21–22 October Schwarzkopf presented a revised plan, a flanking attack around Iraq's front line. Such an offensive option, noted Schwarzkopf, would require a vast increase in the US deployment in the Gulf region of 200,000 troops. For the "warfighting piece" he insisted on double the force planned for the "deterrence piece," including the élite VII Corps of three armored and mechanized divisions then in West Germany. Powell was strongly supportive: "'If we go to war', he promised, 'we will not do it halfway. The United States military will give you whatever you need to do it right'." And they agreed "that February was a possible date for a ground attack" (Schwarzkopf, 1992: 367). The "window of opportunity" for an offensive operation was defined by the generals as 1 January–15 February 1991: first, because the required military buildup would not be ready until the end of 1990; and secondly, because inclement weather conditions, combined with *Ramadan*, would preclude a campaign for many months thereafter.

Bush told Cheney on 24 October that he was inclined to add substantial forces for an offensive option but would not make an announcement until after the 6 November Congressional elections. And the secret decision to prepare for war was made at a meeting of Bush, Quayle, Baker, Cheney, Scowcroft and Powell on 30 October.

Powell fully supported Schwarzkopf's request for a vast increase in American forces, if the US were to move from a "defend Saudi Arabia" posture to a "liberate Kuwait" strategic goal, which he had persistently opposed from August onward. The issue, as Scowcroft observed, was to continue with the policy of "deter-and-defend, or . . . switch to developing the offensive option" (Woodward, 1991: 318). Cheney supported Schwarzkopf and Powell unreservedly. Scowcroft, as always in the Gulf Crisis, was the most hawkish. And Baker, reportedly a dissenter from the "rush to war" line, was now amenable.

The discussion was unstructured. The second-tier Deputies Committee had not met to consider this turning-point issue. At the 30 October meeting of "the Principals," as at all others during the Gulf Crisis, "there was little or no process where alternatives and implications were written down so they could be systematically weighed and argued. . . . There was no feedback . . . , and if there was any kind of organized debate within the inner circle, it was done without the benefit of staff" (Wolfowitz). Powell concurred: "There was no real organization to the proceedings as they weighed the options. Ideas bounced back and forth as one thought or another occurred to one of them" (Woodward, 1991: 318). The decision was not unanimous from the outset. But "Bush and Scowcroft," backed by Quayle and Cheney, "seemed primed to go ahead with the development of the offensive option" (Woodward, 1991: 318). And that was decisive.

Bush and his aides made a two-track decision: to prepare for a mid-January air/naval war, followed by a land campaign in February; and to secure a UN mandate for that strategy. The first track led to the 8 November announcement of a major escalation of US forces, the second to Baker's month-long quest for support for a UN deadline/authorization of force resolution, beginning with a visit to Coalition capitals from 3 to 10 November. The two tracks were intertwined.

That crucial crisis-war decision was taken by the President. Baker, Powell informed Schwarzkopf, was to seek Gulf states' agreement "to offensive operations." "Then we'll take the idea to the U.N. and ask for an ultimatum for Iraq to leave Kuwait. You should be prepared," he advised Schwarzkopf, "to build up the force and go to war." And Powell reiterated: "It will be dramatic. You're gonna get everything you asked for and more, [to] nearly double the force of Desert Shield" (1992: 370). The buildup, Schwarzkopf recalled (1992: 376), "was even more massive than what Powell had described. . . The President had doubled our ground force, tripled our number of tanks, boosted our air power by thirty percent, and doubled our naval force. . ."

As in early August, the pre-requisite to a further US military buildup—and an "offensive option"—was Saudi approval. This was readily granted. "While we all still want peace," Fahd reportedly told Baker on 3 November, "if we must go to war, Saudi Arabia's armed forces will fight side by side with yours." Regarding the increased deployment, "at least 140,000 more troops," the King remarked: "I've never set a limit on troop strength." He also accepted the request that "the commander of the U.S. forces will have final approval authority for all military operations." And finally, to Baker's "amazement," while Arab forces could not "be perceived as allied with Israelis. . . [i]f Israel were to defend itself [against an Iraqi attack], the Saudi armed forces would still fight by our side" (Schwarzkopf, 1992: 372–373).

The strategy underlying the "prepare for war" decision remained compellance. The primary purpose of the 8 November announcement —sending a clear signal of US resolve—was widely recognized: "President Bush sought today to send an unmistakable message to President Saddam Hussein of Iraq that the United States had the will to go to war, that it would soon have the means to go to war and that a war, if it came, would inevitably inflict terrible damage on Iraq." All US decision-makers were hopeful that the massive increase of US forces, "combined with the setting of a deadline, might be enough to scare Mr. Hussein into leaving Kuwait."[33]

Just in case Saddam Hussein did not "get the message," Bush pursued the second track with great vigor, that is, coalition diplomacy and the search for legitimacy intertwined. How difficult was the task of sustaining a coalition became evident during the Baker talks with eight allies in Europe and the Middle East from 3 to 10 November 1990.

For the Arab members of the Coalition—Saudi Arabia, Kuwait, Egypt and Syria—the preferred option was war, with some diversity of opinion on timing. France, China and the Soviet Union preferred coercive diplomacy, that is, the use of the military buildup to compel Iraq's withdrawal from Kuwait without resort to war. They also differed on economic sanctions, as well as on the auspices for resort to force: some, notably the US and the UK, were prepared to use force without an explicit Security Council authorization, arguing that Article 51 of the UN Charter, the "right to self-defense" provision, was sufficient; others, notably China, France and the USSR, were not.

Baker acknowledged this diversity amidst unity and the problems of sustaining a coalition:

> As we wrap up this trip, I feel that we have a very strong consensus on our collective aims, and on the need particularly to resist partial solutions and on the need to work together and stay together in this coalition and on the need to make all of our options credible. . . .
>
> There are some differing views . . . but generally speaking there is an extraordinary unanimity, and cohesiveness. There are differing opinions with respect to how long it would take sanctions to work. Indeed there are some different opinions on

whether sanctions are already having some bite (Friedman, *NYT*, 11/11/90, A1, 14).

In short, Coalition members agreed on objectives but differed on strategy and tactics.

Coalition differences had a profound effect on US behavior in November. The Baker mission, designed partly to "test the waters" on a resolution authorizing force, convinced Washington that a UN umbrella was essential for political if not for legal reasons. In terms of the Unified Model, coalition maintenance required a further expression of global system legitimacy for war. This culminated in Security Council Resolution 678, which set a deadline for Iraq's withdrawal and authorized the use of force by the Coalition.

The evidence on *coping* [see Figure 1.4, Chap. 1] in the US's pre-crisis period is mixed. In the realm of *information*, the US President contacted allies around the world by phone almost immediately—the leaders of Turkey, Japan, Canada, France, West Germany, the UK, and Kuwait, as he informed the press on 5 August. And this pattern of personal communication continued throughout the Gulf Crisis. However, direct telephone communication with foreign leaders was an established practice of the Bush presidency from its inception in January 1989.

Consultation by US decision-makers, notably by the President and the Secretary of State, vastly exceeded the norm during the pre-crisis period: it embraced the 28 members of the anti-Iraq coalition and many other involved states, such as Israel and Jordan. The task of forging a coalition of disparate elements was achieved by peripatetic diplomacy on the part of Baker: he crisscrossed the world frequently—until the outbreak of war. In short, for this dimension of coping the US pattern was that of a crisis period.

Three crisis management techniques were canvassed by US decision-makers during the pre-crisis period: economic sanctions, coercive diplomacy, and force. As such, the search for, and consideration of, *alternatives* more closely resembled that of behavior postulated for the crisis period. The explanation would seem to lie in the very high and multiple value threat and the higher-than-normal likelihood of war that were perceived by US decision-makers very early in the complex Gulf Crisis.

The US *decisional forum* was, as always, an extension of the presidency. There was no formal crisis management unit, as there had been in many earlier international crises, from Cuban Missiles onward. Rather, as noted in the analysis of crucial decisions, the President relied on a small group of advisors, consisting of Baker, Cheney, Scowcroft, Quayle and Sununu and the two dominant military figures throughout the Gulf crisis-war, Powell and Schwarzkopf. Others who participated in decision-making meetings were Deputy National Security Advisor Robert Gates, Brady, Darman, Fitzwater, and NSC Middle East expert, Richard Haass. It was, in short, an *ad hoc* group within the National Security Council. The "Principals" were assisted by a second tier, the Deputies Committee, chaired by Gates, and consisting of Robert Kimmitt (State), Paul Wolfowitz and David Jeremiah (Defense) and Richard Kerr (CIA).

The pattern of Iraq's decision-making during its pre-crisis period was no different from the non-crisis norm. President Saddam Hussein was the preeminent decision-maker. He set the agenda, tone and direction of discussions in the Revolutionary Command Council (RCC) and the *Ba'ath* Party leadership. These institutionalized bodies of Iraqi decision-making since 1968 provided executive legitimacy to his decisions. And the National Assembly, a rubber stamp, was summoned, when necessary, to grant legislative legitimacy to decisions taken by the President or, formally, by the RCC, such as the annexation of Kuwait on 8 August, its formal integration into Iraq as the 19th province on 28 August, and the release of foreign hostages on 6 December 1990.

Yet Hussein did not function entirely in a vacuum or without the influence of any other person in the Iraqi leadership. His inner circle comprised: Izzat Ibrahim, Deputy Chairman of the RCC, who conducted the ill-fated Jidda negotiations with Kuwait's Crown Prince the day before Iraq's invasion; Taha Yassin Ramadan, First Deputy Prime Minister and Head of the *Ba'ath* Party militia of 850,000, an advocate of stringent governmental control over the economy; Sa'adun Hamadi, a University of Wisconsin-educated former Foreign Minister and Oil Minister, who was Deputy Prime Minister at the time of the Gulf Crisis, and who conducted most of the negotiations with Kuwait over money and territory; and Tariq Aziz, the urbane and articulate Foreign Minister, who conducted the negotiations with Baker and Gorbachev throughout the crisis.

Unquestionably, Saddam Hussein held the ultimate power of decision. How much he relied on his colleagues or family associates is unknown to the author. He tried to create the impression of diversity in the RCC-*Ba'ath* leadership, as with his reference to "hawks" and "doves" during a late October 1990 session with the Soviet envoy, Primakov. The latter expressed doubts: "Everything was decided by one man" (*Time*, 4/3/91).

While alternatives to standing fast may have been considered by Iraq in its pre-crisis period, Saddam Hussein was consistent from 12 August 1990 until escalation to war on 17 January 1991 and through the first month of the war: Kuwait was negotiable only if the major powers and the UN would commit themselves to convening an international peace conference to solve the Palestinian problem and terminate the other Middle East occupations—Israel in the West Bank and Gaza, East Jerusalem, the Golan Heights and south Lebanon, and Syria in most of Lebanon.

"Linkage" was the essence of the Iraqi bargaining posture in its pre-crisis period and, indeed, throughout the Gulf Crisis. While Iraq seemed amenable to mediation in disputes with Kuwait at the beginning of the crisis, notably that of Egyptian President Mubarak, it remained impervious to all other efforts at mediation. It was determined not to make unilateral concessions on Kuwait.

Pre-War II (29 November 1990–16 January 1991)

Pre-crisis for the US, it will be recalled, was set in motion by indirect violence, namely, Iraq's invasion of Kuwait on 2 August 1990. For Iraq, the catalyst was condemnation of its conquest by the UN and the US the same day, a verbal act. The trigger to the crisis period differed for both, as noted: an internal act, for the US—the 30 October secret decision; and an external political act, for Iraq—the twelfth Security Council resolution relating to the Gulf Crisis. On 29 November 1990, by a vote of 12–2 (Cuba and Yemen), with one abstention (China), Resolution 678 authorized UN member-states "to use all necessary means to uphold and implement resolution 660 (1990) and all subsequent relevant resolutions and to restore international peace and security in the area"—unless Iraq withdrew its forces from Kuwait, completely and unconditionally, by 15 January 1991 (S/RES/678 [1990], 29/11/90). The making of Resolution 678 is instructive on superpower cooperation in the post-Cold War era and on the return to US primacy in world politics.

In search of a fresh, decisive UN mandate Baker devoted the rest of November to intense lobbying for a new Security Council resolution. The key to success was the USSR, a point that was recognized at once by Bush, Baker and Scowcroft. Although the US and the USSR agreed on the need to compel Iraq's withdrawal from Kuwait, there was a wide gap on preferred procedure and timing. The US initially wanted a UN resolution that would provide the Coalition with maximum flexibility to launch a military strike whenever it saw fit. Gorbachev wanted a "pause for peace" in order to give (Soviet) diplomacy a "last chance" to persuade Iraq to withdraw from Kuwait. Thus he suggested two resolutions: one authorizing the use of force in principle, but conditional on a second resolution to be passed six weeks later that would formally specify a deadline. The US sensed a trap and countered with a single resolution without a deadline, but if necessary, 1 January. Moscow countered with 15 January. And the deal was struck, incorporating Gorbachev's "pause of goodwill" to allow diplomacy one last chance, under the threat of war, to achieve Iraq's withdrawal from Kuwait. This agreement in principle was reportedly hammered out at two sessions, on 8 and 19 November. Yet it took another ten days for the Soviets to accord formal, public approval, at the Security Council session on 29 November.

Persuasion of the lesser powers represented on the Security Council took a different line: if the UN failed to dislodge Iraq from Kuwait, all small states would be at risk of external aggression. In the case of China the technique was purchase—the non-use of its veto would be rewarded by a much-sought invitation to its Foreign Minister for a meeting with the US President. And Saudi Arabia was reportedly encouraged to provide the USSR with $1 billion in aid.[34]

Saddam Hussein was not impressed by the threat of military sanctions. On the morrow of the Security Council discussion and vote on Resolution 678, a combined RCC-*Ba'ath* Party Statement railed against:

> . . . a resolution that gives false legitimacy to its [US] military presence and evil intentions of aggression against Iraq, the Arab nation, and Muslims. The resolution . . . [of] 29 November is illegal and invalid. It is an American resolution . . . a shameful resolution. . . . Iraq rejects ultimatums and threats. . . . . If the evil ones resort to aggression, then the people . . . and their heroic . . . Armed Forces will teach the evil ones a lesson unprecedented in history (*FBIS–NESA*, 30/11/90).

Nothing changed during the next six weeks: Saddam Hussein remained defiant until the air bombardment of 17 January 1991.

The quest for global system legitimacy for military sanctions against Iraq ended with Resolution 678. Halting efforts were made by the USSR and, more actively, by Yemen and Cuba, until 15 January 1991 to require a specific UN mandate for resort to force. But the US successfully held to the position that no further Security Council role was necessary. Indeed, the Council did not meet publicly again until after the end of Gulf War II. The general purpose clause of Resolution 678 was invoked to legitimize the expansion of Coalition war aims in January–February 1991 [see below].

For US perceptions, Resolution 678 had a profound meaning. It was one thing to say that Iraq's invasion of Kuwait "will not stand," that is, to add the "liberation of Kuwait" to the defense of Saudi Arabia as an objective of the US military buildup, which Bush did on 5 August 1990 and, more emphatically—"the immediate, complete, and unconditional withdrawal of all Iraqi forces from Kuwait"—on 16 August, causing concern to both Powell and Schwarzkopf, who reflected, "this did not sound like a leader bent on compromise. . ." (Schwarzkopf, 1992: 316); or to call for the dismantling of Iraq's non-conventional weapons (10 September); or to state on many occasions that the US intended to use force, if necessary, to expel Iraqi forces from Kuwait; or even to signal US resolve to acquire an "offensive military option" by a massive increase of American forces (8 November).

All of these statements of US goals and resolve, and related actions, were calculated steps in an intricate bargaining process. None contained a time element or an irrevocable commitment to wage war against Iraq. Both of these *lacunae* vanished with Resolution 678. The deadline was precise, 15 January 1991. And, while the authorization to use "all necessary means" did not formally commit the Coalition or specify a date, it was perceived by Bush, Baker and Cheney, Gorbachev and Shevardnadze, in fact, by the rest of the world as an irrevocable US commitment to engage Iraq in full-scale war unless it withdrew completely and unconditionally from Kuwait by 15 January.

US credibility was at stake, especially since all knew that Washington had initiated the deadline and authorization of force resolution and had expended energy and political resources to secure the necessary majority, including a consensus by the five permanent members at least not to exercise a veto. In that sense, the "die was cast" for the US with the passage of the twelfth Security Council resolution on 29 November.

Stated in terms of the Unified Model, that event was a crucial escalation point, triggering the change from pre-crisis to crisis period for the US. It indicated the crossing of the upper threshold of war likelihood; for the US, war now became a very high probability. Moreover, time became acutely salient: that resolution started a countdown—47 days until the deadline date was reached. And to all of the values perceived to be under threat by US decision-makers in the pre-crisis period, there was now added the most emotive value of all, the lives of American military personnel.

Large-scale casualties was the nightmare scenario of Bush from the moment war became very likely on 29 November. This is evident from an extraordinary presidential order to Schwarzkopf on 8 December "to accept losses no greater than the equivalent of three companies per coalition brigade, that is, approximately 10 percent of allied ground forces, or 10,000 soldiers (the Pentagon's three-volume *Report on the Gulf War*, 10/4/92, as cited in Cushman, *NYT*, 11/4/92, A4). Heavy casualties could cause a national security disaster by compelling the US to abandon the objective of reversing Iraq's aggression. The potential spillover, from wavering after the UN deadline or yielding to what would certainly be an increasing clamor of American public opinion to withdraw from the Gulf, was awesome: US credibility as a superpower; the post-Cold War "new world order"; the security of US clients in the Gulf region—with their enormous oil resources—and elsewhere, in fact, everywhere in the world. And all this might occur at the time the US had emerged triumphant from a 45-year contest with the Soviet Union for global leadership, if not hegemony, with the latter defeated and no longer a superpower, except for its nuclear armory. In sum, basic US values were now perceived to be at much greater risk as a result of a calculated decision to escalate the Gulf Crisis.

For Iraq, Resolution 678 was even more of a turning point, despite the RCC's derisive comment noted above. When superimposed on the major increase in the US military buildup (8 November), it triggered a more acute sense of value threat, an awareness of time pressure for choice, and a sharply higher probability of war: the "realist" strand in Saddam Hussein's thinking could not have totally dismissed the finiteness of the 15 January deadline and the legitimacy accorded the use of force by the US-led Coalition after that date. And yet Iraq's President still "did not get the message." Only when war erupted was his skepticism swept aside, a theme to be explored later.

CRISIS MANAGEMENT

There was no change of actors in the second pre-war sub-phase of escalation. On one side was the United States-led Coalition of 28 states. On the other was Iraq, supported verbally by several Arab states, notably Jordan and Yemen, the PLO, and the "Arab street," mostly in Jordan, Israel's occupied West Bank and Gaza, and the far-off lands of the *Maghreb*—Algeria, Libya, Morocco and Tunisia.

The US-led Coalition remained intact to the end of the war on 28 February 1991 (and beyond, into deescalation). As in Pre-War I, the preeminence of the US was visible in every aspect of the UN-sanctioned effort to compel Iraq's withdrawal from Kuwait: political and diplomatic leadership — Bush and Baker; military leadership — Schwarzkopf and Powell; and size of armed forces in the Gulf region. It is true that, when war came in mid-January, several members of the Coalition were visible participants, notably the UK, France, Saudi Arabia and Egypt. Nonetheless, in terms of the Unified Model the Gulf Crisis remained a two-actor game — Iraq and the US — throughout the escalation phase. And the behavior of these actors was a continuation of roles played during Pre-War I. How they coped in Pre-War II will be noted briefly.

The military buildup continued unabated, an extension of the tit-for-tat strategy the two main adversaries pursued from the beginning of the Gulf Crisis. The result was that on the eve of the war two (seemingly) formidable military machines were in place. [See the section on *War* for salient details.]

The protagonists also persisted in the task of *coalition maintenance*. For the US, sustaining the polyglot coalition of 28 states was not easy. The UK, to be sure, continued to be a faithful friend and ally. China persisted in the role of passive, loyal maverick, trying to improve its post-"Tienamen Square" image in the West, notably the US, and at the same time to retain its posture as Third World protector against "imperialist" pressure. Most disappointing was the attitude of Germany and Japan — their contribution was solely financial.[35] Parenthetically, by their behavior in the Gulf Crisis, the two post-World War II pariahs demonstrated once more that economic power does not automatically translate into political or military power in world politics.

France and the USSR remained problematic members of the Coalition. Each was determined to protect its far-reaching economic, strategic and political interests in the Arab world by trying to enhance damage control before its client, Iraq, suffered catastrophic defeat. Herein lay the root of attempts at mediation by these two permanent members of the Security Council [see below]. Yet when war erupted on 17 January 1991 France was an active member of the Coalition, placing its forces under overall US command. And the USSR was not opposed to military intervention in Iraq.

The Arab members of the Coalition, notably Egypt and Syria, remained loyal throughout the escalation phase. On the Israel dimension of the Gulf Crisis, Egypt and the lesser Gulf states, too, were accommodating, assuring Bush and Baker that they would not leave the Coalition if Iraq attacked Israel, unprovoked, and Israel retaliated.

In that context, the results of Baker's whirlwind tour of European and Middle East allies from 8 to 13 January were summed up by a "senior Administration official," almost certainly the Secretary of State himself, with a pithy phrase: "no one has balked." Significantly, "France will fight if that is what it comes to." And all but Syria had agreed on the timing and necessity of force to expel Iraq from Kuwait after 15 January (Friedman, *NYT*, 14/1/91, A9). As an exercise in coalition maintenance it was a *tour de force*.

For Iraq, coalition maintenance was much less complex since its allies were confined to a few weak Arab states—Jordan, Yemen and the Sudan, along with the PLO and segments of the mass public. On the whole the attitude of pro-Iraq Arab League members was consistent, with a few modest shifts. In terms of rhetoric, Iraq's supporters, notably King Hussain, were loyal to the end. Pre-War II witnessed a broadening of pro-Iraq sentiment in the "Arab street," notably in the cities of the *Maghreb*.

Iraq's coalition-sustaining efforts were most successful in the declaratory domain: public opinion was mobilized to put pressure on governments, in the West as well as the Arab world. In deeds, by contrast, Iraq's attempt at coalition-maintenance was an utter failure. All peace proposals from its friends—Jordan, Yemen, Algeria, Iran, Cuba and the Non-Aligned Movement—before and after the outbreak of war included Iraq's withdrawal from Kuwait as a necessary component of a solution or a cease-fire, an unacceptable condition for Iraq. Secondly, notwithstanding the persistent call for, and offers of, volunteers to fight alongside the Iraqis, none participated in Gulf War II. Third, none of Iraq's friends provided troops or planes or ships to augment its military capability. Nor did any possess surplus financial resources, high technology, or vital foodstuffs to assist Saddam Hussein in his effort to overcome the worldwide embargo. Jordan was most helpful in breaking the blockade by transshipping supplies from its port of Aqaba across the desert to Baghdad; but it was far from sufficient. In short, unlike the success of US coping in the realm of coalition-maintenance, Iraq's efforts failed.[36]

As postulated in the Unified Model, the main adversaries also continued to engage in elaborate bargaining. It began one day after Resolution 678 was passed: on 30 November Bush, acting on Baker's recommendation, signalled his willingness "to go the extra mile for peace" by offering to invite Iraq's Foreign Minister to Washington "during the latter part of the week of Dec. 10" and to send his Secretary of State to Baghdad between 15 December and 15 January, "to discuss all aspects of the gulf crisis" "within the mandate of the United Nations resolutions" (*NYT*, 1/12/90, A6).

Iraq's RCC responded the next day, 1 December, with a qualified acceptance of "an idea whose purposes are not clear enough." It reaffirmed its willingness, "as always, to hold an in-depth serious dialogue ... instead of ... threats and warnings ... ," based upon Saddam Hussein's 12 August initiative and, pointedly, "linkage" between the Gulf conflict and the Palestinian problem (*FBIS–NESA*, 3/12/90).

Iraq made further conciliatory gestures on the hostage issue in order to influence the bargaining outcome. On 6 December came a dramatic message from Saddam Hussein to Iraq's National Assembly requesting the release of all hostages, "with our apologies for any harm done to any one of them" (*FBIS–NESA*, 6/12/90). Clearly the aim was to gain the high moral ground before the impending Bush/Aziz and Saddam Hussein/Baker meetings. Within days the 2000 Westerners, including 900 Americans, were flown home.

The Aziz/Baker meeting in Geneva on 9 January was the peak of the bargaining process in Pre-War II—and the only direct high-level exchange between Iraq and the US during the Gulf crisis-war. It was courteous but fruitless. Both sides restated their positions. And the outcome was total deadlock.

The Secretary of State told a news conference, resignedly:

"Regrettably, ... I heard nothing today that—in over six hours I heard nothing that suggested to me any Iraqi flexibility whatsoever on complying with the United Nations Security Council Resolutions. ...

There have been too many Iraqi miscalculations. ... the international response to the invasion of Kuwait. ... the response ... to the barbaric policy of holding thousands of foreign hostages. ... [and the belief that] it could divide the international community. ... So let us hope that Iraq does not miscalculate again. ...

[Then came a clear warning to Iraq.] If it should choose—and the choice is Iraq's—if it should choose to continue its brutal occupation of Kuwait, Iraq will be choosing a military confrontation which it cannot win, and which will have devastating consequences for Iraq.

.... The path of peace remains open ..." (*NYT*, 10/1/91, A14).

Iraq's Foreign Minister concurred with Baker's remark that it was "a serious meeting."

Further, "the tone of his [Baker's] language was diplomatic and polite. I reciprocated. But the substance was full of threats. And I told him, also in substance, that we will not yield to threats."

Aziz restated Iraq's insistence on "linkage" between Kuwait and the Palestinian question, the need for a comprehensive settlement of all Middle East disputes. And he called once more for an "Arab solution" (*NYT*, 10/1/91, A15).

The US President was frustrated and angry, especially because Iraq's Foreign Minister had refused to accept a letter from him to Saddam Hussein—according to Aziz "because the language of that letter was contrary to the traditions of correspondence between heads of state . . ." "The letter was not rude," said Bush. "The letter was direct. And the letter did exactly what I think is necessary at this stage."[37]

As so often, Bush bemoaned the fact that Saddam Hussein had still "not gotten the message". . . . (*NYT*, 10/1/91, A16).

In one respect Bush and Baker almost certainly were relieved by the outcome at Geneva. As the countdown to Deadline Day gathered strength, they increasingly feared a Saddam Hussein bargaining gambit that would pose a serious problem for US policy (Friedman, *NYT*, 18/12/90, A1, 8; 19/12/90, A16; and Apple, *NYT*, 19/12/90, A16).

Saddam Hussein had three options in coping with the impending deadline. One was *withdrawal*, whether total and unconditional, as demanded, or partial, and in either case, immediate or phased. Another was to *do nothing*, calculating that Bush and the Coalition were bluffing. And the third was *to wage war*, either defensive war or a strike against Saudi oil fields or Israel or both. Hints and rumors of a Saddam Hussein pre-emptive move in the form of withdrawal continued until the UN deadline, fed largely by officials and the media of Arab Coalition members, notably Egypt. However, despite the bargaining advantage that would accrue, Saddam Hussein made no move in that direction. Nor did he initiate war. Rather, he chose to do nothing.

A persuasive explanation of Iraq's behavior in the Gulf crisis-war was provided by Cigar (1992: 1, 4, 5, 10, 13, 14, 18, 20, 22):

". . . Iraq's basic strategic political and military mindset . . . had a predictable and decisive impact on the outcome of the crisis: first, by predisposing Baghdad to risk the possibility of going to war, and, second, by determining to a large extent how it prepared for and fought that war. Iraq's key strategic assumptions included an underestimation of US national will [because of the 'Vietnam Syndrome' and] the threat of heavy casualties . . . , an underestimation of the cohesion of the United Nations coalition. . . . (that the Arab states were a particularly weak link in the coalition), a misinterpretation of the USSR's role . . . (Baghdad clearly underestimated the magnitude of change in the USSR's foreign policy outlook under Gorbachev), and a misreading of the military balance and of the likely nature of war in the Gulf. . . . Iraqis were obsessed by calculations of pure numbers of men and equipment. . ., underestimated the significance of military technology . . . ., convinced that the advantage of recent combat experience from the Iran-Iraq War would weigh heavily in their favor . . . and grossly underestimated the contribution that air power could make in a conflict. . . .

Iraqi predictions were that it would do even better than Vietnam against the USA. . .

Iraq's interpretation of the Vietnam War and the Iran-Iraq War, in particular, were seminal in shaping its strategic outlook. . . ."

The cost of these miscalculations was very high.

The statements by Baker, Aziz and Bush immediately after the Geneva meeting serve as one of several indicators of the extent to which the Gulf Crisis, like many interstate crises, was *personalized*. From the beginning the two-actor game was, in essence, a two-person game, Bush versus Saddam Hussein, with Baker and Aziz in secondary roles. Mutual strident denunciations by the two Presidents were widespread in the onset and escalation phases, as noted—Hussein likened to Hitler, Bush portrayed as Satan, the enemy of God. Hussein's personal attacks on Bush increased as the Gulf Crisis progressed, and the crisis became increasingly a test of resolve.[38]

Saddam Hussein seemed oblivious to the many signals of Bush's determination to expel Iraqi forces from Kuwait, by force if necessary. His behavior was a classic case of miscalculation by one adversary of the other's resolve to take all measures necessary to achieve its objectives. That miscalculation, in turn, derived from cognitive dissonance, an inability to adapt his contrary expectations to the adversary's verbal threats and accompanying acts to initiate war. Baker's final attempt, at the Geneva meeting on 9 January, to impress upon Aziz the US resolve to go to war once the 15 January deadline passed, fell on deaf ears. Hussein seems to have persuaded himself that the "Vietnam syndrome" would paralyze US decision-makers and prevent war, leaving him with the spoils of conquest.

The Geneva deadlock terminated bilateral Iraq/US bargaining before the war. For the last week (9–16 January 1991), crisis management was dominated by the final Baker mission in pre-war coalition diplomacy, noted above, and multiple efforts at *mediation*, by the UN, the European Community (EC), several Arab states, France, and the USSR. Such intervention by third parties in an essentially two-actor crisis is anticipated in the Unified Model. And third party efforts to resolve the Gulf Crisis without war had the formal approval of the US. "I have said for months," Baker told the 9 January news conference at

Geneva, "we welcome any and all diplomatic efforts to solve this crisis peacefully."

At a meeting with Bush on 5 January the UN Secretary-General raised the idea of his going to Baghdad if the Aziz/Baker meeting proved fruitless. It was neither opposed nor encouraged. Perez de Cuellar met with Iraq's President on the evening of the 13th, to no avail. The next evening he told the Security Council that Saddam Hussein wanted a "package deal" that would solve the region's other problems as well, that is, "linkage." Further, Hussein had said that Iraq was "ready to sacrifice for the cause of peace" if others did so. And he added his belief that Iraq's President was not willing to withdraw from Kuwait unconditionally. The next day the Secretary-General sent Saddam Hussein a final personal appeal to "turn the course of events away from catastrophe." In his first public backing for the "package deal," he told Hussein: "I have every assurance . . . from the highest levels of government that, with the resolution of the present crisis, every effort will be made to address, in a comprehensive manner, the Arab-Israeli conflict, including the Palestinian question. I pledge my every effort to this end." The appeal and the offer of sequential "linkage" fell on deaf ears (Tyler, *NYT*, 14/1/91, A1, 9; P. Lewis, *NYT*, 16/1/91, A13, and "U.N. Secretary General Appeal," *NYT*, 16/1/91, A13).

The EC's foray into mediation had even less effect. After stating its "firm commitment" to "full and unconditional implementation of the relevant [UN] resolutions," it too offered sequential "linkage," but more generally than the Secretary-General's appeal 11 days later (*NYT*, 5/1/91, A5). Baker rejected the EC proposal on the 6th. Iraq did not even respond. As Belgium's Foreign Minister remarked, "Europe is an economic giant, a political dwarf and a military worm" (AP report, *Jerusalem Post*, 15/1/91).

The most serious last-minute attempt at mediation before the war was a six-point peace plan by France circulated on the evening of the 14th to the Security Council. It called for "a last appeal" by the Council to Iraq: to agree to withdraw before the deadline; to announce a timetable for its completion, and to begin "a rapid and massive" evacuation. The benefits for Iraq would be considerable: the dispatch of a UN peacekeeping force to verify the withdrawal and maintain order; a guarantee that Coalition forces would not attack the withdrawing Iraqi troops; negotiation of Iraq's disputes with Kuwait, and a Council commitment to make "an active contribution" to settling the Palestinian problem through an international conference "at the appropriate moment" (Riding, *NYT*, 16/1/91, A13).

The French plan was almost identical to an Algeria–Yemen–Libya six-point plan floated the same day (P. Lewis, *NYT*, 15/1/91, A12). Once more sequential "linkage" was being offered to Saddam Hussein. The US and the UK firmly opposed the clause on "linkage," on the grounds that it would reward aggression; and they accused France of concealing the plan from Washington and London until the last moment. It must be emphasized, however, that there was no substantive difference on "linkage" between France and the EC, on the one hand, and the US and the UK, on the other. All supported sequential, not direct, "linkage." France and the EC did so openly during the crisis.

The US, despite its persistent verbal rejection throughout the crisis, accepted it in words and deeds soon after the war, in the deescalation phase. This is evident in the high priority accorded to a renewal of the Arab/Israel peace process in Bush's "victory" speech to a joint session of the US Congress on 6 March:

> Our commitment to peace in the Middle East does not end with the liberation of Kuwait. . . . We must do all that we can to close the gap between Israel and the Arab states—and between Israelis and Palestinians. . . . The time has come to put an end to the Arab–Israel conflict (*NYT*, 7/3/91, A8).

And this was immediately followed by Baker's indefatigable mediation effort with Arab, Israeli and Palestinian leaders during the eight months following Gulf War II, designed to convene an Arab/Israel peace conference. The result was an open-ended series of bilateral and multilateral negotiations in Madrid, Washington, Moscow, and elsewhere from October 1991 onwards.

At the very last moment the other ambivalent major power in the Coalition tried to avert war. When Baker informed his Soviet counterpart early in the morning of 17 January (Moscow time) that Coalition forces would attack an hour later, Bessmertnykh, at Gorbachev's instruction, contacted Bush "to ask him not to go ahead with this military action and to allow for additional time to undertake a last decisive attempt to influence President Saddam Hussein." The Soviet President then tried but failed to reach Hussein, because of communications problems. Finally, after the war had begun, a message did get through via the Soviet embassy in Baghdad: "Unfortunately, we could not stop the military action. . . . We believe it absolutely vital that you announce urgently the beginning of the withdrawal of troops from Kuwait." Gorbachev also informed France, Germany, the UK, Italy, India, China and Arab states of the Soviet Union's final, failed effort and appealed to them "to take joint and parallel steps to localize the conflict and prevent it from spreading dangerously." It was too late (Whitney, *NYT*, 18/1/91, A13, and Reuters, in *Jerusalem Post*, 18/1/91).

What were the key *decisions* of the main adversaries in Pre-War II and their dates of implementation?

the US:
To offer high-level talks (Bush/Aziz and Saddam Hussein/Baker)—9 January;
To embark on full-scale war against Iraq—17 January.

Iraq:
To reject Resolution 678 and its deadline for withdrawal—30 November;
To accept Bush's offer of high-level talks—1 December, 4 January.

While the probability of war had become very high for Bush and his advisors from 29 November onward, they avoided an irrevocable decision until as late as possible. The Defense Secretary's reported view is instructive:

> Cheney didn't think the decision to go to war had occurred in a definite moment or sequence of moments. There was no single discussion or meeting where it had been made. As best he could piece it together, however, by Christmas Eve it was close; by December 29, when the warning order was sent [to Schwarzkopf to be fully prepared to attack on 17 January at 3.00 a.m. Gulf time], it was solidified; and at this New Year's Day meeting it was finally ratified (Woodward, 1991: 353–354).

Schwarzkopf's recollection about the timing of this decision did not differ in essentials.

"Washington was signalling us [on 11 December] to be ready to attack sooner rather than later" (1992: 393).

After meetings with Cheney and Powell in Riyadh, on 19–20 December, there was "no doubt in my mind that unless Saddam knuckled under, the President would order us to bomb the hell out of Iraq's military shortly after January 15" (395).

Powell reported on 25 December that "the President will probably launch the air campaign as soon as possible after 15 January. The prep time is almost over; we are nearly at war" (399–400).

On 30 December, "we were in a countdown to war" (401).

On 8 January, Powell "passed a verbal warning order to the CINC for launching the air campaign at 0300, 17 January 1991" (407).

Yet it was at the 1 January meeting—of Bush, Quayle, Baker, Cheney, Powell and Sununu—that the President, urged by his Secretary of State, made a final offer to Hussein, leading to the Geneva meeting of Baker and Aziz on the 9th. As a journalist with exceptional access to senior US national security decision-makers observed: ". . . since the start [of the Gulf Crisis there was a] commitment to reverse the Iraqi invasion while hoping that force, with all of its military and political uncertainties, would not be necessary" (Friedman, *NYT*, 18/1/91, A11). Schwarzkopf concurred: although he had "already passed on preliminary attack orders to my senior commanders [on the 9th] we'd still hoped for peace" (1992: 408).

The turning point regarding the necessity of force seems to have been the deadlock at Geneva on 9 January: "Before that meeting, while officials were growing increasingly pessimistic about the prospects of a peaceful Iraqi withdrawal, there was still a feeling that a last-minute 'surprise' from Baghdad was possible, even likely." When Baker phoned Bush to report no flexibility from Aziz, "the President and his advisers decided that war was inevitable" (Friedman, *NYT*, 18/1/91, A11). Schwarzkopf also cited the deadlock at Geneva as crucial: after watching the Baker-Aziz news conference, "I realized this was it: we were going to war" (1992: 408).

After insisting for months on the President's prerogative regarding a decision to wage war, Bush yielded to advice, notably from lawyers: on the 10th he sought a supporting resolution from the Congress. Three days of acrimonious debate culminated in a clear majority in the House of Representatives, 250–183 (164 Republicans and 86 Democrats), with a bare majority in the Senate, 52–47 (42 Republicans and 10 Democrats). It was widely interpreted as a "limited political victory"; but it was sufficient to accord US legislative legitimacy to the resort to force after 15 January. The resolution authorized the President "to use United States Armed Forces pursuant to United Nations Security Council Resolution 678" (Text and Apple, *NYT*, 13/1/91, A1, 11).

On 11 January Baker requested and received King Fahd's unqualified approval for war. He told the Saudi ruler that, although a formal decision had not been taken, war would begin within two or three days after the UN deadline expired. It was on the evening of the 13th that the timing of the attack was formally fixed for 03.00 on 17 January (Gulf time), giving Saddam Hussein a "day of grace" "to signal any intention to withdraw." On the morning of the 15th the President made a formal commitment to war, through a National Security Directive. It is noteworthy that the Directive was to be revoked if Iraq began to withdraw from Kuwait before the end of the 16th, another indicator that the decision was revocable as late as 16 January.

Powell notified Schwarzkopf at 23.30 on the 15th. Baker informed the Saudi and Israeli ambassadors of the decision on the morning of the 16th. Coalition leaders were notified by Bush and Baker that afternoon and, as noted, the Soviet Foreign Minister early in the morning on the 17th. That led to Gorbachev's frantic effort to stem the tide. It was too late, as it was to be again in February 1991 on the eve of the ground campaign (Friedman, *NYT*, 18/1/91, A11).[39]

War (17 January–28 February 1991)[40]

War came to Iraq at 02.40 on 17 January 1991 [Gulf time], five-and-a-half months after its conquest of Kuwait. In terms of the Unified Model, the launching of an air/naval campaign by the Coalition ushered in a new, more dangerous stage of crisis escalation. This view differs from the adage, "the outbreak of war means the end of a crisis," as noted in Chapter 1.

To repeat this novel view: war is one of several crisis management techniques: verbal, political, economic, non-violent military, and violent. War does not eliminate or replace crisis. Rather, crisis is accentuated by war. Both, as indicated in Figure 1.1 [Chap. 1], are also types of international conflict. They are distinct conceptually but are closely related. Not only do crises occur without war; they often precede war. And even when war and crisis erupt simultaneously, or when war occurs during a crisis, a crisis may persist after a war ends. Moreover, crisis is, conceptually, a broader phenomenon than war. *All wars, ipso facto, are interstate crises.* However, *not all crises involve war.*

The distinction between crisis and war and their interrelationship are clearly illustrated by the Gulf Crisis. In conceptual terms, both Iraq and the US attempted crisis management by various techniques: statements of resolve (verbal); coalition diplomacy (political); bargaining (political); mandatory global economic sanctions (economic); and a prolonged military buildup (non-violent military). Only when the decision-makers of the Coalition (really the US) concluded that all the non-violent techniques of crisis management had failed to achieve the primary goal, namely, the complete, unconditional withdrawal of Iraq's forces from Kuwait, did the Coalition resort to violence (war) as the ultimate crisis management technique. And in the last stage the Coalition reverted to the political technique, UN cease-fire resolutions, to "wind down the crisis."

Whether or not war was, in reality, the "last resort" is debatable—and remains controversial: the Coalition could have waited another six months or longer, as many prominent Americans and others in politics, the bureaucracy, the military services, academe and the media advocated, in the hope that economic sanctions would achieve the desired effect; but Coalition and US resolve might have crumbled in the process; and, in that situation, the military option would no longer have been viable.[41]

The link between crisis and war is also illuminated by a temporal overview of the Gulf Crisis. From mid-July 1990 to 16 January 1991 a crisis of global scope unfolded between Iraq and the US-led Coalition. There was no war between the main protagonists: there had, of course, been a six-hour war between Iraq and Kuwait on 2 August 1990. Disruptive interaction and perceptions of harm increased, albeit unevenly. At different times Iraq and the US perceived war as possible, likely, or highly probable. The key point is that a major interstate crisis persisted for half a year without war between the principal adversaries. When war erupted on 17 January 1991, the Gulf Crisis did not end. Rather, it moved to a higher level of escalation, with Iraq's perception of value threat undergoing a qualitative change, as indicated. That perception, along with its awareness of time pressure and consequent high stress, became even more acute when a ground campaign seemed imminent, in mid-February, leading to Iraq's first, qualified acceptance of UN Resolution 660 and the principle of withdrawal from Kuwait [see below]. So too did the US perception of harm: the anticipation of American casualties reached its peak in the last days of the air/naval war and the early hours of the ground campaign.

Finally, as will become evident in the analysis of the deescalation phase, the Gulf Crisis did not terminate with the end of Gulf War II on 28 February. Rather, the crisis continued during the negotiations leading to a temporary cease-fire and then a permanent cease-fire, from the beginning of March until early April. In fact, deescalation and the cessation of *interstate* violence between the main protagonists in the Gulf Crisis generated an upheaval of *intrastate* violence: in southern Iraq, the Shi'ite rebellion; in the North, the Kurdish rebellion; and their consequence—horrific suffering by two million refugees.

In sum, the Gulf Crisis of 1990–91 began without war between Iraq and the US-led Coalition. It continued half a year without violence between them. The coming of war accentuated the crisis. The end of the war left the crisis unresolved.

US objectives in the Gulf crisis-war changed over time. Throughout Pre-War I and II Bush and Baker had almost always spoken of three aims: Iraq's complete, unconditional withdrawal from Kuwait; restoration of Kuwait's legitimate government, and the freeing of all foreign hostages. The last was achieved early in the US's crisis period (6 December). The second was conspicuously absent from Baker's 2 December statement of goals, as well as from many other declarations by the President and the Secretary of State.

When war broke out only the first of these objectives was mentioned by Bush: "Our goal is not the conquest of Iraq. It is the liberation of Kuwait" (NYT, 17/1/91, A14). A month into the air/naval phase of Gulf War II Bush added a personal dimension, namely, the ouster of Saddam Hussein from power:

> . . . there's another way for the bloodshed to stop, and that is for the Iraqi military and the Iraqi people to take matters into their own hands, to force Saddam Hussein, the dictator, to step aside, and to comply with the United Nations resolutions, and then rejoin the family of peace-loving nations (NYT, 16/2/91, A5).

The widening of US war aims was not lost on Iraq or its internal opposition. Nor did it escape the attention of several Coalition members, notably France and the USSR, as well as the US Congress and media. There was dissent from within the Coalition before, during and after the ground campaign (24–28 February). And there was a feeling of betrayal on the part of the Kurds and the Shi'ites during the deescalation phase (March–April) [see below].

In contrast to US decision-makers, Iraq's leadership does not seem to have anticipated the coming of war until the bombs rained down on its cities and armed forces. It was the scope and intensity of the air and naval assault that generated a step-level change in Saddam Hussein's perception of value threat. There was no turning back to peaceful accommodation and conflict resolution. And the road ahead was fraught with the near-certainty of vast damage, if not disaster.

And yet, even during the air and naval campaign (17 January–23 February), Saddam Hussein's behavior suggests that he did not yet perceive the full gravity of the situation then confronting Iraq and himself. He seems not to have accepted the reality of the disaster until the 100-hour ground campaign. At that point he could no longer delude himself about Iraq's crushing defeat; and, as will become clear, he responded accordingly.

The trigger to Gulf War II was a massive aerial bombardment of many parts of Iraq and Kuwait. The air war, with a secondary role for the Coalition's naval flotillas in the Gulf and the Red Sea, was a relentless, daily assault on multiple Iraqi targets: infrastructure—roads, bridges, railways, airports, electric power systems, storage depots,

ammunition dumps, oil installations, etc.; the military-industrial complex that produced the basic (and some advanced) weapons for Iraq's
estimated one-million-man army; command and control centers; communications between Baghdad and the South; the main Scud missile-
launching sites; Iraq's nuclear reactor plants; its facilities for chemical
and biological weapons; the US Central Command estimate of 545,000
Iraqi troops, 4,300 tanks and 3,100 artillery pieces in Kuwait and
southern Iraq (Schwarzkopf 1992: 408); and, especially, the eight
Republican Guard Divisions, the core of Iraq's army—in fact, anything
that contributed to Iraq's capacity to sustain its presence in Kuwait and,
more generally, to wage war.

Although Iraq possessed almost 700 combat aircraft, including
approximately 200 first-line Soviet MIG-29 interceptors and long-range
Su-24 fighter-bombers, they were no match for the air power of the
Coalition, 1350 of the most advanced US aircraft, supplemented by
squadrons of British and French fighter-bombers. Indeed, the Coalition
established its air supremacy within hours. And early in the war most of
Iraq's surviving first-line planes flew to Iran for sanctuary.[42]

With unhindered control of the skies over Iraq, the Coalition air
campaign, running to 100,000 sorties during 38 days, bombed Iraq
"back into the Stone Age." There were very few lapses from the stringent policy of eschewing attacks on civilian targets. Notable was a
highly-publicized incident in which 400 Iraqi civilians were killed by
bombs which were directed to what Coalition spokesmen termed a
command-and-control center, and which Iraq identified as a bomb
shelter for civilians. For the rest, precision bombing was remarkably
accurate, leaving Iraq's urban population desolate, desperate and
depressed, with shortages of food and medicine, contaminated water,
no electricity, and widespread destruction—a veritable wasteland
(Schmitt and Gordon, NYT, 10/3/91, A1, 16); Schwarzkopf, 1992:
414-416, 421, 429-432.

Viewed in terms of the Unified Model, Gulf War II has three meanings. First, it was, as argued, a self-perceived "last resort" technique of
crisis management by the US, when all else had failed. Second, the
air/naval war and, later, the ground campaign, were dramatic escalation
points, in the escalation phase of the Gulf Crisis as a whole and in the
US and Iraq crisis period. Third, the act of war was the ultimate
Coalition bargaining gambit, a bid that Iraq had to match on the battlefield. In this perspective the entire war was an escalation sub-phase of
intense, continuous bargaining.

The Coalition tried to determine the "rules of the game" by calling for unconditional surrender. Accommodation was precluded. Iraq attempted to circumvent or change that unilateral "rule" by withstanding the air/naval assault and thereby delay the decisive ground campaign or even prevent its occurrence by making the likely cost for the Coalition prohibitive. This was the strategy pursued by Baghdad for four weeks into the war.

Finally, Iraq's leadership came to realize during the second week of February that the Coalition could not be swerved from its stated aim —the expulsion of Iraqi forces from Kuwait—by military means alone. At that point Saddam Hussein set in motion a complex process of diplomatic bargaining, to supplement the strategy of military bargaining and to undermine the cohesion of the Coalition. The new path was to dominate the last nine days of the air/naval war.

It began with an unexpected Iraqi bid for accommodation on 15 February 1991, in the form of a conditional offer to withdraw from Kuwait. First, the Revolutionary Command Council declared "Iraq's readiness to *deal with* Security Council resolution No. 660 of 1990, with the aim of reaching an honorable and acceptable political solution, *including withdrawal.*" Then came the crucial conditions: Iraq's pledge to withdraw "will be *linked* to the following": a total cease-fire; immediate abolition of all relevant Security Council resolutions other than 660; withdrawal of all Coalition forces from the Gulf region within a month; Israel's complete withdrawal from the West Bank, Gaza, East Jerusalem, the Golan Heights and South Lebanon; a guarantee of Iraq's "historical" rights; and the dispossession of the al-Sabah family. There were four other demands "linked" to the pledged withdrawal (*FBIS–NESA*, 15/2/91 [emphasis added]).

At first glance the RCC Statement seemed to be a turning point—the first time in more than six months that Iraq indicated a willingness to withdraw, albeit under certain conditions. Within hours the US President publicly rejected the offer as "a cruel hoax . . . full of unacceptable old conditions." The UK's Prime Minister and France's President were no less critical, the former terming it a "bogus sham," the latter, more like "the diplomacy of propaganda" than "a real wish" to adhere to UN resolutions. Critical, too, were the Foreign Ministers of the eight Arab members of the Coalition, then meeting in Cairo. Iraq's sympathizers—Jordan, the PLO, Libya and Iran—welcomed the offer as a ray of hope. More important was the USSR's positive but measured initial response: the RCC Statement was greeted "with satisfaction and hope . . . , an important beginning. . . . We hope that this announcement can become the starting point for peace, and will not be fruitless."[43] Much depended on Tariq Aziz, who was expected in Moscow on the 17th or 18th.

In rejecting Iraq's offer and reaffirming his rigid "rules of the game," Bush was engaging in hard bargaining: "no deal" meant no deviation from unconditional surrender as far as the occupation and annexation of Kuwait were concerned. Did it also mean total unwillingness to accommodate any of Iraq's demands? A definitive answer is not possible. However, from scattered remarks by Baker and Bush, one glimpses hints that a "deal" was possible on such matters as the negotiation of border disputes with Kuwait, Iraqi access to the Persian Gulf, and even on the substance, as distinct from the form, of "linkage" between the Gulf Crisis and the Arab/Israel conflict. But all these could be undertaken only after the Gulf Crisis was resolved.

What was the meaning of the term, "linked," in the RCC Statement? Were the ten points "linked" to Iraq's offer "conditions," as leaders of the Coalition argued, or merely "issues" to be considered by the UN and the parties to the conflict in the course of implementation, as some Iraqi officials and sympathizers asserted? This remains unclear; but the purpose of the ten points does not. The form of the RCC statement and its phraseology strongly suggest deliberate ambiguity by Iraq's leaders. In terms of crisis bargaining, it was a conscious bid to avert a destructive land war. And while it was rejected by the adversary—Baghdad could not possibly have expected otherwise—it inaugurated eight days of furious indirect bargaining through the good offices of the Soviet Union. In fact, the evidence strongly indicates that Moscow was the catalyst for Hussein's initiative. For one thing, the RCC Statement explicitly acknowledged the USSR's role. More important was the time sequence: the Soviet envoy, Primakov, held talks with Iraq's leaders on the evening of 12 February. Three days later came the RCC's conditional offer.[44]

Moscow's attempt to manage the Gulf crisis-war by diplomacy had begun several weeks before its role in the timing of the 15 February RCC Statement. It started with Foreign Minister Bessmertnykh's criticism of the continuing Coalition assault, on 26 January (Friedman, *NYT*, 28/1/91, A7). His Joint Statement with Baker on the 29th legitimized sequential "linkage": "both ministers agreed that . . . in the aftermath of the crisis in the Persian Gulf, mutual U.S.-Soviet efforts to promote Arab–Israeli peace and regional stability . . . will be greatly facilitated. . . ." (*NYT*, 31/1/91, A15). And then came Gorbachev's statement on 9 February, carefully crafted to satisfy many constituencies: a condemnation of Iraq's invasion; a reaffirmation of support for the UN resolutions on the crisis; a warning that "the logic of the military operations . . . [is] creating a threat of going beyond the mandate defined by" the Security Council's resolutions; and an appeal to Saddam Hussein to adopt "realism" and comply with the will of the international community (*NYT*, 10/2/91, A19, and Schmemann, *NYT*, 10/2/91, A1, 19).

Gorbachev's first public statement on the Gulf Crisis since the outbreak of war set the stage for two pairs of intense interrelated bargaining, one between Iraq and the Soviet Union, the other between the USSR and the US. The Primakov mission to Baghdad on 12–13 February was one episode in the first bargaining process. The statement by Iraq's Revolutionary Command Council on the 15th was another. The third was Aziz's missions to Moscow on 18 and 20 February.

Gorbachev cabled Bush on the 14th to report that Primakov discerned "some change in [Hussein's] attitude" regarding unconditional withdrawal from Kuwait. He also requested a delay in the ground campaign—"it might be desirable"—until his talks with Aziz were concluded. "This was not received with enthusiasm." At the same time, Bush was determined not to embarrass Gorbachev or weaken him at home (Friedman and Tyler, *NYT*, 3/3/91, A19). The two pairs of bargaining had now become intertwined, for Gorbachev realized that any Soviet-Iraqi agreement would be stillborn if the US did not approve the terms.

With Aziz's arrival in Moscow the pace of mediation quickened. There were, in fact, three variations of the Soviet terms for war termination, an initial package that was drastically revised twice in the light of emphatic American objections (Primakov, *Time*, 11/3/91; Rosenthal, *NYT*, 20/2/91, A1; P. Lewis, *NYT*, 21/2/91, A1, 13).

Saddam Hussein seemed to muddy the waters with a lengthy, defiant address to his people on 21 February, while Aziz was en route to Moscow with Iraq's reply to Gorbachev's first package. It was full of anger, fury and the determination not to yield (*FBIS–NESA*, 21/2/91). Notwithstanding this negative signal, Gorbachev and Aziz reached agreement in the early hours of the 22nd on a six-point plan—the second Soviet version. Iraq agreed to "full and unconditional withdrawal of its forces from Kuwait." The withdrawal was to begin "on the second day after the cessation of hostilities"; but no date for completion was specified. Economic sanctions would be lifted "after the withdrawal of two-thirds of all . . . Iraqi forces." All UN resolutions would lapse when the withdrawal was completed. All prisoners of war would be released "right after the cease-fire." And the withdrawal would be monitored by forces from non-combatant states responsible to the Security Council (*NYT*, 22/2/91, A6).

Gorbachev communicated the six-point plan to Bush by phone at once. The reaction was evasive and negative. "President Bush thanked President Gorbachev for his intensive and useful eforts, but raised *serious concerns* about several points in the plan" (*NYT*, 22/2/91, A7 [emphasis added]). Those "serious concerns" were clarified by Primakov, who was present at the Bush–Gorbachev telephone conversation: "the fate of the POWs"; "the colossal damage inflicted on Kuwait"; and "the period set for the troop withdrawal."

Tough Soviet–Iraqi bargaining ensued, with some success. All the POWs were to be released three days after the cease-fire went into effect. On the time frame for withdrawal: it was to begin one day after the cease-fire; while the Iraqis at first insisted on six weeks for completion, they settled for three weeks; and Kuwait City would be evacuated within four days. Iraq also made a concession on the lifting of economic sanctions: this was to take place when the withdrawal was completed, when all UN resolutions would cease to operate. There was no agreement on the issue of compensation to Kuwait, Aziz indicating that he had a "rigid mandate" on that point (Primakov, *Time*, 11/3/91, and *NYT*, 23/2/91, A5).

While the third and final version of the Soviet mediation effort was being considered by Iraq's leadership, the US abruptly preempted the bargaining. On Friday morning, 22 February, Bush's spokesman issued an ultimatum to Iraq:

> ". . . the United States . . . declares that a ground campaign will not be initiated against Iraqi forces if, prior to noon Saturday Feb. 23, New York time, Iraq publicly accepts the following terms, and authoritatively communicates that acceptance to the United Nations";

> to *"begin large-scale withdrawal* from Kuwait by noon New York time, Saturday, Feb. 23rd" (EST), that is, by 7.00 p.m. Gulf time;

> withdrawal, including from Bubiyan and Warba islands and "Kuwait's Rumaila oil field," was *to be completed within one week*;

> *Kuwait City* was to be *evacuated within the first 48 hours* of withdrawal; and

> *all POWs* were *to be released within 48 hours* of the beginning of the withdrawal.

> Iraq was also expected *to provide all data on the location of mines*, booby traps, etc., and *to end combat air fire*.

> As for UN *economic sanctions*, "only the Security Council can agree to lift sanctions . . ." and that would require a demonstration of "Iraq's peaceful intentions" (*NYT*, 23/2/91, A4 [emphasis added]).

At first glance, the differences between the Soviet-mediated terms and those of the US may not have seemed unbridgeable: a matter of days or weeks regarding the duration of withdrawal and release of POWs. However, the differences were more far-reaching, as the following point-by-point comparison reveals.

Soviet-Iraq Terms

Withdrawal   to begin one day after the cease-fire;
                to be completed in 21 days;
                evacuation of Kuwait City in four days;
                to be supervised by UN peace-keeping force.

POWs: to be released within three days of the cease-fire.

Economic   all UN resolutions other than 660 to be cancelled after
sanctions: Iraq's withdrawal was completed.

US Terms

Withdrawal: to begin by noon 23 February (EST); no mention of
                    cease-fire;
                to be completed in seven days;
                evacuation of Kuwait City in two days;
                to be supervised by US and Coalition forces.

POWs: to be released within two days.

Economic   to remain in force until Iraq complied with all UN
sanctions: resolutions;
                Security Council resolution required to end sanctions.

Others: al-Sabah Government to return to Kuwait.
                Iraq must assist in removal of mines and booby traps
                    from Kuwait.
                Iraq must end combat flights.
                Iraq must return thousands of Kuwaitis abducted to
                    Iraq.
                Iraq must safeguard Kuwaiti property and civilians.

The differences were real and not insignificant. In the USSR–Iraq package, withdrawal was linked to a prior cease-fire; for the US, withdrawal was to be unconditional, and a cease-fire would follow withdrawal. The difference on the duration of withdrawal was crucial: in 21 days Iraq could evacuate all of its heavy equipment—tanks, artillery, armored personnel carriers—and vast stockpiles of weapons, with which it could fight another day; a complete pullback in seven days would have meant leaving these valuable weapons and supplies in Kuwait and territory occupied by Coalition forces. Supervision of Iraq's withdrawal by a UN peacekeeping force was one thing; supervision by Coalition forces was another.

The difference on sanctions and all UN resolutions other than 660 was fundamental: Iraq and the USSR wanted them to become null and void the moment withdrawal ended; the US ultimatum retained sanctions as a lever against Iraq, and it insisted that Iraq comply with all Security Council demands, including reparations to Kuwait, nullification of Kuwait's annexation, etc. Finally, there were several "other" US terms, cited above, which were conspicuously absent in the USSR initiative.

Beyond the specifics was a more profound, unbridgeable gap in the underlying conception of terms to end the war. Iraq, assisted by the USSR, perceived the cessation of hostilities as an agreement between victorious and defeated armies, not a *diktat*. The US demanded unconditional surrender by the vanquished state, not unlike the "unconditional surrender" doctrine of Roosevelt, Churchill and Stalin, as implemented in 1945 against Germany and Japan.

There is strong evidence that Bush and his advisors produced a war termination package which they knew Iraq could not accept. For one thing, the terms were in the tradition of a "Carthaginian peace." For another, the timing of the ultimatum, as noted, indicates that the US bargaining gambit on 22 February was designed to abort the Soviet initiative, which seemed about to bear fruit.

Iraq's imminent acceptance of Moscow's third version would have confronted the US with a "no win" dilemma: to launch a land campaign when Iraq had made substantial concessions would have seemed to many a flagrant and unnecessary escalation of hostilities; not to do so would have had high political costs. An end to Gulf War II on Gorbachev's terms would have been a major Soviet triumph in the Third World generally and, especially, in the Arab world, restoring the USSR's influence and severely undermining the US claim to primacy in shaping the post-Cold War "new world order." Moreover, an end to the war on Soviet terms would have meant converting a certain military catastrophe for Iraq into a "face-saving" retreat: in fact, it would probably have been perceived as a diplomatic triumph by Saddam Hussein's two main constituencies, the Iraqi people and the "Arab street" generally, not unlike Nasser's political victory in the face of military defeat during the 1956 Suez War. And the consequences for Bush's presidency were certain to be negative. Finally, Bush and his advisors knew that a decision to launch a ground campaign had been made, effective 24 February at 4.00 a.m., Gulf time. For all these *realpolitik* reasons, the Soviet initiative had to be rejected. And so it was.

Iraq's leadership understood the bargaining ploy of its adversary and tried to avoid the necessity of choice between two forms of humiliation, yielding to a 24-hour *diktat* or suffering a crushing defeat. Thus, late on Friday, 22 February, the RCC communicated to Moscow its acceptance of the Soviet six-point plan for war termination (Primakov, *Time*, 11/3/91). Then at noon on Saturday, the 23rd, just before leaving Moscow for Baghdad, Iraq's Foreign Minister reiterated the RCC's approval—in English. "I am here to tell you that the Iraqi Government fully endorses this plan and fully supports it" (*NYT*, 24/2/91, A19). It was too little and too late.

As for Soviet behavior towards the US ultimatum, Gorbachev tried on the 22nd to persuade the US President that the two sets of terms were not far apart. Bush listened politely, thanked the Soviet President for his effort, but would not be moved. At the same time, Bush and his advisors were responsive, adopting a carefully-conceived posture to maintain US control of the process leading to the ground war, without undue political cost to Gorbachev. It indicated that the days of adversarial partnership (from the 1972 Brezhnev–Nixon Basic Principles Agreement to 1985) had long since passed. More important, the new era of competitive partnership between the US and the USSR, ushered in by Gorbachev's *glasnost* and *perestroika*, had withstood the severe test of the Gulf Crisis.

The process leading to the US rejection of Gorbachev's revised terms for war termination is not yet known. However, there is some insight into the concerns of the Bush Administration:

> "The initial feeling was that at the final moment of decision-making [fixing a date for the launching of the ground campaign] this old ghost from the past got up to haunt us," a senior Administration official said. "We were well aware of the wreckage potential. From the start, the President took the view that Gorbachev, for domestic reasons, obviously needed to be seen to be playing a role. We had to reject that role, but not dismiss it in a way that would embarrass him."

> "Essentially from Monday night [18 February] until noon on Saturday [the 23rd], President Bush and his advisers engaged in a dizzying series of phone calls and cables with Moscow to administer a mercy killing to the Soviet peace initiative. Each day Mr. Gorbachev would say he had brought the Iraqis a little closer to an unconditional withdrawal, and each day Mr. Bush would point out the conditional fine print that the Iraqis were adding—particularly their insistence right up to the end that once they withdrew all sanctions, reparations and other demands embodied in the United Nations resolutions would have to be dropped" (Friedman and Tyler, *NYT*, 3/3/91, A19).[45]

With that standoff the complex bargaining during the air/naval phase of Gulf War II reached its *dénouement*: Gorbachev could not extract any further concessions from Iraq; Saddam Hussein could not accept the humiliation of unconditional surrender; and Bush would not accept anything but visible and unqualified victory. Once more, the die was cast in favor of crisis management by war.

The trigger to the 100-hour ground campaign was a combined land, air and sea assault on Iraqi forces in Kuwait and southern Iraq early in the morning of 24 February. By then the concentration of power in the Gulf region was awesome, the result of a relentless *military buildup* since August 1990.

On the eve of the war's escalation the *US-led Coalition* comprised more than 700,000 troops. The largest contingent by far consisted of 527,000 American combat and support personnel, backed by approximately 1500 aircraft, including 1350 advanced fighters and bombers, 1700 helicopters, 2000 tanks, 1900 armored personnel carriers, a mighty naval flotilla of 91 warships, including six aircraft carriers and two battleships, and the most advanced technology in the annals of warfare. Supplementing the 410,000 US ground troops (Army and Marines) were those from Saudi Arabia (45,000), Egypt (38,500), the UK (32,000), Syria (19,000), and France (10,000), along with non-combatant forces from Pakistan (11,000), the emirates and sheikhdoms of the Gulf region (10,000), Bangladesh (2300), Morocco (1700), and Niger and Senegal (500 each). Many other states made symbolic contributions of ground forces or naval support, with some having a medical presence.

Entrenched in Kuwait and southern Iraq were more than half of *Iraq*'s armed forces: there were various estimates — 450,000, 545,000, 625,000. Whichever is correct, they included battle-hardened troops from the Iran/Iraq War (Gulf War I) (1980–88), among them 12 armored divisions, notably eight élite Republican Guard divisions. They were supported by 2595 tanks (of the 4250 tanks on the eve of the air/naval campaign), including 500 T-72s, the most advanced in the Soviet armory, 1945 armored personnel carriers (of the 2870) and 1625 artillery pieces, the remnant of 3110 on 16 January. Iraq also had accumulated Scud-B missiles in large numbers and, probably, chemical weapons.[46]

In numerical terms the military balance favored Iraq, according to the commander of Coalition forces. They were outnumbered by a ratio of 3 to 2; and, for combat troops, the gap was 2 to 1. Moreover, Iraq had many more tanks when Gulf War II began in mid-January — 4700 to

3500. (*NYT*, 28/2/91, A8) After the war, these figures were seriously challenged. A British correspondent (Simpson, 1991) estimated Iraq's forces in early January as 260,000, compared to 525,000 for the Coalition, and by the beginning of the ground campaign, "possibly even lower than 200,000"; that is, a ratio of 2.5:1 in favor of the Coalition. More damaging to the image of a "brilliant victory" was a bipartisan assessment by the US House of Representatives Armed Services Committee that Iraqi forces arrayed against the Coalition the day the land war began totalled 183,000.[47]

Like Schwarzkopf on several occasions, Simpson noted: "US military intelligence . . . was one of the main failures of the entire campaign. It wasn't only the quantity but the quality of the Iraqi army which was inflated" (332–333). The Pentagon's official version of the Gulf War in 1992 concurred: the US intelligence community, it acknowledged, was "not prepared to cope with the volume of intelligence requirements to support the large-scale" military operations; the Department of Defense's intelligence units produced "a very high level of duplicative, even contradictory" intelligence; and the CIA's national intelligence estimates "proved of limited value" to the military. (As quoted in Cushman, *NYT*, 11/4/92, A4.)

The balance of power, incorporating the level of technology in the armed forces of the adversaries, was clearly in favor of the US-led Coalition, even though Iraq appeared to have the compensating advantages of familiarity with desert warfare, years of exposure to battle conditions, and war close to home. Overall, the array of military might in a minuscule theater of operations—Kuwait, southern Iraq and the northern Gulf—was the greatest since the concentrations of Allied and German forces in Western Europe in 1944–45, and Soviet and Axis forces in Eastern Europe in the last 18 months of World War II.

Gulf War II was an uneven contest between the Coalition's post-modern technology and a large, well-equipped Third World army that had survived an eight-year war of attrition against another Third World army. The gap was compounded by the difference between the Coalition's strategy of dynamic offense, and Iraq's strategy of static defense reminiscent of France's Maginot Line in 1939–40. The result in both cases was disaster for the defender (Freedman and Karsh, 1991).

In four days Saddam Hussein's forces in southern Iraq and Kuwait were mauled by Schwarzkopf's flanking maneuver;[48] but the "extraordinary effectiveness" of superior air power, high-tech weapons, and the quality of the US's all-volunteer military force were credited with the

Coalition victory (Pentagon report, April 1992). Iraq's losses of major weapons were estimated as horrendous.[49] And its human costs were initially assessed as staggering: 100,000–120,000 soldiers killed, 300,000 wounded, and 74,000–101,000 civilians dead, compared to 2000–5000 Kuwaitis and 343 killed for all Coalition armies.[50] In that respect, among others, the ground campaign of Gulf War II resembled another Middle East test of arms, namely, Israel's victory over Egypt, Syria and Jordan in the Six Day War of June 1967.[51]

Several early reports on the damage caused to Iraq by Gulf War II agreed that it was enormous: "near-apocalyptic results . . . ," according to a UN study (P. Lewis, *NYT*, 22/3/91, A1, 9); a staggering cost in human life, according to the Greenpeace environmental group, as noted; a CIA estimated cost of "$30 billion to restore Iraq's economy, superimposed upon $80 billions in debt, $8 billion in interest for 1991, and huge war reparations arising from Gulf War II (Tyler, *NYT*, 3/6/91, A1, 8).

Eighteen months after the war, however, Baghdad reportedly had made great strides in material reconstruction: its telephone service had been restored; 120 of 134 bridges were functioning; and the electrical grid had been largely repaired. (P. Lewis, *NYT*, 14/7/92, A1, 6). Moreover, a large part of its oil industry seems to have been re-habilitated, with a daily production of 800,000 barrels, a capability of exporting 1.3–1.6 million barrels a day, a refining capacity to meet all domestic gasoline and heating needs, and partial repairs to pipelines and pumping stations. (Petroleum Intelligence Weekly, reported by Ibrahim [*NYT*, 27/7/92, A7]).

For Kuwait, the damage centered on the burning of many of its oil wells by Iraqi forces (650) and disruption of 749 wells, an estimated cost of $5–10 billion "outside the oil sector" and $10–20 billion to revive the oil industry, with a return to the pre-Gulf War II economic level considered likely in 2–5 years; but, unlike Iraq, Kuwait had about $80 billion in financial assets abroad (Ibrahim, *NYT*, 18/3/91, A1, 9). By early November 1991, long before expected, all burning oil wells had been extinguished and capped; and the official Kuwaiti estimate of the value of lost oil was $12 billion (Wald, *NYT*, 7/11/91, A3).

Perhaps the gravest damage was the displacement of an estimated 5 million people in the Gulf region. There were three waves of refugees—before, during and after the war.[52] Indeed, the 1990–91 exodus from the Gulf was one of the great human upheavals of the century, the largest displacement since the migration of (an estimated 15 million) Hindus and Sikhs from Pakistan to India, and Muslims in the reverse direction in the summer of 1947, accompanying the partition of the sub-continent.

The Gulf War of 1991 was reported in enormous detail in the press and on TV and radio. No doubt, the strategy and tactics of the ground campaign and their implementation will be taught at military academies around the world for decades to come, though not all regarded it as a brilliant victory. Draper (1992b, 42), relying on military accounts and Schwarzkopf himself, was disparaging: ". . . the Iraqi army put up almost no defense at all. The war took the form of forty-two days of allied air bombardment and one hundred hours of ground attack. The sides were so mismatched that it was hardly a war at all." The Coalition's military commander had confirmed this just before the war's end: on the first afternoon of the ground war, ". . . there was nobody between us and Baghdad. If it had been our intention . . . to overrun the country, we could have done it unopposed for all intents and purposes from this position at that time. . . . [w]e certainly did not expect it to go this way" (NYT, 28/2/91, A8). And, on 27 March he told Frost: "They chose not to stand and fight."

For the study of interstate crisis, the war's importance lies elsewhere: the context in which it occurred, especially the bargaining process preceding its eruption, which has been analyzed in depth; the effectiveness of violence as a crisis management technique, which has been noted above; and its outcome of decisive military victory, including the occupation for several months of approximately 15% of Iraq's territory.

Gulf War II ended abruptly. War termination took the initial form of a US-declared unilateral "suspension of offensive combat operations" by Coalition forces effective at midnight EST on 27 February, i.e., at 08.00 on the 28th, Gulf time. In making the announcement, a jubilant US President declared: "Kuwait is liberated. Iraq's army is defeated. Our military objectives are met. Kuwait is once more in the hands of Kuwaitis in control of their own destiny."

Bush also specified several conditions for a formal cease-fire: the immediate release of all Coalition prisoners of war, third-country nationals, the remains of all who had fallen, and all Kuwaiti detainees; information about the location and nature of all land and sea mines; full compliance with all relevant Security Council resolutions; and the designation of military commanders to meet with Coalition commanders within 48 hours "to arrange for military aspects of the cease-fire" (NYT, 28/2/91, A12).

In terms of the Unified Model, the US's crisis period terminated that day: stress for American decision-makers declined sharply, as their perceptions of threat, time pressure and war likelihood (the resumption of war, in that context) moved towards their non-crisis norm. Iraq's leaders retained high stress until a permanent cease-fire, formally approved by the Security Council, went into effect on 12 April. However, their stress level declined after the guns fell silent on 28 February. Thus the interim cease-fire that day marks the change from crisis period to end-crisis period for Iraq as well. The informal cease-fire and the *de facto* cessation of hostilities between Iraq and the Coalition on 28 February also meant a sharp reduction in disruptive interaction. As such, they also mark the end of the escalation phase of the Gulf Crisis.

What were the key *decisions* made by the two main protagonists during the war sub-phase of escalation—and their date of implementation?

the US:
> *To set the day and time of the ground campaign—0400, 24 February (Gulf time)—11 February;*
> To reject Iraq's 15 February offer of conditional withdrawal—15 February;
> *To reject Gorbachev's terms for war termination—22 February;*
> *To issue an ultimatum to Iraq—22 February;*
> *To declare a unilateral cease-fire—27 February.*

Iraq
> To offer a conditional withdrawal from Kuwait—15 February;
> To accept the Soviet six-point plan—22 February;
> To reject the Bush ultimatum—23 February;
> To accept, in principle, all UN resolutions relating to the Gulf Crisis—27–28 February;
> To accept Resolution 686—3 March;
> To accept the formal cease-fire resolution (Res. 688)—6 April.

The *decision-making process* in Iraq during Gulf War II remains shrouded in mystery. As in the onset phase and pre-war sub-phases of escalation, however, it can be surmised that the ultimate decision-maker was Saddam Hussein. But he did not decide alone. As indicated earlier, the Revolutionary Command Council served as the *decisional forum*, at least in form, and the members of its inner circle merit designation as decision-makers: Izzat Ibrahim, Deputy Chairman of the RCC; Taha Yassin Ramadan, First Deputy Prime Minister and Head of the *Ba'ath* Party militia; Sa'adun Hamadi, Deputy Prime Minister, and Foreign Minister Tariq Aziz.

The US decision-making process, too, remained essentially unchanged in the escalation phase. So too did the core group in the informal decisional forum: Bush, Baker, Cheney, Scowcroft and Gates, Powell and Schwarzkopf, and Quayle. One substantial change was reported to have occurred during the war, namely, the emergence of Scowcroft and Gates as the White House rival to Baker and the State Department for primacy in the making of high policy (Rosenthal, *NYT*, 21/2/91, A14).

The decision *to fix the day and time for the ground campaign* was straightforward. On 5 February Bush sent Cheney and Powell to Saudi Arabia, to meet with Schwarzkopf and to assess the need.

> On Monday night Feb. 11 Mr. Cheney visited the White House to tell the President that General Schwarzkopf had asked for a "window" of dates to begin the ground war, with the earliest date being Feb. 21.
>
> The President agreed that would be the planning date. Within a day or two, General Schwarzkopf refined his H-hour as 4 a.m. on Feb. 24 (8 p.m. Feb. 23 EST) (Friedman and Tyler, *NYT*, 3/3/91, A19).

Schwarzkopf confirmed this decision process in his memoirs (1992: 434–435). Responding to Cheney's request for a recommendation, in Riyadh on 8 February, he declared:

> "I think we should go with the ground attack now. We'll never be more ready . . . the optimum time has always been the middle of February."
> As for the precise day: "The twenty-first. But I'll need three or four days of latitude because we've got to have clear weather to kick off the campaign."
> Cheney replied: "I'll take those dates to the President."
> On the 12th Powell informed him that Bush had accepted his dates.
> "You can go anytime after twenty-one February. It'll be your call."

It was this decision and the ensuing countdown that shaped Bush's behavior toward the Gorbachev mediation effort in mid-February and, especially, the US decision to issue an ultimatum on the 23rd. The ground campaign, in short, became irrevocable on 11 February.

As the events unfolded, however, it was not entirely the Coalition commander's "call." "The tension really started to build late Monday, February 18. First, Powell called. 'The National Security Council is saying we may need to attack a little early. Can you let me know by tomorrow if you can manage it.' During the next 24 hours there were four more calls from Powell, with Cheney participating in one of them. Cheney had been one of the fiercest cold warriors while in Congress, and I could sense that Moscow's intervention was not making him happy." The Coalition commander explained that Saddam Hussein would never negotiate directly.

Recalling the 20th of February, Schwarzkopf exploded:

"The increasing pressure to launch the ground war early was making me crazy. I could guess what was going on and figured Cheney and Powell were caught in the middle. There had to be a contingent of hawks in Washington who did not want to stop until we'd punished Saddam. . . . These were guys who had seen John Wayne in *The Green Berets*, they'd seen *Rambo*. . . . Of course, none of them was going to get shot at. . . ."

Then came a tense exchange with Powell late on the 20th. The Chairman of the JCS admitted:

"You don't appreciate the pressure I'm under. I've got a whole bunch of people here looking at this Russian proposal and they're all upset. My President wants to get on with this thing. My Secretary wants to get on with it. We need to get on with this.
Schwarzkopf responded no less bluntly: "I'm under pressure too. My commanders are telling me to wait . . . But you are pressuring me to put aside my military judgment for political expediency. I've felt this way for a long time. Sometimes I feel like I'm in a vise—like my head is being squeezed in a vise. Maybe I'm losing it. . . ."

The two generals calmed down and agreed that it was important to continue to work together. The weather changed; and Schwarzkopf informed Powell: "Tell everybody the twenty-fourth is a go." (Schwarzkopf, 1992: 441–444).

The decision process leading to *Bush's ultimatum* on 22 February was reported as follows:

The turning point came Thursday night [21 February], when the President, having concluded that the Soviet diplomacy was getting out of hand, decided he wanted to put out a statement with his own terms for an Iraqi withdrawal in compliance with "all" the United Nations resolutions. During the White House deliberations, General Powell suggested to the President, "Why not just set a deadline?" on Friday for noon Saturday because a date would be "helpful" for his forces who were poised to attack at the already appointed hour of 8.00 p.m. eastern time on Saturday (Friedman and Tyler, *NYT*, 3/3/91, A19).

The reason for the preemptive act was, then, a sense of loss of control: the USSR and Iraq were now setting the agenda for war termination, despite Iraq's grave military weakness, a situation that was unpalatable to the victor.

Why and when Bush decided *to terminate hostilities through a unilateral cease-fire* remain unclear. The 1992 three-volume Pentagon report was conspicuously silent about this decision and how it was reached. By contrast, Les Aspin, Chairman of the House Armed Services Committee, blamed the decision on an intelligence failure, namely, the incorrect assessment of the damage inflicted on Iraq's forces, especially the Republican Guard (Schmitt, *NYT*, 24/4/92, A6). According to Schwarzkopf, Powell phoned him in the late afternoon of 27 February to say: "We ought to be talking about a cease-fire. The doves are starting to complain about all the damage you're doing." The White House was becoming concerned: "The reports make it look like wanton killing." The Coalition commander responded: " . . . in one more day we will be done. . . the 'Five-Day War'."

Powell phoned again at 22.30: "I'm at the White House. We've been batting around your idea about ending the war in five days." Further, Bush was thinking about announcing a unilateral cease-fire at 9.00 pm EST, that is, six and a half hours later. "Would you have any problem with that?"

> "He waited as I took a minute to think. My gut reaction was that a quick cease-fire would save lives. . . What was more, we'd accomplished our mission. . . . Of course . . . I'd have been happy to keep on destroying the Iraq military for the next six months. Yet . . . we'd won decisively and . . . with very few casualties. Why not end it? Why get somebody else killed tomorrow? That made up my mind.
> 'I don't have any problem with it', I finally answered. 'Our objective was the destruction of the enemy forces, and for all intents and purposes we've accomplished that objective'." Powell phoned again a few hours later to confirm the impending cease-fire to take effect at midnight EST. "'That makes it a hundred-hour war', he added." Schwarzkopf observed wryly: "I had to hand it to them: they really knew how to package an historic event" (1992: 468–470).

Eighteen months earlier, however, soon after the end of Gulf War II, Schwarzkopf stirred a controversy by clearly implying his dissent from the abrupt termination of the war after four days. Using a celebrated analogy from antiquity. Hannibal's victory over the Romans in an historic battle in 216 BC, he declared in a TV interview on 27 March 1991:

> ". . . it was literally about to become the battle of Cannae, a battle of annihilation. Frankly, my recommendation had been, you know, continue the march. I mean **we had them in a rout and we could have continued to . . . reap great destruction upon them.** We could have completely closed the door and made it in fact a battle of annihilation. And the President, you know, made the decision that . . . we should stop at a given time, at a given place that did leave some escape routes. . . I think it was a very humane . . . and a very courageous decision on his part. . . Because it's one . . . of those ones [decisions] that historians are going to second-guess . . . forever."
> Finally, "had the war gone on for another 24 hours, we could have inflicted terrible damage on them with air attacks . . . on the far side of the river."

After being publicly rebuked by an irritated President and the Defense Secretary, the General gracefully apologized.

One reason for the abrupt termination was almost certainly "advice" or pressure from the US's Arab allies, notably Egypt and Saudi Arabia. Their leaders may have feared the backlash in the "Arab street" generally, including public opinion in their own states, if they were seen to be supporting the total destruction of Iraqi forces and, possibly, the dismemberment of a Sunni-ruled Arab state, rather than merely severe defeat in the four-day ground campaign. Further, such punitive behavior towards Iraq in 1991 could become a dangerous precedent for future interventions in the Arab world by non-Arab powers.

The influence of the "Arabists" in the US national security bureaucracy probably reinforced this "advice" from US allies in the Arab world. Their conventional wisdom dictated the maintenance of the "balance of power" in the Gulf region: the "annihilation" of Iraqi forces and the overthrow of Saddam Hussein might have led to the disintegration of Iraq, leaving fundamentalist Iran the dominant power in the Gulf region, with Saudi Arabia and other oil-rich Arab states in the area at its mercy. They may also have argued that Iraq's military defeat was a sufficient precedent to discourage future Iranian adventurism in the Gulf region.

The US calculus probably included other anticipated costs of ousting Saddam Hussein from power: occupation of an Arab capital by Western forces, since Egypt and Syria were unwilling to do so; the prospect of intense fighting, since Iraq's leader had deployed his élite Republican Guard divisions around Baghdad; the problem of a 'quisling' government installed by the Coalition; and the likely sundering of the Coalition, for the Soviet Union and, probably, France would have withdrawn if Coalition forces had occupied Iraq's capital.

One thing is certain: the decision was made in great haste. Whether or not it was wise was vigorously debated in the weeks and months that followed. For many skeptics, including the author, Draper's comment (1992b: 45) is apt: "The decision to permit an Arab Hitler, as President Bush had called Saddam, to remain in power was political abdication and failure of nerve.... It is a perverse, paradoxical outcome for a 'glorious victory'."

Hoffmann (1992) was somewhat more generous. "What makes George Bush's war look good is not only the success it achieved, but also the shakiness of several of the criticisms aimed at it"(55). These comprised the two alternatives to war: sanctions, notably, "punitive containment" of Iraq, advocated by Tucker and Hendrickson (1992: Chaps. 7,8); and negotiation, for in Hoffmann's view, Saddam Hussein was not amenable to a deal. Nor did Hoffmann share Smith's (1992) criticism of

Bush's "policy of minimum candor"; rather, as a Realist, deception was justified by a worthy goal. Hoffmann was more sympathetic to the argument that excessive force was used. Moreover, the Gulf War was, like WWII, an unnecessary war. But in the end, he agreed with Draper and others: given Bush's Saddam Hussein–Hitler analogy, "the only appropriate outcome would have been his fall"(57).

In "Afterthoughts" on the war, the commander of the Coalition forces cited four factors in response to the persistent criticism: "*Why didn't we go all the way to Baghdad and 'finish the job'?*"

> "We had no authority to invade Iraq for the purpose of capturing the entire country or its capital. . .
> . . . the coalition . . . would have fractured . . . Even the French would have withdrawn. . .
> . . . we would have been considered occupying powers . . . responsible for all the costs of maintaining or restoring government, education and other services . . . like the dinosaur in the tar pit, . . . a burden the beleaguered American taxpayer would not have been happy to take on. . . [and]
> . . . . every citizen of the Arab world today would be convinced that what Saddam said was true [namely, that the] western colonialist nations [were] embarking as lackeys of the Israelis in the destruction of the only Arab nation willing to destroy the state of Israel. . . "
> . . . For once we were strategically smart enough to win the war *and* the peace" (Schwarzkopf, 1992: 497–498).

On the related question, "Since Saddam is still alive and in control in Iraq, wasn't the whole war fought for nothing?", he posed the alternative:

> "First, he would now control all of the oil from Kuwait and perhaps from the Arabian peninsula. . .
> . . . the rest of the gulf nations . . . would have been intimidated. . .
> Worse yet . . . his greatly increased oil revenues would have gone to the strenghening of his already strong . . . military force and the expansion of his developing nuclear and biological and existing chemical arsenals . . . [with grave implications for] the future of Israel and the course of world peace. . .
> . . . Instead, a defanged Saddam has been forced to retreat behind his own borders. His nuclear, biological and chemical military capabilities have been destroyed. . . .
> . . . Saddam's military forces . . . are no longer a threat to any other nation . . .
> . . . Saddam's irrational, militant voice is no longer relevant in Arab politics. . .
> . . . the Middle East peace process is moving forward. . .
> . . . and our hostages have been freed.
> Do I think it was worth it? You bet I do" (1992: 499).

Which of Schwarzkopf's versions correctly reflects his view on the abrupt cease-fire *at the time it was decided* remains unknown. However, there can be no doubt that the initiative for this crucial and highly-controversial decision emanated from Washington. Until the documents become available, one can only speculate about the pressures and motives.

Before turning to the winding-down of the Gulf Crisis the escalation phase will be summarized in terms of the concepts and categories of the Unified Model. In general, as the Model postulates, escalation was far more complex than onset. It was, first, of much longer duration, seven months compared to two weeks. There were, as noted, three distinct sub-phases: *Pre-War I*, from Iraq's invasion of Kuwait (2 August 1990) to the eve of Resolution 678 (28 November); *Pre-War II*, from the Security Council's deadline and authorization of force resolution (29 November) to the eve of Gulf War II (16 January 1991); and *War* (17 January–28 February). The number of crisis actors, too, increased enormously, from one to 14: Kuwait, Iraq, Saudi Arabia, the four lesser emirates and sheikhdoms of the Gulf Cooperation Council, the US, the UK, France, Egypt, Syria and the USSR, and Israel. There were also many more involved actors: the other 16 members of the Coalition, and Iraq's politically active sympathizers—Jordan, Yemen, Algeria, and Iran. A third difference relates to the catalyst. The trigger to escalation in the Gulf Crisis was direct violence, compared to a verbal threat in the onset phase. In terms of the sub-phases, there were two violent triggering acts—Iraq's invasion of Kuwait (Pre-War I) and the Coalition's air/naval attack on Iraq (War)—and a political act, namely, UN Resolution 678. Each of these led to more disruptive interaction between the two main protagonists, Iraq and the US, with each sub-phase exhibiting more intense escalation than its predecessor.

Both Iraq and the US employed multiple techniques of crisis management in the escalation phase. One was non-violent military behavior, in the form of sharp increases in the military buildup. Another was bargaining, with clear signals of resolve to defend vital interests —the annexation of Kuwait, for Iraq, and for the US, the expulsion of Iraqi forces from Kuwait. This took the form of frequent speeches by Bush and Hussein, including harsh personal attacks; a dozen US-initiated Security Council resolutions before the war, and two "Carthaginian"-type cease-fire resolutions. This verbal and political bargaining supplemented the military strand of bargaining noted above.

Another technique of crisis management was coalition-building and, later, coalition-maintenance. The US forged and sustained an alliance of 28 states. Its successful search for global legitimacy, in the form of overwhelming support by the UN Security Council for Coalition demands, reinforced the cohesion of the US-led Coalition. Iraq tried to mobilize active support but succeeded in eliciting only expressions of sympathy. Ultimately it stood alone when the Coalition's military assault began. Viewed in these purely *technical* terms, US management of the

Gulf Crisis was highly effective; Iraq's was not. Substantively, Bush's crisis management was inept and, ultimately, failed. This can be traced to two crucial decisions late in the Gulf Crisis, one positive, the other negative: termination of the war, abruptly and prematurely, before some basic US goals were achieved; and aloofness from the Kurd-Shi'ite tragedy in March and early April 1991.[53]

The Unified Model does not postulate a specific number of decisions per phase. In the escalation phase, both Iraq and the US made many decisions of consequence. To recall the most important: in *Pre-War I*, Iraq's decisions to annex Kuwait, to terminate Gulf War I by making important concessions to Iran, and to take thousands of foreigners hostage; and US decisions to defend Saudi Arabia, to liberate Kuwait, to launch a war against Iraq in mid-January if necessary, to double its military presence in Saudi Arabia, and to seek UN authorization for war; in *Pre-War II*, Iraq's decisions to reject Resolution 678, to negotiate with the US at Foreign Minister level, and to reject all UN, EC, Arab, French and Soviet mediation efforts; and US decisions to initiate direct talks with Iraq, to reject all proposals for "linkage" between the Gulf Crisis and the Arab/Israel conflict, and to launch an air/naval campaign almost immediately after the UN deadline; and during the *War*, Iraq's decisions to offer conditional withdrawal from Kuwait, and to accept the Soviet six-point plan to prevent a ground campaign; and US decisions to reject the Soviet terms for war termination, to launch a land campaign on 24 February, and to terminate the war four days later.

Phase-change, it will be recalled from the Unified Model, is step-level in character, that is, a "quantum leap," not an incremental change that occurs as a consequence of most decisions; these are escalation points. Thus, as long as an act, event or environmental change produces incremental change in perceptions of harm and the intensity of disruptive interaction, the actors continue to behave within the "rules" of the crisis period, and the international crisis persists within the "rules" of the escalation phase. Only when a step-level change is triggered by an act, event or environmental change, does period-change or phase change take place.

Applying these "rules" to the escalation phase of the Gulf Crisis, most of the key decisions cited above intensified disruptive interactions between Iraq and the US and the target's perceptions of harm. In terms of the Unified Model, they contributed incrementally to escalation of an international crisis (system/interactor level of analysis) and of a foreign policy crisis (actor level of analysis). However, only the last US decision —war termination—generated phase change, from escalation to deescalation. Period change within the escalation phase was triggered by earlier decisions—from pre-crisis to crisis for the US, its 30 October decision to launch a military attack, and for Iraq, the UN's authorization of force, along with a deadline for Baghdad's withdrawal from Kuwait.

In short, the initiation of war—by Iraq against Kuwait—catalyzed the change from onset to escalation phase, from pre-crisis to crisis period for Kuwait, and from non-crisis to pre-crisis for the US and Iraq. So too, the termination of war—by the Coalition against Iraq—served as the step-level change from escalation to deescalation and, for all crisis actors, from crisis to end-crisis period.

Deescalation

The winding-down of an interstate crisis, as specified in the Unified Model, is characterized by a decline in one or more of the perceptual indicators of crisis and in the intensity of disruptive interaction between the adversaries. Both, as noted, began to be evident in the Gulf Crisis on 28 February 1991. In the next few days this process gathered momentum.

The terms set out in Bush's unilateral proclamation were codified in an interim cease-fire resolution approved by the Security Council on 2 March. **Resolution 686** took note of "the suspension of offensive combat operations," affirmed that the 12 previous Security Council resolutions "continue to have full force and effect," and listed the demands specified by Bush when he suspended military operations, as noted above: these had to be met by Iraq before a "definitive end to the hostilities." Finally, Iraq was reminded that the provision of Resolution 678 (29 November 1990) authorizing the use of force ("all necessary means") would continue to be valid "during the period required for Iraq to comply with" all these demands (S/RES/686 [1991] and P. Lewis, *NYT*, 3/3/91, A16).

The harsh terms imposed by the victor were in accord with the conditions of peace laid down in most interstate wars over the centuries. Iraq had no alternative but to yield, for its armed forces had been decimated, its cities lay in ruins, and its people were suffering from all of the ills of modern war. Thus, on 27–28 February, Iraq agreed to comply with the 12 UN resolutions and to heed the call for a meeting of military commanders (*FBIS–NESA*, 28/2/91). That meeting, about technical details relating to the cease-fire, took place on 3 March (*NYT*, 4/3/91, A8, and Apple, *NYT*, 4/3/91, A1, 8; Schwarzkopf, 1992: 481–491).[54]

On 3 March, Tariq Aziz notified the Council that Iraq accepted the terms of Resolution 686, with a pledge of "meeting [its] obligations ... sincerely and as soon as possible, in an objective and honorable manner" (*FBIS–NESA*, 4/3/91). In a further move toward meeting UN and Coalition demands, Baghdad Radio announced on the 5th that the Revolutionary Command Council had "rescinded" the annexation of Kuwait, making null and void all decrees, laws and regulations affecting Kuwait that were made since 2 August 1990 (*FBIS–NESA*, 6/3/91). It also agreed to return Kuwaiti assets plundered by Iraq during its seven-month occupation (*FBIS–NESA*, 6/3/91). All of these acts reflected deescalation of the Gulf Crisis. Yet it took more than a month for all the terms to be accepted and for a permanent cease-fire to come into effect.

While the interstate dimension of the Gulf Crisis was winding down, its effects within Iraq were explosive. In an end-crisis development that was to haunt Bush and cause disquiet among the US public, Shi'ites in the South and Kurds in the North rebelled against Saddam Hussein's—and Baghdad's—rule, not for the first time. They had been encouraged by the US President's call to overthrow Hussein and were convinced that US aid would be forthcoming. They were crushed; and a flight of hundreds of thousands of Shi'ites and almost two million Kurdish refugees ensued.

After brief local victories, the Shi'ite revolt was suppressed by Hussein's Republican Guards. The Kurds held sway for a week, even in some urban centers, including Kirkuk, center of the oil-producing region in northern Iraq. But the superior firepower of the Republican Guards, aided by helicopter gunships that the Coalition forces carelessly allowed Iraq to retain, rapidly subdued all of the cities and towns of Iraqi Kurdistan. That, in turn, triggered one of the worst refugee calamities of the 20th century, the panic flight of Kurds to Turkey and Iran to escape the vengeance of Saddam Hussein's armed forces.[55]

The US President denied, disingenuously, that he had encouraged rebellion in Iraq or had pledged support to the Shi'ites and Kurds. He also strenuously disclaimed any responsibility for the failure to oust Saddam Hussein or the human tragedy that unfolded. His Defense Secretary tried to fudge the issue at the time but did not conceal Bush's intent—and signal:

> ... the President did not state that Saddam Hussein *has* to go. [But] He *certainly did encourage* the proposition that perhaps Iraqi officials, maybe senior commanders in the army, might want to consider the possibility that they ought to create a new government in Iraq (Rosenthal, *NYT*, 17/2/91, A18 [emphasis added]).

Coalition leaders agreed that to pursue the land war to the point of occupying Baghdad and overthrowing Saddam Hussein would be counter-productive for Middle East stability. At the height of the ground campaign, Coalition forces were 150 miles from the Iraqi capital, which lay defenseless in its path. Unwisely, Bush relied on Iraqi army and *Ba'ath* Party leaders, and the Iraqi public, to oust Hussein from power, following the precedent of Romania and Ceausescu in 1989. Although he did not formally pledge support for rebellion against Saddam Hussein, the persistent call for his ouster, as a precondition to the lifting of UN economic sanctions and the reentry of Iraq into the community of "law-abiding" states, had horrendous consequences, almost immediately after the interim cease-fire resolution of 2 March.

(On the first anniversary of the war, Bush openly called for rebellion and revealed his intent from the outset: "The United States *reiterates* its pledge to the Iraqi people and the Iraqi military that we stand ready to work with a new regime" [Rosenthal, *NYT*, 17/1/92, A8, emphasis added].)

The US decision not to intervene in Iraq's civil war, in support of the Shi'ites and Kurds, was reportedly made by Bush on 26 March (Tyler, *NYT*, 2/4/91, A9). In effect, it meant the abandonment of oppressed minorities in Iraq. The rationale was that to do otherwise would have violated the sacrosanct principle of "non-intervention in the internal affairs of sovereign states." Or, as some in the Bush Administration contended, while the world community would support an attempt to "roll back" an invasion of a sovereign state, Kuwait, it would not countenance "intervention" in the internal affairs of the aggressor, Iraq. That argument sounded hollow to many, including the author, in the light of frequent US interventions in support of pro-US rebellions against legitimate governments of sovereign states, notably the *Contras* in Nicaragua, the *Mujahidin* in Afghanistan, and *UNITA* in Angola.

The real reason for the only substantive US decision in the deescalation phase lay elsewhere. Major-power interests had created a worldwide coalition of states to protect the principle of sovereign statehood and, with it, Western interests in the untrammelled flow of oil—at a reasonable price—to the industrialized economies of Europe, Japan and America. Now those same interests dictated that the culprit, having been humiliated on the battlefield, should be allowed to engage in genocidal acts in order to preserve the territorial integrity of the state that had triggered the Gulf Crisis and had held the world at ransom for seven months, all in order to maintain a viable balance of power in the Gulf region. As one Middle East expert put it, colorfully: "Saddam was like a rampaging bull, whom we shot and wounded but decided not to kill in the name of preserving the balance of power" (Fouad Ajami, as quoted in Friedman, *NYT*, 28/9/91, A6). More soberly, General Powell remarked during Iraq's civil war: "a new set of problems could be introduced if Iraq suddenly broke up into a number of different countries or got Lebanonized, as it has often been called" (Tyler, *NYT*, 23/3/91, A4). Presidents Mubarak and Asad, the leaders of the two most active non-Gulf Arab members of the anti-Saddam Hussein coalition, also opposed the splintering of Iraq; and the latter said so, publicly, at their Cairo meeting on 1 April (Ibrahim, *NYT*, 2/4/91, A8). Such was the "logic" of international relations.

The Bush Administration's indifference to the calamity that befell the Kurds in the aftermath of the US-led war against Iraq was not its "finest hour." And it continued even after the Security Council passed **Resolution 688** on 5 April, which

> "*Condemns* the repression of the Iraqi civilian population in many parts of Iraq
> . . . ,
>
> *Demands* that Iraq . . . immediately ends this repression . . . , [and]
>
> *Insists* that Iraq allow immediate access by international humanitarian organizations to all those in need of assistance in all parts of Iraq and to make available all necessary facilities for their operations" (S/RES/688 [1991]).

Only when the US media and public opinion around the world criticized his insensitivity and shamed him into a humanitarian gesture to save the Kurdish refugees did Bush retreat from his rigid commitment to non-intervention.[56] After two weeks of aloofness the President responded on 11 April with support for a diluted version of a proposal by UK Prime Minister Major and President Ozal of Turkey to establish "safe havens" for the Kurds in northern Iraq, protected by American, British and other Western troops against a possible assault by Hussein's Republican Guards (Tyler, *NYT*, 12/4/91, A1, 6, and 13/4/91, A5; Haberman, *NYT*, 13/4/91, A1, 4; Sciolino, *NYT*, 17/4/91, A1, 12; Rosenthal, *NYT*, 18/4/91, A1, 16). This decision was reportedly made after a frantic phone call from Ozal who emphasized that the burden on Turkey was now unbearable (Sciolino, *NYT*, 18/4/91, A16). It was a limited change in direction.

More than a year later, in the midst of a US presidential campaign, Bush initiated, and the UK and France approved, a 'no-fly' zone south of the 32nd Parallel, to accord protection to Iraqi Shi'ites against Saddam Hussein's use of force to crush this large minority in the South (Gordon, *NYT*, 19/8/92, A1, 6; 27/8/92, A14; Wines, *NYT*, 27/8/92, A1, 14; Miller, *NYT*, 30/8/92, E5).

In sum, effective US crisis management until the last day of the war was followed by grave and callous mismanagement. Decisive military victory gave way to political ineptitude, and the basic goal, the ouster of Saddam Hussein, remained a chimera. More important, in human terms, US behavior led to a post-war tragedy on a grand scale. The rout of Saddam Hussein's army did not prevent a brutal suppression of minorities in Iraq's South and North. Bush, perceiving a threat to US interests from a fundamentalist Iran aspiring to hegemony in the Gulf, stood aside from a dual rebellion which he had encouraged, in fact if not formally, and watched the rebels' extinction from afar.

By that time the interstate Gulf Crisis had come to an end. *Crisis termination* took the form of a conditional cease-fire, embodied in **Resolution 687**: it was adopted on 3 April by a majority of 12–1 (Cuba), with two abstentions (Ecuador and Yemen) (S/RES/687 [1991]). In essence, the second Security Council resolution of the deescalation phase offered Iraq a permanent cease-fire if it accepted and implemented a series of military and financial steps. The most important conditions were as follows:

to cooperate in the elimination of all of its non-conventional weapons;
to pledge never to try to develop or otherwise acquire such weapons again;
to pay billions of dollars in reparations to Kuwait and other states for damage inflicted, and losses suffered, during Gulf War II;
to accept the border with Kuwait as agreed in October 1963;
to renounce terrorism "unequivocally" and pledge that it would deny sanctuary or bases in Iraq to international terrorist organizations; and
to accept a demilitarized zone extending 10 kilometers into Iraq (and five kilometers into Kuwait), to be monitored by a UN military observer force.

These demands were straightforward—and harsh. The complexity of Resolution 687 lay, rather, in a detailed 120-day timetable for Iraq's implementation of its commitments under the terms of this resolution and reciprocal actions to be taken by the Security Council.[57]

Resolution 687 was the longest (4,000 words) and most complex document ever produced by the Council, aptly dubbed the "mother of all resolutions." It was also the most punitive, in the tradition of a Carthaginian peace. The Council's seven non-aligned members—Cuba, Ecuador, India, Ivory Coast, Yemen, Zaire and Zimbabwe—tried to moderate some of its provisions, notably: to call for Iraq/Kuwait negotiations over their border dispute, rather than imposing the 1963 agreement; and to provide for the withdrawal of Coalition forces from southern Iraq as soon as the UN observer unit was in place. However, the major powers resisted any softening of the draft.

Iraq's delegate to the UN denounced its terms as humiliating and accused the US of manipulating the Council so as to create a "new colonial period" (Tyler, *NYT*, 7/4/91, A1, 14; Cowell, *NYT*, 7/4/91, A1, 14). Iraq's new Foreign Minister, Ahmed Hussein, too, railed against the harsh UN resolution, in his letter of acceptance. He also reiterated Hussein's paranoia, that "Iraq was the target of a conspiracy . . .". But this was merely rhetoric accompanying Iraq's unconditional acceptance of Resolution 687 on 6 April 1991 (*NYT*, 8/4/91, A6).

Iraq's two important decisions in the deescalation phase, to accept the interim cease-fire conditions (Resolution 686) and to accept the Carthaginian terms of a permanent cease-fire (Resolution 687), were made swiftly. There can be no doubt that, in terms of personal, party and "national" interests, these were wise decisions. No controversy surrounds Iraq's decisions, unlike the US decision not to intervene in Iraq's civil war, let alone the earlier decision to terminate the ground campaign after four days.

The formal cease-fire took effect on 12 April 1991. With that event, the interstate Gulf Crisis was over. But the goal of driving Saddam Hussein from power remains elusive. And the agony of Iraq's people, especially its Kurdish and Shi'ite minorities, had barely begun.

Several analytic tasks remain in the application of the Unified Model to the Gulf Crisis, 1990–91. One is to measure the intensity (or severity) of this crisis, using the Index of Intensity as elaborated in Chapter 5 and applied to the ten case studies that recur in Chapters 2–5. Another is to evaluate the impact of the Gulf Crisis, following the decision rules of the Index of Impact, as discussed in Chapter 5. A third is to test the hypotheses generated earlier in this book and to report which are supported/not supported by the evidence from the Gulf Crisis. And finally, one must address the question, how does the UMC facilitate an explanation of the first global crisis of the post-Cold War era? To these tasks I now turn.

Intensity

The indicators of intensity, it will be recalled, are: the *number of crisis actors* (direct participants); the extent of major power *involvement* in a crisis; the scope of *geostrategic salience*; the degree of *heterogeneity* between the adversaries; the range of *issues*, and the level of *violence*. Overall intensity is a composite of the scores of these six indicators, measured along a 10-point scale. Only one international crisis from the end of 1918 to the end of 1988, Entry into World War II, scored 10.00; that is, it scored the maximum for number of actors, major power involvement, etc. The question to be addressed here is: how intense was the Gulf Crisis, measured from its outbreak in mid-July 1990 until its termination on 12 April 1991?

During the onset phase (17 July–1 August), Kuwait was the only crisis actor, that is, the only state whose decision-makers perceived a change in the level of value threat. Iraq was the triggering entity, and Egypt, Saudi Arabia and the US were *involved actors*; but they did not yet identify the heightened tension in the Gulf region as an incipient foreign policy crisis for themselves. With Iraq's invasion of Kuwait and its condemnation by the US and the UN on 2 August, the number of crisis actors expanded dramatically: Saudi Arabia and the four lesser Arab states of the Gulf region, Iraq, the US, the UK and France, Egypt and Syria, and later, although inactive in the military domain, Israel and the USSR. So it remained until the end of this international crisis. Only the crisis leading to World War II, with 21 crisis actors, exceeded the Gulf Crisis's 14 direct participants. And there were many involved actors: the other 17 members of the US-led Coalition, and several Arab states that rallied behind Iraq, notably Jordan, Yemen and the Sudan. Since the highest point on the *number of actors* scale is six or more crisis actors, the Gulf Crisis of 1990–91 scored 6 on the six-point scale for the first indicator of intensity.

From the beginning of the escalation phase, too, major power activity was visible and consequential. One of the two superpowers, the US, was fully engaged in support of Kuwait, mobilizing the largest and most powerful American combat force since World War II to back up its president's public commitment to compel the expulsion of Iraq's forces from Kuwait, by force if necessary. The USSR was deeply involved in the crisis, politically. Two paths were followed, at times simultaneously.

One was to play the role of reliable member of the US-led Coalition, especially in the Security Council, where Moscow cast a crucial affirmative vote for all 12 UN resolutions until the outbreak of war. (These, it will be recalled, included severe sanctions against Iraq and authorization of the use of force by the Coalition, if Iraq ignored the Council's deadline of 15 January 1991.) The other track was several highly-visible attempts at mediation, notably in mid-February. Soviet mediation failed to save a longtime client from what it correctly assessed as certain military disaster for Iraq. But Gorbachev played the role of "peacemaker" without alienating the Coalition leader. And, while there was no Soviet military activity in the Gulf Crisis, the USSR met the criteria of a crisis actor. There was a growing perception in Moscow of a threat to Soviet values, notably the safety of its 10,000 technical advisors in Iraq. Moscow also was aware of the steadily increasing probability of war that could spill over its sensitive southern borders and of ever-growing time constraints, after the 15 January deadline was set by the Security Council. In short, both superpowers were crisis actors (as were two other major powers, France and the UK), leading to a score of 5 on the five-point scale for *involvement*.

The term geostrategic salience, as noted in Chap. 5, refers to the scope of potential effects of an international crisis. They may be confined to the crisis adversaries or to the subsystem of which they are members. The consequences may spill over to other subsystems, to the dominant system of world politics, or even to the entire global system. The crucial criteria for assessment of geostrategic salience are the location of the crisis and the resources at stake.

On both counts, the Gulf Crisis of 1990–91 ranked very high. Throughout the Cold War era the Middle East was pivotal, a grey zone of competition between the two contending blocs, straddling the southern rim of the USSR and much of its industrial heartland. Yet location alone does not ensure high salience. Not all Middle East crises and wars have had a wide reach in terms of potential impact, for example, crises involving Syria and Israel over Lebanon or those between the two Yemens from the early 1960s onward. Even the long Iran/Iraq War (1980–88) barely caused a ripple in the chancelleries of the world, after the initial panic over the possible consequences for oil supplies to a dependent world. Oil tankers continued to carry the vital raw material to the advanced industrial economies of Japan and Western Europe, and even to the US. Nor was there a threat of control over the Gulf region's oil reserves by a single state hostile to the interests of the West.

In 1990, the states of the Gulf region produced half of the oil consumed by the world economy and controlled more than half of the known reserves. Saudi Arabia had long achieved primacy in OPEC, whose decisions on prices and production had already revealed their potency in the oil-price shocks of 1973 and 1979. With Iraq's conquest of Kuwait and its massing of troops on the Saudi border, the West in general, and especially US decision-makers, perceived a grave threat to global economic stability if a victorious Iraq were to seize the vast Saudi oil fields, which would have given Saddam Hussein control over 40% of global oil production. And many perceived this to be his next objective, in quest of hegemony in the Gulf region and primacy in the Arab world. In short, the resources at stake in the Gulf Crisis of 1990–91 were awesome, with perceived spillover effects on the entire global system. Thus, on this indicator of intensity, too, the Gulf Crisis scored the maximum, 5 on the five-point scale for *geostrategic salience*.

Heterogeneity, in the Index of Intensity, refers to the number of differences between crisis adversaries, with respect to four attributes: military capability, political regime, economic development, and culture. If this indicator is applied to the initial adversarial pair, Iraq and Kuwait, the score would be modest. Iraq was a major regional power, with a million-man army, considerable air power, and unconventional weapons of mass destruction, while Kuwait, with 16,000 troops, was highly vulnerable to conquest. For all other attributes, however, they were essentially similar. Both states were ruled by authoritarian regimes, one a dual authority of the *Ba'ath* Party and the Iraqi Army under the domination of Saddam Hussein, the other a benign dictatorship of the al-Sabah family in Kuwait. Both were oil-rich, developing economies. And the peoples of Iraq and Kuwait were members of the Arab "family," sharing the same language and belief system. Thus the score for heterogeneity would be 2 on a five-point scale.

However, heterogeneity is measured for any adversarial pair. And in the Gulf Crisis the two principal adversaries were Iraq and the United States. For that pair, differences are evident in all attributes. Despite Iraq's major power status and capability in the Gulf region, the military gap between them was massive—as noted earlier, the difference between a battle-hardened Third World army and an armed force endowed with the most advanced military technology in the air, on land and at sea. Their political systems were at polar opposites, with democracy confronting an unabashed dictatorship. Moreover, Iraq's developing economy contrasted with a post-industrial US economy. And there was nothing in common in the cultural domain. The upshot was a score of 5 on the five-point scale for *heterogeneity*.

Several issues were in dispute between Iraq and the US. Preeminent was the military-security issue area, with a profound difference over (Kuwait's) territory. Of great importance, too, was the economic-developmental issue-area, with control over the Gulf region's vast oil resources at stake. There was also a basic status issue, namely, an unbridgeable gap over the Iraqi historical claim to sovereignty over all of Kuwait. The upshot was a score of 5 on the five-point scale for *issues*.

Finally, the Gulf Crisis of 1990–91 culminated in a full-scale war of an intensity unparalleled since World War II. Its casualties were less than in Gulf War I, but higher in proportion to the war's duration—six weeks versus eight years. And the material damage was much greater. Thus the Gulf Crisis scored the maximum 4 on the four-point scale of *violence*.

The result is an *overall intensity of 10.00*, the theoretical maximum. Thus the Gulf Crisis of 1990–91 is one of the two most intense international crises since the end of 1918, along with Entry into World War II.

Impact

The concept of impact in the Unified Model, it will be recalled [Chap. 6], encompasses various levels and types of change. At the state level, the focus is on the effects of an international crisis on relations between the adversaries, political, economic, military, cultural. At the system level, impact refers to consequences for the subsystem(s) of which the adversaries are members, the dominant system of the major powers, and the global system.

Operationally, as noted, system impact is assessed in terms of four types of change. One is *change in power distribution*, which ranges from no change through change in relative power among the crisis adversaries, to change in ranking among the five most powerful states in the relevant subsystem or the dominant system, to the most drastic shift in power, namely, in the composition of states at the apex of the power pyramid. Another is *change in actors*, ascending from no change through change in regime orientation, to change in regime type, to the most far-reaching effect, the creation, preservation, or elimination of one or more state actors. The extent of *change in alliance configuration*, too, can be measured, from none to an increase/decrease in cohesiveness within an existing alliance, to the entry/exit of actors into/from a formal or informal alliance, to the most drastic shift in alignment, the formation/elimination of an alliance. Finally, a crisis may lead to *change in rules of the game*, from no change to a decline in consensus, to a breakdown in consensus, and, most significantly, to the creation/elimination of codified or tacit rules of the game.

These four indicators of change are combined to generate the Index of Impact which, as noted, facilitates the measurement of the effects of an international crisis along a ten-point scale. What, then, can be discerned from an application of this construct to the Gulf Crisis of 1990–91? Although less than two years have elapsed since the end of this crisis—the preferred time frame for assessment of impact is three years—it is possible to provide a tentative evaluation. I begin with the bilateral level of analysis, for which a comparable index has not been devised.

Many adversarial pairs are evident in the Gulf Crisis, with Iraq and each member of the Coalition comprising a hostile dyad. Suffice it for this analysis to concentrate on three bilateral relationships: Iraq/Kuwait, Iraq/Saudi Arabia, and Iraq/US.

The unanticipated conquest of the emirate and the harshness of Iraq's seven-month occupation—2000–5000 killed; many thousands abducted; large numbers maimed, rendered homeless and dispossessed, and even more forced to flee, and the wanton destruction of the Kuwaiti economy, especially the setting aflame of most of its oil fields—all this traumatized Kuwait as a state and Kuwaitis as a people. It also sundered the tenuous relationship between "Arab brothers," with reconciliation unlikely in the foreseeable future. Superimposed on three decades of Iraq's unconcealed denial of Kuwait's legitimacy as a state—for Baghdad, the emirate was rightfully Iraq's "19th Province"—the Gulf crisis-war of 1990–91 ensured near-universal anger, bitterness and fear of their powerful neighbor among Kuwaitis, both the rulers and the ruled, into the indefinite future.

For Saudi Arabia, the immediate effects of the Gulf crisis-war were much less visible and traumatic. Casualties were few. There was fear in Dhahran and Riyadh for six weeks (mid-January–end February 1991), arising from Iraq's Scud attacks.[58] And the kingdom's financial resources were reduced by some $16 billion to help cover the costs of "Desert Shield" and "Desert Storm." But there was no damage to Saudi Arabia's infrastructure or to its oil fields.

At the same time, the dramatic display of its northern neighbor's military capability—and of Iraq's willingness to use force for purposes of national aggrandizement—was a lesson that penetrated deeply into the mindset of Saudi Arabia's rulers and ruled alike. Specifically, the massing of Iraqi forces on the Saudi border, a brief incursion into Saudi territory early in February—the Battle of Khafji—and near-total dependence on a vast US expeditionary force laid bare, as no other event in the history of the Saudi kingdom, its high vulnerability to grave damage, invasion and occupation by a much more powerful and rapacious Arab neighbor. It is true that Saudi awareness of the gap in military power long preceded the Gulf Crisis of 1990–91. So too did its awareness of Saddam Hussein's ambition to achieve hegemony in the Gulf and the ruthlessness of his regime. But never had Iraq exhibited such overt hostility towards Saudi Arabia, so sweeping a denunciation of inter-Arab borders dating to the Western colonial era, so flagrant a use of force against other Arab states, and such risk-prone behavior that had no compunctions about violating fundamental rules of the game in the Arab state system.

The short-term bilateral impact of the Gulf Crisis has been the total severance of state–state relations between Riyadh and Baghdad. The Saudi regime has strongly supported the US's hard line on the maintenance of punitive UN sanctions against Iraq until Saddam Hussein's rule is terminated, by one means or another. The Saudi treatment of Iraq as a pariah state is likely to continue as long as Saddam Hussein remains in power, probably until a new regime replaces the *Ba'ath* Party–Army dictatorship. Yet Saudi Arabia's long-term vulnerability—a small population and a small, though well-equipped army, the concentration of oil fields in the Eastern province not far from an aggressive, ambitious, powerful and risk-prone Iraq—may well, in the longer term, lead to a bilateral *rapprochement* and a return to the traditional Saudi use of its financial resources to try to tame its dangerous northern neighbor, dangerous to Saudi Arabia no matter which individual, group, party or army faction wields power in Baghdad.

Compared with Kuwait and Saudi Arabia, the costs of the Gulf crisis-war for the US, both material and psychological, were minimal. The small number of military casualties was a source of unconcealed relief to the politicians and the generals whose careful estimate was of the order of 10,000–20,000. There was no physical damage to US installations, no Scud missile attacks on US cities, and not even a financial burden: the contributions of allies exceeded the funds spent by the Pentagon throughout the military buildup and the war. And rather than experiencing a national trauma (Kuwaitis) or an acute awareness of long-term vulnerability (Saudis), Americans witnessed—on their TV sets at home—an unprecedented display of US technological prowess and military power. Operation "Desert Storm" was also the first major victory of the US armed forces since World War II: the Korean War (1950–53) ended in stalemate, and the Vietnam War (1964–73) ended in ignominious defeat. Grenada (1983) and Panama (1989) were hardly tests of US military prowess. In fact, Gulf War II was acclaimed by many American politicians, generals and commentators as marking the demise of the "Vietnam Syndrome."

Since the unilateral US cease-fire on 28 February 1991, the severance of US/Iraq state-to-state relations has been complete. US policy has been channelled through the UN Security Council—the retention of stringent economic sanctions, the persistent attempt to destroy Iraq's weapons of mass destruction, both the stockpiles that survived the 38-day air assault and Iraq's capability to resume production in the future, etc. In sum, like Kuwait and Saudi Arabia, the US has treated Iraq as a pariah state. Total isolation is likely to persist until Saddam Hussein is removed from power. Given the visceral hostility to Iraq's ruler, and the importance of the personal element in US behavior, it is unlikely to be otherwise.

To measure the *systemic* impact of the Gulf Crisis is both easier and more difficult than to assess bilateral effects. It is easier because of the Index of Impact, with its precise scales and scale-points to identify the extent of each of the four types of change noted above. At the same time, the full systemic impact of an international crisis takes longer to unfold, and less than two years have elapsed since the end of the Gulf Crisis, 1990–91. Nonetheless, an interim assessment is possible.

Far-reaching change in the distribution of power is evident as a result of the Gulf Crisis. First, the decimation of Iraq's armed forces meant a shift in relative power between Iraq and Saudi Arabia, though this did not signify that the former was now weaker in absolute terms. But change in this indicator of impact went much further, to include the ranking of the most powerful states within the Gulf subsystem. This point needs elaboration.

At the end of the Iran/Iraq War in 1988 (Gulf War I), Iraq could—and did—claim primacy in the power pyramid of the Gulf region, though the outcome was more akin to stalemate than to victory. Iraq possessed what appeared to be a formidable million-man army, many of the troops battle-hardened; an air force of 700 combat planes, including 200 front-line Soviet fighters and bombers, and growing stockpiles of weapons of mass destruction. Iran, with more than double the population and potentially greater power, was exhausted by the long war of attrition and acquiesced in less than victory, notwithstanding Khomeini's vow to persist as long as Saddam Hussein remained in power. All other Gulf region states were mini-powers, except for Saudi Arabia, whose military capability was vastly inferior to that of Iraq.

The outcome of Gulf War II in 1991 did not eliminate Iraq from the élite of the power pyramid in the Gulf region, which would have meant the maximal impact (point 4 on the scale). But it did change the ranking among the most powerful: Iraq's primacy gave way to Iran, now the beneficiary of most of Iraq's front-line combat aircraft, with a victorious Saudi Arabia a growing military power in the Gulf region. In the larger

Arab subsystem, the Gulf crisis-war led to an even sharper change: Iraq's place in the power pyramid declined, while Syria's and Egypt's rank rose accordingly. And finally, in the Arab/Israel subsystem, Iraq, a bulwark of an Arab "eastern front" in the protracted conflict with Israel, was now, in the aftermath of Gulf War II, preoccupied with internal revolts by Kurds and Shi'ites and, therefore, no longer a grave threat to Israel in the foreseeable future: in that subsystem, too, the ranking of states had been significantly altered by Iraq's defeat in 1991. Thus the Gulf Crisis scores 3 on the four-point scale for *power change*.

There have been few substantive consequences for the politics of Gulf region actors and regimes. In Kuwait, the Gulf crisis-war triggered a renewed demand for democratization, specifically, a call for the restoration of the 1962 constitution, which had created an elected legislature with limited powers to constrain the authoritarian regime of the al-Sabah ruling family. The constitution had been set aside in 1986. Now, under mounting domestic pressure, especially from Kuwaitis who stayed behind, along with low-key expressions of US government support, the Emir yielded, partially. On 2 June 1991 Kuwait's Government announced that elections to a new national assembly would be held in October 1992. In the interim, Kuwait was under martial law (Cushman, *NYT*, 5/6/91, A3).

The election was held on 5 October, but with a severely restricted franchise—only men 21 or over who could trace their families in the emirate before 1921. Thus 81,400 of Kuwait's 606,000 citizens were authorized to elect members of the 50-seat National Assembly, from 278 candidates. And the emir retains ultimate authority over all aspects of public policy. The results were startling: 31 of the elected members identify with the pro-democracy opposition, with 19 Islamic members from competing religious groups (Hedges, *NYT*, 5/10/92, A20; 6/10/92, A6; 7/10/92, A12; 18/10/92, A16).

In Saudi Arabia, "the trauma of Iraq's invasion of neighbouring Kuwait and the Gulf War . . . triggered [far-reaching] reforms" (Azmeh, 3/3/92, 5). These took the form of three royal decrees announced by King Fahd on 1 March 1992. The major innovation was the creation of a 60-member Consultative Council, appointed by the King but with an intended extensive role in the kingdom's future political process. It was granted the right to review all foreign and domestic policy; to initiate proposals leading to a new or revised law; to question any Cabinet minister; and to revise or reject expenditure budgets submitted by the Cabinet.

The new Consultative Council is embedded in an 83-article "Basic System of Government," the first written constitution since the founding of Saudi Arabia in 1932. Also included is a quasi-bill of rights. Moreover, in a move towards decentralization, the Governors and local assemblies of Saudi Arabia's 14 provinces were granted extensive authority to set priorities in development plans for their regions. And finally, new succession procedure was created, to take effect after Fahd's successor, Crown Prince Abdullah: rulers are to be chosen by a group of princes serving as an electoral college, with a broadening of candidates to include the younger generation of princes (Ibrahim, *NYT*, 2/3/92, A1, 8).[59]

The King ruled out free elections (Ibrahim, *NYT*, 30/3/92, A6). And his vast authority remains intact. Nonetheless, this post-Gulf Crisis development set in motion a process of modernization and democratization, with potential spillover effects to the emirates and sheikhdoms of the Gulf region. Among the lesser Gulf states, too, there was talk of political change.[60]

More immediate and tangible was the impact of the Gulf Crisis on Kuwait's existence. Early in the crisis, in fact, serving as the trigger to the escalation phase, Kuwait was eliminated from the "club of nations," an infrequent event in twentieth-century world politics. And the first visible effect of the crisis was Kuwait's restoration as an independent state. As such, the Gulf Crisis scores the maximum on this indicator of impact, 4 on the four-point scale for *actor/regime change*.

As always, changes in rules of the game are the most difficult to discern. Those that long obtained between Gulf region states and outside powers have not changed in the aftermath of the Gulf Crisis. Nor have inter-Arab rules, as evident in the negotiations after the crisis ended. Yet the Gulf Crisis did generate a new rule in the impact phase, with potential far-reaching implications: in mid-April 1991, soon after the formal ending of the Gulf Crisis, the Kurdish revolt—and its savage repression by Baghdad—led the major powers, acting through the UN, to proclaim the right of the international system to intervene in a member state, militarily, on grounds of human rights: in this instance, to protect a defenseless or exposed minority against genocide. This right was extended, as noted, to the Shi'ites of southern Iraq in August 1992 and, less stringently—no provision for immediate enforcement—to besieged Bosnia–Hercegovina two months later (*NYT*, 3/10/92, A5; Gordon *NYT*, 3/10/92, A1, 5; P. Lewis, *NYT*, 8/10/92, A14; 10/10/92, A3). Many regard this as violating the hallowed principle of non-intervention in the internal affairs of a sovereign state. Nonetheless, intervention did occur, with the full sanction of the UN. Because of the creation of this rule, the Gulf Crisis scores 4 on the 4-point scale for *rules change*.

As for change in alliances, the Gulf Crisis had been a watershed. The six oil-rich Arab Gulf states, headed by Saudi Arabia, had created a loose security regime, the Gulf Cooperation Council, in 1981. Although fearful of Iran's fundamentalist Islam and wary of Iraq's ambitions, it insisted on aloofness from any formal entanglement with the US for a decade. And even after the Gulf Crisis had demonstrated the Gulf states' total dependence on the West, there was no rush to formal alignment with the patron state that protected their independence from Iraqi expansionism. The only exception was the *raison d'être* of US intervention in the Gulf Crisis: on 19 September 1991 Kuwait and the US signed a ten-year security pact that allows access to Kuwaiti ports by US navy ships, and provides for prepositioning of US military equipment, training and joint exercises, though not the stationing of US forces (Schmitt, *NYT*, 20/9/91, A10).

By contrast, the centerpiece of US post-Gulf War II strategy, an alliance with Saudi Arabia, seemed to founder on the latter's insistence on creating, with US assistance, an offensive army capable of large-scale mobile warfare (Tyler, *NYT*, 30/9/91, A5; 13/10/91, A1, 18). No less important, a much-heralded realignment of forces within the Arab world quickly disintegrated because of traditional suspicions and rivalries. On 8 March 1991, barely a week after the interim cease-fire in Gulf War II, a Damascus Declaration was signed by the eight Arab states in the US-led Coalition: Egypt and Syria were to provide the bulk of an inter-Arab force of 60,000 to defend Kuwait, Saudi Arabia, and the lesser Gulf states, with the six GOC members financing the force. But these military clauses have not been implemented. Mubarak announced the withdrawal of Egypt's 36,000 troops from the Gulf region; and Syria followed soon after (Tyler, *NYT*, 11/5/91, A1, 4; Cowell, *NYT*, 8/7/91, A2). In short, an incipient inter-Arab realignment was aborted. Nonetheless, the formation of an alliance between an Arab Gulf state and the US, and the growing evidence that more will follow, warrants a score of 4 on the four-point scale for change in *alliance configuration*.

Taken together, the Gulf Crisis of 1990–91 ranks very high for *overall impact*, 8.88 on the ten-point scale.

Hypothesis-Testing

Turning to the third exercise: the propositions and hypotheses that were generated from the phase models can be tested with the evidence from the Gulf Crisis. The data are set out in Table 7.2.

TABLE 7.2   *Gulf Crisis, 1990–1991: Hypothesis-Testing*

PROPOSITIONS[1] Propositions on Crisis Onset	Supported	Not Supported
1. Outbreak of Crisis (int)° the dispute occurs:		
in a polycentric structure	X	
in a subsystem of world politics	X	
in a protracted conflict	X	
there is no power discrepancy between the adversaries		X
the regime pair is non-democratic	X	
the adversaries are territorially contiguous.	X	
2. Initiation of Crisis (fp)† *the initiator:*		
is a young or new state		X
is militarily stronger than its adversary	X	
has a non-democratic regime	X	
confronts domestic instability		X
is territorially contiguous to its adversary	X	
has a large territory.	X	
3. Vulnerability to a Crisis (fp)† *the target:*		
is a young or new state	X	
is in a protracted conflict with its adversary	X	
has little/no power discrepancy with its adversary		X
has different political regime than its adversary		X
confronts domestic instability		X
is territorially contiguous to its adversary	X	
has a regime of recent origin	X	
has a small territory.	X	

HYPOTHESES[1] Escalation		
1. Escalation to Full-Scale International Crisis the crisis occurs in:		
a polycentric structure	X	
a subsystem of world politics	X	
a protracted conflict	X	
the adversaries are geographically contiguous	X	
there are more than two actors[2]		X
the adversaries are heterogeneous[3]		X
there are several issues in dispute.	X	
2. Escalation through Violence (int)° (the conditions in Hyp. 1);	XX XX X	X X

TABLE 7.2   *Continued*

HYPOTHESES Escalation	Supported	Not Supported
and the adversaries have authoritarian regimes	X	
there is high power discrepancy between them	X	
major power activity is high.[4]		X
3. *Change from No/Low Violence to Severe Violence during the Escalation Phase (int)°* (the conditions in Hyp. 1 and 2);	XX XX XX XX	X X
and there is a violent trigger to escalation	X	
the response is reciprocal or stronger.	X	
4. *Escalation to Full-Scale Crisis (fp)†* *the initiator:* is ruled by an authoritarian regime	X	
is engaged in a protracted conflict with the target	X	
has a favorable power relationship with the target	X	
is geographically contiguous to the target	X	
is a young/new political entity		X
confronts acute internal instability.		X
5. *Escalation of Crisis through Violence (fp)†* (the conditions in Hyp. 4)	XX XX	X X
and the initiator is receiving major power military support.	X	
6. *Vulnerability to Crisis Escalation (fp)†* *the target:* is not a dominant system actor	X	
is ruled by an authoritarian regime	X	
is engaged in a protracted conflict with the initiator	X	
is militarily weaker than the initiator	X	
is geographically contiguous to the initiator	X	
is a young or new state	X	
confronts acute internal instability.		X
7. *Vulnerability to Violent Crisis Escalation (fp)†* (the conditions in Hyp. 6);	XX XX XX	X
and the regime is of short duration		X
the target's territory is small.	X	

TABLE 7.2   *Continued*

HYPOTHESES Deescalation	Supported	Not Supported
8. *Termination in Mutual Agreement*[5] *(int)*°		
the crisis occurs in a non-protracted conflict setting	X	
the adversaries have equal capability	X	
there are few crisis actors	X	
major powers are not highly active	X	
the international organization is highly involved		X
the adversaries rely on non-violent crisis management techniques.	X	
9. *Low Intensity Leads to Short Duration*[6] *(int)*°		
there are few actors	X	
there is non-military activity by major powers	X	
the crisis has low geostrategic salience	X	
there is little heterogeneity among the adversaries	X	
there are few issues	X	
the primary crisis management techniques are non-violent.	X	
10. *An Accommodative Strategy Will be Adopted*[7] *(fp)*†		
the crisis occurs in a non-protracted conflict setting	X	
a state is equal to/inferior to its adversary in power		X
it has a democratic regime	X	
it confronts domestic stability	X	
major power support is non-military		X
it receives support from the relevant IO.	X	
11. *Satisfaction with Outcome (fp)*†		
the crisis is not part of a protracted conflict	X	
the state receives military support from a major power	(NR)[8]	
it receives support from the relevant international organization	X	
the perceived outcome is victory.	X	

Impact

	Supported	Not Supported
12. *The Bilateral Effect of International Crisis Higher Tension (fp)*†		
there is a definitive, disharmonious outcome (victory/defeat)	X	
the crisis terminates without mutual agreement[9]	X	
there are several crisis actors	X	
the major powers exhibit intense activity	X	
the crisis has high geostrategic salience	X	

Table 7.2 *Continued*

HYPOTHESES Impact	Supported	Not Supported
there is high heterogeneity between the adversaries	X	
there are several issues in dispute	X	
the crisis is characterized by severe violence.	X	
13. *Higher Intensity Leads to Greater Impact (int)°*		
the crisis is characterized by:		
several crisis actors	X	
high major power activity	X	
high geostrategic salience	X	
high heterogeneity	X	
several issues	X	
severe violence.	X	
14. *Far-reaching Systemic Impact (int)°*		
(the conditions in Hyp. 13;)	XX	
	XX	
	XX	
and there is		
an extreme catalyst	X	
severe violence in crisis management	X	
long duration	X	
an outcome other than formal agreement.		X

°int = international crisis (system/interactor level)
†fp = foreign policy crisis (actor level)

1. Each proposition and hypothesis specifies the conditions in which the dependent variable (e.g., Hyp. 1 – Escalation to Full-Scale International Crisis) is most likely to occur.
2. There were only two adversarial crisis actors, Iraq and Kuwait, until the escalation phase began on 2 August 1990.
3. Heterogeneity until the beginning of the escalation phase refers to the Iraq/Kuwait dyad: they differed only with respect to military capability.
4. Until the escalation phase, no major power was involved in the Iraq/Kuwait bilateral crisis, except for US joint military exercises with the UAE in late July 1990. Thus "high major power activity" is coded as not supported for H. 2. However, this condition did obtain after the beginning of the escalation phase. Thus it is coded as supported for H. 3.
5. The Gulf Crisis ended through a unilateral act, a US–UN-imposed cease-fire, not agreement. Thus the obverse of H. 8 is being tested for this case – termination in Imposed Agreement, using the obverse of the 'most likely' conditions for Mutual Agreement, as indicated above.
6. The Gulf Crisis was highly intense and long (9 months). Thus, as with H.8, the obverse is tested for this case, namely, High Intensity leads to Long Duration, using the obverse of the most likely conditions for short duration, as indicated above.
7. Since neither of the main adversaries, Iraq or the US, adopted an accommodative strategy in the Gulf Crisis, the same procedure as in H.8 and

Notes to TABLE 7.2   *Continued*

9 is being followed for H.10: the obverse is being tested – for Iraq.

8. This element is not relevant (NR) since the state whose crisis is being tested is a major power (the US) – it was satisfied with the outcome, Iraq was not.

9. Iraq accepted both interim and permanent UN cease-fire resolutions, but under duress.

The findings are compelling: one proposition (no. 1) and 12 hypotheses (1–3, 5–9, 11–14) exhibit a very strong fit; two propositions (2, 3) and two hypotheses (4, 10) show a strong match. Among the 123 elements, 99 apply to the Gulf Crisis, 24 do not. Thus the Gulf Crisis of 1990–91 and the behavior of its main adversaries unfolded in accord with most of the Unified Model's expectations at both system and actor levels of analysis: about outbreak, initiation, and vulnerability; escalation, and the role of violence; the winding-down process, extent of satisfaction, and duration; and consequences for the actors and the relevant international systems.

Some may argue that the Gulf Crisis's overwhelming support for the UMC's expectations cannot be generalized—and rightly so. The purpose of hypothesis-testing was not to imply sweeping generalizations from one case, a flawed methodology that is widespread in case studies on crisis, conflict and war. Rather, it was to demonstrate that hypotheses deduced from the UMC and its phase models can be tested with the evidence from any interstate crisis to discover the extent of fit. And throughout this book they have been tested with voluminous evidence drawn from a large number of international and foreign policy crises during most of the twentieth century.

Does this mean that the UMC fully explains the Gulf Crisis? This depends upon the meaning given to "explanation." In formal cause-effect terms, $a, b, c \ldots$ cause $x, y, z \ldots$, it does not, for the hypotheses are not so framed. Rather, for the reasons elaborated in Chapter 2, notably the overwhelming evidence of the ubiquity of crisis, the UMC and its derived hypotheses indicate the "most likely" constellation in which an international crisis such as the Gulf Crisis will emerge and evolve. The explanatory factors of this model are, as noted, *enabling*, not *predictor* variables.

The Unified Model and the Gulf Crisis: Conclusions

What, then, is the contribution of the UMC to an explanation of the Gulf Crisis—or any interstate crisis? First, it is to enhance comprehen-

sion of a complex phenomenon by introducing "order" into "chaos."
Without a framework of analysis, let alone a model, the array of data
about any crisis is devoid of meaning except as a chronological sequence
of events.

Questions relating to Iraq's behavior—why did it initiate a foreign
policy crisis for Kuwait, why in July 1990 and why did it escalate the
crisis, swiftly, by resort to massive violence—cannot elicit a plausible
explanation, except to note that Iraq did not accept the legitimacy of
Kuwait as an independent state from 1961 onwards. But why in July
1990, and not in the 1970s, and why through extreme threats portending rapid escalation by violence? Neither chronological sequence nor
history can answer these questions. Nor can they explain why the US
should respond instantly to the invasion of Kuwait by an unqualified
commitment to the victim; or, in systemic terms, why the Iraq/Kuwait
crisis should have been transformed from a typical bilateral crisis into a
global crisis, abruptly and pervasively. The traditional answer, "oil," is
undoubtedly relevant, but it is not a sufficient explanation.

To state this in positive terms, the likelihood of an international crisis
erupting in the Gulf in 1990 can be assessed more accurately through
an analytic construct, a model that argues, deductively, why conditions
a, b and c are more likely than others to generate an interstate crisis. Let
there be no misunderstanding about what is being argued here. A
model cannot identify the exact time of crisis outbreak; but it can
indicate that, when X conditions are present, crisis occurrence is most
likely. Furthermore, the evolution of the Gulf Crisis over a period of
eight months and, especially, its "turning points" can be explained and
anticipated by filtering the data through a lens which demarcates all
crises into distinct phases, onset, escalation, deescalation and impact,
and, for actors, into pre-crisis, crisis, end-crisis and post-crisis periods.

A crisis is not a unilinear phenomenon; it is characterized by several
breakpoints. It does not evolve over time at the same level of intensity,
of violence or of stress for its actors. What the Unified Model does is to
capture that multilinearity by logically anticipating changing intensity,
violence and stress, and by specifying which conditions are most likely
to generate qualitative changes during a crisis. Moreover, it explains
why those changes occur, from a low stress onset phase to a peak stress
escalation phase to a declining stress deescalation phase. With respect
to the Gulf Crisis, the UMC and its derived propositions and hypotheses help to explain Iraq's initiation of a foreign policy crisis for
Kuwait, and Kuwait's vulnerabilty to crisis, as well as to violent escalation. And the UMC draws attention to the attributes that propelled this

international crisis from low stress to higher stress and then to winding-down towards termination, whether or not by mutual agreement.[61]

Does this type of explanatory schema meet the test of theory? If theory is conceived as a body of propositions capable of explaining all cases of a phenomenon under inquiry, the UMC will be found wanting. If a less stringent view of theory is acceptable, as attempting to capture the essence of a phenomenon and to explain much, though not all, of its empirical diversity and its dynamic process of change, then the Unified Model does qualify as theory. And it is this conception of theory that has permeated the inquiry into the meaning of crises in the twentieth century.

CHAPTER 8

What Have We Learned?

WHAT have we learned about crises in the twentieth century?[1] Can one discern patterns in their eruption, evolution and exit from the landscape of world politics? Are crises comparable in a meaningful sense; or are they unique episodes that defy all attempts at systematic analysis? Do states cope with stress in accordance with the expectations of cognitive psychology or rational choice theory? Are there lessons for decision-makers on foreign and security policy? These core questions serve as the focus of the concluding chapter. I begin with an overview of what has been learned about crisis as a whole and each phase/period.

Concepts and Models

Interstate crisis is a distinct source of disruption in the politics among nations. It is, at the same time, closely related to conflict and war, for all are integral parts of international conflict. In terms of conflict space, war is a subset of crisis; that is, all wars are subsumed in crises, but not all crises involve violence, let alone full-scale war; in fact, half do not. Crises are not spasmodic but, rather, definable, recurrent events. They erupt in pre-war, intra-war and post-war settings. And they occur within or outside a protracted conflict between states [Figure 1.1].[2]

A crisis evolves at two distinct but intricately interrelated levels, system/interactor (international) and actor (foreign policy). It can—and should—be analyzed at both levels, for they provide complementary insights into the phenomenon of crisis as a whole [Figure 1.2]. The essential processes of crisis at the two levels were dissected through general models of international crisis [Model I] [Figure 1.3], and of foreign policy crisis [Model 2] [Figures 1.4, 1.5]. These were integrated later into the Unified Model of Crisis [Model 3] [Figure 6.1].

An international crisis exhibits higher-than-normal disruptive interaction and heightened likelihood of violence or, during a war, change in

500

the military balance. Together, these aspects of reality pose a challenge to system stability and, often, its structure. A foreign policy crisis is identified by three interrelated perceptions: of value threat; of time pressure for response to the threat; and of heightened likelihood of military hostilities before the threat is overcome.

An interstate crisis unfolds in a logical sequence, in four pairs of phase and period: onset/pre-crisis, escalation/crisis, deescalation/end-crisis, and impact/post-crisis [Figures 1.2 and 6.1]. For each, a set of questions was posed, a model was constructed, and propositions/ hypotheses were framed and tested.

Onset/Pre-Crisis

For this domain, attention was focused on crisis outbreak, initiation, and vulnerability [Figure 2.1], along with coping, and the role of violence.[3] A crisis begins at the state level. The trigger is generally external and takes the form of a hostile verbal, political, economic, non-violent military, or violent act, direct or indirect. The catalyst may be an internal challenge to a regime, verbal or physical. It may be an uncertain event or environmental change. Whatever the source, a state's decision-makers perceive a (usually low) threat, but not yet time pressure or heightened probability of war.

The ten crises examined throughout this book, from Munich (the UK) in 1938 to the Falklands/Malvinas (Argentina) in 1982, exhibit great variation in actor attributes during the pre-crisis period. They ranged from one to five strategic decisions, one to six key decision-makers, and from very small to very large decisional forums. Diversity is also conspicuous in attitudinal prisms during the onset phase, the lens through which images were filtered: they comprised Realism, Stalinism, pacifism, anti-racism, socialism, and irredentism.

Crisis triggers took the form of political, economic, non-violent military and violent acts. A wide range of values was perceived to be under threat: reputation for resolve, symbolic presence, military superiority, unity, security, human life, political system, economic development, honor and, in larger terms, existence, influence and territory. Crisis actors generally responded with tit-for-tat or more hostile behavior. And some crises lasted a few weeks, others years [Table 2.8.A].

The same diversity is evident among situational attributes: in structure, polarity, system level, conflict setting, power level, peace/war setting, severity of violence, political regime, level of economic development, and region [Table 2.8.B.1 and 2]. Nonetheless, there was an unambiguous common pattern of coping with low stress in the pre-crisis period. Information processing revealed little or no change from the non-crisis norm with respect to the channels and volume of communication. Consultation was confined to senior decision-makers and their technical advisors. Decisional forums, too, tended to follow non-crisis practice. And there was a minimal search for options, with reliance on standard operating procedures (SOPs) [Table 2.8.C].

The reason for this coping pattern, which the US replicated in the Gulf Crisis, 1990–91 [Chap. 7], was indicated at the close of Chapter 2:

> Stress is a shared challenge, an indicator of impending danger. States have common traits that outweigh their diversity, especially the need to survive and to minimize harm from external foes. And foreign policy decision-makers, in coping with crisis-generated stress, act as humans do in all comparable situations of impending harm. In essence, the commonality of statehood, stress and human response to expected harm, or gain, generates a near-identical pattern of coping in an external crisis.

Escalation/Crisis

Not all incipient crises mature, that is, become full-scale international crises. Some abort and fizzle out, especially when the target's decision-makers perceive a threat as marginal and do not respond.

To explain "step-level" change from onset to escalation, a second phase model was created. In order to tap the several dimensions of this process, the escalation model generated seven hypotheses, three at the system/interactor level, four at the actor level. These specified the conditions most likely to lead to: a full-scale international crisis [Hypothesis (henceforth H.) 1]; its violent escalation [H. 2]; high-severity violence [H. 3]; initiation of a full-scale foreign policy crisis by a state [H. 4]; its violent escalation [H. 5]; vulnerability to a crisis [H. 6]; and vulnerability to violent escalation [H. 7]. [The findings are reported below in the section on Hypothesis-Testing.]

Research on the ten cases uncovered the same pattern of diversity among actor attributes in the crisis period as in pre-crisis: 1–13 strategic decisions; 7–67 decisions; 1–5 key decision-makers; and more conspicuous attitudinal prisms—"Riga Axioms" [the US], "Brezhnev Doctrine" [the USSR], the "Conception" [Israel], appeasement [the UK], irredentism [Argentina] [Table 3.10.A].

As in pre-crisis, too, great variation is evident in situational attributes during the crisis period. Acute threat was perceived for many values, e.g., reputation for resolve [the US], the image of military invincibility [Germany, Israel], territory [India, Argentina], and existence [Zambia].

The awareness of time pressure was high in five cases, increasingly salient in the other five. War likelihood was perceived as higher in four cases, steadily increasing in five others. Triggers included verbal, political, non-violent military, indirect violent, and violent acts, and internal challenge. Response, too, was diverse: economic, political, non-violent military, and violent acts. Periods during a crisis also varied: in duration, from less than two weeks to eight months; in the number of crisis actors; and in violence, from none [the US, the UK, Zambia] to full-scale war [Germany, Israel, India, Argentina] [Tables 3.10.B.1 and 2].

How states coped with high stress, whether or not accompanied by violence, was explored in the same ten cases. Once more, notwithstanding conspicuous variety in actor and situational attributes, there was a distinct pattern of common coping in the peak stress crisis period, reinforcing the key finding about coping with pre-crisis low stress. There was a greater felt need and quest for information in all cases except Stalingrad, the sole intra-war crisis. Consultation was broader and more intense as stress increased. Decisional forums were larger than in the pre-crisis period, in most cases. And there was an extensive search and careful evaluation of alternative options [Table 3.10.C]. Moreover, apart from the common pattern of coping in almost all cases, behavior did not conform with traditional expectations about how decision-makers cope with crisis-generated high stress. [See below, "Cumulative Knowledge on Coping."]

Deescalation/End-Crisis

The winding-down of a crisis may be of long or short duration. It may occur through direct bargaining or third party intervention, or the exercise of superior military power by one of the adversaries. The deescalation process, or how crises end, is a neglected topic in the study of world politics, compared with war termination.[4] The only partial exception is crisis bargaining, which operates in both escalation and deescalation phases.

To overcome this *lacuna*, a model of crisis deescalation was designed, aiming to shed light on the accommodation process [H. 8], crisis duration [H. 9], and crisis outcome [H. 10, 11]. [The findings are reported below in "Hypothesis-Testing."]

As in pre-crisis and the crisis period, diversity in actor attributes is visible in the end-crisis period, e.g., from 1–5 strategic decisions and 3–21 decision-makers. Some situational attributes reveal commonality.

There was a perception of reduced value threat in eight of the ten cases, the exceptions being the US in Berlin Blockade and Argentina in the Falklands/Malvinas case. Time constraint was also perceived as less —in all but one case, the USSR in the Prague Spring. And there was a decline in the expectation of war in all but one case—Syria in Lebanon Civil War I. Other attributes of that period exhibit diversity: trigger—verbal, non-violent military, violent, internal; duration—from one week to 10 months; the number of actors—from one to 13; and the extent of violence, including none, minor clashes, serious clashes and full-scale war.

Coping with the declining stress of the end-crisis period was more blurred than in the other two periods; but two findings merit attention. On the one hand, the case studies reveal more commonality than variety in the behavior of the crisis actors. On the other, there was more continuity with, than change from, the pattern of coping in the high stress crisis period. There was no change in the felt need or quest for information in eight cases. There was no change in consultation in five cases, broader consultation in three, and less in two others. The decisional forum exhibited continuity in seven cases, change in three others. As for alternatives, there was continued careful search in two cases, a decline in six, and no search for options in two cases. Careful evaluation continued in six cases; it was less careful in two, more rigid in one, and non-existent in one case.

The reason for continuity, as noted in Chapter 4, was a psychological time lag. Decision-makers experienced high stress in the crisis period and could not easily adjust their thought and behavior to less stressful conditions.

Impact/Post-Crisis

An interstate crisis has effects on the adversaries and, often, on the system(s) of which they are members. Bilateral effects were assessed in terms of the legacy of higher or lower tension between the adversaries in the aftermath of a crisis. System impact was measured on a ten-point scale (1.00–10.00), based upon the extent of change in four system attributes: its power configuration; actors or their regimes, or their foreign policy orientation; "rules of the game"; and interstate alignments.

A crisis impact model was created to explain the consequences of crisis: specifically, for subsequent relations between the main adversaries [H. 12], the causal link between intensity and impact [H. 13], and the conditions most likely to lead to system transformation [H. 14]. [The findings are reported in "Hypothesis-Testing."]

Of the 390 international crises from the end of 1918 to the end of 1988, 273 were assessed for their impact.[5] The vast majority of these cases led to no power change or to a (usually marginal) change in relative power between the main adversaries, 36% and 57%, respectively. More far-reaching change, in the ranking of the five most powerful members of a system, and a fundamental change in the composition of the power élite in the relevant system, accounted for only 4% and 3%.

Actor change, too, revealed a concentration of crises at low points on the scale. There was no change in actors or regimes in 74% of the cases. Only 11% led to a change in regime orientation, 7%, a change in regime type, and 8%, a change in the formation, maintenance or elimination of a state.

A similar finding relates to rule change. Most cases had no effect on tacit or codified rules (67%). One of six (16%) led to a decline in consensus on tacit rules. Fewer led to a breakdown in consensus on codified rules (10%). And very few (7%) led to the creation or elimination of rules of the game.

As for alliance change, 70% of the 273 international crises had no effect. An increase or decrease in cohesiveness within an existing alliance occurred in the aftermath of 15% of the cases. Only 8% stimulated the entry or exit of a state into or from an alliance. And 7% had the highest possible effect, the formation or elimination of an alliance. In short, only *a small number of international crises catalyzed far-reaching system change.* Yet those that did so, e.g., Entry into World War II, Berlin Blockade, and Six Day War, had transforming effects on the global system, the dominant system, and a subsystem.[6]

The ten case studies reveal great variation with respect to all four attributes of impact: power change—from change in relative power between adversaries to change in ranking among the power élite; actor change—from no change to creation and elimination of actors; rule change—from no change to creation of new rules; and alliance change —from no change fo formation of new alliances.

There was also diversity in overall impact. One case, Rhodesia UDI, had very little impact. Three, Hungarian Uprising, Lebanon Civil War I, and Falklands/Malvinas, led to modest change. One, India/China Border, led to moderate change. Two, Stalingrad and Prague Spring, generated high impact. And three international crises, Munich, Berlin Blockade, and October-Yom Kippur, were ranked as having a very high impact, the first two on the dominant system, the third on the Middle East subsystem.

Other empirical themes will be recalled briefly. Interstate crises have been pervasive in the twentieth century and in all regions. They were not, however, evenly distributed over structure, time and space. Viewed in terms of the North/South divide, crises erupted most frequently in the developing world, two-thirds in Africa, Asia and the Middle East. In that context, the indifference to crises (and wars) in the "peripheries" (Gaddis, 1991) ignores a crucial source of instability in the global system.

There was a steady decline of crisis-type turmoil in Europe since 1945—until its reemergence in 1991. In Africa, by contrast, a spiral of crises is evident, correlating with a steady increase in the number of independent states and, therefore, of potential crisis actors. Elsewhere, in the Americas, Asia and the Middle East, there was little change over time in the number of crises. Crises in Africa were less complex than those in Europe and Asia. One indicator was the smaller combined number of actors in its crises. Violence, too, was a much more frequent catalyst in Africa.

Protracted interstate conflicts have been endemic, 26 since the end of 1918. Some included many international crises, others only one or two. Some concerned a single issue, notably territory, while others encompassed many issues. Intra-war crises, a long-neglected subset of interstate crises, occurred in all system structures, regions and decades.

At the actor level, the vast majority of members of the global system (123 states) experienced interstate crises since the end of World War I. The major powers have been the most crisis-prone; but others, with a shorter existence as independent states, have also been active, notably Angola, Egypt and Israel. Moreover, crisis initiation does not always match proneness to crisis. The USSR, Germany (pre-1945), the US and Israel were the most frequent catalysts; but the most frequent targets relative to initiation were some Third World states, Angola, Zambia, Lebanon, Jordan, Mozambique. And several states experienced fewer crises than they initiated, notably South Africa, Germany, Italy, and the USSR.[7]

Unified Model of Crisis

It became apparent early in this inquiry that interstate crisis is a dynamic whole which requires an integrated model to explain the multidimensional crisis process and crisis behavior, that is, how states cope with varying stress over time.

All models are flawed to some extent; that is, analytic perfection is beyond our grasp, at least in the present state of the art. While recognizing this limitation, the Unified Model of Crisis (UMC, Unified Model) is based upon the premise that social science can uncover the *essential* traits of any object of inquiry.

As indicated earlier, the UMC is, by design, a holistic model: it treats crisis as two distinct but interrelated segments of reality. These are captured by Models I and II (international and foreign policy crisis), which merge into Model III (interstate crisis), the Unified Model of Crisis. Thus the UMC integrates system and actor levels in dynamic, continuous interaction, including post-crisis feedback, and addresses them in all four phases/periods of a crisis. Moreover, this model employs both deductive and inductive methods of analysis, on the grounds that no single method has a monopoly of access to the truth about any phenomenon. Finally, it draws upon several strands of evidence, notably aggregate findings on all international and foreign policy crises from 1918 to 1988, and in-depth evidence from 11 case studies. As such, the Unified Model aspires to an architectonic unity, a synthesis of levels of analysis, methods, and types of evidence, to accord with its holistic perspective and function.

The Unified Model has unravelled many of the mysteries of twentieth-century interstate crises; that is, the model works. What does it mean to say, "the model works"? In the most general sense, the UMC provides a comprehensive explanation of the unfolding of crises from onset to termination and of how crisis actors cope during each phase, with an in-depth application to the Gulf Crisis [Chap. 7]. This view requires elaboration.

The Unified Model first explained crisis eruption and the process through which a state's foreign policy crisis is converted to the onset phase of an international crisis—or is aborted, if the target state does not respond to the value threat. The onset model, the first of four phase models within the overarching UMC, addressed key questions by deducing a set of hypotheses about outbreak and, at the actor level, initiation, the likelihood of violence at both levels, and vulnerability to crisis. Moreover, recognizing the ubiquity of crisis in time and space, the onset model offered "most likely" explanations; that is, it postulated the conditions in which a crisis is most likely to break out and to be initiated, with or without violence. Key concepts of the Unified Model, namely, trigger, value threat, stress, coping and choice, were operationalized for the onset phase. And the crucial process of step-level change from onset to escalation was explained.

The onset phase model set the tone and the form of those that follow. Each of the subsequent phase models—escalation, deescalation, impact—addressed key questions by generating hypotheses on the most likely conditions in which an aspect of the spiral process (escalation), the accommodation process (deescalation), and feedback or consequences (impact) is most likely to occur. The result was 14 hypotheses which were tested with the evidence of 390 international and 826 foreign policy crises during the 70 years after the end of World War I. In short, the necessary confrontation between theory and reality was achieved.[8]

Hypothesis-Testing

Another "cut" on what has been learned about twentieth-century crises is derived from the testing of hypotheses, those generated by the Unified Model and, later, some from cumulative crisis research on coping with stress. I begin with the former: the findings are based upon aggregate data from the end of 1918 to the end of 1988, and from 11 cases from 1938 to 1990–91 that were examined in earlier chapters.

The first seven hypotheses focus on escalation, three at the system/interactor level, followed by four at the actor level.

Hypothesis Test [HT.] 1. The spiral from incipient to fully-crystallized international crisis [H. 1] was found to be most likely to occur in a polycentric structure, in a subsystem setting, when the main actors are territorially contiguous, with high heterogeneity between them; and when more than two adversaries are engaged (mixed support) [Table 3.1].[9]

As evident in Table 8.1, which summarizes the extent of "fit" between the 11 interstate crises that were explored in depth and the hypotheses tested with aggregate data, seven cases fit a majority of the postulated conditions of escalation: October-Yom Kippur, all of them; Rhodesia UDI, Falklands/Malvinas, and the Gulf crisis-war, five of the seven conditions; and Berlin Blockade, Prague Spring, and Lebanon Civil War I, each four conditions (some of these cases fit one or more of the postulated conditions not supported by aggregate data, but not all of those noted above). The other cases fit only two or three of them.

HT.2. From the aggregate data, violent escalation of an international crisis [H.2] was found to be most likely when three fully-supported conditions of H.1 noted above—polycentric structure, subsystem level, and geographic contiguity—are present, along with authoritarian regimes in the main adversaries and a protracted conflict setting [Table 3.2].

None of the 11 cases met all three additional postulated conditions of violent escalation. However, four of them—Prague Spring, Stalingrad, Hungarian Uprising, and the Gulf Crisis—fit two of them.

HT.3. Escalation to high-severity violence during a crisis [H. 3] was found to occur most frequently when eight of the ten conditions specified in H. 1 and 2 are present, along with a violent trigger to escalation, and a reciprocal or stronger response by the target [Table 3.3].

Both trigger and response conditions are evident in five of the eight reported cases—Stalingrad, Lebanon Civil War I, India/China Border, Falklands/Malvinas, and the Gulf Crisis. Three other cases met one of these conditions, namely, a reciprocal or stronger response. Berlin Blockade, Munich and Rhodesia UDI were, as noted, not characterized by violence.

Taking the three system-level hypotheses [H.1–3] together: the Gulf Crisis and October-Yom Kippur fit nine of the 12 postulated conditions of escalation, Falklands/Malvinas, eight of them. Three other cases match seven conditions.

HT.4. The conditions most likely to lead a state to initiate a full-scale foreign policy crisis [H. 4] are: an authoritarian political regime; high positive power discrepancy; territorial contiguity to its adversary; newly-acquired independence; and increasing internal instability [Table 3.5].

As evident from Table 8.1, initiators in four of the 11 cases met most of the six postulated conditions: Egypt, as the catalyst to Israel's October-Yom Kippur Crisis (five conditions); Czechoslovakia, in the Prague Spring Crisis; Rhodesia, the triggering entity for Zambia in Rhodesia UDI; and Iraq, for Kuwait in the Gulf crisis-war (four conditions each). Six other triggering states met three of the conditions. (H. 4 was not relevant to Lebanon Civil War I, for the initiator was a non-state actor.)

HT.5. Violent escalation of a full-scale foreign policy crisis is most likely [H. 5] when all the conditions cited above except positive power discrepancy [HT.4] are present, along with a protracted conflict setting [Table 3.6].

One case, Egypt in October–Yom Kippur, fits six of the seven post-

TABLE 8.1 *Hypothesis-Testing: Aggregate and Case Study Findings*

Hypothesis	Number of Postulated Conditions Supported by Aggregate Data[1]	Number of Postulated Conditions Supported by Case Studies										
		Berlin Blockade 1948–49[2]	Prague Spring 1968	Munich 1938	Stalingrad 1942–43	October – Yom Kippur 1973–74	Lebanon Civil War I 1975–76	India/China Border 1959–63	Hungarian Uprising 1956–57	Rhodesia UDI 1965–66	Falklands/ Malvinas 1982	Gulf 1990–91
1. Escalation – International Crisis	4 of 7	4	4	2	3	7	4	2	2	5	5	5
2. Violent Escalation	5 of 10	NR	6	NR	5	8	5	2	4	NR	6	7
3. High-severity Violence	10 of 12	NR	7	NR	7	9	7	4	5	NR	8	9
4. Escalation – Full-Scale Foreign Policy Crisis	5 of 6	3	4	3	3	5	3	3	3	4	3	4
5. Violent Escalation	5 of 7	NR	4	NR	4	6	3	4	3	NR	3	5
6. Vulnerability to Crisis	4 of 7	4	4	2	3	4	4	3	2	5	2	6
7. Vulnerability to Violent Escalation	8 of 9	4	4	2	3	5	6	3	2	7	3	7

	Conditions supported	1	2	3	4	5	6	7	8	9	10	11
8. *Termination in Agreement*	3 of 6	1	5	4	3	1	3	1	4	2	3	5
9. *Short Duration*	6 of 6	NR	NR	NR	NR	NR	NR	NR	4	NR	4	6
10. *Accommodative Strategy*	5 of 6	3	4	5	4	2	4	2	3	5	1	4
11. *Satisfaction with Outcome*	4 of 4	2	2	2	2	1	4	3	3	3	3	3
12. *Higher Tension Between Adversaries*	7 of 8	6	4	5	6	6	4	3	4	3	4	8
13. *High Intensity – High Impact*	6 of 6	5	2	4	3	6	4	5	4	4	4	6
14. *System Transformation*	10 of 10	6	4	6	7	9	5	5	6	6	5	9

NR = not reported; see Table 3.9, n. 1, Table 4.5, n. 2.
1. "Conditions supported" includes all elements of each hypothesis with some degree of support, from very strong to modest. This column is derived from Tables 3.1–3.3, 3.5–3.8, 4.1–4.4, and 5.4–5.6.
2. The data for the 11 cases in this table are derived from: Table 3.9 (Escalation, H.1–7); Table 4.5 (Deescalation, H.8–11); Table 5.8 (Impact, H.12–14); and Table 7.2 (Gulf Crisis, all hypotheses).
3. As indicated in Table 3.9, since the initiator of Syria's Lebanon Civil War I Crisis was a non-state actor, this case cannot be tested for H.4 and 5.

ulated conditions. Iraq in the Gulf Crisis fits five of them. Three other cases, e.g., Czechoslovakia in Prague Spring, match four conditions. The obverse coding for the non-violent cases—Berlin Blockade, Munich, Rhodesia—was not reported. And this hypothesis was not relevant to Lebanon Civil War I.

HT.6. Vulnerability to a full-scale foreign policy crisis was found to be highest [H. 6] when: a state is not a member of the dominant system; its regime is non-democratic; it is territorially contiguous to the initiator; and it is experiencing increasing internal instability [Table 3.7].[10]

Three cases—Syria in Lebanon Civil War I, Zambia in Rhodesia UDI, and Kuwait in Gulf War II—met three of these four supported conditions of most likely vulnerability. As for the seven postulated conditions, the best fit was Kuwait, six conditions, followed by Zambia, five conditions. The USSR in Berlin Blockade, Poland in the Prague Spring, Israel in October-Yom Kippur, and Syria in Lebanon Civil War I fit four of the conditions.

HT.7. Finally, a state's proneness to violent escalation [H. 7] was found to be most likely when all of the postulated conditions of vulnerability, except increasing instability [HT.6], are present, along with a political regime of short duration and a small territory [Table 3.8].

Only two cases, Syria in Lebanon Civil War I and Zambia in Rhodesia UDI, fit both conditions. Three other cases, Israel in October-Yom Kippur, the UK in Falklands/Malvinas, and Kuwait in the Gulf Crisis, fit one of these conditions.

[The findings from the 11 cases on H. 1–7 were derived from Tables 3.9 and 7.2.]

The next four hypotheses generated by the Unified Model focus on deescalation leading to termination.

HT.8. The winding-down process is not well-explained by the deescalation model: one of the postulated conditions in H. 8, great power activity, is *strongly* supported, with *moderate* support for the number of adversaries, and *modest* support for conflict setting [Table 4.1].

Eight of the 11 cases ended through a unilateral act or an imposed agreement and were therefore assessed for the obverse of this hypothesis. Prague Spring and the Gulf Crisis fit five of the obverse conditions, while Munich and Hungarian Uprising match four of them.

HT.9. By contrast, all six elements of H. 9 that purport to explain the duration of an international crisis are supported by the aggregate evidence, five of them strongly: few adversaries in a crisis; non-military activity by major powers; low geostrategic salience; low heterogeneity between the adversaries; few issues, and non-violent crisis management techniques [Table 4.2].

Since eight of the 11 cases were of long duration, and three of those were "mixed," i.e., low intensity and long duration, the matching exercise focused on the obverse of the elements specified in H. 9 for five cases, along with the three cases of low intensity and short duration. October–Yom Kippur and the Gulf Crisis fit all six conditions. Berlin Blockade fits five of them. And four other cases—Munich, Stalingrad, Hungarian Uprising, and Falklands/Malvinas, match four conditions.

HT.10. A state's adoption of an accommodative strategy in crisis bargaining is more likely [H. 10] when: a foreign policy crisis occurs in a non-protracted conflict setting; the concerned state perceives little power discrepancy *vis-à-vis* its adversary; it has a democratic political regime; and it receives non-military support from a major power, along with the backing of the relevant international organization [Table 4.3].

Five of the 11 state actors assessed for this hypothesis did not adopt an accommodative strategy. Thus, as in similar cases relating to H. 8 and 9, they were scored for the obverse of the postulated conditions. The upshot is that two cases—the UK in Munich and Zambia in Rhodesia UDI—fit five of the six conditions. Four other cases—the USSR in Prague Spring, Germany in Stalingrad, Syria in Lebanon Civil War I, and Iraq in the Gulf Crisis—match four conditions or their obverse.

HT.11. Satisfaction with the outcome of a foreign policy crisis is most likely [H. 11] when: it occurs outside a protracted conflict; the state concerned receives military aid from a major power; and it perceives victory, along with the backing of the relevant IO; that is, all four postulated conditions are supported [Table 4.4].

One of the 11 cases—Syria in Lebanon Civil War I—fits all four conditions of H. 11. Five other cases—the PRC in India/China Border, the USSR in Hungarian Uprising, Rhodesia in Rhodesia UDI, the UK in Falklands/Malvinas, and the US in the Gulf Crisis—fit three of the conditions.

[The findings from the 11 cases on H. 8–11 were derived from Tables 4.5 and 7.2.]

The last three UMC-derived hypotheses focus on the impact of crises.

HT.12. The aggregate data on bilateral effects [H. 12] reveal support for six of the eight postulated sources of higher tension, and part of a seventh. Three show very strong support—crisis termination without agreement; several actors; high activity by the great powers (but not high activity by the superpowers). The others are high geostrategic salience; high heterogeneity between the main adversaries; several issues in dispute, and severe violence [Table 5.4].

One of the 11 cases—the Gulf Crisis—fit all eight conditions of higher tension between the main adversaries. Three matched six of the conditions—Berlin Blockade, Stalingrad and October-Yom Kippur. Munich met five of them. And in four others four conditions applied.

HT.13. A close link between crisis intensity and system impact [H. 13] is discerned from the aggregate data: that is, the presence of several crisis actors, high major power involvement, high geostrategic salience, high heterogeneity between the adversaries, several issues, and severe violence are the conditions most likely to lead to high impact on the relevant international system [Table 5.5.1].

Five of the 11 cases were characterized by low intensity and had a relatively low impact. Thus they were coded for the obverse conditions. Two cases—October–Yom Kippur and the Gulf Crisis—fit all six conditions of high impact. Berlin Blockade and India/China Border fit five of them or their obverse. And five other crises—Munich, Lebanon Civil War I, Hungarian Uprising, Rhodesia UDI and Falklands/Malvinas —met four of the conditions or their obverse; that is, nine cases fit at least two-thirds of the conditions of high or low impact.

HT.14. As for basic system change [H. 14], the most likely conditions were found to be all six elements relating to H. 13, along with: the most extreme catalyst to crisis escalation, that is, direct violence; the use of severe violence in crisis management, and an outcome without agreement [Table 5.6].

As with H.13, five of the 11 cases were coded for the obverse of those conditions. Stalingrad alone met all the four additional postulated conditions specified in H.14. Two other cases—October–Yom Kippur and the Gulf Crisis—fit three of those extra conditions. If one takes the 10 conditions of system transformation supported by aggregate data, that is, the elements of H. 13 and 14 combined, three cases rank high:

October–Yom Kippur and the Gulf Crisis (nine of 10 conditions), and Stalingrad, seven.

[The findings from the 11 cases on H. 12–14 are taken from Tables 5.8 and 7.2.]

Methods and Findings

Another perspective on crisis findings focuses on the perennial controversy over *the* optimal method of analysis in the social sciences. This takes the form of a comparison between aspects of crisis explained by the use of deductive and inductive methods. The results, derived from the Unified Model of Crisis [Table 6.3] and from hypothesis-testing [Table 8.1], are presented in Table 8.2.

The findings are instructive. Six of the 15 independent variables in the UMC [Chap. 6] reveal full empirical support for deductively-derived linkages. Geographic distance was postulated as partly explaining four aspects of crisis; and all four expectations—regarding escalation to full-scale crisis, violent escalation, crisis initiation, and vulnerability—were very strongly supported by the evidence from the end of 1918 to the end of 1988.[11] The data also show very strong support for the deduced link between geostrategic salience and short duration, as well as high systemic impact of a crisis.

Structure and system level address two of five systemic aspects, namely, outbreak of a full-scale international crisis, and violence in the escalation process. The evidence shows very strong support for the effect of system level on both aspects, very strong and strong support for the effect of structure. IO involvement, too, helps to explain all three expected effects, strongly for satisfaction with outcome and moderately for an accommodative strategy and the winding-down process.

Other independent variables with a very close fit between deductively- and inductively-derived linkages are: number of actors, five of six crisis aspects;[12] heterogeneity, regime type and issues, four of five; internal instability, three of four; and major power activity, six of eight. In sum, *12 of the 15 independent variables are closely matched in results derived from the two methods*. The exceptions are conflict setting, capability and violence.

There is further evidence of a close fit. Together, the 15 independent variables generated 66 partial explanations of the nine aspects of crisis from outbreak to impact. Fifty of these, that is, three-fourths of the

TABLE 8.2 *Unified Model and Hypothesis-Testing: Comparison of Findings*

Independent Variable† / Multiple-Phase Variables	Aspects Addressed / Deductively-Derived Linkages°	Aspects Supported / Inductively-Derived Linkages	Inductively-Derived Linkages	Level	Tables
Conflict Setting	7	1 strong	Violent escalation	system	3.2, 3.3
		3 moderate[1]	Vulnerability to violent escalation	actor	3.8
			Winding down to agreement	system	4.1
			Satisfaction with outcome	actor	4.4
Capability	6	1 very strong	Initiation of crisis	actor	3.5
		1 strong	Vulnerability to violent escalation	actor	3.8
		1 moderate[1]	Accommodative strategy	actor	4.3
Regime Type	5	1 very strong	Initiation of Crisis	actor	3.5
		2 strong	Violent escalation	system	3.2, 3.3
			Vulnerability to escalation and violence	actor	3.7, 3.8
		1 moderate[1]	Accommodative strategy	actor	4.3
Internal Instability	4	3 very strong	Initiation of crisis	actor	3.5
			Violent escalation	actor	3.6
			Vulnerability to escalation	actor	3.7
Number of Actors	6	3 very strong	Escalation to full-scale crisis[2]	system	3.1
			Short duration	system	4.2
			System effect – high impact	system	5.5.1
		1 strong	Violent escalation	system	3.3
		1 moderate	Bilateral effect – higher tension	interactor	5.4
Heterogeneity	5	2 very strong	Escalation to full-scale crisis	system	3.1
			Bilateral effect – higher tension	interactor	5.4
		1 strong	System effect – high impact	system	5.5.1
		1 moderate	Short duration	system	4.2

Issues	5	2 very strong	Violent escalation	system	3.3
			Short duration	system	4.2
		2 strong	Bilateral effect – higher tension	interactor	5.4
			System effect – high impact	system	5.5.1
Major Power Activity	8	2 very strong	System effect – high impact	system	5.5.1
			Bilateral effect – higher tension[3]	interactor	5.4
		3 strong	Violent escalation	system	3.3
			Short duration	system	4.2
			Accommodative Strategy[4]	actor	4.3
		1 moderate	Satisfaction with outcome	actor	4.4
Dual-Phase Variables					
Structure	2	1 very strong	Violent escalation[5]	system	3.2
		1 strong	Escalation to full-scale crisis[6]	system	3.1
System Level	2	2 very strong	Escalation to full-scale crisis	system	3.1
			Violent escalation	system	3.2
Geographic Distance	4	4 very strong	Escalation to full-scale crisis	system	3.1
			Violent escalation	system, actor	3.2, 3.3, 3.6
			Initiation of crisis	actor	3.5
			Vulnerability to escalation and violence	actor	3.7, 3.8
Age	4	3 very strong	Initiation of crisis	actor	3.5
			Violent escalation	actor	3.6
			Vulnerability to violent escalation	actor	3.8
Geostrategic Salience	3	2 very strong[1]	Short duration	system	4.2
			System effect – high impact	system	5.5.1

Table 8.2 *Continued*

Independent Variable†	Aspects Addressed Deductively-Derived Linkages°	Aspects Supported Inductively-Derived Linkages		Level	Tables
Multiple-Phase Variables					
Single-Phase Variables					
IO Involvement	3	1 strong 2 moderate	Satisfaction with outcome	actor	4.4
			Winding down to agreement	system	4.1
			Accommodative strategy	actor	4.3
Violence	2	1 strong	System effect, high impact	system	5.5.1
Total	66	50[7]			

†The sequence of independent variables in this table follows that in Table 6.3, with which it is analytically linked; but only 15 of the 24 independent variables are analyzed here.

°There are nine aspects for which causal links were deduced, as distinct from the 17 propositions and hypotheses: crisis outbreak – escalation; violence in crisis; initiation of crisis; vulnerability to crisis; termination; accommodative strategy; satisfaction with outcome; bilateral effect – high tension; systemic effect – high impact;

For the content of deductively-derived aspects, see Table 6.3.

1. There was, too, modest support for the postulated links between: conflict setting and two other aspects – the adoption of an accommodative strategy, and satisfaction with a crisis outcome (Tables 4.3, 4.4); between capability and accommodative strategy (Table 4.3); between regime type and accommodative strategy (Table 4.3); between geostrategy and violence and higher tension (Table 5.4); etc.
2. For involved actors, not crisis actors.
3. There is strong support for great power activity, 1918–39.
4. There is strong support for superpower activity, 1945–88.
5. Very strong for bipolar–polycentric; strong for multipolar–polycentric.
6. Strong-to-very strong for multipolar–polycentric; moderate-to-strong for bipolar–polycentric.
7. There was also very strong support for the expectations of: severe violence during the escalation phase of an international crisis when the trigger was violent, and a response by the target of equal or stronger severity (Table 3.3); and for the link between regime type and vulnerability to violent escalation.

deductively-derived linkages, were supported by the empirical evidence, and forty of those with strong or very strong support.

Among the crisis aspects explored, the most important are: outbreak of a full-scale crisis, that is, the escalation process; the role of violence in escalation; initiation of crisis; vulnerability; the winding-down process, and impact. *Ranked in terms of explanatory power vis-à-vis* these aspects, a core cluster of independent variables emerges. *The most potent are: geographic distance; structure; system level; major power activity, and IO involvement.* Others, notably *number of actors, age, and heterogeneity,* contribute to an understanding of the multi-faceted crisis phenomenon and can be added to this group. However, if parsimony is sought, these five are the crucial variables in the explanation of interstate crisis.

With the completion of the "internal" hypothesis-testing exercise, in which the unified model and its derived hypotheses were tested with aggregate and case evidence, I turn to the "external" exercise. This will take the form of relating findings on coping with crisis, uncovered in this book and the ICB Project as a whole, to hypotheses generated by others.

Cumulation of Knowledge

Earlier in the long quest for knowledge about interstate crises, a fundamental assumption of this inquiry was stated as follows:

> The basic premise that has guided our empirical research . . . is that there are important strands of regularity in the behavior of states in the international [global] system, and that such regularities can be identified through careful and systematic examination of relevant cases over reasonably long periods of time. . . . It is often difficult for policymakers faced with specific situations, or scholars writing from a single case-study approach, to discern [these patterns]. Our role as social scientists is to identify these regularities where they exist, and to attempt to provide adequate explanations for them (Wilkenfeld and Brecher, 1982: 208).

Since the early 1960s an array of hypotheses on crisis has been generated, especially on coping with stress. Its magnitude is evident in the earliest and still the most comprehensive of the compilations, Hermann's (1972b) list of 311 "empirically testable propositions," derived from ten studies for his pioneer volume on the subject. Many more have been added since then. Many are redundant. Some seem, *a priori,* important, and others less so.

The cumulation of knowledge on crisis and, especially, on coping has not been free from controversy, sometimes accompanied by rancor.

Perhaps none has been so bitter as the continuing "war" between political psychologists, e.g., the works of George, O. R. Holsti, Jervis, Lebow, and Stein, individually and jointly, cited earlier in this book, and the proponents of rational actor behavior, e.g., Bueno de Mesquita, Achen and Snidal, Brams and Kilgour, and James, also cited earlier. The former, relying on the findings of cognitive psychology, have asserted the innate limitations on the capacity of decision-makers to cope effectively with high stress in an interstate crisis, acknowledging, at best, a severely "bounded rationality." The latter, with rare exceptions, e.g. Achen and Snidal, 1989, ignore the claims of the psychologists and assume a capacity for unqualified rational calculus by decision-makers.

The difference between the contending views can be highlighted by focusing on the inverted-U curve that relates stress to performance. Political psychologists claim that, in crises, the relationship is past the peak and that high stress leads to diminished performance. Advocates of rational choice claim that stress level correlates with the importance of the task at hand. Thus attentiveness will increase under high stress and enhance performance, except in situations of overwhelming tension, which are assumed to be infrequent, even during crises. Thus the stress-performance link will be at or near the top of the U-shaped curve during a crisis.

This seemingly academic issue has far-reaching practical implications in a world of potentially catastrophic military technology. Are decision-makers able to read correctly the signs of impending crisis and potential escalation to war? Can they calculate the costs and benefits of alternative courses of action, free from the constraining effects of stress? Can they search for and process information, or search for and consider options, unhindered by rising stress? Are they able to brake the thrust to violence and the adverse consequences of a spiral effect that can lead the adversaries into the unknown arena of war in an era of proliferating weapons of mass destruction, e.g., Iraq's stockpiles before, during, and after the Gulf crisis-war of 1990–91? In short, can they cope with value threat, time pressure and the heightened probability of war, so as to achieve their goals without horrendous costs to their adversaries, themselves, neighbors and far-off lands and peoples, and the global commons, that is, the fragile environment for all?

To answer these questions definitively may be beyond the state of the art, competing claims notwithstanding. What is possible, however, is a great leap in the cumulation of knowledge, by drawing on the abundant evidence uncovered in the case studies of how decision-makers coped with crisis at different levels of stress, in some of the celebrated crises of the century, as well as some on the peripheries of the major power dominant system.

There are several methods of cumulating knowledge. The path to be followed here is to select "important" hypotheses on coping and to test them against these and other cases. The main criterion for choosing these hypotheses is their high visibility in research on crisis during the past few decades. Moreover, they tap crucial psychological-political aspects of behavior: the *effects of higher or increasing stress*, and the *effects of decision time*.

The 19 hypotheses, chosen from among hundreds that have been generated by scholars, are designed to contribute further to the cumulation of knowledge about crisis behavior. They focus on the *cognitive* dimension, for individuals and groups, and the *decisional* dimension, including information processing, consultation and communication, the decision-making forum, and the consideration of alternatives. Taken together, they draw attention to what, by consensus, are the most salient questions regarding behavior in interstate crises.

The hypotheses were tested by experts, namely, authors of in-depth case studies associated with the ICB project. The scores—Supported, Not Supported, Mixed, etc.—for each of the 11 cases explored in Chapters 2–5 and 7 are derived from books and unpublished studies noted in the analysis of coping with low stress during the pre-crisis period [Chap. 2 above]. Evidence from six other cases is included in this exercise: Trieste 1953 (Italy); Lebanon 1958 (US); Berlin Wall 1961 (US); Six Day War 1967 (Israel); Syria/Jordan Confrontation 1970 (US); and Nuclear Alert 1973 (US). The sources are specified in the notes to Table 8.3, which presents the results of hypothesis-testing.

In order to make the skeletal "scores" more meaningful, evidence from one or more of the 17 cases will now be cited for each of the hypotheses.

H. 1. "As crisis-induced stress increases, the more concerned the decision-maker(s) will be with the immediate rather than the long-run future."

In the 1961 Berlin Wall Crisis, President Kennedy, the key US decision-maker, adopted an accommodative stance during the rising stress period, in decisions on 15 June, 8 and 19 July, "to employ the mixed options of partial mobilization and overtures for negotiations to settle the question" (Pold, 1991: 32, based upon Schick, 1971: 148; all subsequent findings on this case are from Pold). This posture was

TABLE 8.3 *Testing Hypotheses of Earlier Crisis Research*

Other than Hypotheses 7, 14, 15, 17 and 18, which relate to the effects of Time, the following hypotheses focus on the impact of Stress and are framed in the following terms: The higher the crisis-induced stress, . . . or As crisis-induced stress increases, . . .	Berlin Blockade US	Prague Spring USSR	Munich UK	Stalingrad Germany	October – Yom Kippur Israel	Lebanon Civil War I Syria	India/ China India	Hungarian Uprising Hungary	Rhodesia UDI Zambia	Falklands/ Malvinas Argentina	Gulf US
A. Cognitive Dimension											
1. the more concerned the decision-maker(s) will be with the immediate rather than the long-run future.	NS	NS	Mixed	Mixed	S	NS	S	S	S		NS
2. the greater the felt need, and consequent quest, for information.	S	S	S	S	S	S	S	S	S		S
3. the more closed (conceptually rigid) to new information the decision-maker(s) become.	S	S	NS	S	Mixed	NS	S	S	NS		NS
4. the more the decision-maker(s) will supplement information by relying on past experience as a guide to choice.	S	S	MD	S	S	S	S	S	S		S
5. the more active the information search is likely to become, but also more random and unproductive	NS	S	S/NS°	S	S	S	S	S	S/NS°		S/NS°

	(1)	(2)	(3)	(4)	(5)	(6)	(7)	(8)
6. the more information about a crisis tends to be elevated to the top of the decisional pyramid.	S	S	NS	S	S	S	S	S
B. Decisional Dimension								
a) Consultation/Communication								
7. (The longer the crisis decision time), the greater the consultation with persons outside the core decisional unit.	S	NS	NS	S	S	S	Mixed	S
8. the greater the reliance on extraordinary channels of communication.	S	S	S	S	S	S	S	NS
9. the higher the rate of communication with international actors.	S	Mixed	nr	S	S	S	S	S
b) Decisional Forum								
10. the smaller the decision group tends to become, that is, the greater the tendency to centralized decision-making.	S	NS	S	NS	NS	S	NS	S
11. the greater the tendency for decisions to be reached by *ad hoc* groups.	S	NS	Mixed	NS	NS	S	NS	S
12. the greater the tendency to "groupthink", that is, to conformity with group norms.	NS			S		S	S	NS

TABLE 8.3 *Continued*

	Berlin Blockade	Prague Spring	Munich	Stalingrad	October – Yom Kippur	Lebanon Civil War I	India/ China	Hungarian Uprising	Rhodesia UDI	Falklands/ Malvinas	Gulf
	US	USSR	UK	Germany	Israel	Syria	India	Hungary	Zambia	Argentina	US
13. the greater the felt need for face-to-face proximity among decision-makers.	S	S		NS	S	S	S	S			S
14. (The longer the crisis decision time), the greater the felt need for effective leadership within the decisional unit.	S			S	S	NS	S	S			S
15. (The longer the crisis decision time), the greater the consensus on the ultimate decision.	NS	S		Mixed	S		S	NS			S
c) Alternatives											
16. the less careful the evaluation of alternatives.	NS	NS		MD	NS	NS	S	NS	NS		NS
17. (The shorter the crisis decision time), the greater the tendency to premature closure.	NS			Mixed	NS	NS		Mixed	NS	S	NS

18. (The shorter the crisis decision time), the more likely will decisions be made with inadequate assessment of consequences, that is, with less sensitivity to negative feedback.	NS	NS	NS	NS		S	NS
d) General							
19. High stress is dysfunctional; that is, cognitive and, therefore, decisional performance will be greatly influenced by psychological biases and will deteriorate markedly.	NS	NS	Mixed	Mixed	NS	S	NS / S / NS

Code:

S   = supported
NS = not supported
nr   = not relevant
MD = missing data
Mixed = mixed findings that cancel each other out
A blank set means that the relevant hypothesis was not tested in the specific case.

*When two scores are specified, they refer to the two different parts of the hypothesis being tested.

Supplementary Findings on Hypothesis-Testing [Table 8.3]

The sources for the six additional cases are: Trieste 1953 [Italy] [Croci, 1991]; Lebanon 1958 [US] [Dowty, 1984]; Berlin Wall 1961 [US] [Pold, 1991]; Six Day War 1967 [Israel] [Brecher with Geist, 1980]; Syria/Jordan Confrontation 1970 [US] [Dowty, 1984]; and Nuclear Alert 1973 [US] [Dowty, 1984].

1. H.1 is supported by: Six Day War/[Israel] [hereafter, SDW]; Syria/Jordan Confrontation [US] [hereafter S/J Conf.]; and Nuclear Alert [US]; it is not supported by Berlin Wall [US]; the findings for Lebanon 1958 [US] are mixed [hereafter Lebanon]; this hypothesis was not tested for Trieste [Italy].
2. H.2 is supported by: Trieste; Lebanon; Berlin Wall; SDW; S/J Conf.; Nuclear Alert.
3. H.3 is supported by Lebanon; S/J Conf.; Nuclear Alert; the findings for SDW are mixed; it is not supported by Berlin Wall; this hypothesis was not tested for Trieste.

TABLE 8.3 *Continued*

4. H.4 is supported by: Lebanon; SDW; S/J Conf.; Nuclear Alert; it was not tested for Trieste or Berlin Wall.
5. H.5 is supported by: Trieste [the first part]; Lebanon; SDW [the first part]; S/J Conf.; Nuclear Alert; it is not supported by Trieste or SDW [the second party], and by Berlin Wall.
6. H.6 is supported by: Lebanon; SDW; S/J Conf.; Nuclear Alert; the findings are mixed for Trieste; it was not tested for Berlin Wall.
7. H.7 is supported by: SDW; S/J Conf.; and Nuclear Alert; it is not supported by Lebanon; it was not tested for Trieste or Berlin Wall.
8. H.8 is supported by: Lebanon; SDW; S/J Conf.; Nuclear Alert; it is not supported by Trieste; and it was not tested for Berlin Wall.
9. H.9 is supported by: Lebanon; Berlin Wall; SDW; S/J Conf.; Nuclear Alert; it is not supported by Trieste.
10. H.10 is supported by: Lebanon; Berlin Wall; S/J Conf.; Nuclear Alert; it is not supported by Trieste.
11. H.11 is supported by: Lebanon; Berlin Wall; S/J Conf.; and Nuclear Alert; it is not supported by Trieste and by SDW.
12. H.12 is supported by: SDW; it is not supported by Trieste; it was not tested for the other cases.
13. H.13 is supported by: Lebanon; Berlin Wall; SDW; S/J Conf.; and Nuclear Alert; it is not supported by Trieste.
14. H.14 is supported by: Lebanon; SDW; S/J Conf.; and Nuclear Alert; it is not supported by Trieste; and it was not tested for Berlin Wall.
15. H.15 is supported by: SDW; and Nuclear Alert; it is not supported by Trieste; Lebanon; S/J Conf.; it was not tested for Berlin Wall.
16. H.16 is not supported by: Trieste; Lebanon; Berlin Wall; SDW; S/J Conf.; and Nuclear Alert.
17. H.17 is not supported by: Trieste; Lebanon; Berlin Wall; SDW; S/J Conf.; and Nuclear Alert.
18. H.18 is not supported by: Lebanon; Berlin Wall; SDW; and S/J Conf.; it is supported by Nuclear Alert; and it was not tested for Trieste.
19. H.19 is not supported by: Trieste; Lebanon; SDW; S/J Conf.; and Nuclear Alert; it was not tested for Berlin Wall.

expressed in his nation-wide speech on 25 July. And his decision of 16 August, to dispatch a token battle group of 1500 from West Germany to West Berlin, was a clear signal of his preference for a diplomatic solution and of his long-term perspective: for Kennedy, the Berlin Wall Crisis was an episode in a dangerous protracted conflict; and the avoidance of war with the Soviet Union was more important than an unlikely symbolic "victory" in this East/West crisis. Hence the coding, Not Supported.

In the rising stress stage of its Six Day War Crisis, Israel's decision-makers were preoccupied with immediate challenges rather than long-run goals: after 22 May 1967, the goal of lifting Nasser's proclaimed blockade of the Strait of Tiran; and from 28 May to 4 June, the goal of countering Egypt's massive concentration of forces on Israel's Sinai border. Only Foreign Minister Eban, among Israel's senior decision-makers, emphasized the longer-term goal of support from US and world public opinion in the political struggle that would follow a war (Brecher with Geist, 1980: 248; all subsequent findings on this case are from this source). Thus the coding, Supported.

H. 2. "... the greater the felt need, and consequent quest, for information."

During the UK's Munich Crisis of 1938 there was a dramatic increase in the volume of information, from 7 September onwards, when stress rose steadily. One indicator was the four-fold increase in the average daily number of diplomatic messages transmitted to and from the Foreign Office: from 6.3 during the pre-crisis period of 3 August–6 September—it was 4.8 in the non-crisis months of June and July—to 26.2 in the crisis period, 7–30 September (Woodward, vol. II, 1949, cited in P. Wilson, 1984: section 4, 2; all subsequent findings on this case are from Wilson). Other indicators were Prime Minister Chamberlain's trips to Berchtesgaden (15 September) and Godesberg (22 September), to elicit further information on Hitler's intentions and resolve, and his dispatch of Horace Wilson as a special emissary on 26–27 September to transmit his "last, last word" to Hitler. Hence the coding, Supported.

In Italy's Trieste Crisis, the felt need for information grew markedly from the beginning of the crisis period. As a tangible indicator of the greater quest for information, the number of cables between Rome and the three Western capitals "more than doubled after August 29, reached its peak after October 10 and began to decline after December

5," the starting dates of the three periods of that crisis (Croci, 1991: 419; all subsequent findings on this case are from this source). Hence the coding, Supported.

H. 3. "... the more closed [conceptually rigid] to new information the decision-maker(s) become."

President Kennedy constantly sought new information during the Berlin Wall Crisis. And, while some conceptual rigidity was evident in his early favorable disposition to former Secretary of State Acheson's hard line, his mind was not closed to the accommodative strategy recommended by the US's Soviet experts, which, in fact, he accepted. Thus the coding, Not Supported.[13]

In the UK's Munich Crisis, there was more conceptual flexibility as stress increased, not the reverse. On 20 September 1938 London tried to compel Prague to accept the UK–France proposals, which would have meant abject surrender to German demands. Five days later, with much higher stress, the British Cabinet decided not to press the Czechoslovaks to accept the even harsher Godesberg proposals; and on the 27th the Cabinet announced full mobilization. These acts do not provide evidence of conceptual rigidity. Thus the coding, Not Supported.

H. 4. "... the more the decision-maker(s) will supplement information by relying on past experience as a guide to choice."

This was clearly evident in Israel's 1967 crisis: the decision-makers' initial reading of Nasser's intention as a replay of the brief "Rottem" Crisis between Egypt and Israel in February 1960, that is, a symbolic gesture in support of Syria; the perception of Nasser's closing of the Straits on 22–23 May as a sign of Egypt's continuing goal of politicide, that is, the destruction of Israel as a state; and the interpretation of the Egypt–Jordan Defense Pact on 30 May as the recurrence of the tripartite Arab military pact in October 1956, on the eve of the Sinai–Suez War. Hence the coding, Supported.

From the moment news reached Washington that Iraq had invaded Kuwait, on 2 August 1990, President Bush personalized the Gulf Crisis, with Saddam Hussein cast in the role of Hitler. And he frequently drew an analogy between aggression in Europe in the 1930s and Iraq's aggression in the Middle East in 1990, with the US—and him-self—engaging in a "just war" against the evil represented by Iraq's president [Chap. 7]. Hence the coding, Supported.

H. 5. "... the more active the information search is likely to become, but also more random and unproductive."

Italy's Trieste Crisis in 1953 indicates support for the first part of this hypothesis but not the second. With rising stress, Italy's decision-makers "increased their probe of existing sources. The additional information thus obtained continued to be seen as accurate and reliable." It was neither more random nor less productive: the more active search did not "produce a higher level of 'noise' " (Croci, 1991: 421). Hence the coding, Supported/Not Supported.

In the Lebanon 1958 crisis, the US's "search [for information] was reasonably thorough, and could not be described as random," as evident in the dispatch of Under-Secretary of State Robert Murphy to Lebanon, resulting in "a new and direct source of information from the field to the President himself" (Dowty, 1984: 93; all subsequent findings on this case are from this source). Thus the coding, Not Supported.

H. 6. "... the more information about a crisis tends to be elevated to the top of the decisional pyramid."

In the US's 1973 Nuclear Alert pre-crisis period, "there was a flood of 'raw' data to the top. . . . Communication became mostly 'vertical,' with little or no time for the 'horizontal' circulation and analysis of information." This intensified as stress increased. "In particular, there was a pronounced tendency to channel intelligence directly to the top of the decision-making hierarchy, often in the form of raw and unanalyzed data . . ." (Dowty, 1984: 303–305; all subsequent findings on this case are from this source). Hence the coding, Supported.

H. 7. "The longer the crisis decision time, the greater the consultation with persons outside the core decisional unit."

In the Berlin Blockade pre-crisis period, 1948, US consultation was confined to government officials. ". . . [R]ising stress and the magnitude of the issues facing the nation prompted a Democratic President to seek the involvement of the rival political élite," notably the invitation to Republican Senator Vandenberg and John Foster Dulles to participate in confidential State Department conferences on Berlin (Shlaim, 1983: 277; all subsequent findings on this case are from this source). Hence the coding, Supported.

H. 8. "As stress increases, the greater will be the reliance on extraordinary channels of communication."

In the USSR's Prague Spring Crisis of 1968, the disruption of normal information flows led to Moscow's reliance on "less reliable sources." These included: "[Czechoslovak] individuals who were demoted or threatened by the reforms and who presented a one-sided picture of events"; staff members in the Soviet embassy in Prague; and conservative officials in the Czech political and military élites (K. Dawisha, 1984: 352; all subsequent findings from this case are from this source). Hence the coding, Supported.

H. 9. ". . . the higher the rate of communication with international actors."

In the Berlin Wall Crisis, Kennedy and senior US officials consulted and coordinated policies with the UK and France. That process intensified as stress rose, and crucial decisions had to be made: to counter the erection of the Wall; to prepare for possible direct military hostilities against the GDR and its patron, the USSR, or to seek a diplomatic solution while continuing to make credible the US commitment to West Berlin. Thus the coding, Supported.

H. 10. ". . . the smaller the decision group tends to become, that is, the greater the tendency to centralized decision-making."

In the 1970 Syria/Jordan confrontation, "the size of the [US] decisional unit decreased as the perception of threat increased [during its crisis period]." WSAG (Washington Special Action Group), the special crisis management unit, met continuously; but decision-making passed to the daily meetings of the "Principals"—Nixon, Kissinger, Secretary of State Rogers, Defense Secretary Laird, CIA Director Helms, and Chairman of the Joint Chiefs, Admiral Moorer. (It was an almost identical small group that made the key US decisions during the Gulf crisis-war [Chap. 7].) And at the peak of the crisis, the US decisions were made by Nixon in consultation with Kissinger, the latter conducting most of the negotiations with Israeli Ambassador Rabin. (Dowty, 1984: 187; all subsequent findings on this case are from this source.) Hence the coding, Supported.

Italy's experience in the Trieste Crisis was different. In the "prelude" or pre-pre-crisis period, all the decisions were made by Prime Minister-Foreign Minister De Gasperi. During the three periods of the crisis proper, Prime Minister Pella relied heavily on his diplomatic advisors, the *de facto* crisis managers. Moreover, "there were no variations in this new decision-making pattern among the three periods, notwithstanding variations in the level of stress" (Croci, 1991: 427). Thus the coding, Not Supported.

H. 11. ". . . the greater the tendency for decisions to be reached by *ad hoc* groups."

In the Prague Spring Crisis, "the overwhelming impression . . . is that the Politburo remained the institutional focus for the formal and major decisions made on Czechoslovakia" (K. Dawisha, 1984: 361). Individuals like Defense Minister Grechko and Foreign Mnister Gromyko were also involved. And an inner core of the Politburo acted as the Negotiating Committee, with day-to-day management of the crisis —Brezhnev, Podgorny, Suslov, and Shelest. Yet they acted in the name of the Politburo. And most relevant, that core decisional unit did not change throughout the crisis. Nor was it *ad hoc*. Hence the coding, Not Supported.

H. 12. ". . . the greater the tendency to 'groupthink,' that is, to conformity with group norms."

In the Berlin Blockade Crisis, "the makers of American foreign policy did not become 'victims of groupthink' under the impact of crisis-induced stress, and groupthink certainly did not narrow the perceived range of alternatives in the interest of maintaining group cohesion" (Shlaim, 1983: 418). Among these were: a military defense of Berlin; a land convoy or airlift to sustain the West's presence; and a negotiated solution. Nor were riskier courses of action chosen under the impact of groupthink. Hence the coding, Not Supported.

Similarly, the US decisional forum in the Gulf Crisis exhibited candor and sharp disagreement, notably between a "dovish" and reluctant General Powell, Chairman of the JCS, and the more hawkish National Security Advisor, Scowcroft, and Defense Secretary Cheney. While all members of the *ad hoc* group recognized the President's primacy and closed ranks once a decision was reached, the discussions preceding choice were free, animated and contentious, with no evidence of "groupthink," whether because of fear of peer sanctions or any other reason. Thus the coding, Not Supported.

H. 13. " . . . the greater the felt need for face-to-face proximity among decision-makers."

In Italy's Trieste Crisis there was "a slightly higher pace of activity," but "business continued to be transacted as usual . . . phone calls and written memoranda continued to be the standard means of communication among decision-makers" (Croci, 1991: 425). There is no evidence of a felt need for more direct personal contact. Hence the coding, Not Supported.

H. 14. "[The longer the crisis decision time], the greater the felt need for effective leadership within the decisional unit."

In the US's 1958 crisis over Lebanon, "the immediate reaction to peak crisis on July 14 was to convene a series of large meetings of advisors in an *ad hoc* fashion. But then, and later, the real decisional unit was the President himself. . . . There was a pronounced tendency to consensus both in the decisional unit and among advisors, reflecting perhaps the respect for strong leadership expressed by more than one observer" (Dowty, 1984: 98). Hence the coding, Supported.

H. 15. "The longer the crisis decision time, the greater the consensus on the ultimate decision."

In Germany's Stalingrad Crisis, 1942–43, a tacit consensus developed over time on the inevitability of defeat and the loss of the Sixth Army. ". . . the consensus . . . involved no more than a silent acceptance of an overwhelmingly apparent reality and a turning of attention to other areas where genuine choices could be made . . ." (Jukes, 1985: 196). Thus the coding, Supported.

H. 16. "As stress increases, the less careful is the evaluation of alternatives."

In the Berlin Wall Crisis, "the [US's] evaluation of alternatives became more careful as crisis-induced stress rose: Kennedy became increasingly aware of the danger of Soviet miscalculation and the possibility of a nuclear exchange over the Berlin question" (Pold, 1991: 86). Hence the coding, Not Supported.

In Zambia's Rhodesia UDI Crisis, 1965–66, "what evidence does exist indicates that overall the evaluative process was *more* thorough during the crisis period than in either earlier or late periods" (Anglin, forthcoming, 1993: 318). Thus the coding, Not Supported.

The number of options considered by the USSR was highest in the first two phases of its Prague Spring crisis period: "political exhortations and pressure, positive and negative economic incentives, the permanent stationing of troops as a limited and sufficient objective; the use of these troops to support a comeback by Czechoslovak conservative elements;

and the disposition of [Warsaw] Pact troops in and around Czechoslovakia as a form of minatory diplomacy designed to warn Prague ..." (K. Dawisha, 1984: 315). But while the number declined, the quality of assessment did not. Thus the coding, Not Supported.

H. 17. "The shorter the crisis decision time, the greater the tendency to premature closure."

In Syria's Lebanon Civil War I Crisis, 1975–76, "'as the crisis worsened and the possibility of war increased, the evaluation process was widened and was made more rigorous.' Thus a thorough evaluation-search process seems to have characterized *all* the consequential strategic decisions ..." (A. I. Dawisha, 1980: 179–80, citing Adib al-Dawoodi, then President Asad's Advisor on Foreign Affairs; this view was echoed by Ahmad Iskander Ahmed, then Syria's Minister of Information, and Adnan Omran, then Syria's Ambassador to the UK). Hence the coding, Not Supported.

In Israel's 1967 crisis, too, decision-makers did not make premature choices in the crisis period. Despite rising stress, they deliberated on 23 May and opted for diplomacy. They opted for further delay on the 28th after a marathon all-night session and a 9–9 informal vote on whether or not to initiate war. And on 4 June they decided in favor of preemptive war. Thus the coding, Not Supported.

H. 18. "... the more likely will decisions be made with inadequate assessment of their consequences, that is, with less sensitivity to negative feedback."

The Soviet decision on 17 August 1968 to invade Czechoslovakia on the 20th was made under growing time pressure, the approach of the end of summer. The evidence strongly indicates that, like the other decisions during the Prague Spring Crisis, the Soviet decision-makers made a careful assessment of likely consequences, including possible adverse repercussions within the communist bloc, and hostile reaction from parts of the non-aligned world, as well as from the West, though not including a military response. By the 17th all of the other 15 options (K. Dawisha, 1984: 362–363) had been exhausted, and the time for decisive action to destroy the reform movement in Prague was becoming increasingly short. Hence the coding, Not Supported.

In the Gulf Crisis, too, the US decision to press for a UN-sanctioned ultimatum for Iraq's withdrawal from Kuwait (Resolution 678 on 29 November, setting a deadline of 15 January) exhibited a careful assessment of consequences: there was a clear understanding of the high likelihood of full-scale war against Iraq, with the distinct possibility of high casualties, a US military triumph and the positive benefits at home, excising the "Vietnam Syndrome," and abroad, dramatically asserting US military hegemony in the post-Cold War "New World Order." Thus the coding, Not Supported.

H. 19. "High stress is dysfunctional; that is, cognitive and, therefore, decisional performance will be greatly influenced by psychological biases and will deteriorate markedly."

Given the centrality of this hypothesis in the crisis literature, it will receive more attention. The conventional wisdom was summarized by O. R. Holsti (1979: 405, 410, building on Holsti and George, 1975):

> A vast body of theory and evidence suggests that intense and protracted crises tend to erode rather than enhance . . . cognitive abilities. . . .
> . . . among the more probable casualties of crises and the accompanying high stress are the very abilities that distinguish men from other species: to establish logical links between present actions and future goals; to search effectively for relevant policy options; to create appropriate responses to unexpected events; to communicate complex ideas; to deal effectively with abstractions; to perceive not only blacks and whites, but also to distinguish them from the many subtle shades of grey that fall in between; to distinguish valid analogies from false ones, and sense from nonsense; and, perhaps, most important of all, to enter into the frame of reference of others. . . .
> [Finally,] With respect to these precious cognitive abilities, the law of supply and demand seems to operate in a perverse manner; as crisis increases the need for them, it also appears to diminish the supply.

Holsti proclaimed the dysfunctional effect of high stress most precisely in terms of an inverted-U model: "Low-to-moderate stress may facilitate better performance, but high stress degrades it."

This is a formidable catalogue of high costs of high stress and a dismal portrait of human cognitive and decisional disabilities. If it is accurate, the ability of decision-makers to manage crises effectively is disturbingly deficient, with grave inferences for the stability of interstate politics, given the pervasiveness of crises in the twentieth century and *the likelihood that they will continue to erupt in the decades ahead* [see "Lessons for the Future," below]. What, then, is the record in the crises explored in this book and in the ICB project as a whole?

In the Berlin Blockade Crisis (1948–49), "it is reasonably clear from the actual historical record . . . that stress, as the central concomitant of crisis, can have positive effects which outweigh the negative effects on the performance of selected cognitive and decision-making tasks . . .

there is sufficient evidence here to at least call into question the universal validity of the premise that high and protracted stress seriously and adversely affects decision processes and outcomes. On the whole, the American policymakers stood up to stress well and coped fairly effectively and even creatively with the acute dilemmas posed by the Soviet ground blockade. . . . [It] was in essence a rational and calculated process of decision-making" (Shlaim, 1983: 422). Thus the coding, Not Supported.

In the Trieste Crisis (1953), "these [psychological] biases ["propensity to stereotype and rely heavily on historical lessons"] were also present before the crisis, their frequency did not increase with stress and, even more important, they rarely determined the decision-makers' approach. On the contrary, it was precisely during the period of higher stress (October–November 1953), when the challenge they faced became more complex, that Italian decision-makers operated at their best . . . rising stress did not lead to groupthink. Likewise, there were no clear instances of premature closure. . . . On balance . . . the performance of Italian decision-makers during the Trieste crisis shows no evidence to support [this] hypothesis. The increase in stress . . . cannot be said to have disrupted performance in any significant way" (Croci, 1991: 439–440). Hence the coding, Not Supported.

In the Rhodesia UDI Crisis (1965–66), "the evidence does suggest that crisis-induced stress accounted for some impairment in the cognitive abilities of decision makers in Zambia. Nevertheless, the degree of deterioration was nothing like as catastrophic as implied in Ole Holsti's catalog [cited above]. . . . On the contrary, the level of cognitive performance of Kaunda and his colleagues, despite their limited means and comparative inexperience in the world of high politics, was commendably high" (Anglin, forthcoming, 1993, 326–327). Thus the coding, Not Supported.

In the Six Day War Crisis of 1967, "many (of the Holsti-George [1975] findings) are not supported by Israel's crisis experience. High stress did not lead to a reduced span of attention and, with it, a lower cue awareness. Nor did it create a reduced time perspective, a reduced tolerance for ambiguity, or a tendency to premature closure. . . . And while complex problems were viewed, in part, through predispositional lenses, these did not determine the decision-makers' approach. On balance, then, intense and increasing stress impaired cognitive performance . . . but not drastically or fundamentally" (Brecher with Geist, 1980: 346–347). Hence the coding, Not Supported.

In the Lebanon Civil War I Crisis of 1975–76, "Syrian decision-makers seem to have been aware of the complexity of their environment." Moreover, three of the four crucial decisions of the crisis period were "rational choice decisions . . . , the outcome of lengthy and exhaustive meetings in which all the high-level political interests participated. . . . (And) Syria's decision-making sessions were dominated by a concern for long-term rather than short-lived solutions" (A. I. Dawisha, 1980: 182). Thus the coding, Not Supported.

Suffice it to note the overall finding on this crucial hypothesis: support in two cases, non-support in ten; there were mixed findings in two cases; and H. 19 was not tested in three others (see Table 8.4 below). Parenthetically, Holsti and George sensed that their finding of dysfunctional behavior under high stress might not have universal validity: they noted (1975: 256 n.) that their conclusion was drawn from US experience and might have "more limited applicability for other nations," e.g., "in small countries that have small or virtually non-existent foreign policy bureaucracies." More significantly, their finding is not supported by the experience of many other developed states as well, including Italy, the UK, and the USSR, and often the US as well.

Another perspective on testing hypotheses from the cumulative research on crisis focuses on the extent of support and non-support for each proposition relating to the cognitive and decisional aspects of coping. The findings are presented in Table 8.4.

The findings are instructive. Overall, of the 19 hypotheses, nine are strongly supported, and four strongly disconfirmed; that is, the testing of 70% of the selected propositions generated by earlier research has uncovered convincing results. The evidence on the other six is also salient.

In the cognitive domain, two of the four hypotheses, the felt need for information [H. 2], and the reliance on past history [H. 4], are totally supported by the available evidence. As for information processing, one part of the proposition regarding activity and randomness of the search [H. 5], and another regarding the shift of information to the top of the decisional pyramid [H. 6], are very strongly supported. So, too, are all three hypotheses on consultation and communication [H. 7, 8, 9], and two concerning decisional forums [H. 13, 14].

The three hypotheses on the consideration of alternatives [H. 16, 17, 18] are strongly disconfirmed, as argued in this book. And most important, the widely-assumed view that high stress is dysfunctional, cognitively and in decision-making [H. 19], is also strongly disconfirmed. Indeed it raises a fundamental question, namely, the appropriateness—and the policy cost—of persisting in the belief that high stress

TABLE 8.4   *Hypotheses on Stress, Time Pressure and Coping: Findings From 17 Crises*

	Support	Non-Support	Mixed	Missing Data	Not Relevant	Not Tested
H.1	7	5	4			1
H.2	16	0				1
H.3	8	5	2			2
H.4	13			1		3
H.5 (part a)	13	2		2		
(part b)	9	7	1			
H.6	11	1	1			4
H.7	9	3	1			4
H.8	13	2				2
H.9	11	1	1		1	3
H.10	8	6	1			2
H.11	7	8	1			1
H.12	5	3				9
H.13	12	2				3
H.14	10	2				5
H.15	6	5	1			5
H.16	2	11	1			3
H.17	1	11	2			3
H.18	2	9				6
H.19	2	10	2			3

has severe negative consequences on coping with stress. *The evidence uncovered here points strongly to the need to be much more sanguine about the human capacity for effective crisis management. The traditional view is, simply put, scientifically incorrect.*

What does this hypothesis-testing exercise tell us, in substance, about coping with increasing crisis-induced stress? First, there is now powerful evidence in support of the following expectations about decision-makers from diverse cultural and geographic settings with variations in power, economic development, size, etc.:

cognitive dimension: they will feel a greater need for information and will enlarge their quest accordingly; and they will supplement such information with a growing reliance on personal experience as a guide to choice among options;

information processing: their search for information will become more active; and, as a crisis escalates, information will move swiftly to the senior decision-makers, severely weakening the role of bureaucrats in the decisional process;

consultation: the scope of consultation, outside the core decisional unit, will grow under the impact of increasing stress, not decline; decision-makers will seek extraordinary channels to communicate bids to adversaries in the negotiation process during a crisis; and they will communicate more with allies, adversaries and other international actors;

decisional forum: decision-makers will feel a greater need for face-to-face proximity among themselves (notwithstanding exceptions such as Germany re Stalingrad and Italy re Trieste), resulting in more frequent direct contact and deliberations as stress grows; and, as a crisis escalates, they will feel a greater need for effective leadership from the principal decision-maker.

No less important for an understanding of coping with stress are four negative findings:

alternatives: that increasing time pressure leads to a less careful evaluation of options—it does not; that optimal decision-making will suffer from a greater tendency to premature closure, before all alternatives are carefully assessed and ranked—it will not; that decisions will be reached without an adequate assessment of consequences—they will not; and, finally, the most compelling finding:

general: that high stress is dysfunctional, for cognitive performance and, therefore, the decisional process as well.

All of these findings, positive and negative, are robust. Highly relevant, too, are half a dozen hypotheses on the effects of increasing stress which exhibit mixed results:

that decision-makers will become more concerned with the immediate than the long-run future, with adverse consequences for the quality of choice [H. 1];

that they will become more closed to new information, another constraint on quality decision-making [H. 3];

that the more active search for information will become more random and less productive [H. 5, part b];

that the decisional group will become smaller and the decision process more centralized [H. 10];

that decisions will be reached by an *ad hoc* group [H. 11]; this, together with the contraction in size, is likely to undermine the quality of decision-making;

that such a small, *ad hoc* decisional forum is likely to experience the adverse phenomenon of "groupthink," in which participants feel a strong pressure to conform to group norms, thereby undermining an optimal assessment of options and optimal choice [H. 12]; and

that longer decision time will lead to greater consensus on the ultimate decision [H. 15].

Most of these expectations, if confirmed, would further undermine the quality of decision-making. The results on all of them are split; that is, they are neither supported nor not supported. As such, they are incomplete statements about those aspects of the coping process which they address. Effects are present; but stress interacts with other variables. Stated differently, simple bivariate linkages do not appear in the case of these dependent variables. In sum, these blurred results remove many hitherto-assumed constraints on optimal choice.

It remains to note the central thrust of the combined findings on the question, what have we learned. *In essence, crises are comparable along many dimensions. And patterns do exist: in international and foreign policy crises, that is, at both levels; in phases and periods; in perceptions and behavior; in evolution from outbreak to termination; in intensity and impact, etc. There is, in short, an inner logic to the process in which crises erupt, evolve and exit from the arena of world politics.*[14]

This discovery provides a reliable basis for assessing the likely future pattern of interstate crises. To this final task I now turn, with an added aim, namely, to enhance decision-makers' ability to cope with crises in the years ahead: specifically, to defuse crises when they erupt; to avert the use of violence, or to minimize its severity and scope in crisis management; and thereby to contribute to a more peaceful world.

Lessons for the Future

Forecasting in the social sciences is a risky enterprise. It is especially so in a period of structural change, the kind of change that occurred at the end of the 1980s. Put simply, 1989–90 marks the end of power bipolarity, the preeminent trait of global politics since the guns fell silent in World War II. That year of dramatic events—the dismantling of the Berlin Wall, the Soviet retreat from Central and Eastern Europe, and the reunification of Germany—also marks the close of the (short) twentieth century, an epoch that lasted from the 1914 crisis and World War I until the end of the Cold War and, soon after, the collapse of the USSR.

Despite the "obsolescence" of major power war (Mueller, 1989) and the "long peace" between the superpowers (Gaddis, 1991), crisis, conflict and war remain endemic phenomena. International crises continue to erupt. States have not ceased to initiate crises for other members of the global system and to be targets of hostile behavior—e.g., Iraq/Kuwait, Armenia/Azerbaijan, Serbia/Croatia/Bosnia-Hercegovina, US–UK/Libya, all in 1990–92. Their decision-makers continue to grapple with stress and the problem of choice in an environment of uncertainty and complexity. And interstate crises continue to cause instability.

Moreover, notwithstanding the change from power bipolarity to unipolarity, the fragmented state system continues to function, with more legally autonomous actors that engage in conflictive as well as cooperative behavior. Given that reality, the cumulative experience of crises in most of the twentieth century would seem to be a reliable basis for anticipating the pattern of crisis, conflict and war in the next decade. I begin with the *outbreak of international* crises, the system/interactor level of analysis.

Earlier in this book it was argued that *structure* combines two dimensions, *power polarity* and *decision polarity*. Moreover, the concept of polycentrism was introduced to designate a hybrid structure, denoting bipolarity in terms of power and multipolarity in terms of decisional autonomy. The changes wrought by the end of the Cold War and the dissolution of the Soviet Union transformed the first of these structural elements: the US emerged as the sole military superpower on a global scale. However, the fragmentation of decisional autonomy has not diminished; rather, it has increased, in both scope of issue-areas and number of autonomous units. This theme requires elaboration.

The Gulf crisis-war of 1990–91 consummated the basic change in power polarity: the US initiated, mobilized and sustained a world-wide coalition against Iraq, albeit under the UN umbrella, and furnished most of the military power to compel Saddam Hussein's withdrawal from Kuwait. As such, the US role as sole superpower was dramatically displayed. At the same time, the diffusion of decisional authority was reaffirmed. Germany and Japan provided financial support, reluctantly, and remained aloof from the military alliance against Iraq. A declining Soviet Union attempted to mediate the conflict and did not participate in UN-sponsored military sanctions. Only a few Arab states were persuaded to send troops to the Gulf. And while, formally, 28 UN members joined the US-led Coalition, 130 did not. They decided to stand aside in the first post-Cold War global crisis.

What the Gulf crisis-war also revealed, in structural terms, is that the US's writ is limited. Unlike the 1945–88 era, its military power vastly exceeds that of all other states, and its global superpower status is unchallenged. But in the economic domain, the 1990s continue the trend of the 1980s to intense competition, with several rivals to the US: the European Community, notably Germany, and Japan, along with many lesser but rising centers of economic power, notably in the Pacific rim. The spectacle of US dependence on Germany, Japan, Saudi Arabia, and the Gulf states to finance the Gulf War, noted in Chapter 7, revealed that the structure of global *economic* power is not synonymous with the structure of global *military* power.

Even in the military domain, regional power centres remain in the post-Cold War era of global unipolarity: the Union of South Africa in Southern Africa; India in South Asia; Vietnam in the Indo-China segment of Southeast Asia; China and Japan in East Asia; and Egypt, Israel and Syria in the Middle East. The US status of sole superpower cannot prevent crises—and wars—from being initiated by lesser powers in most regions, especially in the Third World. Moreover, the dissolution of the USSR into 15 independent states has extended the concept of "periphery" to all of these post-Cold war actors, except Ukraine, Bela Rus, and Russia itself. In sum, it would be wrong to extrapolate from structural change in global military power to the likely future frequency of interstate crises in the global system as a whole. Rather, it seems more plausible to argue that polycentrism persists in the sense of decisional autonomy, and that one should anticipate the persistence of such crises, especially in the "peripheries."

Earlier in this chapter, structure was designated an explanatory variable in crisis analysis, based upon both deductive reasoning and inductive findings. The logical inference is that, as long as decisional autonomy pervades the structure of world politics, and this seems likely in the foreseeable future, interstate crisis must be anticipated as a recurrent phenomenon. A unipolar military hierarchy does not alter that likelihood. But where are international crises likely to erupt? What indicators should guide decision-makers in this elusive quest?

The most important indicator lies in the second key explanatory variable in crisis analysis, *system level*. The evidence from 70 years of crises, it will be recalled, located the terrain of international crises as primarily at the subsystem level, with one notable exception, the process leading to Entry into World War II and the global war that followed from 1939 to 1945. Throughout the Cold War (1945–89), the two main protagonists, the US and the USSR, managed their complex relations so as to avoid direct military hostilities in the 11 international crises in which they were the principal adversaries, despite intense rivalry for global hegemony, reinforced by ideological and political sources of conflict (Wilkenfeld and Brecher, 1982). In fact, the only direct military confrontation between any pair of major powers since 1945 involved the US and China in the Korean War, 1950–53.

In the post-Cold War era of power unipolarity, the "long peace" among the major powers is very likely to continue, with one possible exception, the China/Russia border conflict. There were many border incidents in the past and one full-scale military-security crisis (Ussuri River, 1969), in a territorial dispute that dates to the 17th century. And, while it was relatively tranquil during the past half century, China's historic claims and Russia's decline as a global power augur ill for indefinite tranquillity in the vast arc stretching from Central Asia to the Pacific Ocean. This potential source of inter-major power crisis and violence has far-reaching implications for global order.

Future crises are likely to occur mostly at the subsystem level, if the evidence from 1918 to 1988 is any guide: 82% of all cases, compared to 18% in the dominant system. For one thing, Europe, especially the members of the European Community, have attained a degree of cooperation since 1945 that makes resort to force to settle disputes among them virtually unthinkable. In that context, it will be recalled that the frequency of military-security crises in Europe declined drastically after the Berlin Wall Crisis in 1961. For another, major powers tend to be insensitive to crises in the geographic peripheries of the dominant system, with three notable exceptions.

One is a situation in which decision-makers become mesmerized by myth, encased in doctrine, e.g., the "domino theory" that penetrated the mindset of US leaders in the 1960s about the grave consequences in Southeast Asia that would ensue from a North Vietnam victory over South Vietnam. Another is a perception of the profound danger of aggrandizement by a peripheral state which can jeopardize international economic stability, e.g., Iraq's conquest of Kuwait in 1990 and the feared impact on oil supplies to the advanced industrial economies of Western Europe and Japan.

The third source of major power sensitivity is the threat of nuclear proliferation, as evident in US anxiety about, and consequent efforts to thwart, the nuclear weapons programs of Libya, North Korea, and Pakistan from the late 1980s onward. It has also surfaced in embryonic relations with two of the successor states to the USSR, namely, the Ukraine and Kazakhstan, in 1991 and 1992. And this may become more acute if they do not fulfil pledges to eliminate all nuclear weapons on their territory by the year 2000. The problem of proliferation on the periphery would become more acute if Iran's quest for nuclear weapons is assisted by Kazakhstan.

For the rest, crises among lesser powers tend to be allowed to run their course, especially in regions that are distant from the dominant system and/or lack scarce crucial resources, notably Africa, and South and Southeast Asia. Typical was the aloofness of the two superpowers from crisis-wars between India and Pakistan in 1947–48 and 1971, with the USSR playing a mediatory role in 1965–66 (the "Spirit of Tashkent"), and even in the prolonged crisis-war between the two giants of Asia, India and China, from 1959 to 1962. The Americas, too, fall into that category by virtue of the informal recognition of US hegemony in the Western Hemisphere on the part of all other major powers.

One *caveat* must be noted about the subsystem dimension of future crises. Until the disintegration of the Soviet Union in 1991, its entire Eurasian land mass, extending from Tallinn to Vladivostok, and its East European client states were part of the dominant system of world politics, along with Western Europe and the United States. However, the emergence of weak independent states all along the periphery of Russia proper, from the Baltics in northern Europe to the five Central Asian Muslim-majority republics, has drastically altered the meaning of dominant system and subsystem. The dominant system in the early 1990s comprises the US, Russia, despite an economy in distress, the European Community, Japan and China. All the East European states and all the members of the post-USSR Commonwealth of Independent States, other than Russia, have become members of subsystems—East Europe, TransCaucasia, and Central Asia. And it is in these, as well as other, subsystems that international crises are likely to erupt in the years ahead.

One contextual source of anticipated crises is *unresolved conflicts of long duration* in regional subsystems, most of them bilateral territorial disputes. In *Africa*, they include: *Ethiopia/Somalia*, over the Ogaden desert; *Chad/Libya*, with eight international crises since 1971, almost all over control of the uranium-rich Aouzou Strip; the conflict over the

Western Sahara between *Morocco* and the *Polisario* movement, now internationally recognized by most members of the OAU; and the deep-rooted *Burundi/Rwanda* ethnic conflict.

In the *Americas*, the unresolved dispute between *Guyana* and *Venezuela* over the vast Essequibo territory may well give rise to another crisis.

In *Asia*, recurrent high tension between several dyads can be expected to generate fresh crises in the future: between *India* and *Pakistan* over the long-disputed Muslim-majority territory of Jammu and Kashmir and their embryonic nuclear weapons programs; between *Afghanistan* and *Pakistan*, in a still-unresolved conflict over the Durand Line that split the Pushtu-speaking Pathans, who inhabit the latter's North West Frontier Province, and are also the majority ethnic group in Afghanistan; between *North and South Korea*, despite the steps toward *rapprochement* in 1991–92; between *Vietnam* and *Cambodia*, despite the weakness of the former in the aftermath of the collapse of the USSR and the protective role of the UN and the major powers towards the latter; between *China* and *India* over their still-disputed frontiers, stretching for 2500 miles from Ladakh in the "Western Sector" to India's North East Frontier Agency; between the two Chinas, the *PRC* and *Taiwan*, which engaged in three military-security crises over the Taiwan Straits in the 1950s and 1960s; between *China* and *Vietnam*, long wary contiguous neighbors with unsettled territorial disputes; and between *China* and *Russia*, two dominant system members, over parts or all of their border, as noted. To this group of Asian conflicts must be added the *India/Sri Lanka* dyad, in view of the increasingly bitter ethnic conflict between the latter's Sinhalese majority and Tamil minority, towards whom India has long been ambivalent. Powerful pressures in India's state of Tamilnadu might trigger an international crisis over the issue of an independent Tamil state in northern and eastern Sri Lanka.

The *Middle East*, too, remains a subsystem of persistent conflicts in which international crises are almost certain to recur in the next decade: the *Arab/Israel* conflict over many issues—control over the West Bank (Judea and Samaria) and Gaza, the Golan Heights, Israel's "security zone" in southern Lebanon, and Jerusalem, division of the Jordan waters, and Palestinian rights; *Greece/Turkey* over the status of Cyprus and their respective communities, and Aegean seabed resources; *Iran/Iraq* over the Shatt-al-Arab; and *Iraq/Kuwait* over the islands of Bubiyan and Warba, the Rumaila oil field, and Kuwait's existence as an independent state.

In post-Cold War *Europe*, one longstanding dispute may reignite in the aftermath of the Yugoslav upheaval. *Italy* was not satisfied, then or since, with the US–UK-imposed compromise agreement in 1953 and may well seize the opportunity of a weak *Croatia* to undo the partition of the Trieste region and secure control over all of the disputed territory.

Many of these disputes are dormant; some have been for decades. However, as long as mutual agreement on borders, territory, and resources, or ethnic accommodation remain elusive, the possibility exists of recurrent military-security crises. For some dyads this can be assessed as high probability, notably: Ethiopia/Somalia, Chad/Libya, Morocco/Polisario, and Rwanda/Burundi, in Africa; India/Pakistan, Afghanistan/Pakistan, and China/Russia, in Asia; Arab/Israel, Greece/ Turkey, Iran/Iraq, and Iraq/Kuwait, in the Middle East.

To this group of subsystem conflicts must be added another source of potential international crises, namely, post-independence relations among some of the 15 succession states to the USSR and the five states that emerged from the ashes of Yugoslavia. In fact, the reality of instability and crisis is already evident: a long-smoldering ethnic conflict between Armenians and Azeris in the enclave of Nagorno-Karabakh during the last years of the Soviet Union, continuing as a conflict between independent Armenia and Azerbaijan since 1991; civil war between Serbia and Croatia, transformed into an interstate war by the international recognition of the latter's independence in 1992; and civil war among the Croat, Muslim and Serbian communities in Bosnia-Hercegovina, which is likely to persist in the form of interstate crisis and violence as well.

The disintegration of Yugoslavia will almost certainly leave a residue of *irredenta*, especially for *Serbia*, which lost the most and whose leaders retain the vision of a Greater Serbia. Even after independence has been achieved by most of the non-Serbian nationalities, the residue of dissolution—the need to divide resources and debts, pressures for territorial revision, and the (mal)treatment of minorities—is likely to generate crises among the hostile successor states.

Decision-makers of major powers, who assume primary responsibility for the management of interstate tensions when they erupt into crisis, conflict and war, must also anticipate destabilizing conditions in some of the successor states to the USSR, partly because of the resurgence of ethnic tensions, which are likely to draw protector states into a conflict situation, thereby triggering an international crisis. One highly likely source is tension between *Russia* and one or more of the *Baltic* states, if resurgent nationalism in the latter leads to rampant discrimination against their large ethnic Russian communities, whose welfare Russia will regard as a "sacred" responsibility. Others are Russian minorities in the *Ukraine* and the Trans-Dneister region of *Moldova*. This type of crisis may also extend to the Muslim republics of *Central Asia*, whose ethnic Russian minorities will almost certainly look to Moscow for protection of their rights.

There are also embryonic territorial disputes in the former USSR which could lead to interstate crisis. The Crimea, transferred by Stalin in 1944 from Russia to the Ukraine, is a notable example of this potential source of crises between successor states.

There is still another cluster of potential subsystem crises in the post-Cold War era, namely, Central and Eastern Europe. Interstate conflicts in that region lay dormant for 40 years in the apparent monolith of the Soviet bloc which, itself, experienced dramatic crises—the Berlin Uprising in 1953, the Hungarian Uprising in 1956, the Berlin Wall in 1961, and the Prague Spring in 1968. For the most part, however, the USSR successfully suppressed interstate conflicts in its Central-East European "security zone" until its withdrawal in 1989.

Since then, the ethnic/nationalist virus has created a context for other crises in the future. The upsurge of tension between *Hungary* and *Romania* over the latter's mistreatment of its large Hungarian minority is one potential focus of crisis between two former Soviet vassal states. Even the continued viability of a two-nation state in *Czechoslovakia* fell victim to the disease. The model of democracy in inter-World War Central Europe sundered into two independent states at the beginning of 1993; and disputes over territory, resources and debts may generate crises between them.

It would also be unwise to rule out the possibility that a resurgent *Russia*, once its economic malaise has been overcome by massive foreign aid and economic reform, will attempt to reassert Moscow's hegemony in Central and Eastern Europe. This would almost certainly precipitate crises with its former clients, from which other major powers might not be able to remain aloof. And finally, the revival of *Germany* as a major military power—it is already the preeminent economic power in the European Community and Europe as a whole —could generate crises with weaker neighbors and other states to the east, competing with or, once more, cooperating with the new Russia in the historic "great game" of politics in Central and Eastern Europe.

In short, the post-Cold War subsystems retain an abundance of conflicts within which international crises are likely to erupt. Nor is it far-fetched to anticipate the possibility of crises between separatist movements of established Western states and their former metropole if and when they attain independence, such as the *Basques* and *Catalans*, and Spain, *Corsica* and France, *Tamil Eelam* and Sri Lanka, *Flanders* and Belgium, and *Quebec* and Canada.

A third explanatory variable to emerge from this inquiry into twentieth-century crises is *geographic distance*. The reasoning for this expectation was elaborated earlier. And the evidence was overwhelming: the vast majority of international crises occurred betwen immediate neighbors. This is, perhaps, natural, in accordance with the adage, "familiarity (proximity) breeds contempt." More substantively, near-neighbors are more likely to have competing interests—over territory, resources, status, ethnic minorities, etc. Only major powers have the luxury of indulging in distant crises, a role assumed by the few who play the role of global or regional crisis managers. And, indeed, virtually all the conflicting dyads for whom interstate crises are anticipated during the next decade are contiguous pairs of states with common borders, e.g., Chad/Libya, Israel/Syria, India/Pakistan, China/Russia, Guyana/Venezuela.

Some of these exhibit *heterogeneity* along several dimensions, which accentuate other sources of conflict noted earlier. Thus Israel and Syria differ in political regime, economic capability, and culture; their military capability is of the same order of modernity. Most other dyads reveal greater commonality than diversity, e.g., Iran and Iraq, with authoritarian regimes, developing economies, Muslim culture, and military capability of the same order of sophistication. Thus the support for the hypothesis that relates high heterogeneity to crisis outbreak does not apply to the crises anticipated during the coming years.

If this prognosis about future international crises proves to be correct, under what conditions are they likely to erupt in *violence*? One cannot be sure, of course. However, projecting the findings from this inquiry, the most salient features are: geographic contiguity between the adversaries; a military-security-type issue in dispute, notably over territory, or several issues combined; the unfolding of the conflict within a subsystem; a structure of fragmented decisional authority, i.e., polycentrism, whether accompanied by power bipolarity or unipolarity; considerable heterogeneity; and authoritarian regimes (supported elements of H. 2). To what extent do these conditions apply to the group of expected international crises?

In general, there is a strong fit; that is, most of the conditions apply to most of the crises anticipated in the years ahead. This is evident from a brief assessment of the specific pairs. In Africa, all of the conditions are present in the Morocco/Polisario protracted conflict, and all but heterogeneity in the Ethiopia/Somalia, Chad/Libya, and Rwanda/Burundi dyads. The first of this cluster consists of two contiguous states, both governed by authoritarian regimes, in a conflict occurring within the East African subsystem, in a global system of diffuse decisional autonomy, over a military-security issue, ownership of the Ogaden desert. And Chad/Libya exhibits heterogeneity in military capability, economic development, and culture, in a conflict over the Aouzou Strip, unfolding in the Central African subsystem.

In the longstanding Guyana/Venezuela conflict over Essequibo, heterogeneity is present only in part, and the parties, in 1992, shared a commitment to democracy.

A close fit is also evident in Asia. In the India/Pakistan protracted conflict, the exceptions to the postulated conditions of violent crises are heterogeneity and, in 1993, a democratic regime pair. In the Afghanistan/Pakistan conflict there is a mixed (authoritarian/democratic) regime pair. The two Koreas exhibit heterogeneity only with respect to economic capability and a mixed regime pair. The China/Taiwan dyad conforms to all the conditions, except heterogeneity. So too does the India/Sri Lanka pair, except for a shared democratic regime. Only the Russia/China case deviates substantially: the conflict is between major powers in the dominant system, with a mixed regime pair, in 1993, and limited heterogeneity.

In the Middle East, too, the anticipated crisis pairs fit most of the conditions. The only exceptions are: Arab/Israel—a different political regime; Greece/Turkey—heterogeneity in part and, in 1993, democratic regimes; Iran/Iraq, and Iraq/Kuwait—heterogeneity; all are conflicts between contiguous states, most with authoritarian regimes, over several issues in the Middle East sub-system, within a global system of decisional autonomy.

This pattern is replicated in Europe, with few exceptions: Italy/Croatia—a mixed regime pair; Serbia/Croatia and Serbia/Bosnia-Hercegovina—limited heterogeneity; Russia/Ukraine—limited heterogeneity, and mixed regime pair.

The conclusion is disquieting: *most anticipated international crises in the coming years are likely to erupt in violence*, though its severity will vary from minor clashes to full-scale war. So it was in three highly visible post-Cold War crises. The fully-crystallized Gulf Crisis began with Iraq's six-hour invasion and occupation of Kuwait; the escalation to full-scale war occurred more than five months later. In the Balkans and TransCaucasia, the process of military escalation was different. The

Serbia/Croatia and Serbia/Bosnia-Hercegovina crises that accompanied the dissolution of Yugoslavia in 1991–92, and the crisis between Armenia and Azerbaijan over Nagorno-Karabakh, both began with minor violence, but rapidly escalated to war and serious clashes, respectively. Relying on the evidence of the past, violent crises would seem to be the wave of the future.

Using the method of extrapolating from the past, the pattern of future crises can be delineated. First, the phenomenon of military-security crisis is unlikely to disappear; that is, the "end of history" (Fukuyama, 1992), if it has any validity, does not apply to this aspect of world politics. Second, while multi-state crises such as the Gulf crisis-war of 1990–91 may recur, *the vast majority of international crises will take the form of dyadic conflicts over territory, resources or status.* Third, the clusters specified above do not exhaust the possible scope of crises, but they will occupy much of the crisis space in the next decade. Fourth, they are more likely to be triggered by violence than by non-violent acts, with the severity of violence escalating over time, from minor clashes to serious clashes or full-scale war.

The profile of a state that is most likely to *initiate* a foreign policy crisis comprises: a new or recent independent member of the global system; with an authoritarian regime; contiguous to, and more powerful than, its adversary; and experiencing domestic instability (supported elements of H. 4).

All or most of these conditions apply to one or both members of many conflict dyads cited earlier as likely sources of future interstate crises. In Africa, the exceptions are: Somalia, Chad and Polisario, military weakness *vis-à-vis* their adversary; Burundi and Rwanda, power equality; Ethiopia, an old state, one of the very few in Africa; Morocco and Libya, both relatively stable internally. In the Americas, Guyana is militarily weaker than Venezuela; and both have a democratic regime.

In Asia, the fit is less apparent, but extensive for the most part. The exceptions can be noted briefly. Afghanistan is a long-established state. Vietnam and Taiwan are internally stable, and Taiwan is weaker than the PRC. Cambodia is weaker than Vietnam. Sri Lanka is weaker than India, and both are democracies. Finally, at least two of the four conditions do not apply to India, Pakistan, South and North Korea, China and Russia.

In the Middle East, all of the conditions apply to Iraq. Kuwait and Jordan are weaker than their most likely adversaries. Syria is not characterized by internal instability; nor is it stronger than Israel. Lebanon is not governed by an authoritarian regime. At least two of the four conditions do not apply to Israel, Greece, Turkey, and Iran.

In Europe, all the conditions cited above, except capability, apply to Croatia, Bosnia-Hercegovina, Azerbaijan, Moldova. The exceptions for the Baltic states, Ukraine, and Armenia are internal instability and military superiority *vis-à-vis* their likely crisis adversaries. Romania's independence dates to the nineteenth century. At least two conditions do not apply to Italy, Serbia, Russia, Hungary and Czechoslovakia.

Using this criterion alone, future crises are likely to be initiated by any of the eight actors in the four African dyads cited above; by Afghanistan, Vietnam, Cambodia, Taiwan and Sri Lanka, in Asian crises, with uncertainty about which members of the India/Pakistan, China/India, and China/Russia dyads will be more likely to initiate future crises between them, since neither actor within these pairs meets most of these conditions; by Jordan, Syria, Iraq, Kuwait and Lebanon, in the Middle East, with uncertainty about which member of the Greece/Turkey dyad is most likely to initiate future crises between them; and by many of the successor states to Yugoslavia and the USSR, along with Romania, in Europe.

However, as argued throughout this book, the results from hypothesis-testing with aggregate data on crisis initiation must confront other relevant evidence, qualitative and quantitative. Two decades of civil war in Cambodia, a ravaged economy, a deeply-split society, and military weakness make it an unlikely crisis initiator *vis-à-vis* its neighbor. Jordan's dependence on Arab states for financial aid and its military weakness relative to Israel, and Kuwait's experience in Gulf War II, strongly counter the conditions noted above. Israel's record as a frequent initiator of crises from 1948 to 1988 strongly suggests that it will continue in this role in the future. And Serbia, no less a crisis initiator during the disintegration of Yugoslavia and possessed of strong irredentist feelings, must be included among likely catalysts to inter-state crises in the future.

Vulnerability or proneness to military-security crises will be highest when the target: is not a member of the dominant system; is geographically contiguous to its adversary; is governed by an authoritarian regime; and suffers from domestic instability (supported elements of H. 6). It will be vulnerable to a *violent* crisis when these conditions, except internal instability, obtain and when: it is engaged in a protracted conflict with its adversary; it is a new or recently-created independent state; it is militarily weaker than its adversary; its regime is of short duration; and it has a small territory (supported elements of H. 7).

All or most of these conditions fit one or both members of the majority of dyads expected to experience crises in the years ahead, especially in the Third World. Among the African conflict pairs cited above, the states most prone to crisis and violence are Somalia, Chad, Polisario and Burundi. Ethiopia and Rwanda, too, match all four conditions of vulnerability, Libya and Morocco, all but internal instability. However, these states are less likely to be a target of a violent crisis: one of them, Ethiopia, is not a new state; Libya's regime has been in power more than twenty years; and both are militarily stronger than their adversaries.

The conditions of vulnerability and violence do not fit the Essequibo conflict pair, Guyana/Venezuela. In Asia, the most likely targets are Afghanistan, in its protracted conflict with Pakistan over Pushtunistan; both Koreas; Cambodia, *vis-à-vis* Vietnam; and Taiwan, in its long struggle with the PRC. Members of the other dyads do not match many of these conditions. Two examples will suffice. India and Pakistan have democratic regimes, large territory, and relatively equal military capability; and neither suffers from debilitating internal instability. Similarly, China and Russia are members of the dominant system; the latter has moved to a non-authoritarian regime; both are old states with very large territory.

Among Middle East states expected to experience crises in the next decade, the best fit on vulnerability to crisis applies to Iraq, and to a lesser extent, that is, all but one of the four conditions, to Lebanon (not an authoritarian regime), Jordan, Syria, Kuwait and Iran (not internally unstable). The least prone to being a crisis target, in terms of these conditions of vulnerability, are Israel, Greece and Turkey. However, that poor match, derived from aggregate data analysis, is offset by the conditions of the specific cases, namely, active, unresolved multiple-issue conflicts of long standing between Arab states and Israel, and the Greece/Turkey hostile dyad. As for proneness to violent crises, Kuwait, Lebanon and Jordan are the most likely targets, particularly because they are all markedly weaker than their adversary.

In Europe, the actors most vulnerable to crisis and violence among the conflicting dyads cited above are Croatia and Bosnia-Hercegovina, in the South, and Latvia, Lithuania and Estonia, in the North: they are all new states, with an authoritarian regime of short duration, and small territory; and they are militarily weaker than their adversary, Serbia and Russia, respectively. Italy, Serbia and Russia are the least likely targets of crisis or of violent crises.

Projecting from the aggregate evidence on twentieth-century cases, future international crises are most likely to be of *short duration* when they are less intense, that is, when they are characterized by: few adversarial actors; non-military activity by the major powers; little heterogeneity between the main adversaries; low geostrategic salience; few contending issues; and by the parties' resort to non-violent techniques of crisis management (supported elements of H. 9). To what extent do these conditions apply to expected crises in the years ahead?

In the post-Cold War era the African dyads are likely to generate crises of low intensity. With the possible exception of renewed French military involvement in the Chad/Libya conflict, they will be one- or two-actor crises, with little, if any, major power activity, low heterogeneity between the adversaries, minimal geostrategic salience in a system of power unipolarity, and a single issue, namely, a territorial dispute. If so, they are likely to be of short duration. However, their occurrence on the periphery of the dominant system and major power indifference to their outcome may offset the low intensity/short duration link, allowing such crises to "run their course."

If the longstanding Guyana/Venezuela dispute over Essequibo should catalyze another crisis, it is likely to be short. The indicators of low intensity would apply. And, while the hegemonial power in the Americas would not engage in military activity, the US, now the sole global superpower, would have no compunction about pressing the parties, through the OAS and unilaterally, to terminate their crisis quickly through a mediated compromise agreement.

In Asia, both low- and high-intensity crises are likely. Most dyads, including Afghanistan/Pakistan, Vietnam/Cambodia, China/Vietnam, and India/Sri Lanka, would fit the low-intensity profile. A crisis between the two Koreas would tend to high intensity, largely because of North Korea's anticipated nuclear arsenal. A crisis between Russia and China over disputed borders would be of even higher intensity because of the confrontation between two global major powers, both possessing operational nuclear weapons. So too would an India/Pakistan crisis, if both of these enemies of long standing possess even a small stockpile of deliverable nuclear weapons, a very likely development before the year 2000.

All Asian crisis actors in the next decade will have to contend with the "new world order," especially US primacy as a military superpower. But it is highly unlikely that the US would perceive the need to become embroiled militarily in an Asian crisis except, perhaps, in a case of intense violence between North and South Korea. In all the other conflicting dyads the US would probably attempt to play the role of "neutral" crisis manager: in an Indo/Pakistani crisis over Kashmir, an

Afghan/Pakistani crisis over Pushtunistan, a Sino/Indian crisis over Ladakh or NEFA, etc. This role would extend to the nightmare of a China/Russia crisis, especially one involving violence, over their disputed borders in Central and East Asia. The US aim in all these crises would be to hasten the winding-down process, with minimal fallout for global stability.

Most future Middle East crises are likely to replicate the past pattern of high intensity. Arab/Israel crises have rarely been dyadic, given the scope and depth of the conflict, but fewer states are likely to be directly engaged as the network of peace expands. Heterogeneity, as always, would be high. Yet the end of power bipolarity in the global system will reduce the salience of an Israel/Syria crisis, even one triggered by or escalating to war. A renewed Gulf crisis-war between Iraq and Kuwait would qualify for higher intensity because an invaluable resource, oil, would be at stake once more. In fact, that dimension would ensure such a crisis very high geostrategic salience, as it did in 1990–91. A crisis between Greece and Turkey, by contrast, would be marginal to major power interests, as were earlier crises over Cyprus and Aegean seabed resources. Projecting the finding of a link between intensity and duration, Middle East crisis-wars would tend to last longer than in other regions.[15]

In Europe, almost all crisis dyads in the foreseeable future can be traced to the end of the Cold War: Serbia and its neighbors in what was once the Yugoslav federation; Russia and former autonomous republics in the dismantled USSR; Hungary and Romania in the former Soviet bloc; and, possibly, the successor states to a sundered Czechoslovakia. The sole, partial, exception is the conflict dyad over Trieste, with Croatia succeeding to the interests and role of Yugoslavia in its dispute with Italy. All these anticipated crises are likely to be confined to the pair of conflicting actors. Only those between Russia and its immediate neighbors would involve one or more major powers. None is of high geostrategic salience. And all would focus on a territorial or ethnic issue. They would not, in short, be high-intensity crises. And other major powers, notably the US and the European Community, would likely engage in political activity only, attempting to limit the adverse effects of such crises on European stability. Although the crises accompanying the disintegration of Yugoslavia lasted more than a year, successor state crises would tend to be of short duration.

How, and how well, are states and statesmen likely to cope with future crises? The most important lesson in this regard is the essential commonality and rationality of crisis management in the past. At different stages of a crisis, the pattern of information processing and choice—the search for and consideration of alternatives, as well as consultation and the forum for decision-making—revealed the shared impact of stress on coping, overriding cultural, geographic, historical, age and other differences among decision-makers responding to military-security crises. Would-be mediators in future crises, whether major powers or international organizations, would be wise to absorb this compelling counter-traditional finding about coping with crisis, as the point of departure for their attempts to deescalate interstate crises at minimal costs to global system stability.

In this context, under what conditions are decision-makers most likely to adopt an *accommodative strategy* rather than a strategy of coercion in pursuing their objectives during a future crisis? While the findings from the past are only moderately supported, they point to: a non-protracted conflict setting; power inferiority *vis-à-vis* the adversary; the presence of a democratic regime; low activity, that is, non-military support, by a major power; and support for its claims by the relevant international organization.

Only a few of these conditions obtain in the four African dyads discussed earlier. All are protracted conflicts. Somalia, Chad, Polisario and Burundi are weaker than their adversaries. None of the eight actors has a democratic regime. The major powers are aloof from all of these conflicts. And the global organization has withheld support from all parties to these conflicts.

In Asia, the picture is more mixed. There are some protracted conflicts–India/Pakistan, Afghanistan/Pakistan, the Koreas, China/Taiwan; the others are not, as defined by ICB. In the former, then, the adoption of an accommodative strategy by either actor is unlikely, all other things being equal. By contrast, those actors that perceive power inferiority would be more inclined to such a strategy: Pakistan in a crisis with India; Afghanistan *vis-à-vis* Pakistan; Cambodia, in a crisis with Vietnam; Taiwan *vis-à-vis* China; and Sri Lanka in a crisis with India. Among these Asian states, only India, Pakistan and Sri Lanka have democratic regimes, with South Korea and Taiwan moving in that direction. As noted, the major powers are likely to remain aloof from these crises or to become involved only politically. The attitude of international organizations to any of these crises cannot be anticipated.

In the Middle East, most of the postulated conditions of an accommodative strategy do not apply. The setting for all expected crises in that region would be protracted conflict. Most of the states are governed by authoritarian regimes, the exceptions being Greece, Israel and

Turkey. The major powers are likely to continue their active involvement in Arab/Israel crises and a Gulf crisis. And the past performance of the UN does not indicate support for any of the competing claims. In short, the likelihood of an accommodative strategy is remote in future Middle East crises, more so than in any other region.

In Europe, the conditions likely to lead a state to adopt an accommodative strategy in a future crisis find more resonance. Only one of the cases, the struggle over Trieste, would occur in a protracted conflict setting. Several of the conflicting states have a democratic regime in the early 1990s—Italy, Hungary and Czechoslovakia; and others, Russia, the Baltic states, and Romania aspire to the change from authoritarianism. Major power activity will likely be confined to the political arena. And, based upon the UN's intense involvement in crisis management of the Serbia/Croatia and Serbia/Bosnia-Hercegovina crises in 1991–93, the global organization, while not openly supporting the claims of any party, will probably attempt to move future crisis actors in the direction of accommodation. Thus the prospects for an accommodative strategy in future European interstate crises would seem to be greater than in other regions.

Can future crises be *prevented* by UN and/or major power anticipatory crisis management? Probably not, because the issues in conflict have deep roots in history, culture, attitudinal prisms, diverse ideologies, political and social systems, and often, ethnicity. Conflicts over access to limited resources on a shrinking planet, territorial transfers, minority rights, status recognition, etc., are endemic in a global system of fragmented authority and decisional autonomy. Wisdom dictates the recognition of this reality by decision-makers of all international actors: crises and the conflicts from which they erupt are an inevitable trait of the current and foreseeable global landscape.

Can crises be *aborted*, that is, diverted at their incipient, pre-crisis stage, averting escalation to a full-scale international crisis? Possibly, by timely, skilful and coordinated third party intervention [see below]. However, even such early crisis management is not likely to derail the process of escalation in most embryonic interstate crises. Their internal dynamics cannot easily be thwarted by external intervention, even when the costs of runaway escalation and the proffered rewards for accommodative behavior are high. Put simply, the capacity of major powers and international organizations to abort crises is limited. They will have to live with continued eruptions of crises, that is, international political earthquakes.

Does that mean that major powers and international organizations should adopt a policy of aloofness from the hostile interaction among states which can, and often will, lead to military-security crises, even in a unipolar, increasingly cooperative world? Should they extend the post-Cold War orthodoxy of "free markets" for states aspiring to prosperity to interstate relations? To do so would be folly, especially in a system in which the process of nuclear proliferation is likely to add up to a dozen new members to the nuclear weapons club, with a no less dangerous accumulation of other weapons of mass destruction likely among many states. A "free market" philosophy on crises—allow them to run their course—is a prescription for frequent resort to violence among the ever-growing number of independent states, including full-scale war and the danger of spillover to relations among major powers.

What, then, can be done to prevent crises from "getting out of hand," that is, from setting in motion a spiral of violence that would undermine the fragile stability of the post-Cold War global system? This problem has become increasingly acute in an interdependent world characterized by growing diffusion of weapon systems of mass destruction.

Interested third parties can develop an integrated, multi-faceted program of crisis management. A crucial and viable first step would take the form of *continuous monitoring of likely crisis dyads*. As soon as any evidence of incipient crisis, that is, escalating tension, is uncovered, the entire inventory of third party intervention, designed to channel the emerging crisis into a path of non-coercive resolution, should be offered to the disputants—fact-finding, good offices, conciliation, mediation and, if appropriate, arbitration or adjudication, with a skilful use of face-saving devices so as to ease the burden of compromise and concession by both parties. Such a policy, sometime termed preventative diplomacy or war avoidance, can be most effectively implemented by the global organization, with the backing of the major powers, and legitimized through Security Council approval. Consensus on a strategy of war avoidance was impossible throughout the four decades of the Cold War. But with the end of power bipolarity and the far-reaching domestic changes in the former USSR and Eastern Europe, such a consensus seems possible. Indeed, the evidence of major power consensus in the Security Council, and not only during the Gulf crisis-war, has made this a realistic scenario for the rest of the 1990s.

Permanent monitoring is but the first step in a program to direct incipient crisis away from violence. It must be underpinned by a carefully-conceived and skilfully-executed program of *positive and negative sanctions* on the part of the major powers and international organizations, including specialized agencies such as the World Bank and the

International Monetary Fund. Tangible and intangible rewards, in the form of economic aid and assurances of support in future crises over the same issue(s), must be offered to states that pursue an accommodative strategy of negotiation of disputed issues. The obverse, threat of punishment, must also be invoked as part of the on-going process of pressure on reluctant crisis actors to choose the path of negotiation and the avoidance of violence. Negative sanctions may take several forms: withholding economic aid; denial of access to markets; and a threat to use force under the auspices of the global organization, to compel compliance with non-coercive procedures of crisis resolution.

To facilitate the choice of an accommodative strategy by crisis actors, the global organization must be prepared to provide, swiftly and in adequate numbers, *peacemaking forces* and to keep them in place for as long as it takes to bring the disputants to the bargaining table. Peacemakers can not only assist the "winding-down" of a crisis. Their presence can serve as a symbol of global system commitment to a peace-oriented process and to security in the interim. The face-saving element of yielding to the "international community" rather than to the adversary is an important element in redirecting the crisis from violence to negotiation. In short, the mix of positive sanctions (reward), negative sanctions (punishment), peacemakers and/or other separation-of-forces devices, can achieve the desired aim in most crises.

Peacekeeping, undoubtedly valuable, is, however, an *ad hoc* response to the persistent problem of violent or potentially violent crises. To be successful for the next decade or more, it needs to be nested in a complex of global and regional security regimes under the aegis of Chapter 7 of the UN Charter and, operationally, the UN Security Council and its counterpart organs in regional security organizations. This, in turn, must be underpinned by the further development of global and regional functional regimes, especially designed to cope with the ever-growing problems of nuclear proliferation and an uncontrolled arms flow from the dozen major arms producers, mostly industrialized states, to any state that can pay for advanced weapons.

The objective of international crisis management should not be to eradicate conflict or to prevent crises. That path is certain to fail because conflict is part of the human and interstate condition; and crisis is an inevitable concomitant of conflict. Rather, the aim must be to channel conflict from the path of violence to that of non-violent bargaining and negotiation towards a mutually-acceptable compromise agreement, an outcome that will be satisfactory to all but ideal for none.

The central concern of would-be crisis managers should be violence, more precisely, full-scale war. Even if future war is, initially, confined to lesser powers on the periphery, war escalation, involving major powers, will always be a threat to system stability. And in a world of increasing dispersion of weapons of mass destruction, the avoidance of war, everywhere, must remain high on the agenda of global public policy. It is a global imperative, until the "new world order" is transformed into an assured peaceful world, in which resort to violence to achieve goals ceases to be a norm of state behavior.

Many global values demand urgent attention in the years ahead: protection of humankind against the scourge of rampant environmental pollution; the redistribution of material resources between an affluent North and an impoverished South; the protection and enhancement of human rights everywhere; limits to population growth, especially in lands where resources cannot sustain human needs; and effective control over weapons of mass destruction. These must be enhanced simultaneously, along with war prevention, for war in an era of advanced military technology is the gravest direct threat to human survival. And the path to war lies in the eruption of crisis within festering conflict.

It would be folly to assume that the end of the Cold War presages the end of crisis and conflict. To create and sustain a program of conflict and crisis management on a global scale is indispensable to war prevention. And that, in turn, is the precondition for the solution of all other global problems at the close of the twentieth century.

APPENDIX A

Ranking the Variables: Crisis Onset

THE fundamental postulate of the crisis onset model, as indicated in the text, is that the three onset dimensions—*outbreak, initiation* and *vulnerability*—are most likely to occur under specific clusters of system, interactor and actor attributes. Each cluster operates as a composite independent variable. However, the ranking of the attributes was not assessed in Chapter 2.

All other things being equal, a rank order of the attributes of crisis onset based upon deduced cause-effect relations among its constituents has more theoretical value than one obtained through the inductive method. This is so because such a weighing of variables can be better understood in logical than in statistical terms. Thus the *rank* of each independent variable will be derived from its presumed causal effects on the other variables.

Since 10 attributes (independent variables) were specified in the crisis onset model, and these can be causally related to any of the others, there exists a maximum of 90 potential *direct* linkages. (No attempt will be made to incorporate the much larger number of *indirect* links.) The logic underlying the inferred effects will be stated for each attribute, more elaborately for some, in a more cursory manner for others. This analysis will follow the sequence of system, interactor and actor variables specified in Figure 2.1 (p. 54 above).

For system **structure**, *eight* linkages are postulated. First, structure affects *system level*. Bipolarity places a greater emphasis on the struggle for hegemony between the two superpowers in the dominant (and, therefore, the global) system. Multipolarity, too, has the effect of focusing attention on the (more fuzzy) competition among the major powers for dominant and, therefore, global system primacy, in a setting of more uncertainty about coalitions and cross-cutting issues in contention. By contrast, polycentrism accentuates the subsystems of world politics as the arenas for intense turmoil.

Conflict setting, too, is influenced by structure. Bipolarity is inherently more likely than the other polarity configurations to generate rivalry among its major powers that will be manifested as a protracted conflict. Rivalry will focus on the quest for hegemony within their international system—global, dominant or subordinate—and will encompass an array of issues, tangible and intangible, such as territory, military power, economic welfare, status, etc. Rivalry and the struggle for hegemony are likely to be accompanied by periodic outbursts of violence and to spill over to other domains of their relationship. As such, bipolarity is likely to set in motion and sustain a protracted conflict between the two contending poles.

Structure also affects relative *capability*, that is, *power discrepancy vis-à-vis* potential adversaries. For one thing, multipolarity is characterized by flexible alliances, as noted, including the ability to form, or disengage from, an alliance during a crisis. This flexibility spills over to the calculus of relative power, leading to a tendency to *underestimate* power discrepancy. By contrast, bipolarity, with its rigid alliance configuration, exhibits a tendency to *overestimate* power discrepancy *vis-à-vis* the rival bloc. Moreover, polycentrism (and multipolarity), with their diffusion of decisional centers, are more likely to create uncertainty about the distribution of power within the system, other than the balance between the two global leaders, and among the plethora of potential conditions. This means the greater likelihood of uncontrollable arms races in polycentrism and multipolarity; for, while arms races flourish in bipolarity—they may even be more intense and prolonged —they will be fewer in number and more easily limited in scope and damage, since fewer actors are effectively involved in the arms control negotiating process.

Regime type (and *duration*) are also likely to be affected by system structure. This is due to the strong tendency of the two major powers in a bipolar structure to maintain the status quo and to prevent regime change within their bloc, lest such change become contagious and undermine the bloc leader's hegemony, as well as bloc cohesion. The result is that the type of political regime within states in the system is likely to be more rigid, and regime duration longer, than in other polarity configurations.

A link between structure and *geographic distance* can also be discerned. In bipolarity, the geostrategic distance between potential inter-bloc crisis adversaries will decline, because the two major powers possess the interest, as well as the capability, to extend their reach to the peripheries of their respective bloc, controlling all or most of the interaction between its members and those of the competing bloc. Hypothetically, the major powers in a multipolar system would have equal capability, conventional and/or nuclear, to extend their reach throughout the system. However, they lack the pervasive interest of bipolar bloc leaders in controlling clients; and the flexible alliance pattern in multipolarity, including sharp changes in alignment among its major powers, reduces the scope and effectiveness of their control over the behavior of lesser powers in that system.

It can also be argued that polycentrism, because of the diffusion of decisional authority within the system, provides a more conducive structural setting for the emergence of new system members. More precisely, polycentrism accords legitimacy to the quest for legal sovereignty and decisional autonomy on the part of weak but distinct collective entities/nations that are often dependencies of major powers. Bipolarity militates against enlarging the number of states. And multipolarity is less concerned about, and less capable of thwarting, the diffusion of sovereignty through the creation of new system members. Stated in terms of the conditions of the crisis onset model, system structure influences the *age* of states, polycentrism by encouraging the creation of new decisional centers in world politics, bipolarity by discouraging this process.

Finally, bipolarity is less likely than other structures to generate intense *instability* within bloc members, for the two poles have a greater interest and capacity to assist client states confronted with challenges to domestic stability. If unchecked, instability might spill over to other bloc members and thereby undermine bloc unity, as well as its capability to defend or enhance its interests in the struggle for system hegemony.

In sum, there are eight *direct* linkages between structure and other independent variables in the crisis onset model. No effect of structure on territorial size can be deduced.

Six linkages can be discerned between **system level** and other independent variables in the onset model. First, the level of crisis interaction is closely related to *structure*. If a crisis erupts in the dominant system, the major powers, some or all, cannot remain aloof. Thus such a crisis would pose a challenge to the existing hierarchy in the dominant system, as well as to the relationship between the principal adversaries, who may be small or middle powers. That challenge has the potential of changing the hierarchy—and the structure itself. If the major powers are reduced from many or several to two as a result of an interstate crisis (e.g., bipolarity, following Entry into World War II,

1939), the dominant system would be transformed from multipolarity to bipolarity. Or a crisis may change—or contribute to change from —bipolarity to polycentrism, etc. Moreover, because a crisis of such magnitude and intensity poses a challenge to the central subsystem in world politics, it may contribute to basic change in the global system as well. The same line of argument applies to subsystem crises: that is, they, too, may challenge—and change—the power hierarchy and, possibly, the structure of the subsystem in which a crisis occurs.

System level is also linked to *capability*, for, as indicated earlier, states in subsystem crises are relatively weaker and more dependent on the dominant system for military and economic aid.

A third effect of system level relates to *geographic distance*. Adversaries in subsystem crises are more likely to be contiguous or, at least, territorially close to each other. This is so because, all other things being equal, their ability to project power abroad is less than that of their counterparts in the dominant system. In dominant system crises, by contrast, geographic distance is much less important because of the adversaries' higher capability to project power beyond their borders.

The tendency of subsystem actors to military ineffectiveness beyond their neighbors is accentuated by their dependence on the dominant system for inputs of advanced technology. Nor is such dependence confined to minor subsystem powers. A notable example is the intensely conflictive Middle East, where both Israel and Syria have long depended upon their patron for advanced weapons, especially in the midst of grave violent crises such as the 1967 Six Day War and the October-Yom Kippur crisis-war of 1973–74.

System level is also linked to *age*. The dominant system, in any era, is likely to comprise older states than subsystems. The very notion of dominance, in system terms, clearly implies that the major powers, if not all members, have functioned as autonomous actors for a considerable period of time. There are, of course, old states in subsystems, for example, China, Thailand, Iran. However, subsystems in interstate politics generally emerge and function largely as appendages to the dominant system. In the last analysis, the survival of subsystem actors depends upon the goodwill of the major powers in the dominant system.[1] Finally, the tendency of subsystem states to be smaller and less stable entities suggests that system level also affects *size* and *internal instability*.

All other independent variables in the onset model—conflict setting, regime type, and regime duration—are unaffected by the system level at which the crises unfold.

For **conflict setting**, *four* linkages are postulated. As with the logi-cally-inferred effects of structure on conflict setting and on capability, noted above, the fact that arms races flourish in all conflict environ-ments does not, *per se*, prove the latter's irrelevance to *capability*. Rather, all other things being equal, a protracted conflict is likely to accentuate the quest for a favorable balance of power, far more so than in the case of adversaries not burdened by a lengthy, complex conflict, usually over several high-value unresolved issues. Stated differently, a protracted conflict imposes on crisis adversaries a need to assess their relative power, far more than does a non-PC setting: in a protracted conflict, violence must always be anticipated by the rival state, and positive power discrepancy will thus be crucial for a state that might become a crisis actor. A *long-war PC* will exacerbate this cause–effect relationship.

A protracted conflict setting is also likely to affect *regime duration*. One reason is that the challenge posed by crises within a PC tends to become routinized; that is, the burden on a regime's coping capacity is lessened. Thus regime survival is more likely in the face of persistent but anticipated adversity. A PC also increases the likelihood that an authoritarian regime, civil or military, will maintain its power base for a longer period. Not only are dissidents less effective in undermining an existing regime while the state that it rules is engaged in a protracted conflict. The regime can also bolster its power by mobilizing wider support through a "rally around the flag" appeal to its mass public. In short, persistent external threat leads, *inter alia*, to extended regime duration.

Another linkage is between conflict environment and *territorial size*: all other things being equal, a PC setting is more likely to create conditions where territory is continuously lost and gained by adversaries through resort to violence, which is ubiquitous in such conflict.

A final effect of conflict setting is to strengthen the tendency to *internal instability*: in a protracted conflict, a state contends with con-tinuous external pressure to mobilize domestic resources in order to overcome frequent value threats and to cope with costly involvement in military hostilities. Thus, while a protracted conflict tends to generate internal instability, it can also, paradoxically, extend regime duration. All other independent variables—structure, system level, geographical distance, regime type, and age—are unaffected by the conflict environment.[2]

Four linkages are postulated for **capability/power discrepancy**. One is *geographic distance*. All other things being equal, a more advanced military technology will shrink the distance between a state and its potential crisis/war adversary. A dramatic illustration is the effect of air power and, later, missiles on geostrategic distance during most of the twentieth century. Moreover, when a state perceives relative weakness, the psychological distance of the adversary is reduced. This, in turn, is due to the fact that the self-identified target anticipates hostile behavior, including crisis initiation, by the stronger state. In short, distance/proximity is partly a function of the perception of a power gap between the perceiver and its adversary.

Regime duration, too, is likely to be affected by capability. An adverse change in the balance of power will weaken the capacity of an existing political regime to cope with challenges to its authority from domestic opponents and/or hostile states. And a decline in power and coping capacity will, in turn, reduce a regime's ability to survive, that is, to cope with challenges to its authority.

It can also be argued that the stronger a state, the better it can cope with sources of *internal instability*, political, economic and social. Alternatively, negative power discrepancy may provide an incentive for political leaders to transfer large segments of the state budget to defense expenditure. As such, less funds would be available to overcome political unrests, due to unemployment, inflation, high food prices, etc.[3]

Finally, the larger a state's military capability relative to its potential adversary(ies), the less salient will be its *territorial size*; that is, power compensates for size in the quest for security. And positive power discrepancy will be crucial in their choices: whether or not to initiate a foreign policy crisis for another member of the global system; and if so, whether or not to do so by resort to violence.[4]

All other independent variables—structure, system level, conflict setting, regime type, and age—are unaffected by power discrepancy.[5]

Four linkages are also postulated between **regime type** and other independent variables in the crisis onset model. The first is with *conflict setting*. As noted in the elucidation of the model, discordant regimes, notably a democratic/non-democratic pair, are more prone to interstate crisis and to protracted conflict between adversaries. The principal reason is that regime discordance adds another important source of hostile interaction and accentuates others, such as tangible disputes, different economic systems, and competing ideologies.

The same reasoning applies to other regime type linkages. Thus different regime types, e.g., democratic/civil authoritarian or military/democratic, will place an extra burden on coping capacity and, therefore, on *regime duration*.

Civil authoritarian or military regimes will also tend to exaggerate the power of potential adversaries and to understate their own; that is, they are likely to perceive negative *power discrepancy*, as well as adding to the distrust that plays a crucial role in generating arms races. And finally, non-democratic regimes, all other things being equal, are likely to accentuate *internal instability* because of their greater rigidity and lesser capacity to cope with dissent or material problems at home. For the remaining independent variables—structure, system level, geographical distance, age, and territorial size—no effect of regime type is expected.

Geographic distance is likely to affect only *two* other independent variables in the model. One is *conflict setting*: contiguous states are more likely to generate a protracted conflict than those geographically remote from each other; proximity permits, as well as being more likely to induce, on-going pervasive conflictive interaction. It can also be argued that contiguity will also likely increase *internal instability*, due to the greater likelihood of ethnic spillovers and unresolved border disputes.[6] No cause-effect links can be inferred for geographic distance, on the one hand, and, on the other, structure, system level, power discrepancy, regime type, age, regime duration, and size.

The **age** of a state is linked to *five* other independent variables. First, new or young states are more likely than old states to generate a *protracted conflict*. This is due to less security of tenure, an underdeveloped economy, and the lack of social cohesion. One way of expediting the process of state-building is to externalize these obstacles by initiating crises for other states, from which—all other things being equal—protracted conflicts over diverse issues are likely to develop.

Capability/power discrepancy, too, is likely to be affected by age. The older a state, the more time it has to develop its economy by effective mobilization of resources, more precisely, to generate the economic surplus that provides the basis for military power. As a consequence, other things being equal, old, established states are more likely than new states to have a favorable power balance *vis-à-vis* an adversary.

Age will also affect *regime type* and *regime duration*. New states are more likely to be non-democratic because of the struggle, often long and violent, that attends their emergence, whether from the uniting of disparate groups and territories or from foreign rule—or both. Similarly, the younger a state, the less likely it is that it will have created the political, economic and social conditions for a durable regime.

Younger states, too, are more likely than older ones to suffer from *internal*, as well as external, *instability* because of their youth, weakness, lack of experience, and relative military weakness; that is, they will be more prone to a "paranoia syndrome" regarding the intentions of opposition groups, as well as other states. Age does not, however, affect other variables, namely structure, system level, territorial distance, and size.

For **regime duration**, *two* linkages are postulated with other crisis onset variables. The longer a regime lasts, the more likely it is to experience a favorable power balance, that is, positive *power discrepancy* relative to an adversary. This is so because a regime of longer standing is more secure and is capable of more effective mobilization of human and natural resources to protect its interests and enhance its values. Moreover, all other things being equal, a regime of short duration, still uncertain of its legitimacy and authority, is more likely to be confronted with *internal instability*.[7] All other independent variables in the model—structure, system level, conflict setting, regime type, geographic distance, age and size—are not directly affected by regime duration.

Territorial size manifests one linkage, *capability*: all other things being equal, the smaller a state, the fewer will be its natural and human resources; and the more likely it is to operate with negative power discrepancy *vis-à-vis* an adversary.[8] No other independent variable is affected by the attribute of size *per se*.

The last of the independent variables in the crisis onset model to be ranked is **internal instability**. *Three* linkages can be deduced. One is *conflict setting*: in accordance with externalization theory, it can be argued that domestic instability creates a propensity to protracted conflict, for decision-makers seek long-term outlets or compensatory devices to cope with persistent political dissent, social unrest and economic shortcomings at home. Instability also undermines *capability* by generating negative *power discrepancy*: the less stable a state's domestic political, economic and/or social conditions, the more likely it is to suffer from military weakness relative to an adversary. *Regime duration*, too, will be influenced by internal instability. The more unstable a regime, the more likely it is that regime change will occur, in order to cope with the sources of instability.[9] No direct effects can be inferred from internal instability to the other independent variables—structure, system level, territorial distance, regime type, age and size.

The deductive derivation of linkages among the enabling conditions of crisis onset is now complete. Thus it is possible to construct a rank-order of the independent variables, based upon the number of linkage effects.[10]

Rank

1	structure –	8 effects
2	system level –	6
3	age –	5
4	conflict setting –	4
4	capability –	4
4	regime—type (pair) –	4
7	internal instability –	3
8	geographic distance –	2
8	regime—duration –	2
10	territory—size –	1

In sum, 43% of the theoretically possible linkages have been operationalized (39 of 90). Of the six variables with the highest rank, two are system attributes, three interactor, and one actor attribute.

Aggregate Findings on Intensity

THIS descriptive analysis will focus on the distribution of international crises from the end of 1918 to the end of 1988 at each scale point of the six indicators of intensity, beginning with the *number of crisis actors*.

The vast majority of the 390 international crises had only one or two crisis actors, that is, states whose decision-makers perceived value threat, time pressure, and heightened probability of war: a single actor in 157 cases (40.3%), and two actors in 151 cases (38.7%). As the number of actors increased, the proportion of cases declined: three–four actors (16.7%); five and more actors (4.3%).

Single-actor cases occurred in all polarity configurations, regions, etc.:

polarity: multipolarity—19%, World War II—11%, bipolarity—19%, polycentrism—51%;

system level: subsystem—84%, dominant system—16%;

conflict setting: non-PC—58%, PC—42%;

region: Africa—32%, Americas—11%, Asia—15%, Europe—19%, Middle East—22%;

decade: 1919–28—10%, 1929–38—6%, 1939–48—18%, 1949–58—10%, 1959–68—12%, 1969–78—20%, 1979–88—24%.

Examples are: Austria in the Burgenland Dispute (1921) (Central Europe, multipolarity); the US in the Panay Incident (1937) (East Asia, multipolarity); Turkey in Kars-Ardahan (1945–46) (Middle East, bipolarity); Spain in the 1957 Ifni Crisis (North Africa, bipolarity); Bolivia in the Ché Guevara Crisis (1967) (Latin America, polycentrism); Mauritania in Nouakchott I (1976) (West Africa, polycentrism); and Bahrain in the Bahrain/Qatar Dispute (1986) (Middle East, polycentrism).

Several themes emerge from the distribution of crises in terms of major power *involvement*. One is the infrequency of high adversarial involvement by the powers in crises for the 70-year period, except for World War II IWCs (7%). Another is the steady proportional increase of low/no involvement by the major powers from the multipolar to the bipolar to the polycentric systems, 48.1%, 67.7%, and 73.3%, respectively. A third is the difference between superpower activity in crises since the end of World War II, and great power activity in the inter-World War period: the US and the USSR were not involved at all or were only marginally involved in 62.6% of all crises from mid-1945 to the end of 1988; non-involvement or low involvement by the seven major powers from 1918 to 1939 was much less (48.1%). In short, *superpower behavior exhibits much greater caution and concern* about limiting the military fallout from crisis disruption and reducing the attendant risk of uncontrollable escalation in the era of nuclear weaponry.

The *geostrategic salience* of most crises, measured by their distance from major powers and the natural resources of the region in which they occur, also tended to the lower end of the scales: more than half (62.8%) were salient to one subsystem only. If the World War II subset of intra-war crises is excluded, the thrust to minimal salience is only slightly accentuated (63.7%). In terms of system level, the distribution of cases reveals a high concentration of salience to the subsystem (81.8% of all cases), with only 18.2% salient to the dominant system.

The highest point on the geostrategic salience scale was scored by many well-known international crises, among them Entry into World War II (1939), several intra-war crises, such as Battle of Britain (1940), "Barbarossa" (1941), Pearl Harbor (1941–42), Stalingrad (1942–43), and D-Day (1944), along with Suez-Sinai War (1956–57), Cuban Missiles (1962), Six Day War (1967), and October-Yom Kippur (1973–74). Munich (1938) and the Berlin crises (1948–49, 1957–59, 1961) were salient to the then-dominant system of world politics, as well as to the West European and East European subsystems, the latter by virtue of their significance in the struggle for Germany and their symbolic meaning for the future of Europe. So too did the crisis arising from the Soviet Invasion of Afghanistan (1979), affecting the Middle East and South Asia subsystems, as well as the superpower balance. These crises registered point 4 on the scale of geostrategic salience.

Invasion of the Ruhr (1923), the Mukden Incident (1931–32), and the Soviet Bloc/Yugoslavia Crisis (1949–) were all salient to the dominant system and one subsystem, Western Europe, East Asia, and Eastern Europe, respectively (point 3). Even more cases scored point 2 on geostrategic salience, for example, the India/China Border crisis-war: it was salient to South and East Asia but not to the dominant system of world politics. The largest group comprised crises that were salient to one subsystem only (point 1), from the Teschen Crisis between Czechoslovakia and Poland (1919) to those between Chad and Libya (e.g., 1971, 1978, 1986, 1987), mainly over the uranium-rich Aouzou Strip that straddles their disputed border.

To determine *heterogeneity* in international crises with several adversarial pairs, the most heterogeneous pair is used. For example, in the Remilitarization of the Rhineland Crisis (1936), Germany and Yugoslavia, with maximal heterogeneity, was selected, rather than Germany and the UK, which did not differ in military capability or economic development. Maximal heterogeneity among crisis adversaries is evident in two of the Taiwan Straits crises (1954–55, 1958): the US was a superpower in global terms, the PRC a great power; the US had an advanced post-industrial economy, China a very poor developing economy; the two adversaries also differed in political regime—democracy versus civil authoritarianism; and they were far apart in all aspects of culture. Thus those crises were coded 5 on the heterogeneity scale.

In all of their crises, beginning with Rhodesia UDI (1965–66) and ending with Rhodesian Settlement (1979–80), Rhodesia and Zambia differed on three of the four attributes of heterogeneity: a middle power in Southern Africa versus a small power; an economically developed versus an underdeveloped economy; and vast cultural differences between a white-ruled colonial society and a black African society that emerged from foreign rule as part of the "end of empire" phase of twentieth-century international history. The political regime of both was civil authoritarian, wrapped in democratic form. Thus those cases were scored 4 on the heterogeneity scale.

The two crises between Austria and Germany in the thirties (*Putsch* [1934] and *Anschluss* [1938]) exhibit moderate heterogeneity. Germany was a great power, Austria a small power, and Germany was far more developed economically. However, they had a common language and culture, and were ruled by civil authoritarian regimes. The two elements of heterogeneity led to point 3 on the scale.

There was minimal heterogeneity in the Sino-Vietnam War (1978–79) and in lesser crises in the eighties, over the border (1987) and over the Spratly Islands (1988). The PRC and Vietnam shared a communist political regime, underdeveloped economy, and, in the region, great power status. Only in language and culture did they differ, leading to point 2 for these cases.

No heterogeneity is evident in many international crises, for example, in the Saudi/Yemen War (1933–34): both were small powers, economically underdeveloped, with civil authoritarian regimes, and Arab, Muslim, tribal societies. Towards the close of the period of inquiry, a crisis between two oil-rich Persian Gulf states, Bahrain/Qatar, exhibited the same absence of heterogeneity; that is, point 1 for both cases.

Most crises during the period of inquiry exhibited considerable heterogeneity. There were relatively few cases with no attribute differences or one difference, 7.7% and 12.6%, respectively. At the other extreme, almost a third (32.3%) of all crises were characterized by maximal heterogeneity among the adversaries, closely followed by cases with two and three attribute differences (26.2% and 21.3%). This distribution suggests that *adversaries with a high degree of homogeneity*—whether equal military or economic capability, a shared political regime, a common culture, or all of these—*find it easier to negotiate differences* with other states without escalating to crisis interaction, let alone violence. Heterogeneous adversaries, by contrast, are more likely to be incapable of avoiding the eruption of international crises and their attendant high costs.

In the realm of *issues*, a military-security (m-s) issue alone was present in 49.5% of the 390 international crises, such as the two Chaco War cases between Bolivia and Paraguay (1928–29 and 1932–35), and a plethora of crises in Africa during the 1970s and 1980s (e.g., Nagomia Raid [1976] between Rhodesia and Mozambique). Another frequent issue type of international crisis involved two issue-areas, one of them military-security (31%). This was evident in the Chinese Eastern Railway Crisis (1929) between China and the USSR, and Chad/Libya VIII (1986), among Chad, France and Libya. By contrast, only 16 crises (4.1% of the total) affected three issue-areas, such as the *Anschluss* between Austria and Germany (1938) and Rhodesian Settlement (1979–80).

A moderate number of international crises (48, or 12.3%) were concerned with a single, non-military issue (e.g., East Berlin Uprising [1953], which centered on the survival of the communist regime in the GDR). In one of their recurrent crises within a protracted conflict, Greece and Turkey were embroiled in a dispute over claims to the resources of the continental shelf of Greece's Aegean Islands (Aegean Sea II, 1987). In the political-diplomatic issue-area, the survival of Mauritania's regime was the object of an unsuccessful attack by the Polisario Front in Nouakchott I (1976). There were very few crises involving two non-m-s areas (12, or 3.1%) (e.g., two East European crises that focused on political and status issues, namely, Communism in Hungary [1947] and Communism in Czechoslovakia [1948]).

For the period as a whole, there was an almost equal distribution among the four *violence* categories. Full-scale war was present in 89 of the 390 international crises (22.8%), among them, Greece/Turkey War II (1921), the Ethiopian War (1935–36), World War II, the Korean War cases (1950–53), Arab/Israel crisis-wars from 1948–49 to 1982, India/Pakistan crisis-wars from 1947–48 to 1971, and Vietnam War cases from 1954 to 1973. Serious clashes occurred in 100 cases (25.6%), from the Russo/Finnish Border Crisis (1919–20) to Gulf of Syrte II (1986) between Libya and the US. Minor clashes occurred in 25.9% of the cases, from the Persian Border (1920–21) to Indian Intervention in Sri Lanka (1987). And there was no violence in 25.6% of the international crises from 1918 to 1988, from the Aaland Islands Crisis for Sweden (1919–20), to Punjab War Scare II (1987) between India and Pakistan.

If all intra-war cases are deleted—for they distort the distribution sharply in the direction of high violence—the picture is starkly different: no violence (32.8%); minor clashes (30.4%); serious clashes (25.0%); and full-scale war (11.8%); that is, no/low violence (63.2%), and high violence (36.8%). Viewed in terms of a violence/non-violence dichotomy, violence in some form was present in 67.2% of 283 international crises other than those during a war, no violence in 32.8% of the crises.

No less striking, *violent crises increased in frequency as the number of states in the global system increased: multipolarity* was the least violent, with violence in 65% of its cases, compared to 69.8% for the larger *bipolar* system, and 79.3% for the much larger *polycentric* system. Serious clashes were proportionately much more frequent after World War II than in the inter-World War period (88.4% and 11.6%, respectively). Moreover, the *upward trend in violence over the three system-periods* is evident for both serious clashes (14.3%, 24.7%, and 32.3%, respectively), and for high violence (serious clashes and war combined), 40.2%, 40.8%, and 51.3%.[1]

With the completion of the general findings on crisis intensity, attention will now focus on a crucial subset, the *most intense* international crises since 1918.

Most Intense Crises

All intra-war crises are excluded because of the "contamination" created by a context of on-going war. Of the remaining 317 international crises, 20 cases with the highest overall intensity score were selected for comparative analysis. Their scores range from 10, the theoretical maximum (Entry into World War II, 1939) to 6.77 (Prague Spring, 1968) on the 10-point intensity scale.[2] The distribution of cases in time and space, and in terms of the individual indicators of intensity, is presented in Appendix B Tables 1 and 2.

Europe was the preeminent region of intense international crises for the 70 years under inquiry, accounting for nine of the 20 cases. Viewed in terms of time, the most intense crises increased sharply from the multipolar period (five in 21 years) to bipolarity (nine in 17 years), declining in polycentrism (six in 26 years). The largest concentration of these cases was in the years 1956–62, six of the 20 crises, beginning with Suez–Sinai and ending with Cuban Missiles. Among other indicators, this pointed to *a decline in the number of intense crises*, though not of the total number of crises, *from the onset of polycentrism* in 1963.

Many of the most intense international crises were linked to recurring disturbances in the global system arising from a shared issue. Two clusters were located in Europe, one in the 1930s over Germany's challenge to the post-World War I status quo, the other in the East/West protracted conflict, over Berlin. One cluster focused on the Arab/Israel protracted conflict.

Especially instructive is the evidence on *power discrepancy* among adversaries in these crises. Most crises (15) were characterized by high power discrepancy (e.g., Prague Spring, in which there was an overwhelming superiority by the USSR-led Warsaw Pact coalition over dissident Czechoslovakia). However, full-scale war was present in only eight cases (e.g., Korean War I), whereas there was no violence in six cases (e.g., Munich). Conversely, three of five cases with low power discrepancy between the adversaries were accompanied by full-scale war. These findings suggest that *states do not fight when they know, or believe, they will win, or lose, a war. In intense crises, they are more inclined to fight when the power balance is uncertain*, indicating at least a possibility of winning a war.

What do the data on the intensity indicators reveal about the most intense crises during the 70-year period? The minimal number of *crisis actors* was three (e.g., Cuban Missiles), the maximum, 21 (Entry into

APPENDIX TABLE 1 *Most Intense International Crises, 1918–1988: Time, Space, Overall Intensity*[a]

	Africa	Americas	Asia	Europe	Middle East
1918–39				Rhineland (1936) 8.51	
				Spanish Civil War (1936–39) 8.11	
				Munich (1938) 7.98	
				Invasion of Albania (1939) 6.77	
				Entry into World War II (1939) 10.00	
1945–62			Korean War I (1950) 7.58	Berlin Blockade (1948–49) 8.25	Azerbaijan (1945–46) 7.71
				Berlin Deadline (1957–59) 8.51	Suez–Sinai (1956–57) 9.72
		Cuban Missiles (1962) 7.58	Taiwan Straits II (1958) 6.91	Berlin Wall (1961) 9.58	Lebanon/Iraq Upheaval (1958) 6.91
1963–88	Congo II (1964) 7.98			Prague Spring (1968) 6.77	Six Day War (1967) 9.72
	Angola (1975–76) 9.18				October – Yom Kippur War (1973–74) 9.18
	Shaba II (1978) 7.44				

[a] Each of the 20 cases in this table has an overall intensity score larger than 6.76. Intra-war crises of high intensity, e.g., Fall of Western Europe (1940) and Pearl Harbor (1941–42) are excluded.

APPENDIX TABLE 2 *Most Intense International Crises, 1918–1988: Components of Overall Intensity*

International Crisis	Crisis Actors	Major Power Involvement	Geostrategic Salience	Heterogeneity	Issues	Violence	Overall Intensity
Rhineland (1936)	6 (7)*	4	4	5	4	1	8.51
Spanish Civil War (1936)	4	6	3	5	4	4	8.11
Munich (1938)	4	6	5	3	5	1	7.98
Invasion of Albania (1939)	4	4	2	5	4	4	6.77
Entry into World War II (1939)	6 (21)	6	5	5	3	4	10.00
Azerbaijan (1945–46)	4	6	3	5	4	1	7.71
Berlin Blockade (1948–49)	4	6	5	4	5	1	8.25
Korean War I (1950)	4	5	3	5	4	4	7.58
Suez–Sinai War (1956–57)	6	6	5	5	4	4	9.72
Berlin Deadline (1957–59)	5	6	5	4	4	1	8.51
Lebanon–Iraq Upheaval (1958)	4	5	3	5	2	3	6.91
Taiwan Straits (1958)	3	5	3	5	4	3	6.91
Berlin Wall (1961)	6	6	5	5	5	1	9.58
Cuban Missiles (1962)	3	6	5	5	3	2	7.58
Congo II (1964)	4	6	3	5	4	3	7.98
Six Day War (1967)	6	6	5	5	4	4	9.72
Prague Spring (1968)	6	3	3	2	5	2	6.77
October – Yom Kippur (1973–74)	5	6	5	5	4	4	9.18
Angola (1975–76)	6 (7)	6	3	5	4	4	9.18
Shaba II (1978)	5	5	1	5	4	3	7.44

*The scales and scale points for each intensity indicator were specified in the first section of Chap. 5.

World War II). There was high or very high *involvement* by the major powers (scale points 4–6) in all but one of the 20 most intense crises (Prague Spring, 1968). Both superpowers were crisis actors in 10 of these cases (eg., Berlin Blockade, Cuban Missiles); and more than two great powers were crisis actors in three of the most intense inter-World War crises; that is, 13 of the 20 cases registered 6 on the six-point involvement scale. A noteworthy pattern is evident in the four most intense post-World War II crises in which one superpower was a crisis actor, the other highly involved, always the US and the USSR, respectively. *In all cases, the USSR sent military aid to the US's adversary but avoided direct confrontation with its rival for global hegemony.*

As for *geostrategic salience*, all but one of the 20 most intense crises (Shaba II, 1978) had relevance beyond one subsystem; nine of them had maximal salience, that is, to the global system (scale point 5):

Entry into World War II, because of the world-wide location of its 21 crisis actors and the issues of ideological conflict and global hegemony;

Suez-Sinai Campaign, because of the participation of both superpowers and two great powers, France and the UK, and the salience of the Suez Canal to world trade, as well as access to Middle East oil;

Cuban Missiles, because of the nuclear confrontation between the US and the USSR and its potential consequences for peoples and states everywhere; and

Munich, Berlin Blockade, Berlin Deadline, Berlin Wall, Six Day War and October-Yom Kippur, because of the very active involvement of major powers, often in support of their clients and, in the last case, the oil embargo and the second nuclear confrontation between the US and the USSR.[3]

A large majority of the most intense crises was characterized by maximal *heterogeneity* (scale point 5), 16 of 20 cases (e.g., Entry into World War II, with many adversarial pairs, and War in Angola, with the US and Angola differing in military capability, level of economic development, type of political regime, and culture).

The extent of *violence* varied in the most intense crises. Full-scale war was present in eight of the 20 cases, as noted, either initiating an international crisis (e.g., Suez-Sinai) or as the culmination of an escalation process during a crisis (e.g., Entry into World War II). Four of these crises were characterized by serious clashes short of war (e.g., Congo II, 1964). Yet no less than six of the most intense crises were free

from violence (e.g., Remilitarization of the Rhineland, Berlin Blockade), indicating that, contrary to conventional wisdom, *violence is not a
necessary condition of an intense international crisis.*

Key Crisis Dimensions

The most intense international crises from 1918 to 1988 will now be
examined in terms of their frequency distribution along key crisis
dimensions: trigger or breakpoint; value threat; crisis management
technique; centrality of violence; severity of violence; duration; global
organization involvement and its effectiveness; content of outcome; and
form of outcome.

Nine of the 20 cases were catalyzed by violent acts: eight were from
external sources (e.g., the attack on South Korea by North Korean
forces on 25 June 1950, Korean War I); and one was an internal physical
challenge to a state's political regime (the revolt against the Spanish
Republic by the Franco-led Falange army on 17 July 1936). Four
international crises of high intensity were set in motion by non-violent
military acts (e.g., the emplacement of Soviet offensive missiles in Cuba
in 1962, triggering the Missile Crisis). Six cases were initiated by political acts (e.g., the publication by the three Western Powers in June 1948
of their March London Conference recommendation to integrate the
US, British and French occupation zones in Germany, triggering the
Berlin Blockade Crisis). And one crisis was catalyzed by an external
change, the construction of the Berlin Wall in 1961.

One of three basic *values* was perceived to be threatened in 19 of the
20 crises. Existence was at stake in five cases (e.g., for Czechoslovakia in
the Munich Crisis and for Israel in the Six Day War Crisis). Grave
damage was anticipated in eight cases (e.g., by both the PRC and
Taiwan in Taiwan Straits II [1958], and by Egypt and Israel in the
October-Yom Kippur War). And influence was the highest value
threatened in six cases (e.g., by the United States and Britain in the
Azerbaijan Crisis, and by the Soviet Union in the Prague Spring Crisis).
A political threat existed for one case, War in Angola.

Violence was the pervasive *crisis management technique* (CMT) in
this subset of crises. It was the primary CMT in seven of the 20 cases
and was present in six others (e.g., Korean War I and, for violence
as a coequal CMT with one or more others, the Suez-Sinai War).
There were three cases in which non-violent military acts were the
primary CMT (e.g., Cuban Missiles); three others with negotiation or a
combination of pacific CMTs (e.g., Remilitarization of the Rhineland);

and one case with non-military pressure as the primary CMT (Azerbaijan).

As for the *centrality of violence* in crisis management, it was preeminent in seven of the 20 most intense cases (e.g., Six Day War and Shaba [1978]). It was important but supported by other CMTs in six other cases (e.g., Lebanon–Iraq Upheaval). In only one of these cases (Cuban Missiles) did violence play a minor role. And it was absent in six cases (e.g., the three Berlin crises).

Violence was very severe as a crisis management technique in the majority of these 20 cases. Actors resorted to full-scale war in eight cases (e.g., the Spanish Civil War, Korean War I, October-Yom Kippur War). There were serious clashes in four cases (e.g., Lebanon–Iraq Upheaval) and minor clashes only in two (e.g., Prague Spring). The remaining six cases, as noted, were without violence as a CMT.

A majority of the most intense crises, 13 of 20, were of long *duration*, that is, 61 days or more (e.g., Spanish Civil War, almost three years, Berlin Blockade, more than a year, Prague Spring, six months). There were five medium-duration cases, 32–60 days (e.g., Rhineland, Munich, Cuban Missiles). And two of these cases lasted no more than one month (Invasion of Albania [1939], Six Day War).

There was no *involvement by the global organization* in five of the 20 most intense crises (e.g., Munich, Berlin Wall, Shaba II). In three cases, the League of Nations or the United Nations engaged in discussion but did not pass a resolution (e.g., Taiwan Straits II). The global organization did pass an operative resolution in six crises: in two, UN calls for a cease-fire (e.g., Six Day War); two condemnations (Rhineland, Angola); and two calls for action by member-states (e.g., by the USSR and Iran in the Azerbaijan Crisis). There were two cases of mediation (Berlin Blockade, Cuban Missiles). Emergency military forces were dispatched in two others (Korean War I, Suez). An Observer Group was sent in one case (Lebanon–Iraq Upheaval). And there was one case of general UN activity (attempted conciliation by the Secretary-General in Berlin Deadline).

Global organizations were ineffective on the whole in the most intense international crises from 1918 to 1988. As noted, there was no League of Nations/UN involvement in five of 20 cases. In nine others, IO activity did not contribute to crisis abatement (e.g., Rhineland, Berlin Blockade). It had an important, positive effect in three of these crises: in Azerbaijan, the Security Council exerted pressure on the USSR to reach an amicable withdrawal agreement with Iran; in the Suez-Sinai War, the UN passed cease-fire resolutions and, later, dispatched a UN Emergency Force (UNEF I) to Sinai; in Cuban Missiles, mediation was undertaken by the Secretary-General, and the UN supervised the withdrawal of Soviet missiles from the island. However, in the other cases, activity by the global organization escalated the crisis: in Lebanon–Iraq Upheaval, the dispatch of an inadequate Observer Group that was ineffective in curbing infiltration into Lebanon prolonged the crisis; and in Six Day War, the withdrawal of UNEF from Sinai escalated the crisis by removing a ten-year barrier to direct military confrontation between Egypt and Israel. Finally, in one case (October-Yom Kippur War), the UN contributed marginally to crisis deescalation after the two superpowers had, *de facto*, imposed a ceasefire on Egypt and Israel.

A majority of the most intense international crises, 13 of 20, terminated with an ambiguous *outcome*; that is, they resulted in some combination of defeat, victory, stalemate, or compromise between the adversaries other than a strict victory-defeat pairing. The other seven cases ended with a definitive result, that is, with a defeat-victory outcome. Among them were several celebrated crises: Berlin Blockade, with defeat for the USSR and victory for the three Western Powers; Cuban Missiles, with a (thinly-concealed) defeat for the Soviet Union and Cuba and a (self-constrained) victory for the United States; and Six Day War, with a (dramatic) defeat for Egypt, Jordan, and Syria, and a victory for Israel.

Eleven of these 20 crises ended through a formal or semi-formal agreement between the adversaries (e.g., the Munich Agreement among France, Germany, Italy, and the UK; a Soviet-Iran withdrawal of forces agreement, based upon a UN Security Council resolution, in the Azerbaijan Crisis; semi-formal agreements between the Soviet Union and the Western Powers or the United States, ending Berlin Blockade and Cuban Missiles, respectively). There was a tacit agreement in one case (Taiwan Straits II). The other eight cases ended without agreement, usually through a unilateral act.

These are the essential empirical findings about the 20 most intense international crises outside of an on-going war, from the end of 1918 to the end of 1988.

Notes

Complete authors' names, titles, and publication data are given in the References.

Preface

1 Brecher (1953).

2 Brecher (1974), Brecher with Geist (1980).

3 The in-depth case studies are cited in Chapter 1, n. 50, and the aggregate data analyses in Chapter 1, n. 1.

4 Wright (1942); Sorokin (1937); Richardson (1960a,b); Singer and Small (1972); Small and Singer (1982).

5 Choucri and North (1975), among others.

6 McClelland (1961, 1964, 1968, 1972); Robinson (1962, 1968, 1970, 1972); Hermann (1963, 1969a,b, 1972a,b); Holsti (1965, 1972); Young (1967, 1968); Snyder and Diesing (1977). Their work is discussed in Chapter 1, "State of the Art."

7 On these debates, see Bull (1966) and Kaplan (1966); Jervis (1967) and North (1967); Knorr and Rosenau (1969); Dougherty and Pfaltzgraff (1971); Rosenau *et al.* (1972); Bueno de Mesquita (1985), Krasner (1985), and Jervis (1985); Achen and Snidal (1989), and George and Smoke (1989). On the state of the discipline in the mid-1980s see K. J. Holsti (1985).

8 Zinnes (1980).

9 Brecher (1977, 1979).

10 Brecher (1972); George (1979).

11 Eckstein (1975).

12 The sequence of Models I and II, in Chapter 1, is reversed in Chapter 6, which sets out Model III, the Unified Model. The reason may be termed the "two logics," the logic of presentation and the logic of content. In Chapter 1, I proceed from the larger construct, international crisis, to the smaller one subsumed within it, foreign policy crisis. However, crisis take-off or eruption occurs first at the actor level; that is, in content, a foreign policy crisis generates an international crisis, not the reverse. Thus the actor level is discussed first in Chapter 6. The linkage between the two levels of analysis will be elaborated in Chapter 1.

13 Fukuyama (1992).

Chapter 1

1 These examples and all other empirical evidence cited in this book are drawn from the *International Crisis Behavior (ICB) Project* dataset (end 1918–end 1988), much of

which (1929–85) was presented in Brecher and Wilkenfeld, Vol. I (1988), Wilkenfeld and Brecher, Vol. II (1988), and Brecher and Wilkenfeld (1989).

Summary data relating to the 390 crises—over time and region, conflict setting, territorial disputes, the crisis-war link, and overall distributions according to key crisis categories—are presented in Figure 2.2 and Tables 2.1–2.5 [Chap. 2].

2 Yet it is noteworthy that the *Handbook of Political Conflict* (Gurr, 1980) does not discuss "crisis," and *The Social Science Encyclopedia* (Kuper and Kuper, 1985) does not contain an entry for the term, "crisis," unlike the earlier *International Encyclopedia of the Social Sciences* (Robinson, 1968).

3 "Heightened" probability means "higher-than-normal" or "increased"; all three *relative* terms are used interchangeably in this book. The rationale for the selection of "heightened" as preferable to the *absolute* notion, "high," is set out in the "state of the art" critique [p. 19].

4 Conceptually, "international system" ranges across a broad spectrum, from the global system through the dominant system to subsystems.

The *global system* comprises all autonomous actors (state, supranational and transnational) and their interactions (political, economic, military, cultural, etc.). It is cited interchangeably as *the international system*. (Rosenau [1990: 14, 77, 78, 108, 112, 152], by contrast, differentiates these two concepts: the former is the "multi-centric world," comprising all actors, including state bureaucracies, transnational actors, and subgroups; the latter is the "state-centric world," essentially the interstate system, and is part of the global system).

The *dominant system* refers to the power configuration and the interactions among the major state actors in a particular historical era; for example, France, Germany, Italy, Japan, the UK, the US, and the USSR were the acknowledged great powers in the inter-World War global system, 1919–39. It is often cited as the *central subsystem*.

There are two types of *subsystem* (or *subordinate system*), *geographic* and *issue*. For an informative discussion of the early international subsystems literature see Thompson (1973); and, for a selection of that literature, see Falk and Mendlovitz (1973, esp. Part V). M. Haas, in an empirical analysis of 21 subsystems (1974: 336–356), combined geographic and issue criteria. Lampert (1980) was the most direct in asserting the primacy of issue over geography as the basic component of subsystems. On the centrality of issues in world politics generally, see Mansbach and Vasquez (1981) and Vasquez and Mansbach (1983).

5 On the linkage of domestic politics and foreign policy issues, especially crisis and war, see pp. 60–61, 147–148.

6 The definitions of crisis presented here were framed to guide a comprehensive inquiry into twentieth-century crises at both macro (system/interactor) and micro (actor) levels of analysis, the International Crisis Behavior Project (ICB) (Brecher, 1977; Brecher and Ben Yehuda, 1985). See the ICB works cited in notes 1, 50, 51.

The link between foreign policy crisis and international crisis will be elaborated in Chapter 6.

7 For informative surveys of the literature on social conflict see Lasswell (1931), Mack and Snyder (1957), McNeill (1965), Coser (1968), Fink (1968), North (1968), Nicholson (1970), and Gurr (1980). See also the war literature cited in n. 9 below.

8 On the concept of protracted conflict, see also Azar (1979), Azar and Farah (1981), Brecher (1984), Azar (1985), Brecher and Wilkenfeld (1989: Chaps. 9–11), and Hewitt, Boyer and Wilkenfeld (1991).

9 The contemporary literature on war is vast and exhibits an array of approaches, methods, theories, and substantive foci. A selection of works by category is noted here: *pioneering works*: Sorokin (1937), Wright (1942), Richardson (1960a, 1960b);

collections of articles on war: Pruitt and Snyder (1969), Falk and Kim (1980); Vasquez and Henehan (1992);

critical reviews: Zinnes (1980), on quantitative studies of the outbreak of war, Singer (1981), on the "state of the discipline," Eberwein (1981) and Levy (1989c) on the literature relating to the causes of war, Luterbacher (1984), on recent contributions, Vasquez (1987) and Dessler (1991) on the Correlates of War Project, and Midlarsky (1989a) — surveys of theories and findings until the late 1980s;

causes of war: Blainey (1973), Nelson and Olin (1979), Beer (1981), Howard (1984), Brown (1987), Vasquez (forthcoming, 1993);

conflict and war: Rummel (1975–81);

crisis and war: O. R. Holsti (1972), Brecher and Wilkenfeld (1988, 1989), James (1988); Wilkenfeld and Brecher (1988);

deterrence and war: Huth (1988a,b), Stern *et al.* (1989), Lebow and Stein (1990), Huth and Russett (1990);

diversionary theory: Levy (1989a);

domestic aspects of war: A. A. Stein (1978), Levy and Morgan (1986), Levy (1989b);

expected utility theory: Bueno de Mesquita (1981, 1985, 1989), Bueno de Mesquita and Lalman (1992);

game theory: Brams and Kilgour (1987);

hegemonic war: Gilpin (1981, 1989), Levy (1983);

hierarchical equilibria theory: Midlarsky (1986, 1988, 1989b);

historical approach: Stoessinger (1985), Nogee and Spanier (1988), K. J. Holsti (1991);

historical sociology approach: Aron (1957, 1959), S. Hoffmann (1965), Luard (1987);

inadvertent war: George (1991);

initiation of war: Paul (forthcoming, 1994);

lateral pressure theory: Choucri and North (1975, 1989);

levels of analysis: Waltz (1959);

long cycles and war: Modelski and Morgan (1985), Thompson (1986, 1988), Modelski (1987), Goldstein (1988), Modelski and Thompson (1989);

nuclear war: Kahn (1960, 1962, 1965, 1970), Bracken (1983);

obsolescence of major power war: Mueller (1989), Van Creveld (1991);

outcome and consequences: A. A. Stein and Russett (1980);

paradoxes of war: Maoz (1990a);

polarity and war: Levy (1985), Sabrosky (1985), Domke (1988);

political economy of war: Ashley (1980);

power transition theory: Organski and Kugler (1980), Kugler and Organski (1989);

psychological dimension of war: Glad (1990);

quantitative (aggregate data) research (Correlates of War project): Singer and Small (1972), Singer *et al.* (1979a, 1979b, 1980), Small and Singer (1982), Houweling and Siccama (1988), Gochman and Sabrosky (1990);

revolution and war: Walt (1992);

search for patterns: Barringer (1972);

strategic theory: Schelling (1960), Brodie (1973), Luttwak (1987), Harkabi (1990);

technology and war: McNeill (1982), Van Creveld (1989).

See also the critique of the literature on *escalation and war* and *war termination* in Chaps. 3 and 4.

10 Figure 1.1 builds upon two earlier attempts to capture the multiple relationships, James (1988: 8–9), and Brecher and James (1988: 448–449).

Conflict setting has a profound impact on crises. This conceptual link was elaborated in a protracted conflict-crisis model (Brecher, 1984, and Brecher and Wilkenfeld, 1989: Chap. 9). The essence of the argument will be set out in the presentation of the phase models of crisis onset and escalation, in Chaps. 2 and 3.

11 The literature on international and foreign policy crisis is extensive. For earlier instructive reviews, see Robinson (1968: 510–514, 1970, 1972), Hermann (1972b), Candela (1974), Williams (1976: 19–26), Parker (1977), Eberwein (1978), O. R. Holsti (1979, 1989), Tanter (1979), Hopple and Rossa (1981), M. Haas (1986), Oneal (1988). For a harsh critique of crisis theory, see Garfinkle (1986). For a general review of crisis in fields other than world politics, see O'Connor (1987).

12 Apart from McClelland's own writings, see, for the first "wave," Azar (1972), Burrowes and Muzzio (1972), Azar and Ben-Dak (1975). For the second "wave," see Andriole and Young (1977), Azar et al. (1977), Rossa et al. (1980).

There have been fewer attempts at forecasting, using events data, at the actor (state) level of analysis: see Hermann (1975), Hermann and Mason (1980), Raphael (1982). Other techniques for analyzing crisis anticipation are evident in Martin (1977), and Chan and Bobrow (1981).

13 For a sympathetic, insightful critique of the Snyder et al. framework, see Rosenau (1967).

14 For assessments of the literature on crisis management, see Shapiro and Gilbert (1975), Tanter (1975), Gilbert and Lauren (1980), O. R. Holsti (1980, 1989), and Richardson (1988).

15 See also, among others: Zinnes, North and Koch (1961); Holsti, Brody and North (1964); Zinnes (1966, 1968); Holsti, North and Brody (1968). For critiques of the Stanford Studies, see Jervis (1967), North's reply (1967), and Hilton (1969). A comprehensive assessment and bibliography of the Stanford Studies is to be found in Hoole and Zinnes (1976: Chaps. 17–21 and pp. 514–519).

16 See also Zinnes and Wilkenfeld (1971), Phillips (1973, 1978), Wilkenfeld et al. (1980), and Ward (1982).

17 See also Cohen (1979) and M. G. Hermann (1979); and for empirical studies of the effects of cognitive constraints on crisis decision-making, see, for example, Suedfeld and Tetlock (1977), Shlaim and Tanter (1978), J. L. Snyder (1978), Bonham, Shapiro and Trumble (1979).

A very different cognitive conception of crisis, from the perspective of administrative theory, is presented in Jarman and Kouzmin (1991).

18 Some scholars claimed substantial evidence that decision-makers employ the analytic mode, that is, an expected utility calculus, in crisis decision-making (Bueno de Mesquita, 1981, 1985, 1989; Maoz, 1981). For earlier applications of this model, see Horelick (1964) and Sigal (1970).

19 For critiques of alternative models of crisis, see Hermann and Brady (1972), Stein and Tanter (1980: 21–62), and Maoz (1990b: Chap. 5).

20 Later, Holsti (1989: 12) revised his view in the direction of the definition set out at the beginning of this chapter: "There is general agreement that crises are marked by a *severe threat* to important *values* and that *time* for coping with the threat is *finite*. That definition will be adopted here." Although "the behavioral consequences of surprise may be significant," it was deleted as a "necessary condition for the existence of a crisis" because of insufficient evidence. As for the third ICB condition, probability of war, "This requirement may be valid for many foreign policy situations, but it also seems overly restrictive" (emphasis added).

21 There are others who defined "crisis" as a situation that might lead to war. McClelland (1972: 83) viewed "international crisis" as a "transition from peace to war. . . . A crisis refers to both a real prelude to war and an averted approach toward war. Crises are most commonly thought of as interpositions between the prolongation of peace and the outbreak of war". So too did Schelling (1966: 96–97), Young (1967: 10),

and Lebow (1981). The first three of these works focused on crisis at the system/interactor level. Moreover, all identified the *possibility*, not *increasing or heightened probability*, of war.

The *high probability* of war as a crucial condition of military-security crisis is also evident in, Bell (1971), Williams (1976), and Leng and Singer (1988: 159).

The author's—and the ICB's—earlier definition of crisis (Brecher, 1977, 1979, 1980; Brecher and Wilkenfeld, 1988, 1989; Wilkenfeld and Brecher, 1988) combined "high" and "higher" war likelihood. However, in the selection of cases this condition was operationalized in relative terms, that is, the perception of *higher-than-normal* or *heightened* probability of war.

22 While it is possible to explore even further problems of concept formation at the actor level, comparative advantage dictates a shift to other aspects of the literature on crisis.

23 I am grateful to Hemda Ben Yehuda for her contribution to this segment of the "state of the art" review. An earlier, abbreviated version appeared in Brecher and Ben Yehuda (1985: 20–24).

24 The *events data* sets upon which these studies were based, notably WEIS [see p. 8 and n. 12 above], and the Cooperation and Peace Data Bank (COPDAB), directed by Azar, have been severely criticized, on several grounds: that they rely on biased and exaggerated reporting in the press (WEIS relied solely on the *New York Times*); that official statements and official policy often differ; that the accuracy of the cooperation-conflict index, based upon press reports, is questionable; and that the method of content analysis suffers from serious problems. (Burgess and Lawton, 1972; Howell, 1983; Vincent, 1983; Andriole and Hopple, 1984; Goldstein and Freeman, 1990: Chap. 1.). Their great value is the abundant information they compiled on state behavior and interstate interaction.

25 For several scholars with a systems orientation, including M. A. Kaplan (1957), Pruitt (1969)and Waltz (1979), systems are characterized by normal periods of equilibrium and stability, with occasional shifts to disequilibrium and instability. Although they do not explicitly term such situations systemic crises, these transitions are related to the concept of crisis.

26 For an elaboration of the Chinese view of crisis, see Chan (1978), and Bobrow *et al.* (1979). For perceptions of crisis by other non-Western and Western states, see Mahoney and Clayberg (1980), and Gaenslen (1986).

27 For a notable integrative work on the phenomenon of change or *turbulence* in world politics, see Rosenau (1990). Turbulence was defined as "extraordinarily high degrees of complexity and dynamism . . . and interconnectedness at work in the global system." Formally, "Global turbulence can be defined as a worldwide state of affairs in which the interconnections that sustain the primary parameters of world politics are marked by extensive complexity and variability" (65, 78).

28 The term, "interstate crisis," as used throughout this book, applies to any *military-security crisis* between or among legally sovereign members of the global system. It does not include: environmental, political, economic, social or cultural crises within a state or those that extend beyond a state's boundaries but do not generate perceptions of value threat, time pressure, and heightened probability of military hostilities, along with higher-than-normal disruptive interaction between states; inter-ethnic disputes, non-violent or violent; civil strife between non-state actors; or conflict between a state and a non-state actor, as in conflicts between colonial powers and groups aspiring to independence.

Nor does "interstate crisis" apply to domestic upheavals that have potentially large-scale spillover effects on the global system or a subsystem. A notable example is the failed coup attempt to overthrow Soviet President Gorbachev, on 19–21 August 1991. Only if such a crisis escalates to the point of generating perceptions of basic value threat, time pressure and heightened probability of war and, in turn, higher-than-normal disruptive interaction with one or more states, does such a situational change qualify as an interstate crisis.

This evolutionary process is evident in the struggle between the forces of centralization, led by Serbia, and the forces demanding self-determination, led by Croatia and Slovenia, in Yugoslavia's civil war in 1991–92. At first it did not qualify as an interstate crisis. However, by the autumn of 1991, with increasing involvement by the European Community (EC) and, later, the United Nations, the imposition of economic sanctions against Serbia, and the recognition of Croatia and Slovenia as independent states by EC members, the UN and the world community at large, a domestic crisis had been transformed into an international crisis with two principal actors, Serbia and Croatia. The post-Cold War international crisis attending the disintegration of Yugoslavia was accentuated in 1992 by the Serb attempt to frustrate the Bosnia-Hercegovina referendum in favor of independence, leading to civil war, a massive flight of refugees, and UN-EC economic sanctions against Serbia and its ally, Montenegro.

The onset of this crisis is dated back to Croatia's declaration of independence in June 1991. An earlier example of this type is Pakistan's domestic upheaval over East Bengal's demand for independence in 1970 which was transformed into the Bangladesh Crisis, with Pakistan, India and Bangladesh as the crisis actors.

"Interstate crisis" encompasses both "international crisis" and "foreign policy crisis." Conceptually, it is designed to integrate the two levels of analysis, that is, the system/interactor level and the state or actor level. As such, it is part of a continuing central theme of this book, culminating in the Unified Model of Crisis (Model III) [Chap. 6]. This model is designed to integrate the Model of International Crisis (Model I) and the Model of Foreign Policy Crisis (Model II), which are specified later in this chapter.

29 The term, "military hostilities" is much broader than "war." In fact, it encompasses any interstate hostile physical interaction, which is classified as "minor clashes," "serious clashes" or "full-scale war." However, for stylistic convenience, the terms, "war likelihood," "probability of war," "likelihood of (involvement in) military hostilities," and "probability of (involvement in) military hostilities" are used interchangeably throughout this book. They all denote the prospects for any level of military hostilities, from minor clashes to full-scale war.

30 The term, "end-crisis," is intended to identify the period corresponding to the deescalation or winding-down phase of a crisis leading to termination. It should be emphasized that, heretofore, this period had been termed "post-crisis." In the Unified Model of Crisis [Chap. 6], the period corresponding to the impact phase is labelled the "post-crisis" period. This term for the final stage, after or beyond the crisis proper, will be used interchangeably with "beyond crisis."

31 The outer closed lines in Figure 1.2, vertical and horizontal, indicate that the four phases and four periods are an integrated whole. The broken vertical lines between the four phases and the four periods indicate that, while each phase and each period is distinct, they are closely linked, sequentially, from onset to impact, and from pre-crisis to post-crisis.

32 This discrepancy, along with the link between the concepts of phase-change and period-change, will be elaborated in Chapter 7 and Figure 7.1.

33 Figure 1.2 and the accompanying discussion of phases and periods is a brief, tentative formulation designed to inform the reader as to where the analysis is going. The crystallized version of the Unified Model, after the analysis of the four phases and periods, will be presented in Chapter 6 and, schematically, in Figure 6.1.

34 Even though, as indicated earlier in this chapter, an interstate crisis begins with a foreign policy crisis for a state, model specification will begin at the system level. This ordering is derived from the principle that inquiry should begin with the whole (general) and proceed to its component parts (specific). This was, too, the sequence followed in the presentation of the two-volume encyclopedia of crises (Brecher and Wilkenfeld, 1988; Wilkenfeld and Brecher, 1988).

35 A closely-related conceptual link, between *polarity* and *war*, has been the focus of an unresolved major debate in the study of world politics. Among the participants are Deutsch and Singer (1964), Waltz (1964, 1967), Rosecrance (1966), Young (1968), M. Haas (1970), Wallace (1973, 1985), Bueno de Mesquita (1975, 1978), Rapkin, Thompson with Christopherson (1979), Wayman (1984), Garnham (1985), Levy (1985), Gaddis (1986, 1987, 1991), Thompson (1986), Most and Starr (1987), Rapkin (1988), Midlarsky (1989b), and Brecher and Wilkenfeld (1991). For an assessment of the relative stability of the three twentieth-century polarity configurations, see Brecher, James and Wilkenfeld (1990).

36 Most accounts of World War I suggest that its outbreak was largely a product of security dilemmas, mistakes, misperceptions, and spiralling stimulus-response sequences (O. R. Holsti, 1972; Jervis, 1976; Nomikos and North, 1976; Lebow, 1981, among others). However, these explanations are not inconsistent with the above-stated thesis that the great powers have a collective interest, *generally*, in acting as security managers, that is, in sustaining system stability. Rather, the events of 1914 only demonstrate that they were inept security managers in that European crisis.

37 On governmental instability in Africa, see Welch (1987, esp. Table 8.A1 on "Forcible Changes of Government in Africa, 1958–85"), Decalo (1976), and Baynham (1986). On the Italian variant of frequent change in government, see Cioffi-Revilla (1984).

38 The method of operationalizing internal instability, in ICB research, differs from that in the three editions of *World Handbook of Political and Social Indicators* (Russett *et al.*, 1964; Taylor and Hudson, 1972; and Taylor and Jodice, 1983. In all three editions, there is no reference to "internal instability" in the Contents, but it appears in the Index. All three relate to instability only as the converse of stability.

In the first edition, the indicators of stability were: deaths from domestic group violence per one million people; and the rate of turnover in office by the legally designated Chief Executive; that is, stability was considered a function of continuity over time of a regime's personnel. Taylor and Hudson used the same broad categories of stability—political violence and executive change. And Taylor and Jodice used the same indicators but spelled them out in more detail.

Moreover, *internal instability* differs fundamentally from the concept of crisis-generated *system instability*. The Index of Instability, referring to a system, incorporates three dimensions: turmoil, power status and duration. For a discussion of the Index and its application to 251 international crises from 1945 to 1985, see Brecher and Wilkenfeld (1991).

39 While case studies, *per se*, cannot create valid theory, theory is present implicitly in some form before a method is selected and employed. Moreover, hypotheses can be generated from the findings from case studies. And these findings also provide a body of evidence to test propositions derived from deductive reasoning and correlational analysis. As such, they offer a complementary path to aggregate data analysis in testing propositions with empirical evidence. This is a crucial element in theory-building about crises in the twentieth century.

On case study as a method of analysis, see Verba (1967), Russett (1970), Eckstein (1975), George (1979), Ragin (1987), Achen and Snidal (1989), and George and Smoke

(1989). In short, the approach used in this book copes with the methodological issues raised by these scholars by combining deductive theorizing and systematic empirical research in both breadth and depth—the method of *structured empiricism*, first set out in Brecher, 1972: Chap. 1.

40 As understood here, "necessary" and "sufficient," when appearing together as "necessary and sufficient condition(s)," is taken to mean "defining condition(s)." Thus these terms will be used interchangeably throughout the book.

41 The specific set of preconditions most likely to generate an international crisis and the rationale for our expectations will be presented in Chapter 2 (Onset). The preconditions relevant to the other phases will be set out in Chaps. 3 and 4 (Escalation and Deescalation).

The concept of crisis as political earthquake will be elaborated in Chapter 5 (Impact).

42 Creative early works on bargaining are Rapoport (1960) and Schelling (1960). See also p. 11 above.

43 It could be misunderstood that what is being argued here is a connection between power equality and *rapid* accommodation. No time limit is implied.

44 An earlier version of Model I is to be found in Brecher and Wilkenfeld (1989: Chap. 14).

45 For an insightful discussion of the spiral process, see Jervis (1976: 62–113).

46 The following summary of the crisis behavior model is based upon a more elaborate discussion in Brecher (1979).

47 On coping strategies see Lazarus (1966), Holsti and George (1975), Janis and Mann (1977), Lazarus and Folkman (1984), Janis (1989), and Vertzberger (1990).

48 The generality of this definition is somewhat restricted, for the notion of "constantly changing . . . efforts" excludes a cybernetic (SOP) type of coping with minimal change in responding to "demands."

49 The perception of war likelihood—in those crises that have not been accompanied by violence—does not vanish in the end-crisis period. It merely diminishes, as shown in Figure 1.5.

50 Thirteen ICB studies of crisis behavior have been published or are in process:
Israel in the 1967 and 1973 Middle East crises—Brecher with Geist (1980);
Syria in the Lebanon Civil War in 1975–76—A. Dawisha (1980);
the United States in the Berlin Blockade of 1948–49—Shlaim (1983);
the Soviet Union in the 1968 Prague Spring Crisis—K. Dawisha (1984);
the US in the Lebanon civil strife of 1958, the Jordan/Syria Confrontation of 1970, and the nuclear alert crisis of 1973—Dowty (1984);
Germany during and after the 1942–43 Stalingrad Crisis—Jukes (1985);
India in the Sino-Indian Border Crisis of 1959–63—S. A. Hoffmann (1990).
Three others are in process:
Zambia in the Rhodesia UDI Crisis of 1965–66—Anglin (1993, forthcoming);
Hungary in the 1956 Hungarian Uprising—Geist;
Italy in the Trieste Crisis of 1953—Croci.
A large number of unpublished case studies—graduate student research at McGill University prepared under the author's direction—enrich the body of evidence on stress, coping and choice in foreign policy crises. Information on these studies is available from the author.

51 The ICB dataset for the 70-year period, end of 1918–end of 1988, is accessible through the Inter-university Consortium for Political and Social Research at the University of Michigan, Ann Arbor, MI (ICPSR 9286).

52 The findings for this analytical summary are drawn from Brecher with Geist (1980).

53 The official name of Egypt from 1958 to 1971 was the UAR. Since September 1971, it has been the Arab Republic of Egypt.

Chapter 2

1 The concept of initiation refers to *active* effects of the independent variables, that is, effects which induce a state to set a foreign policy crisis in motion. See also n. 12 below.

The concept of vulnerability refers to *passive* effects, that is, effects which make a state a likely target of a foreign policy crisis.

2 The sequence of these explanatory (enabling) variables in Figure 2.1 and in the text follows the attribute clusters—system, interactor, and actor—not their "ranking." See p. 66 and Appendix A for a discussion of the ranking of independent variables, that is, their relative potency.

None of the situational attributes in Figure 1.3 is included in the analysis of onset. The reason is that, while some are relevant to the onset phase/pre-crisis period after the initial outbreak, they do not attain high salience until crisis escalation. Thus they will be introduced in the discussion of the escalation phase/crisis period [Chap. 3].

3 Those who question the postulated greater stability of a bipolar world argue that the closer states are to parity the more protective they will be of their position, and the more likely they are to assume that any change will affect their status adversely. More specifically, according to the logic of *power transition* theory (Organski, 1958; Organski and Kugler, 1980; Kugler and Organski, 1989), when a state is experiencing a dramatic increase in military and economic power, the opportunities for conflict are likely to *increase*, for two reasons: (1) the rising state is likely to resent treatment as a second-class power and is more inclined to demonstrate its newly-acquired strength by "picking a fight"; and (2) existing major powers, fearing that they might be outstripped by the ascending power, might launch a preemptive attack in order to prevent the ascending power from gaining an advantage in the distribution of resources. In other words, conflict and crisis may be less a product of an imbalance in the distribution of resources and power than of uncertainty resulting from rapid change in the distribution of power towards parity.

4 It has been argued, to the contrary, that the proliferation of international regimes during polycentrism (post-1962) has actually served to constrain state behavior. This process would question the inclusion of "lack of system constraints" as a defining trait of polycentrism. However, even if this claim is empirically correct, the postulated link between polycentrism and higher frequency of crises would still apply. International regimes (and the assumed constraints they impose on states) tend to undermine stability because there are more opportunities for failure: the more demands that are placed on a system, in the form of regimes, the more difficult it is for members to adhere to all of the rules, norms and principles—and the more likely it is that tensions will mount and crises result. In other words, national interests may undermine adherence to international regimes and provoke more conflictive interaction than would otherwise occur.

5 The inference about polycentrism and outbreak relates to the *frequency* of crises in different structures, not to their *gravity*, or *impact*, on the global system. On that dimension, some, notably Waltz (1979), have argued that crises in the peripheries (subsystems) contribute to the stability of the dominant bipolar system. This thesis is a twentieth-century variant of the contention that the "Hundred Years Peace" among the great powers in the nineteenth century (1815–1914) was facilitated by competition and

war among the European powers in Asia and Africa, the peripheries of that era. Both arguments are, at best, imaginative speculation. In any event, the focus of the crisis onset model is the likelihood of crisis outbreak, not its impact.

6 This is not to argue the obverse, namely, that multipolarity and/or polycentrism are likely to create conditions that are not conducive to protracted conflict. PCs are not logically incompatible with those structural types; and empirically, they occur. Rather, the linkage is couched in terms of *extent of likelihood*. Rivalry and the struggle for hegemony are to be expected in multipolarity and polycentrism as well, for they, too, are anarchic system structures. But they are more blurred by the uncertainty of alliance patterns and are muted by multiple obstacles to hegemony. In bipolarity, the alliance pattern is unambiguous and there is only one barrier to hegemony—the rival major power.

7 Employing this index, the United States and the Soviet Union scored the highest point on each of the six scales: 4 for population (more than 100 million); 6 for annual GNP (above $200 billion); 4 for territory (above 500,000 square miles); 4 for alliance capability (alliance leader); 4 for military expenditure (above $20 billion per annum); and 4 for nuclear capability (second-strike), making a total of 26, the theoretical maximum. (The US scored the maximum from 1953 onwards, the USSR since 1960.) At the other extreme, Kuwait in 1961 (Kuwait Independence crisis), Burundi in 1964 (Rwanda/Burundi), and Cambodia in 1975 (Mayaguez), among many others, each scored a total of 6, the theoretical minimum of power. The difference between the power scores of adversaries (or the combined power scores for each adversarial coalition) in an international crisis constitutes the power balance for that case. At the actor level, these are collapsed into three categories, *positive*, *nil*, and *negative* power discrepancy.

The ICB indicators and index of power are more comprehensive and precise than the Correlates of War (COW) approach to the measurement of power (capability). For one thing, the COW data were collected, for the most part, at the system level, which renders them unreliable for testing micro-level hypotheses. For another, data collected on war rarely incorporate specific behavioral dynamics that are encompassed in crisis data—regarding trigger-response mechanisms, crisis management techniques, etc.

The Cox-Jacobson power index of five indicators—but not their data—(1974: Appendix A) is similar to the index noted here.

8 It is recognized that the link between geographic distance and crisis outbreak may be partly a function of relative capability; that is, small powers—most members of the global system—cannot project threats or military power beyond their neighbors; by contrast, major powers are more likely to be active in crises distant from their home territory. The overall effect would be to accentuate the number of crises between immediate neighbors.

9 The relationship between domestic and foreign conflict behavior of states remains an unresolved issue. As Levy observed, in a thorough critique of the diversionary theory of war (1989a: 259–288): "Whereas the theoretical and historical literature suggests the importance of the diversionary use of force by political elites to bolster their internal political positions, the quantitative empirical literature in political science has repeatedly found that there is no consistent and meaningful relationship between internal and external conflict behavior of states.

"The basic problem [with the latter] . . . is that there is too poor a fit between the hypotheses supposedly being investigated and the overall research design guiding the empirical analyses" (282). As for the former, Levy and others advocate comparative case studies to test the diversionary theory of war. In this volume an attempt is made to combine correlational and case study methodologies to shed further light on this important aspect of the crisis-conflict-war nexus.

10 For brief summaries of these international crises, see Brecher and Wilkenfeld (1988: 302, 311–312, 145–146, 244, 213, 237–238, 253, 279–280); and, for the Gulf Crisis, Chapter 7 of this book.

11 The above-noted ranking is based upon the *number* of *direct* effects of each explanatory variable on the others. Secondary, tertiary or higher-order effects are excluded. It is recognized that the number of effects says nothing about *intensity*. In sum, 43% of the theoretically possible linkages were operationalized (39 of 90). In addition, all ten variables affected value threat. The six variables with the highest rank are unevenly divided—2 system, 3 interactor, and 1 actor attribute(s).

The sequence of variables in the propositions to follow accords with their ranking as specified above. The logic leading to the above ranking of independent variables is set out in Appendix A. An even greater centrality in the causal nexus is attributed to structure in James's (forthcoming, 1994) structural realist theory of crisis.

12 As noted in the critique of the crisis literature [Chap. 1], there has been little theorizing or research on the *initiation* of interstate crises. Maoz (1982a: 2) correctly attributed this to "inherent normative predispositions in Western scholarship . . . [which] has been primarily defender-oriented or tended to treat initiators and defenders in the same behavioral terms."

For Maoz, initiation is a *process*, not a single act committed by A against B or, perhaps, several targets. He examined and tested three explanatory models:

(a)   the *frustration model*, which argues that a combination of high capability and low diplomatic status, i.e., status inconsistency, generates frustration and leads a state to initiate a dispute;

(b)   the *threat model*, which argues that states perceiving externally-threatening acts, events or changes in the environment are likely to initiate disputes; and

(c)   the *power transition model*, which, as noted, views as a likely crisis initiator a state that is undergoing rapid economic and military growth but is not accorded a corresponding diplomatic status in the international system; it will initiate a crisis in order to change the status hierarchy. The thrust of the argument of (a) and (c) is essentially the same.

Maoz's evidence (Chaps. 4, 5) led him to conclude that there was partial support for the power transition model.

The basic flaw in his analytical and empirical exercise is that none of the three models explains the initiation of all or even most serious interstate disputes. At best, they provide partial explanations of crisis onset, by specifying a single necessary condition. An alternative path, to be followed here, is to specify both the defining condition for crisis onset and the cluster of conditions in which states are most likely to initiate crises for other members of the global system, while, at the same time, recognizing that crises will erupt in a great variety of conditions.

13 For the case study and Gulf Crisis findings on the onset phase/pre-crisis period (Propositions 1–3), see, respectively, Table 2.7 and Table 7.2.

14 The gap is even wider if World War II intra-war crises (24) are excluded: 250 cases in Africa, Asia and the Middle East, 66 in Europe, that is, 68.3% of the total (366 crises), compared to 18%.

15 The largest concentration occurred in the 1920s, 22 of 40 in the world (55%), declining to 4 of 83 in the last decade (4.8%). And for the entire period since 1948, Europe accounted for 20 of 259 international crises, a mere 7.7%.

16 The most lucid statement of the "long peace" thesis is by Gaddis (1986, 1987, 1991). For a dissenting view, see Brecher and Wilkenfeld (1991).

The total number of crises almost doubled from the 1949–58 decade to 1979–88, from 43 to 83. During that period the number of sovereign states trebled, from 50 to more than 150 UN members.

17 There were more than twice as many (104) in Africa and 263 in the other three segments of the Third World—Africa, Asia and the Middle East.

18 The concept, intensity of crisis, will be elaborated in the first section of Chapter 5.

19 Nicaragua issued a postage stamp in August 1937 showing a large part of southeastern Honduras as "territory in dispute," triggering a crisis for the latter. Honduras protested this "affront to her sovereignty." Armed hostilities were prevented by the mediation of Costa Rica, Venezuela and the United States. And the two crisis actors signed an agreement in December 1937. The dispute flared up again in 1957.

20 One, sometimes more, of these or other basic values was perceived to be at risk in the pre-crisis period of all other foreign policy crises analyzed by the ICB Project. The year(s) specified for each case is the year in which the pre-crisis period occurred. Similarly, the year(s) of the crisis and end-crisis periods is indicated in the presentation of findings in Chapter 3 (Escalation) and Chapter 4 (Deescalation).

The value threats are discussed at greater length, as part of the psychological environment of the pre-crisis period, in each of the case studies of coping and choice to follow.

21 Value threat and response apply to the first crisis actor or "target" in the international crisis.

22 The case summaries and analysis benefit greatly from the data and findings uncovered by scholars associated with the ICB Project. It should be emphasized that the analysis of coping with stress in the pre-crisis, crisis and end-crisis periods [Chaps. 2–4] focuses on the foreign policy crisis of a single state.

23 The dates indicated for the ten cases, in this chapter, refer to the international crisis as a whole.

24 All four major powers were crisis actors (direct participants); that is, each perceived, though not at the same time, the defining conditions of a foreign policy crisis: threat to one or more basic values (and, later), finite time for response, and increased likelihood of involvement in military hostilities. Here I examine the US's foreign policy crisis over Berlin.

25 The "Riga axioms" refer to a school of thought about communism and, in particular, the Soviet Union that was developed by American diplomats stationed in the capital of Latvia prior to US recognition of the USSR in 1933. It was also the training ground of an influential generation of US specialists on the Soviet Union, notably George F. Kennan (Kennan, 1967), Llewellyn Thompson, and Chester E. Bohlen (Bohlen, 1969). The "Yalta axioms" derive from the more benign view of Soviet intentions associated with the Big Three Yalta Conference (Churchill, Roosevelt and Stalin) in 1945.

There is a vast literature on the origins of the Cold War and US-Soviet relations. See, especially, Halle (1967: esp. Chaps. XII–XVI); Fontaine (1968: Part II, esp. Chap. 17); Kolko (1972); Sherwin (1975: Part III); Yergin (1978); Gaddis (1982); Larson (1985); and Thomas (1986). For a useful selection of articles see Hoffmann and Fleron (1980: esp. Part IV).

26 The summary of findings about the US's Berlin Blockade pre-crisis period is derived from Shlaim (1983: Chap. 3 and pp. 162–168). The sources for Shlaim's book comprise archival materials from the Truman Library, the National Archives in Washington, the Princeton University Library, the Public Records Office in London, unpublished diaries, oral histories, documents and official publications, and almost 400 books and articles (*ibid.*, 425–443).

27 The Prague Spring also generated foreign policy crises for all other members of the East European bloc other than Romania, namely, in the order of their entry into that international crisis, the German Democratic Republic (GDR), Poland, Bulgaria, Hungary and Czechoslovakia: each perceived value threat, time pressure, and heightened probability of involvement in military hostilities.

28 The summary of findings on the pre-crisis period of the USSR's Prague Spring Crisis are based upon K. Dawisha (1984: Chap. 5). The sources for this book comprise: (1) US documents from the White House, National Security Council, State Department, and the Central Intelligence Agency declassified under the US Freedom of Information Act; (2) archival materials from the Johnson Library; (3) a "Selected Bibliography" of 250 books and articles (*ibid.*, 385–397), along with a large number of Russian, English, and foreign-language newspapers and journals cited in footnotes; and (4) interviews with Czech, American and British officials directly involved in the Prague Spring Crisis.

29 There were four crisis actors in the Munich Crisis—Czechoslovakia, France, the UK and the USSR; that is, each perceived value threat, time pressure, and heightened war likelihood. Three other states were involved actors: Germany, as the triggering entity which generated the perceptions of harm of the four direct participants, and the focal point of all negotiations leading to a settlement; Italy as a signatory to the Munich Agreement; and the US, marginally.

30 This summary of findings about the pre-crisis period of the UK's Munich Crisis is based upon Wilson's unpublished M.A. research paper (1984), which relied on: Foreign Office documents for 1938 (Woodward, 1949); memoirs and apologia by the key decision-makers—Chamberlain (1939), Halifax (1957), Hoare (Templewood, 1954), and Simon (1952); influential civil servants and diplomats—Cadogan (Dilks, 1971), and Henderson (1940); and, among knowledgeable outsiders, A. J. P. Taylor (1961), and T. Taylor (1979). This was supplemented by Beck (1989) and Watt (1989).

31 These decisions are analyzed in detail in Jukes (1985: Chaps. 1–3 and pp. 213–220), the basis for this summary of the pre-crisis period of Germany's Stalingrad Crisis. The sources for this book comprise German and Soviet documents and memoirs, in a bibliography of almost 100 items (*ibid.*, 249–252).

32 There were four other crisis actors in the 1973–74 Middle East Crisis, namely, Egypt, Syria, the US and the USSR.

33 These findings are derived from Brecher with Geist (1980: 51–69 and 78–87). The sources for this analysis comprise 100 books and articles on the phenomenon of foreign policy crisis, and 125 books and articles on Israel's October-Yom Kippur Crisis, including 20 interviews with senior Israeli decision-makers (*ibid.*, 433–438, 445–451).

34 For alternative explanations of the motives for Syria's intervention in Lebanon, see Rabinovitch (1986), and Weinberger (1986).

35 The findings on the pre-crisis period of Syria's Lebanon crisis in 1975–76 are based upon A. I. Dawisha (1980: Chaps. 4, 10). The sources for this meticulous analysis are more than 100 books and articles (*ibid.*, 195–200), and interviews with 11 senior Syrian officials in the President's Office, the Foreign Ministry, and the Ministry of Information.

36 The People's Republic of China (PRC), too, was a crisis actor in this international crisis.

37 The summary of India's pre-crisis period is based upon S. A. Hoffmann (1990, Part II). Because of its extended duration the analysis of this case is slightly longer than the others. The sources for this book comprise: (1) half-a-dozen unpublished primary

sources, including Nehru's "Fortnightly Letters" to the Chief Ministers of the Indian States, 1959–63; (2) 122 interviews with 34 leading Indian politicians and officials, and two British scholars over the period, 1966–1989; (3) 13 volumes of official documents on the border crisis published by the Government of India; and (4) more than 100 books and articles (*ibid.*, 307–315).

38 Hungary and the USSR were the crisis actors in this international crisis.

39 The findings on the pre-crisis period of Hungary's 1956–57 crisis are based upon Geist (forthcoming: Chaps. 2, 4, 10). This study draws upon the vast literature devoted to the Hungarian Uprising, including valuable primary sources published in the aftermath of the overthrow of the communist regime in Budapest in 1989 and of the Soviet regime in 1991. Altogether, 190 sources are cited.

40 President Kaunda differed from some of his senior colleagues, notably Foreign Minister Kapwepwe, in attitudes and personality. He was more of an idealist, a humanist, and an internationalist. He was more willing to sacrifice for the sake of Southern African liberation. He had more faith in Britain, more trust in the Commonwealth. He was more patient and diplomatic, and more disposed to optimism. Kapwepwe was more of a realist, a nationalist, and a Pan-Africanist. He placed more emphasis on "Zambia first." He was more distrustful of Britain, more skeptical of the Commonwealth. He was more impatient and undiplomatic, and more disposed to pessimism (Anglin [forthcoming 1993]: Table 5).

41 The findings on the pre-crisis period of Zambia's Rhodesia UDI Crisis are based upon Anglin [forthcoming, 1993]: 31–50, Chaps. III, IV and IX).

42 Argentina and the UK were the crisis actors in this case.

43 The invasion plan was based on others dating to 1942. The most recent version had been drafted in the late 1960s and refined in 1977 by a naval officer who became one of the key decision-makers in the 1982 crisis, then-Captain Anaya. It had been revived soon after General Galtieri assumed the presidency in late December 1981 and was now given high priority.

44 These misperceptions were reaffirmed and embellished nine years later, in interviews conducted by a BBC correspondent with long-retired members of the junta. BBC World Service, 25 July 1991.

45 The summary of Argentina's pre-crisis period is based upon Bartley's unpublished M.A. paper (1985), along with supplementary research in 1990. It utilized an array of sources, including government documents, a dozen books, and 28 articles on the Falklands/Malvinas Crisis, along with the extensive discussions in five major newspapers.

For a lively critique of the "second wave" of literature on the Falklands/Malvinas Crisis (1987–90), along with extensive comments on the "first wave" (1982–84), see Danchev (1991).

Chapter 3

1 The postulated link between an arms race and the outbreak of war was strongly supported by Wallace (1979, 1981, 1982): on the basis of Correlates of War evidence from 1816 to 1965 (Singer and Small, 1972), he found a strong *association* between the presence/absence of an arms race and war/no war outcomes of serious disputes (more than 90%)—but "the findings do not provide incontrovertible proof of a *causal* link" (1979: 14).

Weede (1980), Altfeld (1983), and Diehl (1983) dissented sharply on methodological grounds. Moreover, Diehl reported that only 25% of the disputes that were preceded by a mutual military buildup escalated to war, and that 77% of wars were not preceded by arms races. And Altfeld found that all arms races led to war—but many wars were not preceded by arms races. Dissent from Wallace's claims was also registered by Houweling and Siccama (1981), Diehl (1985), and Diehl and Kingston (1987).

Dissenting from Wallace's findings on other methodological grounds, Intriligator and Brito (1984) argued that certain arms races can lead to peace, and certain disarmament races can lead to war. This was challenged by Mayer (1986), who contended that arms races are unlikely to generate a stable peace; further, that mutual disarmament will not increase the likelihood of war—and might reduce it.

The controversy remains unresolved, perhaps because, as Siverson and Diehl (1989: 32) observed in a review of the debate: "a primary difficulty in arms race studies is their tendency to look at arms races in isolation from the other relevant conditions for war."

The literature on arms races is vast and complex. For comprehensive surveys, see Moll and Luebbert (1980), Isard and Anderton (1985), Anderton (1985), Intriligator and Brito (1989), and Siverson and Diehl (1989).

For a discussion of formal models and escalation processes, see Luterbacher and Ward (1985: Part 2).

2 For this research project, war was defined in terms of context, following Lebow, rather than in terms of threshold of casualties (Singer). The war initiator was "the side which first made the decision to accept war as a crisis outcome" (64).

3 For other allusions to intra-war escalation in strategic thought during the past two centuries, see Earle (1943) and Paret (1986).

4 In terms of organization theory, *escalation situations* have been defined as "predicaments where costs are suffered in a course of action, where there is an opportunity to withdraw or persist, and where the consequences of persistence and withdrawal are uncertain." Further, persistence and withdrawal can be explained by four clusters of content variables—project, psychological, social and structural determinants (Staw and Ross, 1987: 40, 44). While this definition can be helpful in the analysis of individual decision-making, in foreign policy as in other spheres, it is not salient to the escalation phase (crisis period) of interstate crises.

5 Earlier research on externalization referred to conflict and cohesion or linkage politics. The idea of an integrated process, and causal mechanism, embodied in the terms, "externalize" and "externalization theory," first appeared in James, 1987.

Levy (1989a) draws attention to an important distinction—between "externalization of internal conflict," the meaning used in this book, and "internalization of external conflict."

6 An alternative historical perspective on the causes of war, deriving from conservative, liberal and radical ideologies, and on the causes of World Wars I and II, was provided by Nelson and Olin (1979).

7 For a critical assessment of the power-war debate, see Siverson and Sullivan (1983).

8 For a review of the "contagion" literature, see Most and Siverson (1989: Chap. 5).

Parenthetically, the literature on war is not without counter-intuitive findings on its positive aspects: Stein and Russett (1980) identified war as a stimulus to economic growth and technological progress and as a mechanism of state formation; Organski and Kugler (1980), too, viewed war as an inducement to higher productivity; and Levy (1985) claimed positive effects of war on society and the international system.

9 The crisis-war nexus and the voluminous literature on war were discussed in Chapter 1, pp. 2–8 and n. 9 on pp. 581–582.

10 For other assessments of research on war until 1980, see: Singer (1981), on "the state of the discipline"; Eberwein (1981), on quantitative studies of the causes of war; and Stein and Russett (1980), on outcomes and consequences. For other reviews of

research on war until the late 1980s, see Levy (1989c) and the contributions in Midlarsky (1989a).

11 Viewed from the perspective of game theory, crisis escalation is a product of a bargaining process formalized as games. Models of escalatory—and deescalatory —games will be discussed in Chapter 4.

12 It has been argued (Betts, 1977, 1991) that soldiers in a democratic regime are more reluctant than civilian leaders to employ force. However, once force is used, the military is unlikely to be interested in limits—they seek victory, e.g., US General Schwarzkopf in the Gulf War of 1991 [see Chap. 7].

13 A "not-exhaustive" list of 66 abortive cases from 1929 to 1979 is to be found in Brecher and Wilkenfeld (1988: 32–33, n. 3).

14 The sequence of independent variables presented in this and all other hypotheses follows their relative weight in the "ranking of variables" indicated above.

All the hypotheses in this book are framed in a multi-faceted form. In fact, each of the individual elements within an overarching hypothesis is distinctive and autonomous. Testing will relate each element to one of the dependent variables in a model. The assumption is that the larger the number of constituent parts that is supported, the greater the likelihood that the overarching hypothesis is valid. In short, testing of the individual elements amounts to an indirect evaluation of the overarching hypothesis.

15 The categories for extent of support are as follows:

very strong = at least twice as much support for the postulated linkage than for the alternative "value," e.g., 76% of the cases that escalated to full-scale international crises were "close to home," compared to 24% "more distant" cases; thus the geographic distance postulate is very strongly supported;

strong = 50%–99% higher support for the postulated linkage, e.g., the finding on system level (H. 2), in Table 3.2;

moderate = 25%–49% higher support for the postulated linkage, e.g., the finding on conflict setting (H. 7), in Table 3.8;

modest = 10%–24% higher support for the postulated linkage, e.g., the finding on capability (H. 2), in Table 3.2.

An alternative method was also used to determine the extent of support for each element of an hypothesis, namely, subtracting one proportion from the other to discern the difference: the results were essentially the same.

16 They are also related to the perennial "behavior-begets-behavior" thesis, on which Wilkenfeld (1991) found that crises, like conflict in general, "exhibit a very high degree of matching behavior" with respect to trigger-crisis management technique and trigger-violence links: 75% in the former, and 79% in the latter, when the trigger was non-violent.

17 Value threat applies to the first actor in the full-scale international crisis.

18 Response applies to the first actor in the full-scale international crisis.

19 Research findings on whether some states are more vulnerable than others to foreign policy crises, especially on the link between crisis/conflict/war and political, economic and military institutions, have been summarized in Zinnes (1980) and Singer (1981).

20 This summary of the US's crisis period relating to the Berlin Blockade is based upon Shlaim (1983: Chaps. 5, 6).

21 This summary of the crisis period of the USSR's Prague Spring crisis is based upon K. Dawisha (1984: Part III).

22 This summary of Britain's Munich crisis period is based upon Wilson (1984), *op. cit.*

23 This summary of the Stalingrad crisis period is based upon Jukes (1985), *op. cit.*, Chaps. 4, 5.

24 The perceptions of the other key Israeli decision-makers in the October-Yom Kippur Crisis—Defense Minister Dayan, Foreign Minister Eban, and Deputy Prime Minister Allon—are examined in Brecher with Geist (1980: 182–191). As with the onset phase, the summary of Israel's coping with escalating stress is based on this book, particularly Chaps. 6 and 11.

25 This summary is based upon A. I. Dawisha (1980: Part III).

26 This summary of India's 1962 crisis period is based upon S. A. Hoffmann (1990: Parts III, IV).

27 This decision came perilously close to shattering India's cherished policy of Non-Alignment, the pillar of its foreign policy since independence (Brecher, 1979–80).

28 The quotations from Hegedues and the summary of Hungary's crisis period are from Geist, *op. cit.*, Parts IV and VI.

29 The apparent greater trust of Zambia in the former colonial ruler than in the intentions of fellow African states in the OAU may seem like an anomaly; but its authenticity is beyond question.

30 The data on perceptions by Zambia's decision-makers and the summary of Zambia's behavior in its Rhodesia UDI crisis period are based upon Anglin (forthcoming, 1993: Chaps. V, VI, IX).

31 James Markham, *NYT*, 16/5/82, cited in Bartley (1984), the source for this summary of Argentina's crisis period.

32 This analytical exercise is not a statistical test. Rather, it is an indication of the extent to which the conditions attending a select group of ten international crises, the focus of case study analysis in this book, match or "fit" the postulated conditions of crisis escalation, crisis violence, initiation of, and vulnerability to, crisis, that were derived from the phase model of escalation. This note applies equally to the matching exercises for the deescalation and impact phase-domains, the findings of which are set out in Tables 4.5 and 5.8 and the related analysis, in Chaps. 4 and 5 below.

Chapter 4

1 On the social sciences' neglect of war termination, relative to the attention given to war initiation, see Fox (1970: 1, 2, 6), and Carroll (1970: 15–16). This neglect included the major works on strategy in the early 1960s, by Schelling (1960), Rapoport (1960), and Boulding (1962), as well as *The Journal of Conflict Resolution*, since its founding in 1957, and the *Journal of Peace Research*, since its founding in 1964, with a few exceptions cited later in the text.

2 A cease-fire refers to a (usually brief and finite) cessation of hostilities. An armistice incorporates a cease-fire but (usually) specifies the terms for a longer renunciation of hostilities, often as a prelude to a peace treaty or agreement. The last concept connects the parties to indefinite non-belligerency and the restoration (or creation) of normal diplomatic, economic and cultural relations between the adversaries.

3 The dispersion around the average is unavailable.

4 For a critical assessment of Wittman's expected utility model, see Mitchell and Nicholson (1983). In essence, they called for "qualifications" in that model "in order to cope with the problem of the nonunitary decision maker," citing decision-making on war termination in the Anglo/Boer War case (1899–1902) as not unusual (496).

5 Other mixed motive symmetric games discussed by Snyder and Diesing are Hero

(the UK and Zambia in Rhodesia UDI, 1965–66), and Leader (Germany and Austria in 1914). These are alliance games during a crisis, in that the adversaries value the alliance's continuation over their preferred strategy towards their opponent. In Deadlock, a symmetric but not mixed motive game, both players prefer firmness to appeasement or compromise with the opponent (the US vs. Japan in 1941).

Other asymmetric games are: Big Bully, with one player Chicken, the other preferring no agreement, in fact, preferring war over any compromise (Munich, 1938, Germany vs. Czechoslovakia); and Protector, an alliance game between two unequal partners, in which the client must make concessions demanded by its patron as the condition for the latter's support (Taiwan Straits II, 1958, the US and Taiwan).

6 The other games are escalatory:

Fight—both adversaries use coercive influence strategies or they combine bullying with tit-for-tat; and this leads to a conflict spiral (e.g., 1967 Arab/Israel Six Day War);

Resistance—a variation of Fight, in which one adversary adopts a coercive strategy, the other stands firm; this too is escalatory (Ethiopian War, 1935); and

Put Down—one player uses coercive bargaining, with severe threats; the other yields, after an attempt to display resolve (UK/Russia Crisis, 1878).

7 The deescalation model, too, attempts to meet the test of parsimony by using the same core independent variables (with a few additions for duration), to explain all the dimensions of this crisis domain.

8 This positive role of third party intervention can also be played by a major power, a regional organization, a prominent public figure, etc. (Touval and Zartman, 1985).

9 For an elaboration of the concept of intensity, see the first section of Chap. 5.

10 The summary of the US's end-crisis period is based upon Shlaim, *op. cit.*, Part IV.

11 The summary of Soviet coping with end-crisis in the Prague Spring Crisis is based upon K. Dawisha, *op. cit.*, Part IV.

12 The summary of Germany's Stalingrad end-crisis period is based upon Jukes, *op. cit.*, Chapter 6.

13 There is a remarkable similarity in the US role during the peace process of 1978–79 and in the continuing quest for peace a dozen years later, with Baker replicating Kissinger's shuttle diplomacy in 1991, actively supported by President Bush.

14 The summary of Israel's October-Yom Kippur end-crisis period is based upon Brecher with Geist, *op. cit.*, Part III.

15 The summary of Syria's end-crisis behavior in the Lebanon crisis is based upon A.I. Dawisha (1980), *op. cit.*, Parts IV, V.

16 *White Papers* (Government of India), Vol. 8, p. 19, as cited in S. A. Hoffmann, *op. cit.*, p. 213. The following summary of India's end-crisis period is based upon S. A. Hoffmann (1990: Part 5 and Chapter 16).

17 *United Nations: Report of the Special Committee on the Problem of Hungary*, Doc. A/3592, New York, June 1957, as quoted in Geist, *op. cit.*, 182. This summary of Hungary's end-crisis period is based upon Geist, Part V.

18 On 10 November 1956 the General Assembly called for the withdrawal of all Soviet forces from Hungary and free elections under UN auspices. Ten days later it decided to send an inquiry mission to Hungary. Its June 1957 report, based on testimony from refugees, was endorsed by 60 to 10, with 10 abstentions: it termed the events in Hungary a national uprising that was suppressed by the USSR. It had no effect on the outcome of the Hungarian Uprising.

19 The summary of Zambia's end-crisis period is based upon Anglin (forthcoming, 1993: Chapter VII).

20 As indicated in Notes to Table 4.5, many of the ten international crises cannot be coded for H. 8, 9, 10 and 11, since the dependent variables of these hypotheses—mutual agreement, short duration, adoption of an accommodative strategy, and satisfaction with the crisis outcome—did not apply to these cases. Thus these cases were coded for the obverse dependent variable—imposed agreement, long duration, conflictive strategy, and dissatisfaction with crisis outcome, using the obverse of the independent variables of these hypotheses as cited in Table 4.5.

Chapter 5

1 *Equilibrium* may be defined as the steady state of a system, denoting change below the threshold of reversibility. *Disequilibrium* designates change beyond the threshold of reversibility. These concepts are operationalized in terms of the significance of change in structure, process, or both, varying from total reversibility to total irreversibility.

Steplevel (irreversible) change indicates disequilibrium which leads to system transformation, that is, a fundamental change in potential actors and/or the distribution of power between them. Violence *per se*, even violence that exceeds the bounds of normal fluctuation, constitutes instability—but not disequilibrium, unless this violence challenges the structure of the system. Disequilibrium, *ipso facto*, denotes a high level of instability, that is, acute distortion in an existing structure, process or both, but the reverse does not necessarily apply (Brecher and James, 1986: 17).

For a different conception of instability, as "a period . . . of violent-ridden or violent-prone interactions among states" (227) and the relationship between outcomes and stability, see Maoz (1984).

2 There were other well-known cases with six crisis actors: Israel Independence (1948–49); Suez–Sinai War (1956–57); Berlin Wall (1961); Six Day War (1967); and Prague Spring (1968).

3 There was only one crisis actor in 40.3% of the 390 cases. However, every state whose decision-makers perceive basic value threat, acute time pressure and heightened likelihood of war has at least one adversary, usually the state that triggers its foreign policy crisis. It is their disruptive interaction that, as noted, generates an international crisis.

4 The Berlin crises, and, indirectly, Azerbaijan, October-Yom Kippur, and the Angolan War.

5 The Gulf Crisis of 1990–91 was of grave concern to the US and other major powers, not because of access through the Strait of Hormuz but because of possible Iraqi control over the oil reserves and production facilities of the region [see Chap 7].

6 Geostrategic salience, it must be emphasized, is not synonymous with major power involvement: the former taps the salience of location and resources for the global system; the latter taps one element of crisis actor capability to determine crisis outcomes.

7 Illustrations are provided in Appendix B.

8 The US and the USSR since 1945, in global terms, along with some regional powers, such as Japan in East Asia (1931–45), the Union of South Africa in Southern Africa (1948–88), and India in South Asia (1971–88). The assessment criteria vary between dominant system and subsystem, and among regional subsystems; that is, India, a middle power in global terms, is designated a superpower in South Asia because it was qualitatively superior to all other states in that subsystem along the four criteria of

military capability. This variation in assessment criteria applies to great powers and middle powers as well.

France, Germany, Italy, Japan, the UK, as well as the US and the USSR, were great powers in the inter-World War period, China from 1949 onward, with Italy and Japan dropped from the group, and the US and the USSR elevated to superpower status; there were also several regional great powers, such as India and Pakistan in South Asia, 1947–71 and, in the Middle East, Egypt, Israel, Syria, Iraq and Iran, at different times from 1947 to 1988.

Middle powers included China until 1949, when it acquired great power status, Argentina, Brazil, Canada, Indonesia.

9 Illustrations range from Afghanistan and the UK in the Third Afghan War (1919) to India and Sri Lanka in the India Intervention Crisis (1987).

10 Examples range from the UK and Turkey in the Mosul Land Dispute (1924) (a wide economic gap), to Morocco and Algeria in all their crises over the Western Sahara, most recently in 1987 (the same level).

11 Heterogeneity regarding political regime was present in all US/USSR crises from 1945 to 1988, all Arab/Israel crises since 1948, most India/Pakistan crises, during lengthy periods when Pakistan was ruled by the military, etc. By contrast, heterogeneity was absent or minimal in most African and Latin American crises because of the ubiquity of military or civil authoritarian regimes in that continent until the late 1980s.

12 Crises between the two superpowers exhibited heterogeneity on this dimension, as did all crises between Muslim Arab states and the Jewish state of Israel, between Hindu India and Muslim Pakistan, between European and Third World States, all US crises in Latin America, etc.

13 See Appendix B for the procedure of determining heterogeneity and illustrations of each scale point.

14 Illustrations of cases at the various scale points for issues are noted in Appendix B.

15 For the distribution of international crises by violence, with examples, see Appendix B.

16 Violence may keep uninvolved states aloof; but it may also exacerbate strife and trigger the entry of states hitherto outside an international crisis. Heterogeneity, too, can be enhanced or diminished by crisis violence. And while violence may raise new issues and expand the domain of crisis, it may focus attention on a single issue. In short, since arguments can be made either way, there is no rationale for linking violence to any of these indicators directly.

17 An alternative method of measuring intensity, applied to war, was devised by the Correlates of War project. See Singer and Small (1972: Chap. 6); Small and Singer (1982: Chap. 5).

18 This operational method for measuring intensity was used to determine the overall intensity of the other nine cases analyzed throughout this book—and, in fact, of the entire set of 390 international crises from the end of 1918 to the end of 1988.

19 So it was when the US was a crisis actor in its spheres of influence. The Soviet Union remained aloof or was minimally involved in, among other crises, since the end of World War II, Truman Doctrine (1947), China Civil War (1948–49), then still a predominantly US zone of primacy, Korean War III (1953), Dien Bien Phu (1954), Taiwan Straits I (1954–55), Bay of Pigs (1961), Pathet Lao Offensive II (1962), Panama Canal (1964), Dominican Republic (1965), several Vietnam War cases, Grenada (1983) and Invasion of Panama (1989). The reverse roles are evident in Communism in Poland (1946–47), Communism in Hungary (1947), Marshall Plan (1947), Communism in Czechoslovakia (1948), East Berlin Uprising (1953), Poland Liberalization (1956),

Hungarian Uprising (1956–57), and others. And so it was to be in Polish Solidarity (1980–81). In all these cases the USSR was a crisis actor, and US involvement was nil or was limited to criticism of Soviet behavior or, on occasion, to some other form of low involvement (e.g., an offer of economic aid, in the crisis over the Marshall Plan). On the behavior of the two superpowers in international crises generally, see Blechman and Kaplan (1978), Kaplan (1981), and Wilkenfeld and Brecher (1982).

20 General Prchlik, head of the Defense and Security Department of the Czechoslovak Communist Party Central Committee, severely criticized the Warsaw Pact structure on 15 July. He also advocated a shift of control over security affairs and the military from the party to the state. And most explosive, he called for resistance to "any violation of our state sovereignty." Ten days later Prague yielded to Moscow's demand for Prchlik's removal from his key post, signalling that the Czechoslovak Party had rejected the path of military resistance to invasion.

21 Like their date of entry, the values perceived to be at risk varied among the crisis actors: existence as an independent state, for Czechoslovakia; the ability to deter a German attack, and influence in world politics, for France; peace in Europe and its status as a major power, for the UK; and for the USSR, the threat of grave damage to the territory and population, if war with Germany ensued, including the possible overthrow of the communist regime.

22 For a discussion of this subset of 20 cases, see Appendix B.

23 In that context, contrary to conventional wisdom about violence and international crises, only 8 of the 20 most intense crises during the 70-year period exhibited full-scale war (Spanish Civil War; Invasion of Albania; Entry into World War II; Korean War I; Suez-Sinai Campaign; Six Day War; October-Yom Kippur War, and War in Angola). Six were without violence (Remilitarization of the Rhineland; Munich; Azerbaijan; and the three Berlin crises—the Blockade, the Deadline, and the Wall) (see Appendix B).

24 Illustrations of these changes in relative power are as follows:
victory/defeat—victory for the USSR and its Warsaw Pact allies, defeat for Czechoslovakia, in the Prague Spring Crisis of 1968;
victory/stalemate—victory for Turkey, since Bulgaria withdrew its memo to the League of Nations charging Turkey with aggression, and stalemate for Bulgaria, since the outcome of Bulgaria/Turkey I (1935) was a standoff;
victory/compromise—victory for the USSR in the Changkufeng Incident (1938), for Japan decided to withdraw its forces from the battlefield and to settle their dispute by negotiation, with Japan perceiving the truce in the fighting as a compromise;
compromise/stalemate—compromise for Mexico, when Guatemala ceased strafing its fishermen with planes in disputed fishing waters, while it made concessions for a peaceful settlement of the dispute, and stalemate for Guatemala, in that it could not establish its self-proclaimed 12-mile territorial water limit, in Mexico/Guatemala Fishing Rights (1958–59); and
compromise/defeat—compromise for Saudi Arabia, which later withdrew its forces but acquired predominant influence in the Government of Yemen, and defeat for Egypt, for its forces were withdrawn from Yemen under the terms of an agreement with Saudi Arabia ending the lengthy Yemen War, in Yemen War IV (1966–67).

25 An example of all adversaries perceiving victory was Taiwan Straits II (1958): the US, because talks with the PRC were resumed in Warsaw, after Secretary of State Dulles threatened military intervention, not excluding the use of nuclear weapons; the PRC, because Dulles publicly called for the evacuation of Nationalist forces from the "offshore islands," Quemoy and Matsu; and Taiwan, because a tacit understanding was reached with the PRC.

Mutual compromise was perceived in Trieste II (1953), with the partition of the disputed territory between Italy (Zone A) and Yugoslavia (Zone B).

Both the PRC and the USSR perceived a stalemate in their Ussuri River border clash (1969).

There are no cases with a mutual perception of defeat.

26 The contributing crises to this phenomenon were: Communism in Romania (1945); Communism in Poland (1946–47); Communism in Hungary (1947), with a modified replay of regime change later—Hungarian Uprising (1956). The reverse process occurred in these and other Central and Eastern European states in 1989–90, but it was not the consequence of international crises.

27 Several East European states entered the Soviet-led bloc soon after World War II as a result of international crises in which the USSR played the crucial role in bringing about regime- and alliance-change, as noted: Communism in Romania (1945); Communism in Poland (1946–47); and Communism in Hungary (1947). In the Middle East, Iran entered the US-led Western alliance as a result of the Azerbaijan Crisis (1945–46).

28 Actor changes are not expected to influence rules of the game, which are relatively static. Stated differently, behavioral norms in world politics will rarely be affected by changes in attributes or traits of individual system members.

29 Rules do not affect power directly; they reflect it; that is, in anarchic world politics, authority and its legitimizing rules are determined, in the first instance, by the most powerful actors.

30 A causal link from alliance change to actor change is ruled out: first, because a state's political regime is not a product of coalitional commitments; and second, entry into or exit from a system is not the result of any alliance links. Rather, the reverse obtains: actor change is likely to lead to shifting alliances.

Nor are rules affected by changing alliances, for system norms tend to be impervious to short-term disruptions. Historically, the self-help, anarchic character of world politics has persisted amidst drastic shifts in alliances among the major powers.

31 A more elaborate discussion of the index of impact was presented in Brecher and James (1986: Part 2).

32 Parenthetically, the "beginning of the end" of the Cold War was also associated with Berlin, namely, the dismantling of the Wall in November 1989, the construction of which had catalyzed still another Cold War crisis, Berlin Wall (1961).

33 This operational method for measuring impact was used to determine the overall impact of the other nine cases analyzed throughout this book—and of most of the 390 international crises from 1918 to 1988 [see n. 34 below].

34 Munich and the two other "blurred" cases illustrate a larger theme, namely, the discrepancy between the assessment of intensity and impact. Of the 390 international crises for 1918–1988, all are scored for overall intensity, but only 273 are accorded an overall impact score. The reason for this difference is the existence of several kinds of clusters that act together as a catalyst to system change.

Long-war crises are a striking example, notably those that occurred in World War II (1939–45), Korea (1950–53), Yemen (1962–67), Vietnam (1964–75), and the Gulf War (1980–88). Since impact gauges the consequences of a crisis for several years after its termination, the effects of each crisis within a long war are most accurately assessed as the impact of the entire cluster, not of any component part. For example, the impact score for World War II cases is attached to the last crisis within that cluster, namely, End of World War II, not Fall of Western Europe, "Barbarossa", El Alamein, D-Day, etc. In other words, the impact of the cluster and of each crisis within it is assessed from the end of World War II as a whole.

There are also *clusters* of crises *that occur in close proximity in space and time and focus on a common issue*. For example, the three India/Pakistan crises in 1947–48, namely, Junagadh, Hyderabad and Kashmir I, derived from the partition of the subcontinent into two independent states in August 1947. Thus only Kashmir I, the last to terminate, was given an impact score; it represents the combined impact of this three-case, single-issue cluster.

Some international crises are parts of *unfinished clusters*, the impact of which cannot yet be measured, such as the Chad/Libya and Polisario (Morocco/Algeria/Mauritania) cases in the 1970s and 1980s: those conflicts continue unabated. The crises in these unfinished clusters were therefore not scored for impact. For an explanation of the decision rules related to recognition of an "unfinished cluster," see Brecher and James (1986: 128–129) and James, Brecher and Hoffman (1988).

35 Another noteworthy power change flowing from October-Yom Kippur was the effect on the balance of superpower influence in the region. The US was the main beneficiary. It gained more credibility as a mediator. And, while its commitment to Israel's survival remained intact, its "honest broker" role in the negotiations leading to both disengagement agreements, along with arms sales to Arab states, enhanced its influence in the Middle East subsystem as a whole. By contrast, the Soviets lost their primacy in Egypt.

36 There were also consequences for UK domestic politics, notably, enhanced popular support for Prime Minister Thatcher and the Conservative Party and their return to power in the general election of 1983. Norpoth (1987) gave several reasons for this effect. First, Britain won the war. Second, the UK acted in response to what most Englishmen considered a blatant act of aggression. Third, it "allowed Thatcher to demonstrate her blend of decisiveness and perseverance" (957). And fourth, the war was brief and cost very little.

Chapter 6

1 These examples of catalysts to foreign policy crises are not always synonymous with the trigger to the international crisis of which they are a part, for the state noted may not have been the first crisis actor in that cluster. Thus the Berlin Blockade Crisis began earlier than the US crisis, as noted: on 6 March 1948 the three Western Powers indicated their intention of merging their zones into what later became West Germany (FRG), triggering a foreign policy crisis for the USSR. That hostile act marked the beginning of the first international crisis over Berlin [see Chap. 2, pp. 83–84].

2 As will be apparent from Table 6.3 [see below], two of the enabling variables, capability and geographic distance, purport to explain all three aspects of crisis onset, namely, outbreak, initiation and vulnerability. Others relate to two of these dimensions, e.g., regime type and age. And still others are linked to only one aspect of onset, e.g., structure and system level, which focus on the outbreak of an international crisis.

For the findings on onset/pre-crisis, see Table 2.7 (case studies) and Table 7.2 (Gulf Crisis).

3 The logic for selecting these variables, as well as for the expectation of fewer decisions in the pre-crisis period, will be presented in the discussion of the crisis period of the Unified Model.

4 As with crisis onset, not all enabling variables are relevant to an explanation of all aspects of escalation. Their scope ranges from conflict setting (all aspects) to trigger and response (only the role of violence in escalation). [See Table 6.3.]

For the aggregate, case study, and (later) Gulf Crisis findings on the escalation phase/crisis period, see, respectively, Tables 3.1–3.3 and 3.5–3.8; Table 3.9; and Table 7.2.

5 The neglect of the deescalation phase of interstate crisis is analogous to the preoccupation of globalists with the superpowers in world politics, to the exclusion of the 160-odd states that constitute the peripheries of major power politics, as well as all interstate conflicts and crises other than major power wars. A glaring illustration of this flawed view of the world is the "long peace" thesis of Gaddis (1986, 1987, 1991) which focuses on the absence of war between the US and the USSR since 1945 as the central, almost exclusive, fact of post-World War II international politics. For a conceptual and empirical critique of this thesis see Brecher and Wilkenfeld (1991).

6 The holistic approach to crisis analysis pervades this book, as evident in the presentation of the phase models [Chaps. 2–5], the summaries of the ten case studies from 1938 to 1982, and the earlier sections of the Unified Model. It will also be apparent in the in-depth study of the Gulf Crisis, 1990–91 [Chap. 7].

7 For deescalation/end-crisis, too, there is considerable variation in the explanatory reach of the enabling variables, from major power activity (all aspects) to geostrategic salience, heterogeneity and issues (duration, only [Table 6.3]).

For the findings on deescalation/end-crisis see Tables 4.1–4.4 (aggregate), Table 4.5 (case study), and Table 7.2 (Gulf Crisis).

8 The aggregate and case study evidence on H. 12–14 was presented in Tables 5.4–5.6 and 5.8, respectively. And the testing of these hypotheses for the Gulf Crisis, 1990–91, is reported in Table 7.2 [Chap. 7].

9 For the findings relating to these nine variables, see the relevant tables in Chaps. 3–5.

Chapter 7

1 *FBIS–NESA* is used throughout this chapter to indicate *Foreign Broadcast Information Service*, a US Government publication. This is a valuable primary source for the English-language version of the texts of all important speeches, statements, letters, decisions, and newspaper editorials emanating from Iraq (and other Middle East states) from April 1990 to April 1991, most of them broadcast on Baghdad Radio's Domestic Service in Arabic. The full citation for each abbreviated reference in the text is to be found at the end of the book under *REFERENCES: THE GULF CRISIS 1990–91: PRIMARY SOURCES: Foreign Broadcast Information Service, Daily Report/Near East and South Asia.*

For the background and early developments of the Gulf Crisis see also "Kuwait: How the West Blundered," *The Economist* (London), 29/9/90, 19–20, 22; and Miller and Mylroie (1990).

OPEC = Organization of Petroleum Exporting Countries.

2 The trigger to Kuwait's crisis occurred on 25 June 1961, six days after it was granted independence by Britain: Iraq's Prime Minister reaffirmed a claim that Kuwait was an integral part of Iraq. Kuwait responded on the 30th by formally requesting assistance from Britain under the provisions of their defense treaty. This catalyzed a crisis for the UK. On 1 July London responded by rapidly building up its troops and airborne forces in Kuwait: within one week British forces numbered 6000. Kuwait appealed to the UN Security Council, but a proposed resolution was vetoed by the USSR. An Egyptian appeal for the withdrawal of British troops did not secure a Security Council majority. In July 1961 the League of Arab States accepted Kuwait as a member, in the face of Iraqi protests, and established a pan-Arab force, consisting mostly of Jordanians and Saudi Arabians, to defend Kuwait.

The Kuwait Independence Crisis ended on 13 July when Iraq's Military Attaché in the UK denied allegations that Iraq intended to attack Kuwait or had concentrated troops on the border. With the recognition of the Arab world, the Emir of Kuwait requested British troops to leave; the evacuation was completed by October 1961. After the downfall of General Qassem, Iraq's ruler, in February 1963, Iraq recognized Kuwait's independence—but not the finality of the Iraq/Kuwait border. Iraq withdrew its claim to all of Kuwait in the autumn of 1963. (Bartlet, 1977; Fitzsimmons, 1964; Macmillan, 1973; Northedge, 1974.

The fundamental differences between the 1961 and 1990–91 crises over Kuwait —short (3 weeks) vs. lengthy duration (9 months), non-violent military acts vs. full-scale war, Iraq's acquiescence in Kuwait's independence vs. Iraq's conquest of Kuwait, etc.—were due to the differences in relative power and resolve. Iraq was militarily weak in 1961, and its leaders lacked resolve in the face of the UK's immediate military buildup and all-Arab opposition. In 1990 Iraq had a seemingly formidable military machine, reputedly the fourth largest in the world; and its leader's resolve could not be shaken, not even by a massive US-led Coalition military buildup.

In this context, it is possible to combine the insights from comparative case studies with the rigor and quest for generalization of social science in order to improve our ability to anticipate future recurrent crises in conflicts of this type and to cope more effectively with them when they arise. [See Chap. 8 below, "Lessons for the Future."] However, a detailed comparison of the 1961 and 1990–91 crises over Kuwait is beyond the scope of this chapter.

3 On US aid to Iraq from 1982 to 1990 see pp. 411–412 and n. 13 and 14 on pp. 607–608.

4 British Prime Minister Chamberlain's comment on Czechoslovakia at the height of the Munich Crisis, as noted; see p. 190.

5 Aziz reportedly sent a memorandum to Kuwait on 16 July, demanding this $2.4 billion, along with $12 billion as compensation for the depressed oil prices created by Kuwait's alleged over-production; forgiveness of Baghdad's (Iran/Iraq) war debt of $10.5 billion, and a lease on Kuwait's island of Bubiyan (Boustany and Tyler, *Washington Post*, 31/7/90, 16, 22, and Thedoulou, *The Times* (London), 2/8/90, 1, 11)

6 According to Schwarzkopf (1992: 292–293), the State Department initially opposed acceding to the UAE request and relented a few days later only after pressure from the newly-appointed Chairman of the Joint Chiefs of Staff (JCS), General Powell, urged on by Schwarzkopf, and from Defense Secretary Cheney.

7 A month after Iraq's invasion there was an unconfirmed report that, at the Jidda talks, "Kuwait agreed to write off Iraq's $15 billion war debt and to lease Warba Island to Iraq as an oil outlet for the Rumaila field" (Cockburn, *Wall Street Journal* [New York], 6/9/90), A15.

At the Jidda meeting, Iraq reportedly demanded a new $10 billion loan from Kuwait, to which the latter agreed on condition the long-disputed boundary question was addressed. Iraq refused. (Cooley, 1991, 128, based upon interviews with King Hussain and Jordan's then–Foreign Minister.)

Before the outbreak of war Aziz declared, in an interview, that Iraq's deteriorating economy was the trigger to its invasion of Kuwait (Viorst, *The New Yorker*, 24/9/90, 90). And *after* the military debacle, he claimed that the massing of troops on Kuwait's border was designed to extract concessions from Kuwait, a bargaining ploy, not a signal of intent to invade (Viorst, *The New Yorker*, 24/6/91, 66).

8 *NYT* is the abbreviated citation, used throughout this chapter, for *The New York Times*, a valuable primary source for the texts of statements, speeches, news conferences, interviews, etc. of US and other Coalition leaders and their governments throughout the Gulf Crisis. When *NYT* is cited without an author it refers to the text of

a speech, statement, news conference, document, etc. All of these are listed in the *REFERENCES* at the end of this book, under *PRIMARY SOURCES: NEW YORK TIMES (NYT) DOCUMENTS.*

9 The pervasiveness of surprise was acknowledged by three senior US officials soon after the Iraqi invasion. John H. Kelly, Assistant Secretary of State for the Near East and South Asia, told a Congressional hearing: "The Kuwaitis didn't think that they were going to be attacked the night that they were attacked. Nobody in the Arab world thought he [Saddam Hussein] was going to do it." (*Joint Hearings,* August–December 1990, 126.) Assistant Secretary of Defense for International Security Affairs, Henry S. Rowen, declared before the same forum (*ibid.*, 126–127): "The Kuwaitis, of course, who had the most to lose, did not understand his [Saddam Hussein's] intentions . . . they [the Arabs] were all working on a different theory, and we indeed were, to a large extent, ourselves, . . . that he would coerce the Kuwaitis into paying a great deal of money . . . and that turned out to be wrong." And US Ambassador to Iraq, April Glaspie, took comfort in the fact that "[e]very Kuwaiti and every Saudi, every analyst in the Western world was wrong too" (to a *New York Times* correspondent; Sciolino, 1991: 177).

A notable exception to skepticism in Washington seems to have been the Defense Intelligence Agency (DIA)'s specialist on the Middle East, Pat Lang. His 30 July assessment was unambiguous on the prospects of war: "He [Saddam] has created the capability to overrun all of Kuwait and all of Eastern Saudi Arabia. If he attacks . . . we will have no warning. I do not believe he is bluffing. I have looked at his personality profile. He doesn't know how to bluff. It is not in his past pattern of behavior. . . . In short, Saddam Hussein has moved a force disproportionate to the task at hand. . . . Then there is only one answer: he intends to use it."

This assessment was rejected by the Director of the DIA, Lieutenant-General Soyster. General Powell, Chairman of the Joint Chiefs of Staff (JCS), was skeptical. The Administration played down reports of an Iraqi military buildup. Then, early in the morning of 1 August, Lang, in writing, forecast an Iraqi attack on Kuwait that night or the next morning. Powell remained skeptical. General Schwarzkopf, at a briefing of the Joint Chiefs and the Defense Secretary that afternoon "did not predict an invasion or border crossing." Finally, on the basis of irrefutable evidence from the DIA that Iraq's three divisions had moved to within three miles of the Kuwait border, Powell reluctantly accepted the near-certainty of invasion. Even then, General Tom Kelly, Chief of Operations for the JCS, remained unconvinced. And the President's National Security Advisor, Brent Scowcroft, remained skeptical to the end: he "was astonished. He had been sure it was all bluster" (Woodward, 1991: 205–223; the quotations are from 216–217, 220, 223).

Schwarzkopf wrote later that his Central Command intelligence staff, too, anticipated an Iraqi attack on Kuwait:

> ". . . at first we thought this might be merely another exercise . . . But by the end of July . . . [t]here was no way to mistake what we were seeing for a mere show of force: this was a battle plan taking shape. . . Shortly after noon on the last day of July, we notified Washington that war between Iraq and Kuwait appeared imminent. . . ."

However, he acknowledged being "half right and half wrong": on 1 August, in response to Cheney's query, what would Iraq do, "I think they're going to attack," but he expected a "limited incursion"—to take Kuwait's part of the Rumaila oil field and Bubiyan island, not the conquest of the entire emirate. "Everybody was surprised—an Arab had attacked a brother Arab" (1992: 293–296).

Surprise is evident in many other crisis-wars in the twentieth century: among others, the USSR before "Barbarossa" (Germany's attack) in June 1941; the US on the eve of Japan's attack on Pearl Harbor in December 1941; India until China's attack in October

1962, and Israel during the crisis leading to the October-Yom Kippur War in 1973. For reference to the abundant literature on surprise attack in interstate crises, see Chapter 1, pp. 8–9 above.

10 The border dispute originated in the imperious demarcation of the Iraq/Nejd (Saudi Arabia)/Kuwait borders by the UK High Commissioner in Iraq, Sir Percy Cox, in November 1922. In essence, he drew a red line on a map of the area, which granted Iraq much of the territory it claimed from Nejd, the forerunner of Saudi Arabia; and he compensated Ibn Saud by transferring two-thirds of the territory of Kuwait to Nejd. He also created two "neutral zones," which were to be additional bones of contention for decades. At the same time, Iraq was given a minuscule 30-mile coastline along the Gulf, while Kuwait, with one-tenth of Iraq's population, received a 310-mile coastline and the islands of Bubiyan and Warba. Dickson, 1956: 270–279. See also Schofield, 1991. (The two islands had been assigned to Kuwait, not the Basra Province, in a 1913 UK/Turkey agreement that recognized Kuwait, now a British protectorate, as an autonomous region within the Ottoman Empire.)

The arbitrary British-defined frontiers seventy years ago created the geographic source of the unresolved Iraq/Kuwait conflict: coastal space; control over the two islands at the head of the Gulf; and a disputed land border, especially an Iraq/Kuwait boundary marker that left the enormously rich Rumaila oil field another issue of conflict. Parenthetically, the Cox "Line" was typical of British colonial behavior in the Middle East and South Asia during the late nineteenth and early twentieth centuries. It was preceded by a similar *diktat* on the part of two Foreign Secrtaries of the Government of India: the Durand Line of 1893, a source of continuing territorial dispute and three crises between Afghanistan and Pakistan since 1946 (Dupree, 1980: 425–428, 444–445, 538–554); and the McMahon Line of 1914 that delineated the boundaries between China and Tibet, and in what came to be known as the "Eastern Sector" of the still-unresolved border dispute between China and India, including the border crisis-war from 1959 to 1963 (Lamb, 1966, and S. A. Hoffmann, 1990: 19–22, 38–39, 69–70, 231–232).

11 Since the invasion of Kuwait was the catalyst to the Gulf Crisis, a brief overview of the emirate is appropriate here.

Kuwait was a marginal pearl-diving and trading settlement on the edge of the Arabian peninsula until World War II. The current ruling family, the al-Sabahs, was chosen in 1756 by migrant Bedouin tribes from the Nejd Desert to administer the realm. Kuwait became a British protectorate in 1899. And the British acquired what became an extraordinarily valuable oil concession in 1934.

On the eve of the Gulf Crisis Kuwait had a population of about 2.2 million, of whom 700,000 were Kuwaitis. Two-thirds were Sunni Muslim, one-third Shi'ite. Almost all menial work and three-fourths of managerial and professional jobs were in the hands of foreigners—Palestinians, Egyptians, Jordanians, and immigrants from all over Southern Asia.

Kuwait was the only Gulf state with a semblance of democracy—a parliament that functioned from 1962 to 1985, and a free press. However, according to the suspended 1962 constitution, only literate males over 21, whose families resided in Kuwait before 1920, were eligible to vote, that is, 62,000 or less than 10% of the Kuwaiti citizens.

An oil boom in the 1950s transformed the emirate into the wealthiest state in the world, per capita, by the 1970s. The concentration of wealth, including an estimated $80–100 billion in investments and foreign exchange reserves abroad, facilitated free education and high standards of health care and other social services. It also led to the creation of a new class of intellectuals and civil servants, which became the core of political opposition in the 1980s to the al-Sabah domination of politics in Kuwait. Shimoni, 1987: 281–285, and Kifner, *NYT*, 31/3/91, A1, 8.

For an insightful analysis of the political economy of Kuwait (and Qatar), two of the

Gulf "accidental states," see Crystal (1990). For a novel, political economy analysis of Kuwait in the twentieth century, based upon the concept of "international cliency," "a strategic relationship between a strong state and a weak state" (567), see Tetrault (1991).

12 This process, typical of interstate crises, casts serious doubt on the validity of the sharp distinction between opportunity and threat crises attributed to China's conception of crisis (Bobrow, Chan and Kringen, 1977: Table 2, point 2).

There is a larger issue in dispute, namely, whether or not a universally-valid definition of interstate crisis, the basis of this inquiry, is flawed because of cultural differences (Bobrow, Chan and Kringen, 1979, and area specialists). The Gulf case, it is argued here, provides further evidence against this contention. The theoretical grounds for dissent were presented in the "State of the Art" review [Chap. 1 above].

13 One of the earliest embarrassing indicators of US aid to Iraq was the "Kloske affair": on 8 April 1991, Dennis E. Kloske, Under-Secretary of Commerce for Export Administration, told a House of Representatives sub-committee that the US Government, especially the State Department, ignored his recommendation in the spring of 1990 "to reduce the flow of advanced American technology to Iraq, because the Administration wanted to encourage better relations with Baghdad." The White House ordered his dismissal by 1 June! (Farnsworth, *NYT*, 10/4/91, A1, D2).

On US military and technological aid to Iraq see, in addition to Waas, and Hersh's in-depth reports, and Farnsworth: Emerson, *NYT Magazine*, 21/4/91, 30–32, 56–57, 68–69; Sciolino, 1991: Chap. 7, "The Arming of Iraq"; A. Lewis, *NYT*, 15/3/92, A17; Milhollen and Edensword, *NYT*, 24/4/92, A35; Baquet, *NYT*, 27/4/92, A1, D4; *NYT*, 29/5/92, A3; Gelb, *NYT*, 4/5/92, A17; a "Special Report" on "Iraqgate," *U.S. News and World Report* (New York), 18/5/92, 42–51; Tisdall, *Guardian Weekly* (Manchester), 31/5/92, 9; Sciolino, *NYT*, 7/6/92, A1, 16; Sciolino and Wines, *NYT*, 27/6/92, A1, 8; Wines, *NYT*, 2/7/92, A1, 6; Sciolino, *NYT*, 5/7/92, A8; Gelb, *NYT*, 9/7/92,A21; Safire, *NYT*, 6/7/92. A13; Sciolino with Baquet, *NYT*, 26/7/92, A1,8; Frantz and Waas, *Los Angeles Times*, in *Jerusalem Post*, 7/8/92; Sciolino, *NYT*, 9/8/92, E18; Safire, *NYT*, 10/9/92, A23; 8/10/92, A35; A. Lewis, *NYT*, 26/10/92, A17; Sciolino, *NYT*, 27/10/92, A15; Tolchin, *NYT*, 28/10/92, A15; Baquet with Sciolino, *NYT*, 2/11/92, A8; Waas and Unger, *New Yorker*, 2/11/92, 64–83; and Baquet, *NYT*, 10/11/92, A1, 13.

Other Western powers, notably France, Germany and the UK, also poured large supplies of weaponry and advanced technology into Iraq. For a sweeping condemnation of "How the West Armed Iraq," see Timmerman, *NYT*, 25/10/91, A33, and 1992. In fact, Timmerman argued that the primary motive of "Desert Storm" was to destroy Iraq's formidable military power, to which the West had contributed significantly, not to protect Saudi oil or liberate Kuwait. See also P. Lewis, *NYT*, 15/1/92, A1, 12 (on Germany's aid to Iraq's nuclear weapons program); Schmidt, *NYT*, 17/1/92, A8 (on the UK's role in the "supergun" affair); and Baquet, *NYT*, 27/10/92, A1, 13 (on UK arms & manufacturing equipment to Iraq).

14 See also Sciolino, *NYT*, 16/9/92, A6, and frequent investigative reports in September and October 1992; Tolchin, *NYT*, 6/10/92, A8; Sciolino with Baquet, *NYT*, 18/10/92, A36.

There were even reports of plans for military cooperation between the US and Iraq, specifically, Central Command proposals for military training and exchange programs with Iraqi forces, eight months before the invasion of Kuwait and, again, as late as May 1990. As with US economic aid to Iraq, these were rationalized as part of a policy to 'moderate' Saddam Hussein's behavior at home and abroad. (Gordon, *NYT*, 5/8/92, A9).

Notwithstanding the decision of the US Attorney General to reject demands for an independent prosecutor (Johnston, *NYT*, 10/12/92, A1, B13), the "BNL affair" remained firmly on the agenda of American politics at the close of the Bush Administration. This is evident from President–elect Clinton's remark, ". . . we need to know more about it than we now know" (N.A. Lewis, *NYT*, 11/12/92, A32), as well as the fact that several investigations by Congress and the CIA continued into 1993.

15 In the midst of Gulf War II, Bush acknowledged his failed policy of "constructive engagement" (a term used by the US to describe its [more successful] policy against *apartheid* in South Africa): "Well, we tried the peaceful route. We tried working with him [Saddam] and changing [him] through contact. . . . The lesson is clear in this case—that that didn't work." (Weekly Compilation of Presidential Documents, 5/2/91, 131, as quoted in Draper, 1992b: 38). He reiterated this theme just after the war (Weekly Compilation of Presidential Documents, 8/3/91, 288, as quoted in *ibid.*). And, amidst the gathering storm of criticism of Bush's pre-Gulf crisis-war policy, in the spring of 1992 ("Iraqgate," see n. 13), senior officials, notably Deputy Secretary of State Eagleburger, accused the critics of distorting the record (Sciolino, *NYT*, 22/5/92, A6).

16 Hussein reportedly clarified his fiery statement on 5 April: "I want to assure President Bush and His Majesty King Fahd that I will not attack Israel," he told the Saudi Ambassador to the US, Prince Bandar. "It's a message from me to the President," with a request that it be communicated personally to Bush. Bandar conveyed Hussein's message to the President on 9 April. Bush reportedly responded: "Well, if he doesn't intend it, why on earth does he have to say it?" (Woodward, 1991: 200–204). Apparently, Iraq's leader sought a reciprocal assurance that Israel would not attack Iraq (Seib, *Wall Street Journal* [New York], 22/10/90, A10; Oberdorfer, *Washington Post Magazine*, 17/3/91, 23, 36.

17 "Excerpts from Iraqi Transcript of Meeting With U.S. Envoy," translated from Arabic by ABC News. *NYT*, 23/9/90, A19.

Almost eight months after the Glaspie–Saddam Hussein meeting, the former US Ambassador to Iraq gave a spirited defense of her warnings to Iraq's leader a week before the invasion of Kuwait. She confirmed, before an informal meeting of the Senate Foreign Relations Committee on 20 March 1991, that she had conveyed to Hussein a neutral US stance on inter-Arab conflicts. But she added: "I told him orally we would defend our vital interests, we would support our friends in the Gulf, we would defend their sovereignty and integrity." (These words did not appear in Iraq's version, cited above. Nor is there evidence that Glaspie ever clarified the meaning of the phrase, "border disagreement.")

At the time of its publication the Government of Iraq transcript was termed "essentially correct" by an unidentified official in the State Department, though the Department did not comment. By contrast, Glaspie claimed before the Senate committee: "This is a fabrication. It is disinformation. It is not a transcript. This is the kind of thing the Iraqi Government has done for years and not very subtly." And she claimed that 20% of the actual content of their exchange was distorted, falsified or omitted.

Neither Bush nor Baker, or anyone else in authority, said that the Iraqi version was false or allowed Glaspie to clear her name for eight months. Nor was Glaspie invited to participate in the group of advisors accompanying Baker to his crucial Geneva meeting with Foreign Minister Tariq Aziz on 9 January 1991 [see pp. 447–448]. (The Glaspie testimony before the Congressional committees and the quoted passages are taken from Friedman, *NYT*, 21/3/91, A1, 15, and 22/3/91, A1, 9.)

The "Glaspie Affair" remained blurred until the State Department made public the relevant cables, including her report to the Department on what transpired during her (unscheduled) meeting with Saddam Hussein on 25 July. Their publication a year after the event was revealing. Suffice it to note the essential points.

19 July 1990: Glaspie was instructed by the State Department to emphasize US friendship with Iraq but to make clear that Washington was "committed to ensure the free flow of oil from the gulf and to support the sovereignty and integrity of the gulf states." Further, "we will continue to defend our vital interests in the gulf . . . [and are] strongly committed to supporting the individual and collective self-defense of our friends in the gulf. . . ."

24 July: a second cable to Glaspie directed her to reiterate that the US had "no position" on inter-Arab border disputes, but to warn that the solving of disputes by force was "contrary to UN Charter principles."

25 July: Glaspie's cable to Secretary of State Baker, summarizing her meeting with Hussein that day, did not convey the US commitments, as instructed in the 19 July cable to her; she merely asked, "in the spirit of friendship, not confrontation, the simple question: What are your intentions?" She did, however, report Saddam Hussein's threat to "respond" to Kuwait's and the UAE's intransigence, especially, "If Iraq is publicly humiliated by the US G[overnment]," "however illogical and self-destructive that would prove." And she conveyed at some length Hussein's litany of woes, e.g., Iraq's $40 billion foreign debt and its grievances, notably against Kuwait, the UAE, and "some circles" in US government agencies, the CIA, the State Department and the USIA.

28 July: a cable from Under-Secretary of State Eagleburger to Glaspie conveyed a conciliatory message from Bush to Hussein—cited on pp. 413–414. The warnings and strong commitments of the 19 July cable were not reiterated. And there was no reference to Iraqi troops near Kuwait's border.

(Excerpts from these cables are given in Hoffman, *Washington Post*, 12/7/91, A1, 26, Hoffman and Dear, *Washington Post*, 13/7/91 A1, 14, and in *NYT*, 13/7/91, A4.)

The sharp discrepancy between Glaspie's assertive version of her meeting with Hussein, as conveyed to the Congressional committees in March 1991, and the clear indication of effusive friendship and conciliation, in her 25 July cable to Baker, led to blunt criticism of the former US Ambassador by several senators as having misled Congress (Sciolino, *NYT*, 13/7/91, A1, 4).

18 There is a noteworthy similarity between the exclusion of Kuwait (and the Gulf region generally) from an official statement of US security commitments in the Middle East, in July 1990, and Secretary of State Acheson's exclusion of South Korea (and Taiwan) from the US "defensive perimeter" in East Asia, in a speech in January 1950. That *lacuna* was not lost on North Korea which, from its subsequent behavior, also seemed to have perceived a "green light": it attacked South Korea on 25 June 1950. As an authority on US Far Eastern policy observed: ". . . the uncertainty of what American action would be and the weakness of the South Korean regime tempted the Communists [North Korea] to act promptly and decisively." Latourette, 1952: 181.

19 The "Masada complex" theme was mentioned several months before Primakov's experience by a senior Jordanian official: "You cannot push him. If he is cornered and feels he must die, he would welcome the opportunity to take a great many of us along with him." Miller, *NYT*, 28/11/90, A14. For informative biographical studies of Saddam Hussein and his regime before the Gulf Crisis see al-Khalil (1989) and Matar (1981).

20 Social scientists have a predilection for precision and schemas—regarding categories, dates, events, etc. I recognize that most, if not all, decision-makers do not think in a linear way. Thus Saddam Hussein, like Bush, almost certainly vacillated on the likelihood of war. Some days he might have thought, "there is going to be war." On other days he would be more sanguine, persuading himself that Iraq's military concentration in Kuwait and southern Iraq, with half a million troops, would deter the US. However, on balance, the evidence supports the above-noted delineation of changes in his perception. The crucial point remains that he was not fully persuaded that war would erupt—until it did.

21 There were several *escalation points* for Kuwait during its crisis period, which continued until the end of Gulf War II, notably:

8 August—its annexation by Iraq;
28 August—its formal integration as Iraq's 19th province;
17 January 1991—the outbreak of war between the US-led Coalition and Iraq; and
24 February 1991—the launching of a ground campaign by the Coalition.

Kuwait's role in the Gulf Crisis was symbolic: diplomatic activity at the UN and in Coalition capitals; and nominal participation of planes and troops of the Kuwaiti Government-in-Exile in Saudi Arabia in Gulf War II, January–February 1991.

22 In Schwarzkopf's view (1992: 313), this "trapping [of] more than thirteen thousand westerners and other foreigners. . . [changed] the entire nature of the crisis."

23 This remained Iraq's consistent bargaining position throughout the Gulf Crisis. But Saddam later softened his notion of "linkage." On 5 October he told Gorbachev's special envoy: "I want to make one thing clear [about his 12 August statement]. The time linkage and the process leading to a solution of the Palestinian problem are to be discussed at negotiations." Primakov, *Time*, 4/3/91.

24 Two "discrepancies" in this application of the Unified Model to the Gulf Crisis may be puzzling for some readers: (a) between termination dates for the pre-crisis period of the main adversaries; and (b) between actual and known changes in perception. These require clarification.

Termination of the US's pre-crisis period is designated as 29 October 1990 because thereafter its decision-makers experienced all three perceptions of harm, even though awareness of time pressure and heightened probability of war was self-induced. However, the US decision on 30 October to launch a war against Iraq in January 1991 remained unknown to the adversary—and to all but a few American decision-makers—throughout the Gulf crisis-war. Thus it did not trigger a "perceptible leap" to the crisis period, for Iraq. That came a month later with the UN deadline-cum-authorization of force.

25 The goals, said Thatcher in an hour-long, private monologue with Gorbachev's envoy on 20 October 1990, should be "not to limit things to a withdrawal of Iraqi forces from Kuwait but to inflict a devastating blow at Iraq, 'to break the back' of Saddam and destroy the entire military, and perhaps industrial, potential of that country. Mrs. Thatcher did not mince any words. No one should interfere with this objective, she declared. . . . No one should even try to ward off the blow against the Saddam regime." And she saw no option other than war. Primakov, *Time*, 4/3/91.

26 The US yielded on both points: the Military Staff Committee met six times by the end of October; and the Security Council passed the authorization of force resolution (Resolution 678), on 29 November 1990.

27 The text of the Bush-Gorbachev Joint Statement, and News Conference, and several articles on the Helsinki summit (Keller, Friedman) are in *NYT*, 10/9/90, A1, 6–9.

28 Primakov recalled his several-hour session with Iraq's Foreign Minister, Tariq Aziz, on the 4th, as "probably the toughest I've ever had with an Iraqi official. . . . In Aziz's monologue [about Iraq's rightful claim to Kuwait] one could easily hear the sharp note of displeasure and dissatisfaction with the policy of the Soviet Union, which 'should have acted in a different way,' considering its [1972] treaty [of friendship] with Iraq" (*Time*, 4/3/91).

Aziz reportedly conveyed this anger and feeling of abandonment to Baker as well, at their Geneva meeting on 9 January 1991 [to be analyzed below]: "We don't have a patron anymore." Correctly, he added: "If we still had the Soviets as our patron, none of this would have happened. They would have vetoed every U.N. resolution." As quoted in Friedman and Tyler, *NYT*, 3/3/91, A18.

29 There are many such statements. See, for example: on rallying the poor, Saddam Hussein's "Victory Day" Message, 7/8/90, *FBIS–NESA*, 8/8/90; on mobilizing the poor Arab states against the rich states, Saddam's speech, "to save Mecca," 10/8/90, *FBIS–NESA*, 13/8/90; and on championing the Palestinians, the National Assembly Statement urging *Jihad*, 11/8/90, *FBIS–NESA*, 13/8/90.

30 The following account of the NSC meetings and the making of the US decision to deploy troops to the Gulf region is based upon Woodward (1991: 224–229, 236–238, and 247–253), Friedman and Tyler, *NYT*, 3/3/91, A18, and Schwarzkopf (1992: 297–302), except where other specific references are cited.

31 Kuwait was no less ambivalent. A half hour after the Iraqi invasion began, Kuwait's Crown Prince asked the US Embassy for immediate military assistance—but insisted that this "not be made public or treated as official." An hour later the request was renewed officially, to no avail (Friedman and Tyler, *NYT*, 3/3/91, A18).

32 This account of the "prepare for war" decision is based mainly upon Woodward (1991: 303–321), supplemented by Friedman and Tyler, *NYT*, 3/3/91, A18, and Schwarzkopf (1992: 356–370).

33 The text of Bush's "offensive military option" statement is in *NYT*, 9/11/90, A12. The comments are from Apple, *NYT*, 9/11/90, A13, and Friedman and Tyler, *NYT*, 3/3/91, A18.

34 This analysis of the making of Resolution 678 is based upon Friedman, *NYT*, 2/12/90, A1, 19. See also Sciolino, *NYT*, 15/1/91, A10.

US/USSR cooperation on Resolution 678 was not the first time these powers intervened jointly to cope with a Middle East crisis that threatened to undermine the global order. The classic precedent was the joint US/USSR *démarche* to end the October-Yom Kippur War, agreed-upon at Secretary of State Kissinger's meetings with President Brezhnev on 19–20 October 1973. (See Kissinger, 1982: Chap. XII, and Brecher with Geist, 1980: 219–224.)

US/USSR cooperation in the Gulf Crisis generally points to an important, neglected theme: without the end of the Cold War, it is doubtful that the US-led military assault on Iraq in January 1991 could have been launched. Tariq Aziz correctly lamented the demise of Soviet power in that context, during his meeting with Secretary of State Baker in Geneva on 9 January (see n. 28 above).

On the persistence of US global primacy, even before the demise of Soviet power, see Strange (1982) and Russett (1985). They were responding to the claim of many theorists of interdependence, especially of "hegemonic stability," that the US position in the global *power* hierarchy had declined irrevocably, partly because of its declining prominence in the global *economy* (e.g. Krasner, 1982). Not for the first time, incorrect inferences may have been drawn about changes in *power* status from apparent changes in *economic* status.

35 Yet, according to Schwarzkopf (1992: 365), "[h]ad it not been for the Japanese, Desert Shield would have gone broke in August. . . . the Japanese embassy in Riyadh quietly transferred tens of millions of dollars into Central Command's accounts."

36 On the behavior of Middle East states during the Gulf Crisis, as a case study of theories of international alignment, see Garnham (1991). The most notable case of pro-Iraq policy, namely, Jordan, was attributed by Brand (1991) primarily to "two key domestc factors . . . , the ongoing process of political liberalization . . . [and] the emergence of new political coalitions that bridged both significant ideological . . . and communal . . . divides [following the 1989 economic riots]" (2).

37 The eight-paragraph letter was drafted by the Deputies Committee. Although not yet published, it reportedly said: "We stand today at the brink of war between Iraq and

the world." The failure to withdraw would mean "calamity," "tragedy," and "further violence" for Iraq. In another attempt to convey US resolve, while offering no war, the last sentence read: "I hope you weigh your choice carefully and choose wisely, for much will depend upon it." Woodward, 1991: 354.

38 On the personal dimension of Iraq/US bargaining and the credibility of resolve, see Friedman, *NYT*, 16/12/90, sec. 4, p. 2.

Bush persisted with his personal focus on Iraq's president: "The American people and I," he declared in a formal statement on the first anniversary of the launching of the air war, "remain determined to keep the pressure on Saddam until a new leadership comes to power in Iraq" (Rosenthal, *NYT*, 17/1/92, A8).

The extent to which Bush personalized the Gulf Crisis has been documented by Smith (1992): "I've had it," "I'm getting increasingly frustrated," were typical. "It was as if foreign policy had become presidential autobiography" (quoted in Will, *International Herald Tribune* [Paris], 11–12/1/92, 4; see also A. Lewis, *NYT* [12/1/92, section 4, E19]).

Smith argued that Bush personally maneuvered the US into war—from 5 August onward; it was a "superlative performance" in the exercise of unbridled power by the President, whom he accused of being persistently disingenuous and less than candid. From the evidence of Bush's behavior and US decision-making cited in the earlier pages of this chapter, such a unilinear, one-person, conspiratorial interpretation of how the US went to war against Iraq in January 1991 is open to serious doubt.

39 Only when the memoirs of decision-makers, thus far limited to Schwarzkopf, and later, the secret documents are available will it be possible to reconstruct in detail the US decision for war.

40 In the interest of parsimony, all aspects of Gulf War II will be examined as one sub-period and one sub-phase of escalation, rather than two. The rationale is that the launching of the Coalition's ground campaign on 24 February 1991 was a logical extension of the decision for war. And indeed they were so conceived in the "preparation for war" decision by the US on 30 October 1990, analyzed earlier.

41 The debate within the US over economic sanctions versus resort to force was highly visible in the national security-foreign policy establishment. On 28 November two former Chairmen of the Joint Chiefs of Staff, Admiral William Crowe and General David Jones, testified before the Senate Armed Forces Committee and strongly advocated allowing economic sanctions extended time—up to a year—to take effect. William Webster, director of the CIA, adopted a similar view early in December. So too did most former Secretaries of Defense, most Democrats in Congress, and one academic-turned National Security Advisor, Brzezinski. The other, Kissinger, along with most Republicans in Congress and sundry middle-level former officials, urged resort to force when the UN deadline for Iraq's withdrawal expired. The op-ed commentators were also split on this issue. For these and other views on the Gulf Crisis, see Sifry and Cerf, 1991.

42 Eighteen months later, Saudi and Kuwaiti officials reported that Iran had decided to expropriate 132, mostly military, Iraqi aircraft (more than double the initial estimate) that had sought refuge from a Coalition attack: this was viewed in Teheran as a first "payment" of Iran's claim to hundreds of billions of dollars for damages in Gulf War I. (Ibrahim, *NYT*, 31/7/92, A6).

43 The remarks by Bush, Major, Mitterand and Soviet spokesmen are as quoted in *NYT*, 16/2/91: Tyler, A1, 4; "Excerpts From 2 Statements by Bush . . . ," A5; "World Reaction . . . ," A7; and Schmemann, A7; and Schmemann, *NYT*, 17/2/91, A1.

44 Two versions of those talks are available: an Iraqi account broadcast on Baghdad Radio the same evening (*FBIS–NESA*, 13/2/91); and Primakov's initial reaction followed by a memoir (Schmemann, *NYT*, 14/2/91, A19, and *Time*, 11/3/91).

45 The 'dovish' views of the two senior US military commanders is noteworthy in this context. Schwarzkopf "expressed mixed feelings" to Powell on 18 February about "the Gorbachev mediation effort and the military implications of [an Iraqi] withdrawal." He was preoccupied with US casualties: "It comes down to a question of lives. We have probably inflicted a hundred thousand casualties on the Iraqis at the cost of one hundred for us. Why should we inflict a hundred and fifty thousand casualties at a cost of five thousand for us? We could lose that many in the first two days of the [land] attack." He also noted the "heavy damage to Iraq's war machine." Powell agreed: "If they withdraw from Kuwait, it is a [US] victory. . . . At bottom, neither Powell nor I wanted a ground war. We agreed that if the United States could get a rapid withdrawal we would urge our leaders to take it." (Schwarzkopf, 1992: 442, 445). This 'soft' line was clearly at variance with the White House, State Department and Pentagon civilian chiefs, who pressed for an [earlier] ground campaign.

46 Sources for the military balance in the Gulf region in mid-January 1991 are the United States Naval Institute, Jane's All the World's Aircraft, the International Institute for Strategic Studies, and the Center for Defense Information, as summarized in *NYT*, 20/1/91, sec. 4, p. 2; and an elaborate Associated Press report, "The War's Confronting Forces," as presented in *Jerusalem Post*, 18/1/91, p. 6. The updated estimate on the eve of the ground war is to be found in *NYT*, 25/2/91, A12. A post-war Reuters/AP estimate of military or medical contributions by all states in the Coalition is in *NYT*, 24/3/91, A18.

47 The report, "Defense For A New Era: Lessons of the Persian Gulf War," arrived at this figure by the following estimates:

42 Iraqi divisions, at full strength	547,000
(the figure cited by US spokesmen during the war);	
the actual 42 divisions, 185,000 below strength, thus	362,000
of these, 9000 killed	
17,000 injured	
153,000 deserted during the air war	−179,000
Thus in southern Iraq and Kuwait on 24 February 1991	183,000

Of these, 63,000 were estimated to have been taken prisoner and 120,000 escaped or were killed during the ground war; the estimate of killed was less than 60,000 (Porth, 23/4/92, 4–5; and Schmitt, *NYT*, 24/4/92, A6).

48 On the planning of the offensive campaign, including the sweep to the west, outflanking Iraq's forces, see Schwarzkopf, 1992: 354–362, 382–385, 388–392.

49 A post-war assessment, based upon satellite photographs of the battlefield and the southern part of Iraq, led to a considerable downward adjustment of material hardware damage in an initial estimate the day the war ended (*NYT*, 1/3/91, A12): 700 of 4550 tanks escaped the encirclement, not 280 of 4280, about half of them T-72s; 1430 of 2880 armored personnel carriers escaped, not 1014, as noted above; but fewer artillery pieces escaped than believed earlier, only 340 of 3257, not 970 of 3110. (This consensus view of the CIA, the Pentagon's DIA and the National Security Agency [NSA] left Saddam Hussein much weaker but with an ample armory to crush the Shi'ite and Kurdish revolts in March–April [see below])(Gordon and Schmitt, *NYT*, 25/3/91, A1, 8). And, a year after the outbreak of Gulf War II, the CIA Director told a Congressional committee that Iraq could restore its nuclear, chemical and biological weapons capability, and its ballistic missile program, within a few years (Sciolino, *NYT*, 16/1/92, A9).

50 Estimates of Iraqi casualties are from a Greenpeace report (Thomma, *Philadelphia Inquirer*, 30/5/91, 5A), and a Pentagon DIA report, which acknowledged an "error factor of 50 percent or higher" (Tyler, *NYT*, 5/6/91, A5). For a severe criticism of "needless deaths in the Gulf," see Middle East Watch (1992).

The US suffered 148 killed in combat, including 35 by "friendly fire" and 28 of them in a Scud missile attack on an American base in Saudi Arabia, and 467 wounded, including 72 by "friendly fire," of whom 90 were at that base (Schmitt, *NYT*, 10/8/91 A4, and the massive, three-volume Pentagon report of April 1992, "Conduct of the Persian Gulf War").

The actual US casualties contrasted sharply with the expectation of as much as 10% of ground combat troops, that is, upwards of 10,000 Coalition soldiers. The actual duration of the war, too, differed from the expectation: an air campaign of six weeks and a land war of four days, compared to an anticipated 18 days and two weeks (Pentagon report, 1992).

51 A vivid, instantaneous account of the ground campaign is to be found in Schwarzkopf's news conference on 28 February at his HQ in Saudi Arabia. *NYT*, 28/2/91, A8. A more elaborate description, much more detailed than his account of the air war, was presented in his autobiography (1992: 451–472).

The commander of Saudi forces in Gulf War II, Prince Khaled bin Sultan, openly disputed Schwarzkopf's version of the war, accusing him of "concocting" stories and "distorting" facts in order "to give himself all the credit for the victory over Iraq while running down just about everyone else." (Miller, *NYT*, 21/10/92, A8). For the texts of Schwarzkopf's briefings in Saudi Arabia throughout the war, see Pyle (1991). For instructive studies of Gulf War II, see Dunnigan and Bay (1991); N. Friedman (1991); Hiro (1992); Sackur (1991), Summers (1992); Simpson (1991); US News and World Report (1992); and the Pentagon's official report on the war; see Gordon, *NYT*, 23/2/92, A1, 12); and for a laudatory biography of Schwarzkopf and his role in the war, Cohen and Gatti (1991).

52 From the invasion of Kuwait until the beginning of the air/naval war, more than 1.5 million people were uprooted from Iraq and Kuwait, notably 380,000 Kuwaitis, 700,000 Egyptians, 250,000 Palestinians/Jordanians, and 350,000 South Asians from India, Pakistan, Bangladesh and Sri Lanka. Before the war, too, an estimated one million Yemenis fled/were expelled from Saudi Arabia. During the war, in fact, until mid-March 1991, about 65,000 fled, 35,000 Shi'ite Iraqis to Iran, and 28,000 Asians or other Middle Easterners. In late March 1991 a human avalanche was unleashed by Iraq's civil war: two million fled to neighboring Turkey and Iran, 1.5 million Kurds in the North, half a million Shi'ites in the South. Most of them returned, but only after a belated Western re-involvement through the creation of "safe havens" for the Kurds [see below] (Miller, *NYT*, 16/6/91, IE 3).

53 George (1991: 573–574), too, was critical of US behavior in the Gulf Crisis, using *war avoidance* as the exclusive criterion of successful crisis management. Unlike Kennedy during the Cuban Missile Crisis, he wrote, "the type of coercive diplomacy the Bush administration employed relied almost exclusively on the stick. . . . [It] rejected any negotiation with Hussein and any compromise settlement." However, he acknowledged US success in achieving the goals of crisis management emphasized here, namely, coalition-building, coalition-maintenance and international system legitimacy to manage a crisis by violence, if necessary.

Stein (1992) assessed US compellance strategy as a failure; but she placed the onus entirely on Iraq's leader:

". . . There is only one plausible explanation . . . It is clear in retrospect that Saddam preferred to retain Kuwait without war, but that he preferred war to unconditional withdrawal from Kuwait. . . ."

Several factors were cited to explain "why Saddam ranked his preferences that way."

First, "Saddam believed that the Soviet Union would not endorse American coercion nor agree to UN resolutions authorizing the use of force."

Second, he "behaved at times as though he were not certain that the United States would attack:"

Third, he "calculated that Iraq could survive the military consequences of the war and win a political victory."

Fourth, he "doubted the resolve of the United States to sustain the large numbers of casualties expected in ground fighting."

"Far more important . . . was the weight Saddam gave to political factors in the Arab world. He expected that [pro-Coalition] Arab governments . . . would not survive . . . and that the coalition . . . would rupture . . ."

In short, "[t]he explanation for the failure to avoid war lies largely in the strategic judgment of Saddam Hussein." (173, 175–177).

Deibel (1991) offered a somewhat different mixed assessment of US behavior in the Gulf crisis-war ("Mastery and Inaction"). While commending the Bush Administration's tactical competence, he charged it with strategic failure and quoted, approvingly, the London *Economist*'s pre-war judgement: "Bush is rather good at crises: he is by nature reactive. What he is not good at is strategy and forethought"(9).

Leng (1993, forthcoming) was critical of both protagonists, expecially the US: "In the critical last month of the crisis . . . the U.S. offered no line of retreat for Iraq . . . Bush's message to Iraq was clear: choose between submission or war . . . the fault, if there is one, in the bargaining of the two sides lies not in the choice of influence strategies, but in the inflexibility with which they were implemented. On both sides, an unswerving focus on the need to demonstrate resolve excluded the consideration of potential peaceful solutions. . .

Saddam Hussein . . . woefully misjudged Iraq's power and the motivation of his adversaries . . . [His] only reasonable way out of the [self-created] trap . . . was through a face-saving retreat. His refusal to make a serious diplomatic effort to do so is an inexcusable diplomatic failure. . .

By publicly committing himself to reject any face-saving way out for Iraq, Bush may have thrown away the only feasible possibility of achieving their stated objectives without war."

Whether or not a "face-saving peaceful solution" was desirable or feasible," Leng concluded that "in a situation fraught with a high probability of war, the bargaining of the two sides contributed nothing to its avoidance." (283–287).

54 Schwarzkopf, in his memoir (1992: 489), acknowledged a serious blunder on his part, namely, agreeing to an Iraqi request to be allowed to fly helicopters anywhere in Iraq where there were no Coalition forces. That enabled the Saddam Hussein regime to employ "helicopter gunships to suppress rebellions in Basra and other cities," including the entire area of Iraqi Kurdistan, in March–April 1991.

55 The Kurds are an ancient Middle Eastern people, mostly Sunni Muslim, with an Indo-European language similar to Persian. There are varying estimates of their numbers, with Kurdistan spilling over the territory of five states: Turkey, with 3–10 million; Iraq (2–3 million); Iran (2–6 million); Syria (300,000–700,000); and the USSR, with 100,000–200,000; that is, a maximum population of 20 million.

The Kurdish "problem" in modern international relations is as old as the state of Iraq, which was carved out of the Ottoman Empire after World War I. The Treaty of Sèvres between the victorious Allied powers and a shattered Turkey, in 1920, promised the Kurds a "scheme of local autonomy" in eastern Anatolia and the oil-rich Mosul province of Iraq, with an option for independence later. However, the treaty was rejected by a renascent Turkey under Kemal Ataturk. Its successor, the Treaty of Lausanne, in 1923, made no reference to Kurdish national rights.

The Kurds of Iraq revolted persistently, almost every year since 1922. They never succeeded in overthrowing an Iraqi Government, though a short-lived Kurdish

Republic of Mahabad was established in northern Iran in 1946, with Soviet assistance.

An agreement recognizing the Kurds as one of "the two nations of Iraq" and granting limited autonomy was reached in 1970. Saddam proclaimed his intent at unilateral implementation in March 1974. He reneged in 1975, following the Iran/Iraq agreement to fix their border midway in the Shatt-al-Arab. Kurdish rebellions persisted during the eight-year Iran/Iraq War (Shimoni, 1987: 277–281, and Rejwan, *Jerusalem Post*, 14/4/1991).

56 Among many others, the preeminent US newspaper, the *New York Times*, and virtually all of its commentators, from Left to Right, directed scathing criticism at Bush's "hands-off" policy. See Gelb, and F. Lewis, 3/4/91, A21; A. Lewis, and A. M. Rosenthal, 5/4/91, A25; and editorials, 5/4/91 and 9/4/91.

For a merciless criticism of Bush's abandonment of the Kurds, see Safire, *NYT*, 4/4/91, op-ed page: "The enormity of the dishonor brought on the United States by President Bush's decision to betray the Kurdish people . . .".

A more balanced—but less than kind—assessment is to be found in Gelb, *NYT*, 14/4/91, IE7: "Mr. Bush proved himself to be a master of the old game of power politics—and a man insensitive to and out of place in the new world his own actions are helping to create."

For a sweeping condemnation of US "Realpolitik in the Gulf" from 1972 onwards, including its consistent indifference to the fate of the Kurds, see Hitchens (1991).

57 By *6 April* the Secretary-General was to submit a plan to the Security Council for a UN observer force to monitor the demilitarized zone;

as soon as he certified that the force was deployed, Coalition forces were to complete their withdrawal from the zone occupied by them during Gulf War II;

by *18 April* (15 days after the adoption of Res. 687) Iraq had to submit details on the location, amounts and types of all its chemical and biological weapons, Scud and other ballistic missiles with a range over 150 kilometers, and all its "nuclear-weapons-usable" materials;

by *3 May* (30 days after adoption) the Secretary-General was to seek Council approval of a plan to create a special fund, financed by an unspecified percentage of Iraq's oil revenues in the future, to pay reparations for war damages and losses; Iraq's needs and its foreign debt then would be considered by the commission administering the fund;

by *18 May* (45 days after adoption) the Secretary General and the International Atomic Energy Agency were to submit a proposal to the Council to create a special commission which, in turn, was to develop a plan within 45 days to inspect, take possession of, and eliminate all Iraq's weapons of mass destruction;

at an unspecified date, *after* Iraq had transferred all of its weapons of mass destruction to the special commission, and *after* the Council approved the reparations plan, the Council was to lift its ban on Iraq's exports, including oil, and free its frozen financial assets abroad;

by *2 June* (60 days after adoption of Res. 687), the Secretary-General was to submit guidelines to the Council for supervising a continuing arms embargo on Iraq;

by *2 June* and *every 60 days thereafter* the Security Council was to review the embargo on non-military imports into Iraq and could modify it "in the light of" Iraq's "policies and practices," including its implementation of Council resolutions;

(Resolution 687 lifted, at once, the trade sanctions relating to food, medicine and other essential materials and supplies for civilian use); and

by *20 August* (120 days after adoption), and regularly thereafter, the Council was to review the ban on conventional arms sales to Iraq, in the light of Iraq's compliance with the terms of Resolution 687 and progress towards arms control in the Gulf region (S/RES/687 [1991]); P. Lewis, *NYT*, 4/4/91 A1, 10, and 7/4/91, A14.

58 There is a continuing controversy over the effectiveness of the Coalition's anti-

Scud campaign. The US Air Force claimed that many missiles and mobile launchers had been destroyed. And Schwarzkopf (1992: 417) asserted: "our bombers had obliterated every known Scud site in western Iraq, destroying thirty-six fixed launchers and ten mobile ones." But an American UN ballistic missile analyst declared categorically that none had been destroyed (Schmitt, *NYT*, 24/6/92, A6; and Miller, *NYT*, 24/6/92, A21).

59 King Fahd's decrees were severely criticized by the US human rights group, Middle East Watch. Its report, "Empty Reforms, Saudi Arabia's New Basic Laws," argued that the "reforms" strengthened King Fahd's near-absolute power, did not provide for elections or democracy, and did not meet recognized international standards on basic human rights (Miller, *NYT*, 17/5/92, A13). At the other extreme of the political spectrum, Muslim fundamentalists in Saudi Arabia condemned the reforms and demanded stricter Islamic norms in public life. (Ibrahim, *NYT*, 9/3/92, A1, 7: 8/10/92, A6).

60 Even Iraq felt the need to appear to favor change: on 2 September 1991 the RCC promulgated a law permitting the formation of political parties, though not on the basis of race, regionalism, sectarianism or atheism; and political activity in the armed forces remained exclusively the province of the ruling *Ba'ath* Party (Reuters, *NYT*, 4/9/91, A6). No one inside or outside Iraq was impressed. In reality, the *Ba'ath* Party–Army dictatorship in Iraq, under the domination of Saddam Hussein, remained firmly in power.

61 A more elaborate discussion of what has been learned from the United Model, especially from the testing of its hypotheses with the evidence of many international crises, and the lessons from its application to the Gulf crisis-war for future crises in the Middle East, is provided in Chapter 8.

Chapter 8

1 This book has focused primarily on states and the interstate dimension of crises. However, the roles of IOs and non-state actors have not been excluded from the analysis.

2 During the 70 years from the end of 1918 to the end of 1988 there were, as noted, 390 international crises and 826 foreign policy crises. From the end of 1918 to 1980, the Correlates of War (COW) Project uncovered 31 interstate wars and 15 extra-systemic wars (Singer and Small, 1982: Appendix A). A subsidiary COW-generated data set, known as "militarized interstate disputes," is much closer to the ICB data set in volume and to crisis as a concept. It reported an average number of 6.7 "disputes begun per year," for 1919–45, and 12.7 for 1946–76 (Gochman and Maoz, 1984: Table 1, 92). The comparable figures for international crises are 4.1 (1919–45) and 6.5 (mid-1945–end 1988).

3 Since the evidence regarding the first three of these questions, framed as Propositions 1–3, was extrapolated from the escalation phase/crisis period, it will be reported in that context.

4 The latter, too, is neglected relative to the causes of war. See the critique of the literature on crisis, in Chapter 1.

5 The discrepancy is due to *long-war* and *close proximity* crises, two types of cluster whose crises act together as a catalyst to system change. Thus they were treated as single cases for purposes of measuring impact; for example, the impact of all 31 crises during World War II was assessed *en bloc* from the end of that war. There are also *unfinished clusters*, whose effects cannot yet be measured. See Chap. 5, n. 34 for an elaboration of this point.

6 As in many other respects, this finding on crisis parallels an important generalization on war, namely, that "the frequency of war is inversely related to its seriousness

..." This hypothesis was tested and confirmed by evidence from the "modern great power system", 1500–1975 (Levy and Morgan, 1984: 746).

7 These and other findings were elaborated in the discussion of Tables 2.1–2.6 [Chap. 2], Table 3.4 [Chap. 3], and (will be) in Appendix B, on crisis intensity.

8 The Unified Model of Crisis, summarized here, was delineated at length in Chapter 6 above.

9 The expectation relating to protracted conflict setting is not supported. The finding for number of actors is supported for adversaries, not for crisis actors.

As noted (Chap. 3, n.15), "Support," for purposes of this analysis, refers to some degree of support by the aggregate data for a specific element of an hypothesis, ranging from "very strong" to "modest":

"very strong" support = at least twice as high a proportion of cases in support of the postulated element as its alternative, e.g., new states vs. old states, democracy vs. authoritarian regime;

"strong" = 50%–99% higher support for the postulated element;

"moderate" = 25%–49% higher support;

"modest" = 10%–24% higher support.

10 The expectation of a link between vulnerability to crisis escalation and conflict setting, capability and age is not supported.

11 On the related themes of geographic contiguity and territory as sources of *war*, see, respectively: Bremer, 1992, 312–313, 321–322; Diehl, 1985; Diehl and Goertz, 1988, and Vasquez, 1993 (forthcoming), Chaps. 1,4, 9.

12 On the related theme of the link between the number of actors and the propensity to *war*, see Vasquez, 1993 (forthcoming), Chap. 4.

13 Conceptual rigidity (or a "closed mind") depends not only on stress but also on such contextual factors as personality and decision-making style. It may also depend on the level of stress. Thus the extent of rigidity will depend upon the interaction between stress and other conditions. However, for this exercise, the hypothesis is being tested as framed, namely, the link between rigidity and stress.

14 On a crucial related question, namely, who is right about crisis behavior, Realists or political psychologists, a forthcoming study (Leng, 1993: 262–267) concludes that the findings from a sample of 40 crises between 1816 and 1980 "support a middle ground explanation. . . ." Three types of evidence support the classical Realist contention: the "strong association . . . between the crisis structure and war or nonwar crisis outcomes . . ."; "the association between major power involvement and peaceful crisis outcomes"; and "some evidence in support of the [coercive] bargaining prescriptions of conflict strategists . . .".

The latter is seriously challenged by "the high degree of tit-for-tat found in the responses to both coercive and cooperative influence attempts, and in the tendency of escalating coercive Bullying influence strategies to lead to war." In sum, "there is some validity to both . . . perspectives, but . . . neither can offer a sufficient description [of reality] on its own." The best approach to crisis bargaining is a prudent application of the precepts of both schools, Realism and Reciprocity.

15 On the related, general theme of crisis management by states, as distinct from the role of third parties, Stern and Sundelius (1992) cautioned, as has this book, against the bias in much of the crisis literature in favor of major power crises and cases characterized by power symmetry. The "wave of the future," as suggested above, is most likely to be asymmetrical crises in power terms or crises between small states. Thus their advice to devote more attention to these types of crisis is salutary.

Appendix A

1 The interstate politics of subsystems, as noted, are more permissive than those of the dominant system. This extends to the eruption of crises and the use of violence by crisis adversaries. As such, the level of *value threat* perceived by the antagonists is likely to be higher: existence will rarely be perceived to be at risk in the dominant system, except in cataclysmic system wars; but a threat to existence is not abnormal in subsystem conflicts, wars and crises. This is compounded by the greater tendency of subsystem states to be newer, weaker, smaller and less stable entities.

2 Conflict setting also affects perceptions of *value threat* by the contending parties. In a protracted conflict, rivalry, mistrust, disputes, and the persistent expectation of violence from adversaries leads to perceived value threat at the outset, and to escalation from low to high values, especially if a conflict persists for an extended period.

3 The argument can be extended by establishing links between domestic instability, caused by power discrepancy, and both *regime duration* and *conflict setting*, the latter through a propensity of unstable regimes to protracted conflict. However, both of these are *indirect* linkages and are therefore excluded from this ranking exercise.

4 Capability has an interesting indirect effect on conflict setting which is worth noting. States with a negative power discrepancy will avoid a protracted conflict where possible. Stated differently, PCs are more likely between states with power parity. This, in turn, helps to explain why a protracted conflict tends to be chronic, rather than being resolved decisively through military confrontation.

5 Power discrepancy is also linked to *threatened values*. All other things being equal, a state will feel less threatened by hostile external acts, events or situational changes, the more favorable its power relative to its adversary(ies); that is, the greater security derived from superior power will make a state more impervious to value threats. The obverse is equally true: the weaker a state relative to an adversary, the graver will be its perceived value threat from that adversary. Moreover, weakness is also likely to lead decision-makers of the target state to adopt change in order to cope with the power discrepancy and the identified value threat.

6 Proximity is also more likely to generate a perception of *value threat* from a hostile (near)-neighbor than from one far from one's borders. Contiguity will sharpen such a perception.

7 The decision-makers of a new or recently-formed regime will be more prone than those of older regimes to perceive value threats from abroad.

8 A small state is more likely than a large one to perceive a high *value threat*—because of its diminished capacity to cope with external sources of threat.

9 The perception of *value threat* will also be affected for the same reason. Instability at home will undermine the self-confidence of an unstable state's rulers. Among other consequences, they will be more likely to exaggerate threatening acts or events that pose a danger to one or more basic values of the less secure, unstable state.

10 The centrality of *values* among the conditions of crisis onset is also evident in the fact that, as evident from the assessment of variables, they are affected by nine of the ten independent variables in the onset model.

Appendix B

1 Despite the end of the Cold War and military bipolarity in 1989–91, as noted, violence continued to flourish in Third World interstate crises. Moreover, it was massively employed in the Gulf Crisis 1990–91. It reappeared in Europe—in Yugoslavia.

And its ambit widened and deepened in the former USSR—in Armenia/Azerbaijan over the enclave of Nagorno-Karabakh, Georgia and Moldova, in 1991–93. The earlier trend in violence has not changed fundamentally. Yet several high-violence protracted conflicts terminated, e.g., Angola/South Africa, Indo-China. The explanation would seem to lie in the global shift to US-USSR cooperation and the emergence of quasi-unipolarity (US domination), a process sharpened by the demise of the USSR (1991) and its replacement by a much weaker Commonwealth of Independent States in 1991–92.

2 The choice of 6.77 as the lower threshold was based upon the criterion of the subset of "most intense cases", 20 international crises: 6.77 was the lowest overall intensity score among these cases.

3 Two intra-war crises also had global geostrategic salience: Pearl Harbor (1941–42), because of the physical globalization of World War II and the struggle for world mastery between the Axis and the Allied Powers; and Korean War III (1953), because of the US threat to use tactical nuclear weapons against Chinese and North Korean forces on the battlefield and its implications for members of the global system.

References

Books and Articles

ACHEN, Christopher H. and Duncan SNIDAL. "Rational Deterrence Theory and Comparative Case Studies," *World Politics*, **41**, 2 (1989), 143–169.

ADOMEIT, Hannes. *Soviet Risk-Taking and Crisis Behavior: A Theoretical and Empirical Analysis.* London: Allen and Unwin, 1982.

ALLAN, Pierre. *Crisis Bargaining and the Arms Race: A Theoretical Model.* Cambridge, MA: Ballinger, 1983.

ALLISON, Graham T. *The Essence of Decision: Explaining the Cuban Missile Crisis.* Boston: Little, Brown, 1971.

ALTFELD, Michael F. "Arms Races?—And Escalation? A Comment on Wallace," *International Studies Quarterly*, **27**, 2 (1983), 225–231.

ANDERTON, Charles H. "A Selected Bibliography of Arms Race Models and Related Subjects," *Conflict Management and Peace Science*, **8**, 2 (1985), 99–122.

ANDRIOLE, Stephen J. "The Levels-of-Analysis Problems and the Study of Foreign, International, and Global Affairs: A Review Critique and Another Final Solution," *International Interactions*, **5**, 2–3 (1978), 113–133.

ANDRIOLE, Stephen J. and Gerald W. HOPPLE. "The Rise and Fall of Event Data: From Basic Research to Applied Use in the U.S. Department of Defense," *International Interactions*, **10**, 3–4 (1985), 293–309.

ANDRIOLE, Stephen J. and Robert A. YOUNG. "Toward the Development of an Integrated Crisis Warning System," *International Studies Quarterly*, **21**, 1 (1977), 107–150.

ANGLIN, Douglas G. *Zambian Crisis Behavior: UDI in Rhodesia, 1965–66.* Montreal: McGill–Queen's Press (forthcoming, 1993).

ANGLIN, Douglas G. "Zambian Crisis Behavior: Rhodesia's Unilateral Declaration of Independence," *International Studies Quarterly*, **24**, 4 (1980), 581–616.

ARON, Raymond. *Peace and War.* New York: Doubleday, 1966.

ARON, Raymond. *On War.* New York: Doubleday, 1959.

ARON, Raymond. "Conflict and War from the Viewpoint of Historical Sociology," in *The Nature of Conflict.* Paris: UNESCO, 1957.

ASHLEY, Richard K. *The Political Economy of War and Peace.* London: Frances Pinter, and New York: Nichols, 1980.

AXELROD, Robert (ed.). *Structure of Decision: The Cognitive Maps of Political Elites.* Princeton, NJ: Princeton University Press, 1976.

AZAR, Edward E. "Protracted International Conflicts: Ten Propositions," *International Interactions*, **12**, 1 (1985), 59–70.

AZAR, Edward E. "Peace Amidst Development: A Conceptual Agenda for Conflict and Peace Research," *International Interactions*, **6**, 2 (1979), 123–143.

AZAR, Edward E. "Conflict Escalation and Conflict Reduction in an International Crisis: Suez, 1956," *Journal of Conflict Resolution*, **16**, 2 (1972), 183–201.

AZAR, Edward E. and Joseph D. BEN-DAK (eds.). *Theory and Practice of Events Research: Studies in International Actions and Interactions*. New York: Gordon and Breach, 1975.

AZAR, Edward E., Richard BRODY and Charles A. MCCLELLAND. "International Events Interaction Analysis: Some Research Considerations," *Sage Professional Papers in International Studies*, 02–001. Beverly Hills, CA: Sage, 1972.

AZAR, Edward E. and Nadia FARAH. "The Structure of Inequalities and Protracted Social Conflict: A Theoretical Framework," *International Interactions*, **7**, 4 (1981), 317–335.

AZAR, Edward E., Paul JUREIDINI and Ronald MCLAURIN. "Protracted Social Conflict: Theory and Practice in the Middle East," *Journal of Palestine Studies*, **8**, 1 (1978), 41–60.

AZAR, Edward, E. *et al.* "A System for Forecasting Strategic Crises: Findings and Speculations about Conflict in the Middle East," *International Interactions*, **3** (1977), 193–222.

BARRINGER, Richard E. *War: Patterns of Conflict*. Cambridge, MA: MIT Press, 1972.

BARTLEY, Allan. "The Malvinas/Falklands Crisis: A Case Study of Argentina in Crisis" (Unpub. M.A. paper), 1984.

BAYNHAM, Simon J. (ed.). *Military Power and Politics in Black Africa*. London: Croom Helm, 1986.

BECK, Peter J. "The Future of the Falkland Islands: A Solution Made in Hong Kong?" *International Affairs* (London), **61**, 4 (1985), 643–660.

BECK, Robert J. "Munich's Lessons Reconsidered," *International Security*, **14**, 2 (1989), 161–191.

BEER, Francis. *Peace Against War*. San Francisco: Freeman, 1981.

BELL, Coral. *The Conventions of Crisis: A Study in Diplomatic Management*. London: Oxford University Press, for the Royal Institute of International Affairs, 1971.

BEN-ZVI, Abraham. "Hindsight and Foresight: A Conceptual Framework for the Analysis of Surprise Attacks," *World Politics*, **28**, 3 (1976), 381–395.

BEN-ZVI, Abraham. "American Preconditions and Policies Toward Japan, 1940–41: A Case Study in Misperception," *International Studies Quarterly*, **19**, 2 (1975), 228–248.

BERGESEN, Albert. "Crises in the World-System: An Introduction," in Albert BERGESEN (ed.), *Crisis in the World-System*. Beverly Hills, CA: Sage, 1983, 9–17.

BERKOWITZ, Leonard. *Aggression: A Social Psychological Analysis*. New York: McGraw-Hill, 1962.

BETTS, Richard K. "Surprise, Scholasticism, and Strategy: A Review of Ariel Levite's *Intelligence and Strategic Surprises*," *International Studies Quarterly*, **33**, 3 (1989), 329–343.

BETTS, Richard K. *Surprise Attack*. Washington, D.C.: Brookings Institution, 1982.

BETTS, Richard K. "Analysis, War and Decisions: Why Intelligence Failures Are Inevitable," *World Politics*, **31**, 1 (1977), 61–89.

BETTS, Richard K. *Soldiers, Statesmen, and Cold War Crises*. Cambridge, MA: Harvard University Press, 1977; New York: Columbia University Press, 1991.

BLAINEY, Geoffrey. *The Causes of War*. New York: Free Press, 1973.

BLECHMAN, Barry M. and Stephen S. KAPLAN. *Force Without War: U.S. Armed Forces as a Political Instrument*. Washington, D.C.: Brookings Institution, 1978.

BOBROW, Davis B., Steve CHAN and John A. KRINGEN. *Understanding Foreign Policy Decisions: The Chinese Case*. New York: Free Press, 1979.

BOBROW, Davis B., Steve CHAN and John A. KRINGEN. "Understanding How Others Treat Crises: A Multimethod Approach," *International Studies Quarterly*, **21**, 1 (1977), 199–223.

BOHLEN, Charles E. *The Transformation of American Foreign Policy*. New York: Norton, 1969.

BONHAM, G. Matthew and Michael J. SHAPIRO. "Explanation of the Unexpected: The Syrian Intervention in Jordan in 1970," in Robert AXELROD (ed.), *Structure of Decision: The Cognitive Maps of Political Elites*. Princeton, NJ: Princeton University Press, 1976, 113–141.

BONHAM, G. Matthew and Thomas L. TRUMBLE. "The October War: Changes in Cognitive Orientation Toward the Middle East Conflict," *International Studies Quarterly*, **23**, 1 (1979), 3–44.

BOULDING, Kenneth E. *Conflict and Defense: A General Theory*. New York: Harper, 1962.

BOULDING, Kenneth E. *The Economy of Peace*. New York: Prentice-Hall, 1946.

BRACKEN, Paul. *The Command and Control of Nuclear Forces*. New Haven, CT: Yale University Press, 1983.

BRADY, Linda P. *Threat, Decision Time and Awareness: The Impact of Situational Variables on Foreign Policy Behavior*. (Unpub. Ph.D. Diss.), Ohio State University, 1974.

BRAMS, Steven J. *Superpower Games: Applying Game Theory to Superpower Conflict*, New Haven, CT: Yale University Press, 1985.

BRAMS, Steven J. and D. Marc KILGOUR. *Game Theory and National Security*. New York: Basil Blackwell, 1988.

BRAMS, Steven J. and D. Marc KILGOUR. "Winding Down if Preemption or Escalation Occurs," *Journal of Conflict Resolution*, **31**, 4 (1987), 547–572.

BRECHER, Michael. "Turning Points: Reflections on Many Paths to Knowledges," in J. KRUZEL and James N. RASENAU (eds.). *Journeys Through World Politics*. Lexington, MA: Lexington Books, 1989, 119–135.

BRECHER, Michael. "International Crises and Protracted Conflicts," *International Interactions*, **11**, 3–4 (1984), 237–297.

BRECHER, Michael. "Non-Alignment Under Stress: The West and the India-China Border War," *Pacific Affairs*, **52**, 4 (1979–80), 612–630.

BRECHER, Michael. "State Behavior in International Crisis: A Model," *Journal of Conflict Resolution*, **23**, 3 (1979), 446–480.

BRECHER, Michael. "Toward a Theory of International Crisis Behavior," *International Studies Quarterly*, **21**, 1 (1977), 39–74.

BRECHER, Michael. *Decisions in Israel's Foreign Policy*. London: Oxford University Press, and New Haven, CT: Yale University Press, 1974.

BRECHER, Michael. *The Foreign Policy System of Israel: Setting, Images, Process*. London: Oxford University Press, and New Haven, CT: Yale University Press, 1972.

BRECHER, Michael. *The Struggle for Kashmir*. Toronto: Ryerson Press, 1953.

BRECHER, Michael and Hemda BEN YEHUDA. "System and Crisis in International Politics," *Review of International Studies*, **11**, 1 (1985), 17–36.

BRECHER, Michael with Benjamin GEIST. *Decisions in Crisis: Israel, 1967 and 1973*. Berkeley and Los Angeles: University of California Press, 1980.

BRECHER, Michael and Patrick JAMES. "Patterns of Crisis Management," *Journal of Conflict Resolution*, **32**, 3 (1988).

BRECHER, Michael and Patrick JAMES. *Crisis and Change in World Politics*. Boulder, CO: Westview Press, 1986.

BRECHER, Michael and Jonathan WILKENFELD. "International Crises and Global Instability: The Myth of the 'Long Peace'," in Charles W. KEGLEY, Jr. (ed.). *The Long PostWar Peace*. New York: HarperCollins, 1991, 85—104.

BRECHER, Michael and Jonathan WILKENFELD. *Crisis, Conflict and Instability*. Oxford: Pergamon Press, 1989.

BRECHER, Michael and Jonathan WILKENFELD. *Crises in the Twentieth Century, Vol. I: Handbook of International Crises*. Oxford: Pergamon Press, 1988.

BRECHER, Michael, Patrick JAMES and Jonathan WILKENFELD. "Polarity and Stability: New Concepts, Indicators and Evidence," *International Interactions*, **16**, 1 (1990), 69–100.

BREMER, Stuart A. "Dangerous Dyads," *Journal of Conflict Resolution*, 36, 2 (1992), 309–341.

BREMER, Stuart A. "The Contagiousness of Coercion: The Spread of Serious International Disputes, 1900–1976," *International Interactions*, **9**, 1 (1982), 29–55.

BRODIE, Bernard. *War and Politics*. New York: MacMillan, 1973.

BROWN, Seyom. *The Causes and Prevention of War*. New York: St. Martin's Press, 1987.

BUENO de MESQUITA, Bruce. "The Contribution of Expected-Utility Theory to the Study of International Conflict," in Manus I. MIDLARSKY (ed.), *Handbook of War Studies*. Boston: Unwin Hyman, 1989, Chap. 6.

BUENO de MESQUITA, Bruce. "Toward A Scientific Understanding of International Conflict: A Personal View," *International Studies Quarterly*, **29**, 2 (1985), 121–136, 151–154.

BUENO de MESQUITA, Bruce. "The War Trap Revisited: A Revised Expected Utility Model," *American Political Science Review*, **79**, 1 (1985), 156–177.

BUENO de MESQUITA, Bruce. *The War Trap*. New Haven, CT: Yale University Press, 1981.

BUENO de MESQUITA, Bruce. "System Polarization and the Occurrence and Duration of War," *Journal of Conflict Resolution*, **22**, 2 (1978), 241–267.

BUENO de MESQUITA, Bruce. "Measuring Systemic Polarity," *Journal of Conflict Resolution*, **19**, 2 (1975), 187–216.

BUENO de MESQUITA, Bruce and David LALMAN. *War and Reason*. New Haven, CT: Yale University Press, 1992.

BUENO de MESQUITA, Bruce, Robert W. JACKMAN and Randolph M. SIVERSON (eds.). "Democracy and Foreign Policy: Community and Constraint," *Journal of Conflict Resolution*, **35**, 2 (1991), 181–381 (Special Issue).

BULL, Hedley. "International Theory: The Case for a Classical Approach," *World Politics*, **18**, 3 (1966), 361–377.

BURGESS, Phillip M. and Raymond W. LAWTON. *Indicators of International Behavior: An Assessment of Events Data Research*, Sage Professional Papers, International Studies, Vol. 1. Beverly Hills, CA: Sage, 1972.

BURKE, John P. and Fred I. GREENSTEIN. *How Presidents Test Reality: Decisions on Vietnam, 1954 and 1965*. New York: Russell Sage Foundation, 1989.

BURROWES, Robert and Douglas MUZZIO. "The Road to the Six Day War: Aspects of an Enumerative History of Four Arab States and Israel, 1965–67," *Journal of Conflict Resolution*, **16**, 2 (1972), 211–226.

BUTOW, Robert J. C. *Tojo and the Coming of War*. Princeton, NJ: Princeton University Press, 1961.

BUTOW, Robert J. C. *Japan's Decision to Surrender*. Stanford, CA: Stanford University Press, 1954.

CALAHAN, H. A. *What Makes a War End*. New York: Vanguard Press, 1944.

CANDELA, C. *Decision-Making During Crises: A Literature Review*. Baltimore, MD: Bendix Corporation, Applied Sciences Technology Division, 1974.

CARR, Edward H. *The Twenty Years Crisis, 1919–1939*. London and New York: Macmillan, 1939.

CARROLL, Berenice A. "War Termination and Conflict Theory: Value Premises, Theories and Policies," in W. T. R. FOX (ed.), *How Wars End*. The Annals, **392** (Nov. 1970), 14–29.

CARROLL, Berenice A. "How Wars End: An Analysis of Some Current Hypotheses," *Journal of Peace Research*, **4** (1969), 295–321.

CHAMBERLAIN, Neville. *The Struggle for Peace*. London: Hutchinson, 1939.

CHAN, Steve. "Mirror, Mirror on the Wall . . . Are the Freer Countries more Pacific?" *Journal of Conflict Resolution*, **28**, 4 (1984), 617–648.

CHAN, Steve. "The Intelligence of Stupidity: Understanding Failures in Strategic Warning," *American Political Science Review*, **73**, 1 (1979), 171–80.

CHAN, Steve. "Chinese Conflict Calculus and Behavior: Assessment from a Perspective of Conflict Management," *World Politics*, **30**, 3 (1978), 391–410.

CHAN, Steve and Davis B. BOBROW. "Horse Races, Security Markets and Foreign Relations: Some Implications and Evidence for Crisis Prediction," *Journal of Conflict Resolution*, **25**, 2 (1981), 187–236.

CHARLTON, Michael. *The Little Platoon: Diplomacy and the Falklands Dispute*. Oxford: Basil Blackwell, 1989.

CHASE-DUNN, Christopher K. "Comparative Research on World-System Characteristics," *International Studies Quarterly*, **23**, 4 (1979), 601–623.

CHOUCRI, Nazli and Robert C. NORTH. "Lateral Pressure in International Relations: Concept and Theory," in Manus I. MIDLARSKY (ed.), *Handbook of War Studies*. Boston: Unwin Hyman, 1989, Chap. 12.

CHOUCRI, Nazli and Robert C. North. *Nations in Conflict: National Growth and International Violence*. San Francisco: W. H. Freeman, 1975.

CIMBALA, Stephen J. *Nuclear Endings: Stopping War on Time*. New York: Praeger, 1987.

CIOFFI-REVILLA, Claudio. "The Political Reliability of Italian Governments: An Exponential Survival Model," *American Political Science Review*, **78**, 2 (1984), 318–337.

CLAUDE, Inis L., Jr. *Power and International Relations*. New York: Random House, 1962.

CLAUSEWITZ, Karl von. *On War*. Trans. and ed. Michael HOWARD and Peter PARET. Princeton, NJ: Princeton University Press, 1976. (First published in German, 1832).

COHEN, Raymond. *Threat Perception in International Crisis*. Madison, WI: University of Wisconsin Press, 1979.

CONVERSE, Elizabeth. "The War of All Against All: A Review of The Journal of Conflict Resolution, 1957–1968," *Journal of Conflict Resolution*, **XII**, 4 (1968), 471–532.

CORSON, Walter H. *Conflict and Cooperation in East-West Crises*. (Unpub. Ph.D. Diss.), Harvard University, 1970.

COSER, Lewis A. "Conflict: Social Aspects," in David A. SILLS (ed.), *International Encyclopedia of the Social Sciences*, **3**, 232–236. London: Collier-Macmillan, 1968.

COSER, Lewis A. "Termination of Conflict," *Journal of Conflict Resolution*, **V**, 4 (1961), 347–353.

COX, Robert W. and Harold K. JACOBSON. *The Anatomy of Influence*. New Haven, CT: Yale University Press, 1974.

CRAIG, Gordon A. *The Politics of the Prussian Army, 1640–1945*. New York: Oxford University Press, 1955.

CROCI, Osvaldo. *The Trieste Crisis, 1953*. (Unpub. Ph.D. Diss.), McGill University, 1991.

DANCHEV, Alex. "Life and Death in the South Atlantic," *Review of International Studies*, **17**, 3 (1991), 305–312.

DAVIS, Paul K. and Barry WOLF. "Behavioral Factors in Nuclear Crisis De-escalation," in Joseph E. NATION (ed.), *The De-escalation of Nuclear Crises*. New York: St. Martin's Press, 1992, 77–102.

DAWISHA, Adeed I. *Syria and the Lebanese Crisis*. London: MacMillan, 1980.

DAWISHA, Karen. *The Kremlin and the Prague Spring*. Berkeley and Los Angeles: University of California Press, 1984.

DE RIVERA, Joseph H. *The Psychological Dimension of Foreign Policy*. Columbus, OH: C. E. Merrill Publications Co., 1968.

DECALO, Samuel. *Coups and Army Rule in Africa: Studies in Military Style*. New Haven, CT: Yale University Press, 1976.

DESSLER, David. "Beyond Correlations: Toward a Causal Theory of War," *International Studies Quarterly*, **35**, 3 (1991), 337–355.

DEUTSCH, Karl W. *Politics and Government*. Boston: Houghton Mifflin, 1974.

DEUTSCH, Karl W. and J. David Singer. "Multipolar Power Systems and International Stability," *World Politics*, **XVI**, 3 (1964), 390–406.

DEUTSCH, Morton. *The Resolution of Conflict: Constructive and Destructive Processes*. New Haven, CT: Yale University Press, 1973.

DIEHL, Paul F. "Arms Races to War: Testing Some Empirical Linkages," *The Sociological Quarterly*, **26, 3** (1985), 331–349.

DIEHL, Paul F. "Arms Races and Escalation: A Closer Look," *Journal of Peace Research*, **20**, 3 (1983), 205–212.

DIEHL, Paul F. and Gary GOERTZ. "Territorial Changes and Militarized Conflict," *Journal of Conflict Resolution*, 32, 1 (1988), 103–122.

DIEHL, Paul F. and Jean KINGSTON. "Messenger or Message? Military Buildups and the Initiation of Conflict," *Journal of Politics*, **49**, 4 (1987), 789–799.

DILKS, David (ed.). *The Diaries of Sir Alexander Cadogan, O.M., 1938–1945*. London: Macmillan, 1971.

DOLLARD, John, Leonard W. DOOB, Neal E. MILLER, *et al. Frustration and Aggression*. New Haven, CT: Yale University Press, 1939.

DOMKE, William K. *War and the Changing Global System*. New Haven, CT: Yale University Press, 1988.

DOUGHERTY, James E. and Robert L. Pfaltzgraff, Jr. *Contending Theories of International Relations*. Philadelphia: J. B. Lippincott Co., 1971.

DOWNS, George W. "The Rational Deterrence Debate," *World Politics*, **41**, 2 (1989), 225–37.

DOWTY, Alan. *Middle East Crisis: US Decision-Making in 1958, 1970 and 1973*. Berkeley and Los Angeles: University of California Press, 1984.

DOYLE, Michael W. "Liberalism and World Politics," *American Political Science Review*, **80**, 4 (1986), 1151–69.

EARLE, Edward M. (ed.). *Makers of Modern Strategy: Military Thought from Machiavelli to Hitler*. Princeton, NJ: Princeton University Press, 1943.

EBERWEIN, Wolf-Dieter. "The Quantitative Study of International Conflict: Quantity and Quality?" *Journal of Peace Research*, **XVIII**, 1 (1981), 19–38.

ECKHARDT, William and Edward E. AZAR. "Major World Conflicts and Interventions, 1945–1975," *International Interactions*, **5**, 1 (1978), 75–110.

ECKSTEIN, Harry. "Case Study and Theory in Political Science," in Fred I. GREENSTEIN and Nelson W. POLSBY (eds.), *Handbook of Political Science: Strategies of Inquiry*. Vol. VII. Reading, MA: Addison, Wesley, 1975, 79–137.

EIBL-EIBESFELT, Irenaus. *The Biology of Peace and War*. New York: Viking, 1979.

ELLSBERG, Daniel. "The Theory and Practice of Blackmail" (Unpub. lecture, Lowell Institute, Boston, 1959, discussed in Snyder and Diesing [1977]: 48–52, 191–192).

EMBER, Carol R., Melvin EMBER and Bruce RUSSETT. "Peace Between Participatory Polities: A Cross-Cultural Test of the 'Democracies Rarely Fight Each Other' Hypothesis," *World Politics*, **44**, 4 (1992) 573–599.

FALK, Richard A. and Samuel S. KIM (eds.). *The War System: An Interdisciplinary Approach*. Boulder, CO: Westview Press, 1980.

FALK, Richard A. and Saul H. MENDLOVITZ (eds.). *Regional Politics and World Order*. San Francisco: W. H. Freeman, 1973.

FALKOWSKI, Lawrence S. *Presidents, Secretaries of State, and Crisis in US Foreign Relations: A Model and Predictive Analysis*. Boulder, CO: Westview Press, 1979.

FARNHAM, Barbara (ed.). "Prospect Theory and Political Psychology," *Political Psychology*, 13, 2 (1992), 167–329. (Special Tone).

FERRIS, Wayne H. *The Power Capabilities of Nation-States*. Lexington, MA: Lexington Books, 1973.

FINER, Samuel E. *The Man on Horseback: The Role of the Military in Politics*. London: Pall Mall Press, 1962.

FINK, Clinton F. "Some Conceptual Difficulties in the Theory of Social Conflict," *Journal of Conflict Resolution*, **XII**, 4 (1968), 412–459.

FONTAINE, André. *History of The Cold War*. New York: Pantheon, 1968.

FOX, William T. R. "The Causes of Peace and Conditions of War," in W. T. R. FOX (ed.), *How Wars End. The Annals*, **392** (November 1970), 1–13.

FREI, Daniel (ed.). *Managing International Crises*. Beverly Hills, CA: Sage, 1982.

FREUD, Sigmund. *Great Political Thinkers: Plato to the Present*. Geneva: League of Nations: International Institute of Intellectual Cooperation (September 1932), 804–810.

FROMM, Erich. *The Anatomy of Human Destructiveness*. New York: Holt, Rinehart and Winston, 1973.

FROMM, Erich. *Escape from Freedom*. New York: Holt, Rinehart and Winston, 1941.

FUKUYAMA, Francis. *The End of History and the Last Man*. New York: Free Press, 1992.

GADDIS, John L. "Great Illusions, the Long Peace, and the Future of the International System," in Charles W. KEGLEY, Jr. (ed.), *The Long PostWar Peace*. New York: HarperCollins, 1991, Chap. 2.

GADDIS, John L. *The Long Peace: Inquiries into the History of the Cold War*. New York: Oxford University Press, 1987.

GADDIS, John L. "The Long Peace: Elements of Stability in the Postwar International System," *International Security*, **10**, 4 (1986), 99–142.

GADDIS, John L. *Strategies of Containment: A Critical Appraisal of Postwar American National Security Policy*. New York: Oxford University Press, 1982.

GAENSLEN, Fritz. "Culture and Decision Making in China, Japan, Russia and the United States," *World Politics*, **39**, 1 (1986), 78–103.

GALTUNG, Johan. "Institutionalized Conflict Resolution," *Journal of Peace Research*, **4** (1965), 348–397.

GAMBA, Virginia. *The Falklands/Malvinas War*. London: Allen and Unwin, 1987.

GARFINKLE, Adam M. "Crisis Decision Making: The Banality of Theory," *Orbis*, **30**, 1 (1986), 12–41.

GARNHAM, David. "The Causes of War: Systemic Findings," in Alan Ned SABROSKY (ed.), *Polarity and War: The Changing Structure of International Conflict*. Boulder, CO: Westview Press, 1985, 7–23.

GEIST, Benjamin. *Hungary 1956: Crisis Decision-Making in a Socialist State* (forthcoming).

GEORGE, Alexander L. (ed.). *Avoiding War: Problems of Crisis Management*. Boulder, CO: Westview Press, 1991.

GEORGE, Alexander L. "Crisis Management: The Interaction of Political and Military Considerations," *Survival*, **24**, 1 (1984), 223–234.

GEORGE, Alexander L., "Case Studies and Theory Development," in Paul G. LAUREN (ed.), *Diplomacy: New Approaches in History, Theory and Policy*. New York: Free Press, 1979, 43–68.

GEORGE, Alexander L. "The Operational Code: A Neglected Approach to the Study of Political Leaders and Decision Making," *International Studies Quarterly*, **13**, 2 (1969), 190–222.

GEORGE, Alexander L. and Juliet L. GEORGE. *Woodrow Wilson and Colonel House*. New York: Dover Publications, 1964.

GEORGE, Alexander L. and Richard SMOKE. "Deterrence in Foreign Policy," *World Politics*, **41**, 2 (1989), 170–182.

GEORGE, Alexander L. and Richard SMOKE. *Deterrence in American Foreign Policy*. New York: Columbia University Press, 1974.

GEORGE, Alexander L., D. K. HALL and W. E. SIMONS. *The Limits of Coercive Diplomacy*. Boston: Little, Brown, 1971.

GILBERT, Arthur N. and Paul G. LAUREN. "Crisis Management: An Assessment and Critique," *Journal of Conflict Resolution*, **24**, 4 (1980), 641–664.

GILPIN, Robert. "The Theory of Hegemonic War," in Robert I. ROTBERG and Theodore K. RABB (eds.), *The Origin and Prevention of Major Wars*. Cambridge: Cambridge University Press, 1989, 15–37.

GILPIN, Robert. *War and Change in World Politics*. Cambridge: Cambridge University Press, 1981.

GLAD, Betty (ed.). *Psychological Dimensions of War*. Newbury Park, CA: Sage, 1990.

GLASSMAN, Jon D. *Arms for the Arabs: The Soviet Union and War in the Middle East*. Baltimore, MD: John Hopkins University Press, 1975.

GOCHMAN, Charles S. and Zeev MAOZ. "Militarized Interstate Disputes, 1816–1976: Procedures, Patterns, Insights," *Journal of Conflict Resolution*, **28**, 4 (1984), 585–615.

GOCHMAN, Charles S. and A. Ned SABROSKY (eds.). *Prisoners of War? Nation-States in the Modern Era*. Lexington, MA: Lexington Books, 1990.

GOLAN, Galia. "Soviet Decisionmaking in the Yom Kippur War, 1973," in Jiri VALENTA and William C. POTTER (eds.), *Soviet Decisionmaking for National Security*. Boston: George Allen & Unwin, 1984, Chap. 8.

GOLAN, Galia. *Yom Kippur and After: The Soviet Union and the Middle East Crisis*. Cambridge: Cambridge University Press, 1977.

GOLDSTEIN, Joshua S. *Long Cycles: Prosperity and War in the Modern Age*. New Haven, CT: Yale University Press, 1988.

GOLDSTEIN, Joshua S. and John R. FREEMAN. *Three-Way Street: Strategic Reciprocity in World Politics*. Chicago: University of Chicago Press, 1990.

GURR, Ted R. (ed.). *Handbook of Political Conflict: Theory and Research*. New York: Free Press, 1980.

HAAS, Ernst B. *Why We Still Need the United Nations*. University of California Policy Papers in International Affairs, No. 26. Berkeley, CA: Institute of International Studies, 1986.

HAAS, Ernst B. "Regime Decay: Conflict Management and International Organizations, 1945–1981," *International Organization*, **37**, 2 (1983), 189–256.

HAAS, Michael. "Research on International Crisis: Obsolescence of an Approach?" *International Interactions*, **13**, 1 (1986), 23–58.

HAAS, Michael. *International Conflict*. Indianapolis, IN: Bobbs-Merrill, 1974.

HAAS, Michael. "International Subsystems: Stability and Polarity," *American Political Science Review*, **64**, 2 (1970), 98–123.

HALIFAX, Lord Edward. *Fulness of Days*. London: Collins, 1957.

HALLE, Louis J. *The Cold War as History*. New York: Harper, Row, 1967.

HALPER, Thomas. *Foreign Policy Crises: Appearance and Reality in Decision-Making.* Columbus, OH: Charles Merrill, 1971.

HANDEL, Michael I. *War Termination—A Critical Survey.* Jerusalem Papers on Peace Problems, 24. Jerusalem: Hebrew University, 1978.

HANDEL, Michael I. "The Yom Kippur War and the Inevitability of Surprise," *International Studies Quarterly*, **21**, 3 (1977), 461–502.

HARKABI, Yehoshafat. *War and Strategy.* Tel Aviv: Maarachot, 1990 (Hebrew).

HARVEY, Frank and Patrick JAMES. "Nuclear Deterrence Theory: The Record of Aggregate Testing and an Alternative Research Agenda," *Conflict Management and Peace Science*, 12, 1 (1992), 17–45.

HASTINGS, Max and Simon JENKINS. *The Battle for The Falklands.* London: Michael Joseph, 1983.

HAZLEWOOD, Leo, John J. HAYES and James R. BROWNELL, Jr. "Planning for Problems in Crisis Management: An Analysis of Post-1945 Behavior in the U.S. Department of Defense," *International Studies Quarterly*, **21**, 1 (1977), 75–106.

HEAD, Richard G., Frisco W. SHORT and Robert C. McFARLANE. *Crisis Resolution: Presidential Decision-Making in the Mayaguez and Korean Confrontations.* Boulder, CO: Westview Press, 1978.

HENDERSON, Sir Neville. *Failure of a Mission.* London: Hodder and Stoughton, 1940.

HEREK, Gregory M., Irving L. JANIS and Paul HUTH. "Decision-Making During International Crises: Is Quality of Process Related to Outcome?," *Journal of Conflict Resolution*, **31**, 2 (1987), 203–226.

HEREK, Gregory M., Irving L. JANIS and Paul HUTH. "Quality of U.S. Decision-Making During the Cuban Missile Crisis: Major Errors in Welch's Reassessment," *Journal of Conflict Resolution*, **33**, 3 (1989), 446–459.

HERMANN, Charles F. "Enhancing Crisis Stability: Correcting the Trend Toward Increasing Instability," in Gilbert R. WINHAM (ed.), *New Issues in International Crisis Management.* Boulder, CO: Westview Press, 1988, 121–149.

HERMANN, Charles F. "Indicators of International Political Crises: Some Initial Steps Toward Prediction," in Edward E. AZAR and Joseph D. BEN-DAK (eds.), *Theory and Practice of Events Research.* New York: Gordon and Breach, 1975, 233–243.

HERMANN, Charles F. "Threat, Time and Surprise: A Simulation of International Crisis," in Charles F. HERMANN (ed.), *International Crises: Insights from Behavioral Research.* New York: Free Press, 1972a, 187–211.

HERMANN, Charles F. (ed.). *International Crises: Insights from Behavioral Research.* New York: Free Press, 1972b.

HERMANN, Charles F. *Crises in Foreign Policy: A Simulation Analysis.* Indianapolis, IN: Bobbs-Merrill, 1969a.

HERMANN, Charles F. "International Crisis as a Situational Variable," in James N. ROSENAU (ed.), *International Politics and Foreign Policy*, rev. ed., New York: Free Press, 1969b, 409–421.

HERMANN, Charles F. "Some Consequences of Crisis which Limit the Viability of Organizations," *Administrative Science Quarterly*, **VIII**, 1963, 61–82.

HERMANN, Charles F. and Linda P. BRADY. "Alternative Models of International Crisis Behavior," in Charles F. HERMANN (ed.), *International Crises: Insights From Behavioral Research.* New York: Free Press, 1972, 281–303.

HERMANN, Charles F. and Robert E. MASON. "Identifying Behavioral Attributes of

Events That Trigger International Crises," in Ole R. HOLSTI, Randolph M. SIVERSON, and Alexander L. GEORGE (eds.), *Change in the International System*. Boulder, CO: Westview Press, 1980, 189–210.

HERMANN, Margaret G. "Indicators of Stress in Policymakers During Foreign Policy Crises," *Political Psychology*, 1 (1979), 27–46.

HERSH, Seymour M. *The Samson Option: Israel's Nuclear Arsenal and American Foreign Policy*. New York: Random House, 1991.

HERZ, John H. *Political Realism and Political Idealism*. Chicago: University of Chicago Press, 1951.

HERZ, John H. "Idealist Internationalism and the Security Dilemma," *World Politics*, II, 2 (1950), 157–180.

HEWITT, J. Joseph, Mark A. BOYER and Jonathan WILKENFELD. "Crisis Interactions Among States in Protracted Conflict" (Unpub. paper, 1991).

HILTON, Gordon. "The 1914 Studies: A Reassessment of the Evidence and Some Further Thoughts," *Peace Research Society (International) Papers*, 13 (1969), 117–141.

HOFFMANN, Eric P. and Frederic J. FLERON, Jr. (eds.). *The Conduct of Soviet Foreign Policy*. New York: Aldine Pub. Co., 2nd ed., 1980.

HOFFMANN, Stanley. *The State of War*. New York: F. A. Praeger, 1965.

HOFFMANN, Steven A. *India and the China Crisis*. Berkeley and Los Angeles: University of California Press, 1990.

HOLST, Johan J. "Surprise, Signals and Reaction: The Attack on Norway, April 9, 1940—Some Observations," *Cooperation and Conflict*, 1, 1 (1966), 31–45.

HOLSTI, Kalevi J. *Peace and War: Armed Conflicts and International Order, 1648–1989*. Cambridge: Cambridge University Press, 1991.

HOLSTI, Kalevi J. "Resolving International Conflicts: A Taxonomy of Behavior and Some Figures on Procedures," *Journal of Conflict Resolution*, X, 3 (1966), 272–296.

HOLSTI, Kalevi J. *The Dividing Discipline: Hegemony and Diversity in International Theory*. Boston: Allen and Unwin, 1985.

HOLSTI, Ole R. "Crisis Decision Making," in Philip E. TETLOCK, Jo L. HUSBANDS, Robert JERVIS, Paul C. STERN and Charles TILLY (eds.), *Behavior, Society, and Nuclear War*. Vol. I. New York: Oxford University Press, 1989, 8–84.

HOLSTI, Ole R. "Historians, Social Scientists and Crisis Management: An Alternative View," *Journal of Conflict Resolution*, 24, 4 (1980), 665–682.

HOLSTI, Ole R. "Theories of Crisis Decision-Making," in Paul G. LAUREN (ed.), *Diplomacy: New Approaches in History, Theory and Policy*, Chap. 5. New York: Free Press, 1979.

HOLSTI, Ole R. *Crisis, Escalation, War*. Montreal: McGill-Queen's University Press, 1972.

HOLSTI, Ole R. "The 1914 Case," *American Political Science Review*, 59, 2 (1965), 365–378.

HOLSTI, Ole R. and Alexander L. GEORGE. "The Effects of Stress on the Performance of Foreign Policy Makers," *Political Science Annual*, 6 (1975), 255–319.

HOLSTI, Ole R., Richard H. BRODY and Robert C. NORTH. "The Management of International Crises: Affect and Action in American-Soviet Relations," *Journal of Peace Research*, 3–4 (1964), 170–190.

HOLSTI, Ole R., Robert C. NORTH and Richard H. BRODY. "Perception and Action in the 1914 Crisis," in J. David SINGER (ed.), *Quantitative International Politics*. New York: Free Press, 1968, 123–158.

HOOLE, Francis W. and Dina A. ZINNES. *Quantitative International Politics: An Appraisal*. New York: Praeger, 1976.

HOPKINS, Terence K. and Immanuel WALLERSTEIN. "Cyclical Rhythms and Secular Trends of the Capitalist World-Economy," *Review*, **2** (1979), 483–500.

HOPPLE, Gerald W. and Paul J. ROSSA. "International Crisis Analysis: Recent Developments and Future Directions," in Terrence HOPMANN, Dina A. ZINNES and J. David SINGER (eds.), *Cumulation in International Relations Research*. Denver, CO: Monograph Series in World Affairs, vol. 18, book 3, 1981, 65–97.

HORELICK, Arnold L. "The Cuban Missile Crisis: An Analysis of Soviet Calculations and Behavior," *World Politics*, **XVII**, 3 (1964), 363–389.

HOUWELING, Henk W. and Jan G. SICCAMA. *Studies of War*. Dordrecht, The Netherlands: Martinus Nijhoff, 1988.

HOUWELING, Henk W. and Jan G. SICCAMA. "The Epidemiology of War, 1816–1980," *Journal of Conflict Resolution*, **29**, 4 (1985), 641–663.

HOUWELING, Henk W. and Jan G. SICCAMA. "The Arms Race-War Relationships: Why Serious Disputes Matter," *Arms Control*, **2** (September 1981), 157–197.

HOWARD, Michael. *The Causes of War*. Cambridge, MA: Harvard University Press, 2nd ed., 1984.

HOWELL, Llewellyn D. "A Comparative Study of the WEIS and COPDAB Data Sets," *International Studies Quarterly*, **27**, 2 (1983), 149–59.

HUDSON, Michael C. *Arab Politics: The Search for Legitimacy*. New Haven, CT: Yale University Press, 1977.

HUDSON, Michael C. *The Precarious Republic: Political Modernisation in Lebanon*. New York: Random House, 1968.

HUNTINGTON, Samuel P. *The Soldier and the State*. New York: Vintage Books, 1957.

HUTH, Paul. *Extended Deterrence and the Prevention of War*. New Haven, CT: Yale University Press, 1988a.

HUTH, Paul. "Extended Deterrence and the Outbreak of War," *American Political Science Review*, **82**, 2 (1988b), 423–443.

HUTH, Paul and Bruce M. RUSSETT. "Testing Deterrence Theory: Rigor Makes a Difference," *World Politics*, **42**, 4 (1990), 466–501.

HUTH, Paul and Bruce M. RUSSETT. "Deterrence Failure and Crisis Escalation," *International Studies Quarterly*, **32**, 1 (1988), 29–45.

HUTH, Paul. and Bruce M. RUSSETT. "What Makes Deterrence Work? Cases from 1900 to 1980," *World Politics*, **36**, 4 (1984), 496–526.

HYBEL, Alex R. *The Logic of Surprise in International Conflict*. Lexington, MA: Lexington Books, 1986.

IKLE, Fred C. *Every War Must End*. New York: Columbia University Press, 1971.

INTRILIGATOR, Michael D. and Dagobert L. BRITO. "Richardsonian Arms Race Models," in Manus I. MIDLARSKY (ed.), *Handbook of War Studies*. Boston: Unwin Hyman, 1989, Chap. 9.

INTRILIGATOR, Michael D. and Dagobert L. BRITO "Can Arms Races Lead to the Outbreak of War?" *Journal of Conflict Resolution*, **28**, 1 (1984), 63–84.

ISARD, Walter and Charles H. ANDERTON. "Arms Race Models: A Survey and Synthesis," *Conflict Management and Peace Science*, **8**, 2 (1985), 27–98.

JACKSON, Robert H. and Carl G. ROSBERG. "Why Africa's Weak States Persist," *World Politics*, **35**, 1 (1982), 1–24.

JAMES, Patrick, *Structure and Crisis at the International Level*, (in process).

JAMES, Patrick. *Crisis and War*. Montreal: McGill-Queen's University Press, 1988.

JAMES, Patrick. "Conflict and Cohesion: A Review of the Literature and Recommendations for Future Research," *Cooperation and Conflict*, **22**, 1 (1987), 21–33.

JAMES, Patrick and Frank HARVEY. "The Most Dangerous Game: Superpower Rivalry in International Crises, 1948–1985," *Journal of Politics*, **54**, 1 (1992), 25–51.

JAMES, Patrick, Michael BRECHER and Tod HOFFMAN. "International Crises in Africa, 1929–1979: Immediate Severity and Long-Term Importance," *International Interactions*, **14**, 1 (1988), 51–84.

JANIS, Irving L. *Crucial Decisions: Leadership in Policy-making and Crisis Management*. New York: Free Press/Macmillan, 1989.

JANIS, Irving L. *Victims of Groupthink: A Psychological Study of Foreign Policy Decisions and Fiascos*. Boston: Houghton, Mifflin, 1972.

JANIS, Irving L. and Leon MANN. *Decision-Making: A Psychological Analysis of Conflict, Choice and Commitment*. New York: Free Press, 1977.

JARMAN, Alan and Alexander KOUZMIN. "Decision Pathways from Crisis," in Uriel Rosenthal and Bert Pijnenburg (eds.), *Crisis Management and Decision Making*. Dordrecht, The Netherlands: Kluwer Academic Publishers, 1991, 123–157.

JERVIS, Robert. "Rational Deterrence: Theory and Evidence," *World Politics*, **41**, 2 (1989), 183–207.

JERVIS, Robert. "Pluralistic Rigor: A Comment on Bueno de Mesquita," *International Studies Quarterly*, **29**, 2 (1985), 145–149.

JERVIS, Robert. "Cooperation Under The Security Dilemmas," *World Politics*, **30**, 2 (1978), 167–214.

JERVIS, Robert. *Perception and Misperception in International Politics*. Princeton, NJ: Princeton University Press, 1976.

JERVIS, Robert. "The Costs of the Scientific Study of Politics: An Examination of the Stanford Content Analysis Studies," *International Studies Quarterly*, **11**, 4 (1967), 366–393.

JERVIS, Robert, R. Ned LEBOW and Janice G. STEIN (eds.). *Psychology and Deterrence*. Baltimore, MD: Johns Hopkins University Press, 1985.

JUKES, Geoffrey. *Hitler's Stalingrad Decisions*. Berkeley and Los Angeles: University of California Press, 1985.

KAHN, Herman. "Issues of Thermonuclear War Termination," in W. T. R. FOX (ed.), *How Wars End. The Annals*, **392** (November 1970), 133–172.

KAHN, Herman. *On Escalation: Metaphors and Scenarios*. New York: F. A. Praeger, 1965.

KAHN, Herman. *Thinking About the Unthinkable*. New York: Horizon Press, 1962.

KAHN, Herman. *On Thermonuclear War*. Princeton, NJ: Princeton University Press, 1960.

KAHNEMAN, Daniel, and Amos TVERSKY. "Prospect Theory: An Analysis of Decision Under Risk," *Econometrica*, **47**, 2 (1979), 263–291.

KAM, Ephraim. *Surprise Attack: The Victim's Perspective*. Cambridge, MA: Harvard University Press, 1988.

KAPLAN, Morton A. "The New Great Debate: Traditionalism vs. Science in International Relations," *World Politics*, 19, 1 (1966), 1–20.

KAPLAN, Morton A. *System and Process in International Politics*. New York: John Wiley, 1957.

KAPLAN, Stephen S. *Diplomacy of Power: Soviet Armed Forces as a Political Instrument*. Washington, D.C.: Brookings Institution, 1981.

KAUFMAN, Edy. *Crisis in Allende's Chile*. New York: Praeger, 1988.

KECSKEMETI, Paul. "Political Rationality in Ending War," in W. T. R. FOX (ed.), *How Wars End. The Annals*, 392 (November 1970), 105–115.

KECSKEMETI, Paul. *Strategic Surrender*. Stanford, CA: Stanford University Press, 1958.

KENNAN, George F. *Memoirs: 1925–1950*. Boston: Atlantic-Little, Brown, 1967.

KENNAN, George, F. "The Sources of Soviet Conduct," *Foreign Affairs*, XXV, 4 (1947), 566–582.

KEYNES, John Maynard. *The Economic Consequences of the Peace*. New York: Harcourt, Brace and Howe, 1920.

KISSINGER, Henry. *Years of Upheaval*. Boston: Little, Brown, 1982.

KLINGBERG, Frank L. "Predicting the Termination of War: Battle Casualties and Population Losses," *Journal of Conflict Resolution*, X, 2 (1966), 129–171.

KNORR, Klaus. "Failures in National Intelligence Estimates: The Case of the Cuban Missiles," *World Politics*, XVI, 3 (1964), 455–467.

KNORR, Klaus and James N. ROSENAU (eds.). *Contending Approaches to International Politics*. Princeton, NJ: Princeton University Press, 1969.

KOLKO, Joyce and Gabriel. *The Limits of Power*. New York: Harper and Row, 1972.

KRASNER, Stephen. "Toward Understanding in International Relations," *International Studies Quarterly*, 29, 2 (1985), 137–144.

KRATOCHWIL, Friedrich V. *Rules, Norms, and Decisions*. Cambridge: Cambridge University Press, 1990.

KUGLER, Jacek and A. F. K. ORGANSKI. "The Power Transition: A Retrospective and Prospective Evaluation," in Manus I. MIDLARSKY (ed.), *Handbook of War Studies*. Boston: Unwin Hyman, 1989, Chap. 7.

KUPER, Adam and Jessica KUPER (eds.). *The Social Science Encyclopedia*. London: Routledge and Kegan Paul, 1985.

LAKATOS, Imre. "Falsification and the Methodology of Scientific Research Programmes," in Imre LAKATOS and Alan MUSGRAVE (eds.), *Criticism and the Growth of Knowledge*. Cambridge: Cambridge University Press, 1970, 91–196.

LAKE, David A. "Powerful Pacifists: Democratic States and War," *American Political Science Review*, 86, 1 (1992), 24–37.

LAMPERT, Donald E. "Patterns of Transregional Relations," in Werner J. FELD and Gavin BOYD (eds.), *Comparative Regional Systems*. New York: Pergamon Press, 1980, 429–481.

LANIR, Zvi. *Fundamental Surprise: The National Intelligence Crisis*. Tel Aviv: Hakibbutz Hameuhad, for the Center of Strategic Studies, Tel Aviv University, 1983.

LARSON, Deborah W. *Origins of Containment: a psychological explanation*. Princeton, N.J.: Princeton University Press, 1985.

LASSWELL, Harold D. "Conflict: Social," in E. R. SELIGMAN and A. JOHNSON (eds.), *Encyclopedia of the Social Sciences*, IV. New York: Macmillan, 1931, 194–196.

LAZARUS, Richard S. "Stress," in David A. SILLS (ed.). *International Encyclopedia of the Social Sciences*, 15. New York: Collier-Macmillan, 1968, 337–348.

LAZARUS, Richard S. *Psychological Stress and the Coping Process*. New York: McGraw-Hill, 1966.

LAZARUS, Richard S. and Susan FOLKMAN. *Stress, Appraisal, and Coping*. New York: Springer Publishing Co., 1984.

LEBOW, R. Ned. *Nuclear Crisis Management: A Dangerous Illusion*. Ithaca, NY: Cornell University Press, 1987.

LEBOW, R. Ned. *Between Peace and War: The Nature of International Crisis*. Baltimore, MD: Johns Hopkins University Press, 1981.

LEBOW, R. Ned and Janice G. STEIN. "Deterrence: The Elusive Dependent Variable," *World Politics*, **42**, 3 (1990), 336–369.

LEBOW, R. Ned. and Janice G. STEIN. "Rational Deterrence Theory: I Think, Therefore I Deter," *World Politics*, **41**, 2 (1989), 208–224.

LEBOW, R. Ned. and Janice G. STEIN. "Beyond Deterrence" and "Beyond Deterrence: Building a Better Theory," *Journal of Social Issues*, **43**, 2 (1987), 5–72, 155–170.

LENG, Russell J. *Interstate Crisis Behavior: 1816–1980: Realism vs. Reciprocity*. Cambridge: Cambridge University Press (forthcoming, 1993).

LENG, Russell J. "Crisis Learning Games," *American Political Science Review*, **82**, 1 (1988), 179–194.

LENG, Russell J. "Structure and Action in Militarized Disputes," in Charles F. HERMANN, Charles W. KEGLEY, Jr. and James N. ROSENAU (eds.), *New Directions in the Study of Foreign Policy*. Boston: Allen and Unwin, 1987, 178–199.

LENG, Russell J. "When Will They Ever Learn? Coercive Bargaining in Recurrent Crises," *Journal of Conflict Resolution*, **27**, 3 (1983), 379–419.

LENG, Russell J. and Charles S. GOCHMAN. "Dangerous Disputes: A Study of Conflict Behavior and War," *American Journal of Political Science*, **26**, 4 (1982), 664–687.

LENG, Russell J. and J. David SINGER. "Militarized International Crises: The BCOW Typology and its Applications," *International Studies Quarterly*, **32**, 2 (1988), 155–173.

LENG, Russell J. and G. G. WHEELER. "Influence Strategies, Success and War," *Journal of Conflict Resolution*, **23**, 4 (1979), 655–684.

LENIN, V. I. *Imperialism: The Highest Stage of Capitalism*. New York: International Publishers, 1939 (first published in 1917).

LEVITE, Ariel. "*Intelligence and Strategic Surprises* Revisited: A Response to Richard K. Betts' 'Surprise, Scholasticism, and Strategy'," *International Studies Quarterly*, **33**, 3 (1989), 345–349.

LEVITE, Ariel. *Intelligence and Strategic Surprises*. New York: Columbia University Press, 1987.

LEVY, Jack S. "An Introduction to Prospect Theory," *Political Psychology*, **13**, 2 (1992a), 171–186.

LEVY, Jack S. "Prospect Theory and International Relations: Theoretical Applications and Analytical Problems," *Political Psychology*, **13**, 2 (1992b), 283–310.

LEVY, Jack S. "The Diversionary Theory of War," in Manus I. MIDLARSKY (ed.), *Handbook of War Studies*. Boston: Unwin Hyman, 1989a, 257–286.

LEVY, Jack S. "Domestic Politics and War," in Robert I. ROTBERG and Theodore K. RABB (eds.), *The Origin and Prevention of Major Wars*. Cambridge: Cambridge University Press, 1989b, 79–97.

LEVY, Jack S. "The Causes of War: A Review of Theories and Evidence," in Philip E. TETLOCK, JO L. HUSBANDS, Robert JERVIS, Paul C. STERN and Charles TILLY (eds.), *Behavior, Society, and Nuclear War*. Vol. I. New York: Oxford University Press, 1989c, 209–333.

LEVY, Jack S. "Organizational Routines and the Causes of War," *International Studies Quarterly*, **30**, 2 (1986), 193–222.

LEVY, Jack S. "The Polarity of the System and International Stability: An Empirical Analysis," in A. Ned SABROSKY (ed.), *Polarity and War*. Boulder, CO: Westview Press, 1985, Chap. 4.

LEVY, Jack S. *War in the Modern Great Power System, 1495–1975*. Lexington, KY: University Press of Kentucky, 1983.

LEVY, Jack S. "The Contagion of Great Power War Behavior, 1945–1975," *American Journal of Political Science*, **26**, 3 (1982), 562–584.

LEVY, Jack S. and T. Clifton MORGAN. "The War Weariness Hypothesis: An Empirical Test," *American Journal of Political Science*, **30**, 1 (1986), 26–49.

LEVY, Jack S. and T. Clifton MORGAN. "The Frequency and Seriousness of War: An Inverse Relationship," *Journal of Conflict Resolution*, **28**, 4 (1984), 731–749.

LORENZ, Konrad. *On Aggression*. New York: Harcourt Brace and World, 1966.

LUARD, Evan. *War in International Society*. New Haven, CT: Yale University Press, 1987.

LUTERBACHER, Urs. "Last Words About War?" *Journal of Conflict Resolution*, **28**, 1 (1984), 165–182.

LUTERBACHER, Urs and Michael D. WARD (eds.). *Dynamic Models of International Conflict*. Boulder, CO: Lynne Rienner, 1985.

LUTTWAK, Edward N. *Strategy: The Logic of War and Peace*. Cambridge, MA: Belknap Press of Harvard University Press, 1987.

MACK, Raymond W. and Richard C. SNYDER. "The Analysis of Social Conflict — Toward an Overview and Synthesis," *Journal of Conflict Resolution*, **1**, 2 (1957), 212–248.

MAHONEY, Robert B. Jr. and Richard P. CLAYBERG. "Images and Threats: Soviet Perceptions of International Crises, 1946–1975," in Patrick J. McGOWAN and Charles W. KEGLEY, Jr. (eds.), *Threats, Weapons, and Foreign Policy*. Beverly Hills, CA: Sage, 1980, 55–81.

MANSBACH, Richard W. and John A. VASQUEZ. *In Search of Theory: A New Paradigm for Global Politics*. New York: Columbia University Press, 1981.

MANTOUX, Etienne. *The Carthaginian Peace or The Economic Consequences of Mr. Keynes*. New York: Scribner's, 1952.

MAOZ, Zeev. *Paradoxes of War: On the Art of National Self-Entrapment*. Boston: Unwin Hyman, 1990a.

MAOZ, Zeev. *National Choices and International Processes*. Cambridge: Cambridge University Press, 1990b.

MAOZ, Zeev. "Peace by Empire? Conflict Outcomes and International Instability, 1816–1976," *Journal of Peace Research*, **21**, 3 (1984), 227–241.

MAOZ, Zeev. "Resolve, Capabilities, and the Outcomes of Interstate Disputes, 1816–1976," *Journal of Conflict Resolution*, **27**, 2 (1983), 195–230.

MAOZ, Zeev. *Paths to Conflict, International Dispute Initiation 1816–1976*. Boulder, CO: Westview Press, 1982a.

MAOZ, Zeev. "Crisis Initiation: A Theoretical Exploration of a Neglected Topic in International Crisis Theory," *Review of International Studies*, **8**, 4 (1982b), 1–17.

MAOZ, Zeev. "The Decision to Raid Entebbe: Decision Analysis Applied to Crisis Behavior," *Journal of Conflict Resolution*, **25**, 4 (1981), 677–707.

MAOZ, Zeev and N. ABDOLALI. "Regime Types and International Conflict, 1816–1976," *Journal of Conflict Resolution*, **33**, 1 (1989), 3–35.

MARRA, Robin F. "A Cybernetic Model of the U.S. Defense Expenditure Policy-Making Process," *International Studies Quarterly*, **29**, 2 (1985), 121–136.

MARTEL, William C. "Non-Superpower Nuclear Crisis De-escalation," in Joseph E. NATION (ed.), *The De-escalation of Nuclear Crises*. New York: St. Martin's Press, 1992, 198–225.

MARTIN, Wayne R. "The Measurement of International Military Commitments for Crisis Early Warning," *International Studies Quarterly*, **21**, 1 (1977), 151–178.

MAY, Ernest R. *"Lessons" of the Past: The Use and Misuse of History in American Foreign Policy*. New York: Oxford University Press, 1973.

MAYER, Thomas F. "Arms Races and War Initiation," *Journal of Conflict Resolution*, **30**, 1 (1986), 3–28.

McCLELLAND, Charles A. "The Anticipation of International Crises," *International Studies Quarterly*, **21**, 1 (1977), 15–38.

McCLELLAND, Charles A. "The Beginning, Duration, and Abatement of International Crises: Comparisons in Two Conflict Arenas," in Charles F. HERMANN (ed.), *International Crises: Insights From Behavioral Research*. New York: Free Press, 1972, 83–105.

McCLELLAND, Charles A. "Access to Berlin: The Quantity and Variety of Events, 1948–1963," in J. David SINGER (ed.), *Quantitaive International Politics: Insights and Evidence*. New York: Free Press, 1968, 159–186.

McCLELLAND, Charles A. "Action Structures and Communication in Two International Crises: Quemoy and Berlin," *Background*, **7** (1964), 201–215.

McCLELLAND, Charles A. "The Acute International Crisis," in Klaus KNORR and Sidney VERBA (eds.). *The International System: Theoretical Essays*. Princeton, NJ: Princeton University Press, 1961.

McCLELLAND, Charles A. "Systems and History in International Relations: Some Perspectives for Empirical Research and Theory," *General Systems: Yearbook of the Society for General Systems Research*, III (1958), 221–47.

McCLELLAND, Charles A. "Applications of General Systems Theory in International Relations," *Main Currents in Modern Thought*, **12** (1955), 27–34.

McCORMICK, David M. *Decisions, Events and Perceptions in International Crises, Vol. I: Measuring Perceptions to Predict International Conflict*. Ann Arbor, MI: First Ann Arbor Corp., 1975.

McCORMICK, James M. "International Crises: A Note on Definition," *Western Political Quarterly*, **31**, 3 (1978), 352–358.

McCORMICK, James M. "Evaluating Models of Crisis Behavior: Some Evidence from the Middle East," *International Studies Quarterly*, **19**, 1 (1975), 17–45.

McNEIL, Elton (ed.). *The Nature of Human Conflict*, Englewood Cliffs, N.J.: Prentice-Hall, 1965.

MCNEILL, William H. *The Pursuit of Power: Technology, Armed Force, and Society since A.D. 1000.* Chicago: University of Chicago Press, 1982.

MIDLARSKY, Manus I. (ed.). *Handbook of War Studies.* Boston: Unwin Hyman, 1989a.

MIDLARSKY, Manus I. "Hierarchical Equilibria and the Long-Run Instability of Multipolar Systems," in Manus I. MIDLARSKY (ed.). *Handbook of War Studies.* Boston: Unwin Hyman, 1989b.

MIDLARSKY, Manus I. *The Onset of World War.* Boston: Unwin Hyman, 1988.

MIDLARSKY, Manus I. "A Hierarchical Equilibrium Theory of Systemic War," *International Studies Quarterly*, **30**, 1 (1986), 77–105.

MILBURN, Thomas W. "The Management of Crisis," in Charles F. HERMANN (ed.), *International Crises: Insights from Behavioral Research.* New York: Free Press, 1972, 259–277.

MILBURN, Thomas W. and Michael NICHOLSON. "Rational Models and the Ending of Wars," *Journal of Conflict Resolution*, **27**, 3 (1983), 495–520.

MODELSKI, George. *Long Cycles in World Politics.* Seattle, WA: University of Washington Press, 1987.

MODELSKI, George. "Long Cycles of Global Politics and the Nation-State," *Comparative Studies in Society and History*, **20**, 2 (1978), 214–235.

MODELSKI, George and Patrick M. MORGAN. "Understanding Global War," *Journal of Conflict Resolution*, **29**, 3 (1985), 391–417.

MODELSKI, George and William R. THOMPSON. "Long Cycles and Global War," in Manus I. MIDLARSKY (ed.), *Handbook of War Studies.* Boston: Unwin Hyman, 1989, Chap. 2.

MOLL, Kendall D. and Gregory M. LUEBBERT. "Arms Race and Military Expenditure Models: A Review," *Journal of Conflict Resolution*, **24**, 1 (1980), 153–185.

MORGAN, Patrick M. "Reconsidering Crisis Decision Making." Presented to the annual meeting of the International Studies Association, March 1991.

MORGAN, Patrick M. *Deterrence: A Conceptual Analysis.* Beverly Hills, CA: Sage, 1977.

MORGENTHAU, Hans J. *Politics Among Nations.* New York: Knopf, 5th ed. 1973, 1st ed. 1948.

MORGENTHAU, Hans J. *Scientific Man vs. Power Politics.* Chicago: University of Chicago Press, 1946.

MORSE, Edward L. "Crisis Diplomacy, Interdependence, and the Politics of International Economic Relations," in Raymond TANTER and Richard H. ULLMAN (eds.), *Theory and Policy in International Relations.* Princeton, NJ: Princeton University Press, 1972, 123–150.

MOST, Benjamin A. and Randolph M. SIVERSON. "The Logic and Study of the Diffusion of International Conflict," in Manus I. MIDLARSKY (ed.). *Handbook of War Studies.* Boston: Unwin Hyman, 1989, Chap. 5.

MOST, Benjamin A. and Harvey STARR. "Polarity, Preponderance and Power Parity in the Generation of International Conflict," *International Interactions*, **13**, 3 (1987), 225–262.

MOST, Benjamin A. and Harvey STARR. "Case Selection, Conceptualization and Basic Logic in the Study of War," *American Journal of Political Science*, **26**, 4 (1982), 834–856.

MUELLER, John. *Retreat from Doomsday: The Obsolescence of Major War.* New York: Basic Books, 1989.

NELSON, Keith L. and Spencer C. OLIN, Jr. *Why War? Ideology, Theory, and History.* Berkeley and Los Angeles: University of California Press, 1979.

NEUSTADT, Richard E. and Ernest R. MAY. *Thinking in Time: The Uses of History for Decision-Makers.* New York: Free Press, 1986.

NICHOLSON, Michael. *Conflict Analysis.* London: English Universities Press, 1970.

NICOLSON, Harold G. *Peace-Making 1919.* London: Constable, 1933.

NOGEE, Joseph L. and John SPANIER. *Peace Impossible—War Unlikely.* Glenview, IL: Scott, Foresman/Little, Brown, 1988.

NOMIKOS, Eugenia V. and Robert C. NORTH. *International Crisis: The Outbreak of World War I.* Montreal: McGill-Queen's University Press, 1976.

NORPOTH, Helmut. "Guns and Butter and Government Popularity in Britain," *American Political Science Review*, **81**, 3 (1987), 949–959.

NORTH, Robert C. "Conflict: Political Aspects," in David A. SILLS (ed.). *International Encyclopedia of the Social Sciences*, 3. New York: Collier-Macmillan, 1968, 226–232.

NORTH, Robert C. "Research Pluralism and the International Elephant," *International Studies Quarterly*, **11**, 4 (1967), 394–416.

NORTH, Robert C., Richard A. BRODY and Ole R. HOLSTI. "Some Empirical Data on the Conflict Spiral," *Peace Research Society (International) Papers*, **I** (1964), 1–14.

O'CONNOR, James. *The Meaning of Crisis: A Theoretical Introduction.* Oxford: Basil Blackwell, 1987.

OLSON, Mancur. *The Logic of Collective Action.* Cambridge, MA: Harvard University Press, 1965.

ONEAL, John R. "The Rationality of Decision Making During International Crises," *Polity*, **20**, 4 (1988), 598–622.

ONEAL, John R. *Foreign Policy-Making in Times of Crisis.* Columbus, OH: Ohio State University Press, 1982.

OPPENHEIM, Franz L. *International Law: Disputes, War and Neutrality.* Vol. 2. ed. Hersh LAUTERPACHT. London: Longmans 7th ed., 1952.

ORGANSKI, A. F. K. *World Politics.* New York: Knopf, 1958.

ORGANSKI, A. F. K. and Jacek KUGLER. *The War Ledger.* Chicago: University of Chicago Press, 1980.

PAIGE, Glenn D. "Comparative Case Analysis of Crisis Decisions: Korea and Cuba," in Charles F. HERMANN (ed.), *International Crises: Insights from Behavioral Research.* New York: Free Press, 1972, 41–55.

PAIGE, Glenn D. *The Korean Decision.* New York: Free Press, 1968.

PARET, Peter. *Clausewitz and the State: The Man, His Theories, and His Times.* Princeton, NJ: Princeton University Press, 1985.

PARET, Peter (ed.). *Makers of Modern Strategy: from Machiavelli to the Nuclear Age.* Princeton, NJ: Princeton University Press, 1986.

PARKER, Richard W. "An Examination of Basic and Applied International Crisis Research," *International Studies Quarterly*, **21**, 1 (1977), 225–246.

PAUL, T. V. *Assymetric Conflicts: War Initiation By Weaker Powers.* Cambridge: Cambridge University Press, (forthcoming, 1994).

PHILLIPS, Warren R. "Prior Behavior as an Explanation of Foreign Policy," in Maurice A. EAST, Stephen A. SALMORE and Charles F. HERMANN (eds.), *Why Nations Act.* Beverly Hills, CA: Sage, 1978, 161–172.

PHILLIPS, Warren R. "The Conflict Environment of Nations: A Study of Conflict Inputs to Nations in 1963," in Jonathan WILKENFELD (ed.), *Conflict Behavior and Linkage Politics*. New York: David McKay, 1973, 124–147.

PHILLIPSON, Coleman. *Termination of War and Treaties of Peace*. London: T. F. Unwin, 1916.

POLD, Garrick. *The Berlin Wall Crisis of 1961: A United States Decision-Making Perspective*. (Unpub. M.A. Research Paper), McGill University, 1991.

POST, Jerrold M. "The Impact of Crisis-Induced Stress on Policy-Makers," in Alexander L. GEORGE (ed.), *Avoiding War: Problems of Crisis Management*. Boulder, CO: Westview Press, 1991, 471–494.

PRUITT, Dean G. and Richard C. SNYDER. *Theory and Research on the Causes of War*. Englewood Cliffs, NJ: Prentice-Hall, 1969.

QUATTRONE, George A. and Amos TVERSKY. "Contrasting Rational and Psychological Analyses of Political Choice," *American Political Science Review*, **82**, 3 (1988), 719–736.

RABINOVITCH, Itamar. *The War for Lebanon, 1970–85*. Ithaca, NY: Cornell University Press, 1986.

RAGIN, Charles C. *The Comparative Method: Moving Beyond Qualitative and Quantitative Strategies*. Berkeley and Los Angeles: University of California Press, 1987.

RAPHAEL, Theodore D. "Integrative Complexity Theory and Forecasting International Crises, Berlin, 1946–1972," *Journal of Conflict Resolution*, **26**, 3 (1982), 425–450.

RAPKIN, David P. and William R. THOMPSON, with Jon A. CHRISTOPHERSON. "Bipolarity and Bipolarization in the Cold War Era," *Journal of Conflict Resolution*, **23**, 2 (1979), 261–295.

RAPOPORT, Anatol. "Conflict Escalation and Conflict Dynamics," in Raimo VAYRYNEN (ed.). *The Quest for Peace*. Beverly Hills, CA; Sage, 1987, 163–178.

RAPOPORT, Anatol. *Fights, Games and Debates*. Ann Arbor, MI: University of Michigan Press, 1960.

RAPOPORT, Anatol. "Lewis F. Richardson's Mathematical Theory of War," *Journal of Conflict Resolution*, **I**, 3 (1957), 282–298.

RICHARDSON, James L. "Crisis Management: A Critical Appraisal," in Gilbert R. WINHAM (ed.), *New Issues in International Crisis Management*. Boulder, CO: Westview Press, 1988, 13–36.

RICHARDSON, Lewis F. *Arms and Insecurity*. Pittsburgh, PA: Boxwood Press, 1960a.

RICHARDSON, Lewis F. *Statistics of Deadly Quarrels*. Pittsburgh, PA: Boxwood Press, 1960b.

RICHARDSON, Lewis F. "War Moods," *Psychometrika*, **13**, 3 and 4 (1948), 147–174, 197–232.

ROBINSON, James A. "Crisis: An Appraisal of Concepts and Theories," in Charles F. HERMANN (ed.), *International Crises: Insights from Behavioral Research*. New York: Free Press, 1972, 20–35.

ROBINSON, James A. "Crisis Decision-Making: an Inventory and Appraisal of Concepts, Theories, Hypotheses and Techniques of Analysis," in James A. ROBINSON (ed.), *Political Science Annual: An International Review*, 1, Indianapolis, IN: Bobbs-Merrill, 1970, 111–148.

ROBINSON, James A. "Crisis," in David L. SILLS (ed.), *International Encyclopedia of the Social Sciences*. London and New York: Collier-Macmillan, 1968, Vol. 3, 510–514.

ROBINSON, James A. *The Concept of Crisis in Decision-Making*. Washington, DC: National Institute of Social and Behavioral Science, Symposia Study Series No. 11, 1962.

ROMANO, Patricia E. *War Initiation: Opportunity and Vulnerability*. (Unpub. M.A. Research Paper), McGill University, 1991.

ROSECRANCE, Richard N. "Bipolarity, Multipolarity, and the Future," *Journal of Conflict Resolution*, **X**, 3 (1966), 314–327.

ROSECRANCE, Richard N. *Action and Reaction in World Politics*. Boston: Little, Brown, 1963.

ROSENAU, James N. *Turbulence in World Politics*. Princeton, NJ: Princeton University Press, 1990.

ROSENAU, James N. "The Premises and Promises of Decision-Making Analysis," in James C. CHARLESWORTH (ed.), *Contemporary Political Analysis*. New York: Free Press, 1967, Chap. 11.

ROSENAU, James N., Vincent DAVIS and Maurice A. EAST (eds.). *The Analysis of International Politics*. New York: Free Press, 1972.

ROSENTHAL, Uriel, Michael T. CHARLES and Paul T. HART (eds.). *Coping with Crises: The Management of Disasters, Riots and Terrorism*. Springfield, IL: Charles C. Thomas, 1989.

ROSS, Marc H. "Internal and External Conflict and Violence: Cross-cultural Evidence and a New Analysis," *Journal of Conflict Resolution*, **29**, 4 (1985), 547–579.

ROSSA, Paul J., Gerald W. HOPPLE and Jonathan WILKENFELD. "Crisis Analysis: Indicators and Models," *International Interactions*, **7**, 2 (1980), 123–163.

RUBINSTEIN, Alvin Z. *Red Star on the Nile: Soviet-Egyptian Influence Relationship Since the June War*. Princeton, NJ: Princeton University Press, 1977.

RUBINSTEIN, Alvin Z. "Libertarian Propositions on Violence Between and Within Nations: A Test Against Published Research Results," *Journal of Conflict Resolution*, **29**, 3 (1985), 419–455.

RUBINSTEIN, Alvin Z. "Libertarianism and International Violence," *Journal of Conflict Resolution*, **27**, 1 (1983), 27–71.

RUBINSTEIN, Alvin Z. *Understanding Conflict and War*. Beverly Hills, CA: Sage, 1975–81 (5 volumes).

RUBINSTEIN, Alvin Z. "Dimensions of Conflict Behavior Within and Between Nations," *General Systems*, **8** (1963), 1–50.

RUSSETT, Bruce M. *Controlling the Sword: The Democratic Governance of National Security*. Cambridge, MA: Harvard University Press, 1990.

RUSSETT, Bruce M. *What Price Vigilance? The Burdens of National Defense*. New Haven, CT: Yale University Press, 1970.

RUSSETT, Bruce M. "International Behavior Research: Case Studies and Cumulation," in Michael HAAS and Henry S. KARIEL (eds.), *Approaches to the Study of Political Science*. Scranton, PA: Chandler, 1970, 425–443.

RUSSETT, Bruce M. "The Calculus of Deterrence," *Journal of Conflict Resolution*, **7**, 1 (1963), 97–109.

RUSSETT, Bruce M. *et al. World Handbook of Political and Social Indicators*. New Haven, CT: Yale University Press, 1964.

SABROSKY, A. Ned (ed.). *Polarity and War*. Boulder, CO: Westview Press, 1985.

SABROSKY, A. Ned. "From Bosnia to Sarajevo: A Comparative Discussion of Interstate Crises," *Journal of Conflict Resolution*, **XIX**, 1 (1975), 3–24.

SCHELLING, Thomas C. *Arms and Influence*. New Haven, CT: Yale University Press, 1966.

SCHICK, Jack M. *The Berlin Crisis, 1958–1962*. Philadelphia: University of Pennsylvania Press, 1971.

SCHUMPETER, Joseph. *Imperialism and Social Classes*. New York: Meridian Books, 1955 (first published in 1919).

SCHWARZENBERGER, Georg. *International Law: The Law of Armed Conflict*. Vol. 2. London: Stevens & Sons Ltd., 1968.

SCHWELLER, Randall L. "Domestic Structure and Preventive War: Are Democracies More Pacific?" *World Politics*, **44**, 2 (1992), 235–269.

SEABURY, Paul and Angela CODEVILLA. *War: Ends and Means*. New York: Basic Books, 1989.

SEMMEL, A. K. "Small Group Dynamics in Foreign Policy Making," in Gerald W. HOPPLE (ed.), *Biopolitics, Political Psychology, and International Politics*. London: Frances Pinter, 1982, 94–113.

SERGEEV, V. M., V. P. AKIMOV, V. B. LUKOV and P. B. PARSHIN. "Interdependence in a Crisis Situation: A Cognitive Approach to Modeling the Caribbean Crisis," *Journal of Conflict Resolution*, **34**, 2 (1990), 179–207.

SHAPIRO, Howard B. and Marcia A. GILBERT. *Crisis Management: Psychological and Sociological Factors in Decision-Making*. MacLean, VA: Human Science Research Inc., 1975.

SHERWIN, Martin J. *A World Destroyed: The Atomic Bomb and the Grand Alliance*. New York: Knopf, 1975.

SHLAIM, Avi. *The United States and the Berlin Blockade, 1948–1949: A Study of Crisis Decision-Making*. Berkeley and Los Angeles: University of California Press, 1983.

SHLAIM, Avi. "Failures in National Intelligence Estimates: The Case of the Yom Kippur War," *World Politics*, **28**, 3 (1976), 348–380.

SHLAIM, Avi and Raymond TANTER. "Decision Process, Choice and Consequences: Israel's Deep Penetration Bombing in Egypt, 1970," *World Politics*, **30**, 4 (1978), 483–516.

SIGAL, Leon V. "The 'Rational Policy' Model and the Formosa Straits Crises," *International Studies Quarterly*, **14**, 2 (1970), 121–156.

SIMON, Sir John (Viscount). *Retrospect*. London: Hutchinson, 1952.

SINGER, J. David. "Accounting for International War: The State of the Discipline," *Journal of Peace Research*, **XVIII**, 1 (1981), 1–18.

SINGER, J. David (ed.). *The Correlates of War: II*. New York: Free Press, 1980.

SINGER, J. David. *The Correlates of War: I*. New York: Free Press, 1979a.

SINGER, J. David et al. *Explaining War: Selected Papers from the Correlates of War Project*. Beverly Hills, CA: Sage, 1979b.

SINGER, J. David and Melvin SMALL. *The Wages of War 1816–1965: A Statistical Handbook*. New York: John Wiley, 1972.

SIVERSON, Randolph M. and Paul F. DIEHL. "Arms Races, the Conflict Spiral, and the Onset of War," in Manus I. MIDLARSKY (ed.), *Handbook of War Studies*. Boston: Unwin Hyman, 1989, Chap. 8.

SIVERSON, Randolph M. and Harvey STARR. *The Diffusion of War*. Ann Arbor, MI: University of Michigan Press, 1991.

SIVERSON, Randolph M. and Michael P. SULLIVAN. "The Distribution of Power and the Onset of War," *Journal of Conflict Resolution*, **27**, 3 (1983), 473–494.

SMALL, Melvin and J. David SINGER. *Resort to Arms: International and Civil Wars, 1816–1980*. Beverly Hills, CA: Sage, 1982.

SMALL, Melvin and J. David SINGER. "The War-Proneness of Democratic Regimes, 1816–1965," *Jerusalem Journal of International Relations*, **1**, 4 (1976), 50–59.

SMOKE, Richard. *War: Controlling Escalation*. Cambridge, MA: Harvard University Press, 1977.

SNYDER, Glenn H. "Conflict and Crises in the International System," in James N. ROSENAU, Kenneth W. THOMPSON and Gavin BOYD (eds.), *World Politics: An Introduction*. New York: Free Press, 1976, 682–720.

SNYDER, Glenn H. "Crisis Bargaining," in Charles F. HERMANN (ed.). *International Crises: Insights from Behavioral Research*. New York: Free Press, 1972, 217–256.

SNYDER, Glenn H. *Deterrence and Defense: Toward a Theory of National Security*. Princeton, NJ: Princeton University Press, 1961.

SNYDER, Glenn H. and Paul DIESING. *Conflict Among Nations: Bargaining, Decision-Making and System Structure in International Crises*. Princeton, NJ: Princeton University Press, 1977.

SNYDER, Jack L. "Rationality at the Brink: The Role of Cognitive Processes in Failures of Deterrence," *World Politics*, **XXX**, 3 (1978), 345–365.

SNYDER, Richard C., H. W. BRUCK and Burton SAPIN. "Decision-Making as an Approach to the Study of International Politics," in Richard C. SNYDER, H. W. BRUCK and Burton SAPIN (eds.), *Foreign Policy Decision-Making: An Approach to the Study of International Politics*. New York: Free Press of Glencoe, 1962.

SOROKIN, Pitirim A. *Social and Cultural Dynamics: Fluctuations of Social Relationships, War and Revolution*. Vol. III. New York: Bedminster, 1937.

STARR, Harvey and Benjamin A. MOST. "The Forms and Processes of War Diffusion: Research Update on Contagion in African Conflict," *Comparative Political Studies*, **18**, 2 (1985), 206–227.

STARR, Harvey and Benjamin A. MOST. "Contagion and Border Effects on Contemporary African Conflict," *Comparative Political Studies*, **16**, 1 (1983), 92–117.

STAW, Barry M. and Jerry ROSS. "Behavior in Escalation Situations: Antecedents, Prototypes, and Solutions," *Research in Organization Behavior*, **9** (1987), 39–78.

STEIN, Arthur A. *The Nation at War*. Baltimore, MD: Johns Hopkins University Press, 1978.

STEIN, Arthur A. and Bruce M. RUSSETT. "Evaluating War: Outcomes and Consequences," in Ted R. GURR (ed.), *Handbook of Political Conflict: Theory and Research*. New York: Free Press, 1980, Chap. 10.

STEIN, Janice G. "The Managed and the Managers: Crisis Prevention in the Middle East," in Gilbert R. WINHAM (ed.), *New Issues in International Crisis Management*. Boulder, CO: Westview Press, 1988, 171–198.

STEIN, Janice G. "War Termination and Conflict Reduction or, How Wars Should End," *Jerusalem Journal of International Relations*, **I**, 1 (1975), 1–27.

STEIN, Janice G. and Raymond TANTER. *Rational Decision-Making: Israel's Security Choices, 1967*. Columbus, OH: Ohio State University Press, 1980.

STEINBERG, Blema S. "Psychoanalytic Concepts in International Politics: The Role of Shame and Humiliation," *International Review of Psycho-Analysis*, **18**, 1 (1991a), 65–85.

STEINBERG, Blema S. "Shame and Humiliation in the Cuban Missile Crisis: A Psychoanalytic Perspective," *Political Psychology*, **12**, 4 (1991b), 653–690.

STEINBRUNER, John D. *The Cybernetic Theory of Decision*. Princeton, NJ: Princeton University Press, 1974.

STERN, Eric and Bengt SUDELIUS. "Managing Asymmetrical Crisis: Sweden, the USSR, and U-137," *International Studies Quarterly*, **36**, 2 (1992), 213–239.

STERN, Paul C., Robert AXELROD, Robert JERVIS and Ray RADNER (eds.). *Perspectives on Deterrence*. New York: Oxford University Press, 1989.

STOESSINGER, John G. *Why Nations Go To War*. New York: St Martin's Press, 1985 (4th ed.).

STONE, Julius. *Legal Controls of International Conflict*. New York: Rinehart, 1954.

SUEDFELD, Peter and Philip E. TETLOCK. "Integrative Complexity of Communications in International Crises," *Journal of Conflict Resolution*, **21**, 1 (1977), 169–184.

TANTER, Raymond. "International Crisis Behavior: An Appraisal of the Literature," in Michael BRECHER (ed.), *Studies in Crisis Behavior*. New Brunswick, NJ: Transaction Books, 1979, 340–374.

TANTER, Raymond. "Crisis Management: A Critical Review of Academic Literature," *Jerusalem Journal of International Relations*, **1**, 1 (1975), 71–101.

TANTER, Raymond. *Modelling and Managing International Conflicts: The Berlin Crises*. Beverly Hills, CA: Sage, 1974.

TAYLOR, A. J. P. *The Origins of the Second World War*. London: Hamish Hamilton, 1961.

TAYLOR, Charles L. and Michael C. HUDSON. *World Handbook of Political and Social Indicators* (2nd ed.). New Haven, CT: Yale University Press, 1972.

TAYLOR, Charles L. and David A. JODICE. *World Handbook of Political and Social Indicators* (3rd ed.). New Haven, CT: Yale University Press, 1983.

TAYLOR, Telford. *Munich: The Price of Peace*. New York: Doubleday, 1979.

TEMPLEWOOD, Viscount (Sir Samuel Hoare). *Nine Troubled Years*. London: Collins, 1954.

THOMAS, Hugh. *Armed Truce: The Beginnings of the Cold War, 1945–46*. London: Hamilton, 1986.

THOMPSON, William R. *On Global War*. Columbia, SC: University of South Carolina Press, 1988.

THOMPSON, William R. "Polarity, the Long Cycle, and Global Power Warfare," *Journal of Conflict Resolution*, **30**, 4 (1986), 587–615.

THOMPSON, William R. "The Regional Subsystem: A Conceptual Explication and a Propositional Inventory," *International Studies Quarterly*, **17**, 1 (1973), 89–117.

THUCYDIDES. *The Peloponnesian War*. Trans. by Rex Warner. Harmondsworth, UK: Penguin, 1954.

TOUVAL, Saadia and I. William ZARTMAN (eds.). *International Mediation in Theory and Practice*. Boulder, CO: Westview Press, 1985.

VALENTA, Jiri. *Soviet Intervention in Czechoslovakia, 1968: Anatomy of a Decision*. Baltimore, MD: Johns Hopkins University Press, 1979, 1991.

VALENTA, Jiri. "Soviet Decisionmaking on Czechoslovakia, 1968," in Jiri VALENTA and William C. POTTER (eds.), *Soviet Decisionmaking for National Security*. Boston: George Allen & Unwin, 1984, Chap. 7.

VAN CREVELD, Martin. *The Transformation of War*. New York: Free Press, 1991.

VAN CREVELD, Martin. *Technology and War*. New York: Free Press, 1989.

VASQUEZ, John A. *The War Puzzle*. Cambridge: Cambridge University Press. (forthcoming, 1993.)

VASQUEZ, John A. "The Steps to War: Toward a Scientific Explanation of Correlates of War Findings," *World Politics*, **XL**, 1 (1987), 108–145.

VASQUEZ, John A. and Marie T. HENEHAN (eds.), *The Scientific Study of Peace and War: A Text Reader*. New York: Lexington Books, 1992.

VASQUEZ, John A. and Richard W. MANSBACH. "The Issue Cycle: Conceptualizing Long-Term Global Political Change," *International Organization*, **37**, 2 (1983).

VERBA, Sidney. "Some Dilemmas in Comparative Research," *World Politics*, **XX**, 1 (1967), 111–127.

VERTZBERGER, Yaacov Y. I. *The World in Their Minds: Information Processing, Cognition, and Perception in Foreign Policy Decision-Making*. Stanford, CA: Stanford University Press, 1990.

VERTZBERGER, Yaacov Y. I. "Foreign Policy Decision-Makers as Practical-Intuitive Historians: Applied History and Its Shortcomings," *International Studies Quarterly*, **30**, 2 (1986), 223–247.

VERTZBERGER, Yaacov Y. I. *Misperception in Foreign Policymaking*. Boulder, CO: Westview Press, 1984.

VINCENT, Jack. "Freedom and International Conflict: Another Look," and "On Rummel's Omnipresent Theory," *International Studies Quarterly*, **31**, 1 (1987), 103–112, 119–126.

VINCENT, Jack. "WEIS vs. COPDAB: Correspondence Problems," *International Studies Quarterly*, **27**, 2 (1983), 161–168.

WALLACE, Michael D. "Polarization: Towards a Scientific Conception," in A. Ned SABROSKY (ed.), *Polarity and War*. Boulder, CO: Westview Press, 1985, 95–113.

WALLACE, Michael D. "Armaments and Escalation: Two Competing Hypotheses," *International Studies Quarterly*, **26**, 1 (1982), 37–56.

WALLACE, Michael D. "Old Nails in New Coffins: The Para Bellum Hypothesis Revisited," *Journal of Peace Research*, **XVIII**, 1 (1981), 91–95.

WALLACE, Michael D. "Arms Races and Escalation: Some New Evidence," *Journal of Conflict Resolution*, **23**, 1 (1979), 3–16.

WALLACE, Michael D. "Alliance Polarization, Cross-Cutting, and International War, 1815–1964," *Journal of Conflict Resolution*, **17**, 4 (1973), 575–604.

WALLACE, Michael D. "Status, Formal Organization, and Arms Levels as Factors Leading to the Onset of War, 1820–1964," in Bruce M. RUSSETT (ed.), *Peace, War and Numbers*. Beverly Hills, CA: Sage, 1972, 49–70.

WALLACE, Michael D. and Peter SUEDFELD. "Leadership Performance in Crisis: The Longevity-Complexity Link," *International Studies Quarterly*, **32**, 4 (1988), 439–451.

WALLERSTEIN, Immanuel. "Crises: The World-Economy, The Movements, and The Ideologies," in Albert BERGESEN (ed.), *Crises in the World-System*. Beverly Hills, CA: Sage, 1983, 21–36.

WALT, Stephen M. "Revolution and War," *World Politics*, **44**, 3 (1992), 321–368.

WALTZ, Kenneth N. *Theory of International Politics*. Reading, MA: Addison-Wesley, 1979.

WALTZ, Kenneth N. "International Structure, National Force, and the Balance of World Power," *Journal of International Affairs*, **XXI**, 2 (1967), 215–231.

WALTZ, Kenneth N. "The Stability of a Bipolar World," *Daedalus*, **XCIII**, 3 (1964), 881–909.

WALTZ, Kenneth N. *Man, the State and War*. New York: Columbia University Press, 1959.

WARD, Michael D. and Ulrich WIDMAIER. "The Domestic-International Conflict Nexus: New Evidence and Old Hypotheses," *International Interactions*, **9**, 1 (1982), 75–101.

WASSERMAN, Benno. "The Failure of Intelligence Prediction," *Political Studies*, **VIII** (1960), 156–169.

WATT, Donald C. *How War Came: The Immediate Origins of the Second World War, 1938–39*. New York: Pantheon Books, 1989.

WAYMAN, Frank W. "Bipolarity and War: The Role of Capability Concentration and Alliance Patterns Among Major Powers, 1816–1965," *Journal of Peace Research*, **21**, 1 (1984), 61–78.

WEEDE, Erich. "Democracy and War Involvement," *Journal of Conflict Resolution*, **28**, 4 (1984), 649–664.

WEEDE, Erich. "Arms Races and Escalation: Some Persisting Doubts," *Journal of Conflict Resolution*, **24**, 2 (1980), 285–287.

WEEDE, Erich. "Overwhelming Preponderance as a Pacifying Condition Among Contiguous Asian Dyads 1950–69," *Journal of Conflict Resolution*, **20**, 3 (1976), 395–411.

WEINBERGER, Naomi J. *Syrian Intervention in Lebanon*. New York: Oxford University Press, 1986.

WELCH, Claude, Jr. "The Military and the State in Africa: Problems of Political Transition," in Zaki ERGAS (ed.), *The African State in Transition*. London: Macmillan, 1987, 191–215.

WELCH, David A. "Crisis Decision-Making Reconsidered," *Journal of Conflict Resolution*, **33**, 3 (1989), 430–445.

WHALEY, Barton. *Codeword BARBAROSSA*. Cambridge, MA: MIT Press, 1973.

WIEGELE, Thomas C., *et al. Leaders Under Stress: A Psychophysiological Analysis of International Crises*. Durham, NC: Duke University Press, 1985.

WIEGELE, Thomas C. "Decision-Making in an International Crisis: Some Biological Factors," *International Studies Quarterly*, **17**, 3 (1973), 295–335.

WIENER, Anthony J. and Herman KAHN (eds.). *Crisis and Arms Control*. Hudson, NY: Hudson Institute, 1962.

WILKENFELD, Jonathan. "Trigger-Response Transitions in Foreign Policy Crises, 1929–1985," *Journal of Conflict Resolution*, **35**, 1 (1991), 143–169.

WILKENFELD, Jonathan and Michael BRECHER. "A Time-Series Perspective on Conflict in the Middle East," in Patrick J. McGOWAN (ed.), *Sage International Yearbook of Foreign Policy Studies*. Beverly Hills, CA: Sage, 1975, Vol. 3, 177–212.

WILKENFELD, Jonathan. "Models for the Analysis of Foreign Conflict Behavior of States," in Bruce M. RUSSETT (ed.), *Peace, War and Numbers*. Beverly Hills, CA: Sage, 1972, 275–298.

WILKENFELD, Jonathan. "Some Further Findings Regarding the Domestic and Foreign Conflict Behavior of Nations," *Journal of Peace Research*, **2** (1969), 147–156.

WILKENFELD, Jonathan. "Domestic and Foreign Conflict Behavior of Nations," *Journal of Peace Research*, **1** (1968), 56–69.

WILKENFELD, Jonathan and Michael BRECHER. *Crises in the Twentieth Century. Vol. II: Handbook of Foreign Policy Crises*. Oxford: Pergamon Press, 1988.

WILKENFELD, Jonathan. "Superpower Crisis Management Behavior," in Charles W. KEGLEY, Jr., and Pat MCGOWAN (eds.), *Foreign Policy: USA/USSR*. Beverly Hills, CA: Sage Publications, 1982, Chap. 8.

WILKENFELD, Jonathan, Gerald W. HOPPLE, Paul J. ROSSA and Stephen J. ANDRIOLE. *Foreign Policy Behavior: The Interstate Behavior Analysis Model*. Beverly Hills, CA: Sage, 1980.

WILLIAMS, Phil. *Crisis Management: Confrontation and Diplomacy in the Nuclear Age*. London: M. Robertson, 1976.

WILSON, Edwin O. *On Human Nature*. Cambridge, MA: Harvard University Press, 1978.

WILSON, Peter. "The United Kingdom and the Munich Crisis, 1938." (Unpub. M.A. paper), McGill University, 1984.

WINHAM, Gilbert R. (ed.). *New Issues in International Crisis Management*. Boulder, CO: Westview Press, 1988.

WITTMAN, Donald. "How a War Ends: A Rational Model Approach," *Journal of Conflict Resolution*, **23**, 4 (1979), 743–763.

WOHLSTETTER, Roberta. *Pearl Harbor, Warning and Decision*. Stanford, CA: Stanford University Press, 1962.

WOODWARD, Ernest L. (ed.). *Documents on British Foreign Policy*. Third Series, Vols. I and II (1938). London: His Majesty's Stationery Office, 1949.

WRIGHT, Quincy. "How Hostilities Have Ended: Peace Treaties and Alternatives," in W. T. R. FOX (ed.), *How Wars End. The Annals*, 392 (1970), 51–61.

WRIGHT, Quincy. "Escalation of International Conflicts," *Journal of Conflict Resolution*, **IX**, 4 (1965), 434–449.

WRIGHT, Quincy. *A Study of War*, Vols. I, II. Chicago: University of Chicago Press, 1942; rev. ed., 1965.

YOUNG, Oran R. *International Cooperation: Building Regimes for Natural Resources and the Environment*. Ithaca, NY: Cornell University Press, 1989.

YOUNG, Oran R. *The Politics of Force*. Princeton, NJ: Princeton University Press, 1968.

YOUNG, Oran R. *The Intermediaries: Third Parties in International Crises*. Princeton, NJ: Princeton University Press, 1967.

ZAGARE, Frank C. *The Dynamics of Deterrence*. Chicago: University of Chicago Press, 1987.

ZINNES, Dina A. "Three Puzzles in Search of a Researcher," *International Studies Quarterly*, **24**, 3 (1980), 315–342.

ZINNES, Dina A. "Why War? Evidence on the Outbreak of International Conflict," in Ted R. GURR (ed.), *Handbook of Political Conflict: Theory and Research*. New York: Free Press, 1980, Chapter 8.

ZINNES, Dina A. "The Expression and Perception of Hostility in Prewar Crisis: 1914," in David SINGER (ed.), *Quantitative International Politics: Insight and Evidence*. New York: The Free Press, 1968.

ZINNES, Dina A. "A Comparison of Hostile Behavior of Decision-Makers in Simulate and Historical Data," *World Politics*, **XVIII**, 3 (April 1966), 474–502.

ZINNES, Dina A. and Jonathan WILKENFELD. "An Analysis of Foreign Conflict Behavior of Nations," in Wolfram F. HANRIEDER (ed.), *Comparative Foreign Policy*. New York: McKay, 1971, 167–213.

ZINNES, Dina A., Robert C. NORTH and Howard E. KOCH, Jr. "Capability, Threat and the Outbreak of War," in James N. ROSENAU (ed.), *International Politics and Foreign Policy*. New York: Free Press, 1961, 469–482.

The Gulf Crisis 1990–91

Primary Sources

UN DOCUMENTS

S/RES/660 (1990), 2/8/90
S/RES/661 (1990), 6/8/90
S/RES/662 (1990), 9/8/90
S/RES/664 (1990), 18/8/90
S/RES/665 (1990), 25/8/90
S/RES/666 (1990), 13/9/90
S/RES/667 (1990), 16/9/90
S/RES/669 (1990), 24/9/90
S/RES/670 (1990), 25/9/90
S/RES/674 (1990), 29/10/90
S/RES/677 (1990), 28/11/90
S/RES/678 (1990), 29/11/90
S/RES/686 (1991), 2/3/91
S/RES/687 (1991), 3/4/91
S/RES/688 (1991), 5/4/91

(The text of these resolutions is to be found in UN Security Council documents, as well as in the *New York Times*, usually the day after they were approved, and in Sifry and Cerf, 1991: 137–156.)

US DOCUMENTS

Joint Hearings of the Committee on Foreign Affairs and the Joint Economic Committee, House of Representatives, August 8–December 11, 1990. *The Persian Gulf Crisis.*

Subcommittee on Europe and the Middle East of the Committee on Foreign Affairs, House of Representatives. *Developments in the Middle East*, July 1990.

FOREIGN BROADCAST INFORMATION SERVICE
DAILY REPORT/NEAR EAST and SOUTH ASIA (FBIS–NESA)

"President Warns Israel, Criticizes U.S.," 2/4/90, *FBIS–NESA*, 3/4/90, 32–36.
"Saddam Speech Marks Revolution's 22nd Anniversary," 17/7/90, *FBIS–NESA*, 17/7/90, 20–23.
"Aziz Assails Kuwait, UAE in Letter to Klibi," 18/7/90, *FBIS–NESA*, 18/7/90, 21–24.

"Saddam's 30 May Speech on OPEC Oil Guidelines," 18/7/90, *FBIS–NESA*, 19/7/90, 21.

"Harm to Iraq, Kuwait to be Returned 'Manifold'" [*Al-Jumhuriyah* editorial, 7/8/90], *FBIS–NESA*, 7/8/90, 28–29.

"Saddam Husayn Issues 'Victory' Day Message," 7/8/90, *FBIS–NESA*, 8/8/90, 29–31.

"RCC Approves 'Merger' Decision with Kuwait," 8/8/90, *FBIS–NESA*, 9/8/90, 26–27.

"Saddam Calls Arabs, Muslims to 'Save' Mecca," 10/8/90, *FBIS–NESA*, 13/8/90, 45–47.

"National Assembly Statement Urges 'Jihad'," 11/8/90, *FBIS–NESA*, 13/8/90, 47–48.

"Text of Saddam Husayn Initiative on Situation," 12/8/90, *FBIS–NESA*, 13/8/90, 48–49.

"Saddam Sets Conditions for Foreigners' 'Release'," 19/8/90, *FBIS–NESA*, 20/8/90, 12–14.

"'Guests' Allowed to Leave Beginning 25 Dec." 18/11/90, *FBIS–NESA*, 19/11/90, 9.

"Saddam Husayn Calls Up 250,000 More Troops," 19/11/90, *FBIS–NESA*, 19/11/90, 9.

"RCC, Ba'th Party Statement on UN Resolution," 30/11/90, *FBIS–NESA*, 30/11/90, 17–18.

"RCC Responds to Bush Offer of Negotiations," 1/12/90, *FBIS–NESA*, 3/12/90, 20–21.

"Saddam Calls for Release of All Foreigners," 6/12/90, *FBIS–NESA*, 6/12/90, 13–14.

"Saddam Spells Out Position," 12/2/91, *FBIS–NESA*, 13/2/91, 17.

"RCC Issues Statement of Terms for Peace," 15/2/91, *FBIS–NESA*, 15/2/91, 17–19.

"Saddam Addresses Nation on Initiative 21 Feb.," 21/2/91, *FBIS–NESA*, 21/2/91, 21–24.

"Aziz Informs UN of 'Approval' of Resolutions," 28/2/91, *FBIS–NESA*, 28/2/91, 18.

"Government Accepts UNSC Resolution 686," 3/3/91, *FBIS–NESA*, 4/3/91, 31.

"Aziz Letter to UN on Return of Kuwaiti Assets," 5/3/91, *FBIS–NESA*, 6/3/91, 26.

"Decisions Regarding Kuwait Rescinded," 5/3/91, *FBIS–NESA*, 6/3/91, 26.

NEW YORK TIMES (NYT) DOCUMENTS

"Transcript of News Conference Remarks by Bush on Iraq Crisis," *New York Times* (henceforth *NYT*), 6/8/90, A7.

"Excerpts From Bush's News Conference on the Iraqi Invasion of Kuwait," *NYT*, 9/8/90, A1, 15.

"Excerpt from Shevardnadze's Speech," *NYT*, 5/9/90, A17.

"Text of Joint Statement: 'Aggression Will Not Pay'," *NYT*, 10/9/90, A6.

"Transcript of Bush–Gorbachev News Conference at Summit," *NYT*, 10/9/90, A8, 9.

"Text of President Bush's Address to Joint Session of Congress," *NYT*, 12/9/90, A20.

"Excerpts From Iraqi Transcript of Meeting with U.S. Envoy," *NYT*, 23/9/90, A19.

"Transcript of President's Address to U.N. General Assembly," *NYT*, 2/10/90, A12.

"Bush Talks of Atrocities," *NYT*, 16/10/90, A19.

"Excerpts From Bush's Remarks on His Order to Enlarge U.S. Gulf Forces," *NYT*, 9/11/90, A12.

"Excerpts From President's News Conference on Crisis in Gulf," *NYT*, 1/12/90, A6.

"Europe's Statement Urging a Total Pullout," *NYT*, 5/1/91, A5.

"Remarks by Baker at News Conference in Geneva on Standoff in the Gulf," *NYT*, 10/1/91, A14.

"Excerpts From Iraqi Foreign Minister's News Session After Geneva Talks," *NYT*, 10/1/91, A15.

"Excerpts From Bush's Remarks on Baker's Mission and Diplomacy's Fate," *NYT*, 10/1/91, A16.

"Excerpts of Resolutions Debated by Congress," *NYT*, 13/1/91, A11.

"Text of Statement by U.N. Chief in Appeal to Iraq," *NYT*, 16/1/91, A13.

"Transcript of the Comments by Bush on the Air Strikes Against the Iraqis," *NYT*, 17/1/91, A14.

"Major Military Units in the Persian Gulf Area," *NYT*, 20/1/91, E2.
"Text of the Joint Statement by Baker and Bessmertnykh," *NYT*, 31/1/91, A15.
"Excerpts From the Statement by Gorbachev on Gulf War," *NYT*, (TASS version), 10/2/91, A19.
"Bush's 'Remarks to the American Academy for the Advancement of Science'," *NYT*, 16/2/91, A5.
"World Reaction: Bitter Rejection From Foes of Iraq; Quick Praise From Some Supporters," *NYT*, 16/2/91, A7.
"Moscow's Statement on the Iraqis' Response," *NYT*, 22/2/91, A6.
"Transcript of White House Statement and News Conference on Soviet Plan," *NYT*, 22/2/91, A7.
"Transcripts of Statement by Bush and Fitzwater on Unconditional Pullout," *NYT*, 23/2/91, A4.
"Transcript of the Statement on Moscow Peace Proposal," *NYT*, 23/2/91, A5.
"Transcript of Statement by Iraqi in Moscow," *NYT*, 24/2/91, A19.
"Forces in Place in the Gulf," *NYT*, 25/2/91, A12.
"Excerpts From Schwarzkopf News Conference on Gulf War," *NYT*, 28/2/91, A8.
"Transcript of President's Address on the Gulf War," *NYT*, 28/2/91, A12.
"Iraq's Weapons Losses," *NYT*, 1/3/91, A12.
"A Hard-Faced Schwarzkopf Sets Terms at Desert Meeting," *NYT*, 4/3/91, A1, 8.
"President Bush's Address to Congress on End of the Gulf War," *NYT*, 7/3/91, A8.
"Gulf Allies and the Forces Deployed," *NYT*, 24/3/91, A18.
"Excerpts From the Schwarkopf Interview," *NYT*, 28/3/91, A18.
"Excerpts From Letter to UN: Iraqis 'Accept This Resolution'," *NYT*, 8/4/91, A6.
"U.S. Messages on the July Meeting of Saddam Hussein and American Envoy," *NYT*, 13/7/91, A4.

Books and Articles

AL-KHALIL, Samir. *Republic of Fear*. New York: Pantheon, 1989.
APPLE, R. W., Jr. "Message To Iraq: The Will and The Way," *NYT*, 9/11/90, A1, 13.
APPLE, R. W., Jr. "U.S. 'Nightmare Scenario': Being Finessed by Iraq," *NYT*, 19/12/90, A16.
APPLE, R. W., Jr. "Bush's Limited Victory," *NYT*, 13/1/91, A1, 11.
APPLE, R. W., Jr. "U.S. Says Iraqi Generals Agree To Demands 'On All Matters'; Early P.O.W. Release Expected," *NYT*, 4/3/91, A1, 8.
AZMEH, Youssef. "Fahd puts Saudi Arabia on road of reform" (Reuters), *Jerusalem Post*, 3/3/92, 5.
BAQUET, Dean. "Documents Charge Prewar Iraq Swap: U.S. Food for Arms," *NYT*, 27/4/92, A1, D4.
BAQUET, Dean. "Investigators Say U.S. Shielded Iraqis From Bank Inquiry," *NYT*, 20/3/92, A1, 9.
BAQUET, Dean. "Britain Traded Export Permits for Iraqi Arms Data," *NYT*, 27/10/92, A1, 13.
BAQUET, Dean. "Britain Drops a Case Against 3 Charged With Arms Sales to Iraq, *NYT*, 10/11/92, A 13.
BAQUET, Dean with Elaine SCIOLINO. "European Suppliers of Iraq Were Known to Pentagon," *NYT*, 2/11/92, A8.
BARTLET, Christopher J. *A History of Postwar Britain, 1945–74*. London: Longman, 1977.
BOUSTANY, Nora and Patrick E. TYLER. "Iraq Expands Force Near Kuwait Border," *Washington Post*, 31/7/90, A16, 22.
BRAND, Laurie A. "Liberalization and Changing Political Coalitions: The Bases of

Jordan's 1990–1991 Gulf Crisis Policy," *Jerusalem Journal of International Relations*, **13**, 4 (1991), 1–46.

CIGAR, Norman. "Iraq's Strategic Mindset and the Gulf War: Blueprint for Defeat," *The Journal of Strategic Studies*, 15, 1 (1992), 1–29.

CIOFFI-REVILLA, Claudio. "On the Likely Magnitude, Extent, and Duration of an Iraq-UN War," *Journal of Conflict Resolution* **35**, 3 (1991), 387–411.

CLINES, Francis X. "Soviets Suggest Conference Combining Issues of Mideast," *NYT*, 5/9/90, A17.

COCKBURN, Alexander. "West Vacationed While Saddam Burned," *Wall Street Journal*, (New York) 6/9/90, A15.

COOLEY, John K. "Pre-war Gulf Diplomacy," *Survival*, 33, 2 (1991), 125–139.

COWELL, Alan. "Baghdad Formally Agrees to Unjust U.N. Conditions For Permanent Cease-Fire: Truce is Official," *NYT*, 7/4/91, A1, 14.

COWELL, Alan. "Arab Nations Put off Talks to Create a Kuwait Force," *NYT*, 8/7/91, A2.

COHEN, Roger and Claudio GATTI. *In the Eye of the Storm: The Life of General H. Norman Schwarzkopf.* New York: Farrar, Straus and Giroux, 1991.

CRYSTAL, Jill. *Oil and Politics in the Gulf: Rulers and Merchants in Kuwait and Qatar.* Cambridge: Cambridge University Press, 1990.

CUSHMAN, John H. Jr. "A Thousand Kuwaitis Attend Protest," *NYT*, 5/6/91, A6.

CUSHMAN, John H. Jr. "Pentagon Report on the Persian Gulf War: A Few Surprises and Some Silences," *NYT*, 11/4/92, A4.

DEIBEL, Terry L. "Bush's Foreign Policy: Mastery and Inaction," *Foreign Policy*, **84** (1991), 3–23.

DEIBEL, Terry L. "Pentagon Report on Persian Gulf War: a Few Surprises and Some Silences," *NYT*, 11/4/92, A4.

DAVIS, Paul K. and John ARQUILLA. *Deterring or Coercing Opponents in Crisis: Lessons from the War with Saddam Hussein.* Santa Monica, CA: Rand, 1991.

DICKSON, H. R. P. *Kuwait and Her Neighbors.* London: Allen and Unwin, 1956.

DRAPER, Theodore. "The Gulf War Reconsidered," *The New York Review of Books*, **XXXIX**, 1 & 2, 16/1/92, 46–53.

DRAPER, Theodore. "The True History of the Gulf War," *The New York Review of Books*, **XXXIX**, 3 & 4, 30/1/92, 38–45.

DUNNIGAN, James F. and Austin BAY. *From Shield to Storm: High-Tech Weapons, Military Strategy, and Coalition Warfare in the Persian Gulf.* New York: Morrow, 1991.

DUPREE, Louis. *Afghanistan.* Princeton, NJ: Princeton University Press, 1980.

EMERSON, Steven. "Capture of a Terrorist," *New York Times Magazine*, 21/4/91, 30–32, 56–57, 68–69.

FARNSWORTH, Clyde H. "Official Reported To Face Ouster After His Dissent on Iraq Exports," *NYT*, 10/4/91, A1, D2.

FARNSWORTH, Clyde H. "Military Exports to Iraq Come Under Scrutiny," *NYT*, 25/6/91, A11.

FITZSIMMONS, Matthew A. *Empire by Treaty: Britain and the Middle East in the Twentieth Century.* Notre Dame, IN: University of Notre Dame Press, 1964.

FREEDMAN, Lawrence and Efraim KARSH. "How Kuwait Was Won: Strategy in the Gulf War," *International Security*, **16**, 2 (1991), 5–41.

FRANTZ, Douglas and Murray WAAS. "Bush OK'd Close Ties to Iraq despite CIA Warnings," *Los Angeles Times*, reprinted in *Jerusalem Post*, 7/8/92.

FRIEDMAN, Norman. *Desert Victory: The War for Kuwait.* Annapolis, Md.: Naval Institute Press, 1991.

FRIEDMAN, Thomas L. "Signal Loud and Unclear," *NYT*, 10/9/90, A1, 6.

FRIEDMAN, Thomas L. "Baker Trip Shows Coalition Discord on War with Iraq," *NYT*, 11/11/90, A1, 14.

FRIEDMAN, Thomas L. "The Iraq Resolution: A U.S.-Soviet Collaboration," *NYT*, 2/12/90, A1, 19.

FRIEDMAN, Thomas L. "For Bush and Hussein, A High-Stakes Game of Resolve and Intent," *NYT*, 16/12/90, sec. 4, p. 2.

FRIEDMAN, Thomas L. "Major Iraqi 'Ploy' Can Be Expected, Baker Tells NATO," *NYT*, 18/12/90, A1, 8.

FRIEDMAN, Thomas L. "Baker Hints at War to Thwart Partial Pullout," *NYT*, 19/12/90, A16.

FRIEDMAN, Thomas L. "Baker Says Anti-Iraq Allies, Except Syria, Agree on Force," *NYT*, 14/1/91, A9.

FRIEDMAN, Thomas L. "The Decision: Setting the Hour for the War to Start: Bush Gave Iraqis One Day of Grace," *NYT*, 18/1/91, A11.

FRIEDMAN, Thomas L. "Soviets Said to Hedge on War with Future in Mind," *NYT*, 28/1/91, A7.

FRIEDMAN, Thomas L. "Envoy to Iraq, Faulted in Crisis, Says She Warned Hussein Sternly," *NYT*, 21/3/91, A1, 15.

FRIEDMAN, Thomas L. "U.S. Revises Image of Envoy to Iraq," *NYT*, 22/3/91 A1, 9.

FRIEDMAN, Thomas L. "Explaining Saddam: Hard Gambling," *NYT*, 28/9/91, A6.

FRIEDMAN, Thomas L. and Patrick E. TYLER. "From the First, U.S. Resolve to Fight: The Path to War," *NYT*, 3/3/91, A1, 18, 19.

GARGAN, Edward A. "Kuwaitis Pushing for Ouster of 2 Cabinet Ministers," *NYT*, 24/5/91, A5.

GARGAN, Edward A. "The Causes of War: Systemic Findings," in A. Ned SABROSKY (ed.). *Polarity and War*. Boulder, CO: Westview Press, 1985, Chap. 2.

GARNHAM, David. "Explaining Middle Eastern Alignments During the Gulf War," *Jerusalem Journal of International Relations*, **13**, 3 (1991), 63–83.

GELB, Leslie H. "Iraq: Drawing the Line," *NYT*, 3/4/91, A26.

GELB, Leslie H. "White House Guilt?" *NYT*, 14/4/91, E7.

GELB, Leslie H. "Mr. Bush's Fateful Blunder," *NYT*, 17/7/91, A21.

GELB, Leslie H. "Bush's Iraqi Blunder," *NYT*, 4/5/92, A17.

GELB, Leslie H. "Cuddling Saddam," *NYT*, 9/7/92, A21.

GELB, Leslie H. "A Bush Green Light to Iraq?" *NYT*, 22/10/92, A27.

GORDON, Michael R. "When To Threaten Iraq," *NYT*, 13/11/90, A1, 14.

GORDON, Michael R. "Schwarzkopf Leaves Gulf, Describing the Mission as Completed," *NYT*, 21/4/91, A12.

GORDON, Michael R. with Eric SCHMITT. "Much More Armor Than U.S. Believed Fled Back to Iraq," *NYT*, 25/3/91, A1, 8.

GORDON, Michael R. "Pentagon Study Cites Problems with Gulf Effort," *NYT*, 23/2/92, A1, 12.

GORDON, Michael R. "Pentagon Plan To Train Iraqis In '90 Revealed," *NYT*, 5/8/92, A9.

GORDON, Michael R. "British, French and U.S. Agree To Attack Iraqi Planes in South," *NYT*, 19/8/92, A1, 6.

GORDON, Michael R. "Bush Would Use Force to Ban Bosnia War Flights," *NYT*, 3/10/92, A1, 5.

GORDON, Michael R. "Pentagon Objected to a Message Bush Sent Iraq Before Its Invasion," *NYT*, 25/10/92, A1, 14.

HABERMAN, Clyde. "U.S. Military Takes Over Relief For Kurdish Refugees in Iraq," *NYT*, 13/4/91, A1, 4.

HEDGES, Chris. "Kuwait Vote Today Reopens Democracy Fight," *NYT*, 5/10/92, A10.

HEDGES, Chris. "Voters in Kuwait Elect Legislators," *NYT*, 6/10/92, A6.

HEDGES, Chris. "Kuwaiti Opposition Wins Legislative Election," *NYT*, 7/10/92, A12.

HEDGES, Chris. "Kuwait's Opposition Victors Trying to Unite," *NYT*, 18/10/92, A16.

HEDGES, Stephen J. and Brian DUFFY. "Iraqgate," *U.S. News & World Report*, 18/5/92, 42–51.

HERSH, Seymour M. "U.S. Secretly Gave Aid to Iraq Early in Its War Against Iran," *NYT*, 26/1/92, A1, 12.

HIRO, Dilip. *Desert Shield to Desert Storm: The Second Gulf War*, New York: Routledge, 1992.

HITCHENS, Christopher. "Why We Are Stuck in the Sand," *Harper's Magazine*, January 1991, 70–75, 78.

HOFFMAN, David. "US Envoy Conciliatory to Saddam," *Washington Post*, 12/7/91, A1, 26.

HOFFMAN, David and Helen DEAR. "State Department, Panel, Spar Over Envoy," *Washington Post*, 13/7/91, A1, 14.

HOFFMANN, Stanley. "Bush Abroad", *The New York Review of Books*, XXXIX, 18, 5/11/92, 54–59.

IBRAHIM, Youssef M. "Quick Kuwaiti Recovery Is Seen, With the Cost Less Than Thought," *NYT*, 18/3/91, A1, 9.

IBRAHIM, Youssef M. "Assad and Mubarak Meet and Oppose Breakup of Iraq," *NYT*, 2/4/91, A8.

IBRAHIM, Youssef M. "Saudi King Issues Decrees to Revise Governing System," *NYT*, 2/3/92, A1, 8.

IBRAHIM, Youssef M. "Saudi Rulers Are Confronting Challenge by Islamic Radicals," *NYT*, 9/3/92, A1, 7.

IBRAHIM, Youssef M. "Saudi King Rules Out Free Elections," *NYT*, 30/3/92, A6.

IBRAHIM, Youssef M. "Iraq Is Said to Rebuild a Big Part Of Its Bomb-Damaged Oil Industry," *NYT*, 27/7/92, A7.

IBRAHIM, Youssef M. "Teheran to Seize the Planes Iraq Sent to Iran for Safety," *NYT*, 31/7/92, A6.

IBRAHIM, Youssef M. "Saudi Clergymen Seek Tighter Islamic Rule," *NYT*, 8/10/92, A6.

JOHNSTON, David. "U.S. Will Not Seek New Investigation In Loans To Iraq," *NYT*, 10/12/92, A1, B13).

KELLER, Bill. "Moscow Joins U.S. in Criticizing Iraq," *NYT*, 4/8/90, A6.

KELLER, Bill. "Bush and Gorbachev Say Iraqis Must Obey U.N. and Quit Iraq," *NYT*, 10/9/90, A1, 6.

KIFNER, John. "Arabs Vote To Send Troops To Help Saudis," *NYT*, 11/8/90, A1, 6.

KIFNER, John. "Power Struggle in Kuwait Blocks New Government," *NYT*, 31/3/91 A1, 8.

KRASNER, Stephen D. (ed.). "International Regimes," *International Organization*, **36**, 2 (1982) [special issue].

LAMB, Alastair. *The McMahon Line* (2 vols.). London: Routledge and Kegan Paul, 1966.

LAMB, David. "How Saddam Brought War Clouds to the Gulf," *Los Angeles Times*, reprinted in *The Gazette* (Montreal), 1/12/90, B5.

LATOURETTE, Kenneth S. *The American Record in the Far East, 1945–1951*. New York: Macmillan, 1952.

LEWIS, Anthony. "The New World Order," *NYT*, 5/4/91, A25.

LEWIS, Anthony. "'On His Word Alone'," *NYT*, 12/1/92, E19.

LEWIS, Anthony. "Who Fed This Caesar?" *NYT*, 15/3/92, A17.

LEWIS, Anthony. "Trust," *NYT*, 26/10/92, A17.

LEWIS, Flora. "America Deserts the Rebels Cynically," *NYT*, 3/4/91, A21.

LEWIS, Paul. "The U.N.: France and 3 Arab States Issue an Appeal to Hussein," *NYT*, 15/1/91, A12.

654   REFERENCES

LEWIS, Neil A. "Clinton Says He'll Consider Inquiry Into Bank Case Involving Iraq," *NYT*, 11/12/92, A32.

LEWIS, Paul. "The U.N.: Last-Minute Debating, Then Final Plea to Iraq," *NYT*, 16/1/91, A13.

LEWIS, Paul. "U.S. and Britain Insist on Deadline," *NYT*, 21/2/91, A1, 13.

LEWIS, Paul. "U.N. Poised to Approve U.S.-Backed Gulf Draft," *NYT*, 3/3/91, A16.

LEWIS, Paul. "U.N. Survey Calls Iraq's War Damage Near-Apocalyptic," *NYT*, 22/3/91, A1, 9.

LEWIS, Paul. "U.N. Votes Stern Conditions For Formally Ending War; Iraqi Response is Uncertain," *NYT*, 4/4/91, A1, 10.

LEWIS, Paul. "Iraq Approval Starts Peace Schedule," *NYT*, 7/4/91, A14.

LEWIS, Paul. "Iraq Admits Buying German Materials to Make A-Bombs," *NYT*, 15/1/92, A1, 12.

LEWIS, Paul. "Despite U.N. Embargo, Baghdad Heals Its Wounds," *NYT*, 14/7/92, A1, 6.

LEWIS, Paul. "U.S. Agrees to Compromise on Bosnia Flight Ban," *NYT*, 8/10/92, A14.

LEWIS, Paul. "U.N. Bans Flight in Bosnia But Is Silent on Enforcement," *NYT*, 10/10/92, A3.

MACMILLAN, Harold. *At the End of the Day, 1961–1963*. New York: Harper & Row, 1973.

MATAR, L. Fuad. *Saddam Hussein: The Man, the Cause, and the Future*. London: Third World Center, 1981.

MIDDLE, EAST WATCH. *Needless Deaths in the Gulf: Civilian Casualties During the Air Campaign and Violations of the Laws of War*. New York: Human Rights Watch, 1992.

MILLER, Judith. "Arab Countries in the Middle: Leverage with the Adversaries is Growing," *NYT*, 28/11/90, A14.

MILLER, Judith. "Displaced in the Gulf War: 5 Million Refugees," *NYT*, 16/6/91, IE3.

MILLER, Judith. "Limited Shifts in Cabinet Disappoint Many Saudis," *NYT*, 6/8/91, A5.

MILLER, Judith. "Saudi Reform Plan Is Called 'Empty,'" *NYT*, 17/5/92, A13.

MILLER, Judith and Laurie MYLROIE. *Saddam Hussein and the Crisis in the Gulf*. New York: Times Books, 1990.

MILLER, Judith. "Show of Force on Iraq Signals New Direction," *NYT*, 30/8/92, E5.

MILLER, Judith. "Saudi Prince Disputes Schwarkopf Book on War," *NYT*, 21/10/92, A8.

MILLER, Mark C. *Spectacle: Operation Desert Storm and the Triumph of Illusion*. New York: Poseidon Press, 1992a.

MILLER, Mark C. "Operation Desert Sham," *NYT*, 24/6/92, A21 (1992b).

NORTHEDGE, Frederick S. *Descent from Power: British Foreign Policy, 1945–1973*. London: Allen & Unwin, 1974.

OBERDORFER, Don. "Missed Signals in the Middle East," *Washington Post Magazine*, 17/3/91, 19–41.

PORTH, Jacquelyn S. "Coalition May Have Had Five-Fold Advantage in Gulf War," United States Information Agency, *The Wireless File*, 23/4/9, 4–5.

PRIMAKOV, Evgeni M. "The Inside Story of Moscow's Quest for a Deal," *Time* (European edition), 4/3/91, 32–38.

PRIMAKOV, Evgeni M. "My Final Visit with Saddam Hussein," *Time*, 11/3/91, 48–49.

PYLE, Richard. *Schwarzkopf: The Man, The Mission, The Triumph*. New York: Signet, 1991.

REJWAN, Nissim. "What the Kurds Want," *Jerusalem Post*, 14/4/91.

RIDING, Alan. "Paris Says Its Last-Ditch Peace Effort Has Failed," *NYT*, 16/1/91, A13.

ROSENTHAL, Andrew. "Latest Buildup Called a Signal On Use of Force," *NYT*, 10/11/90, A1, 6.

ROSENTHAL, Andrew. "The Thinking Behind Bush's Call for Iraqi's Ouster," *NYT*, 17/2/91, A18.

ROSENTHAL, Andrew. "Bush Criticizes Soviet Plan as Inadequate to End War: Iraqi May Revisit Moscow," *NYT*, 20/2/91, A1.

ROSENTHAL, Andrew. "Scowcroft and Gates: A Team Rivals Baker," *NYT*, 21/2/91, A14.

ROSENTHAL, Andrew. "A Risky Undertaking," *NYT*, 18/4/91, A1, 16.

ROSENTHAL, Andrew. "Seeking Voter Reward, Bush Still Predicts Fall of Hussein," *NYT*, 17/1/92, A8.

ROSENTHAL, A. M. "The Jews of Iraq," *NYT*, 5/4/91, A25.

RUSSETT, Bruce M. "The Mysterious Case of Vanishing Hegemony; or, Is Mark Twain Really Dead?," *International Organizations*, **39**, 2 (1985), 207–231.

SACKUR, Stephen. *On the Basra Road*. London: London Review of Books, 1991.

SAFIRE, William. "Bush's Bay of Pigs," *NYT*, 4/4/91, op-ed page.

SAFIRE, William. "Digging Deeper in Iraqgate," *NYT*, 6/7/92, A13.

SAFIRE, William. "A Smoking Gun?" *NYT*, 10/9/92, A23.

SAFIRE, William. "Bush on Iraqgate," *NYT*, 8/10/92, A35.

SCHMEMANN, Serge. "Gorbachev Warns Against Exceeding U.N. War Mandate," *NYT*, 10/2/91, A1, 19.

SCHMEMANN, Serge. "Gorbachev's Envoy Sees 'Glimmers' of Hope After Talks with Iraqi Leader," *NYT*, 14/2/91, A19.

SCHMEMANN, Serge. "Moscow Welcomes Baghdad's Offer," *NYT*, 16/2/91, A7.

SCHMEMANN, Serge. "Moscow Tempers Its Satisfaction At Baghdad Offer," *NYT*, 17/2/91, A1.

SCHMEMANN, Serge. "Soviets Say Iraq Accepts Kuwait Pullout Linked to Truce and An End to Sanctions," *NYT*, 22/2/91, A1, 6.

SCHMIDT, William E. "Britain is Accused on Iraqi 'Supergun'," *NYT*, 17/1/92, A8.

SCHMITT, Eric. "U.S. Says Its Fire Killed 20 Americans in the Gulf," *NYT*, 10/8/91, A4.

SCHMITT, Eric. "U.S. and Kuwait Sign Pact on Troops," *NYT*, 20/9/91, A10.

SCHMITT, Eric. "Study Lists Lower Tally of Iraqi Troops in Gulf War," *NYT*, 24/4/92, A6.

SCHMITT, Eric. "Pentagon Claims on Scuds Disputed," *NYT*, 24/6/92, A6.

SCHMITT, Eric and Michael R. GORDON. "Unforeseen Problems in Air War Forced Allies To Improvise Tactics," *NYT*, 10/3/91, A1, 16.

SCHOFIELD, Richard. *Kuwait and Iraq: Historical Claims and Territorial Disputes*. London: Royal Institute of International Affairs, 1991.

SCHWARZKOPF, H. Norman. *It Doesn't Take A Hero*. New York: Linda Grey Bantam Books, 1992.

SCIOLINO, Elaine. *The Outlaw State: Saddam Hussein's Quest for Power and the Gulf Crisis*. New York: Wiley, 1991.

SCIOLINO, Elaine. "Finally, An Arbitrary Deadline Becomes Quite Threatening," *NYT*, 15/1/91, A10.

SCIOLINO, Elaine. "U.S. Troops To Build Camps In North Iraq To Aid Kurds; Bush Sees 'Temporary' Role," *NYT*, 17/4/91, A1, 12.

SCIOLINO, Elaine. "How Bush Overcame Reluctance and Embraced Kurdish Relief," *NYT*, 18/4/91, A16.

SCIOLINO, Elaine. "Envoy's Testimony on Iraq Is Assailed," *NYT*, 13/7/91, A1, 4.

SCIOLINO, Elaine. "Iraqis Could Pose a Threat Soon, C.I.A. Chief Says," *NYT*, 16/1/92, A9.

SCIOLINO, Elaine. "Bush Aides Attack Democrats on Iraq," *NYT*, 22/5/92, A6.

SCIOLINO, Elaine. "'89 Bush Order Says Ply Iraq With Aid," *NYT*, 29/5/92, A3.

SCIOLINO, Elaine. "U.S. Documents Raise Questions Over Iraq Policy," *NYT*, 7/6/92, A1, 16.

SCIOLINO, Elaine. "Documents Warned in '85 of Iraqi Nuclear Aims," *NYT*, 5/7/92, A8.

SCIOLINO, Elaine. "Iraq Policy Still Bedevils Bush as Congress Asks: Were Crimes Committed?" *NYT*, 9/8/92, E18.

SCIOLINO, Elaine. "Iraqi Bank-Fraud Scheme Described," *NYT*, 16/9/92, A6.

SCIOLINO, Elaine. "A Budding Scandal, in Brief: A Primer on the 'B.N.L. Affair'," *NYT*, 18/10/92, E4.

SCIOLINO, Elaine. "Export of Computers to Iraq Was Backed By the U.S. in 1989," *NYT*, 27/10/92, A15.

SCIOLINO, Elaine with Dean BAQUET "An American Front Company Was Cog in Baghdad's Buildup," *NYT*, 26/7/92, A1, 8.

SCIOLINO, Elaine and Dean BAQUET. "Review Finds Inquiry Into Iraqi Loans Was Flawed," *NYT*, 18/10/92, A36.

SCIOLINO, Elaine with Eric PACE. "How U.S. Got U.N. Backing for Use of Force in the Gulf," *NYT*, 30/8/90, A1, 15.

SCIOLINO, Elaine with Michael WINES. "Bush's Greatest Glory Fades As Questions on Iraq Persist," *NYT*, 27/6/92, A1, 8.

SEIB, Gerald F. "Saddam Hussein Takes Pains to Spin Conspiracy Tales," *Wall Street Journal* (New York), 22/10/90, A10.

SHIMONI, Yaacov. *Political Dictionary of the Arab World*. New York: Macmillan, 1987.

SIFRY, Micah L. and Christopher CERF (eds.). *The Gulf War Reader: History, Documents, Opinions*. New York: Times Books, 1991.

SIMPSON, John. *From the House of War*. London: Arrow Books, 1991.

SMITH, Jean E. *George Bush's War*. New York: Henry Holt, 1992.

STEIN, Janice G. "Deterrence and Compellance in the Gulf, 1990–91," *International Security*, 17, 2 (1992), 147–179.

STRANGE, Susan. "Still an Extraordinary Power: America's Role in a Global Monetary System," in Raymond E. LOMBRA and William E. WITTE (eds.), *Political Economy of International and Domestic Monetary Relations*. Ames, IO: Iowa State University Press, 1982.

SUMMERS, Harry G.Jr. *A Critical Analysis of the Gulf War*. New York: Dell, 1992.

TETREAULT, Mary A. "Autonomy, Necessity, and the Small State: Ruling Kuwait in the Twentieth Century," *International Organization*, **45**, 4 (1991), 565–591.

THEDOULOU, Michael, "Kuwait Fears Invasion over Iraqi Demands," *The Times* (London), 2/8/90, 1,11.

THOMMA, Steven. "Greenpeace: War's Toll is 175,000," *Philadelphia Inquirer*, 30/5/91, 5A.

TIMMERMAN, Kenneth R. *The Death Lobby: How the West Armed Iraq*. New York: Houghton Mifflin, 1992.

TIMMERMAN, Kenneth R. "Surprise! We Gave Hussein the Bomb," *NYT*, 25/10/91, A33.

TISDALL, Simon. "Desert Storm Two," *Guardian Weekly* (Manchester), 31/5/92, 9.

TOLCHIN, Martin. "U.S. Is Criticized On 'Lavoro' Case," *NYT*, 6/10/92, A8.

TOLCHIN, Martin. "Exports by U.S. Aided 'Super Gun,' House Banking Chief Says," *NYT*, 28/10/92, A15.

TUCKER, Robert W. and David C. HENDRICKSON. *The Imperial Temptation: The New World Order and America's Purpose*. New York: Council on Foreign Relations Press, 1992.

TYLER, Patrick E. "U.N. Chief's Talks With Iraqis Bring No Sign of Change," *NYT*, 14/1/91, A1, 9.

TYLER, Patrick E. "Iraqis Speak Of A Withdrawal But Impose List of Conditions; Bush Denounces 'Cruel Hoax'," *NYT*, 16/2/91, A1, 4.

TYLER, Patrick E. "The Powell-Cheney Relationship: Blunt Give-and-Take Early in Crisis," *NYT*, 15/3/91, A14.

TYLER, Patrick E. "Powell Says U.S. Will Stay in Iraq For Some Months," *NYT*, 23/3/91, A1, 4.

TYLER, Patrick E. "Bush Aims Rebuke At Schwarzkopf For Truce Remark," *NYT*, 28/3/91, A1, 18.

TYLER, Patrick E. "Scowcroft Went to Talk with Saudis, U.S. Says," *NYT*, 2/4/91, A9.

TYLER, Patrick E. "Baghdad Formally Agrees to 'Unjust' U.N. Conditions For Permanent Cease-Fire: Punished But Hanging On," *NYT*, 7/4/91, A1, 14.

TYLER, Patrick E. "Bush Sees Accord on 'Safe Havens' For Kurds In Iraq," *NYT*, 12/4/91, A1, 6.

TYLER, Patrick E. "U.S. Juggling Iraq Policy," *NYT*, 13/4/91, A5.

TYLER, Patrick E. "U.S. Effort for Postwar Alliance Suffers Setbacks, Officials Say," *NYT*, 11/5/91, A1, 4.

TYLER, Patrick E. "U.S. Officials Believe Iraq Will Take Years To Rebuild," *NYT*, 3/6/91, A1, 8.

TYLER, Patrick E. "Iraq's War Toll Estimated by U.S.," *NYT*, 5/6/91, A5.

TYLER, Patrick E. "U.S.-Saudi Alliance Against Iraq Faces Obstacles," *NYT*, 30/9/91, A5.

TYLER, Patrick E. "Gulf Security Talks Stall Over Plan for Saudi Army," *NYT*, 13/10/91, A1, 18.

US News and World Report. *Triumph Without Victory: The History of the Persian Gulf War*. New York: Times Books, 1992.

VIORST, Milton. "Report from Baghdad," *The New Yorker*, 24/9/90, 89–97.

VIORST, Milton. "Report from Baghdad," *The New Yorker*, 24/6/91, 55–73.

WAAS, Murray. "What We Gave Saddam for Christmas: The Secret History of How the United States and Its Allies Armed Iraq," *Village Voice* (New York), 18/12/90, 27–37.

WAAS, Murray and Craig UNGER, "In the Loop: Bush's Secret Mission," *New Yorker*, 2/11/92, 64–83.

WALD, Matthew L. "Amid Ceremony and Ingenuity, Kuwait's Oil-Well Fires Are Declared Out," *NYT*, 7/11/91, A3.

WHITNEY, Craig R. "Soviets Wanted U.S. Delay But Plea To Iraq Was Late," *NYT*, 18/1/91, A13.

WILL, George F. "Gulf War: The Jewel in Bush's Crown Has Lost Its Gleam," *International Herald Tribune* (Paris), 11–12/1/92, 4.

WINES, Michael. "President Angrily Contests Charges Over Loans to Iraq," *NYT*, 2/7/92, A1, 6.

WINES, Michael. "U.S. And Allies Say Flight Ban In Iraq Will Start Today," *NYT*, 27/8/92, A1, 14.

WOODWARD, Bob. *The Commanders*. New York: Simon and Schuster, 1991.

(Associated Press) "The War's Confronting Forces," *Jerusalem Post*, 18/1/91, p. 6.

(Reuters) "Moscow Sought Last-Minute Delay," *Jerusalem Post*, 18/1/91, p. 20.

(Reuters) "Iraq Law Allows Opposition Groups," *NYT*, 4/9/91, A6.

(Reuters) item in NYT 14/10/92

(Reuters) "Kuwaiti Names Heir Premier," *NYT*, 14/10/92, A10.

ECONOMIST. "Kuwait: How the West Blundered," *Economist* (London), 29 September 1990, 19–20, 22.

Name Index

Subject Index